Instructor's Resource

MW01702224

Biology
The Unity and Diversity of Life

THIRTEENTH EDITION

Cecie Starr

Ralph Taggart

Christine Evers

Lisa Starr

Prepared by

Laura Ritt
Burlington County College

Tara Philips-Durr
Radford University

BROOKS/COLE
CENGAGE Learning

Australia • Brazil • Japan • Korea • Mexico • Singapore • Spain • United Kingdom • United States

BROOKS/COLE
CENGAGE Learning

ISBN-13: 978-1-111-57911-1
ISBN-10: 1-111-57911-3

Brooks/Cole
20 Davis Drive
Belmont, CA 94002-3098
USA

Cengage Learning is a leading provider of customized learning solutions with office locations around the globe, including Singapore, the United Kingdom, Australia, Mexico, Brazil, and Japan. Locate your local office at: **www.cengage.com/global**

Cengage Learning products are represented in Canada by Nelson Education, Ltd.

To learn more about Brooks/Cole, visit **www.cengage.com/brookscole**

Purchase any of our products at your local college store or at our preferred online store **www.cengagebrain.com**

Printed in the United States of America
1 2 3 4 5 6 7 15 14 13 12 11

CONTENTS

PREFACE

We believe the material in this manual will help teachers save time with the organization of their lectures. The information included covers the most important topics from each chapter section as well as important key terms to review for students. This manual corresponds to *Biology: The Unity and Diversity of Life, thirteenth edition* by Starr/Taggart/Evers/Starr. An electronic version of this manual is available on the PowerLecture through your local Cengage Learning representative.

Each chapter of the manual includes:

Chapter Outline: An outline of the headings within each chapter of the textbook giving an overview of its contents.

Objectives: General objectives related to the main headings of each chapter.

Key Terms: A listing of the most important boldface and italic terms in the chapter.

Lecture Outline: A detailed outline of the chapter to aid instructors in preparing lecture notes.

Suggestions for Presenting the Material: Helpful suggestions for presenting topics covered in the textbook.

Classroom and Laboratory Enrichment: A collection of visual or verbal demonstrations to help make the lecture a lively learning experience for students.

***Impacts, Issues* Classroom Discussion Ideas:** These correspond to the Impacts, Issues written directly for each chapter in the text. They are designed to get your students thinking critically about the topics.

Additional Ideas for Classroom Discussion: These are additional topics that correspond to the subject matter in the chapter. These are useful as critical thinking discussions.

***How Would You Vote?* Classroom Discussion Ideas:** This is linked to the *Impacts, Issues* topics and reminds the teacher to monitor the voting on-line. Discussion ideas for the topic are given.

Term Paper Topics, Library Activities, and Special Projects: These give the teachers a great way to expand on the topics in the chapter. These activities and topics will allow students to further their knowledge of the material.

Possible Responses to *Critical Thinking* Questions: This is an additional response to the *Critical Thinking* questions in the chapter. Responses are given in the textbook; however, this is yet another option for discussion.

We hope you find our Instructor's Resource Manual to be a helpful tool in your lesson preparation.

1

INVITATION TO BIOLOGY

Chapter Outline

THE SECRET LIFE OF EARTH
LIFE IS MORE THAN THE SUM OF ITS PARTS
HOW LIVING THINGS ARE ALIKE
- Organisms Require Energy and Nutrients
- Organisms Sense and Respond to Change
- Organisms Use DNA

HOW LIVING THINGS DIFFER
ORGANIZING INFORMATION ABOUT SPECIES
- A Rose by Any Other Name. . .

THE SCIENCE OF NATURE
- Thinking About Thinking
- How Science Works

EXAMPLES OF EXPERIMENTS IN BIOLOGY
- Potato Chips and Stomach Aches
- Butterflies and Birds

ANALYZING EXPERIMENTAL RESULTS
- Sampling Error
- Bias in Interpreting Results

THE NATURE OF SCIENCE
- The Limits of Science
- The Secret Life of Earth (Revisited)

SUMMARY
DATA ANALYSIS EXERCISE
SELF-QUIZ
CRITICAL THINKING

Objectives

1. List the levels of organization in the living world, from an atom to a biosphere.
2. Describe the general pattern of energy flow through Earth's life forms, and explain how Earth's resources (nutrients) cycle around a system.
3. Describe the biodiversity that exists among living things, and show how these organisms are categorized based on the presence or absence of a nucleus.
4. Explain that all living organisms grow and reproduce, transmitting inherited traits (coded in DNA) from parents to offspring.
5. Explain how taxonomy utilizes the combination of a genus and a specific epithet to designate a particular species.
6. Describe the steps of scientific inquiry and emphasize the importance of critical thinking.
7. List the limitations imposed on science and scientists in problem-solving and hypothesis-testing.

Key Terms

atom
biology
molecule
cell
tissues
organs
organ systems
population
community
ecosystem
biosphere
emergent properties
energy
growth
nutrient
producer
photosynthesis
consumer
homeostasis
DNA
inheritance
reproduction
development
species
genus, genera
Bacteria
Archaea
nucleus
prokaryote
eukaryote
protist
plant
fungus, fungi
animal
critical thinking
science hypothesis
prediction
model
experiment
scientific method
variable
control group
experimental group
sampling error
taxonomy
traits
inductive reasoning
deductive reasoning
independent variable
dependent variable
data
biodiversity

Lecture Outline

1.1 The Secret Life of Earth

A. Are there any places left on Earth that have not been explored?
   1. Yes: a 2005 trip to New Guinea discovered many new plant and animal species.
   2. New species, mostly smaller organisms, continue to be discovered every day.

B. The more we learn about nature, the more we realize how much more there is to learn.

C. This text helps students discover "life," that is, how organisms are constructed, how they live, etc.

1.2 Life Is More Than the Sum of Its Parts

A. Pattern in Life's Organization
   1. Biologists examine all aspects of life, from the smallest atom to global communities.
   2. Biologists present us with a glimpse of nature's organization.
   3. Cells are the fundamental building blocks of life.
   4. The levels of organization grow in complexity: atoms → molecules → cells → organism.
   5. Multicelled organisms have increasingly complex levels of organization that result in tissues → organs → organ systems → organisms → populations → communities → ecosystems → biosphere.
   6. At each successive level of organization emergent properties can be detected.

1.3 How Living Things Are Alike

A. Organisms Require Energy and Nutrients
   1. Energy, the capacity to do work, moves through the universe in a series of transfers.
   2. Higher levels of organization would cease without energy inputs from the environment.
   3. Energy flows from the sun.
      a. Producers (plants and other photosynthetic organisms) make their own food by converting sunlight to usable energy.
      b. Consumers (animals and decomposers) cannot make food, but use other organisms to obtain their energy and molecular building blocks (carbohydrates, fats, and proteins).
   4. Producers and consumers cycle nutrients among themselves.
   5. Energy flows one way through producers, consumers, and back to the environment.
   6. Energy flow is not 100 percent efficient, as heat (a form of energy) is lost at each transfer stage.

B. Organisms Sense and Respond to Change

1. Receptors and the stimuli they receive allow organisms to make controlled responses to heat and cold, harmful substances, and varying food supplies.
2. All organisms undergo homeostasis, a state in which the conditions of the "internal environment" are maintained within tolerable limits.
   a. Increased sugar causes insulin release, which stimulates cells to take up sugar.
   b. Decreased blood sugar causes another hormone to call on stored sugar reserves.

C. Organisms Use DNA

1. Deoxyribonucleic acid, or DNA, is considered the signature molecule of life.
   a. DNA carries the hereditary instructions that allow organisms to grow and reproduce.
2. Inheritance is the acquisition of traits through the transmission of DNA from parents to offspring.
   a. Each organism arises through reproduction—the mechanism by which offspring are produced by one or more parents.
   b. DNA also guides development—the orderly transformation of a new individual into a multicelled adult.

1.4 How Living Things Differ

A. Organisms may vary greatly, which we call the Earth's biodiversity.

B. Animals are classified depending on whether their DNA is contained in a nucleus.

1. Bacteria and archaea are single-celled organisms whose DNA is not located within a nucleus.
2. Eukaryotes are organisms whose DNA is housed within a nucleus.
   a. Protists are simple eukaryotes that are often single-celled organisms.
   b. Fungi are eukaryotes that often act as decomposers.
   c. Plants are photosynthetic eukaryotes that serve as food for many other organisms.
   d. Animals are multicellular eukaryotes that act as consumers.

1.5 Organizing Information About Species

A. Taxonomy is a system of naming and classifying species.

1. Carolus Linnaeus developed the two-part naming system that is still in use today.
   a. The first part of the name is the genus.
   b. The second part of the name is known as the specific epithet.
2. Recently species are classified into taxa, which are groups of organisms that share a unique set of features.

B. A Rose by Any Other Name. . . .

1. Traits can vary and are used to classify organisms.
   a. Traits may be based on morphology or processes, such as DNA analysis.
   b. Ernst Mayr developed the biological species approach, which is based on the ability of organisms to produce fertile offspring.

1.6 The Science of Nature

A. Thinking About Thinking

1. All scientific research involves critical thinking—judging information before accepting it.
2. Students should avoid accepting information without question, or failing to consider recognized biases, when processing new scientific information.

B. How Science Works

1. Common research practices follow a step-by-step approach known as the scientific method.
   a. Observe an aspect of nature.

b. Research this aspect of nature, and then frame a question or problem relating to the observation.
c. Develop hypotheses (testable explanations) of the observed phenomenon or process.
d. Make a prediction of what the outcome would be if the hypothesis were valid (deductive, "if-then" reasoning).
e. Test predictions by experiments, models, and observations.
f. Any experimentation should involve changing only a single variable.
g. A control group where no variable is altered should be included in any experiment.
h. Assess the results of such tests.
i. Report objectively on the tests and conclusions.

1.7 Examples of Experiments in Biology

A. Potato Chips and Stomach Aches

1. A Chicago theater was chosen as a "laboratory" to determine if the synthetic fat called Olestra® caused gastrointestinal cramps.
2. Both control and experimental groups were random samples of moviegoers who had no idea which fat-impregnated chips they were eating.
3. Later, the moviegoers were called at home to determine the extent of gastrointestinal distress.
   a. The results were: 15.8 percent of people who consumed Olestra had discomfort vs. 17.5 percent that did not consume Olestra.
   b. As a result of this study, it does not appear that Olestra causes abdominal distress.

B. Butterflies and Birds

1. Researchers of peacock butterflies observed two actions.
   a. When a peacock butterfly rests, it folds its wings so only the dark underside shows.
   b. When a butterfly sees a predator, it repeatedly flicks its paired forewings and hindwings open and closed, a movement that both makes wingspots visible and produces hissing and clicking sounds.
2. Noises when predators approach—may help peacock butterflies avoid predation.
3. The combination of both activities—camouflage at rest and owl-like eyes (wingspots); ion experiments, in which experimenters manipulated the presence of wingspots or the ability to make the clicking and hissing sounds, revealed that birds are indeed deterred by peacock butterfly sounds, and even more so by wingspots.

1.8 Analyzing Experimental Results

A. Sampling Error

1. Research projects typically cannot survey an entire population and must instead rely on data collected from a subset of the population.
2. Sampling errors occur when conclusions inferred from the subset differ from results from the whole population.
   a. Sampling errors occur most often when sample sizes are small.
   b. Selecting a larger population subset or repeating the experiment many times may reduce sampling error.

B. Bias in Interpreting Results

1. It is often difficult to study the change in a single variable in human populations.
   a. For example, the participants in the Olestra study also varied in age, gender, health status, etc.
2. Researchers should use critical thinking skills to remove bias from their studies.

1.9 The Nature of Science

A. When the hypothesis of an experiment is proven via years of collecting evidence, it is called a scientific theory.

1. A scientific theory can be disproven by a single finding or observation.

B. A law of nature is an observed phenomenon for which there is no current scientific explanation.

C. The Limits of Science

1. Science does not address moral, spiritual, or supernatural events, or other intangibles.

a. Galileo was punished for supporting Copernicus' model of the solar system, as it was viewed as a violation of morality.

1.10 The Secret of Life of Earth (Revisited)

A. Over 100 million species exist on Earth today.

1. New species are still being discovered and classified each year.

Suggestions for Presenting the Material

- Although Chapter 1 is a general introduction to biology and to this textbook, it will be viewed very differently by instructor and student. For the instructor, this chapter is a *review* rather than a *preview.* That means the instructor must take extra care not to "intimidate" the students during early lectures by offering more terms and definitions than the student can reasonably absorb.
- A casual glance at the chapter contents will reveal terms unfamiliar to most students. These might include: *emergent properties, prokaryotic,* and *homeostasis.* Individual instructors should decide if these terms need explanation now or are to be deferred until later. This decision may depend on the time available.
- Figure 1.2 (levels of organization) is an excellent "road map" and can be used throughout the course to guide the progression along the organizational ladder. It can also be used in the exercise listed in the Enrichment section below.
- The diagram in Figure 1.3 (energy and nutrient movement in/around a system) also has relevance to future lectures. When introducing it here, you should stress the *flow* of *energy* through a system versus the *recycling* of nutrients and other *raw materials.*
- Sometimes students think the methods of scientific investigation in section 1.6 are used only by scientists. Show that this is not true by discussing the use of these methods in a routine investigation of "Why won't the car start?" (See the Enrichment section below.)
- Some students may think that the scientific method is the only way scientists conduct experiments. Give examples of natural history-based observational studies, or even discuss "The Human Genome Project"—both types of studies are very useful in today's world.
- Explain carefully the necessity for "control" groups in scientific investigations. Point out the difficulty of determining which groups of human patients will *not* receive a valuable drug (the controls) and who will receive a possibly life-saving medication.

Classroom and Laboratory Enrichment

- Generate interest in "discovery" science by showing a slideshow of animals and plants that have been discovered by scientists in the past five years. Examples may include: a horned toad (genus *Proceratophrys*) in Brazil (2008); a giant elephant-shrew called the gray-faced sengi (*Rhynchocyon udzungwensis*) in Tanzania (2008); the floral-banded wobbegong shark (*Orectolobus floridus*), discovered off the coast of Australia (2008); and the Togian white-eye bird (*Zosterops somadikartai*), discovered on a small Indonesian island (2008). A quick search of the internet for photos of these animals would provide much fodder for discussion.

- Bring several organisms into the classroom or lab and various nonliving things (e.g., rocks, candle with flame, even dirt). Ask your students to name characteristics that identify each item as living or nonliving (for some organisms, this may be difficult to do without specialized equipment, such as a microscope). Ask the students to identify equipment or experiments that would help to determine if an item is a living organism. Challenge them to think about how they would classify dirt—living or nonliving—and why.
- Obtain an overhead transparency of levels of organization in nature (Figure 1.2). With the labels of the figure covered, ask your students to help you name each higher level from simple to complex. You can also show the animation of this figure from the CD-ROM if you have computer links in your classroom.
- Select several transparencies from your collection that show a representative variety of plants, animals, and decomposers. Ask students to characterize them as *producer, consumer,* or *decomposer.* This can also be done in a PowerPoint slide presentation.
- Show the videotape *Life on Earth* by David Attenborough (available at retail outlets) as a general introduction to biological diversity.
- Take the time to discuss how scientific names were developed—with Latin as a basis—and present scientific names for local plants and animals that are well known to the students. Interpret the meaning of each Latin-specific epithet. An example would be the raccoon, *Procyon lotor*. The Latin translation means "early-dog" (*Procyon*: an ancestor of the dog) "swimming" (*lotor*: often found along waterways, often "plays" with its food in the water before eating it). A second example might be the house mouse, a common household pest. Its scientific name, *Mus musculus,* means "mouse tiny-mouse" or often translated as "thief tiny-thief," likely related to its ability to steal food from homes!
- Show a phylogenetic tree of vertebrates (or any other group of organisms for which a phylogenetic tree is available) to demonstrate the phylogenetic system of classification. Present students with a set of diverse organisms; ask them how they would classify these organisms. You can add as much detail in the classification as you prefer: grouped by domain, kingdom, phylum, or more. You may wish to hold off going to further levels of classification until students have gone through the diversity chapters and have a better feel for classification.
- Present fossil evidence showing how a group of related organisms or a single genus has evolved and changed through time (for example, the horse, *Equus*, and its ancestors show a complete fossil record).
- Briefly list the steps of the scientific method in the wrong order. Ask the class to place them, one by one, in the correct order.
- Show how we use the scientific method in everyday problem solving, as illustrated by this example:

Event		*Method Step*
a. .... Auto will not start	a.	Observation
b. .... Battery dead	b.	Hypothesis
...................................Ignition problem		Hypothesis
.... Out of gas		Hypothesis
c................................ Turn on headlights	c.	Experiment
...................................Check spark plug		Experiment
.....................................Check gas gauge		Experiment
.... Dip long stick into gas tank		Experiment

d. Headlights burn brightly (battery OK)	d.	Analyze results
.... Strong ignition spark		Analyze results
Gauge says half tank, but no gas on stick		Analyze results
e. Gas gauge is not accurate; car needs gas .... to run	e.	Generalize; form principle

- Present an observation to the class. Divide them into groups of three or four, and give them 10 minutes to devise an experiment, making sure they address each step of the scientific method. Example observations might include: 1) My cell phone does not work; 2) My bread gets moldy faster if I leave it on the counter, as opposed to placing it in the refrigerator; 3) It has rained more this year than it has in the previous five years.
- Present a number of hypotheses to your class, and have students determine if they are scientifically testable. Examples might include: 1) Coke tastes better than Pepsi (not testable, an opinion question); 2) All bats carry rabies (testable); 3) Fish take up oxygen from water through their skin (testable); 4) It snows more at the North Pole than at the South Pole (testable); 5) It is wrong for humans to keep pets on leashes (not testable, a moral/ethical question).

Classroom Discussion Ideas

- Why is it important that we taxonomically catalog all organisms that are discovered?
- Where would you like to travel to search for new organisms, and why?
- Why is "discovery" science, which often lacks standard hypotheses, just as important to biology as true experimental studies?
- Are discoveries of insects and plants less important, as important, or more important than discoveries of more charismatic animals, like birds and mammals?
- A carnivorous sponge was recently discovered near Antarctica—why might nature "select" for such an odd combination?

Additional Ideas for Classroom Discussion

- How does our modern definition of "life" differ from the definition of life that a seventeenth-century biologist might have used? Ask students if they would consider viruses to be "alive." Why or why not?
- What are some examples of homeostasis? Why must living organisms be able to maintain it?
- Human activities, like the use of tanning beds, can have direct effects on our DNA. For example, the concentrated UV rays from the tanning beds may cause mutations in our DNA. We know that mutations may lead to natural selection, the mechanism for evolution. So, is using a tanning bed good or bad for our species? Justify your answer.
- Can the plethora of shows about the supernatural or paranormal be considered scientific?
- Recently, an Australian ecologist suggested that scientific bias toward the cute, unique, or spectacular may be helping condemn a substantial portion of the world's plants and animals to extinction. Do you agree with this statement? Why or why not?
- Have your students list 10 random organisms (you can also do this). Identify ways in which all of the organisms are similar, then ways in which all of the organisms are different. How would you classify these organisms (that is, place into meaningful groups)?

- Why is it important for a species to be able to change? Wouldn't a species be more successful if it could be assured of remaining the same from one generation to the next? Can students relate this answer to current topics, like global warming or habitat fragmentation?
- Name some organisms you might find in a grassy area nearby. Using arrows, arrange the organisms in a diagram depicting energy flow and the cycling of materials (for help, see Figure 1.3). What are some organisms that may be invisible to the eye but are essential for the recycling of nutrients during decomposition?
- An animal carcass infested with insect larvae is not an attractive sight. Yet it is a biological necessity. Explore the role of these and other "recyclers."
- Humans are able to manipulate certain aspects of nature for their own benefit. However, it is often said that "humans are the only animals that engineer their own destruction." Give examples to support this allegation.
- How is a theory different from a truth? Does the use of "theory" in biology mean the concept is in doubt? Explain using examples.
- Why is it difficult to obtain a control group when selecting volunteers to test a new anticancer drug?
- A recent study estimated that the percentage of fabricated experimental data in biomedical scientific literature is 5–10 percent. What can we do as scientists to decrease this percentage and to "catch" the frauds who are publishing this material?

How Would You Vote? Classroom Discussion Ideas

- Monitor the voting for the online question. Divide the room into halves and ask each portion to argue for or against the idea of protecting endangered species before all areas of Earth are surveyed.

Term Paper Topics, Library Activities, and Special Projects

- Discover more about how the first cells are thought to have evolved. How do biologists "draw the line" between that which is living and that which is nonliving?
- Have students choose five animals or plants that interest them. Tell them to look up each scientific name and discern its English-translated literal meaning. Does the translation still describe the organism as it fits into today's world?
- Tell students to watch one 30-minute program on television this week. Have them keep track of every event in the show that depicts the scientific method being implemented.
- Tell students to watch 10 commercials this week. Have them keep track of every claim made about the products for sale. How many claims can be tested, and therefore supported or refuted, scientifically? How many cannot?
- The field of taxonomy is constantly changing. Describe how any one of several modern scientific investigative tools (such as electron microscopy, radioactive labeling, gas chromatography, gel electrophoresis, or polymerase chain reaction (PCR) techniques) has made it possible to discover similarities and differences among living organisms. Why can't we base taxonomic status on "looks" alone? Furthermore, how do these technologies affect our categorization of fossil specimens?
- The origin of life on this planet has always fascinated humankind. Several explanations have been advanced. Search for the principal ones that are still in contention today.

- The supply of easily obtainable energy sources is a matter of debate today. Some persons see a bleak future; others are optimistic. What issues do each of these camps see?
- Have the students think of other examples in history when individuals were punished due to their scientific beliefs.

Possible Responses to *Critical Thinking* Questions

1. The cells of a complex multicellular organism, such as a human, are specialized. This means that different cells develop functions that are unique to that cell type and contribute to the overall homeostasis of the organism. Therefore, if cells that relate to vital life-sustaining processes are destroyed, the organism may die.
2. In a single-celled organism, that one cell performs all of the functions necessary for the organism to successfully survive. This differs from an individual cell from a multicellular organism, since that cell may have a specialized function that depends highly on the functioning of other cells.
3. The specific epithet (species) is not unique, and gives no hint as to what type of organism is being described. This part of the scientific name is typically an adjective, perhaps describing where the organism was first discovered (e.g., *americanus* = America) or who discovered it (e.g., *Lepus townsendii*, the white-tailed jackrabbit, is named after a biologist named Townsend); but these names give no indication as to the type of organism or taxonomic status. (e.g., To whom is it most closely related? A bear? A fish? A sponge? A termite?)
4. Obviously, scientific research should not be eliminated. The "goodness" theory described by the turkey (?!?) appears to be a moral question, not one solely based on scientific observation—so it was never a true scientific theory from the start. Additionally, the evidence collected had a sample size equaling one turkey, certainly not representative of all turkeys (obvious sampling error) or of all organisms in the world.
5. It is disappointing to read about a peer-reviewed article that turns out to be a fraud. However, these cases appear very rarely. The positive side of this story is that, in science, experiments must be repeatable—and because no other labs could successfully repeat such an amazing feat, the fraud was quickly discovered.

Possible Responses to *Data Analysis Exercise* Questions

With all scientific experiments, it is necessary to run a control to insure the accuracy of your findings. In the experiment with the peacock butterflies, researchers were uncertain as to which characteristic frightened away birds: the large "eyes" on the wings, the noise made by fluttering the wings, or both. The butterflies in A had their wings painted so that no "eyes" were visible. The control population for this experiment was represented by D, in which the butterflies were painted but eyes were still visible. The butterflies in group B had wing "eyes," but the parts of the wings that make sounds were removed. The control group in this case was group E, because their wings were cut but not silenced. Finally, we have group C, in which the spots were painted and the wings were silenced. The control for this group was represented by letter F, and the butterflies used as a control had their wings painted yet "eyes" were visible. In addition, their wings were cut but not silenced. By exposing these different groups to their primary predator, the blue tit bird, accurate conclusions could be drawn.

2

LIFE'S CHEMICAL BASIS

Chapter Outline

Objectives

1. Understand how protons, electrons, and neutrons are arranged into atoms and ions.
2. Understand the properties of isotopes and how these properties can be useful to researchers.
3. Explain how the distribution of electrons in an atom or ion determines the number and kind of chemical bonds that can be formed.
4. Know the various types of chemical bonds, the circumstances under which each forms, and the relative strengths of each type.
5. Understand the essential chemistry of water and some common substances dissolved in it.
6. Discuss the unique properties of water that make it vital to living organisms.
7. Understand the pH scale and the relationships between acids, bases, and buffers.

Key Terms

atom	radioactive decay	ionic bond	temperature
protons	tracer	covalent bond	evaporation
neutrons	PET scan	double covalent bond	cohesion
electrons	orbital	triple covalent bond	hydrogen ions (H^+)
charge	shell model	nonpolar covalent bond	hydroxide ions (-OH)
nucleus	ion	polar covalent bond	pH
atomic number	free radical	polarity	acids, acidic
elements	electronegativity	hydrogen bond	bases, basic
isotopes	chemical bond	solvent	salt
mass number	molecule	solutes	buffer system
periodic table	compounds	hydrophilic	
radioisotopes	mixture	hydrophobic	

Lecture Outline

2.1 Mercury Rising

A. Mercury combines with carbon to form methylmercury.

1. Mercury in this form enters the tissues of fish and shellfish.
   a. Humans who consume organisms containing mercury may have adverse effects.
   b. The FDA recommends that ingested mercury levels not exceed 7 micrograms per day.

2.2 Start with Atoms

A. An atom is the smallest unit of matter that is unique to a particular element.

1. Atoms are composed of three subatomic particles.
   a. *Protons* (p^+) are part of the atomic nucleus and have a positive charge. Their quantity is called the atomic number (unique for each element).
   b. *Neutrons* are also a part of the nucleus; they are neutral. Protons plus neutrons = atomic mass.
   c. *Electrons* (e^-) have a negative charge. Their quantity is equal to that of the protons. They move around the nucleus.
2. Charge is an electrical property that attracts or repels other subatomic particles.
3. Elements consist only of atoms with the same number of protons in their nucleus.

B. The periodic table is an arrangement of elements based on their chemical properties.

1. The symbols for different elements are often derived from Greek or Latin words.
2. Elements are arranged based on their chemical properties.

C. Isotopes and Radioisotopes

1. Atoms with the same number of protons (for example, carbon with six), but a different number of neutrons (carbon can have six, seven, or eight), are called isotopes (^{12}C, ^{13}C, and ^{14}C).
2. Radioisotopes are unstable and break down while emitting radiation.
   a. Radioactive tracers can be used to monitor biological processes (e.g., using radioactive carbon to study photosynthesis in plants).
   b. Radioisotopes can be used to gather important medical information (e.g., PET scans).

2.3 Why Electrons Matter

A. Electrons and Energy Levels

1. Electron behavior influences atom bonding.
   a. Electrons are attracted to protons but are repelled by other electrons.
   b. Orbitals are like volumes of space around the atomic nucleus in which electrons are likely to be at any instant.
   c. Each orbital contains one or two electrons.

B. Orbitals can be thought of as occupying shells around the nucleus.

1. The shell closest to the nucleus has one orbital holding a maximum of two electrons.
2. The next shell can have four orbitals with two electrons each for a total of eight electrons.

C. About Vacancies

1. If an atom's outmost shell is filled, it is chemically stable and will not tend to interact with other atoms.
2. Atoms with "unfilled" orbitals in their outermost shell tend to be reactive with other atoms.
   a. Atoms with unfilled outer shells are called free radicals.
   b. Free radicals may be a health risk.
3. The number or distribution of its electrons changes when an atom gives up, gains, or shares electrons.
   a. Any atom with an unequal number of protons and electrons is called an ion.
   b. All ions carry a positive or negative charge.

2.4 Chemical Bonds: From Atoms to Molecules

A. A chemical bond is a union between the electron structures of atoms.

B. A molecule is a bonded unit of two or more (same or different) atoms.

C. A compound is a substance in which the relative percentages of two or more elements never vary.

D. Ionic Bonds

1. When an atom loses or gains one or more electrons, it becomes positively or negatively charged—an ion.
2. In an *ionic bond,* (+) and (–) ions are linked by mutual attraction of opposite charges—for example, NaCl.
    a. The term *polarity* refers to the separation of charge into positive and negative regions.
    b. Electronegativity refers to the atom's ability to obtain electrons from another atom.

E Covalent Bonding

1. A *covalent bond* holds together two atoms that share one or more pairs of electrons.
    a. Two atoms sharing one pair of electrons is a *single bond.*
    b. Two atoms sharing two pairs of electrons is a *double bond.*
    c. Two atoms sharing three pairs of electrons is a *triple bond.*
2. In a *nonpolar covalent bond,* atoms share electrons equally.
3. In a *polar covalent bond,* because atoms share the electron unequally, there is a slight difference in charge between the two poles of the bond; water is an example.
    a. Most covalent bonds are polar.

2.5 Hydrogen Bonds and Water

A. Hydrogen Bonding

1. In a *hydrogen bond,* an atom of a molecule interacts weakly with a hydrogen atom already taking part in a polar covalent bond.
2. These bonds impart structure to liquid water and stabilize nucleic acids and other large molecules.

B. Water's Special Properties

1. Water Has Cohesion
    a. Hydrogen-bonding of water molecules provides *cohesion* (capacity to resist rupturing), which imparts surface tension.
    b. Cohesion is especially important in pulling water through plants.
2. Water Stabilizes Temperature
    a. Water tends to stabilize temperature because it can absorb considerable heat before its temperature changes.
    b. In evaporative processes, the input of heat energy increases the molecular motion so much that hydrogen bonds are broken and water molecules escape into the air, thus cooling the surface.
    c. In freezing, the hydrogen bonds resist breaking and lock the water molecules in the bonding pattern of ice.
3. Water is an excellent solvent.
    a. The *solvent properties* of water are greatest with respect to the polar molecules with which they interact.
    b. Solvents are usually liquids and can dissolve other substances.
    c. Solutes are the substances that are dissolved.
    d. Solvents cluster around the solute (dissolved) molecules, keeping them separate.
    e. Polar substances are hydrophilic (water loving); nonpolar ones are hydrophobic (water dreading) and are repelled by water.

2.6 Acids and Bases

A. The pH Scale

1. pH is a measure of the H^+ concentration in a solution; the greater the H^+ the lower the pH value.
2. The scale extends from 0 (acidic) to 7 (neutral) to 14 (basic).

B. How Do Acids and Bases Differ?

1. A substance that releases hydrogen ions (H^+) in solution is an *acid*—for example, HCl.
   a. Products of combustion bring about a change in the pH of water in the atmosphere known as acid rain.
2. Substances that release ions (such as OH^-) that can combine with hydrogen ions are called *bases*—for example, NaOH.
3. The closer to 7 (neutral), the weaker the acid or base; the farther from 7 (neutral), the stronger the acid or base.

C. Buffers Against Shifts in pH

1. Buffer molecules combine with, or release, H^+ to prevent drastic changes in pH.
2. Bicarbonate is one of the body's major buffers.

2.7 Mercury Rising (Revisited)

A. It is estimated that the amount of mercury in the Pacific Ocean will double within the next 40 years.

1. Mercury can be found in humans, largely due to the ingestion of fish from the Pacific Ocean.

Suggestions for Presenting the Material

- There is no escaping the fact that Chapter 2 is chemistry. And chemistry can be intimidating — especially to non-science majors. The material in the book is elementary and written in a lucid manner, but the quality of presentation is up to the individual instructor.
- Perhaps a quick survey of class members who have and have not had high school chemistry will aid in adjusting your level of presentation. Students who took physical science in high school have also been exposed to basic chemical principles.
- One approach that might help your students in organizing this material is to write it in outline form on an overhead transparency or PowerPoint presentation. This may work especially well for this chapter because a large portion of the material consists of definitions.
- Stress the importance of learning biology from the smallest building blocks up. Living beings are more than the sum of their parts, so it is important to see how those "parts" arrange to form the basis for life. Use the example of a picture collage that takes thousands of small pictures of an object (like the space shuttle) to make a big picture of that same object.
- The use of ball-and-stick models (see the Enrichment section below) is very helpful. If the lecture room is large, you may have to "tour" the room with the models for better viewing or use a document camera to facilitate viewing for all students. Try using magnets to illustrate ionic bonding.
- Remind students frequently that atoms work to complete their outer electron shells. They accomplish this by bonding or by forming ions.
- If students become discouraged, assure them that several of these topics will be reinforced in future chapters (hopefully before the next exam). They need to understand the basic chemistry that drives cellular processes, and this information will help them. Tie future discussions in later chapters back to the basic principles of this chapter as much as possible.

- The text gives careful attention to useful examples of isotopes, electron excitation, bonding, buffers, and water.
- Use Figure 2.12 as your visual reference to help explain acid, base, and pH scale. Note particularly the pH values of common household products. Emphasize that acids and bases are not necessarily terms that describe *corrosive* substances! Point out the pH of the soda some students may be drinking (hopefully not in class!). Ask the students if they ever performed the childhood experiment where a tooth is left in soda for a few days or weeks to study the effects of the acids on tooth enamel.
- The properties of water are vital to life on Earth. After describing the polarity of water molecules, elaborate on the influence that water molecules have on cells and cellular environments. Tie the concepts to events that the students have likely experienced themselves. Use local examples (beach water temperature variance in the summer or fish survival through winter in a frozen-over pond) in discussing the properties of water.

Classroom and Laboratory Enrichment

- Students often approach even basic chemistry with considerable trepidation, especially if they lack sufficient high school background in this area or have been out of school for several years. Emphasize that studying biology includes studying chemistry, physics, math, etc. Explain how the lines between the scientific disciplines are now blurred. An elemental knowledge of chemistry is essential to understanding the structure and function of living things. Give students frequent opportunities to use new terms. Using overheads, diagrams, or PowerPoint presentations, pause often and interject questions to gauge their level of understanding.
- If you are teaching in a room with a "periodic table of the elements" hanging on the wall, point out the major elements, or use a diagram to show the same items. Refer back to the importance of filling the outer electron shells when forming molecules.
- Students frequently have trouble visualizing atoms and molecules as real entities. To help them get a clearer mental picture of some of the basic atoms and molecules, use ball-and-stick models that are very large and easy to see from the back of the room. These models will help students understand the size relationships among molecules. Overhead transparencies of ball-and-stick diagrams will also help. Such models and diagrams will be especially useful when covering the larger carbon compounds. You can also use foam-and-stick models of orbitals if you wish to emphasize electron orbitals.
- Marshmallows and inexpensive plastic straws or coffee stirrers may be used to have students make their own "molecules."
- Present sketches of polar covalent molecules and nonpolar covalent molecules. Ask students to identify which molecules are polar and which are nonpolar, and to explain their choices.
- Ball-and-stick models or a well-drawn diagram or slide, like the ones from the textbook in Figure 2.11, are also useful for demonstrating the hydrogen bonding that occurs between water molecules and the latticework structure of ice.
- Fill a large jar with water then add salad oil. Shake the bottle then allow it to sit on the front desk. Ask students to explain what has happened. Add a few drops of methylene blue (a polar dye) and sudan III fat stain (a nonpolar dye) to the jar and shake. Students will note that the water layer is blue and the oil layer is red; ask them why this is so.
- To help students connect the more inanimate "chemistry" from this chapter with living organisms, bring to class (season permitting) a pond water-filled jar with a live water strider or other surface-

tension dwelling aquatic insect, so students can see cohesion in biology in action. You can also show slides of these organisms as you discuss this property of water.

- Draw a pH scale on the board (or use an overhead transparency or slide of Figure 2.13), and discuss pH values of familiar substances.
- Cover a raw chicken egg with vinegar in a small cup or plastic container. After three or four days the weak acid (vinegar) will eat away the shell, leaving the cell membrane and egg contents intact. With care, one can handle the shell-less egg and illustrate how even weak acids must be buffered by living organisms.
- If your class is small, demonstrate the use of a pH meter. For larger groups, pH paper can be used to give each student a chance to quickly determine the pH of some sample solutions.
- Have students list common acids they consume on a regular basis. Salsa, lemonade, soda, etc. are common examples. Ask why and how antacids work to neutralize these substances.
- Lead a class discussion on why our digestive systems can withstand such wide variation in pH, whereas internal tissues cannot. List areas of the body that are commonly more acidic or basic and why: stomach, arterial blood, etc. Also emphasize the advantages of having an acidic environment in the stomach.
- Initiate a class discussion on acid rain. What is it? Is acid rain a problem where you live? Ask students to come up with a chemical formula for acid rain. What are some of the effects of this kind of precipitation?
- Prepare a glass of iced tea (instant mix) with added sugar and lemon. Ask students to identify which ingredients are compounds. What are the components of this mixture?
- Bring a package of "buffered" and "regular" aspirin to class. Ask students to discover the difference(s) in ingredients.
- Using the names of the active ingredients on an antacid package, explain how they act as *buffers* to stomach acid.
- You may wish to show *Atoms* (PBS, 1987, Video, 1 hour, *Ring of Truth Series*). Philip Morrison leads a tour through the atom, elaborating on its properties and the quest for proof of its existence. New techniques in electron microscopy can visualize atoms, and Quantum Theory outlines behaviors within the atom. Put a full jar of colored water on paper towels in front of the class. Ask several students to predict how many pennies can be added to the water before it overflows onto the paper towel. Most likely the students' guesses will be too low, since they may underestimate the cohesive properties of water. Show how the water bulges over the top of the jar before it spills.
- Illustrate how students can make their own pH indicator at home. Add several finely diced purple cabbage leaves to very hot water. Let the cabbage remain in the water for approximately one hour. Once you filter out the cabbage leaves, you are left with a purple liquid that acts as a simple pH indicator. Add various household substances (such as vinegar, tea, ammonia, oven cleaner, etc.) to small quantities of the liquid. The color changes (acids–pink, bases–green) are impressive. Have the students add buffered substances to a small sample of the liquid to see its effect.
- Design a Jeopardy-style quiz to test the students' knowledge of the chemistry terms in this chapter. A template for this format can be found at: http://jeopardylabs.com/.

Classroom Discussion Ideas

- Which food molecules are comprised of the main elements C, H, O, and N?
- What does the word "trace" mean when speaking of trace elements?
- The difference between a trace element being toxic and actually beneficial to the body is often a matter of __________.

- If humans are made of the same elements as are found in the earth and non-living things, what is it that makes us "alive"?
- Why is it important to understand the building blocks of molecules that form living things?
- Is it necessary for living things to have ALL these elements? Why is the combination so important?
- How is the handling of mercury different than it was in a past? How has the structure of thermometers changed? What substance has replaced mercury in dental fillings?

Additional Ideas for Classroom Discussion

- Distinguish between a compound and a mixture, an atom and a molecule.
- What chemicals are in the human body? Ask students to name as many as they can; help them complete their list.
- What is the difference between polar and nonpolar covalent bonds?
- Why do soft drinks have such a low pH? What ingredient is responsible for this low pH?
- Why is the insulating effect of frozen water so important to living organisms? What would happen to aquatic organisms living in temperate climates if water sank when it froze instead of floated?
- Lots of people go to the beach in the summer. Why is the water still very cool in early summer but still warm well into fall?
- What is the difference between the composition of a *molecule* of a substance and an *atom* of that substance?
- If atoms are beyond the reach of visualization even by "super" electron microscopes, how then do we know so much about their structure?
- Why is it important to understand both physics and chemistry when studying living things?
- How does the regular usage of the term "buffering the blow" relate to the function of buffers? Do both attempt to reduce drastic changes?
- Water is the "universal solvent" on Earth. Do you know of any other compound that would serve as well or better? If life existed on a remote waterless planet, could another substance replace it as an effective solvent?
- Some pain relievers are advertised as "tribuffered." Is this a real advantage or just a sales gimmick?
- Television commercials portray the "acid stomach" as needing immediate R-O-L-A-I-D-S®. Is the stomach *normally* acidic? How do you know when there is too much acid down there?
- There are different kinds of antacids—some work quickly and others work more slowly. Under what circumstances would you use each type of antacid?
- Why do alcohols dissolve in water?
- Why are some medications packaged in gel caps of mineral oil?
- What is the difference between methyl alcohol and ethyl alcohol? How is each of these alcohols processed by the human body?

How Would You Vote? Classroom Discussion Ideas

- Monitor the voting for the online question. Canvas the class to determine their opinions on the issue. Have some students in the class prepare a "warning statement" that could appear on tuna cans. Should the warning be aimed at just women of childbearing age or all populations? Research the literature to see if the effects of increased levels of mercury have been studied on varying ages of participants.

- If the class agrees that warning labels should be placed on tuna cans, are there other foods that should carry warning labels? Alcohol? Soda?
- What human activities could be curtailed to reduce mercury emissions? Should certain industries be targeted?

Term Paper Topics, Library Activities, and Special Projects

- How are hydrophobic substances such as fats broken down in the human digestive tract? What chemicals are released by the body to assist with fat breakdown?
- Why are the cells lining the stomach able to withstand pH ranges between one and two? What is an ulcer and why does it produce a burning feeling after eating?
- How does the body measure blood pH? What are the homeostatic mechanisms that help the human body regulate blood pH? Research causes, symptoms, and treatments for acidosis and alkalosis.
- Discuss strategies currently being considered by the United States and other nations to remedy acid precipitation. What suggestions would you make to help solve this problem?
- Describe some of the roles played by ions in the human body. Note: These ions may be referred to as electrolytes in a clinical setting.
- Why are buffers critical to maintaining homeostasis in living things? What happens when the capacity of a buffer is exceeded?
- How does conservation of temperature in large bodies of water on Earth affect weather? Does this same principle apply on a smaller scale in living things?
- How are different pH levels maintained in different places in the human body? Why are these pHs advantageous in certain areas of the body?
- Many elements have radioactive isotopes that are useful as tracers in biological systems. Show how $^{14}CO_2$ can be used to follow the fate of carbon as it is incorporated into carbohydrate. In addition, make the connection between thyroid studies and the use of radioactive iodine.
- The structure of atoms can be deduced using nuclear magnetic resonance (NMR) and mass spectrometer machines. Report on the principles underlying the performance of each of these instruments.
- Using a pH meter, test the degree of acidity/alkalinity of common household products. If the substance is not a liquid, mix it with water according to package directions before testing.
- Most of the content of human blood is water. However, synthetic blood has been made and tested. What is the base in this fluid? Is it a feasible substitute? Report on its advantages and disadvantages.
- Describe the effects of alcohol on the human body.

Possible Responses to *Critical Thinking* Questions

1. Lead and gold have different numbers of protons. To change the element, one must change the number of protons in each and every atom of the substance. It is impossible to change the number of protons by chemical means. Today physicists have the ability to add or remove

protons by extraordinary means, but this was not possible in ancient time. Also, lead is a very stable substance. Enticing lead to give up three protons would require a huge amount of energy, and the cost involved in doing this would far outweigh the profit realized from changing the lead into gold.

2.

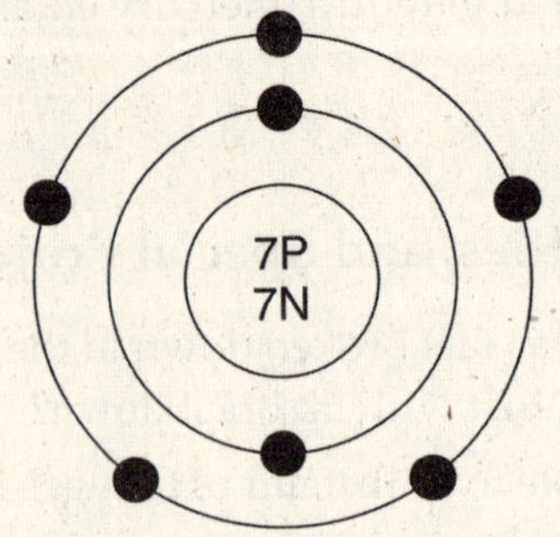

3. Polonium has a half-life of 138 days and decays to form ^{206}Pb (a stable form of lead) after emitting an alpha particle.

4. When an acid is mixed with water, it dissociates and becomes more reactive. Therefore, it is prudent to remove the majority of the acid before washing the area with water.

Possible Responses to *Data Analysis Exercise* Questions

Mercury emissions are a dangerous source of air pollution and are produced by various industries worldwide.

1. Approximately 2200 tons of mercury were released worldwide in 2006.
2. The source that released the most mercury was the combustion of fossil fuels, and the next greatest emissions resulted from artisanal and small-scale gold production.
3. Asia produced the most mercury from cement production.
4. Approximately 150 tons of mercury were released from South America in 2006 due to gold production.

3

MOLECULES OF LIFE

Chapter Outline

Objectives

1. Understand how small organic molecules can be assembled into large macromolecules by condensation. Understand how large macromolecules can be broken into subunits by hydrolysis.
2. Learn the functional groups presented and know the properties they confer when attached to other molecules.
3. Know how more complex carbohydrates are formed from simple monosaccharides.
4. Learn the structure of lipids and know the characteristics of fats, triglycerides, fatty acids (both unsaturated and saturated), phospholipids, waxes, and steroids.
5. Know the structure of proteins and how it obtains its shape.
6. Understand how proteins denature and can form prion diseases.
7. Learn how nucleotides make up the important nucleic acids, DNA and RNA.

Key Terms

organic
functional group
hydroxyl group
alcohols
methyl group
carbonyl group
carboxyl group
amine group
phosphate group
sulfhydryl group
metabolism
condensation
hydrolysis
monomers
polymers
hydrocarbon
carbohydrate
saccharide
reaction
sugar
monosaccharides
glucose
oligosaccharide
disaccharide
sucrose
polysaccharide
starch
cellulose
glycogen
chitin
lipids
fatty acid
fats
triglyceride
saturated fatty acids
unsaturated fatty acids
trans fats
phospholipid
lipid bilayers
waxes
steroids
cholesterol
estrogens
testosterone
proteins
amino acid
peptide bond
R group
polypeptide chain
primary structure
secondary structure
domain
tertiary structure
quaternary structure
globular proteins
hemoglobin
enzymes
glycoproteins
keratin
fibrous proteins
actin
myosin
heme group
globin chains
denature
prion
nucleotide
ATP
nucleic acids
RNA
DNA

Lecture Outline

3.1 Fear of Frying

A. Americans tend to consume much more fat than we need to remain healthy. "Super-sized" meals are common.
   1. This may explain why so many Americans are overweight.
   2. Obesity is a risk factor for many diseases and health conditions.

B. Fats are major constituents of cell membranes and contribute greatly to cell function. Cells require fats, but in appropriate amounts.

C. Fatty acids are typical fat molecules with three long carbon fatty acid "tails."
   1. Small amounts of trans fats are naturally found in red meat and dairy products.
   2. Hydrogenated fats are manufactured trans fats, which have been widely marketed and are consumed in the American diet.
   3. Cholesterol levels are increased rapidly by trans fats, particularly hydrogenated fats used as ingredients and in preparation of food.

D. Many diseases common to overweight Americans are caused by high consumption of hydrogenated fats.
   1. Arteriosclerosis is hardening of the arteries and may be caused by even small amounts of hydrogenated fats.
   2. Heart attacks are a possible result of atherosclerosis (plaque build-up) due to blockage of cardiac arteries.
   3. Diabetes is exacerbated by obesity.

3.2 Organic Molecules

A. Carbon—The Stuff of Life
   1. Oxygen, hydrogen, and carbon are the most abundant elements in living things.
      a. Carbon and hydrogen are primary constituents of the molecules of life—complex carbohydrates, lipids, proteins, and nucleic acids—all organic compounds.

b. Organic compounds were on Earth long before organisms, but can also be made in the laboratory. Organic compounds contain carbon and hydrogen.

2. The orientation of the atoms attached to a carbon backbone gives rise to the three-dimensional shape and functions of biological molecules.

B. Representing Structure of Organic Molecules

1. A ball-and-stick model depicts bonding of atoms; space-filling models convey a molecule's size and surfaces.

2. Larger molecules are best visualized using ribbon models, such as those generated by computer programs, and even more complex computer models that show local differences in electric charge across molecular surfaces.

3.3 Molecules of Life—From Structure to Function

A. Simple sugars, fatty acids, amino acids, and nucleotides are monomers, the building blocks of larger molecules.

1. Monomers may be joined to form polymers, or polymers may be broken down into monomers for a release of energy.

B. What Cells Do to Organic Compounds

1. Metabolism is cellular activity.

a. Energy is required for cellular reactions.

b. Metabolism requires enzymes to allow reactions to proceed quickly.

2. Enzymes are a special class of proteins that speed up chemical reactions but remain unchanged.

3. In a condensation reaction, one molecule is stripped of its H^+, another is stripped of its OH^-; then the two molecule fragments join to form a new compound, and the H^+ and OH^- form water.

4. Hydrolysis is the reverse: one molecule is split by the addition of H^+ and OH^- (from water) to the components.

C. Functional Groups

1. Functional groups are atoms or groups of atoms covalently bonded to a carbon backbone.

a. Common functional groups in biological molecules are hydroxyl, methyl, carbonyl, carboxyl, amino, phosphate, and sulfhydryl.

2. Functional groups convey distinct properties, such as solubility and chemical reactivity, to the entire molecule.

3.4 Carbohydrates

A. Carbohydrates are organic compounds made of carbon, hydrogen, and oxygen in a 1:2:1 ratio.

B. Carbohydrates in Biological Systems

1. Simple Sugars

a. Monosaccharides—one sugar unit—are the simplest carbohydrates.

b. They are characterized by solubility in water and have at least two ^-OH groups and one aldehyde or ketone group.

c. Ribose and deoxyribose (five-carbon backbones) are building blocks for nucleic acids.

d. Glucose (six-carbon backbone) is used by cells as instant energy.

e. Other important molecules derived from sugar monomers include glycerol and vitamin C.

2. Short-Chain Carbohydrates
   a. An oligosaccharide is a short chain of two or more sugar monomers.
   b. Oligosaccharides with three or more sugar monomers are attached as short side chains to proteins where they participate in membrane function.
   c. Disaccharides—two sugar units—are the simplest (e.g., sucrose {glucose + fructose} is the most plentiful sugar in nature).
3. Complex Carbohydrates
   a. A polysaccharide is a straight or branched chain of hundreds or thousands of sugar monomers.
   b. Starch is a plant storage form of energy, arranged as coiled chains, that is easily hydrolyzed to glucose units.
   c. Cellulose is a fiber-like structural material—tough, insoluble—used in plant cell walls.
   d. Glycogen is a highly-branched chain used by animals to store energy in the muscles and liver.
   e. Chitin is a specialized polysaccharide with nitrogen attached to the glucose units; it is used as a structural material in arthropod exoskeletons and fungal cell walls.

3.5 Greasy, Oily—Must Be Lipids

A. Lipids are nonpolar hydrocarbons that do not dissolve in water.
   1. A fatty acid is a long, unbranched hydrocarbon with a $^{-}COOH$ group at one end.
      a. *Unsaturated* fatty acids are liquids (oils) at room temperature because one or more double bonds between the carbons in the tails limit their flexibility.
      b. *Saturated* fatty acids have only single C–C bonds in their tails and are solids at room temperature.

B. Lipids in Biological Systems
   1. Fats have one, two, or three fatty acids attached to one glycerol molecule.
   2. Triglycerides, such as butter, lard, and oils, are the body's most abundant and richest source of energy and insulation.
      a. These lipids have three fatty acid tails attached to a molecule of glycerol.

C. Phospholipids
   1. Phospholipids have a glycerol backbone, two fatty acids, a phosphate group, and a small hydrophilic group.
   2. They are important components of cell membranes, where the hydrophilic heads face toward the inner and outer surfaces and the hydrophobic tails face inward (bilayer).

D. Waxes
   1. Waxes have long-chain fatty acids attached to long-chain alcohols or carbon rings.
   2. All are firm and repel water; examples include plant cuticles, bee honeycombs, and animal coverings.

E. Steroids
   1. Steroids have a backbone of four carbon rings, but no fatty acids.
   2. Cholesterol, the most common steroid, is found in the cell membranes of animals.
      a. Cholesterol can be modified to form sex hormones (testosterone and estrogen), bile salts, and vitamin D.

3.6 Proteins—Diversity in Structure and Function

A. Proteins function as enzymes, in cell movements, as storage and transport agents, as hormones, as anti-disease agents, and as structural material throughout the body.

B. From Structure to Function
   1. Amino Acids

a. Amino acids are small organic molecules with an amine group, an acid group, and one or more "R" groups.

2. Peptide Bonds
   a. Amino acids are joined in condensation reactions to form peptide bonds.
   b. Most enzymes are proteins.

C. The Structure-Function Relationship
   1. *Primary structure* is defined as the chain (polypeptide) of amino acids each linked together in a definite sequence by peptide bonds between an amino group of one unit and an acid group of another.
   2. *Secondary structure* is the helical coil or sheet-like array into which the polypeptide chain is formed by the interaction of hydrogen bonds, which join the side groups of the amino acids.
   3. *Tertiary structure* is the result of interactions among R groups that produce a complex three-dimensional shape, such as is found in globular proteins.
   4. *Quaternary structure* describes the interaction between two or more polypeptide chains.
   5. Some proteins form larger structures such as keratin in fingernails or actin and myosin in muscle cells.

3.7 Why Is Protein Structure So Important?

A. High temperatures or chemicals can cause the three-dimensional shape of proteins to be disrupted in an event known as denaturation.
   1. Normal protein function is lost upon denaturation, which is usually irreversible (e.g., cooking an egg).

B. Prion diseases result from misfolded proteins.
   1. Mad cow and Creutzfeldt-Jakob diseases are examples of prion diseases.

3.8 Nucleic Acids

A. Each nucleotide has a five-carbon sugar (ribose or deoxyribose), a nitrogen-containing base (single- or double-ringed), and a phosphate group.
   1. ATP (adenosine triphosphate) has three phosphate groups attached to its ribose sugar.
   2. ATP is a molecule that provides energy for cellular metabolism.

B. In nucleic acids, a covalent bond forms between the sugar of one nucleotide and the phosphate group of the next.
   1. DNA is double-stranded; genetic messages are encoded in its base sequences: adenine, guanine, cytosine, and thymine.
   2. RNA is single-stranded; it functions in the assembly of proteins based on the code in DNA.

3.9 Fear of Frying (revisited)

A. Processed foods often contain *trans* fatty acids.
   1. We can break down *cis* fatty acids, but have more difficulty with *trans* fatty acids.
   2. Unprocessed foods do not contain *trans* fatty acids, so they are a better food choice.

Suggestions for Presenting the Material

- It is valuable to point out that carbon, hydrogen, and oxygen are the principal atoms in the "molecules of life." Sulfur and nitrogen also participate in proteins and nucleotides.
- Your students will recognize the macromolecules in this chapter as major food groups. You can capitalize on this to generate student interest. Have the students research the ways these varying food groups are digested in the human body.

- The extent to which each instructor requires the learning of molecular structure will vary. Perhaps you will ask your students to be able to draw the molecules, but recognition will usually suffice for the student who is a non-science major.
- Make extensive use of the excellent overhead transparencies or slides available for this chapter. Soon your students will be able to recognize these molecules on sight.
- Note that "bad foods" may be good in certain situations. For example, dairy foods contain trans fat, but have huge benefits in providing calcium and other nutrients necessary for good health.
- Stress that "shape determines function." If a protein does not fold properly, it may not function properly (or at all) in the body.
- Carbohydrates are easy to describe because they are built by assembling monomers into polymers. Lipids are a more diverse group and will need to be defined according to *solubility* rather than *common structural features.*
- Proteins are complex because of: (a) their number of amino acid subunits, and (b) the levels of structure, that is, primary to quaternary. Use a string of beads and a Slinky® to help here (see the Enrichment section below).
- You can preview the future lecture(s) on protein synthesis by stating, "Amino acids are in a precisely defined sequence from one end of a protein to the other." How does the cell select, from the 20 amino acid choices, the proper one at the proper time? Perhaps this will whet the students' interest in the upcoming topic of protein synthesis. At this point, the more adept students may realize that the substitution of a different amino acid in the construction of a protein may have disastrous consequences.
- The *nucleotide* and *nucleic acid* section is only a preview of more extensive information found in Chapters 12 and 13. It is imperative that the students master some of these basic terms, such as nucleotides and nucleic acids, so that subsequent chapters will be more easily understood.
- Students usually recognize DNA and RNA as nucleic acids but may not realize that energy carrier molecules like ATP are also nucleic acids. Be sure to stress that nucleic acids have multiple functions.
- Some instructors may also want to include two more of the molecules of life, namely, *vitamins* and *minerals*. If so, these are discussed in Chapter 36.
- Once again stress the importance of Table 3.1 as a useful summary of the primary functional groups found in biological molecules.

Classroom and Laboratory Enrichment

- Show a video on "atoms and molecules" that will animate these.
- Use ball-and-stick models that are very large and easy to see to illustrate some of the basic carbon compounds. Overhead transparencies of ball-and-stick diagrams or "straight-stick" line drawings will also help students get a mental picture of each molecule.
- Use models, diagrams, or transparencies to demonstrate the functional groups you wish to emphasize. Stress the importance of knowing several characteristic functional groups by identifying those functional groups present in diagrams or models of real molecules.
- To illustrate amino acid structure, draw a generalized amino acid stem (as shown in Figure 3.14 but with an empty spot at the R-group location) on an overhead transparency. Create different amino acids by changing the R groups, each sketched on a small piece of transparency material.
- Use the analogy of a Swiss army knife to illustrate how different functional ("R") groups determine the use of a protein even though the basic structure remains the same.

- Show a ball-and-stick diagram or three-dimensional model of any protein. An enzyme would be a good example; ball-and-stick diagrams of enzymes are readily available. Students will be amazed at the large size of proteins when compared to carbohydrates and lipids.
- Protein *primary structure* can be demonstrated by a string of beads or a Christmas tree garland. Individual beads can be colored with felt-tip markers for greater clarity and distinction. Secondary structure (alpha helix) is adequately illustrated by use of a Slinky®. You can demonstrate tertiary structure by *carefully* folding a portion of the "expanded" Slinky. Even quaternary structure can be visualized by using two (or more?) Slinkies.
- Show the students the amino acid sequence of an important protein in the human body, insulin. Mention that a diabetic patient must administer insulin as an injection, because stomach acids would denature the protein structure.
- Slip a rubber band over two pencils then twist the pencils in opposite directions. As the rubber band coils and then coils on top of itself, make the analogy to the levels of protein structure.
- Students have been exposed to many words related to the ones in this chapter, whether in print or broadcast media. Use this opportunity to explain complex carbohydrates, polyunsaturated fats, cholesterol, fiber, high-fructose syrup, dextrose, anabolic steroid, and no- or low-carb diets.
- Select a variety of food products from your pantry and bring them to class. Ask students to check the ingredients list for forms of sugar. Can they find it in some very unlikely places, such as table salt or ketchup? Have students keep a food log for several days. Can they successfully categorize the major foods they have eaten according to the divisions studied in this chapter? Would they categorize any of these food choices as unhealthy based on the information reviewed in this chapter? What substitutions could be made?
- Help students understand nucleotide structure with models or diagrams. If students can get a good grasp of nucleotides now, they will have a better understanding of ATP and nucleic acids when these topics are covered in later chapters.

Classroom Discussion Ideas

- Your parents and grandparents very likely ate many trans fats as they were growing up. Is today's typical diet so different? How so, and should this be a concern?
- Modern technologies have allowed us to quantify amounts of trans fats in food very accurately. Is this being used to improve diets or as scare tactics to promote the health-food industry?
- If governmental agencies weren't watching, do you think fast-food establishments would voluntarily cease using trans fats or follow the least expensive route?
- Consider the benefits of trans fat foods such as red meats and dairy products. Are there dangers in limiting these foods in different age groups, such as in children? Benefits?

Additional Ideas for Classroom Discussion

- What happens if the proteins that form enzymes are misshapen? How is this like a key in a lock?
- Research some diseases where an amino acid substitution takes place, such as sickle-cell anemia. What are the consequences?
- Researchers have discovered an inappropriate protein in the muscles of patients with muscular dystrophy. Read up on this development and discuss its implications.
- Compare the calorie contents of carbohydrates, lipids, and proteins.
- Why do alcohols dissolve in water?

- What is the difference between methyl alcohol and ethyl alcohol? How is each of these alcohols processed by the human body?
- What is a complex carbohydrate?
- Why don't animal cells contain cellulose? Can you think of at least one reason why cellulose in an animal cell could be considered a drawback?
- Why are saturated fatty acids solid at room temperature while unsaturated fatty acids are liquid?
- What is the difference between a globular protein and a fibrous protein?
- Why is sugar (in various forms) so prevalent as an additive in our packaged food products?
- Which yields more energy, a pound of carbohydrate or a pound of fat?
- Cellulose and starch both consist of chains of glucose units. One is a useful source of energy to humans, the other is not. Identify which is which and why they differ.
- Where is glycogen stored in the human body? What regulates interconversions of glucose and glycogen?
- Steroid misuse is often in the headlines in relation to sports figures and celebrities. Have the students discuss the important functions of steroids in the human body.
- Television advertising implies that the ideal diet would include *zero* carbohydrates. Is this feasible? Would it even be *desirable*? What about the health benefits of a *no*-carb diet?
- A common adage is "everything in moderation." How has the current American fast-food industry modified our expectation of proper quantities in meals?
- Why are canned foods usually high in sodium? How does high sodium affect the body?
- Why do athletes eat high carbohydrate meals before they perform?
- Discuss the effects of nutritional deficiencies on the body. Why is a balanced diet so critically important?
- The term *cholesterol* has a negative connotation in the minds of the typical American. Although we want to keep serum cholesterol values in check, discuss how cholesterol participates in the development of steroid hormones.
- Prepare a Jeopardy-style template based on the information presented in this chapter (http://jeopardylabs.com/). Some of the categories for the questions could be proteins, carbohydrates, lipids, nucleic acids, etc.

How Would You Vote? Classroom Discussion Ideas

- Monitor the voting for the online question. Have the students participate in a lively debate on the positive and negative aspects of limiting the amount of trans fats in the American diet.
- Do the students in your classroom feel that foods containing large amounts of trans fats should be packaged with a warning label? If so, what deleterious conditions could occur due to the ingestion of large amounts of trans fats? Would the trans fats be detrimental to some populations more than others? Should places such as school cafeterias restrict items containing large amounts of trans fats from their diets?
- Do you feel that additional legislation is necessary? Should foods containing large quantities of trans fats be banned? Do any of your students feel this would be a violation of their individual rights?

Term Paper Topics, Library Activities, and Special Projects

- How are hydrophobic substances such as fats broken down in the human digestive tract? What chemicals are released by the body to assist with fat breakdown?
- Describe the effects of alcohol on the human body.
- How are termites able to digest wood products?

- How is the digestive system of a cow designed to digest a plant-based diet?
- Where are the enzymes that facilitate digestion produced? List the common enzymes for digestion of carbohydrates, proteins, and fats and which organs contribute to these processes.
- What is aspartame? How is it processed by the body? Describe studies that have been done regarding its safety as a food additive.
- What is dietary fiber? Describe its possible role as an anticarcinogen.
- What is Olean©? Why is this being marketed as a healthy alternative to foods high in fats and oils? How is Olean processed by the body?
- How does the dietary aid Alli® reduce the amount of fat absorbed?
- Why do women have a higher percentage of body fat than men do? Can you think of any adaptive value for this characteristic?
- Discuss the role of cholesterol in the diet. Approximately what percentage of your cholesterol level is controllable through diet?
- Describe how scientists discovered the structure of hemoglobin.
- Search the "body building" magazines currently available for diet supplement advertising that might be misleading or outright false. Report on the distortions you find.
- Prepare a history report on the cultivation and use of plant fibers (cellulose) from various sources in the construction of clothing.
- After searching for background information on the extent and variety of steroid use by athletes, interview persons who can give a "local and inside" perspective. Can you document any damage to heavy users?
- How is "super-sizing" of American meals affecting cholesterol levels in the body? Why is this a health risk? Have a student view the movie "Supersize Me" and give a report to the class.

Possible Responses to *Critical Thinking* Questions

1. One would accurately predict that the phospholipids would be on the outside of the lipoprotein clump. The phospholipids are well-suited to this function because they are amphipathetic (having both a polar and non-polar end). The polar portion, which is hydrophilic, faces outward so that it is compatible with the surrounding watery environment.
2. Since the literature from experimental studies states that 92.8 percent of the sucralose passes through the body unchanged, it does not appear that significant quantities of chlorine would be released. In addition, toxicity is unlikely because chlorine is highly reactive and a major element in sodium chloride (NaCl), or salt. Living things are mostly saltwater, so any small amount of chlorine from the sucralose would likely be bound to sodium very quickly. Additionally, it would take massive amounts of sucralose consumed on a daily basis to release enough chlorine to even be noticeable.

Possible Responses to *Data Analysis Exercise* Questions

The two densities of lipoproteins react differently in the body. High-density lipoproteins (HDL) carry cholesterol to the liver for disposal, but the cholesterol transported by the low-density lipoproteins (LDL) tends to accumulate in arteries as plaque.

1. The LDL was highest from the group that consumed 10 percent saturated fats.
2. The HDL was lowest in the individuals that consumed 10 percent *trans* fatty acids.
3. The group with the highest LDL-to-HDL ratio is the experimental group that consumed 10 percent of their diet as *trans* fatty acids.
4. The diets, ranked from best to worst, are: *cis* fatty acids, saturated fats, and *trans* fatty acids.

4

CELL STRUCTURE AND FUNCTION

Chapter Outline

Objectives

1. Understand the basic tenets of the cell theory.
2. Understand the implications of how the surface-to-volume ratio constrains cell size.
3. Contrast the general features of prokaryotic and eukaryotic cells.
4. Be able to distinguish the organelles and structures typical of eukaryotic plant and animal cells.
5. Describe the nucleus of eukaryotes with respect to structure and function.
6. Describe the organelles associated with the endomembrane system, and tell the general function of each.
7. Contrast the structure and function of mitochondria and chloroplasts.
8. List several surface structures of cells and tell how they help cells survive.
9. Describe the cytoskeleton of eukaryotes and distinguish it from the endomembrane system.

10. Discuss the various mechanisms that enable a cell to move.
11. Describe the structure and functions of the three types of cell junctions.
12. List the properties possessed by all living things.

Key Terms

bacteria
animalcules
cell theory
cell
eukaryotic cell
prokaryotic cells
plasma membrane
nucleus
nucleoid
cytoplasm
ribosomes
surface-to-volume ratio
lipid bilayer
phospholipids
phase-contrast microscope
fluorescence microscope
wavelength
compound light microscope
transmission electron microscope
scanning electron microscope
prokaryotes
domain Bacteria
domain Archaea
cell wall
flagella
pili, pilus
cyanobacteria
biofilms
plasmid
organelle
nucleus
nuclear envelope
nucleoplasm
nucleolus
chromatin
chromosomes
endomembrane system
endoplasmic reticulum
rough ER
smooth ER
vesicles
peroxisomes
vacuoles
Golgi bodies
lysosomes
mitochondrion
plastids
chloroplasts
photosynthesis
stroma
thylakoid membrane
chromoplasts
amyloplasts
central vacuole
primary wall
secondary wall
lignin
cuticle
extracellular matrix
cell junctions
plasmodesmata
tight junctions
adhering junctions
gap junctions
cytoskeleton
microtubules
microfilaments
cell cortex
myosin
actin
intermediate filaments
motor proteins
eukaryotic flagella
cilia
9+2 array
centriole
basal body
pseudopods

Lecture Outline

4.1 Food for Thought

A. Bacteria are found in nearly every environment on Earth.

B. *Escherichia coli* is a common intestinal bacteria in warm-blooded animals.
   1. Most are not harmful to humans.
   2. Strain O 157: H7 is harmful to humans.
      a. This strain is not harmful to most animals raised for human consumption.
      b. O 157: H7 sticks to and contaminates meat during grinding in meat processing.
      c. Cooking meat to at least 160°F destroys the bacteria.

C. Food contamination outbreaks are costly on many levels.
   1. People die of complications from food contamination.
   2. Recall of potentially-contaminated foods costs growers millions of dollars.
   3. Recent outbreaks have prompted testing for pathogens before sale.

4.2 Cell Structure

A. The cell is the smallest unit with the properties of life: metabolism, response to environment, growth, and reproduction.

B. Components of All Cells
   1. A plasma membrane separates each cell from the environment, permits the flow of molecules across the membrane, and contains receptors that can affect the cell's activities.
   2. A nucleus or nucleoid region localizes the hereditary material, which can be copied and read.
   3. The cytoplasm contains membrane systems, particles (including ribosomes), filaments (the cytoskeleton), and a semifluid substance.
   4. DNA: within a nucleus in eukaryotes and directly in the cytoplasm in prokaryotes.

C. Constraints of Cell Size
   1. Cell size is constrained by the surface-to-volume ratio.
      a. If a cell expands in diameter during growth, its volume will increase more rapidly than its surface area will.
      b. A cell that is too large will not be able to move materials into and out of the cell interior.
   2. The smaller the cell, the more efficiently materials cross its surface and become distributed through the interior.

D. Cell Theory
   1. Early observations revealed an unseen world.
      a. Leeuwenhoek observed several types of living cells.
      b. Robert Hooke saw small compartments in cork, which he named cells.
      c. Robert Brown identified a plant cell nucleus.
      d. Schleiden and Schwann proposed the idea that all living things are composed of cells.
      e. Virchow concluded that all cells come from cells.
   2. These observations and many others led to the cell theory.
      a. All organisms are composed of one or more cells.
      b. The cell is the smallest unit having the properties of life.
      c. The continuity of life arises directly from the growth and division of single cells.

4.3 How Do We See Cells?

A. Research with modern microscopes supports the three generalizations of the cell theory.

B. Microscopes use waves of light to make images.
   1. Compound light microscopes use two or more sets of glass lenses to enlarge cells.
      a. Phase microscopes utilize various stains to visualize internal parts of a cell.
      b. Fluorescence microscopes use a laser beam to measure energy emitted from a cell.
   2. Transmission and scanning electron microscopes (TEM and SEM) use magnetic lenses to bend and diffract beams of electrons to resolve details that are 100,000 times smaller than seen with light microscopes.
      a. TEMs pass electrons through the specimen to provide images of internal details.
      b. SEMs direct a beam of electrons back and forth across a surface of a metal-coated specimen, causing electrons and x-rays to be emitted that are converted to an image of the specimen's surface.

4.4 Introducing "Prokaryotes"

A. Prokaryotes are the smallest known cells and are the most metabolically diverse forms of life on Earth.

B. Two domains of prokaryotes exist: Bacteria and Archaea.

1. The term *prokaryotic* ("before the nucleus") indicates the existence of bacteria before evolution of cells with a nucleus.
   a. A somewhat rigid cell wall supports the cell and surrounds the plasma membrane, regulating transport into and out of the cell.
   b. Sticky polysaccharides help cells attach to surfaces, such as teeth.
   c. Bacterial flagella project from the membrane and permit rapid movement; pili filaments aid in attachment to surfaces.
   d. Many bacterial species have plasma membrane infoldings embedded with photosynthetic machinery, as do the cyanobacteria.
   e. Ribosomes (protein assembly sites) are dispersed throughout the cytoplasm.
   f. The bacterial chromosome is a single circular DNA molecule; other smaller circles of DNA called plasmids are present in some bacteria.

C. Biofilms
1. A biofilm occurs when single-celled organisms share a layer of polysaccharides and glycoproteins.
   a. Most biofilms are combinations of multiple species intertwined together.
   b. Microenvironments within the biofilm support the different species of the community.
2. Biofilms form as different species sense the presence of other species.
   a. Conditions must be right to support formation of the biofilm and to maintain the different species within the community.
   b. When conditions are not conducive to forming a biofilm, the different cells separate and live independently.

4.5 Introducing Eukaryotic Cells

A. Eukaryotic cells (true nucleus) are larger and generally more complex, with a nucleus and other membrane-bound organelles.
B. Interactions between organelles keep cells functioning and metabolizing.
C. Typical organelles in eukaryotic cells include the nucleus, ribosomes, and a cytoskeleton; specialized cells contain additional organelles specific to cellular function.
D. Plant cells contain many of the same organelles as animal cells. Organelles specific to plant cells include the cell wall, chloroplasts, and a central vacuole.
E. Centrioles are specific to animal cells and are important in cell division.

4.6 The Nucleus

A. Nuclear Envelope
1. A *nuclear envelope* (double-membrane) encloses the semifluid interior of the nucleus, called *nucleoplasm*.
2. The outer surface of the nucleus is loaded with pores, which serve as gateways in or out of the cell.

B. Nucleolus
1. Located within the nucleus, the *nucleolus* appears as a darker globular mass where subunits of ribosomes are prefabricated before shipment out of the nucleus.
2. Every nucleus has at least one nucleolus, which is responsible for producing the large and small subunits of ribosomal RNA.

C. The DNAs
1. *Chromatin* refers to the cell's total collection of DNA and associated proteins.
2. A *chromosome* is a double-stranded DNA molecule and its associated proteins.

4.7 The Endomembrane System

A. A Series of Interacting Vessels

1. Endoplasmic Reticulum (ER)
   a. The endoplasmic reticulum is a collection of interconnected tubes and flattened sacs that begin at the nucleus and ramble throughout the cytoplasm.
   b. There are two types, distinguished by the presence or absence of ribosomes.
      i. *Rough ER* consists of stacked, flattened sacs with many ribosomes attached; oligosaccharide groups are attached to polypeptides as they pass through on their way to other organelles or to secretory vesicles.
      ii. *Smooth ER* has no ribosomes; it is the area from which vesicles carrying proteins and lipids are budded; and it also inactivates harmful chemicals.
2. Vesicles
   a. Vesicles are commonly used by the cell as transporters to and from the plasma membrane.
   b. *Peroxisomes* are vesicles containing enzymes that break down fatty acids and amino acids; the hydrogen peroxide released is degraded by another enzyme.
   c. Animal cells have *vacuoles* to house debris and toxic materials within the cell.
   d. The *central vacuole* of mature plant cells accumulates a watery solution of ions, amino acids, sugars, and toxic substances.
3. Golgi Bodies
   a. In the *Golgi bodies*, proteins and lipids undergo final processing, sorting, and packaging.
   b. The membranes of the Golgi are arranged in stacks of flattened sacs whose edges break away as vesicles.
   c. *Lysosomes* are vesicles that bud from Golgi bodies; they carry powerful enzymes that can digest the contents of other vesicles, worn-out cell parts, or bacteria and foreign particles.

4.8 Lysosome Malfunction

A. *Tay-Sachs* disease is caused by a nonfunctional enzyme responsible for ganglioside breakdown, a lipid that accumulates around nerve cells when breakdown fails.

B. Infants with *Tay-Sachs* begin showing symptoms at about 6 months of age and rarely live five years.

C. *Tay-Sachs* disease is more common in Jews of Eastern European descent and currently is incurable.

4.9 Other Organelles

A. Mitochondria

1. Mitochondria are the primary organelles for transferring the energy in carbohydrates to ATP under oxygen-plentiful conditions.
2. Each mitochondrion has two membranes, an inner folded membrane (*cristae*) surrounded by a smooth outer membrane.
3. Inner and outer compartments formed by the membranes are important in energy transformations.
4. Mitochondria resemble bacteria in size and biochemistry.
   a. Like bacteria, they have their own DNA and divide on their own apart from the cell.
   b. They have ribosomes.
   c. Endosymbiosis is a theory that explains that mitochondria may have once been independent ancient prokaryotic cells that were engulfed by another cell but became permanent, remaining with the host cell as an endosymbiont.

B. Plastids

1. Plastids (chloroplasts, chromoplasts, amyloplasts) are important for storage in plants and in photosynthesis.
2. Chloroplasts are oval or disk-shaped organelles bounded by a double membrane and specialized for photosynthesis.
   a. In the innermost membrane, stacked disks (*thylakoids*), pigments, and enzymes trap sunlight energy to form ATP and NADPH.
   b. Sugars and starches are formed in the fluid substance (stroma) surrounding the stacks.
   c. Pigments such as chlorophyll (green) confer distinctive colors to the chloroplasts.
   d. Chloroplasts are like photosynthetic bacteria and may have evolved through endosymbiosis, like mitochondria.
3. Chromoplasts store red and brown pigments that give color to flowers, autumn leaves, fruits, and roots.
4. Colorless amyloplasts lack pigments, store starch grains, and are abundant in stem cells, tubers, and seeds.

4.10 The Dynamic Cytoskeleton

A. Components of the Cytoskeleton

1. The cytoskeleton of eukaryotic cells forms an interconnected system of bundled fibers, slender threads, and lattices that extends from the nucleus to the plasma membrane.
2. The main components are microtubules, microfilaments, and intermediate filaments—all assembled from protein subunits that give cells their internal organization, shape, and capacity to move.

B. Microtubules

1. Microtubules, the largest structural elements in the cytoskeleton, are composed of long, hollow tubulin cylinders; they are responsible for the movement of chromosomes during cell division.
2. Microtubules of animal cells grow in all directions from the anchoring centrosomes and are not permanent structures, assembling and disassembling when needed.

C. Microfilaments

1. Microfilaments, the thinnest elements, consist of two helically twisted polypeptide chains assembled from actin monomers.
2. Microfilaments are particularly important in movements that take place at the cell surface; the cell cortex contributes to the shape of animal cells.
3. Cytoplasmic streaming proceeds as microfilaments loosen, causing local gel-like regions to become more fluid and flow strongly, which then causes substances and cell components to be redistributed within the cell.

D. Intermediate Filaments

1. Intermediate filaments are the most stable of the cytoskeleton elements
2. Their primary functions are to reinforce membranes and add structure to the cell.

E. Cilia, Flagella, and False Feet

1. Both flagella and cilia are motile structures that extend from the surface of many cells and are completely sheathed by an extension of the plasma membrane.
   a. Cilia are short and numerous, and provide locomotion for free-living cells or may move surrounding water and particles if the ciliated cell is anchored.
   b. Flagella are quite long, not usually numerous, and are found on one-celled protists and animal sperm cells.
2. Microtubular extensions of the plasma membrane have a 9 + 2 cross-sectional array that arises from a centriole extending below the array as a basal body.

3. Pseudopods (false feet) are temporary lobes that project from the cell, used in locomotion and food capture.

4.11 Cell Surface Specializations

A. Matrices Between and Around Cells

1. The extracellular matrix (ECM) between animal cells includes cell secretions and materials drawn from the surroundings between cells.
2. Cell walls are carbohydrate frameworks for mechanical support in bacteria, protistans, fungi, and plants; cell walls are not found in animals.
   a. In growing plant parts, bundles of cellulose strands form a primary cell wall that is pliable enough to allow enlargement under pressure.
   b. Later, more layers are deposited on the inside of the primary wall to form the secondary wall.
3. Lignin composes up to 25 percent of the secondary wall in woody plants; it makes plant parts stronger, more waterproof, and less inviting to insects.
4. Cell secretions form a protective covering in plants called *cuticle* that functions to reduce water loss and protect exposed surfaces.

B. Cell Junctions

1. In plants, tiny channels called plasmodesmata cross the adjacent primary walls and connect the cytoplasm.
2. Animal cells display three types of junctions.
   a. *Tight junctions* occur between cells of epithelial tissue in which cytoskeletal strands of one cell fuse with strands of neighboring cells, causing an effective seal.
   b. *Adhering junctions* are like spot welds at the plasma membranes of two adjacent cells that need to be held together during stretching, as in the skin and heart.
   c. *Gap junctions* are small, open channels that directly link the cytoplasm of adjacent cells.

4.12 The Nature of Life

A. Properties of living organisms.

1. Make and use organisms of life.
2. Made of one or more cells.
3. Undergo processes such as metabolism and homeostasis.
4. Grow and change throughout their lifetime.
5. Utilize DNA.
6. Can evolve by adapting to their environment.

4.13 Food for Thought (Revisited)

A. Much of our food is sterilized to kill *E. coli* bacteria.

1. Some sterilization involves exposure to chemicals.
2. Irradiation is also used as a sterilization procedure in foods.

Suggestions for Presenting the Material

- For many readers, Chapter 4 represents the true entry into the realm of biology. A discussion of the cell is fundamental to all future lectures.
- Often students entering into the healthcare fields have a difficult time understanding the relevance of cellular physiology to their studies. Be sure to stress that some diseases, such as Tay-Sachs disease, occur on the cellular level.
- Because of the extent of knowledge concerning the cell, it is impossible to include all of it in one chapter. Therefore, Chapter 4 presents an overview that includes a fair amount of cell part de-

scription and a glimpse of functions, the details of which are explained in several successive chapters.

- Most students are familiar with *E. coli* contamination in hamburger or spinach from recent events reported in the media. Research the literature to investigate the causes of these deadly contamination events. Were most of these outbreaks traced back to a particular farming or food preparation facility? This is a good way to discuss the ubiquitous nature of bacteria.
- This is also an excellent time to review the use of the word *theory* as explained in Chapter 1.
- A clear distinction between prokaryotic and eukaryotic cells should be made (see the Enrichment section below for visual aid suggestion). Additional details on prokaryotes are contained in Chapter 21.
- As you begin the litany of cell organelles, use the overhead or slide of Figure 1.2 (the "road map") to remind students of the progress they are making.
- Although the descriptions and diagrams of the cell organelles occupy only a small number of textbook pages, it is best to proceed carefully and deliberately. There is a dizzying array of unfamiliar terms here.
- It's helpful to make the analogy that organelles are like the different departments/agencies within a town. Not all the organelles will fit into this analogy, but it makes the point that each organelle has a function in the overall workings of the cell as a whole.
- When describing each cell structure, a visual representation of some type should be constantly in view of the students. Each time a new cell part is introduced, Figure 4.12a or 4.12b should be shown for reference purposes to help students visualize where the organelle belongs within the cell.
- Stress the fact that several cell parts are so complex in function that greater detail will follow in future lectures. Examples and chapters are: cell membranes in Chapter 5, chloroplasts in Chapter 7, mitochondria in Chapter 8, and nucleus and chromosomes in Unit II.

Classroom and Laboratory Enrichment

- In the lab, students can view what Robert Hooke saw by looking at cork cells under a microscope. Explain that what they are seeing is the dead cell walls of the cork plant. They can also look at a small *Elodea* leaf to view the chloroplasts, nucleus, and a few other plant cell features. Place the leaf in a small drop of distilled water on a microscope slide. Cover it with a cover slip. Now prepare a second slide, only this time mounting an *Elodea* leaf in a drop of 10 percent NaCl solution. Compare the cells of the second slide to those of the first slide.
- Have the students examine common representative cells with different magnification levels. Which magnification strength is best for viewing the cellular structures? Do the students know how to calculate the magnification of a light microscope?
- The students should familiarize themselves with Table 4.1. Name some common objects and decide if they could be best measured using meters, centimeters, millimeters, micrometers, or nanometers.
- Use sketches or models drawn to scale to demonstrate the size difference between prokaryotic and eukaryotic cells.
- Show an overhead transparency or slide of a diagram or an electron micrograph of any cell. Ask if the cell is prokaryotic or eukaryotic. Is it an animal cell? A plant cell? Some other type of cell? How can they tell?
- Ask students to match "organelle" with "cellular task" at the board or on an overhead.
- If you present the historical sketch of the cell theory, include slides of the researchers you are discussing. These photos can usually be found in a variety of introductory biology texts or special texts on the history of biology, as well as with any Internet search engine.

- Construct a table (overhead or handout) listing side-by-side comparisons of prokaryotic and eukaryotic cells.
- Most departments possess some type of cell model. These are especially helpful in perception of the 3-D aspects of cell structure. They can also be useful in oral quizzing.
- Arrange for students to see an electron microscope and learn about specimen preparation and the operation of the microscope.
- If you have access to electron micrographs generated by your colleagues, bring some to class to pass around, or prepare 2x2 transparencies. Students will be impressed by the "home grown" aspect of these micrographs.
- Show a video or slide/sound set that reviews cell structures and functions.
- Have the students match each organelle to its function in plant and/or animal cells. For those organelles found only in a plant or animal cell, discuss why that organelle is only necessary in that one type of cell.
- Design a Jeopardy-type grid to ensure that the students have mastered the specific functions of the components of the cell (http://jeopardylabs.com/)

Classroom Discussion Ideas

- What are the benefits of irradiated meats being sold in supermarkets? What might be some risks?
- How would you develop a public service announcement on TV to reduce concerns about irradiated meats?
- Should **all** foods be irradiated? What logistical problems might this cause? Would it affect the cost and "freshness" of produce and meats?
- Do you think it would help the public to accept irradiated foods if a pamphlet described the procedure using basic terminology? Could you design such a publication? What information should it contain?

Additional Ideas for Classroom Discussion

- What are some organelles that contain internal compartmentalizations? How do internal compartments assist in the functioning of the organelle?
- List the tasks that a cell must perform.
- Why are there no unicellular creatures one foot in diameter?
- Why do bacteria have ribosomes when they lack other organelles?
- What is the difference between scanning electron microscopy and transmission electron microscopy?
- Why do you think most plant cells have a central vacuole while animal cells lack this organelle?
- What is the significance of the word *theory* in reference to the basic properties of the cell?
- Does the cytoplasm have any functions of its own, or is it just a "filler" matrix in which other organelles float? What are the major chemical components of cytoplasm?
- In which cells might you find a high concentration of peroxisomes? What would be the function of the peroxisomes?
- Show the class some slides of representative cells. Can the class determine the cell type by identifying the cellular components it contains? Often the presence of large quantities of particular structures in a cell can indicate its function. For example, show a slide of a sperm cell. The students may notice a large amount of mitochondria in the midpiece area. This indicates that this cell has a high energy demand. How does this relate to the presence of a flagellum? Next look at a

slide of a mature red blood cell. The students may be surprised to see that it does not contain a nucleus. This explains the fact that a red blood cell cannot divide. Explain that the function of a red blood cell is to carry oxygen, so it expels the nucleus to allow for more room for the transportation of oxygen.

- Why is the term *nucleus* used to describe the center of an atom and the organelle at the center of the cell when these are such different entities?
- In measurement of length, what are the largest cells (when mature) in the human body? What fundamental property of all cells is denied to these?
- What feature makes a eukaryotic cell a "true" cell?
- Why aren't there one-celled organisms as big as beach balls? What modifications would have to be made in distribution within the cell for such an event to occur?
- What organelle could be compared to the "control center" of an assembly line in a factory?
- Describe the interrelationship(s) of the individual members comprising the *endomembrane system* (see Figure 4.15).
- Compare the functions of mitochondria and chloroplasts.

How Would You Vote? Classroom Discussion Ideas

- Monitor the voting for the online question. Many medicines are used without fully understanding the long-term effects. Which is the bigger risk: eating irradiated foods or risking contamination by *E. coli* bacteria?
- Investigate current regulations relating to the preparation and sterilization of food products. Do you think more legislation is necessary?
- When did the irradiation of food begin? Do you feel there has been enough time to look for any ill effects from the practice?
- Irradiation is used to destroy cancerous cells. How does the amount of radiation used for this purpose differ from that used to irradiate food?
- Look up statistics to see how many individuals are sickened by food infected with *E. coli* and how many die annually.

Term Paper Topics, Library Activities, and Special Projects

- Who first coined the term *organelle?* When did biologists discover that eukaryotic cells contained organelles?
- Learn more about plant tissue culture. What mechanisms govern cell differentiation *in vitro*?
- Discuss the development of electron microscopy. What are some of the advances in cell biology that electron microscopy has made possible? How are biological specimens prepared for examination with an electron microscope?
- How do antibiotics such as penicillin stop bacterial growth? Discuss the different methods antibiotics employ to destroy bacteria.
- Design a hypothetical cell that would function with maximum efficiency under conditions of extreme drought.
- Describe the function of liver-cell smooth ER in the metabolism of drugs and alcohol. How might the liver cells of an alcoholic differ from those of a moderate imbiber or nondrinker?
- Prepare brief biographies of the researchers who are credited with early discoveries of cell structure and function.

- Search the library shelves for biology texts of 20, 30, 40, and 50 years ago. Find the diagrams of cell structure. Prepare a sequential composite of these, and compare each to the others and to your present text. What instrument made the difference in the drawings?
- Using a special dictionary of Latin and Greek root words, search for the literal meanings for each of the cell parts discussed in this chapter. (Be careful with Golgi—it is a man's name!)
- Many bacteria live in our digestive tract and are important in producing vitamins and enhancing absorption of nutrients. Antibiotics can kill both "good" and "bad" bacteria. What are some of the effects of antibiotics killing good bacteria? How does consuming acidophilus influence your normal intestinal flora?
- When was the endosymbiont hypothesis developed? What are the facts that led to this conclusion? Are there any other cellular components that could have also been incorporated into a cell via this same mechanism?
- As you learned in the chapter, Tay-Sachs disease is the result of defective lysosomes. There is also a group of diseases that relate to mitochondrial malfunction. Research the possible etiology of some particular mitochondrial diseases. Do you think there may be other conditions that relate to defective cellular components?

Possible Responses to *Critical Thinking* Questions

1. The idea of a gigantic cell of any kind, or a gigantic creature of any kind, has fascinated Hollywood movie-makers for decades. Movie-goers love this sort of thing. But wet-blanket scientists have to spoil the fun by pointing out the impossibility of gigantic cells based on that surface-to-volume ratio thing. Simply put, a huge cell would have so much volume that the distance from the deepest reaches of the interior of the cell would be too far for nutrients and oxygen to diffuse in, and for carbon dioxide and metabolic waste to diffuse out, not to mention the woefully inadequate surface area for all that diffusion to take place. As for encountering a giant amoeba in space, it would be impossible. You have already seen they can't exist and even if one did, it would have to survive in the vacuum of space!
2. The secondary plant cell wall, which is often deposited inside the primary cell wall as a cell matures, sometimes has a composition nearly identical to that of the earlier-developed wall. Because additional substances, especially lignin , are found in the secondary wall, it must be deposited from the inside where it is produced by the cell. The microfibrils of the secondary cell wall are aligned mostly in the same direction, and communication is possible by pits in the secondary cell wall that allow plasmodesmata to connect to the cell.
3. The image at the right is an example of Euglena, a common Protist, taken with an electron microscope.
4. Euglena is a eukaryotic cell, which one knows from the presence of the distinct nucleus. These single-celled protists may have plant or animal characteristics. This particular electron micrograph is of a Euglena that performs plantlike functions, since there are chloroplasts evident. Other structures that can be identified in the image are flagellum, vacuoles, and the cell membrane.

Possible Responses to *Data Analysis Exercise* Questions

In a normal flagellum, one sees a pattern of nine pairs of microtubules arranged in a circle, with the protein dynein located between each pair. Abnormal dynein would affect the movement of both flagella and cilia. This would result in sperm that could not swim normally to perform fertilization and cilia that would have trouble sweeping the respiratory tract free of debris.

5

GROUND RULES OF METABOLISM

Chapter Outline

Objectives

1. State two laws that govern the way energy is transferred from one substance to another.
2. Provide an example of a metabolic pathway and explain what kinds of substances regulate activity of the pathway.
3. Tell exactly what enzymes do and how they do it.

4. Explain how enzymes can be controlled.
5. Understand "redox" reactions.
6. Explain how a molecule can "carry" energy.
7. Understand the essential structure and function of the plasma membrane.
8. Familiarize yourself with the main membrane proteins (Figure 5.6) and their functions in a cell.
9. Know the forces that cause water and solutes to move across membranes passively (without energy).
10. Know the mechanisms by which substances are moved across membranes against a concentration gradient (actively, with energy).
11. Understand the importance of osmosis to all cells including hypo-, hyper-, and isotonic solutions.
12. Understand how material can be imported into or exported from a cell by being wrapped in membranes.

Key Terms

ethanol
alcohol dehydrogenase
alcoholic hepatitis
alcoholic cirrhosis
binge drinking
metabolism
energy
kinetic energy
first law of thermodynamics
entropy
second law of thermodynamics
potential energy
heat
kilocalorie
reaction
reactants
products
endergonic
exergonic
activation energy
ATP
ADP
phosphorylation
ATP/ADP cycle
enzymes
catalysis
substrates
activation energy
active sites
transition state
binding
induced-fit model
cofactors
coenzymes
antioxidants
free radicals
NAD^+
$NADP^+$
metabolic pathways
enzymatic reactions
feedback mechanisms
allosteric
feedback inhibition
oxidation-reduction reactions (redox)
electron transfer chains
adhesion protein
fluid mosaic
receptor protein
recognition protein
transport protein
diffusion
concentration
concentration gradient
hypotonic
hypertonic
isotonic
osmosis
turgor
osmotic pressure
passive transport
active transport
calcium pump
exocytosis
endocytosis
phagocytosis
pinocytosis

Lecture Outline

5.1 A Toast to Alcohol Dehydrogenase

A. The liver is the body's detoxification center.
   1. Beverage alcohol (ethanol) is degraded to non-toxic acetate with the help of catalase, alcohol dehydrogenase, and other enzymes present in the liver.
   2. Excessive amounts of alcohol over a lifetime can lead to liver disease and liver failure.

B. The liver is the largest gland in our body; it performs other functions relative to food utilization, including synthesis of plasma proteins.

C. Binge drinking is considered the most serious drug problem on U.S. campuses.
   1. Fourty-four percent of 17,600 students in 140 surveyed colleges report averages of five alcoholic drinks per day.
   2. Binge drinking kills suddenly, with over 1,400 students killed every year.

5.2 Energy and the World of Life

A. Energy Disperses
   1. *First law of thermodynamics* states that the total amount of energy (capacity to do work) in the universe is constant; it cannot be created nor destroyed; it can only change form.

2. As systems lose energy they become more disorganized; the measure of this disorder is called *entropy*.
3. Systems work toward maximum entropy.
4. *Second law of thermodynamics* states that the spontaneous directional energy flow is from high- to low-quality forms.

B. Energy's One-Way Flow

1. Each conversion produces energy (usually heat) that is unavailable for work.
2. The collective strength of chemical bonds resists the spontaneous direction of energy flow.
3. The world of life (plant and animal) maintains a high degree of organization because it is replenished with energy from the sun.

5.3 Energy and the Molecules of Life

A. Chemical Bond Energy

1. The energy required to break or form chemical bonds is measured in *kilocalories*.
2. Starting substances are called *reactants* and those remaining at the end of the reaction are the *products*.
3. *Endergonic* ("energy in") reactions require energy input resulting in products with *more* energy than the reactants had; for example, photosynthesis.
4. *Exergonic* ("energy out") reactions release energy such that the products have *less* energy than the reactants; for example, aerobic respiration.
5. *Cofactors* are metal ions or coenzymes that aid the enzymes by accepting and donating electrons, atoms, and functional groups.
6. *Transport proteins* affect concentrations of substances by aiding solute movement across membranes, which influences reactions.

B. Why the World Doesn't Go Up in Flames

1. Energy is required to overcome the strength of chemical bonds in reactants.
2. Every single reaction has a characteristic activation energy, which is the minimum amount of energy needed to start a reaction.

C. Energy In, Energy Out

1. Plant cells store free energy during photosynthesis.
2. During aerobic respiration, glucose and oxygen are converted to carbon dioxide and water.

5.4 How Enzymes Work

A. The Need for Speed

1. *Enzymes* are the catalysts that work to speed up specific reactions by lowering activation energy.
2. Enzymes can be reused.
3. Enzymes, at least some of them, can recognize both reactants and products in order to catalyze a reaction in both directions.
4. Enzymes are very selective about the substrates to which they will bind and thereby bring about change.
5. Enzymes have *active sites*, which are areas that allow a chemical binding of the *substrate* to the enzyme; the substrate is complementary in size, shape, solubility, and charge to the active site.

B. The Transition State

1. The transition state occurs when reactions overcome activation energy and run spontaneously to product.

C. Helping Substrates Get Together

1. The closer the substrates are, the greater the likelihood that they will react.

D. Orienting Substrates in Positions That Favor Reaction

1. The substrates are aligned to encourage a reaction.

E. Inducing a Fit Between Enzyme and Substrate

1. The enzyme changes shape to provide for better fit between the enzyme and the substrate.

F. Shutting Out Water Molecules

1. Some enzymes have active sites that repel water so that it does not interfere with the reaction.

G. Effects of Temperature, pH, and Salinity

1. Because enzymes operate best within defined temperature ranges, very high temperatures decrease reaction rate by disrupting the bonds that maintain three-dimensional shape (denaturation).
2. Most enzymes function best at a pH near seven (pepsin in the stomach is an exception); higher or lower values disrupt enzyme shape and halt function.
3. There is a range of salinity tolerance for most enzymes; if enzymes are dissolved in fluids exceeding that tolerance, the hydrogen bonds are disrupted, thus inactivating the enzyme.

5.5 Metabolism—Organized, Enzyme-Mediated Reactions

A. Types of Metabolic Pathways

1. Metabolic pathways are enzyme-mediated sequences of reactions in cells.
2. Some pathways are linear (reactant to produce directly); others have cyclic components (last step regenerates the reactant molecule of first step); and still others have branches (reactants or intermediates are channeled into two or more different sequences).

B. Controls Over Metabolism

1. The direction of reaction depends on concentrations and the collision of molecules.
2. Some controls regulate the number of enzyme molecules available by inhibiting or activating their synthesis; cells are able to produce only what conditions require.
3. *Allosteric* enzymes have regulatory sites (in addition to active sites) where the inhibitor or activator binds, altering the enzyme's configuration of the active site.
4. When this control substance is the end product in the enzyme's metabolic pathway, *feedback inhibition* occurs and shuts down its own synthesis until it becomes needed.
5. Chemical reactions can proceed from reactants to products, which, if they are allowed to accumulate, will convert back to reactants.

C. Redox Reactions

1. Oxidation-reduction reactions ("redox") are simply electron transfers between molecules.
   a. The donor molecule loses an electron and is oxidized.
   b. The receptor molecule gains an electron and is reduced.
2. In electron transfer chains, molecules accept and give up electrons in an orderly, stepwise manner to control the release of energy.
   a. Electrons are at a higher energy level when they enter the chain than when they leave.
   b. Think of the electrons as descending a staircase and losing some energy at each step.

5.6 Cofactors in Metabolic Pathways

A. Cofactors are metal ions or coenzymes that bind to many enzymes and make them more reactive.

1. Coenzymes are organic compounds that may or may not have vitamin components.

2. Metal ions readily give up and accept electrons, and are able to help products form by shifting electron arrangements in substrates.

B. ATP—A Special Coenzyme

1. Energy input links phosphate to ADP to produce ATP (phosphorylation).
2. ATP can, in turn, donate a phosphate group to another molecule, which becomes primed and energized for specific reactions.
3. ATP is like currency in an economy; ATP is earned during exergonic reactions and spent in endergonic ones.
4. ADP can be recycled to ATP very rapidly in the ATP/ADP cycle.

5.7 A Closer Look at Cell Membranes

A. Membrane Lipids

1. The "fluid" portion of the cell membrane is made of phospholipids.
   a. A phospholipid molecule is composed of a hydrophilic head and two hydrophobic tails.
   b. If phospholipid molecules are surrounded by water, their hydrophobic fatty acid tails cluster and a bilayer results; hydrophilic heads are at the outer faces of a two-layer sheet.
2. Bilayers of phospholipids are the structural foundation for all cell membranes.

B. Membrane Proteins

1. Plasma membrane proteins can be peripheral (on the surface) or integral (often through the entire bilayer).
2. Proteins in the plasma membrane have varying functions.
   a. Adhesion proteins hold cells together.
   b. Recognition proteins help cells distinguish "self" from "non-self."
   c. Receptor proteins serve as attachment sites for hormones or toxins.
   d. Transport proteins help move substances across the plasma membrane.

5.8 Diffusion and Membranes

A. The net movement of like molecules down a concentration gradient is called *diffusion;* each substance diffuses independently as illustrated by dye molecules in water.

B. The Rate of Diffusion

1. Several factors influence the rate and direction of diffusion.
   a. *Size.* Smaller molecules diffuse faster than larger ones. (smaller = faster)
   b. *Temperature.* More heat energy makes molecules move faster. (higher = faster)
   c. *Steepness of the concentration gradient.* Rates are high with steep gradients.
   d. *Charge.* A difference in electric charge between adjoining regions.
   e. *Pressure.* A difference in exerted force per unit area in two adjoining areas.
2. When gradients no longer exist, there is no *net* movement (dynamic equilibrium).

C. Semipermeable Membranes

1. Osmosis is the passive movement (diffusion) of water across a differentially permeable membrane in response to solute concentration gradients, pressure gradients, or both.
2. For example, if a bag containing a sugar solution is placed in pure water, the water will diffuse *inward* (higher to lower).
3. Tonicity denotes the relative concentration of solutes in two fluids—extracellular fluid and cytoplasmic fluid, for example.
4. Three conditions are possible.
   a. A *hypotonic* fluid has a lower concentration of solutes than the fluid in the cell; cells immersed in it may swell.

b. A *hypertonic* fluid has a greater concentration of solutes than the fluid in the cell; cells in it may shrivel.

c. An *isotonic* fluid has the same concentration of solutes as the fluid in the cell; immersion in it causes no net movement of water.

5. Most free-living cells counteract shift in tonicity by selectively transporting solutes across the cell membrane.

D. Turgor

1. *Hydrostatic pressure* is a force directed against a membrane by a fluid; the greater the solute concentration, the greater the hydrostatic pressure it will exert. In plants, hydrostatic pressure is called *turgor*.
2. This force is countered by *osmotic pressure*, which prevents any further increase in the volume of the solution.
3. When plants lose water there is shrinkage of the cytoplasm, called *plasmolysis*.

5.9 Membrane Transport Mechanisms

A. When water-soluble molecules bind to transport proteins, they trigger changes in shape that "ease" the solute through the protein and hence through the membrane.

B. Passive Transport

1. A concentration gradient and/or electric gradient drive diffusion of a substance across a cell membrane through a transport protein—a passive process expending no energy.
2. Passive transport will continue until solute concentrations are equal on both sides of the membrane or other factors intervene.
3. The net direction of a solute's movement depends on how many of its molecules are randomly colliding with the transporters.

C. Active Transport

1. To move ions and large molecules across a membrane against a concentration gradient, special proteins are induced to change shape (in a series), but only with an energy boost from ATP.
2. An example of active transport is the sodium-potassium pump of the neuron membrane and the calcium pump of most cells.
   a. The sodium-potassium pump is a cotransport that moves two substances at the same time.
   b. ATP energy is used to move sodium ions against the concentration gradient to the inside of the cell. At the same time, potassium ions are moved against the concentration gradient to the outside of the cell.

5.10 Membrane Trafficking

A. Endocytosis and Exocytosis

1. In exocytosis, a cytoplasmic vesicle moves substances from cytoplasm to plasma membrane, where the membranes of the vesicle and cell fuse.
2. Endocytosis encloses particles in small portions of plasma membrane to form vesicles that then move into the cytoplasm.
   a. *Phagocytosis* is an active form of endocytosis by which a cell engulfs microorganisms, particles, or other debris; this is seen in protistans and white blood cells.
   b. In *receptor-mediated* endocytosis, specific molecules are brought into the cell by specialized regions of the plasma membranes, which form coated pits that sink into the cytoplasm.
   c. In *bulk-phase* endocytosis, a vesicle forms around a small volume of extracellular fluid without regard to what substances might be dissolved in it.

B. Membrane Cycling

1. Even as exocytosis and endocytosis disrupt the plasma membrane, the rates are such that the plasma membrane is continually replaced.
2. For example, in neurotransmitter release, an episode of exocytosis was immediately followed by counterbalancing endocytosis.

5.11 A Toast to Alcohol Dehydrogenase (Revisited)

A. In the average human, alcohol dehydrogenase (ADH) can detoxify approximately 7–14 grams of alcohol per hour.

1. Some individuals have overactive ADH and exhibit an adverse feeling while drinking alcohol.
2. Others may have underactive ADH and may not feel adverse effects while drinking.

Suggestions for Presenting the Material

- Because students may be unfamiliar with the first and second laws of thermodynamics, it is important to distinguish clearly between the two laws; emphasize the central role of the sun in sustaining life on Earth.
- Acknowledge that this chapter speaks in *generalities* and defines terms that will be used to describe *specific* metabolic reactions in subsequent chapters.
- If you prefer to teach from specific examples, you may want to choose a specific metabolic pathway (of your own or from elsewhere in the book). Draw it on an overhead transparency, and use it to explain the various terms found in the text. This is especially helpful in explaining feedback inhibition.
- After presentation of the various capabilities of enzymes, students may think of them as "miracle workers." Remind the students that these are nonliving molecules—albeit, amazing ones. Also emphasize the limitations and vulnerability of enzymes, including causes and effects of denaturation.
- Because of their similarity, NAD and NADP need special emphasis to distinguish each in terms of structural and functional identity. Compare and contrast both terms with ATP.
- Tie endergonic reactions to energy storage and phosphorylation of ADP to ATP, exergonic reactions to ATP breaking the outer phosphate bond to form ADP and release energy.
- Encourage students to bring their textbook to class and refer frequently to the excellent figures in it.
- This chapter provides a good opportunity to introduce the idea that oxidations release energy, reductions require energy, and NADH and NADPH contain more potential energy than their oxidized counterparts. Students should have some idea of oxidation/reduction from chemistry classes, but it may help them remember if you teach this mnemonic acronym: LEO says GER (Lose Electrons Oxidation; Gain Electrons Reduction).
- This chapter provides a good opportunity to introduce the idea that oxidations release energy while reductions require energy. For example: NADH and NADPH contain more potential energy than NAD+ and NADP+.
- This is the first of several chapters that will expand on topics introduced in the cell overview chapter (Chapter 4).
- Don't assume students know, or remember, the definitions of *hydrophilic* and *hydrophobic*.
- Using a transparency, carefully distinguish between which portion of the plasma membrane is the "fluid" (that is, lipid bilayer) and which is the "mosaic" (that is, proteins).

- The various methods by which molecules move, either through space or through membranes, can be confusing to students because of the subtle differences that distinguish each method. Perhaps you could begin with general, non-membrane-associated phenomena such as diffusion. Then proceed to membrane-associated mechanisms such as osmosis, facilitated diffusion, and active transport. (See the Enrichment section below for ideas on introducing diffusion.)
- Note that each of the transport phenomena topics is accompanied by an illustration, which should be used to reduce the "abstract quality" of the mechanism.
- Use the analogy of canoeing down a river to illustrate passive transport. One can sit back and let the current move the canoe down the river and get to the desired destination without using energy to paddle the canoe. Likewise, if one is traveling up-river, it takes a lot of paddling energy to move the canoe against the current to the desired destination. Active transport is like trying to paddle up-river. It is possible to give an even more relevant example for the students. Imagine trying to get in the door of your classroom before the previous class has totally exited. This would represent active transport. Once all of the previous class' students have left, you can enter the classroom by going with the "flow" of students, which represents a passive process.
- Having various photographs of endocytosis and exocytosis from actual cells or protists can help students begin to understand the complexities involved in the processes. Include photographs of receptor-mediated processes and explain how some pathogens are able to "trick" our cell membrane receptors in order to "dock" and gain access to our cells.
- Students are very interested in genetic disorders such as cystic fibrosis (CF). Upon introducing them to the mechanics of the cell membrane, mention how CF patients have mutations that cause one of their transporters to malfunction. Later, you can include CF in your discussion of why harmful genes (like the mutation for CF) remain in a population. Having "threads" like this running through your lectures helps students form ideas and get a bigger picture view of biology.
- Students have much difficulty grasping and applying the concepts of hypertonic, hypotonic, and isotonic. Give them practice by asking them questions about the direction of movement of water in various cells placed in these solutions.
- To help students remember hypotonic, stress that it's hypOtonic, like a beach ball. Water enters the cell and swells the cell like a giant "O."
- Sometimes students can understand isotonic, hypertonic, and hypotonic easier if you look at the concentration of water rather than the concentration of solutes. Work several problems in class, and then assign a few problems for the students to try on their own. Work those trial problems at the very next class, and then assign a few for credit (or extra credit). Students aren't expecting working math problems in biology, so this is a good time to remind them that biology includes chemistry, physics, math, etc.
- Use the adage, "Water follows salt" to help the students determine where water moves in isotonic, hypertonic, and hypotonic solutions.

Classroom and Laboratory Enrichment

- The action of an enzyme (salivary amylase) can be easily demonstrated by the following procedure:
  a. Prepare a 6 percent starch solution in water and confirm its identity by a spot plate test with iodine solution (produces blue-black color).
  b. Collect saliva from a volunteer by having the person chew a small piece of Parafilm and expectorate into a test tube.
  c. Place diluted saliva and the starch solution in a test tube and mix.

d. At suitable intervals, remove samples of the digestion mixture and test with iodine on the spot plate (lack of dark color indicates conversion of starch to maltose).

e. Variations can include heating the saliva to destroy the enzyme or adding acid or alkali.

- Show a videotape or slide/sound set depicting the role and function of enzymes.
- Use tennis balls to represent electrons. Ask five students to line up in front of the class then pass the tennis balls, one at a time, from one student to the next. As a student receives a tennis ball (electron) have them say "reduced." As a student passes an electron, have them say "oxidized." With a little practice the point becomes obvious to the participating students and the class that movement of electrons defines redox reactions.
- Demonstrate the two models of enzyme-substrate interactions in the following ways:

  a. *Rigid "lock and key" model:* Use preschool-size jigsaw puzzle pieces or giant-size Lego blocks.

  b. *Induced-fit model:* Use a flexible fabric or latex glove to show how the insertion of a hand (substrate) induces change in the shape of the glove (active site).
- The relationship between ATP, ADP, energy, enzymes, and phosphorylation may be illustrated by the use of a toy dart gun with rubber suction cup-tipped darts. It is helpful to have acetate transparencies of ADP and ATP structures that can be projected on a screen as the following demonstration is performed:

  a. Tell the students that the unloaded dart gun represents ADP and the dart represents inorganic phosphate (P). Show the structure of ADP on the screen.

  b. As you insert the dart into the gun, emphasize the need for the expenditure of energy to do this. Tell the students that the addition of P to ADP is, therefore, an endergonic reaction; it is also called a phosphorylation reaction. At this time show the structure of ATP on the screen. Also point out that the spring inside the dart gun is under much tension and as such has a great deal of potential energy. The same can be said for the P group that has been added to ADP.

  c. Next, demonstrate the hydrolysis of ATP. The trigger finger represents the necessary enzyme. Aim the gun at some vertical smooth surface (window or aquarium works well) and depress the trigger. Hopefully the dart will adhere to the surface (a substrate molecule being energized by phosphorylation). The reaction is thus exergonic and some of the energy has been transferred to the substrate molecule.
- You can also demonstrate the action of amylase breaking down starches into sugars as the first step of digestion in your mouth. Give each student (or selected volunteers) a saltine cracker and ask them to chew it without swallowing it, keeping it in their mouth as saliva does its work. Ask them what they can taste after it has been in their mouths for a bit—it should begin to taste sweet. Amylase has broken the starch in the cracker into sugar. Students can easily begin to think about the action of enzymes with this demonstration.
- A great way to introduce students to the idea of diffusion is to not tell them anything about it, but to bring out a canister (covered, so they will have no idea of what to look for) of scented air freshener (cinnamon works well). Then spray for several seconds (longer if you have a large lecture hall with many students) into one corner of the room in one position. Ask students to raise their hands when they notice the scent. Continue until every student has raised his/her hand. They will get a visual idea of the molecules of scent moving from area of high concentration throughout the room until they are equally distributed (unless the air conditioner is on—discuss this possibility after students have commented on the patterns of dispersal). After this demonstration, proceed to discussing diffusion and osmosis.
- To show how molecules move from points of greater concentration to regions of lower concentration, pour red ink or dye along one side of a container of water. The liquid will diffuse through a

liquid. Try this with different water temperatures to illustrate the effect of temperature on diffusion.

- Discuss the terms *isotonic, hypotonic,* and *hypertonic* by showing students three sketches of semipermeable bags in beakers of distilled water (these can be drawn ahead of time on an overhead transparency if you wish). You could even set up a good visual aid, yourself, with dialysis tubing and beakers with colored dye to demonstrate diffusion. Vary the concentrations of the sugar solutions shown in the bags. Ask students what the direction of water movement would be in each case. Then ask what direction the sugar molecules will move in. Many students will believe that the sugar molecules will move across the membrane, even though they previously learned these sugar molecules are too large to cross the plasma membrane readily.
- Use raisins as an analogy for a cell. Place raisins in pure water (hypotonic solution), a high sugar solution (hypertonic), and a low sugar solution (isotonic) for an hour before class. Compare the condition of the raisins and discuss how cell membranes work much like the surface of the raisins.
- To demonstrate that some molecules will pass through membranes and some will not, prepare two test tubes as follows: In one tube pour dilute Lugol's iodine solution until it is about nine-tenths full; in another tube pour 1 percent starch paste until it is about nine-tenths full. Cover the mouth of each test tube with a wet goldbeater's membrane; then secure it tightly by tying with thread or a tight rubber band. Invert the starch paste test tube into a beaker about one-half full of dilute Lugol's solution; invert the test tube containing dilute Lugol's solution into a beaker containing a 1 percent starch paste. Ask students why the well-known blue-black color appears in the starch solution and not in the Lugol's solution. Students may decide that the starch requires digestion to a more soluble form before it can pass through the membrane.
- Set up two or more osmometer tubes (glass or plastic thistle tubes covered with a selectively permeable membrane) at the front of the room. Compare rates of osmosis by filling each tube with a colored sugar (you may use corn syrup) or salt solution (vary the concentrations) and placing the base of the tube into a beaker of distilled water.
- In the classroom, demonstrate the loss of turgor pressure by flooding a small potted tomato plant with salt water at the beginning of the class period. You can do the same thing to celery branches in distilled water, salt water, and regular tap water to see how the plant responds to each. Discuss hypo-, hyper-, and isotonic solutions as you look at each celery stalk.
- Half-fill a large washtub with water. Float ping-pong balls on the surface of the water. Drop a coin into the tub and ask a student to retrieve the coin. Note what happens to the ping-pong balls when you reach through to retrieve the coin. What happens when you remove your arm? Use this as analogy for the fluid mosaic model.
- Use models or overhead transparencies/slides to show how channel proteins and transport proteins function during passive transport and active transport, respectively.
- In the lab, students can observe the reaction of an Elodea leaf to both water and saline, as follows: Obtain a small *Elodea* leaf and place it in a small drop of distilled water on a microscope slide. Cover it with a cover slip. Now prepare a second slide, only this time mounting an *Elodea* leaf in a drop of 10 percent NaCl solution. Compare the cells of the second slide to those of the first slide.
- Watch hemolysis by diluting several drops of fresh animal blood with distilled water. Compare the resulting solution with one in which the same number of red blood cells were diluted with physiological saline (0.09% NaCl). The suspension that has undergone hemolysis will be clear (red blood cells have burst), while the solution made with physiological saline will be visibly cloudy (red blood cells remain intact in the solution).

- Demonstrate the diffusion of a liquid in a solid. Prepare three Petri dishes, each filled with a layer of plain agar. Use a cork borer to carefully make three equidistant holes in the agar. Turn the dish over and number each hole. Put three or four drops of the following solutions in each of the appropriately numbered holes: (1) 0.02M potassium dichromate, (2) 0.02M potassium permanganate, (3) 0.02M methylene blue. View results after at least one hour. Because the solutions have identical molarities, the rate of diffusion depends on the molecular weight of each compound. Methylene blue (MW = 373) diffuses at the slowest rate, while potassium permanganate diffuses fastest (MW = 158). Potassium dichromate (MW = 294) diffuses at an intermediate rate.
- At least one day before lecture, dissolve gelatin in water and pour into a screw-top test tube; leave a small space between the top of the gelatin and the top edge of the test tube. Cool the tube in the refrigerator until the gelatin solidifies. At the beginning of the lecture, pour in a small amount of a bright-colored dye on top of the gelatin; replace and tighten the screw top. Allow the dye to diffuse through the gelatin until it reaches the bottom of the glass thread area of the test tube. At this time, turn the test tube to a horizontal position and place it so that students can observe progress of the dye through the gelatin. If one wishes to time the progress of the dye, begin timing when the tube is turned to the horizontal position.
- The diffusion of a gas through other gases (air) can be demonstrated easily as follows: Wet a circle of filter paper with phenolphthalein and insert it into the bottom of a large test tube. Next, invert the test tube over an open bottle of ammonium hydroxide. Ask students to explain the rather rapid color change of the filter paper to red. Set up a control with filter paper soaked in water.
- Place a thin strip of raw potato in a pure-water solution and another strip in a high-salt solution. After 30 minutes note the flexibility of the potato strips. If you're cooking French fries, in what solution would you soak your potatoes before frying if you like crispy fries? What about soft, fluffy fries?
- Demonstrate the diffusion of a gas in a gas using a glass tube at least one-half inch wide and 18 inches in length. Plug one end of the tube with a cotton wad saturated with HCl (hydrochloric acid); plug the opposite end with a cotton wad saturated with NH_4OH (ammonium hydroxide). Label each end appropriately. Hydrochloric acid and ammonium hydroxide react together to produce ammonium chloride and water. Students will be able to see a ring of ammonium chloride that has formed closest to the HCl end of the tube; the ammonium ion (NH_4^+) has a smaller molecular weight than the chloride ion (Cl^-) and thus diffuses faster, meeting the Cl^- ion about two-thirds of the way down the tube.

Classroom Discussion Ideas

- What might be some physiological reasons for long-term alcoholics being chronically sick?
- What are the limiting factors that allow an enzyme to process only a certain amount of substrate in a given time period? Why might this be a problem in binge drinking?
- *Exactly* what causes the liver of a heavy alcohol drinker to diminish in its capacity to metabolize alcohol over a lifetime of drinking?
- What factors are involved in how much alcohol each individual can process?

Additional Ideas for Classroom Discussion

- The second law of thermodynamics is often used as the basis for an argument against evolution. According to the argument, the second law depicts a world that must become more disordered, while evolution depicts a world that is becoming more ordered. Evaluate this argument. Is it valid?

- Pose several "what if" questions concerning enzyme action, such as: What if the body temperature of humans mutated to 105°F? Or body pH rose to 9.5?
- Compare the energy "hill" that an enzyme must overcome to a ski slope. Does an enzyme act more like a chairlift or a bulldozer?
- It is theorized that an asteroid collision caused a global dust cloud that blocked sunlight to the Earth and ultimately caused the extinction of the dinosaurs. Discuss what would have caused the extinction.
- Discuss why heat is the most common form of entropy.
- Discuss what would happen to life on Earth if the flow of sunlight energy stopped.
- Preview genetic disorders—the "inborn errors of metabolism"—by examining how a faulty enzyme blocks or diverts a metabolic pathway, as in phenylketonuria (PKU).
- Name some of the different forms of energy. Are they inter-convertible? Give some examples. For example, trace the energy inter-conversions involved in cooking your breakfast on an electric stove. Begin with how your electricity is generated in the first place (for example, the dam over a hydroelectric plant).
- What happens in arid climates when salts accumulate in cropland soils?
- How do cells "recognize" other cells of the same type during tissue formation?
- Learn more about the functions of the sodium-potassium pump and the calcium pump.
- Investigate how active transport pumps are used to regulate metabolic processes in humans.
- How are saltwater fish species able to cope with their extremely salty surroundings?
- Investigate the loss of estuaries in the Gulf Coast region of the United States. What effect is this having on the wildlife in and around the estuary environment?
- Investigate human autoimmune diseases. How are membrane proteins that identify cells as "self" involved? Look up HLA (human leukocyte antigens)—how do they contribute to a cell's idea of "self"?
- Look up the composition of "physiological saline." Are there different varieties of this preparation for different animal species? How did scientists decide on the appropriate concentration for normal saline that is administered via IV sites in the hospital?
- The diffusion and transport phenomena discussed in the chapter are based on a property called Brownian movement, which is demonstrated by all molecules whether alive or not. What is the physical manifestation of this property, and what is the derivation of its name?
- Design a hypothetical cell that would function with maximum efficiency under conditions of extreme drought.

How Would You Vote? Classroom Discussion Ideas

- Monitor the voting for the online question. The question of who should be eligible for a liver (or any organ for that matter) transplant is a controversy that sparks many ethical debates. Ask groups of students to defend the decision on the basis of: (1) medical need; (2) first-come, first-served; (3) lifestyle; (4) ability to pay; (5) age; and (6) contribution (real or potential) to society. Which of these should be upheld in legal transplant decisions?
- Have the students vote. Should a patient whose alcoholism was the cause of the liver disease be granted a transplant?
- Read about Mickey Mantle's liver transplant. Should a celebrity be placed ahead of a non-famous patient on the transplant list?

- Often liver transplants are delayed because large blood supplies are needed during surgery. Do you think the technology is progressing ahead of needed resources?
- Liver tissue is one of the only tissues capable of regeneration. In some cases, patients can receive a lobe of a lung from a living donor. How would this change the transplantation process?

Term Paper Topics, Library Activities, and Special Projects

- Research the basis for the first and second laws of thermodynamics. On the basis of what observations did scientists formulate these laws? What experiments can be done in the laboratory to confirm the laws?
- Explain the defect in the metabolic pathway that results in the condition known as phenylketonuria (PKU). How can this condition be treated? Is it curable?
- Construct clay models depicting an enzyme, a substrate, the enzyme-substrate complex, and induced fit.
- Explain why nuclear fusion reactors produce such a large amount of energy.
- Investigate the effects of alcoholic hepatitis and alcoholic cirrhosis on the liver.
- Explain the role of the B vitamins in human metabolism.
- Discuss some of the ways coenzymes and inorganic cofactors participate in enzymatic reactions.
- Research an actual organ transplant. What are the factors involved in making the decision? Make a chart of enzymes that are involved in human digestion. What is the function of each of these enzymes? Where are they produced?
- Research the literature to see how a simple model can be designed to simulate a specialized form of diffusion—dialysis. How does this model relate to the medical procedure called dialysis?

Possible Responses to *Critical Thinking* Questions

1. The quantity of energy in the universe comes from the first law, which states that matter (energy) is neither created nor destroyed but remains constant, merely changing forms. You can't gain or "win" energy because there is a finite amount in the universe. The second law deals with the quality of that energy since most of the energy is lost as heat in the transformations. The quality of energy at the beginning of a reaction is not the same as at the end. Entropy measures how much and how far the form of energy disperses after an energy change. Energy tends to flow from concentrated to less concentrated forms spontaneously. So, one cannot "break even" and end up with the same amount of usable energy at the end of energy conversions; much is lost to entropy.
2. Diffusion increases entropy, because the substance goes from a high concentration to a lower concentration. Therefore, this process can be seen as dispersing the energy more.
3. It is a difficult concept for most students to understand that the concentration of water can be changed. It is best to begin by mentioning that a standard solution contains a solute and a solvent (often water). Therefore, if you change the concentration of the solute, you are also changing the concentration of the solvent. For example, if you increase the concentration of the solute, the concentration of the water decreases and, likewise, a decrease in the solute brings about an increase in the water concentration.
4. Pineapple contains the enzyme bromelain, which breaks down protein, preventing the JELL-O from setting.
5. Trypsin is an enzyme that is typically produced in the pancreas. Its function is to finish the digestion of proteins that begins in the stomach. If you take food with trypsin, the digestion of proteins will instead begin in your mouth.

6. Catalase is able to use hydrogen peroxide to oxidize toxins, including alcohol. The following formula shows how: $H_2O_2 + RH_2$ to $2H_2O + R$. Catalase is able to bind and inactivate the alcohol because it has an –OH at the end of its structure: C_2H_5OH. This hydroxyl group would be exposed, much like that of hydrogen peroxide, and thus would be bound to the active site of catalase.
7. The gas is oxygen gas (O_2). $H_2O_2 + H_2O_2 +$ catalase $\rightarrow 2H_2O + O_2 +$ catalase
8. Hydrogen peroxide bubbles when placed on an open cut because it is reacting with enzymes of the blood and tissues—catalase. When the catalase comes in contact with hydrogen peroxide it turns the hydrogen peroxide into water and oxygen gas (the bubbles): $2H_2O_2$ --> $2H_2O + O_2$. Intact skin does not have the enzymes exposed.

Possible Responses to *Data Analysis Exercise* Questions

Some species of Ferroplasma are able to survive in, and even prefer, an acidic environment.

1. The dashed line indicates the optimum enzyme activity for each enzyme.
2. All of the four enzymes have an optimum pH of less than 5. Only two of the enzymes show a significant function at a pH of 5.
3. The optimum pH for carboxylesterase is around 1.5.

6

WHERE IT STARTS—PHOTOSYNTHESIS

Chapter Outline

BIOFUELS
SUNLIGHT AS AN ENERGY SOURCE
Pigments: The Rainbow Catchers
EXPLORING THE RAINBOW
OVERVIEW OF PHOTOSYNTHESIS
LIGHT-DEPENDENT REACTIONS
The Noncyclic Pathway
The Cyclic Pathway
ENERGY FLOW IN PHOTOSYNTHESIS
LIGHT-INDEPENDENT REACTIONS
ADAPTATIONS: DIFFERENT CARBON-FIXING PATHWAYS
Photorespiration
C4 Plants
CAM Plants
BIOFUELS (REVISITED)
SUMMARY
DATA ANALYSIS EXERCISE
SELF-QUIZ
CRITICAL THINKING

Objectives

1. Understand the basic properties of light and how sunlight specifically affects pigments in plants.
2. Understand the main pathways by which energy from the sun enters photosynthetic organisms and passes from organism to organism and back into the environment.
3. Know the steps of the light-dependent and light-independent reactions. Know the raw materials (reactants) needed to start each step, the products made by each step, and where in the plant cell each step occurs.
4. Explain how autotrophs use the intermediates as well as the products of photosynthesis in their own metabolism.
5. Discuss the impact the autotrophs living in the oceans and on land have on global processes such as carbon cycling. Understand how this activity influences the global climate, and discuss the role humans play in these events.

Key Terms

biomass	switchgrass	photons	pigment
biodiesel	visible light	photosynthesis	reflected light
methane seeps	electromagnetic spectrum	white light	chlorophyll *a*
ethanol		prism	phycobilins
cellulose	wavelength	radiant energy	carotenoids

xanthophylls
anthocyanin
retinal
Theodor Engelmann
Cladophora
absorption spectrum
chloroplasts
stroma
thylakoid membrane
photosystems
light-dependent reactions
light-independent reactions
light-harvesting complexes
P700, type I photosystem
P680, type II photosystem
electron transfer chains
ATP synthases
Photolysis
NADP+
NADPH
electron transfer phosphorylation
photolysis
photosystem
cyclic pathway
noncyclic pathway
photophosphorylation
cyanobacteria
Calvin-Benson cycle
carbon fixation
rubisco
RuBP
PGA
PGAL
C3 plants
stomata
photorespiration
C4 plants
CAM plants
autotrophs
heterotrophs
photoautotroph
chemoautotrophs
aerobic respiration
ozone (O_3)
radioisotope dating techniques

Lecture Outline

6.1 Biofuels

A. Photosynthesis uses sunlight as an energy source and stores the energy in chemical bonds of organic molecules.
   1. Autotrophs make their own food via photosynthesis.
   2. Heterotrophs obtain energy by breaking down molecules made by autotrophs or by consuming other heterotrophs.
   3. As organic material dies and decays it compacts and becomes fossil fuels. These fuels — coal, petroleum, and natural gas—are limited.
   4. Biomass (organic matter that is not fossilized) is a renewable source of energy converted from sunlight.

B. Releasing the energy from biomass (organic matter that is not fossilized) is more difficult to process.
   1. Biodiesel is processed from algae, soybeans, rapeseed, flaxseed, and oils used in restaurants.
   2. Methane seeps of manure ponds, landfills, and cows are sources of biomass energy.
   3. Ethanol is made from corn, sugar beets, and sugarcane.

C. High cellulose biomass such as switchgrass, wood chips, wheat straw, cotton stalks, and rice hulls are being researched now as energy sources. Currently these sources are merely burned.

6.2 Sunlight as an Energy Source

A. Properties of Light
   1. Organisms use only a small range of wavelengths for photosynthesis, vision, and other processes.
   2. Most of these wavelengths are the ones we see as visible light, a small part of the electromagnetic spectrum from the sun.
   3. Light energy is packaged as photons, which vary in energy as a function of wavelength. (The shortest are gamma rays, with the highest energy; the longest are radio waves, with the lowest energy.)
   4. Only a small range (380–750 nm) of wavelengths is used for photosynthesis.

B. Pigments: The Rainbow Catchers
   1. The light reflected from each pigment gives the pigment its color. For example, red pigment absorbs all colors of visible light except red light.

2. There is more than one kind of chlorophyll. Chlorophyll *a* is the most common pigment used in photosynthesis by plants, photosynthetic protists, and cyanobacteria.
3. Carotenoid pigments absorb blue-violet and blue-green but reflect yellow, orange, and red.
4. Xanthophylls reflect yellow, brown, purple, or blue light; anthocyanins reflect red and purple light in fruit and flowers; phycobilins reflect red or blue-green light and are accessory pigments found in red algae and cyanobacteria.
5. The chlorophylls in green leaves mask the accessory pigments until autumn, when the chlorophyll content declines.
6. A pigment absorbs light of specific wavelengths by acting as an antenna for receiving photon energy.
7. Photosynthesis begins when photosynthetic pigments absorb a photon of light.

6.3 Exploring the Rainbow

A. Photosynthetic pigments work together to harvest light of different wavelengths.

B. In an elegant experiment with photosynthesizing algae and aerobic bacteria, Engelmann determined that violet and red light were the wavelengths best suited for photosynthesis.

C. Today, an absorption spectrum is used to determine the wavelength most suited for a given pigment.

D. Phycobilins are pigments that absorb light from 500–600 nm. These pigments are common to deep-water algae because this range of light is not absorbed well by water.

6.4 Overview of Photosynthesis

A. A Look Inside the Chloroplast

1. Both stages of photosynthesis occur in the chloroplast.
   a. The semifluid interior (stroma) is the site for the second series of photosynthesis reactions.
   b. Flattened sacs, thylakoids, interconnected by channels weave through the stroma; the first reactions occur here.
2. In the thylakoid membranes, pigments are organized in clusters called photosystems, each consisting of 200–300 pigment molecules capable of trapping energy from the sun.

B. Two Stages of Reactions

1. Light-dependent reactions convert light energy to chemical bond energy of ATP.
   a. Water is split to release oxygen.
   b. NADP+ picks up electrons to become NADPH to be used later.
2. The light-independent reactions assemble sugars and other organic molecules using ATP, NADPH, and CO_2.
3. Overall, the equation for glucose formation is written:

$$6H_2O + 6CO_2 \xrightarrow{\text{light energy \& enzymes}} 6O_2 + C_6H_{12}O_6$$

6.5 Light-Dependent Reactions

A. Capturing Energy for Photosynthesis

1. The pigments in the thylakoid membrane "harvest" photon energy from sunlight.
   a. Absorbed photons of energy boost electrons to a higher level.
   b. The electrons quickly return to the lower level and release energy.
   c. Released energy is trapped by chlorophylls located in the photosystem's reaction center.
      i. A photosystem refers to the groups of chlorophylls, accessory pigments, and other molecules necessary to undergo photosynthesis.

B. The Noncyclic Pathway
   1. Light energy causes electrons to exit from a photosystem II.
   2. Electrons are pulled from water, which separates into oxygen and hydrogen ions.
      a. The oxygen is released.
   3. The electrons enter the electron transfer chain in the membranes of the thylakoids.
   4. The energy lost by the electrons moves hydrogen ions from the stroma into the thylakoid compartment.
      a. There is the formation of a hydrogen ion gradient across the thylakoid membrane.
   5. Light energy forces electrons out of photosystem I.
      a. An electron chain in the thylakoid membrane serves as a source of replacement electrons.
   6. Electrons from step 5 move through another electron transport chain.
      a. The electrons then combine with NADP+ and H+ to form NADPH.
   7. Hydrogen ions in the thylakoid compartment travel through the interior of ATP synthases because of the gradient across the thylakoid membrane.
   8. This movement of hydrogen ions makes ATP synthases attach phosphate to ADP, forming ATP.

C. The Cyclic Pathway
   1. The cyclic pathway occurs when oxygen levels are high, or when NADPH accumulates in the stroma.
   2. This process deals with photosystem I and an electron transfer chain that feeds electrons back into itself.
   3. In this method, NADPH and oxygen are not formed.

6.6 Energy Flow in Photosynthesis

A. Most photosynthetic organisms use the cyclic pathway.
   1. This system evolved before the noncyclic method.
   2. Eventually photosystem II also became part of this pathway.

B. Both the cyclic and noncyclic pathways utilize electron energy to move hydrogen ions across the thylakoid membrane.

C. It is an advantage to have both cyclic and noncyclic pathways.
   1. Cells can make either NADPH and ATP or just ATP.
   2. When NADPH accumulates, the cyclic pathway is the dominant process.
   3. When NADPH is used rapidly, as during sugar production, the noncyclic pathway is the dominant process.

6.7 Light-Independent Reactions

A. These reactions constitute a pathway known as the Calvin-Benson cycle.
   1. The participants and their roles in the synthesis of carbohydrates are:
      a. ATP, which provides energy.
      b. NADPH, which provides hydrogen atoms and electrons.
      c. Atmospheric air, which provides the carbon and oxygen from carbon dioxide.
   2. The reactions take place in the stroma of chloroplasts and are not dependent on sunlight.

B. Carbon dioxide diffuses into a leaf across the plasma membrane of a photosynthetic cell.
   1. Taking carbon from an inorganic source and incorporating that carbon into an organic molecule is called *carbon fixation*.

2. Rubisco joins carbon dioxide to RuBP to produce an unstable intermediate that splits to form two molecules of PGA.
3. Each PGA then receives a P_i from ATP plus H^+ and electrons from NADPH to form PGAL (phosphoglyceraldehyde).
4. Most of the PGAL molecules continue in the cycle to fix more carbon dioxide, but two PGAL join to form a sugar-phosphate, which will be modified to sucrose, starch, and cellulose.

6.8 Adaptations: Different Carbon-Fixing Pathways

A. Photorespiration
1. Plants in hot, dry environments close their stomata to conserve water, but in so doing retard carbon dioxide entry and permit oxygen buildup inside the leaves.
2. C3 plants are named so because the *three*-carbon PGA is the first stable intermediate of the Calvin-Benson cycle. Thus, oxygen—not carbon dioxide—becomes attached to RuBP to yield one PGA (instead of two) and one phosphoglycolate (not useful), and photorespiration dominates.
3. C3 plants such as beans do not grow well without irrigation in hot, dry climates.

B. C4 Plants
1. To overcome this fate, crabgrass, sugarcane, corn, and other C4 plants fix carbon twice (in mesophyll cells, then in bundle-sheath cells) to produce oxaloacetate (a *four*-carbon compound), which can then donate the carbon dioxide to the Calvin-Benson cycle.
2. Photorespiration hampers growth in C3 plants, but natural selection has not eliminated it from the population, perhaps because the gene coding for rubisco structure is linked to carbon fixation—rubisco's primary role.

C. CAM Plants
1. CAM (Crassulacean Acid Metabolism) plants, such as cacti, open their stomata and fix CO_2 only at night, storing the intermediate product for use in photosynthesis the next day.
2. CAM plants use the C4 cycle to break down crassulacean acid to CO_2 once the stomata close. The CO_2 then enters the Calvin-Benson cycle.

6.9 Biofuels (Revisited)

A. The first cells on Earth were chemoautotrophs that took energy and molecules from the environment.
1. Then cyclic photophosphorylation evolved in the first species that directly used the energy from the sun.
2. Organisms that utilized the cyclic pathway were successful.
   a. Oxygen became plentiful in the atmosphere.

B. The atmosphere on Earth is changing.
1. The level of carbon dioxide in the atmosphere is rising.
   a. Over 8,000 years ago, humans burned the forests.
   b. Today we have combustion engines in cars and factories.

C. Man has upset the natural balance between carbon dioxide and oxygen.
1. By studying layers of snow in Antarctica, scientists can compare the atmosphere in the past with conditions that are present today.
   a. The percentage of carbon dioxide in the atmosphere was consistent until the industrial revolution.
2. The pattern of global warming mirrors the rise of carbon dioxide in the atmosphere.
   a. There is an emphasis on reducing the use of fossil fuels as a power source.
   b. The use of biofuels is a better option since they simply recycle the carbon that is already in the atmosphere.

Suggestions for Presenting the Material

- Many students think that the only autotrophic organisms are those with green pigments, which are, of course, capable of using light for food manufacture. Point out the existence of the many *chemoautotrophs,* which derive their energy from chemicals.
- Most students have heard of geothermal vents. Discuss where this energy source originates and how it is ultimately tied to photosynthesis.
- Students may have previously learned to refer to the two divisions of photosynthesis as the "light" and "dark" reactions. Starr and Taggart use the more accurate and currently acceptable terms *light-dependent* and *light-independent,* respectively. You may wish to explain why "dark reactions" is a poor designator and no longer used (since the reactions can occur in both the dark and the light).
- A discussion of the reason why colored objects appear the color they do may facilitate the students' understanding of why, for example, green light is ineffective for photosynthesis (not absorbed).
- Note that different species perceive colors differently. For example, honey bees see extremely bright colors where we see white and blue. This is the basis for insect-pollinating flowers. Print some photos that show the difference between the way we see flowers and the way insects do. Scientists believe that these patterns on flowers serve as a signal to attract the same species of pollinator.
- Show a diagram of the electromagnetic spectrum, and discuss how the wavelength of the radiation is related to its energy content.
- ATP and NADPH were introduced earlier as carrier molecules. Their connection between the light-dependent and light-independent reactions is an excellent opportunity for reinforcement of these molecules as bridges.
- The term *granum* dates from the days when microscopes revealed "grains" within the chloroplast. Now we realize that these grains consist of complex thylakoid membranes.
- Photosynthesis is much more complicated than the usual simple equation that a student may have seen in a previous course. Perhaps the best approach to presenting this topic is to follow a step-wise outline and rely heavily on transparencies and slides of the figures in the chapter.
- Even though *cyclic photophosphorylation* is presented *prior* to the noncyclic pathway in the text, note that this is done in deference to its position as the first to evolve. Point out that most existing plants use the noncyclic pathway.
- Tell the students to master each phase of photosynthesis before going to the next. Compartmentalizing the overall process will make the material less overwhelming to students and allow them to "connect the dots" when each phase is mastered.
- You may wish to note the similarities and differences between the ATP synthase mechanism in chloroplasts and mitochondria.
- Although the diagram of the Calvin-Benson cycle (Figure 6.10) is intimidating, the most important features are the entry of *carbon dioxide* and the production of the sugar phosphate, driven by *ATP* and *NADPH* from the light-dependent reactions.
- Bring in plant examples of C3, C4, and CAM plants. Note which plants are typical in the area where you are teaching and how that ties to climate.
- The emphasis on C3, C4, and CAM plants can be moderated according to the interests of the instructor. Omitting it will not affect future discussions in the book.
- Illustrate the mechanism by which guard cells open and close the stomata to regulate moisture loss.
- Discuss the idea of examining your "carbon footprint." The following website helps you calculate your own "footprint": http://www.nature.org/greenliving/carboncalculator/

Classroom and Laboratory Enrichment

- You can demonstrate the production of oxygen by plants with the following:
  a. Place *Elodea* (an aquarium plant) in a bowl and expose it to bright light.
  b. Invert a test tube over the plant and collect the bubbles.
  c. Remove the tube and immediately thrust a glowing wood splint into the tube.
  d. Result: The splint burns brightly in the high-oxygen air.
- Separate the pigments in green leaves by using paper chromatography. (Consult a botany or biology laboratory manual for the correct procedure.)
- When teaching in the fall, bring in leaves of different fall colors. Have the students identify the pigments that remain once chlorophyll has been degraded. Have the student speculate as to whether these pigments are present when leaves are green in the summer? If so, why can't you see them?
- Many students have never seen the action of a prism of separating white light into its component colors; a demonstration would most likely be appreciated.
- If a greenhouse facility is readily accessible, a brief tour and explanation of the devices used to control light, water, air, and heat are very instructive.
- Use a light microscope to view living *Euglena*. Note the chlorophyll in this photosynthetic protist.
- Show a video on photosynthesis.
- Provide a model of a chloroplast.
- Show an electron micrograph of a chloroplast and indicate where light-dependent reactions and light-independent reactions occur.
- Cut out separated leaf pigments from a paper chromatogram and elute each pigment from the paper with a small amount of alcohol. Using a spectrometer, determine the absorption spectrum for each pigment, and graph the results. (Consult a biology or botany laboratory manual for the procedure.)
- Remove two leaves from a plant and put each in a separate flask. Add sodium hydrogen carbonate to one flask and potassium hydroxide solution to the other. Seal each flask so it is air tight. Wait several days and examine the leaves. The leaf with the sodium hydrogen carbonate looks okay, but the leaf with the potassium hydroxide solution appears to be very weak. This is because the potassium hydroxide solution removed all of the carbon dioxide, so photosynthesis could not occur.
- Have a student make large posters of both phases of photosynthesis and explain the processes to the class.

Classroom Discussion Ideas

- C3 plants grow very quickly, where C4 plants grow more slowly. CAM plants grow even more slowly still. Discuss the trade-off of slower growth for high temperature and drought tolerance in these three categories of plant.
- There is so little moisture in the air of desert environments that temperatures drop suddenly at night. In the winter, particularly, how does this affect CAM plants?
- How might altitude affect what kind of plants predominate an area? Look into the plants found at each level of Mt. Washington in New Hampshire. You will see a vast difference in the plants that exist at each altitude level of this tall mountain!
- Use a map to draw a 10 mile circle around your location. What differences in plant-life do you see? How about in at 100 mile circle? 300 miles? What accounts for these differences?

Additional Ideas for Classroom Discussion

- In what ways could the "greenhouse effect" hurt agriculture? In what ways could it possibly *help*, especially in Canada and the countries of the former Soviet Union?
- Suppose you could purchase light bulbs that emitted only certain wavelengths of visible light. What wavelengths would promote the most photosynthesis? The least?
- Assume you have supernatural powers and can stop and start the two sets of photosynthesis reactions. Will stopping the light-independent affect the light-dependent, or vice versa?
- What conflicting "needs" confront a plant living in a hot, dry environment? What is the frequent result in C3 plants? How is the problem avoided in C4 plants?
- What colors of the visible spectrum are absorbed by objects that are black? What about white objects? Does it really matter if you wear light colors when it is hot outside?
- The website http://photoscience.la.asu.edu/photosyn/study.html has great ideas for discussing the importance of photosynthesis with students. The article "Why Study Photosynthesis" provides good argument for calling photosynthesis the most important biological process on Earth. The website also contains explanations for using reaction centers of chloroplasts as microscopic models for exploring technologies that use light as an energy source.
- Global warming has caused a rise in the world's oceans. How is this affecting world coastlines? How is this affecting the coastline closest to you? Can you envision some popular tourist locations that might be endangered by a rising ocean?
- What effect is global warming having on wildlife in the Arctic and in Antarctica?
- Are "greening" efforts like using biofuels and low-carbon imprint practices too little, too late?
- If global warming continues, will the areas where tropical diseases are prevalent expand northward?
- Investigate the original research performed in Antarctica, where the layers of snow tell the story of the increase in carbon dioxide in the atmosphere over time.

How Would You Vote? Classroom Discussion Ideas

- Monitor the voting for the online question. Poll your students: would they pay more for biofuel that is better for the environment? If so, how much more?
- How is production of ethanol from corn affecting the price of corn for food?
- Should biofuel-burning vehicles be mandated? What would happen if fossil fuel-burning vehicles were suddenly banned?
- Many businesses are going to four-day work weeks due to the increase in gas prices. Would switching to biofuels solve this problem? Why or why not?
- Research different forms of biofuels. Which form seems the most reasonable choice: Biomass? Biogas?
- Look into biofuel use in Brazil. Do you think the United States should use their program as a template?

Term Paper Topics, Library Activities, and Special Projects

- One of the hottest and driest summers in North America in recent years (1988) affected the production of food and grain crops. Prepare an analysis of the effect(s) of that summer's drought (or future ones) on food availability and its cost to the consumer.
- Full-spectrum lights are used to grow plants indoors. It's suggested that humans are less prone to illness when exposed to full-spectrum lights when indoors. Investigate this discovery.

- Consult a biochemist or advanced plant physiology text to learn of a laboratory technique that would clearly indicate whether the oxygen produced by plants is derived from *water* or from *carbon dioxide.*
- Prepare a detailed diagram of the Calvin-Benson cycle showing the introduction of radioactively labeled carbon dioxide and its subsequent journey through several "turns" of the cycle.
- Of the total amount of sunlight energy impinging on a green plant, what percentage of the energy is actually converted into glucose?
- Compare the mechanisms of C3 and C4 photosynthesis and give examples of plants that fit into each category.
- Discuss why radiation with greater or lesser wavelengths than visible light is not generally used in biological processes.
- Investigate "green" practices being used in your city or town. Research what practices might be used in the future. Are "green" practices being mandated in your state?
- Look up the original research performed by Calvin, Benson, and Bassham at the University of California. How did they discover the mechanisms of the Calvin-Benson cycle?
- Are there any fuel stations in your area that sell biofuel? If so, find out about how it is manufactured.
- Investigate the research performed by Engelmann to determine the colors of light that are most useful. Do you think his experiment could be reproduced easily today?
- What species might be endangered by global warming?

Possible Responses to *Critical Thinking* Questions

1. Let's look at the possibilities. The gain in weight of the tree *might* have been water simply absorbed through the roots and retained unchanged in the plant tissues, but not 164 pounds of it! Furthermore, we know that the water molecules are not going to combine *directly* with any other molecules in the tree. Of course we now know much more about the reactions of photosynthesis than van Helmont did, so we can conclude that the gain in weight was from the synthesis of carbohydrate (specifically, cellulose) in the chloroplasts of the leaf cells due to the reacting of carbon dioxide from the air and water from the soil.
2. If you notice bubbles coming from an aquatic plant, the bubbles would contain oxygen, an end-product of photosynthesis.
3. If a C3 plant absorbs a carbon radioisotope, it would first appear as a three-carbon substance known as PGA (phosphoglycerate). If a C4 plant absorbs that same isotope, it would be initially incorporated into a four-carbon acid, oxaloacetate.

Possible Responses to *Data Analysis Exercise* Questions

It is helpful when growing crops for use as biofuel to measure the net energy output, which is equal to the energy output minus the energy input.

1. The ethanol from one hectare of corn produced approximately 23 kcal X 10^6. It took approximately 18 kcal X 10^6 to grow the corn used to make ethanol.
2. The grass grown for synfuel had the highest ratio of energy output to energy input.
3. Corn would require the least amount of land to produce a given amount of biofuel energy.

7

HOW CELLS RELEASE CHEMICAL ENERGY

Chapter Outline

Objectives

1. Understand the relationship of food molecules to glucose, and thus to glycolysis.
2. Know the fundamental differences between glycolysis, fermentation (anaerobic respiration), and glycolysis followed by aerobic respiration.
3. Know the factors that determine whether an organism will carry on fermentation or aerobic respiration.
4. Know the raw materials (reactants) and products of each of these processes: glycolysis, fermentation, the Krebs cycle, and electron transfer phosphorylation.
5. Compare the function and composition of fast- and slow-twitch muscle fibers.
6. Describe how carbohydrates, fats, and proteins can enter the pathways of energy release.

Key Terms

mitochondrion
ATP
Luft's syndrome
Friedreich's ataxia
aerobic
anaerobic
aerobic respiration
fermentation
glycolysis
pyruvate
coenzyme
NAD^+, NADH
FAD, $FADH_2$
glycolysis
substrate-level phosphorylation
ATP-requiring
ATP-generating
Krebs cycle
pyruvate
acetyl Co-A
oxaloacetate
PGAL
electron transfer phosphorylation
coenzymes
ATP synthase
fermentation pathways
alcoholic fermentation
lactate fermentation
slow-twitch
fast-twitch
glycogen
triglycerides

Lecture Outline

7.1 Mighty Mitochondria

A. Mitochondria are the organelles responsible for releasing the energy stored in foods.
   1. In Friedreich's ataxia, too much iron in the mitochondria causes an accumulation of free radicals that attack valuable molecules of life.

B. Proper or improper functioning of mitochondria is the difference between health and disease.

7.2 Overview of Carbohydrate Breakdown Pathways

A. ATP is the prime energy carrier for all cells, both autotrophic and heterotrophic.

B. Aerobic Respiration
   1. Aerobic respiration (with oxygen) is the main energy-releasing pathway leading to ATP formation in eukaryotes; it occurs in the mitochondria.
   2. Every cell begins its energy-releasing pathways with glycolysis, which occurs in the cytoplasm and produces two molecules of pyruvate.

C. Overview of Aerobic Respiration
   1. The aerobic route is summarized:
      $C_6H_{12}O_6 + O_2$ ———> $CO_2 + H_2O$
   2. Three series of reactions are required for aerobic respiration.
      a. *Glycolysis* is the breakdown of glucose to pyruvate; small amounts of ATP are generated.
      b. The *Krebs cycle* degrades pyruvate to carbon dioxide and water, ATP is produced, and NAD and FAD accept H^+ ions and electrons to be carried to the electron transfer chain.
      c. *Electron transfer phosphorylation* processes the H^+ ions and electrons to generate high yields of ATP; oxygen is the final electron acceptor.

D. Anaerobic Fermentation Pathways
   1. Many bacteria, archea, fungi, and protists undergo fermentation to release energy from carbohydrates.
      a. Fermentation is an anaerobic (without oxygen) process that occurs in the cytoplasm.
      b. Anaerobic respiration is not as efficient as aerobic processes.
   2. Fermentation begins with glycolysis.
   3. Electron transport chains do not occur in this process.

7.3 Glycolysis—Glucose Breakdown Starts

A. Enzymes in the cytoplasm catalyze several steps in the breakdown of a six-carbon sugar glucose into two molecules of pyruvate, a three-carbon sugar.

B. Glycolysis begins as *energy-requiring* reactions.
   1. Glucose is first phosphorylated, and then split to form two molecules of PGAL using two ATP molecules in the beginning process.
   2. The two molecules of PGAL are ready to enter the next reaction.

C. Glycolysis continues as *energy-releasing* reactions.
   1. Enzymes remove H^+ and electrons from PGAL to change NAD^+ to NADH (which is used later in electron transfer).
   2. By substrate-level phosphorylation, four ATPs are produced.

D. The end products of glycolysis are (for each glucose molecule): two pyruvates, two ATPs (net gain), and two NADH.

7.4 Second Stage of Aerobic Respiration

A. Acetyl-CoA Formation
   1. As each pyruvate enters the mitochondria, one carbon is removed and attaches to oxygen, forming carbon dioxide; the two-carbon fragment remaining joins coenzyme A to form Acetyl-CoA.
   2. Two NAD^+ are reduced.

B. The Krebs Cycle
   1. Each three-carbon Acetyl-CoA molecule enters the Krebs cycle separately and joins oxaloacetate, already present from a previous "turn" of the cycle.
   2. H^+ and e^- are transferred to NAD^+ and FAD to become NADH and $FADH_2$, respectively; important potential energy for the cell comes from the eight NADH and two $FADH_2$ coenzyme molecules produced during the Krebs cycle.
   3. Two molecules of ATP are produced by substrate-level phosphorylation.
   4. Most of the molecules are recycled to conserve oxaloacetate for continuous processing of acetyl-CoA.
   5. Carbon dioxide is released as a by-product.

7.5 Aerobic Respiration's Big Energy Payoff

A. Electron Transfer Phosphorylation
   1. NADH and $FADH_2$ give up their electrons to transfer (enzyme) systems embedded in the mitochondrial inner membrane.
      a. The energy is used to pump hydrogen ions out of the inner compartment.
      b. When hydrogen ions flow back through the ATP synthases in the channels, the coupling of P_i to ADP yields ATP.
   2. Oxygen joins with the "spent" electrons from the glucose molecule and H^+ to yield water.
      a. Without oxygen, electrons back up the electron transfer chains, and no H^+ gradients form.
      b. No gradient means no ATP; complex cells cannot survive long without enough ATP for their processes.

B. Summing Up: The Energy Harvest
   1. Electron transfer yields 32 ATPs, glycolysis yields two ATPs, and Krebs yields two ATPs for a grand total of 36 ATPs per glucose molecule.
   2. Normally, for every NADH produced within the mitochondria and processed by the electron transfer chain, three ATP are formed; $FADH_2$ yields two ATPs.

a. In most cells (skeletal, brain), NADH from the cytoplasm cannot enter the mitochondrion and must transfer its electrons to FAD, yielding two ATP (for a total of 36).

b. However in the liver, heart, and kidney cells, NAD^+ accepts the electrons to yield three ATP; two NADH are produced per glucose giving a total yield of 38 ATP.

7.6 Fermentation

A. Anaerobic pathways operate when oxygen is absent (or limited); pyruvate from glycolysis is metabolized to produce molecules other than acetyl-CoA.

B. Two Fermentation Pathways

1. Organisms that carry on fermentation (fermenters) are diverse; many die when exposed to oxygen, while others use oxygen but switch when it becomes scarce.
2. Fermentation yields enough energy for many single-celled anaerobic organisms and is sufficient for some aerobic cells when oxygen levels drop, but it is insufficient for large, multicelled organisms.

C. Alcoholic Fermentation

1. Fermentation begins with glucose degradation to pyruvate.
2. Cellular enzymes convert pyruvate to acetaldehyde, which then accepts electrons from NADH to become alcohol.
3 Yeasts are valuable in the baking industry (carbon dioxide by-product makes dough "rise") and in alcoholic beverage production.

D. Lactate Fermentation

1. Certain bacteria (as in milk) and muscle cells have the enzymes capable of converting pyruvate to lactate.
2. No additional ATP beyond the net two from glycolysis is produced, but NAD^+ is regenerated.
3. When muscle cells are very active, they convert to producing lactate temporarily.
   a. Slow-twitch muscle fibers (dark red) support steady, prolonged activity because they have many mitochondria making large quantities of ATP.
   b. Fast-twitch muscle fibers (light color) have few mitochondria and produce small amounts of ATP by lactate fermentation, supporting quick, non-sustained demands for energy.

7.7 Alternative Energy Sources in Food

A. Complex Carbohydrates

1. After eating a meal, glucose is absorbed into the blood.
   a. Insulin levels rise, causing greater uptake of glucose by cells for entry into glycolysis.
   b. Excess glucose is converted into glycogen for storage in muscles and the liver.
2. Between meals blood glucose levels fall.
   a. The hormone glucagon prompts liver cells to convert glycogen back to glucose.
   b. Glycogen levels are adequate but can be depleted in 12 hours.

B. Fats

1. Excess fats (including those made from carbohydrates) are stored away in cells of adipose tissue.
2. Fats are digested into glycerol, which enters glycolysis, and fatty acids, which enter the Krebs cycle.
3. Because fatty acids have many more carbon and hydrogen atoms, they are degraded more slowly and yield greater amounts of ATP.
4. Excess glucose can be converted to fat by a diversion of acetyl-CoA into a pathway that synthesizes fatty acids.

C. Proteins
   1. Amino acids are released by digestion and travel in the blood.
   2. After the amino group is removed, the amino acid remnant is fed into the Krebs cycle.

7.8 Mighty Mitochondria (Revisited)

A. Approximately 1 in every 5,000 people has a mitochondrial disease.
   1. Problems with mitochondrial functions may be responsible for additional disease, such as Alzheimer's and Parkinson's diseases.
   2. Researchers are more apt to try to cure diseases that affect more individuals.

Suggestions for Presenting the Material

- Stress the elegance of the cycle that connects photosynthesis and aerobic respiration. The products of photosynthesis are the reactants of aerobic respiration, and the products of aerobic respiration are the reactants of photosynthesis. How has man offset the natural balance of this cycle?
- The critical role of ATP must be emphasized. Distinguish clearly between the *transfer* of energy from carbohydrates to ATP (this chapter) and the *synthesis* of the ATP molecule (Chapter 6).
- The material in this chapter is most easily and logically presented by skillful use of the figures on the overhead transparencies or slides.
  a. Begin with the flowchart of glycolysis (aerobic respiration), the Krebs cycle, and electron transfer. Point out the entry molecules, exit molecules, and key intermediates as well as the total energy yield (36 ATPs).
  b. Next, examine the graphics that depict more of the details of glycolysis, Krebs cycle, and electron transfer.
- As you progress deeper into the pathway discussions, it is advisable to refer frequently to the overview graphic so that you keep the "big picture" in mind. You will need to indicate that fermentation begins with glucose and proceeds from pyruvate.
- The synthesis of ATP by electron transfer phosphorylation is perhaps beyond the scope of some courses for nonscience majors. It may be omitted without detriment to the overall presentation.
- Summing up the total energy yield is important.
- You can emphasize the roles of other foods (proteins and lipids) and their relationship to carbohydrates by following the arrows of Figure 7.12. This especially appeals to students interested in nutrition.
- Emphasize that plants do carry on aerobic respiration. Many students have the mistaken idea that plants *only* photosynthesize.
- Have students work on learning the reactants and products for each step of cellular respiration first. For example, glucose and two ATPs are the reactants for glycolysis; two pyruvates and four ATPs are the products. Once they have the reactants and products learned the intermediate reactants are easier to learn and understand.
- Stress to students the importance of knowing the *processes* rather than memorizing all the various *reactions*.
- Although the focus in this chapter is the generation of ATP, you may wish to explain to your students that another major function of respiration is the production of intermediates for biosynthetic reactions.
- Design an exercise for the class where you divide the class into team A and team B. Name a characteristic of glycolysis, the Krebs cycle, or electron transfer phosphorylation. Whichever team guesses the correct category of the three, scores a point. Make the winning team a congratulatory

certificate! Perhaps in the spirit of competition, the students will master the specific details of each process.

- Often students get so caught up in learning the processes, they miss the big picture. Don't miss the forest for the trees. Keep repeating to students at every opportunity that the entire purpose of all the steps of anaerobic respiration, fermentation, and aerobic respiration is conversion of stored energy into usable energy.

Classroom and Laboratory Enrichment

- Show a video on cellular respiration.
- Demonstrate a computer simulation whereby basal metabolism rate (BMR) is calculated by measuring oxygen consumption.
- Select several persons who differ in physical stature and exercise conditioning. Allow them to exercise vigorously for several minutes; then determine heart rate and the length of time before breathing rate returns to normal (indicates extent of oxygen debt).
- Explain the purpose of lactic acid in muscle fatigue. Be sure to mention that once the oxygen debt has been repaid, the lactic acid breaks down into the harmless byproducts water and carbon dioxide, and physical activity can resume.
- Explain the difference between slow-twitch and fast-twitch muscles by comparing marathon runners and sprinters.
- Flow-chart the steps of cellular respiration in class, stressing the reactants and products of each step.
- Ask an exercise physiologist to talk to the class about the effect(s) of exercise on body metabolic rate.
- Discuss some animal examples of "red" and "white" types of muscles. A goose is an animal that seems to have almost unlimited endurance. If we cooked a goose for dinner, it would contain primarily dark meat. On the other hand, much of the tuna fish's meat is light in color, representing its ability to move in quick spurts of rapid movement.
- Show an electron micrograph of a mitochondrion and point out the matrix (inner compartment), cristae (inner membranes), and outer compartment. Relate this to the drawings in the text.
- If there is a brewery or winery nearby, arrange for a field trip. Brew masters and winemakers generally are happy to conduct a tour through the facilities and explain the processes involved.
- Perform Activity 1 on the following website, http://www.accessexcellence.org/LC/SS/ferm_activity.php, which provides a fermentation experiment involving yeast.

Classroom Discussion Ideas

- Certain diseases more common in the elderly have been tied to mitochondrial defects. Could mitochondrial degradation be a part of normal aging? How might you detect this in patients?
- Tell how the measurement of oxygen consumption by a human patient is related to metabolic rate.
- In *Luft's syndrome* the mitochondria are not producing sufficient amounts of ATP. What series of reactions could be most responsible for the deficiency? What are some other conditions that are thought to involve mitochondrial malfunction?
- Mitochondria are critical for normal metabolism. From which parent did each human being's original mitochondria come from at conception?
- Why are so many diseases attributed to defective mitochondria?

Additional Ideas for Classroom Discussion

- Table wines, those that have *not* been fortified, have an alcoholic content of about 10–12 percent. What factors could limit the production of alcohol during fermentation? Is it self-limiting, or do the vintners have to stop it with some additive?
- Your text lists two types of fermentation: one leads to alcohol, the other to lactate. Which occurs in yeasts and why? Which pathway is reversible? What would be the consequences of nonreversible lactate formation in muscle cells?
- Yeast is added to a mixture of malt, hops, and water to brew beer—a product in which alcohol and carbon dioxide are desirable! Why is yeast added to bread dough?
- What happens to lactate produced during periods of intense muscle activity? Why is it important that the lactate is broken down quickly?
- What effect do large amounts of lactic acid have on muscle tissue?
- Analyze the simple equation for cellular respiration by telling exactly *at what place* in the aerobic metabolism of glucose each item in the equation is a participant.
- Think about which parts of a chicken are "dark meat." Considering the mitochondrial content of dark versus white meat, why does this make sense?
- What is "metabolic water"?
- Why is fermentation necessary under anaerobic conditions? That is, why does the cell convert pyruvate to some fermentation product when it does not result in any additional ATP production?
- What is the benefit of lactate fermentation to our bodies? What happens if we fail to "repay" our oxygen debt?

How Would You Vote? Classroom Discussion Ideas

- Monitor the voting for the online question. One's response to this question depends on whether you have great compassion for humankind or are more interested in successful business ventures. Obviously, pharmaceutical companies are in business to make money—lots of money. Therefore, they cannot profitably invest time and money in developing a drug/treatment for a small number of persons who will be grateful, but not make the company rich. The only alternative is for the government to give researchers and companies financial incentives, such as tax breaks, to pursue such research.
- One additional factor to keep in mind is that discoveries made while investigating "orphan" diseases (those affecting only a small amount of patients) can ultimately provide useful information for the study of other conditions. For example, if a researcher were investigating Friedreich's ataxia, inroads might be forged in the treatment of other diseases that could be related to mitochondrial malfunctions (e.g., Alzheimer's and Parkinson's diseases). This exact scenario has occurred in the study of seizure disorders.

Term Paper Topics, Library Activities, and Special Projects

- Rotenone is a fish poison and insecticide. Its mode of action is listed on container labels as "respiratory poison." Research exactly where and how it disrupts cellular respiration.
- Prepare a fermentation vat with grape juice and yeast (don't seal it!). Allow the process to proceed for a few days, then strain the fluid into a flask and distill it. What gas is produced during fermentation? What product distills at 78.5°C?

- Certain flour beetles and clothes moths can live in environments where exogenous water is virtually unobtainable, yet they thrive. What are the mechanisms they use for the synthesis and retention of water?
- How is it possible that some organisms can survive in both aerobic and anaerobic environments? Make a list of some of these organisms. Do any of these serve as health risks to humans?
- Investigate obligate anaerobes. Why can't these organisms convert energy aerobically?
- Use diagrams to show how radioactive carbon-14 in glucose fed to rats could end up in body fat and proteins.
- Because ATP is the direct source of energy for body cells, why not bypass the lengthy digestion and cellular metabolism processes necessary for carbohydrate breakdown and eat ATP directly?
- Investigate how the liver stores glucose as glycogen. How are these reactions reversible?
- Which byproducts of cellular metabolism are disposed of in the urine? Can an examination of urine determine any metabolic disorders?
- Damaged, swollen cans of food should be thrown away because of the danger that they have been infected with botulism. Investigate this pathogen and how it grows in such an environment.
- Hydrogen cyanide is the lethal gas used in gas chambers. How does it cause death?

Possible Responses to *Critical Thinking* Questions

1. Altitude sickness results from a lack of oxygen, but more specifically, it results from the deficiency of oxygen needed to "pull" the train of electrons along the electron transfer chain, which provides the energy necessary to produce ATP. This would explain why the symptoms of altitude sickness would mimic those of cyanide poisoning, namely the inability to produce enough ATP to power the muscle cells necessary for breathing and pumping blood.
2. Prokaryotes use the plasma membrane for electron transfer phosphorylation.
3. The journey of the bar-tailed godwit is indeed an amazing feat! This is accomplished by the majority of the flight muscles being of the dark meat variety. The darker color of the muscle is due to an abundance of myoglobin, which stores oxygen. This type of muscle is designed for prolonged activity due to its better endurance level.
4. The *E. coli* bacteria in an aerobic environment will produce more bacteria than the sample in an anaerobic environment over the same time period. This is due to the fact that *E. coli* is classified as a facultative anaerobe, which means that it can survive in either the presence or absence of oxygen—but it prefers an aerobic environment.

Possible Responses to *Data Analysis Exercise* Questions

The disease Tetralogy of Fallot (FT) is characterized by low oxygen levels and subsequent mitochondrial damage.

1. The abnormality in this study that was most strongly associated with TF was the number of mitochondria.
2. The percentage of TF patients that had mitochondria that were abnormal in size was 25 percent.
3. From the data provided, it appears that those patients that have both abnormal numbers and shapes of mitochondria are the most affected by the disease.

8

DNA STRUCTURE AND FUNCTION

Chapter Outline

A HERO DOG'S GOLDEN CLONES
EUKARYOTIC CHROMOSOMES
- DNA Packaging
- Chromosome Number
- Autosomes and Sex Chromosomes

THE DISCOVERY OF DNA'S FUNCTION
- Early Clues of DNA's Function
- Confirmation of DNA's Function

THE DISCOVERY OF DNA'S STRUCTURE
- Evidence of DNA's Structure
- DNA's Base-Pair Sequence

DNA REPLICATION
- How Ss DNA Duplicated?
- A Host of Participants

MUTATIONS: CAUSE AND EFFECT
- DNA Repair Mechanisms
- Environmental Causes of Mutations
- The Short Story of Rosalind Franklin

ANIMAL CLONING
- Reproductive Cloning
- Somatic Cell Nuclear Transfer
- Therapeutic Cloning

DATA ANALYSIS EXERCISE
SUMMARY
SELF-QUIZ
CRITICAL THINKING

Objectives

1. Understand how experiments using bacteria and viruses demonstrated that instructions for producing heritable traits are encoded in DNA.
2. Understand the people and events leading up to the discovery of DNA's structure.
3. Describe the key features of a DNA molecule.
4. Know the parts of a nucleotide and how they are linked together to make a DNA molecule.
5. Understand how DNA is replicated and repaired.
6. Discuss the processes involved in cloning mammals.
7. Distinguish between the different types of cloning.

Key Terms

clone
telomeres
DNA
bacteriophages
nucleotides
deoxyribose
adenine
guanine
thymine
cytosine
pyrimidines
purines
x-ray diffraction images
base pairing
double helix
semiconservative replication
DNA replication
helicases
replication enzymes
DNA polymerases
DNA ligases
DNA proofreading mechanisms
repair enzymes
embryo cloning
artificial twinning
adult cloning
therapeutic cloning
somatic cell nuclear transfer (SCNT)
stem cells

Lecture Outline

8.1 A Hero Dog's Golden Clones

A. The History of Trakr the Search Dog

1. Search dog from Nova Scotia handled by Constable James Symington.
2. Found the fifth and final survivor of the World Trade Center attacks.
3. Trakr collapsed from smoke and chemical inhalation, burns, and exhaustion.
4. Trakr later suffered from a degenerative neurological disease that was likely linked to toxic smoke exposure at the World Trade Center. Trakr died in April 2009.

B. Preserving Trakr's DNA

1. Constable James Symington wrote an essay about Trakr and won a contest to find the world's most clonable dog.
2. Trakr's DNA was sent to Korea and inserted into donor egg cells.
3. Five puppies, all clones of Trakr, were sent to Symington in July 2009.

8.2 Eukaryotic Chromosomes

A. Chromosome Structure

1. DNA must be tightly packaged in order to fit into the nucleus of a cell.
2. Each chromosome consists of one strand of DNA during most of the cell's life.
3. During cell division, DNA replicates and the chromosomes consists of two identical strands of DNA.
4. Condensed, duplicated coils of DNA molecules (chromosomes coiled) are wrapped around histone proteins.

B. Chromosome Number

1. The number of chromosomes is species specific.
2. Human cells are diploid, meaning they contain two of each chromosome.
3. The number of chromosomes can be analyzed by a karyotype.

C. Autosomes and Sex Chromosomes

1. Autosomes are chromosomes that are the same in males and females.
2. Sex chromosomes differ between males and females.
   a. Human females have two X chromosomes.
   b. Human males have an X and Y chromosome.

8.3 The Discovery of DNA's Function

A. Early and Puzzling Clues

1. Johann Miescher is credited with the discovery of DNA in the late 1800s.

2. In 1928, Fred Griffith was working with S (pathogenic) and R (nonpathogenic) strains of a pneumonia-causing bacterium.
3. Griffith performed four experiments.
   a. Injected mice with R cells; mice lived.
   b. Injected mice with S cells; mice died, and blood samples contained many live S cells.
   c. S cells were heat-killed, then injected into mice; mice lived.
   d. Live R cells plus heat-killed S cells were injected into mice; mice died, and live S cells were found in the blood.
4. Some substance from the S cells had transformed the R cells.
   a. Both proteins and nucleic acids were candidates.
   b. In 1944, Oswald Avery showed that the substance was DNA.

B. Confirmation of DNA Function
1. Viruses called bacteriophages use bacterial cells for reproduction.
2. Because they consist of only a protein coat and a nucleic acid core, these viruses were used in experiments by Hershey and Chase to prove which of these was the hereditary material. (It was the nucleic acid.)
   a. ^{35}S-labeled proteins in the bacteriophage coat did not enter the bacteria and thus were not participating in providing directions for new virus assembly.
   b. ^{32}P-labeled DNA in the viral core did enter the bacteria and directed new virus assembly.

8.4 The Discovery of DNA's Structure

A. DNA's Building Blocks
1. DNA is composed of four kinds of nucleotides, each of which consists of:
   a. A five-carbon sugar—deoxyribose.
   b. A phosphate group.
   c. One of four bases—adenine (A), guanine (G), thymine (T), or cytosine (C).
2. The nucleotides are similar, but T and C are single-ring pyrimidines; A and G are double-ring purines.
3. In 1949, Edwin Chargaff noted two critical bits of data.
   a. The four kinds of nucleotide bases making up a DNA molecule differ in relative amounts from species to species.
   b. The amount of A = T, and the amount of G = C.
4. Rosalind Franklin used x-ray diffraction techniques to produce images of DNA molecules.
   a. X-ray diffraction uses a beam of electrons directed at a molecule, which scatters the x-ray in a pattern.
   b. Franklin used x-ray diffraction with a "wet" form of DNA.
   c. DNA exists as a long, thin molecule of uniform diameter.
   d. The structure is highly repetitive.
   e. DNA is helical.
5. Enter James Watson and Francis Crick.
   a. They used numerous sources of data (including Franklin's and Chargaff's) and built various models of DNA.
   b. In 1953, they discovered and published the structure of DNA.

B. Patterns of Base Pairing
1. The following features were incorporated into their models.

a. Single-ringed thymine was hydrogen bonded with double-ringed adenine, and single-ringed cytosine with double-ringed guanine, along the entire length of the molecule.
b. The backbone was made of chains of sugar–phosphate linkages.
c. The molecule was double stranded and looked like a ladder, with a twist to form a double helix.

2. The base pairing is *constant* for all species, but the sequence of base pairs in a nucleotide strand is *different* from one species to the next—the basis for life's diversity.

8.5 DNA Replication

A. How DNA Is Duplicated
1. Semiconservative replication.
a. First, the two strands of DNA unwind and expose their bases.
b. Each unwound strand of DNA serves as a template for the synthesis of a new strand.
c. Unattached nucleotides unbound in cytoplasm are paired with exposed bases of the template strands.
d. Thus, replication results in DNA molecules that consist of one "old" strand and one "new" strand; this is designated "semiconservative replication."
2. Replication enzymes.
a. Initiator proteins specify where DNA replication begins.
b. Helicases unzip the weak hydrogen bonds, causing the DNA molecule to unwind.
c. A specific enzyme adds RNA primers, which are needed for the DNA polymerase to attach and begin replication.
d. Beginning at the primers, DNA polymerases attaches free nucleotides to the growing strand in a 5′ → 3′ direction.
e. DNA ligases seal new short stretches of nucleotides into one continuous strand.
f. The end result is two new molecules of DNA, each consisting of an "old" strand and a "new" strand, and each identical in sequence.

8.6 DNA Repair

A. DNA repair mechanisms.
1. Mutations cause a DNA molecule to have a different sequence than the parent molecule.
2. DNA proofreading mechanisms fix most errors that occur during DNA replication.
3. DNA polymerases "proofread" the new bases for mismatched pairs, which are replaced with the correct bases.
4. If DNA polymerases cannot correct the mismatch, the mutation is past on during subsequent rounds of DNA replication.
5. Unrepaired mutations can cause cancer.
6. Some mutations are beneficial and give rise to genetic variation, which is the source of evolution.

B. Environmental Causes of Mutations
1. X-rays, gamma rays, and UV light can cause mutations.
a. UV light causes adjacent thymines to covalently bond (pyrimidine dimer).
b. Pyrimidine dimers form a kink in the DNA, resulting in DNA replication errors.
2. Natural and synthetic chemicals lead to mutation by modifying bases and causing DNA mismatches during DNA replication.

C. Rosalind's Story
1. Rosalind Franklin was a superb practitioner of x-ray crystallography.
2. Despite intense competition with a co-worker, she worked on taking pictures of DNA and theorizing about its structure.

3. At one of her talks, she correctly presented information regarding the number of strands of DNA, the helical nature, the diameter and the distance between bases. She did not, however, understand how her data could be used to create a model of DNA.
4. Franklin's boss, Maurice Wilkins, was not present for the presentation, but Watson was.
5. Watson and Crick ultimately used Franklin's data to build their Nobel Prize-winning model of DNA.
6. Franklin died at the age of 38 from ovarian cancer, likely caused by exposure to x-rays.
7. Franklin died before the Nobel Prize was awarded to Watson, Crick, and Wilkins.

8.7 Animal Cloning

A. Embryo Cloning
1. Embryo splitting is a natural process that results in identical twins.
2. Embryo splitting can also be artificially induced for research and animal breeding purposes.
    a. The embryos are produced by *in vitro* fertilization, allowed to develop to the eight-cell stage, and then separated.
    b. Small clusters of cells are implanted into surrogate mothers, where they grow into identical clones.

B. Adult Cloning
1. The nucleus from an adult animal's differentiated cell (say liver) replaces an unfertilized egg's nucleus by microinjection in a process known as *somatic cell nuclear transfer (SCNT).*
2. The cell is induced to divide by chemicals or electric shock.
3. Soon a cluster of embryonic cells is implanted into a surrogate mother.

C. Therapeutic Cloning
1. The embryos generated by SCNT can be used to harvest undifferentiated stem cells.
2. These cells could be instructed to differentiate into cell types of specific tissue and organs, and ultimately could aid those who suffer from fatal diseases.

Suggestions for Presenting the Material

- This chapter amplifies the information on nucleic acids presented at the close of Chapter 3. Depending on the amount of information you presented in your lectures at that time, some of this chapter could be repetitious.
- For best success in presenting this chapter, use diagrams, models, and figures when discussing the structure and replication of DNA.
- Students find it hard to understand and identify the components of DNA, so begin this section of the text by making sure that understand what deoxyribose (the five-carbon sugar in DNA), phosphate groups, and the four nitrogen-containing bases each look like. Briefly show figures of the molecular structures of each of these three major players, and then introduce the term *nucleotide.*
- This is a good time to remind students that scientists need to be aware of the social impact of their work. At various times, the United States government has placed limits on stem cell research. This chapter provides the opportunity to have a discussion about the rights a government should have over such areas of research, the ethics of stem cell research, and/or the ethics of using stem cells to treat diseases.
- Ask students to think about the benefits and drawbacks of DNA as a genetic material.
- Search online for computer software that allows the user to build and/or manipulate DNA models on the screen.

Classroom and Laboratory Enrichment

- Use large three-dimensional models to show DNA structure.
- Ask students to work in teams of two. Give each student a set of labeled paper shapes representing the sugars, phosphate groups, and each of the four bases present in DNA. Ask each student to construct a short segment of a DNA strand while his or her partner builds the complementary strand of the DNA double helix. Then ask students to demonstrate the semiconservative replication of DNA.
- Use a video to demonstrate the semiconservative nature of DNA replication. There is also an excellent website by the Howard Hughes Medical Institute Foundation (HHMI) that includes some of the best interactive clips of DNA replication, transcription, and translation I have ever used. This information can be used here and in Chapter 12: http://www.dnai.org.
- DNA is described as a "double helix" or "twisted ladder." An inexpensive device that can show this structure very well is a plastic parakeet ladder that is flexible enough to be twisted from "ladder" configuration to "helix."
- If you search for DNA replication on the Internet you will find many great animations. Here are two of the many I have found: http://www.johnkyrk.com/DNAreplication.html and http://www.umass.edu/molvis/bme3d/materials/jtat_080510/exploringdna/contents/contents.htm (interactive).
- Another website of interest featuring tutorials along with problem sets based on DNA's structure is: http://www.biology.arizona.edu/biochemistry/activities/DNA/DNA.html.
- Prepare a chronological listing of the dates, people, and significant contributions to the discovery of the structure of DNA.
- A distinction in the 1956 edition of the popular high school text *Modern Biology* by Moon, Mann, and Otto was the complete absence of any mention of DNA. Use this as an example of how much we know now compared to then.

Classroom Discussion Ideas

- Why are so many nuclear transfers in cloning experiments not successful?
- Why don't the *different species* of single-celled and multicellular organisms have *different nucleic acids* for coding hereditary information? Why do they all use DNA as the hereditary material?
- One of the problems consistently encountered with cloned organisms is their rapidly declining health. Why do you think this is happening?
- What are the benefits touted by those who advocate cloning? What are the objections raised by those who oppose cloning?

Additional Ideas for Classroom Discussion

- What are some reasons DNA is double-stranded instead of single-stranded?
- When during the cell cycle does DNA replication occur?
- What are some advantages of semiconservative replication?
- Of the experiments done before the structure of DNA was known, which ones demonstrated that nucleic acid was the carrier of heredity?

- How did the Hershey and Chase experiment settle the question of which molecule—DNA or protein—carries heredity?
- Why should the term *DNA relative* replace the more popular term *blood relative* when referring to human kinship?
- Which of the following is a more likely source of altered DNA sequences?
  a. A new copy has an error made during replication from a correct original.
  b. A new copy has an error faithfully copied from an incorrect original.
- A *casual* reading of any one of a number of biology texts would imply that Fred Griffith was a pioneer in DNA research. Is this an accurate assessment?
- What would the shape of a DNA molecule be like if purines paired with purines and pyrimidines paired with pyrimidines?
- Why do eukaryotic cells "need" *histones, nucleosomes,* and *looped regions?*

How Would You Vote? Classroom Discussion Ideas

- Monitor the voting for the online question. Have the students explore the ramifications of banning research on animal cloning. What arguments could researchers use to continue their cloning experiments? Can the ban be enforced by a "cloning ethic"? How might scientists "get around" the ban? When would you consider cloning to be unethical?

Term Paper Topics, Library Activities, and Special Projects

- What happens if DNA is damaged? How does a cell "recognize" an error in base pairing? Does an organism have ways of repairing such damage?
- Describe the research tools (such as radioactive labeling) that have been used in the past and are being used today to learn about DNA structure and function.
- Describe how the semiconservative nature of DNA replication was discovered.
- Learn more about the collaborative nature of scientific discovery, using the discovery of DNA as an example. Could such a discovery have been made at the time by only one individual working alone?
- The shape and structure of bacteriophages is reminiscent of a piece of hardware designed for outer space exploration. To make it more visually appealing, construct a model from inexpensive materials.
- Prepare a synopsis of James Watson's account of the discovery of DNA as recorded in the book *The Double Helix,* published by Atheneum.
- Rosalind Franklin collected data critical to the elucidation of DNA structure. However, she is hardly mentioned in textbook accounts. Locate a biography of her and speculate on why she is lesser known than her collaborators.
- Using the diagram in Figure 8.9 as a starting point, show how copies of DNA from your great-grandparents are present in you.
- Explain in simple language how animals can be cloned.
- Learn more about the animals that have been successfully cloned in various worldwide procedures. What is the status of these animals? For example: Dolly is no longer living, but her lambs are still alive.

- Research the current status of cloning in the United States. Are any university programs dedicated to the procedure? What animals (if any) have been successfully cloned? What are the restrictions or bans on cloning in the United States?

Possible Responses to *Critical Thinking* Questions

1. The replication would look like this (dark lines = ^{15}N; light lines = ^{14}N)

2. As submitted in the movie *Jurassic Park*, something always goes wrong when you mess with nature. Therefore, the con to cloning a woolly mammoth, first of all, would be the question; "Why do we wish to do this?" If the animal went extinct, it is for a good reason through the processes of natural selection. What benefit is there in bringing back an animal that has been selected out of existence? I would also add another question to the con side—how much money would this cost, and can this be justified in light of other ongoing medical research needs? The pro side might argue that in science we are always learning, and to see a slice of the history of Earth preserved and then made whole again in the woolly mammoth would provide valuable details about the conditions necessary for its survival in prehistoric times. The process would be a way of gathering data, which science is always doing. It would be fascinating to study a living mammoth: for example, to be able to examine its physiological makeup and compare this to its descendants, the African and Asian elephants.
3. Normally, when exposed to UV radiation, the thymine dimers in the DNA molecule are identified and excised, then replaced with undamaged nucleotides produced during protein synthesis of interphase. The corrected copy is passed on during DNA replication. Individuals with XP have no enzymes available to repair the thymine dimers. With defects in the repair processes, the resulting mutations lead to defects in the corresponding gene products, which lead to all the symptoms of XP.

Possible Responses to *Data Analysis Exercise* Questions

The Hershey-Chase experiment was designed to detect which portion of a virus entered infected bacteria. The protein coat of the virus was labeled with sulfur and the DNA was labeled with phosphorus.

1. Before blending, the percentage of ^{35}S was approximately 5 percent and the percentage of ^{32}P was around 16 percent.
2. After four minutes, there was 80 percent of ^{35}S and 30 percent of ^{32}P.
3. The researchers knew that the radioisotopes in the fluid did not come from broken bacteria, because the number of bacteria remained fairly constant.
4. The extracellular concentration of ^{35}S increases the most with blending. These results indicate that viruses inject DNA into the bacteria, because the percentage of extracellular ^{32}P stays low in extracellular fluid. This shows that the phosphorus, which labels DNA, is largely inside the infected bacteria.

9

FROM DNA TO PROTEIN

Chapter Outline

Objectives

1. Compare and contrast mRNA, tRNA, and rRNA.
2. Describe the post-transcriptional modifications mRNA must go through to exit the nucleus.
3. Discuss the role of tRNA in translation and how nucleotides are added.
4. Be able to differentiate between codon and anticodon.
5. Discuss the role of codons in the genetic code.
6. Explain how transcription is initiated.
7. Describe the modifications that occur before eukaryote mRNAs are exported from the nucleus.
8. Describe in detail the three stages of translation.
9. Diagram the overall process of transcription and translation.
10. Differentiate between transcription and DNA replication.
11. Differentiate between insertions, deletions, transposons, base-pair substitutions, and frameshift mutations.

Key Terms

transcription
translation
base sequence
messenger RNA
ribosomal RNA
transfer RNA
ribose
uracil
RNA polymerase
promoter
mRNA transcripts
guanine "cap"
poly-A tail
introns
exons
alternative splicing
amino acids
codons
genetic code
anticodon
ribosomes
initiation
elongation
termination
AUG start codon
peptide bond
stop codon
release factors
gene mutations
base-pair substitution
frameshift mutation
insertions
deletions
transposable elements
mutation rate
gene expression
gene

Lecture Outline

9.1 The Aptly *Acronymed* RIPs

A. Ribosome-inactivating proteins (RIPs) prevent protein synthesis in a cell by inactivating the protein-building machinery (ribosomes).
   1. Since proteins are critical to all cellular processes, a loss of protein synthesis causes death.
   2. Not all RIPs efficiently enter cells, but those that do are very toxic.

B. Ricin is a highly toxic RIP found in the seeds of the castor-oil plant.
   1. Although banned as a weapon in most countries, ricin is simple to obtain from raw materials, and is commonly sought by assassins and terrorists.
   2. One molecule of ricin can inactivate 1000 ribosomes per minute.
   3. Someone who inhales ricin can die from low blood pressure and respiratory failure within a few days.

C. Other RIPs include enterotoxin, which causes food poisoning, and Shiga toxin, which causes dysentery.

9.2 DNA, RNA, and Gene Expression

A. DNA stores all the genetic information in a cell and passes it to the offspring.

B. There are several types of RNA in a cell.
   1. Messenger RNAs (mRNAs) carry the information from the DNA to the ribosomes, where the information is made into a protein.
   2. Transfer RNAs (tRNAs) are involved in protein synthesis. They deliver the appropriate amino acid to the ribosomes as the mRNA is read.
   3. Ribosomal RNAs (rRNAs) are also involved in protein synthesis. They are the main structural component of a ribosome.
   4. MicroRNAs (miRNAs) regulate gene expression.

C. RNA is structurally different from DNA.
   1. RNA has the sugar ribose; DNA has deoxyribose.
   2. In RNA, the base thymine is replaced by uracil.
   3. RNA is typically single-stranded; DNA is double-stranded.

D. The path from genes to proteins (gene expression) has two steps.
   1. In *transcription,* molecules of mRNA are produced on the DNA templates in the nucleus.
   2. In *translation,* mRNA molecules shipped from the nucleus to the cytoplasm are used as templates for polypeptide assembly.

E. The overall plan is expressed as:

$$\text{DNA} \xrightarrow{\textit{transcription}} \text{mRNA} \xrightarrow{\textit{translation}} \text{proteins}$$

9.3 How Is RNA Transcribed from DNA?

A. The Nature of Transcription

1. Transcription differs from DNA replication in three ways.
   a. Only *one* region of *one* DNA strand is used as a template.
   b. RNA polymerase is used instead of DNA polymerase.
   c. The result of transcription is a single-stranded mRNA.
2. Transcription begins when RNA polymerase binds to a promoter region (a base sequence at the start of a gene) and then moves along to the end of a gene; after free ribonucleotides are complementary bonded to the template, an mRNA transcript is created.
   a. Transcription ends when RNA polymerase reaches "the end" signal.
   b. mRNA transcript is then released.

B. Finishing Touches on the mRNA Transcripts

1. Newly formed mRNA is an unfinished molecule, not yet ready for use.
2. mRNA transcripts are modified before leaving the nucleus.
   a. The 5′ end is *capped* with a modified guanine that serves as a "start" signal for translation; the cap will also help bind the mRNA to a ribosome.
   b. A "poly-A tail" of about 100–200 molecules of adenine ribonucleotides is added to the 3′ end.
   c. Noncoding portions (*introns*) are snipped out, and actual coding regions (*exons*) are spliced together to produce the mature transcript; both are transcribed before the transcript reaches cytoplasm.
   d. *Alternative splicing* of exons mixes up different parts of the same gene, resulting in differing proteins that increase the cell's capacity to make diverse proteins.
   e. One gene can specify two or more proteins that differ slightly in form and function.

9.4 The Genetic Code

A. Every three bases in mRNA (a triplet) specify an amino acid to be included into a growing polypeptide chain.

1. Both DNA and its RNA transcript are linear sequences of nucleotides carrying the hereditary code.
2. The complete set of triplets is called the *genetic code*.

B. The genetic code consists of 61 triplets that specify amino acids and three that serve to stop protein synthesis.

1. Each base triplet in RNA is called a *codon*.
2. AUG (specifies methionine) is the "start" codon for all new polypeptide chains.
3. Certain codons specify more than one kind of amino acid.
4. With few exceptions, the genetic code is universal for all forms of life, and its near-universal use leaves little tolerance for variation.

C. mRNAs are translated into proteins with the help of tRNAs and rRNAs.

1. Each kind of tRNA has an *anticodon* that is complementary to an mRNA codon; each tRNA also carries one specific amino acid.
   a. After the mRNA arrives in the cytoplasm, an anticodon on a tRNA bonds to the codon on the mRNA, and thus a correct amino acid is brought into place.

b. The first two bases of the anticodon must pair up with the codon by the usual rules of base pairing (A with U and G with C), but there is some latitude in the pairing of the third base (called the "wobble effect").

2. A ribosome has two subunits (each composed of rRNA and structural proteins) that come together only during translation.
   a. Ribosomes are built in the nucleus.
   b. Small and large subunits come together during translation.

9.5 The Three Stages of Translation

A. Translation proceeds through three stages.
   1. In *initiation,* a complex forms in this sequence:
      initiator tRNA + small ribosomal subunit + mRNA + large ribosomal subunit.
   2. In *elongation,* a start codon on mRNA defines the reading frame; a series of tRNAs deliver amino acids in sequence by codon-anticodon matching; a peptide bond joins each amino acid to the next in sequence.
   3. In *termination,* a stop codon is reached and the polypeptide chain is released into the cytoplasm or enters the cytomembrane system for further processing.

B. What happens to the new polypeptides?
   1. The three steps just outlined can be repeated many times on the same mRNA because several ribosomes may be moving along the mRNA at the same time (polysome).
   2. Some polypeptides join the cytoplasm's pool of free proteins; others enter the rough ER of the cytomembrane system.

9.6 Mutated Genes and Their Protein Products

A. A gene mutation is a change in one or several bases in the nucleotide sequence of DNA, altering the message encoded in mRNA, which can result in a change in the protein synthesized.

B. Common Gene Mutations
   1. Spontaneous mutation can cause sickle-cell anemia, which is the result of a single "base-pair substitution," which places valine as the sixth amino acid in the hemoglobin chain instead of glutamate.
   2. In a "frameshift mutation," there may be an insertion or deletion of several base pairs, causing a misreading of the mRNA during translation.
   3. A rather dramatic mutation occurs when transposable elements, which are regions of movable DNA, "jump" to a new location in DNA.
   4. Transposable elements land in genes and alter the timing, duration, or loss of the genes' activity altogether.

C. How does a mutation affect protein function?
   1. Hemoglobin is a molecule that carries oxygen in red blood cells; each hemoglobin molecule consists of two beta globin and two alpha globin proteins.
   2. Sickle-cell anemia is a genetic disorder caused by a base-pair substitution mutation in the gene that encodes the beta globin protein.
   3. The base-pair substitution causes a change in the amino acid sequence of the beta globin protein; the sixth amino acid (glutamic acid) is changed to a valine.
   4. Glutamic acid has hydrophilic chemical properties; Valine has hydrophobic chemical properties.
   5. The change in amino acid chemical properties causes individuals with sickle-cell anemia to have crescent-shaped red blood cells that clump and blood vessels that disrupt the flow of blood to organs.
   6. Over time, sickle-cell anemia causes damage to organs because they do not receive enough oxygen.

Suggestions for Presenting the Material

- The subject of protein synthesis is a difficult one even when presented on an introductory level.

  Begin by very briefly summarizing the process: DNA $\xrightarrow{\text{transcription}}$ RNA $\xrightarrow{\text{translation}}$ protein. You may also want to review protein structure (Chapter 3).
- Students find it hard to understand and identify the components of DNA, so begin this section of the text by making sure they have a clear picture of deoxyribose (the five-carbon sugar in DNA), phosphate groups, and the four nitrogen bases. Briefly show diagrams of the molecular structure of these three major players, and then introduce the term *nucleotide*.
- Students should be able to achieve a good understanding of protein synthesis if they begin by visualizing it as two major steps, transcription and translation, rather than getting lost in complex details. The events of protein synthesis can be effectively presented with visual aids such as diagrams, animations, and models. Students need to have some kind of mental picture in order to understand what happens during the making of a protein.
- Stress the role that mutations play in producing "new" genes and "new" proteins.
- To show how insertions and deletions might affect a reading frame, write this sentence on the board: THE RED FOX RAN FAR. To show the effects of insertions, insert a letter after "T" and have your class read the sentence (try A). It should read TAH ERE DFO XRA NFA R. Try deleting a letter, such as the letter "D," showing the effects of a deletion. The new sentence should read THE REF OXR ANF AR.

Classroom and Laboratory Enrichment

- Use models, figures, and animations to show protein synthesis.
- Ask students to think about the benefits and drawbacks of DNA as genetic material.
- Give students a "dictionary" of the genetic code (Figure 9.7) either as a handout or as transparency slide. Then ask them to identify the codons within a linear stretch of mRNA that you give them. They should be able to tell which amino acid each codon will specify. This can also be part of a quiz or exam.
- Using the overhead transparency of Figure 9.11, cover several of the labels and ask students to review the steps of protein synthesis aloud in class.
- The following items may help your students remember the difference between "transcription" and "translation."
  a. *Transcription* involves the transfer of information from one form to another *in the same* language, for example, an office memo in shorthand transcribed into typed copy but both in English; likewise, a section of genetic code in DNA is copied to RNA (both nucleic acids).
  b. *Translation* is the transfer of information in *one language* to *another language,* for example, a story in French to English; likewise, genetic code in RNA is transferred to amino acids (nucleic acid to protein).
- As an aid to the understanding of protein synthesis, the following analogy in which the process is compared to the construction of a building may be useful.

a. DNA "sealed" in the nucleus .... a. Master blueprints that never leave the architect's office

b. mRNA that leaves nucleus to go to ribosome........b. Blueprint copies taken to the job site

c. Ribosomes and rRNA... c. The construction site

d. Enzymes ....d. Construction workers

e. tRNA carrying amino acids.................................... e. Trucks carrying materials

f. Amino acids ....f. Building materials

- Discuss the various causes and agents of mutations to help students become aware of how easy it is to be exposed to mutagens. You can refer back to the topic of cancer at this time, as many mutagenic agents are known to also be carcinogenic. A common cancer that occurs when an individual is overexposed to UV radiation is skin cancer.

Classroom Discussion Ideas

- Why is ricin so incredibly deadly?
- Why are ribosomes essential to protein synthesis?
- How might alterations in DNA structure be harmful to a species? How might such alterations be beneficial? What type of genetic change is most important for evolution?
- Ask students to compare and contrast: transcription and translation; codons and anticodons; rRNA, mRNA, and tRNA.
- Why is transcription necessary? Why don't cells use their DNA as a direct model for protein synthesis?
- Describe the three stages of translation.
- In what ways are the instructions encoded in DNA sometimes altered?
- In most species, mutation is usually not considered a driving evolutionary force. Why?
- Using the blackboard or document camera, demonstrate how gene mutations, such as a base substitution or a transposition, will produce abnormal proteins.
- In what ways does RNA differ from DNA?
- Which of the RNAs is "reusable"?
- Why do you think DNA has *introns,* which are transcribed but removed before translation begins?
- How does a *chromosomal variation* (Chapter 13) differ from a *gene mutation?*
- If all DNA is made of the same basic building units (sugar, phosphate, and nitrogenous bases), how can DNA differ in, say, a human and a bacterium?
- This chapter refers to the participants and process involved in protein synthesis as if they have been *seen* doing their work; have they? How then do we know all this information is accurate?
- How can you explain the occurrence of birth defects (caused by altered genes) in children and grandchildren of the victims of the atomic bombs that destroyed Hiroshima and Nagasaki, Japan, when the victims themselves were only mildly affected?
- How is the movement of a portion of DNA in the process called *transposition* different from *translocation*?

How Would You Vote? Classroom Discussion Ideas

- Monitor the voting for the online question. Invite your students to consider the value of mass immunization versus the risks. Remind them that even with a long history of successful immunization for such common diseases as measles, there are still minimal risks. Should the general public be vaccinated for something they are not likely to encounter, like ricin or even anthrax? Would immunizing everyone make the threat less likely?

Term Paper Topics, Library Activities, and Special Projects

- Describe experiments performed by Khorana, Nirenberg, Ochoa, Holley, and others to decipher the genetic code.
- Discover why repeated applications of a single drug or pesticide can result in resistance among bacterial strains and species of insects. Why does this pose a problem? What steps can be taken to avoid resistant strains of pathogenic bacteria and disease-carrying insects?
- Learn more about the discovery and treatment of sickle-cell anemia.
- What kinds of substances act as chemical mutagens? What are some of the effects mutagenic substances can have? What kinds of mutagenic agents might be found in industrial waste?
- Prepare a chart that graphically depicts the series of errors (in DNA, mRNA, tRNA, and amino acids) that lead to the production of the abnormal hemoglobin in sickle-cell anemia.
- The progress in molecular biology has proceeded from deciphering genetic codes to the construction of man-made genes by machine. Report on the construction and use applications of such devices.
- In addition to its importance in protecting development of fetuses, folic acid has been claimed to prevent many different types of cancers, as well as neurodegenerative disorders such as Alzheimer's disease and Parkinson's disease. Folate is involved in photorepair, where thymine dimers are corrected. Research folic acid and find out its role in cellular processes and why a deficiency in folic acid can lead to disorders and disease.
- Investigate reports of "gene replacement" as a preventative of possible genetic abnormalities. In what organism has it been tried? Was it successful? What are the difficulties of this procedure?
- What are some common substances that act as mutagens? How are some of these mutagens known to cause cancer? Are there substances that will block the effects of mutagens?
- Learn more about the research of Barbara McClintock.
- Do some research to find out more about ricin. By what mechanism does ricin inactivate a ribosome?
- Find out more about the castor oil plant that produces ricin. Why might a plant need to store a toxin as lethal as ricin in its tissues and seeds? (Hint: You can discuss the "evolutionary arms race" here and expand your discussion when you discuss evolutionary adaptations in Unit 3.)

Possible Responses to *Critical Thinking* Questions

1. Antisense drugs interact with their intended target based on information in the genetic code. Overproduction or abnormal production of proteins is implicated in cancer and many diseases. Antisense drugs will stop the translation of these proteins by preventing the mRNA coding for them from reaching the ribosome. They do this by binding (hybridizing) to the target mRNA, which is degraded by enzymes and thus not translated.

2. Nucleic acid sequences are traditionally written in a 5′→3′ direction, so the anticodon sequence is 5′-GCG-3′. This anticodon would bind to 5′-CGC-3′, which according to figure 9.7 encodes arginine. If the C of the anticodon were changed to a G, the tRNA would still carry the arginine amino acid; but the anticodon now binds to a 5′-CCC-3′ codon, which encodes proline. In this case, the mutant tRNA would be competing with the normal proline tRNA, and in some cases an arginine would be inserted instead of proline.
3. You could not have fewer than the three-base codons that exist. If you had a two-base codon, the maximum number of different codons would be 16 (4x4=16). The three-base codons allow for 64 different codons (4x4x4=64). This is more than the 20 amino acids and allows for redundancy, meaning that multiple codons encode some amino acids. If you look closely at Figure 9.7, you will notice that, in most cases, the redundancy is in the third base of the codon. Thus, if a mutation occurs in the third base of a codon, it will not change the amino acid sequence of the protein.
4. This is the given RNA segment (hyphens have been added for easier reading):

   5′-GGU-UUC-UUC-AAG-AGA-3′

   Consult Figure 9.7 (genetic code) to see which amino acid matches each codon to produce the finished amino acid sequence of the polypeptide:

   glycine-phenylalanine-phenylalanine-lysine-arginine

5. If translation begins at the second base, the codons are as follows:

   5′-GUU-UCU-UCA-AGA-GA-3′

   The resulting protein is:

   valine-serine-serine-arginine

6. The "stem-loop" structure would interfere with the RNA polymerase because it is working in a linear fashion as it "ratchets" down the DNA strand. The polymerase is pulled away from its working position because of an incorrect fit as the hydrogen bonds between the AU base pairs are disrupted.

Possible Responses to *Data Analysis Exercise* Questions

1. The skin cancer cells show the greatest response to the engineered RIP. Notice that the cell survival decreases as the concentration of the RIP increases in concentration.
2. At 10^{-7} grams/liter, all the cells survive.
3. The breast cancer cells. At this concentration, the skin cancer cells are greatly reduced in survival, and the liver and prostate cells are slightly reduced in survival.
4. The data points linked by straight lines are cells that do not have a dose-dependent response to the concentration of RIP.

10

GENE CONTROL

Chapter Outline

Objectives

1. Know the various ways that gene activity (transcription and translation) are turned on (activated) and off (inactivated).
2. Know the difference between promoters and enhancers.
3. Describe the controls before transcription, during processing and translation, and after translation.
4. Describe how cells differentiate by selective gene expression.
5. Know what X-chromosome inactivation is and how it relates to dosage compensation.
6. Explain the ABC model and how it relates to flower formation.
7. Describe how homeotic genes were discovered and how they control body-plan formation.
8. Know what an operon is and how they are controlled.
9. Explain the regulation of the Lac Operon.
10. Describe in detail how humans develop lactose intolerance.
11. Explain what epigenetic marks are and how they can be passed to offspring.
12. Understand how cancer may result when regulatory genes are altered.

Key Terms

radical mastectomy
cancer
BRCA1, BRCA2
gene controls
regulatory proteins
hormones
negative control
positive control
promoters
enhancers
methylation
activator
polytene chromosomes
introns
exons
cell differentiation
X chromosome inactivation
Barr body
mosaic tissue effect
dosage compensation
anhidrotic ectodermal dysplasia
XIST gene
ABC model
Drosophila
homeotic genes
SRY gene
knockout experiments
pattern formation
selective gene expression
Escherichia coli
lactose
promoter
operator
operon
repressor
lactose intolerance
transcription factor
master gene
Arabidopsis

Lecture Outline

10.1 Between You and Eternity

A. There are about 200,000 new cases of breast cancer each year.

B. Cancer occurs when cell division is not properly regulated; most commonly cancer is due to a mutation in a gene that regulates cell division.

C. BRCA1 and BRCA2 are tumor suppressor genes involved in breast and ovarian cancers.

1. BRCA1 and 2 help maintain the structure and number of chromosomes in a dividing cell.
2. They also bind to hormone receptors and repress genes that cause cell division.

10.2 Switching Genes On and Off

A. Because all cells in your body have the same genetic instructions, only a relatively small number of genes are active at any given time in any given tissue.

1. Which genes are expressed depends on the type of cell, its responses to chemical signals, and built-in control systems.
2. Regulatory proteins interact with DNA, RNA, or actual gene products.

B. Some Control Mechanisms

1. In *negative control systems,* a repressor protein binds to the DNA to block transcription; it can be removed by an inducer.
2. In *positive control systems,* an activator protein binds to an enhancer and promotes initiation of transcription.
3. Promoters are short stretches of base sequences in DNA where regulatory proteins control transcription of specific genes.
4. Enhancers are the binding sites in DNA where regulatory proteins are found to be increasing transcription rates.
5. Control can be exerted by chemical modification—methylation and acetylation—of DNA.

C. Points of Control

1. There are five ways that genes in multicelled organisms are turned off and on to maintain homeostasis.
   a. Controls before transcription include: histone interactions that limit access of RNA polymerase to genes; methylation and acetylation of DNA functional groups; polytene chromosome formation; and duplication and rearrangement of DNA sequences.
   b. Control of transcript processing includes: removal of part of the RNA transcript (introns); modification of the RNA, so it can pass through the nuclear pores; special

codes in the mRNA that determine where in the cell's cytoplasm it will be used; and Y-box proteins that can bind to a transcript to block its translation.

c. Control of mRNA transport includes: proper binding of proteins to a sequence near the poly-A tail that direct the mRNA out of the nucleus and to the proper location in the cell.

d. Controls of translation include: interactions of ribosomal subunits and initiation factors and the stability of mRNA transcripts before degradation begins.

e. Controls after translation include: addition of phosphate to the Y-box proteins and allosteric control of enzymes in metabolic pathways.

D. Same Genes, Different Cell Lineages

1. All body cells have the same genes, but the cells of different tissues are differentiated (specialized) because of selective gene expression.
2. For example, red blood cells transcribe genes for hemoglobin; genes in the eye make crystallin for the transparent lens.

10.3 Master Genes

A. Master genes encode proteins that regulate the expression of many other genes.

B. The interaction between the maternal mRNAs and the master genes determines the pattern formation of the embryo.

C. Homeotic genes are a type of master genes that control the formation of specific body parts.

1. Homeotic genes interact with one another and with control elements to bring about the formation of tissues and organs in accordance with the basic body plan.
2. These genes code for regulatory proteins that can bind to promoters and enhancers to control transcription.
3. For example, an *antennapedia* gene will normally be transcribed in the thorax of an insect, where legs form, but a mutated form of this gene can produce a leg on the head!

D. Knockout Experiments

1. Knockout experiments, in which individual genes are deleted, have identified many genes by the *absence* of function due to the missing gene. Genes are named based on what happens in their absence; for example, *tinman* is necessary for heart development; *groucho* prevents overproduction of whisker bristles.
2. By adding special promoters to genes, researchers can control the expression of external cues, such as temperature.
3. These genes are not restricted to fruit flies; the eyeless gene has counterparts in humans, mice, and squid that point to a shared ancestry among such animals.

10.4 Examples of Gene Control in Eukaryotes

A. X Chromosome Inactivation

1. In mammalian females, the gene products of only one X chromosome are needed; the other is condensed and inactive—called a Barr body.
2. Because in some cells the paternal X chromosome is inactivated, while in other cells the maternal X chromosome is inactivated, each adult female is a mosaic of X-linked traits called mosaic tissue effect.
3. Dosage compensation is the name for the process that shuts down one X of the female so that the overall expression of the remaining X of the female is equivalent to the lone X of the male.

B. Male Sex Determination in Humans

1. The human Y chromosome carries the SRY gene—the master control gene for male sex determination.
2. SRY triggers the formation of testis, which make the sex hormone testosterone.

3. XY individuals with mutations in the SRY gene form female reproductive organs instead of male reproductive organs.

C. Gene Control of Flower Formation

1. Plants must also regulate gene expression.
2. Studies of gene mutations in *Arabidopsis thaliana* support an ABC model of floral development and specialization.
   a. Three sets of master genes (A, B, C) guide flower development in a predictable pattern.
   b. Cell differentiation in the plant depends on which genes of the ABC group are activated.

10.5 Examples of Gene Control in Prokaryotes

A. Prokaryotes regulate gene expression in response to environmental changes.

B. The Lac Operon

1. *E. coli* bacteria (common in the human digestive tract) can metabolize lactose because of a series of three genes that code for lactose-digesting enzymes.
   a. The three genes are preceded by a promoter and an operator—together called an operon.
   b. A regulator gene nearby codes for a repressor protein, which binds to the operator when lactose concentrations are low and effectively blocks RNA polymerase's access to the promoter.
2. When milk is consumed the lactose binds to the repressor, changing its shape and effectively removing its blockage of the promoter; thus RNA polymerase can now initiate transcription of the genes.

C. Lactose Intolerance

1. In humans, the enzyme lactase breaks down lactose.
2. In many individuals, the lactase enzyme becomes inactivated around the age of five.
3. When lactase is inactivated, any lactose consumed is not broken down in the small intestine; lactose ends up in the large intestine where it is processed by *E. coli*.
4. *E. coli* releases by-products due to lactose processing; the gaseous by-products cause pain while other by-products disrupt the solute-water balance, causing diarrhea.
5. Individuals who are not lactose intolerant likely have a mutation in a gene that shut down lactase; thus their lactase gene remains active.

D. Riboswitches

1. Riboswitches are short RNAs that bind to, and prevent, translation of a target sequence.
2. Vitamin B_{12} synthesis is regulated by a riboswitch.

10.6 Epigenetics

A. Methylation of CG dinucleotides suppresses gene expression.

B. Methylation is a common mechanism to suppress genes required only during early development.

C. Methylation can be environmentally influenced.

1. Individuals whose grandfathers endured a famine have undermethylated DNA; these individuals lived longer than individuals whose grandparents ate well.
2. Cigarette smoking adds more methyl groups to DNA.

D. Most, but not all, methylation is "reset" when an organism reproduces; the inherited regulation of gene expression due to DNA methylation is an example of epigenetic inheritance.

Suggestions for Presenting the Material

- This chapter builds on information that students learned in previous chapters about gene structure and function. Terms such as DNA, mRNA, transcription, and translation must be familiar before beginning this chapter.
- Emphasize to the students that the control of gene expression is an extremely complex subject area, one which is best approached by first studying some fairly simple and well-understood examples in prokaryotes.
- Give students opportunities to learn and use new words such as promoter, operator, and operon. Gene control among eukaryotes will be easier to understand if students view it as a series of levels.
- Students have a difficult time relating to and understanding gene regulation because it is so foreign to their life experiences. Using analogies might help them relate to the information. Here is an analogy you can try involving a car:
  Repressors are the parking brakes; they inhibit any movement on transcription until they are released.
  The binding of inducers, like lactose, is analogous to releasing the parking brake. Now the car is able to move forward—but RNA polymerase must bind to the promoter.

Classroom and Laboratory Enrichment

- Use visual aids such as overhead slides to illustrate the lactose operon (Figure 10.10).
- Use models to show induction and repression of gene expression in the operon.
- Have the students compare and contrast prokaryotic and eukaryotic gene control.
- If you can arrange a demonstration of chromosome puffs in fruit flies by geneticists, do so; it is a good visual aid for seeing transcription in action. If the timing is inconvenient for students to actually see the process, make a visual recording of the procedure to show later.
- Modify Figure 10.10 (lactose operon) by obscuring the labels. Ask students to identify each item on the figure.
- Prepare a summary table that lists the following:

Type of Control	Specific Example	Found In:		
		Prokaryote	Eukaryote	Both
a. Transcriptional				
b. Transcript processing				
c. Translational				
d. Post-translational				

Classroom Discussion Ideas

- What are some of the possible environmental agents that could trigger cancer?
- Why do you think the disease cancer and deaths from cancer receive so much attention by Americans?
- Evaluate this comment, "Cancer is the disease of those people who live too well."
- What are the benefits of learning you have a gene that may lead to cancer? What are the disadvantages of receiving such knowledge?
- What is the likelihood that there will be a breakthrough cure for cancer in your lifetime?

- How might alterations in DNA structure be harmful to a species? How might such alterations be beneficial? What type of genetic change is most important for evolution?
- What is the role of gene control in causing cancer? How are some viruses known to be linked to cancer?
- Scientists know much more about controls over gene expression among prokaryotes than among eukaryotes. What are some reasons why research in this area is more difficult among eukaryotic species than it is among prokaryotic species?
- Do you think cancer-causing genes could someday be repaired?
- There is much more DNA in eukaryotic cells than scientists call necessary. Why do *you* think it is there?
- Why do eukaryotic cells "need" *histones, nucleosomes,* and *looped domains*?
- What would be the hypothetical effect on the lactose operon of a modified lactose molecule? Do you think it would still bind to the repressor?
- What is the "economic" advantage to a prokaryotic cell of possessing inducible enzymes?
- Distinguish between negative gene control and positive gene control.
- Why are so many of the homeotic genes similar among animal groups? What group would have homeotic genes the most similar to those of humans?

How Would You Vote? Classroom Discussion Ideas

- Monitor the voting for the online question. The decision by some high-risk women to have their breasts removed to *prevent* the possibility of developing cancer could be a truly life-altering decision. At first glance, this decision could make sense for those women who are at elevated risk due to genetic or family history factors. Counter that with living in a society that seems to be moving toward even greater obsession with female breasts at earlier ages (e.g., breast implants for 16th birthdays!)

Term Paper Topics, Library Activities, and Special Projects

- Learn more about current research efforts attempting to uncover the mysteries of development and differentiation.
- Describe the operon and its function.
- Learn more about oncogenes and cancer.
- Discover more about the discovery and diagnostic uses of the Barr body in female mammalian cells. What is the current research saying about X inactivation?
- What are some common substances that act as mutagens? How are some of these mutagens known to cause cancer? Are there substances that will block the effects of mutagens?
- Learn more about tumor cell lines used to study cancerous cell growth *in vitro* in the laboratory.
- Locate the original article by Francois Jacob and Jacques Monod proposing the lac operon. How have the details changed?
- Likewise, see if you can locate the original research publications of Murray Barr and Mary Lyon. Notice the dates of these publications. Were they before or after the publication of DNA structure by Watson and Crick in 1953?
- Research current work of evolutionary geneticists with homeotic or Hox genes in humans.

Possible Responses to *Critical Thinking* Questions

1. In adult humans, many genes that were required for proper development are no longer needed and are permanently turned off (not expressed). For example, hemoglobin, the protein that carries oxygen in the blood, is a large protein that consists of four smaller proteins. Since a developing fetus lives in a reduced oxygen environment, fetal hemoglobin must bind oxygen at a high affinity. Fetal hemoglobin contains two copies of alpha globin protein and two copies of gamma globin protein. Thus the genes that encode alpha and gamma globin are expressed during early development. At birth, a newborn enters an environment that is higher in oxygen, and different globin genes are expressed to match the changing environmental conditions. Beginning at birth and continuing through adulthood, hemoglobin is made of two alpha globin proteins and two beta globin proteins. Thus, at birth, the gamma globin gene is turned off and the beta globin gene is turned on. In this example, gene expression changes to match a change in environmental conditions.

   Genes are also differentially expressed because different tissues perform different functions and thus require different proteins to be made. For example, muscle cells require the expression of genes that encode proteins necessary for muscle contraction. Pancreatic cells require the expression of genes that encode proteins necessary for making insulin. Since these are specialized tissues, muscle cells do not express genes that make insulin and pancreatic cells do not express the genes for muscle contraction. It should be noted that there are genes that are expressed in all tissues. These genes encode proteins that are required for basic cellular function (for example; DNA replication, transcription, and translation).

2. Individuals that are starving express genes that encode proteins that will increase fat production. This is a survival mechanism that allows the individual to produce as much fat as possible under famine conditions. These fat production genes may be regulated epigenetically. In a starving parent, the fat production genes are turned on because they have less DNA methylation than an individual living in normal conditions. The offspring of the starving parents could inherit the low methylation state, and even if the child is raised in a normal environment, the child's fat production genes are overactive because of the inherited methylation state.

3. No. Three types of gene controls are: (1) control by histone organization of the DNA; (2) transcriptional control by regulatory proteins in operons; and (3) control of the transport of mRNA out of the nucleus. Those not found in prokaryotes are: (1) because the single, circular DNA of prokaryotes is not organized around histone proteins and (3) because there is no nucleus in prokaryotes. Of course, (2) is very typical of prokaryotes; the same mechanism is not found in eukaryotes.

4. According to the data, individuals with *BRCA1* are diagnosed with cancer at an earlier age and have the highest percentage of death. While there are far fewer individuals who have the *BRCA2* mutation, the percentage that die is much lower. Thus *BRCA1* is the more dangerous breast cancer gene.

   To determine the effectiveness of the preventative surgeries, one would have to evaluate how many of those who died from breast cancer had the surgeries and how many did not. In addition, it would be helpful to know the age that the individuals died and their age of diagnosis. This information might reveal that the preventative surgery increases survival time even if it does not prevent death.

Possible Responses to *Data Analysis Exercise* Questions

1. A girl whose grandmother experienced a famine at age two is one and one-half times more likely to die early.
2. The data shows that, in general, when a grandmother experienced a famine, her grandchildren are at an increased risk of mortality. If a grandmother was well-fed, her grandchildren are at decreased risk of mortality. However, this trend is reversed around age nine. If a maternal grandmother was well-fed around age nine, her grandchildren have an increased risk of early mortality. If a maternal grandmother experienced a famine at age nine, her grandchildren have a reduced risk of early mortality.
3. This data suggests that the sex chromosomes are involved in the epigenetic changes being inherited. It could be that the epigenetic changes are located on the sex chromosomes. Alternatively, the sex chromosomes could simply be influencing epigenetic changes on the non-sex chromosomes (autosomes).

11

HOW CELLS REPRODUCE

Chapter Outline

HENRIETTA'S IMMORTAL CELLS

MULTIPLICATION BY DIVISION

- The Cell Cycle
- Chromosome Number
- Cell Cycle Controls

A CLOSER LOOK AT MITOSIS

THE ROLE OF TELOMERES

WHEN MITOSIS BECOMES PATHOLOGICAL

SUMMARY

DATA ANALYSIS EXERCISE

SELF-QUIZ

CRITICAL THINKING

Objectives

1. Describe the role of cell division and the factors that cause cells to reproduce.
2. Describe the structural organization of a chromosome and the appearance of DNA during mitosis and interphase.
3. Understand what is meant by *cell cycle* and explain where mitosis fits into the cell cycle.
4. Be able to describe each phase of mitosis.
5. Contrast between cytokinesis and mitosis in a dividing cell.
6. List some of the problems in cell division when cell cycle control mechanisms do not work and control is lost.
7. Explain how cancer cells are different from normal cells in the body.
8. Compare and contrast cytokinesis in plant and animal cells.
9. Be able to describe what occurs during each stage of the cell cycle.
10. Describe how telomeres limit the number of cell divisions a cell can undergo.

Key Terms

HeLa cells
mitosis
somatic cells
meiosis
germ cells
chromosome
sister chromatids
centromere
kinetochores
cell cycle
interphase
G_1, S, G_2, M
chromosome number
diploid number
prophase
metaphase
anaphase
telophase
bipolar mitotic spindle
microtubules
centrioles
centrosome
cytoplasmic division
cytokinesis
contractile ring mechanism
cleavage furrow
cell plate formation
growth factors
proto-oncogenes
tumor
tumor suppressors
neoplasms
benign
cancers
malignant
metastasis

Lecture Outline

11.1 Henrietta's Immortal Cells

A. Researchers at Johns Hopkins cultured a line of immortal cells in 1951.

1. They are referred to as HeLa cells after their source—a woman named Henrietta Lacks.
   a. HeLa cells are rapidly dividing cancer cells.
   b. HeLa cells are involved in identifying viral strains, developing vaccines, cancer research, etc.
2. Her cellular descendants are still dividing today and continue to provide for research around the world.

B. Understanding why cancer cells are immortal, and why normal cells are not, may help researchers develop new drugs to treat cancer.

11.2 Multiplication by Division

A. The cell cycle is a recurring sequence of events that extends from the time of a cell's formation until each division is completed.

B. The cell cycle consists of interphase and mitosis.

1. Interphase is the longest portion of the cell cycle and is subdivided into three phases.
   a. During G_1, cells assemble most of the carbohydrates, lipids, and proteins needed by the cell and for export.
   b. During the S phase the DNA replication occurs.
   c. During G_2, further protein synthesis drives the cell toward mitosis.
2. During mitosis, the chromosomes divide.

C. Mitosis and the Chromosome Number

1. All somatic cells of a particular species have the same number of chromosomes; for example, humans have 46.
   a. Chromosomes come in pairs—one member from each parent.
   b. Chromosome pairs carry genes for the same traits.
2. Chromosome number (n) tells how many of each type of chromosome is present in a cell; 2n represents having two of each type of chromosome in a cell, termed "diploid."
3. Checkpoint proteins regulate the cell cycle.
   a. Checkpoint proteins will stall the cell cycle if the DNA was not properly replicated or if it has been damaged.
   b. When the damage is repaired, the checkpoint proteins allow the cell cycle to proceed.
   c. If the DNA cannot be repaired, the checkpoint proteins instruct the cell to self-destruct.

11.3 A Closer Look at Mitosis

A. Mitosis begins with prophase.

1. Duplicated chromosomes become visible as rodlike units, each consisting of two sister chromatids.
2. Microtubules move one pair of centrioles to opposite poles of the cell.
3. The nuclear envelope begins to disintegrate.
4. Microtubules of the spindle extend from the centrioles and attach to the centromeres (kinetochore area) of the duplicated chromosomes.

B. The transition to metaphase occurs as the chromosomes begin an orderly arrangement.

1. Sister chromatids are each attached separately to microtubules *from opposite poles.*
2. When all the chromosomes are aligned at the cell's equator halfway between the poles, the cell is said to be in *metaphase*.

C. Metaphase: Duplicated chromosomes line up midway between the spindle poles.

1. Opposing microtubules play tug of war and chromosomes arrive at the spindle equator.

2. Chromosomes consisting of two sister chromatids are aligned at the middle of the cell.

D. During anaphase the chromosomes (consisting of one chromatid) migrate to opposite poles.
   1. Sister chromatids separate and move toward opposite poles.
      a. Microtubules attached to the centromeres *shorten* and pull the chromosomes toward the poles. This action pulls sister chromatids apart at the centromere.
      b. Other microtubules at the spindle poles *ratchet* past each other to push the two spindle poles apart, elongating the cell.
   2. Once separated, each chromatid is now an independent chromosome.

E. Telophase gets underway when the chromosomes reach the respective poles.
   1. Each half of the cell now contains two clusters of chromosomes that are identical and equal in number.
   2. The chromosomes relax and return to the threadlike form typical of interphase.
   3. The nuclear envelope forms from the fusion of small vesicles; mitosis is complete.
   4. Two new nuclear envelopes form from fusion of small vesicles. Each envelope surrounds a set of chromosomes in the two daughter cells.

11.4 Cytoplasmic Division Mechanisms

A. How Do Animal Cells Divide?
   1. Cytoplasmic division (cytokinesis) in animals is by means of a cleavage furrow.
      a. The flexible plasma membrane of animal cells can be squeezed in the middle to separate the two daughter cells.
      b. Parallel arrays of contractile microfilaments slide past one another at the cleavage furrow, pulling the plasma membrane inward.
   2. Each daughter cell ends up with a nucleus, some cytoplasm (with organelles), and a plasma membrane.

B. How Do Plant Cells Divide?
   1. Because of the rather rigid cell wall, the cytoplasm of plant cells cannot just be pinched in two.
   2. Instead, vesicles produced by the Golgi, containing remnants of the microtubular spindle, form a disk-like structure called a cell plate between the two new cells.

C. Appreciate the Process!
   1. Failure of chromosomes to duplicate precisely or distribute properly can result in genetic disorders and cancer.
   2. This failure may start in body cells and in germ cells.

11.5 Marking Time with Telomeres

A. Telomeres are non-coding DNA located at the ends of chromosomes.
   1. In vertebrates, the telomeres consist of the sequence 5′-TTAGGG-3′.
   2. This sequence can be repeated thousands of times at the ends of a chromosome.

B. With each round of DNA replication, about 100 bases of telomere DNA is lost; the loss of telomere sequence prevents the loss of more valuable and internally located coding DNA.

C. Checkpoint proteins monitor the length of the telomeres and prevent the cells from dividing once too much telomere DNA is lost, and the more valuable DNA is in jeopardy.

D. A few adult stem cells retain the ability to divide indefinitely because they have an enzyme (telomerase) that counteracts the loss of telomere sequence due to DNA replication.

E. Abnormally short telomeres cause premature aging.
   1. Mice with mutations in the gene that encodes telomerase have a shortened life span.
   2. Dolly, the first cloned animal, had abnormally short telomeres; at the age of five Dolly looked like a typical twelve-year-old sheep.

11.6 When Control Is Lost

A. The Cell Cycle Revisited
   1. The cell cycle has built-in checkpoints where proteins can advance, delay, or block forward progress of the cycle.
   2. For example, kinases can signal the end of DNA replication; growth factors signal the start of mitosis.

B. Checkpoint Failure and Tumors
   1. When checkpoint mechanisms fail, a cell loses control over its replication cycle. A checkpoint gene inhibits mitosis and is called a tumor-suppressor gene.
      a. In some cases, mitosis repeats over and over.
      b. In others, the cells do not die as they are supposed to.
   2. Proto-oncogenes code for proteins that stimulate mitosis.
      a. Neoplasms are abnormal masses of cells that have lost control over their growth and cell division. They can be benign or malignant.
      b. Benign growths pose no threat to the body and typically remain in their home tissue.

C. Characteristics of Cancer
   1. Cancers are abnormally growing and dividing cells of a malignant neoplasm.
   2. All cancer cells display four characteristics.
      a. They grow and divide abnormally.
      b. The cell membrane is leaky, and the cytoskeleton is disorganized.
      c. Cells have a weakened capacity for adhesion and may break away to move to other sites in the body (metastasis).
      d. Cancer cells have lethal effects.

Suggestions for Presenting the Material

- This is the first of two chapters concerning cell reproduction. The present one explains mitosis—division in which the number of chromosomes remains the same in the identical daughter cells. The next chapter explains a more complicated type of cell division in which the number of chromosomes is reduced during the production of cells destined to become gametes—meiosis. Students need to have a solid understanding of mitosis before learning meiosis.
- Emphasize the cell cycle, stressing that cells are not dividing all of the time. Students should be aware of the fact that the steps of cell division are part of a continuum. Our separation of the process into four stages is an artificial one, and it may be hard to say where one stage ends and the next begins when looking at a dividing cell. You may compare it to the showing of a "game tape" that athletes watch to see the errors committed during the big game.
- Students often have trouble following the number of chromosomes throughout the stages of mitosis. To help them, remind them that each chromosome has one centromere, and that it is not until centromeres divide in anaphase that *sister chromatids* are considered *chromosomes*. Make certain that students understand where and when mitosis occurs in any organism.
- Another approach to explaining the *number* of chromosomes before and after mitosis is to abandon all mention of chromosomes and simply keep track of the number of DNA molecules present at each stage. It would look like this for a human somatic cell: G_1 (46); S (92); G_2 (92); prophase (92); metaphase (92); anaphase (46 moving to each pole); telophase (46 each cell).
- Emphasize to the student that the "secret" to preserving the chromosome number in the two daughter cells of mitosis and cutting the chromosome number in half in the four daughter cells of meiosis (next chapter) is the same—DNA duplication during interphase!
- A good way for students to count chromosomes in the diagrams is to count the centromeres of the chromosomes.

- Ask students what would happen if cytokinesis did not occur.
- Use the example of a waistband on a pair of sweats, and the tightening of the waistband to demonstrate cytokinesis in an animal cell.

Classroom and Laboratory Enrichment

- Show a video of time-lapse photography of cells undergoing actual cell division.
- Ask students (working individually or in small groups) to use chromosome simulation kits (available from biological supply houses) to demonstrate chromosome replication during the stages of mitosis. If kits are unavailable, make your own chromosomes using a pop-it bead (or bead and cord) for each chromatid and a magnet for each centromere.
- View ready-made squashes of mitotic material, such as onion root tip, under a microscope or project slides of such material. Ask students to estimate the length of each mitotic phase after counting the number of cells in each phase in several fields of view.
- Using photos of the stages of mitosis, project each stage (not in correct sequence) and ask students to identify each phase. Additionally, you could ask students to give one or two major events happening in each phase.
- Perhaps the following analogy can help students visualize chromosomes during mitosis:

  2 chromatids = 2 nearly matched socks
  1 centromere = 1 clothespin
  spindle fiber = clothesline
- Prepare an overhead of your own sketch, or use one from Chapter 8, to explain how one DNA molecule (that is, chromosome) becomes two identical DNA molecules (that is, daughter chromosomes) during replication.

Classroom Discussion Ideas

- Loosely speaking, the process of one cell becoming two cells is often referred to as mitosis, but to be completely accurate, what does mitosis *specifically* refer to?
- Why do cells undergoing mitosis require one set of divisions but cells undergoing meiosis need two sets of divisions?
- Why are the HeLa cells considered to be immortal?
- Using a generation time of 20 minutes, calculate the size of a bacterial population that has arisen from a single bacterium growing under optimum conditions for eight hours (for example, *salmonella* in a bowl of unrefrigerated potato salad at a picnic on a warm summer day).
- Many of the drugs used in chemotherapy cause loss of hair in the individual being treated. Ask students if they can figure out why such drugs affect hair growth.
- Biologists used to believe that interphase was a "resting period" during the life cycle of the cell. Why did this appear to be so? What do we now consider interphase to be?
- Ask students how cell division in plant cells differs from that in animal cells.
- How can there be 46 chromosomes in a human cell at metaphase and also 46 chromosomes after the centromere splits in anaphase? Hint: Focus on the name change of chromatids to daughter chromosomes.
- What is there about the composition of an animal cell versus a plant cell that necessitates different methods of cleavage?

How Would You Vote? Classroom Discussion Ideas

- Monitor the voting for the online question. The very question of whether a person (or his relatives) should be compensated for being the source of tissue is very much a topic of debate today. Various court cases have decided the issue both for and against. However, in a strictly ethical sense, compensating the family of Henrietta Lacks for the contribution she made to science even in her death would seem the right thing to do.

Term Paper Topics, Library Activities, and Special Projects

- Much progress in studying human disease has been made using the research technique of tissue culture. Describe techniques of tissue culture, explaining how cells can be induced to grow and divide *in vitro*.
- Explore diseases (such as cancer) that involve cell growth gone wrong. How do such diseases affect the mechanism of cell division? What drugs are used to halt runaway cell growth? How do these drugs work, and what are their side effects?
- Why do some cells of the human body (for example, epithelial cells) continue to divide, yet other cells (for example, nerve cells) lose their ability to replicate once they are mature? Describe some of the latest research efforts to induce cell division in nerve cells.
- Colchicine is a chemical used to treat dividing plant cells to ensure that chromosomes of cells undergoing mitosis will be visible. How does colchicine achieve this effect? What is the natural source of colchicine?
- The 1956 edition of the high school biology text *Modern Biology* by Moon, Mann, and Otto was the last to state the human chromosome number as 48. This was not a misprint. What investigations resulted in assigning the correct number of 46 to humans?
- The preparation of a karyotype (picture of chromosomes) is a simple but multi-step procedure. Provide a procedural outline for making such a preparation of chromosomes for publication in a book.
- There is some question as to exactly how chromosomes move to opposite ends of the cell in concert with the bipolar mitotic spindle fibers. Investigate the various theories, and report on their strengths and weaknesses.
- As a student project, encourage the construction of a model of the chromosome. Perhaps some wire and plastic spools could be the building materials. Research one of the human autosomes and illustrate or model the chromosome by showing the names and locations of the genes that have been identified.

Possible Responses to *Critical Thinking* Questions

1. No. Cells can remain in the G_1 state of the cell cycle. Instead of preparing to divide and produce more cells, the cell simply performs its specialized function. For example, a pancreatic cell may receive instructions to produce insulin. Ultimately the cell will die and need to be replaced by other cells that have been instructed to undergo cell division.
2. The mystery cell is an animal cell. It is evident due to the presence of a contractile ring. Plant cells do not have the contractile ring mechanism, but instead deposit vesicles of cellulose to form the cell plate. See figure 11.6 for further details.

3. Radiation has the greatest effect on cells with high rates of mitosis, such as those in hair follicles and the lining of the gut. Cancer cells can be killed by disrupting their mitosis using radiation since they are dividing all the time.

4. One way to measure the amount of DNA in the cell is to count the number of DNA molecules at each point in the cell cycle. It would look like this for a human somatic cell: G_1 (46); S (92); G_2 (92); prophase (92); metaphase (92); anaphase (46 moving to each pole); telophase (46 each cell). Thus you would see a change in the amount of DNA per cell during the S and M phases of the cell cycle.

Possible Responses to *Data Analysis Exercise* Questions

1. 82
2. 36. A normal human cell has 46 chromosomes.
3. Since there is no Y chromosome, this cell is from a female.

12

MEIOSIS AND SEXUAL REPRODUCTION

Chapter Outline

Objectives

1. Contrast asexual and sexual types of reproduction that occur on the cellular and multicellular organism levels.
2. Understand the effect that meiosis has on chromosome number.
3. Describe the events that occur in each meiotic phase.
4. Compare mitosis and meiosis; cite similarities and differences.
5. Contrast meiosis in plant and animal life cycles.
6. Describe the various processes that contribute to genetic variation.

Key Terms

asexual reproduction
genes
clones
sexual reproduction
gametes
allele
meiosis
chromosome number
diploid number
homologous chromosomes
germ cells
haploid number
centromere
sister chromatids
spindle apparatus
meiosis I
meiosis II
prophase I
crossing over
nonsister chromatids
genetic recombination
metaphase I
maternal chromosomes
paternal chromosomes
spores

sporophytes	sperm	egg
gametophyte	oocyte	fertilization
primary spermatocyte	polar body	haploid
	ovum	somatic

Lecture Outline

12.1 Why Sex?

A. Asexual reproduction is quick and efficient.
   1. Asexual reproduction does not require the participation of a partner.
   2. But the offspring are all clones—no variation!
   3. Offspring produced by asexual reproduction are all adapted the same way to an environment.

B. Sexual reproduction is more costly energetically.
   1. Male and female partners must find each other and exchange genetic material.
   2. But the offspring are genetically diverse—a lot of variation!
   3. The variation introduced by sex has selective advantages for survival in changing environments.

12.2 Meiosis Halves the Chromosome Number

A. Introducing Alleles
   1. Sexually reproducing organisms are typically diploid; they contain pairs of chromosomes.
   2. The members of a chromosome pair are slightly different in DNA sequence; thus the two copies of a gene located on homologous chromosomes may vary slightly.
   3. The different forms of the same genes are called alleles; a single gene may have hundreds of different alleles in a *population*, but a diploid *individual* can have a maximum of two different alleles.
   4. The offspring of sexually reproducing species inherit a new combination of traits; this is why the offspring do not look identical.

B. What Meiosis Does
   1. Meiosis begins with diploid ($2n = 46$) germ cells and produces haploid gametes ($n = 23$).
   2. At the beginning of meiosis, the chromosomes are duplicated during interphase to form sister chromosomes held together at the centromere.
   3. Chromosomes are moved by the microtubules of the spindle apparatus.
   4. During meiosis I, homologous chromosomes pair, separate, and cytoplasm divides, giving rise to two daughter cells.
   5. In meiosis II, the sister chromatids of each chromosome separate; the cytoplasm divides again, resulting in four haploid cells (gametes).
   6. Each gamete produced by meiosis has *one of each pair* of homologous chromosomes (i.e., haploid).

12.3 Visual Tour of Meiosis

A. This section is the two-page Figure 12.5 depicting meiosis I and II, with explanatory captions.

12.4 How Meiosis Introduces Variations in Traits

A. Crossing Over in Prophase I

1. Homologous chromosomes pair up.
   a. Nonsister chromatids exchange segments in a process called crossing over.
   b. Because alleles for the same trait can vary between homologues, new combinations of genes in each chromosome can result; this is one source of genetic variation.
2. Crossing over leads to genetic recombination in gametes.

B. Chromosome Segregation

1. During metaphase I, homologous chromosomes randomly line up at the spindle equator.
2. During anaphase I, homologous chromosomes (still duplicated) separate into two haploid cells, each of which with a *random* mix of maternal and paternal chromosomes.
3. Every time a human sperm or egg forms, the possible combinations of chromosomes equal 2^{23} (8,388,608).

12.5 From Gametes to Offspring

A. Gamete Formation in Plants

1. Plants have two types of multicellular tissue; sporophytes produce the spores by meiosis and gametophytes produce the gametes by mitosis.
2. Haploid spores germinate into haploid gametophytes.
3. Gametes fuse to produce the diploid sporophyte tissue.

B. Gamete Formation in Animals

1. In males, meiosis and gamete formation are called spermatogenesis.
   a. Germ cell ($2n$) ——> primary spermatocyte ($2n$) ——> MEIOSIS I ——> two secondary spermatocytes (n) ——> MEIOSIS II ——> four spermatids (n).
   b. Spermatids change in form; each develops a tail to become a mature sperm.
2. In females, meiosis and gamete formation are called oogenesis.
   a. Germ cell ($2n$) ——> primary oocyte ($2n$) ——> MEIOSIS I ——> secondary oocyte (n, and large in size) plus polar body (n, and small in size) ——> MEIOSIS II ——> one large ovum (n) plus three polar bodies (n, small).
   b. The single ovum is the only cell capable of being fertilized by a sperm; the polar bodies wither and die.

C. Fertilization

1. The diploid chromosome number is restored at fertilization when two very different gamete nuclei fuse to form the zygote.
2. Variation present at fertilization is from three sources.
   a. Crossing over occurs during prophase I.
   b. Random alignments at metaphase I lead to millions of combinations of maternal and paternal chromosomes in each gamete.
   c. Of all the genetically diverse gametes produced, chance will determine which two will meet at fertilization.

12.6 Mitosis and Meiosis—An Ancestral Connection?

A. Mitosis and Meiosis are similar but different.

1. Mitosis maintains the chromosome number; meiosis halves the chromosome number.
2. Mitosis produces genetically identical cells; meiosis produces genetically different cells.
3. Mitosis is complete after one round of DNA replication and cell division; meiosis also has one round of DNA replication, but two rounds of cell division.

B. Meiosis likely evolved from mitosis.

1. All organisms have certain gene codes for DNA repair and to regulate the cell cycle; these genes function during mitosis and meiosis.
2. Mutations in genes encoding cell cycle checkpoint proteins may have been part of the evolution of sexual reproduction and the processes of meiosis.

Suggestions for Presenting the Material

- This is a crucial subject area for beginning biology students. Students must have a good understanding of meiosis to comprehend the workings of inheritance, explained in subsequent chapters.
- Before beginning this chapter, ask questions to make sure students are well grounded in the events and purpose of mitosis. Because it was covered in the previous chapter, students should still recall the terms used to describe the parts of the cell involved in cell division.
- Learning and understanding the terminology is critical for students to comprehend the differences between meiosis and mitosis. Make sure to review the difference between germ cells and somatic cells, germ cells and gametes, haploid and diploid, homologous and homolog chromosomes, autosomes and sex chromosomes, etc.
- The events of meiosis can be confusing. Emphasize that meiosis makes it possible for organisms to undergo sexual reproduction. Remind students that the benefit of sexual reproduction is genetic diversity. This will help them understand why a process as complex as meiosis has evolved.
- Students often find it hard to understand when and how the chromosome number changes during meiosis, so be sure they understand that the two chromatids of one chromosome are each considered a chromosome in their own right *after* the centromere splits during meiotic anaphase II.
- Meiosis will be easier to grasp if students can become thoroughly acquainted with a typical animal life cycle (use the human life cycle as a familiar example). Before finishing with this chapter, be sure to question the students about the events of meiosis and its consequences to the organism.
- Be sure to show and explain the excellent comparison of mitosis and meiosis in Figure 12.11.

Classroom and Laboratory Enrichment

- Demonstrate the phases of meiosis, using a series of progressive slides or a video.
- Show students a slide of a karyotype of a normal man or woman to introduce the concept of homologous pairs.
- Compare a human karyotype to that of another organism.
- Ask students (working individually or in small groups) to use chromosome-simulation kits (available from biological supply houses) to demonstrate chromosome replication and reduction of chromosome number during the stages of meiosis. If kits are unavailable, make your own chromosomes using a pop-it bead (or bead and cord) for each chromatid and a magnet for each centromere. A cheap and easy alternative is using colored craft sticks (available in all craft stores). The color denotes maternal or paternal origin, and you can create various sizes of chromosome by cutting the sticks.
- Show slides of adult plants or animals, and ask students to point out where meiosis occurs in each organism.
- Illustrate crossing over by using lengths of different colored string. Snip and tie the ends to create the products of a crossover (see Figure 12.6). Another option is to use colored modeling clay. After rolling out strips of two different colors (maternal versus paternal), form homologous pairs and

then select the chromatids to participate in the crossing-over event. Tear the dough and reassemble it to show the exchange. Students can also do this in a lab setting.

- Place Figure 12.5 on the screen and have students indicate the number of *human* chromosomes present at each stage. Use the centromere hint in the Additional Ideas section below. Repeat the exercise with Figure 12.11.
- Point out the subtle differences between the generalized life cycles of plants and animals shown in Figure 12.8.
- If you can locate a segment of video depicting the union of gametes and subsequent cleavage, it will provide visual presentation of what mitosis and meiosis accomplish in a living cell.
- Show the effects of crossing over through pop-bead kits. Use round stickers for the six different pairs of alleles and place them along two sets of chromosomes (stick each one to one of the pop beads). Have students initiate a random crossover while finishing modeling meiosis. Have students write down their allele combination in their gametes. Have them do the crossover differently each time, while still writing their allele combination for each of their gametes. Ask the class for the different allele combinations they saw in their gametes. Remind students that crossing over does not have to occur, but in humans it typically occurs twice along each chromosome.

Classroom Discussion Ideas

- Why do cells undergoing mitosis require one set of divisions, but cells undergoing meiosis need two sets of divisions?
- All but the most primitive species of organism have the ability to reproduce sexually. Can you explain why sexual reproduction is considered a hallmark of evolutionary advancement? What are the advantages over asexual reproduction?
- What would be an advantage of parthenogenesis?
- Do more advanced organisms have more chromosomes than primitive organisms? Review chromosome numbers of some common plants and animals.
- Division of the cell cytoplasm is equal during spermatogenesis but unequal during oogenesis. Can you think of at least one reason why?
- If bacteria reproduce asexually and give rise to clones, how do antibiotic-resistant bacteria develop? Why do bacteria not die out when their environment changes?
- Why is it impossible for a horse and donkey to give rise to offspring?
- Why are mules considered infertile?
- An old-fashioned name for meiosis is "reduction division." Why?
- What would happen in the formation of the zygote if meiosis did not halve the chromosome number?
- Why does crossing over occur in prophase of *meiosis* and not in *mitosis*?
- One of the meiotic series is very much like mitosis. Is it meiosis I or II?
- Does the reduction in chromosome number occur in meiosis I or II? Hint: To conveniently count the number of chromosomes (whether doubled as chromatids or newly formed daughter chromosomes), simply count the number of centromeres (or portions thereof) present in any particular stage.
- When do the processes of human spermatogenesis and oogenesis begin? Are they the same in males and females?
- What is the derivation of the prefix "chrom-" as used in describing the threadlike bearers of hereditary instructions?

- Ask students to compare an animal life cycle to a complete land-plant life cycle. How is the life cycle of a human different from that of a plant?
- The generalized life cycle of complex land plants is often described as "alternation of generations." Describe the meaning of this phrase.

How Would You Vote? Classroom Discussion Ideas

- Monitor the voting for the online question. The type of research described here, in which an all-female DNA zygote was produced, is certainly not routine (600 attempts). So, there is little worry at this time that it will become commonplace. Nevertheless, many people are concerned that this type of research is dabbling in a "forbidden zone" due to ethical issues. Two questions might be asked: (1) does this type of research have a goal that will lead to some advance in medicine, or (2) is it being done just to say, "We did it"?

Term Paper Topics, Library Activities, and Special Projects

- How are human karyotypes prepared? Discover the laboratory steps required in this procedure.
- Use the karyotypes of related species (for example, primates) to describe evolutionary relationships, if any, between the species.
- Meiosis precisely reduces the chromosome number so the union of several gametes restores the diploid number. How many extra or fewer chromosomes can a human body cell have and survive? Are there consequences? Does the same hold true for plants?
- What are the latest theories and evidence relative to the blockage of entry into the egg of all sperm subsequent to the first one?
- Select from the library shelves several biology texts from the past 50 years. Compare the formal definitions of *gene,* and prepare a historical résumé of the changes.

Possible Responses to *Critical Thinking* Questions

1. Below, the chromosomes are shown during the various phases of meiosis. For simplicity, crossing over and independent assortment are not indicated in the figures.

For 2N=4:

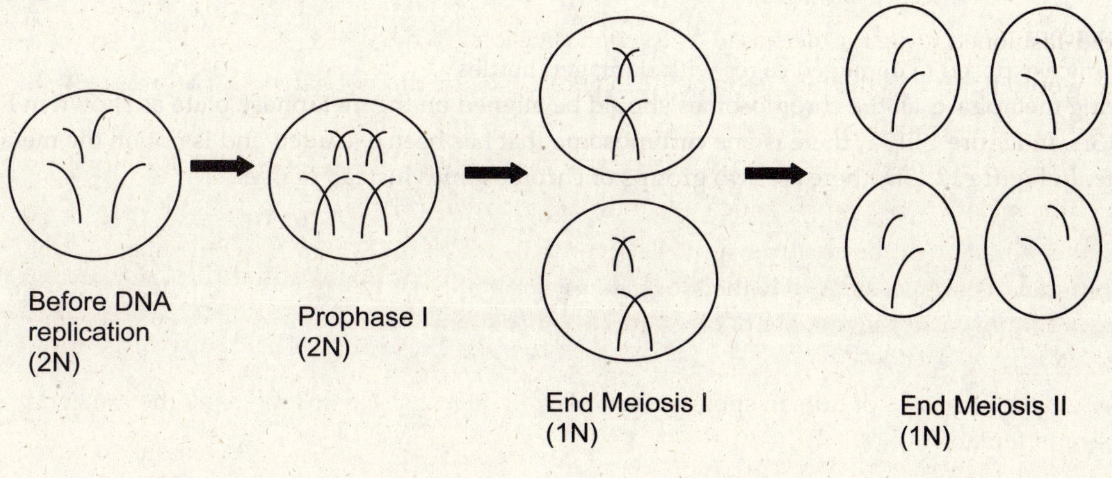

For 2N=2+1 (there is an extra copy of one chromosome):

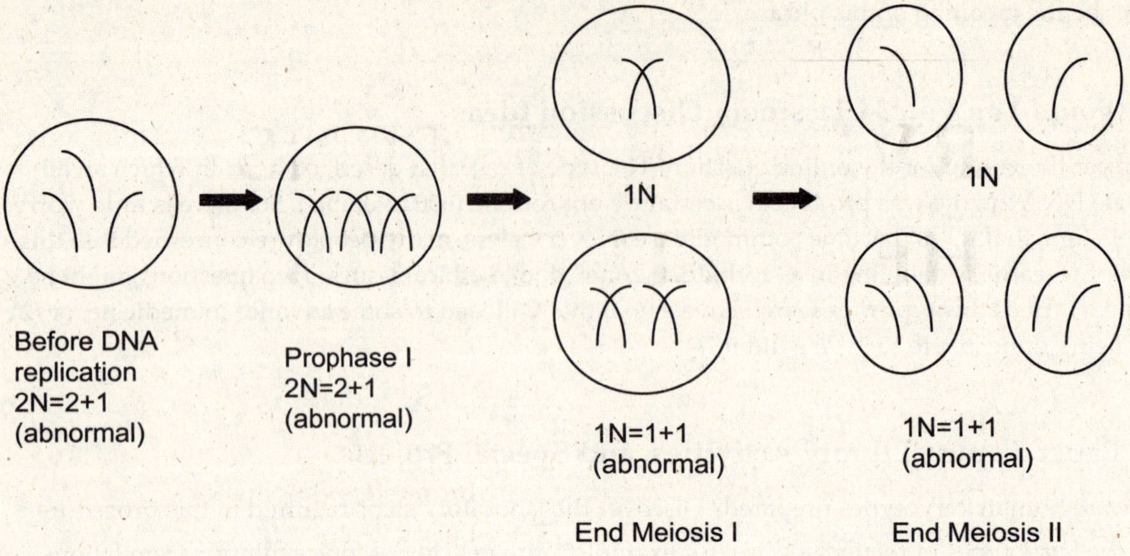

2. If meiosis fails in generation 1, the gametes would have 26 chromosomes (instead of 13). If these abnormal gametes combine, the individuals in generation 2 would contain 52 chromosomes. If meiosis fails in generation 2, those individuals would have gametes that contain 52 chromosomes. If these gametes combine, the individuals in generation 3 would contain 104 chromosomes.
3. Label Figure 12.9 to help you. In the primary spermatocyte (*m*), the DNA has already been replicated. The two cells produced by meiosis I have the chromosome number reduced by one-half and thus contain ½ *m*. In the four haploid spermatids the chromatids have separated, thus further reducing the *mass* of DNA by one-half and thus contain ¼*m*. Therefore, each mature gamete (sperm and egg) formed after meiosis would have a DNA mass of ¼*m*. When the gametes fuse, the DNA mass in (1) zygote would be ½ *m*, and (2) after the first duplication the zygote would contain *m* amount of DNA.

Possible Responses to *Data Analysis Exercise* Questions

1. 1.8 percent
2. The mice exposed to damaged cages with damaged bottles.
3. During metaphase, all the chromosomes should be aligned on the metaphase plate as shown in Figure 12.13A. In Figure 12.13C, there is one chromosome that has been excluded and is not on the metaphase plate. In Figure 12.13D, there are two groups of chromosomes instead of one.

13

OBSERVING PATTERNS IN INHERITED TRAITS

Chapter Outline

Objectives

1. Know Mendel's principles of dominance, segregation, and independent assortment.
2. Be able to describe and differentiate between genes and alleles, diploid and haploid, hybrid and true breeding, homozygous and heterozygous, genotype and phenotype, and self fertilizing and cross breeding.
3. Understand the relationship between P, F1, and F2 generations.
4. Be able to explain what a testcross is and when it is used.
5. Understand how to solve genetics problems that involve monohybrid and dihybrid crosses, and how they determine probability.
6. Describe and differentiate between codominance, incomplete dominance, epistasis, and pleiotropy and multiple alleles.
7. Be able to explain how polygenic inheritance gives rise to continuous variation.
8. Discuss how the environment contributes to variations in gene expression.
9. Describe how a bell curve emerges from a population.
10. Provide *all* the factors (genetic and environmental) contributing to an individual's phenotypic expression.

Key Terms

genes
locus
diploid
mutation
alleles
true-breeding lineage
hybrids
homozygous
heterozygous
dominant allele
recessive allele
homozygous dominant
homozygous recessive
heterozygous
genotype
phenotype
P, F_1, F_2
monohybrid cross
probability
Punnett-square method
testcross
Mendel's theory of segregation
dihybrid cross
Mendel's theory of independent assortment
codominance
ABO blood typing
multiple allele system
incomplete dominance
epistasis
pleiotropy
Marfan syndrome
linkage group
camptodactyly
continuous variation
polygenic inheritance
bell curve

Lecture Outline

13.1 Menacing Mucus

A. Cystic fibrosis is the most common fatal disorder in the United States.
   1. This disorder occurs when a mutation prevents the CFTR protein from reaching the cell surface.
   2. The CFTR protein is normally located on the surface of epithelial cells and functions to maintain the salt and water balance between cells by transporting chloride ions out of epithelial cells (water follows).
      a. Normal individuals have a thin film of water between sheets of epithelial cells.
      b. In cystic fibrosis patients, thick globs of mucus accumulate in the smaller airways of the lungs; the thick mucus occurs because not enough chloride ions (and water) leave the cells.
   3. The normal functioning CFTR protein also helps the body defend itself against bacteria.
      a. In normal individuals the CFTR protein binds bacteria and initiates cellular defenses.
      b. Cystic fibrosis patients do not have a CFTR protein on the cell surface; bacteria are not recognized and destroyed, thus chronic bacterial infections are a problem in these individuals.

B. About 1 in 25 people carry the CFTR mutation in one of their two copies of the gene; in about 1 in 3300 births, both copies of the CFTR are mutated, causing cystic fibrosis.

13.2 Mendel, Pea Plants, and Inheritance Patterns

A. Blending Inheritance versus Particulate Inheritance of Genes
   1. By the late nineteenth century, natural selection suggested that a population could evolve if members were to show variation in heritable traits. Variations that improved survival chances would be more common in each generation—in time, the population would change or evolve.
   2. The theory of natural selection did not fit with the prevailing view of inheritance—blending.
      a. Blending would produce uniform populations; such populations could not evolve.
      b. Many observations did not fit blending—for example, a white horse and a black horse did not produce only gray ones.
   3. Gregor Mendel used experiments in plant breeding and knowledge of mathematics to form his hypotheses.

B. Mendel's Experimental Approach
   1. Mendel used the garden pea in his experiments.
      a. This plant can fertilize itself; true-breeding varieties were available to Mendel.
      b. Peas can also be cross-fertilized by human manipulation of the pollen.
   2. Mendel cross-fertilized true-breeding garden pea plants that had clearly contrasting traits (e.g., white versus purple flowers).
   3. Mendel hypothesized that clearly observable differences might help him track the trait and identify inheritance patterns and heredity.

C. Terms Used in Modern Genetics
   1. *Genes* are units of information about specific traits, each located at a particular *locus* on a chromosome.
   2. Diploid cells have two genes (a gene pair) for each trait—each on a *homologous chromosome.*
   3. *Mutation* alters a gene's molecular structure; *alleles* are various molecular forms of a gene for the same trait.
   4. *True-breeding lineage* occurs when offspring inherit identical alleles, generation after generation; non-identical alleles produce *hybrid offspring.*
   5. When both alleles are the same, the condition is called the *homozygous* condition; if the alleles differ, it is the *heterozygous* condition.
   6. When heterozygous, one allele is *dominant* (*A*), and the other is *recessive* (*a*).
   7. Homozygous dominant = *AA;* homozygous recessive = *aa;* and heterozygous = *Aa*
   8. *Genotype* is the particular alleles an individual carries; *phenotype* is how the genes are expressed physically (what you observe).
   9. P = true-breeding parental generation; F_1 = first-generation offspring; F_2 = second-generation offspring of self-fertilized or intercrossed F_1 individuals.

13.3 Mendel's Theory of Segregation

A. Alleles and Meiosis
   1. Each member of a chromosome pair contains one allele of a gene; individuals have two copies of each chromosome and thus two copies of every gene.
   2. During meiosis, the chromosomes pair and separate such that each gamete contains one copy of each chromosome, and thus one copy of every gene (law of segregation).

B. Testcrosses
   1. Individuals that have a dominant trait, which genotypically could be homozygous or heterozygous, are crossed to individuals that have the recessive trait, which are known to be homozygous.
   2. If the progeny segregate 1:1 for the dominant and recessive trait, then the parent with the dominant trait was a heterozygote.
   3. If the progeny all have the dominant trait, the parent with the dominant trait was a homozygote.

C. Monohybrid Experiment Predictions
   1. Mendel's first experiments were monohybrid crosses.
      a. Monohybrid crosses have two parents that are true-breeding for contrasting forms of a trait (white versus purple flowers).
      b. One form of the trait (white) disappears in the first generation offspring (F_1), only to show up in the second generation (F_2).
      c. We now know that all members of the F_1 offspring are heterozygous (*Aa*) because one parent could produce only an *A* gamete and the other could produce only an *a* gamete.

2. Mendel had a strong mathematic background and knew about sampling error, so he crossed thousands of offspring.
3. In the F_2 generation, the white flowers reappeared.
   a. The numerical ratios of crosses suggested that genes do not blend.
   b. For example, the F_2 offspring showed a 3:1 phenotypic ratio of purple to white.
   c. Mendel assumed that each sperm has an equal probability of fertilizing an egg. This can be seen most easily by using the Punnett square.
   d. Thus, each new plant has three chances in four of having at least one dominant allele.

13.4 Mendel's Theory of Independent Assortment

A. Dihybrids are the offspring of parents that breed true for different versions of two traits.
   1. Mendel also performed experiments involving two traits—a dihybrid cross.
   2. A dihybrid cross is started by first crossing two true-breeding parents, each exhibiting two forms of two different traits. The resulting F_1 hybrids were allowed to self-fertilize, giving rise to offspring of 16 different combinations.
      a. Mendel correctly predicted that all F_1 plants would show both of the dominant alleles (e.g., all purple flowers and all tall plants).
      b. Mendel wondered if the genes for flower color and plant height would travel together when two F_1 plants were crossed.
   3. The F_2 results showed nine-sixteenths were tall and purple-flowered (both dominant forms of the trait), and one-sixteenth were dwarf and white-flowered (both recessive forms of the trait)—as were the original parents; however, there were three-sixteenths each of two new combinations: dwarf purple-flowered and tall white-flowered.
B. Mendel's theory of independent assortment states that as meiosis ends genes on different pairs of homologous chromosomes are sorted into gametes independently of each other; the same is true for genes located far apart on the same chromosome.
C. Genes located close together on the same chromosome do not independently assort; instead they are frequently inherited together (linked).

13.5 More Patterns Than Mendel Thought

A. Codominance in ABO Blood Types
   1. Codominance is when a pair of nonidentical alleles affecting two phenotypes are both expressed at the same time.
   2. In codominance, both alleles are expressed in heterozygotes.
   3. Blood type is determined by markers produced by three genes.
   4. The occurrence of more than three alleles for a single gene locus available to individuals in the population is called a multiple allele system.
      a. I^A and I^B are each dominant to i, but are codominant to each other.
      b. Therefore, some persons can express both genes and have AB blood.
B. Incomplete Dominance
   1. In *incomplete dominance*, a dominant allele cannot completely mask the expression of another.
   2. Phenotype will be an intermediate between the two traits.
   3. For example, a true-breeding red-flowered snapdragon crossed with a white-flowered snapdragon will produce *pink* flowers because there is not enough red pigment (produced by the dominant allele) to completely mask the effects of the white allele.
C. Epistasis
   1. Many phenotypes are due to the action of multiple gene products.
   2. In Labrador retrievers, one gene pair codes for the *quantity* of melanin produced while another codes for melanin *deposition*.

3. Still another gene locus determines whether melanin will be produced at all—absence of melanin produces an albino (recessive).
4. Two interacting gene pairs can give rise to a phenotype in which neither produces by itself.
5. Another example: there are four comb shapes in chickens; these four different shapes are due to the interaction between two genes (R and P); the phenotypes are walnut comb (R-P-), rose comb (R-pp), pea comb (rrP-), and single comb (rrpp).

D. Single Genes with a Wide Reach
1. Sometimes the expression of alleles at one location can have effects on two or more traits; this is termed pleiotropy.
2. Marfan syndrome is caused by an autosomal-dominant mutation of the gene for fibrillin, a protein found throughout the body in connective tissue.
3. Marfan syndrome is characterized by these effects: lanky skeleton, leaky heart valves, weakened blood vessels, deformed air sacs in lungs, pain, and lens displacement in the eyes.

13.6 Genes and the Environment

A. The environment contributes to variations in gene expression among individuals in a population; the inheritance of chromatin modifications likely plays a role.
1. The fur of the snowshoe hare varies by season: brown in the summer, white in the winter.
2. Cuttings from yarrow plant clones grew differently at three different altitudes.
3. Water fleas have different phenotypes depending on the presence or absence of predators.
4. Some people tolerate stress better than others, perhaps due to differences in the gene for a serotonin-transporting protein. Serotonin compromises response to stress.

B. Environmentally driven changes in gene expression can be inherited due to epigenetic changes in gene expression (see section 10.6).

13.7 Complex Variations in Traits

A. Continuous Variation in Populations
1. A given phenotype can vary, by different degrees, from one individual to the next in a population as a result of interactions with other genes and environmental influences.
   a. This feature is known as polygenic inheritance, where many genes along a particular chromosome affect one trait.
   b. In humans, eye color and height are examples.
2. Most traits are not qualitative, but show continuous variation and have an additive effect on phenotype.

B. Regarding the Unexpected Phenotype
1. Tracking even a single gene through several generations may produce results that are different than expected.
2. Camptodactyly (immobile, bent fingers) can express itself on one hand only, both hands, or neither due to the possibility that a gene product is missing in one of the several steps along the metabolic pathway.

Suggestions for Presenting the Material

- Students are usually naturally curious and interested in genetics. Start first with the simple examples of Mendel's monohybrid and dihybrid crosses before fielding questions on human traits such as height or eye color. Emphasize the remarkable nature of Mendel's work; remind the students that he knew nothing of chromosomes and their behavior, and that the term *gene* did not exist until several years after his death.

- Use Mendel's experiments and his conclusions as real-life examples of the scientific method at work. Ask questions to make sure students understand monohybrid and dihybrid crosses and testcrosses.
- Emphasize genetic terms and the figures that make use of these terms. Use Fig. 13.5 to ensure that students can visualize homologous chromosomes, gene loci, alleles, and gene pairs.
- Students should be able to relate the events of meiosis to the concepts of segregation and independent assortment; if their understanding of meiosis is weak, they will have trouble doing this.
- Many students come into college biology classes with the misconception that dominant alleles are "better" or more common than the recessive alleles. This misconception also makes it difficult for these students to understand non-Mendelian patterns of inheritance discussed at the end of Chapter 13. Stress to your students that dominant does not mean the most abundant or most advantageous trait. Give some examples of complete dominance with alleles that are harmful, undesirable, or lethal, such as polydactyly (extra digits), achondroplasia (dwarfism), and Huntington's disease (lethal degenerative neurological disorder).
- Beginning with this chapter, students will be quick to ask questions about human traits, many of which are governed by mechanisms more complex than those postulated by Mendel. Answer questions in this area during (or after) the discussion of variations on Mendel's themes, presented in the second half of this chapter.
- Remind students that the statistical probabilities obtained from Punnett squares are not absolute. There will be some variance, but large sample sizes reduce the likelihood.

Classroom and Laboratory Enrichment

- Ask groups of students to conduct coin tosses. Demonstrate the importance of large sample size by having the students vary the number of tosses before calculating variation from expected ratios.
- Distribute PTC tasting paper to your students, and calculate the number of tasters and nontasters in the classroom. You can also use different physical traits such as tongue rolling or earlobe attachment.
- Expand the biographical sketch of Mendel, including his education and practice as a clergyman. Enliven your presentation with as many slides of photos as you can find.
- Hand out a partially completed pedigree, and show students how to assign squares and circles for their family. Then ask them to select a trait and complete the pedigree after surveying the family members for presence/absence of the trait.
- Select a portion of the class to reenact the photo in Figure 13.16. If the quantity of students chosen does not provide a bell-shaped curve, use this as an illustration of how the greater number of trials/subjects/experiments tends to increase probability.
- Prepare photos of the examples of "variations on Mendel's themes." This will remove some of the "abstractness" of these topics.
- Show a video on genetics.
- Have students do a couple of quick practice Punnett squares (Tt X tt). Students should try to explain the given probabilities and describe possible phenotypes.
- There are many interesting websites that give possible phenotypes of offspring from parents that have different eye color; this shows students the complexity of polygenic inheritance.
- Demonstrate cross fertilization by bringing two large ornamental flowers to class and performing the cross in front of the students.
- An activity to help demonstrate how genotype governs phenotype can be a nice break from lecture. Using the example of fictitious genes may seem oversimplified and silly to you, but

students will enjoy the break. To show incomplete dominance: The "L" gene codes for laughter, the "L" allele codes an enzyme producing very loud laughter, and the "l" allele codes for an enzyme that produces no laughter.

Without explaining what you are demonstrating, hand two students papers with *L* and have them come to the front of the class. Hand two other students papers with *l* and have them come to the front, too. Point out that each student represents one chromosome that is carrying an allele for the *L* gene. Pair the chromosomes (students) by grouping like alleles (*LL* and *ll*). Then have the students demonstrate their phenotypes: *LL* students laugh loudly and *ll* students remain silent. Now, illustrate segregation by having the alleles (student groups) separate; show fertilization when an *L* and an *l* come together. Within each new group, have the *L* students laugh while the *l* students remain silent. Point out that the volume of laughing in the *Ll* individual is *about half* what it was in the *LL* individual. This is how a trait showing incomplete dominance works.

You can extend this to include epistasis: CCHH, CCHh, CcHH, CcHh—no hand clapping despite the "C" allele, because the "H" allele is present and inhibits the "C" allele from expressing (student can hold the clappers' hands); CChh, Cchh—hand clapping; no inhibitor is present; ccHh, ccHH, cchh—no hand clapping because no "C" allele is present.

Classroom Discussion Ideas

- Describe the behavior of one trait with regard to its inheritance in a particular cross; then ask students to identify the genetic mechanism at work (simple dominance, recessive inheritance, incomplete dominance, codominance, epistasis, pleiotropy, polygenic inheritance).
- Cystic fibrosis has been targeted for gene therapy. Discuss the pros and cons of using gene therapy to help cystic fibrosis patients.
- Discuss the pros and cons of requiring individuals to be genetically screened for disorders such as cystic fibrosis. Ask the students to think about how their opinion on having children might change if they knew they were carriers.
- List some human traits that you would guess are governed by a single gene.
- Give several reasons why Mendel's pea plants were a good choice for an experimental organism in genetics. Give an example of an organism that would be a poor choice for genetic research and explain your choice.
- Conduct a quick review in class of the various inheritable traits. Ask the students what kind of inheritance pattern the trait is an example of.
- Describe several different crosses using organisms such as Mendel's pea plants. Then ask students to calculate phenotypic and genotypic ratios for each cross.
- Discuss the significance of Mendel's use of mathematical and statistical analysis in his research.
- Why do you think Mendel was not immediately recognized as the discoverer of a new area of biology—genetics?
- Why does the gene interaction (incomplete dominance) NOT support the blending theory? How does it resemble the blending theory?
- What conclusions might Mendel have made if he had chosen *snapdragons* instead of *peas* for his study material?
- Why are the traits of human skin color and height not suitable for explaining the concept of simple dominance?
- There are four possible blood types in the ABO system. But how many *different* alleles are in the human population for this marker?

- What is the subtle difference between *incomplete dominance* and *codominance*?
- What is the significance of using upper- and lower-case versions of the same letter (for example, *A* and *a*) for the dominant and recessive trait, respectively, rather than a capital *A* for dominant and the letter *B* (or *b*) for recessive?

How Would You Vote? Classroom Discussion Ideas

- Monitor the voting for the online question. Genetic tests are available online and in some drugstores. Ask the students to consider this: insurance companies already charge increased rates or deny coverage for individuals who have a medical history, so how is charging a higher premium or denying coverage based on genetic testing any different? The students should also consider the mental health of an individual who discovers through genetic testing that they will die at an early age (for example, Huntington's disease). Should there be legislation that requires counseling for those individuals who wish to undergo genetic testing?

Term Paper Topics, Library Activities, and Special Projects

- What organisms are used most frequently in modern genetic research, and why?
- Describe the legal role now played by blood-type evidence in paternity cases. Are other aspects of blood genetics (other than the ABO series) now used in deciding such cases?
- How do you think Charles Darwin's writings on his theory of evolution might have changed had he read about Mendel's work?
- Describe examples of how modern knowledge of genetics has led to improved agricultural strains of plants and animals.
- Search for details of Mendel's life and work. Seek answers to the allegations that his results may have been "too good."
- When studying genetics, it is easy to discover variations in plants and animals that result in organisms that, even though related, are very different in appearance. How does a researcher prove whether or not the variants are or are not the "same species"?
- Research and describe other examples of epistasis in organisms.
- Prepare an update on the extent of Marfan syndrome in the United States and the world. Include in your report the consequences for those persons who are recessive and those who are carriers.
- Sickle-cell anemia is an example of pleiotropy that results from an abnormal hemoglobin in which valine is substituted for glutamate. Research the symptoms and explain the mechanism.
- Research recent reports that scientists may be able to reactivate the production of fetal hemoglobin to offset the effects of sickle-cell anemia.

Possible Responses to *Data Analysis Exercise* Questions

1. Approximately 600,000 bacteria enter normal cells and 80,000 enter mutated cells. Therefore, about 7.5 times more bacterium enter the normal cells.
2. Ty2 enters most easily. Approximately 600,000 Ty2 bacteria enter the normal cells compared to approximately 75,000 of strain 167 and 200,000 of strain 7251.
3. All of the strains have about an eight-fold reduction in number of bacteria that enter the cells. The differences in numbers of bacteria internalized into unmutated versus mutated cells are as follows: Ty2, 600,000 versus 80,000 (7.5-fold reduction); strain 167, 75,000 versus 10,000 (7.5-fold reduction) and strain 7251, 200,000 versus 25,000 (8-fold reduction). Thus, all the strains are similarly inhibited by the CFTR mutation.

14

CHROMOSOMES AND HUMAN INHERITANCE

Chapter Outline

SHADES OF SKIN
HUMAN CHROMOSOMES
EXAMPLES OF AUTOSOMAL INHERITANCE PATTERNS
- Autosomal Dominant Inheritance
- Autosomal Recessive Inheritance

EXAMPLES OF X-LINKED INHERITANCE PATTERNS
- Red-Green Color Blindness
- Duchenne Muscular Dystrophy

HERITABLE CHANGES IN CHROMOSOME STRUCTURE
- Main Categories of Structural Change
  - Duplication
  - Deletion
  - Inversion
  - Translocation
- Does Chromosome Structure Evolve?

HERITABLE CHANGES IN THE CHROMOSOME NUMBER
- Autosomal Change and Down Syndrome
  - Female Sex Chromosome Abnormalities
  - Male Sex Chromosome Abnormalities

GENETIC SCREENING
- Prenatal Diagnosis
- Preimplantation Diagnosis

SUMMARY
DATA ANALYSIS EXERCISE
SELF-QUIZ
GENETICS PROBLEMS

Objectives

1. Understand how to interpret a pedigree.
2. Know characteristics of autosomal-dominant and autosomal-recessive inheritance patterns and give examples of disorders for each.
3. Know characteristics of X-linked dominant and X-linked recessive inheritance patterns and give examples of disorders for each.
4. Name some ordinary and extraordinary chromosomal events that can create new phenotypes (outward appearances).
5. Understand how changes in chromosome structure and number can affect the outward appearance of organisms.
6. Compare and contrast duplication, deletion, inversion, and translocation.
7. Understand the variety of genetic screening options that are available.

Key Terms

gene
alleles
diploid
sex chromosomes
autosomes
pairs of homologous chromosomes
karyotype
spectral karyotypes
autosomal dominant inheritance
achondroplasia
Huntington disease
autosomal recessive inheritance
galactosemia
Hutchinson-Gilford progeria syndrome
SRY gene
testosterone
X chromosome
Y chromosome
XX, XY
nonsexual traits
linkage groups
wild-type
mutant
reciprocal crosses
X-linked inheritance
red–green color blindness
hemophilia A
Duchenne muscular dystrophy (DMD)
duplication
inversion
deletion
cri-du-chat
translocation
crossing over
genetic recombination
aneuploidy
polyploidy
nondisjunction
trisomy 21
Down syndrome
Turner syndrome
XXX syndrome
Klinefelter syndrome
XYY condition
pedigree
genetic abnormality
genetic disorder
syndrome
phenotypic treatments
phenylketonuria, PKU
genetic screening
prenatal diagnosis
embryo
fetus
amniocentesis
chorionic villi sampling
fetoscopy
genetic counseling
abortion
preimplantation diagnosis
in vitro fertilization

Lecture Outline

14.1 Shades of Skin

A. In human skin cells, organelles called melanosomes produce pigments (melanin) that cause skin color.

B. Skin color varies because the kinds and amount of melanin vary in individuals.

1. Dark skin is advantageous in high-sunlight regions because melanin acts as a natural sunscreen that prevents folic acid from breaking down; folic acid is essential for embryo and sperm development.
2. Light skin is advantageous in cooler climates with less sunlight because some UV light must enter the skin cells so that vitamin D is made.

C. More than 100 genes are involved in the synthesis of melanin.

1. One gene, *SLC24A5*, encodes a protein that transports melanin into skin cells.
2. Nearly all individuals of European descent carry a mutation in this gene.

D. Individuals of mixed ethnicity may produce gametes that produce offspring with darker or lighter skin than the parents, due to complexity of the trait.

14.2 Human Chromosomes

A. A Rest Stop on Our Conceptual Road

1. *Genes* are units of information about heritable traits.
2. Diploid organisms possess pairs of *homologous chromosomes*, which are alike in length, shape, and gene sequence.
3. *Alleles* are slightly different molecular forms of the same gene, which are shuffled during meiosis.
4. A *wild-type* allele is a gene's most common form; a less common form of the gene is the *mutant* allele.

5. Genes on the same chromosome are physically connected, but genes from one homolog may exchange places with those on the other homolog in *crossing over*, which produces genetic recombination.
6. A chromosome's structure may change during mitosis or meiosis, as can the parental chromosome number (quantity).

B. Autosomes and Sex Chromosomes
   1. *Sex chromosomes* determine gender.
      a. Human females have two X chromosomes.
      b. Males have one X and one Y.
   2. Most of the chromosomes are of the same quantity and type in both sexes and are called *autosomes* (44 present in humans).

C. Sex Determination in Humans
   1. Each human egg will contain 22 autosomes plus one X, but sperm will carry 22 autosomes plus *either* an X or a Y.
      a. An X-bearing egg plus an X-bearing sperm produces female offspring.
      b. An X-bearing egg plus a Y-bearing sperm produces male offspring.
   2. The Y chromosome carries a male-determining *(SRY)* gene, which leads to formation of the testes, which secrete testosterone. Absence of the male gene in females results in formation of ovaries.
   3. The X chromosome obviously codes for sexual traits, but it also carries many genes for nonsexual traits.

14.3 Human Chromosomes

A. Humans are difficult to study genetically.
   1. Unlike organisms raised under laboratory conditions, individuals live under variable conditions.
   2. Humans have a long life span.
   3. Individuals choose their own mates and reproduce whenever they choose.
   4. The number of progeny produced is small.

B. Pedigrees are used to determine the pattern of inheritance for traits in human families.
   1. Autosomal-dominant traits typically appear in every generation of a family.
   2. Autosomal-recessive traits typically skip generations; unaffected parents may have affected children.
   3. X-linked recessive traits are caused by genes located on the X chromosome; these traits are typically more common in males than females.
   4. X-linked dominant traits are also caused by genes located on the X chromosome; these traits are typically more common in females than males.

14.4 Examples of Autosomal Inheritance Patterns

A. Autosomal Dominant Inheritance
   1. The dominant allele is nearly always expressed, even in heterozygotes.
   2. If one parent is heterozygous and the other homozygous recessive, there is a 50 percent chance that any child will be heterozygous.
   3. If the gene (and its resulting disorder) reduces the chance of surviving or reproducing, its frequency should decrease, but may not due to mutations, nonreproductive effects, and postreproductive onset.
      a. *Achondroplasia* (dwarfism) is a benign abnormality that does not affect persons to the point that reproduction is impossible; the gene is passed on in heterozygotes.

b. *Huntington's disease* is a serious degeneration of the nervous system with an onset past the mid-30s, by which time the gene has (usually) been passed from parent to offspring unknowingly.

c. *Hutchinson-Gilford progeria syndrome* is characterized by dramatically accelerated aging; these individuals have defective lamin A, a protein required for nuclear functions including membrane support, DNA synthesis, DNA repair, and mitosis; individuals suffering from the disorder usually die in their early teens.

B. Autosomal Recessive Inheritance

1. Characteristics of this condition:
   a. Either parent can carry the recessive allele on an autosome.
   b. Heterozygotes are symptom-free carriers; homozygotes are affected.
   c. Two heterozygous parents have a 50 percent chance of producing heterozygous children and a 25 percent chance of producing a homozygous-recessive child. When both parents are homozygous, all children can be affected.
2. Examples
   a. Albinism is a condition caused by a mutation in a gene responsible for melanin production; these individuals lack pigment in the skin, eyes, and hair and are at risk for skin cancer because they have a reduced amount of melanin to protect the skin.
   b. Tay-Sachs is caused by a mutation in a gene that encodes an enzyme required for lysosome function; these individuals usually die in early childhood after suffering from neurological disorders caused by a buildup of toxic compounds in the brain.

14.5 Examples of X-linked Inheritance Patterns

A. X-Linked Recessive Pattern

1. Because males have only one copy of the X chromosome, the disorder appears more frequently in males.
2. In females one of the two copies of the X chromosome is inactivated in every cell; however, females can still be heterozygous; those cells that have the dominant X chromosome active cover up the effects of those cells where the recessive X chromosome is active.

B. Examples

1. Red-green colorblindness.
   a. *Color blindness* is the inability to distinguish some or all of the colors in the visible light spectrum; mutated genes change the light-absorbing capacity of sensory receptors of the eyes.
   b. Red-green color-blind people can see fewer than 25 of the 150 differences in color seen by normal individuals. It is 12 times more common in men than women.
2. *Duchenne muscular dystrophy* (DMD) is characterized by rapid degeneration of muscles early in life (one in 3,500 males), and is caused by a recessive allele for a structural protein called dystrophin.
   a. When dystrophin is abnormal or absent, muscle cells progressively die (in an unstoppable manner).
   b. Diagnosed between ages three and seven, the affected boy generally dies before he reaches age 25.
3. Hemophilia A
   a. A serious X-linked recessive condition is *hemophilia A* (affecting 1 in 7,000 males), which is the inability of the blood to clot because the genes do not code for the necessary clotting agent(s).
   b. The disorder's frequency was high among the royal families of Europe and Russia in the 19th century.

14.6 Heritable Changes in Chromosome Structure

A. Main Categories of Structural Change

1. *Duplication* occurs when DNA sequences are repeated two or more times; unequal crossovers at prophase I can cause duplications resulting in neural problems and physical abnormalities.
2. A *deletion* is the loss of a portion of a chromosome by unequal crossovers, inversions, or chemical attack, usually causing serious disorders or death in mammals; an example is the loss of a portion of chromosome 5, causing a disorder called *cri-du-chat*, which carries symptoms of crying and mental retardation.
3. An *inversion* alters the position and sequence of the genes so that gene order is reversed.
4. A *translocation* occurs when a part of one chromosome becomes attached to another chromosome; most are reciprocal exchanges.

B. Does Chromosome Structure Evolve?

1. Changes in chromosome structure tend to be selected against rather than conserved over evolutionary time.
2. However, gene regions for the polypeptide chains of hemoglobin have duplicated to produce different hemoglobins with different oxygen-transporting efficiencies.
3. A mutation that interfered with crossing over is thought to have initiated the structural differences between the X and Y chromosomes in mammals.

14.7 Heritable Changes in the Chromosome Number

A. Abnormal events occur before or during cell division, causing a change in the chromosome number.

1. Aneuploidy is a condition in which the gametes or cells of an affected individual end up with *one extra* or *one less* chromosome than is normal.
2. Polyploidy is the presence of *three or more* of each type of chromosome in gametes or cells. It is common in plants but fatal in humans.
   a. A chromosome number can change during mitotic or meiotic cell division or during the fertilization process.
   b. Tetraploid germ cells can result if cytoplasmic division does *not* follow normal DNA replication and mitosis.
3. *Nondisjunction* at anaphase I or anaphase II frequently results in a change in chromosome number.
   a. If a gamete with an extra chromosome ($n + 1$) joins a normal gamete at fertilization, the diploid cell will be $2n + 1$; this condition is called *trisomy*.
   b. If an abnormal gamete is missing a chromosome, the zygote will be $2n - 1$; this is *monosomy*.

B. Autosomal Change and Down Syndrome

1. Down syndrome results from trisomy 21; it is the most frequent type of altered chromosome number in humans, occurring once in every 800 to 1,000 births.
2. About 95 percent of all cases come from nondisjunction at meiosis; most children with Down syndrome show mental retardation and have heart defects.
3. Down syndrome occurs more frequently in children born to older women.

C. Change in the Sex Chromosome Number

1. Female Sex Chromosome Abnormalities
   a. *Turner syndrome* involves females whose cells have only one X chromosome (designated XO).
      1) Affected individuals (1 in 2,500–10,000 newborn girls) are infertile and have other phenotypic problems such as premature aging and shorter life expectancy.

2) About 75 percent of the cases are due to nondisjunction in the father; furthermore, about 98 percent of all XO zygotes spontaneously abort.

b. The XXX condition is an inheritance of multiple X chromosomes.

1) About 1 in 1,000 females inherits 3, 4, or 5 X chromosomes.

2) Most of these girls are taller and slimmer than average, but are fertile and fall within the normal range of appearance and social behavior.

2. Male Sex Chromosome Abnormalities

a. Klinefelter syndrome is caused by a nondisjunction, which results in an extra X chromosome in the cells (XXY) of these affected males (1in 500–2,000 live-born males).

1) About 67 percent of these result from nondisjunction in the mother, 33 percent in the father.

2) Sterility, slight mental retardation, and body feminization are symptoms.

b. In the XYY condition, the extra Y chromosome in these males (1 in 1,000) does not affect fertility, but they are taller than average and slightly mentally retarded.

14.8 Genetic Screening

A. Genetic screening is early detection of genetic disorders; newborns are routinely screened for many genetic disorders.

B. Many disorders, if detected early, can be controlled by diet, surgery, drugs, and hormone replacement therapy.

C. Newborn screening

1. *Phenylketonuria* (PKU) is a disorder in which the amino acid phenylalanine is not properly metabolized and builds up to toxic levels.

2. PKU can be controlled by restricting the intake of the amino acid phenylalanine.

D. Pre-Pregnancy Screening

1. Prospective parents may want to prepare for the possibility that their future child may inherit a serious genetic disorder.

2. Genetic counseling includes diagnosis of parental genotypes, pedigrees, and genetic testing for many metabolic disorders; Counselors help prospective parents evaluate risks in bringing a child into the world.

E. Prenatal Screening

1. Non-invasive ultrasounds provide detailed images of physical abnormalities that may be associated with a genetic disorder.

2. Amniocentesis is a procedure in which small amounts of fluid from inside the amnion sac are removed and analyzed for the presence of abnormal cells that have been shed from the fetus; it raises risk of miscarriage by 1–2 percent.

3. Chorionic villi sampling (CVS) is also a sampling of cells from the fetus, but in this case from the chorion; it can be done weeks earlier than amniocentesis; CVS may disrupt the placenta's development.

4. Fetoscopy uses a fiberoptic device with pulsed sound waves that scans the contents of the uterus; it increases risk of miscarriage by 2–10 percent.

F. Preimplantation Diagnosis

1. For couples relying on *in vitro fertilization* for conception, they may ask for an analysis to be done on the embryos before insertion into the female for implantation.

2. Embryos with no detectable genetic defects are implanted; those with defects are discarded; again, some may consider this a type of abortion.

Suggestions for Presenting the Material

- Students should be well grounded in their understanding of chromosomal structure before attempting to tackle the material in this chapter. The use of sketches, diagrams, and slides will greatly assist in making this material as clear as possible.
- They also must understand the events of meiosis, or they will have difficulty comprehending crossing over and changes in chromosome number resulting from nondisjunction.
- Remind students that crossing over and genetic recombination create variability among sexually reproducing organisms; challenge students to think about the role this plays in evolution.
- Describe the steps of Thomas Hunt Morgan's work to show how X-linkage was discovered. Ask students to solve the genetics problems that deal with X-linked genes at the end of the chapter. To assess how well students understand this material, work on as many of these problems together in class as time allows.
- Explain how karyotypes are prepared before showing a human karyotype. Otherwise, students might think that human chromosomes naturally occur paired up.
- Ask students to view some popular science videos (or show a short sequence) on possible future negative implications of genetic testing on newborns, such as in the movie *Gattaca.* This always brings forth lots of personal opinions and great questions from the students.
- Students need practice to learn how the different types of inheritance (autosomal recessive, autosomal dominant, and X-linked recessive) actually influence the inheritance of a trait in real-life examples. Review, if necessary, basic genetic terms such as *homozygous, heterozygous, dominant,* and *recessive.* To see how well students understand these types of inheritance, begin by working through some simple examples (as shown in Figures 14.2 and 14.7) of autosomal-dominant inheritance, autosomal-recessive inheritance, and X-linked recessive inheritance at the blackboard. Ask students to predict the possible phenotypic outcomes in each example.
- During lectures, use the genetics problems at the end of the chapter as they apply. Work through one or two examples at the blackboard with your class as a whole, and then ask students to complete the rest in class (possibly as part of a quiz) or on their own time. Students will enjoy the puzzle-solving aspects of pedigree analysis, while at the same time measuring their level of understanding of the different types of inheritance.
- Many of the genetic disorders and abnormalities mentioned in this chapter are ones whose names students have heard, but whose mechanisms of inheritance were unknown to them before reading this chapter. To lend more meaning to the conditions described here, ask students to think about the social and ethical problems associated with some of the diseases mentioned in this chapter.

Classroom and Laboratory Enrichment

- Ask students (working individually or in small groups) to use chromosome-simulation kits (available from biological supply houses) to review chromosome structure, homologous pairing, crossing over, and independent assortment during gamete formation. If kits are unavailable, make your own chromosomes using a pop-it bead (or bead and cord) for each chromatid and a magnet for each centromere, or use the craft sticks mentioned in the Enrichment section for Chapter 10.
- Show karyotypes of males and females of different species without revealing the sex of the individual. Ask students to identify the sex.
- Discuss gene mapping in humans using the Human Genome Project's website to show some of the known locations of particular genes (http://www.ncbi.nlm.nih.gov/mapview/map_search.cgi). A free poster is available upon request to the Human Genome Landmarks Poster website

(http://www.ornl.gov/sci/techresources/Human_Genome/posters/chromosome/).

- Project images of chromosomes with labeled gene sequences to demonstrate deletions, duplications, inversions, and translocations.
- Ask a local health unit or testing lab if you can copy (anonymously, of course) some karyotypes that show chromosomal defects. Show these to the class, and ask if the students can spot the defect before it is revealed to them.
- Prepare a slide to illustrate the relationship between DNA, genes, and chromosomes.
- Show the students unlabeled karyotypes from individuals with chromosomal abnormalities such as Turner syndrome, Klinefelter syndrome, or Down syndrome. Ask students if the karyotype appears normal; if not, what is wrong?
- Ask a genetic counselor to speak to your class about his/her job.
- Draw a pedigree for an unnamed genetic condition. Ask students if the disorder is autosomal dominant, autosomal recessive, sex-linked dominant, or sex-linked recessive.
- Obtain from your local health unit several brochures that explain the various genetic problems that can be inherited. Ask the students to discuss this information.
- From the same source mentioned above, you may be able to obtain a list of those genetic "diseases" for which there is mandatory testing in your state (usually of newborns). What voluntary testing programs are available?

Classroom Discussion Ideas

- Why do harmful genes remain in the human population?
- If it becomes possible to easily and inexpensively choose the sex of your child, how will this change the male-to-female ratio among newborns? Do you think it is ethically correct to select the sex of your children? What about the effect of China's "one-child" policy on sex ratios?
- What is genoism? What will happen if we open Pandora's box and are able to read all the secrets found in DNA? What if we can tell how long your child could possibly live? What if you could genetically engineer your offspring (e.g., eye color, hair color, height, and elimination of all genetic disorders)?
- Do you think any of the traits Mendel followed in the garden pea were linked? Why or why not?
- If male and female offspring occur at a ratio of approximately 50:50, why do some couples have only boys or only girls?
- What is the distinction between the terms *gene* and *allele?*
- Why do individual chromosomes present at the conclusion of meiosis not have the same genetic constituency as they did before meiosis?
- If one sex of offspring tends to exhibit a trait more frequently than the other sex, of what is this an indication?
- What is the physical relationship of *genes* to *chromosomes* to *DNA?*
- What is the difference between a *translocation* of chromosomal segments and *crossing over*?
- Discuss the risks and benefits of amniocentesis. Would you elect to undergo this procedure (or urge your spouse to do so) if you had a history of genetic abnormalities in your family, or if you or your spouse were over 35? Why or why not?
- Why is hemophilia more threatening to the life of a female victim than to a male victim?
- Why do so many people insist that girls cannot be red-green color blind (an X-linked inherited condition)?

- Can you think of some of the ethical questions involved in performing genetic research on humans? As our society learns more about genetic diseases, do you think couples who plan to have children should be required to have genetic counseling or undergo genetic screening?
- Why does the incidence of Down syndrome increase with the mother's age?
- When would you recommend genetic counseling to a couple, and when would you recommend genetic screening? Is there a difference?

How Would You Vote? Classroom Discussion Ideas

- Monitor the voting for the online question. Race is a term that defines a population of individuals that are genetically similar to one another but differ from another population (another race). The twin with the lighter skin color is not genetically different enough from her family to be considered a different race. This twin is simply at the extreme end of phenotypic variation produced by a complex, quantitative trait.

Term Paper Topics, Library Activities, and Special Projects

- How do the sex chromosomes actually determine the sex of the individual? What are some of the characteristics governed by genes of the X and Y chromosomes?
- What human disorders have been determined and mapped? Which chromosome is encoded with the most disorders/diseases?
- Because the sex of an individual is determined by the sperm at the moment of conception, is it possible to select the sex of a child by separating sperm with X chromosomes from those with Y chromosomes? Discuss recent experimental techniques that attempt to do this.
- How are human karyotypes prepared? Discover the laboratory steps required in this procedure.
- Find specific examples of how irradiation, chemical action, or viral attack can cause chromosome breakage.
- Are any human traits Y-linked?
- Describe how (and why) artificially induced changes in chromosome number have been used to create new varieties of fruits and vegetables.
- The predicted ratio of newborns should show a 50-50 sex ratio. Ask a local hospital to provide statistics on the sex ratio in order to confirm or deny this prediction.
- Prepare a protocol for rearing *Drosophila* in the lab and making simple crosses.
- Construct a pedigree for your own family using a trait governed by simple Mendelian inheritance.
- Describe the history of the discovery and treatment of victims of any one of the human genetic abnormalities or disorders described in your text.
- Discover information about some of the tests now available for some genetic diseases (for example, Huntington disorder) to determine if one is a carrier for that disease. What are some of the ethical questions raised by such tests?
- Learn more about hemophilia. Discuss its history, its role in the downfall of the Russian monarchy, and modern treatments for the disease.
- Contact your local health unit for statistics on the incidence of Down syndrome and other genetic disorders whose causes are known.
- Consult a book on medical ethics to learn of the objections that have been raised to genetic screening programs.

Possible Responses to *Data Analysis Exercise* Questions

1. Kenya receives the most (354.21 UVMED). Ireland receives the least (52.92 UVMED).
2. People indigenous to Australia have the darkest skin color (19.30 skin reflectance). People indigenous to the Netherlands have the lightest skin color (67.37 skin reflectance).
3. In general, people indigenous to countries that receive higher amounts of UV radiation will have darker skin.

15

STUDYING AND MANIPULATING GENOMES

Chapter Outline

Objectives

1. Know how DNA can be cleaved, spliced, cloned, and sequenced.
2. Understand what plasmids are and how they may be used to insert new genes into recombinant DNA molecules.
3. Know the role of restriction enzymes and DNA ligase in forming recombinant DNA.
4. Understand what a cDNA library is and how it is created, and the role RNA transcriptase plays in this process.
5. Explain how gene libraries are produced, and describe the role of probes, primers, and nucleic acid hybridization in this procedure.
6. Explain what PCR is and describe its use in replicating genes.
7. Describe automated DNA sequencing and explain how it reveals the sequence of PCR-amplified DNA.
8. Understand what DNA profiling is, and how it can be used for medical and forensic purposes.
9. Understand how the Human Genome Project has paved the way for the field of genomics.
10. Explain how genomics furthered the development of human gene therapy.
11. Describe how SNP chips are used to detect genomic differences between individuals.

12. Explain what genetic engineering is and how it is used to manufacture drugs and clean up the environment.
13. Describe how genetic engineering has helped the agricultural community.
14. Explain how transgenic animals are used in medical research.
15. Name the ethical issues concerning transgenics.
16. Describe the safety concerns and precautions taken in DNA research.
17. Describe eugenics and eugenic engineering, and the pros and cons of human gene therapy.
18. Explain the types of genetic experiments that nature has been performing for billions of years.
19. Understand how one organism can produce the products of another.
20. Be aware of several limits and possibilities for future research in genetic engineering.

Key Terms

GM organisms
Human Genome Project
restriction enzymes
DNA ligase
recombinant DNA technology
plasmids
cloning vector
reverse transcriptase
cDNA
DNA clone
gene library
genomic library
cDNA library
probe
nucleic acid hybridization
primer
PCR
automated DNA sequencing
gel electrophoresis
DNA fingerprint
short tandem repeats
genomics
human gene therapy
DNA chips
genetic engineering
transgenic
xenotransplantation
eugenic engineering
genome
SNPs
DNA profiling

Lecture Outline

15.1 Personal DNA Testing

A. Human Genome Structure

1. Of the 2.97 billion nucleotides that make up your genome, only about 30 million differ between individuals.
2. The genomic differences between individuals are usually single base changes (SNPs) that are scattered throughout the genome.
3. SNPs give rise to different alleles of a gene; therefore, the SNPs that vary between individuals are largely responsible for making all individuals phenotypically unique.

B. The Importance of Understanding SNPs

1. A single SNP in the *APOE* gene increases the chance of individuals developing Alzheimer's later in life.
2. Understanding how each SNP affects gene function may allow physicians to offer customized health care.
3. Physicians could analyze all of your SNPs, assess your risk of developing a genetic disorder (e.g., diabetes), and customize a healthcare plan that would minimize the risk of developing the disorder by reducing the environmental risks (becoming overweight) or offer preventative treatment if available.

15.2 Cloning DNA

A. The Scissors: Restriction Enzymes

1. Bacteria possess restriction enzymes whose usual function is to cut apart foreign DNA molecules.
2. Each enzyme cuts only at sites that possess a specific base sequence.

a. The wide variety of restriction enzymes and their specificity makes it possible to study the genome of a particular species.
b. Many times the "sticky ends" that result from the cut can be used to pair up with another DNA fragment cut by the same enzyme.

3. DNA fragments produced by restriction enzymes are treated with DNA ligase to splice the DNA fragments (from same or different species) together to form a recombinant DNA molecule.

B. Cloning Vectors
1. Plasmids are circular DNA molecules in bacteria that carry only a few genes and can replicate independently of the single "main" chromosome.
2. Modified plasmids that are capable of accepting, replicating, and delivering DNA to another host cell are called cloning vectors.
3. When the plasmid is replicated, any foreign DNA that might have become incorporated into it is also replicated, producing a *DNA clone*.

C. cDNA Cloning
1. Since eukaryotic genes contain introns; those who wish to study gene expression often choose to work with mRNA since the cell has removed the introns (see section 9.3).
2. mRNA is difficult to work with; therefore, many researchers choose to transcribe the mRNA into DNA using the enzyme reverse transcriptase.

15.3 Isolating Genes

A. DNA Libraries
1. A *gene library* is a collection of bacteria that houses different cloned DNA fragments, including one that is of interest; it may be the entire genome or *cDNA*, which is free of introns.
2. A particular gene of interest can be isolated from other genes by use of probes.
   a. DNA probes, short DNA sequences assembled from radioactive nucleotides, can pair with parts of the gene to be studied.
   b. This nucleic acid hybridization technique can be used with other procedures to select cells and their DNA, which may be of interest to the researcher.
3. If researchers know the desired gene sequence, they use it to construct a primer by synthesizing the single-stranded DNA; if the sequence is unknown, they use DNA from the same gene of a closely related species that has already been isolated.

B. Big-Time Amplification—PCR
1. The polymerase chain reaction (PCR) can be used to make millions of copies of cDNA.
2. What is needed for the reaction?
   a. Primers are short nucleotide sequences that are made in the laboratory.
   b. They are recognized by DNA polymerases as the START tags for building complementary sequences of DNA, dictated by computer programs stored in the machines.
3. What are the reaction steps?
   a. Researchers mix primers, DNA polymerase, cellular DNA from an organism, and free nucleotides.
   b. Precise temperature cycles cause the DNA strands to separate, exposing the bases.
   c. Primers become positioned on the exposed nucleotides to form new copies of the original DNA.
   d. Each round of reactions doubles the number of DNA molecules to eventually produce billions of molecules from very tiny amounts of original DNA.

15.4 Automated DNA Sequencing

A. Currently, laboratories use automated DNA sequencing to determine the unknown sequence of bases in a DNA sample.
   1. The machine builds DNA molecules but uses eight kinds of bases; four normal and four that are modified to fluoresce in laser light.
   2. When a modified base is incorporated, DNA synthesis is halted, producing tagged fragments of different lengths.
B. The automated DNA sequencer separates the sets of fragments by gel electrophoresis.
   1. The "tag" base at the end of each fragment in the set is identified by the laser beam.
   2. The computer program in the machine assembles the information from all the nucleotides in the sample to reveal the entire DNA sequence.
C. The Human Genome Project
   1. With the invention of PCR and automated sequencing, scientists argued for the sequencing of the human genome in 1986.
   2. Beginning in 1988, NIH directed the public effort in many laboratories to sequence the human genome.
   3. In the late 1990s, Craig Venter launched his effort at genome sequencing using powerful automated sequencing machines.
   4. Sequencing was officially completed in 2003.
      a. Ninety-nine percent of the coding of human DNA has been deciphered with accuracy; researches found far fewer genes than they expected—just over 20,000.
      b. The next step is to determine what the genes encode; fewer than 2 percent of our genome is protein-encoding genes, and there are many inactivated pseudogenes.

15.5 Genomics

A. Anyone can now pay to have their entire genome sequenced; however scientists do not understand the significance of all the sequences in the human genome.
B. Genomics is the study of genome sequences isolated from different organisms.
   1. Gene structure and sequence variation between organisms can provide many clues into the evolutionary relationship between organisms.
   2. Genomics has many medical benefits; our understanding of the function of many human genes has been discovered by studying the gene in other organisms.
C. DNA Profiling
   1. SNP chips are a way of genotyping single nucleotide differences in the genome.
      a. DNA of a known sequence is spotted onto a glass slide.
      b. DNA of an unknown sequence is washed over the glass slide.
      c. Base pairing between the DNA of unknown and known sequence is detected by fluorescent probes.
      d. The SNPs can be fluorescently labeled such that homozygosity and heterozygosity can be determined.
   2. Short tandem repeats.
      a. Tandem repeats are copies of the same short DNA sequences that are highly variable from one person to the next.
      b. The differences in tandem repeats can be detected by PCR and gel electrophoresis, a technique that pulls molecules through a block of gelatin by electric current; different size molecules travel at different speeds.
      c. Tandem repeats are the basis for DNA fingerprinting, now a widely accepted and valuable tool for forensic scientists to identify criminals, victims, and innocent suspects.

15.6 Genetic Engineering

A. Genetic engineering is a laboratory process where genes are cloned, often altered, and then reinserted into an organism; sometimes the gene is isolated from one species and reinserted into another species.

B. Genetic engineering requires the use of plasmid-taking bacteria, which are now widely used in basic research, agriculture, medicine, and industry.

1. Genetically engineered bacteria make useful amounts of synthetic insulin for humans, in addition to growth hormone, hemoglobin, interferon, and other drugs and vaccines.
2. Environmental remediation uses modified bacteria to clean-up environmental messes, such as oil spills, heavy metals, or even radioactive wastes.

15.7 Designer Plants

A. There is worldwide pressure to produce more food at lower cost and with less damage to the environment.

1. Some farmers are turning to genetically engineered crop plants, accomplished by transferring a gene from one species to another.
   a. Cotton plants are engineered to have an insecticide gene that kills only the insects that feed on it.
   b. Genetically modified wheat has greater yield per acre.
   c. Transgenic tomato plants survive in unusually salty soils.
2. Engineering plant cells starts with vectors that can carry genes into plant cells.
   a. An early experiment showed that a plasmid from a bacterium that normally causes tumors in plants could be modified by replacing the tumor gene with desirable genes.
   b. Such modified bacteria have been injected into plant cells where they expressed their "foreign" genes.
3. Due to an increasing vulnerability of the world's food supply, botanists have collected seeds of the wild ancestors of crop plants and older, diverse varieties of plants and have sent them to seed banks to store and safely preserve plant genetic diversity.

15.8 Biotech Barnyards

A. Transgenic Animals

1. In 1982, the rat gene for somatotropin production was introduced into mouse eggs; the mice, which subsequently expressed the rat gene, grew larger than their littermates.
2. Genetically engineered animals have been used as sources of pharmaceuticals.
   a. Goats have produced TPA for diminishing the severity of heart attacks, and CFTR, used in the treatment of cystic fibrosis.
   b. Rabbits produce interleukin-2, which stimulates divisions of T-lymphocytes in the immune response.
3. Genetic engineering could also lead to healthier animals, just as natural breeding practices have for thousands of years.

B. Knockout Cells and Organ Factories

1. Xenotransplantation is the transferring of an organ from one species to another.
2. Pigs can be engineered to lack certain genes that would cause rejection problems when their organs are transplanted to humans.

C. Genes responsible for human disorders (e.g., cancer) are frequently identified in animals; the animal gene is mutated in order to study the disorder in humans.

1. These animals suffer from the same conditions that humans do and for many people this raises many ethical concerns.
2. However, researchers do gather tremendous amounts of information by studying animal models, and often this research leads to new treatments for humans.

15.9 Safety Issues

A. There is an ongoing debate about potential dangers of transgenic organisms entering the environment before rigorous testing.
   1. Scientists reached a consensus on the safety guidelines for DNA research, which was adopted by the NIH (National Institutes of Health).
   2. No pathogenic or toxic organisms can be used for recombinant experiments without proper containment facilities.
   3. A "fail-safe" lethal gene is built into genetically engineered bacteria that is turned on if the bacteria escape from the controlled lab into the environment.

B. Still, things can go wrong, as in the example of the rabbit virus in Australia that escaped from controlled laboratory facilities and is now out in the wild rabbit population.

15.10 Modified Humans?

A. Are they better off?
   1. Gene therapy was initially successful in a trial against SCID-X1 (severe immune deficiency) in which 10 of 11 patients benefited.
   2. Two from the group later developed leukemia, which has raised questions about future treatments.

B. Where do we draw the line?
   1. Eugenic engineering is based on the idea of being able to select desirable human traits, including behaviors.
   2. Who decides what is "desirable"? Forty percent of surveyed persons in the U.S. said it would be alright to use gene therapy to make people smarter and better looking.

Suggestions for Presenting the Material

- Help students see the relevance of this subject by telling them about some of the products (such as insulin) that are produced as a result of genetic engineering.
- Begin by reminding students that genetic recombination occurs naturally in all organisms during meiosis. Emphasize that even though examples of genetic research in bacteria may seem obscure and of little relationship to more complex eukaryotic genomes, such experimentation yields results of great value to humans.
- Ask questions to ensure that students are indeed knowledgeable about the use of plasmids and restriction enzymes. Visuals are very helpful with this rather abstract and unseen procedure.
- Genetic engineering has the potential to truly capture the students' interest. You may wish to devote extra class time to this subject in order to allow students the opportunity to become involved and invested in it. More than likely there will be issues about genetic engineering they will be voting on in the future.
- One class activity you might wish to consider while discussing Section 15.10 is showing clips from the movie *Gattaca* (1997). Parents meet with their geneticist to select *which* egg and sperm they wish to unite through fertilization to become their child. In this meeting, they are able to select for sex, intelligence, diseases, physical appearance, and abilities, if they so choose—in fact, the exact date and cause of natural death for every human can be determined from a single drop of blood. Such a clip can be a good discussion-launcher into future possibilities in eugenic engineering.

Classroom and Laboratory Enrichment

- Illustrate the cleavage and splicing steps of recombinant DNA formation, using slides or models.
- Demonstrate transfer of a plasmid for antibiotic resistance from one strain of bacteria to another using selected strains of *E. coli.* (Laboratory kits containing all necessary materials are available.)
- Fabricate workable models of cloning as depicted in Figure 15.4.
- Prepare a summary table of the genome modification methods listed in this chapter. Include the following information:
  a. Natural versus manmade
  b. Examples of organisms
  c. Usefulness
- Ask two groups of students to prepare brief arguments *for* and *against* the continuation of genetic engineering research and development.
- Arrange for a classroom presentation on the use of SNP chips and DNA fingerprinting.
- Arrange for students to visit a colleague's laboratory where PCR is regularly performed to get an idea of the technology through a demonstration.

Classroom Discussion Ideas

- Where and when does genetic recombination naturally occur?
- What are some characteristics of an organism ideally suited for research in genetic engineering?
- Discuss the benefits of genetic engineering versus potential risks.
- What (if any) might be the objections to growing and distributing the "golden rice" in third-world countries experiencing food shortages?
- Would *you* eat your tacos if you knew the corn produced for their shells was from a GM plant?
- Why are restriction enzymes useful tools for genetic engineering? How is DNA ligase used in genetic engineering?
- Do you think that new genomes resulting from genetic engineering should be patented? Who should receive monetary benefits from such discoveries—the research scientists performing the work or their academic institutions?
- What advantages would insulin produced by genetic engineering have over preparations from animal sources in the treatment of human diabetes mellitus?
- Is genetic engineering a new concept in nature or just the human application of a natural mechanism already in operation? Explain with examples.
- Is it dangerous to eat foods that have genes from another organism?

How Would You Vote? Classroom Discussion Ideas

- Monitor the voting for the online question. One way to address this issue is to help the students understand the devastating effects of Huntington's disease. Make sure the students understand that this is a dominant, lethal disease and many who suffer from the disease die in their 40s. Ask the students if and how they would change their future plans if they discovered they were likely to die of Huntington's. Would they plan to have children? Would they worry about having a successful career? Would they get married? Expand the discussion to include other disorders: How do the students' answers change if they found out they are likely to suffer from cancer, Alzheimer's, or diabetes? Why do their answers change?

Term Paper Topics, Library Activities, and Special Projects

- Compile a history of research efforts in genetic engineering.
- Describe problems that have resulted from the standard prophylactic use of antibiotics among farm animals such as poultry, pigs, and cattle.
- Describe the safeguards currently followed in labs doing work in genetic engineering.
- List and describe companies currently doing research in genetic engineering. Investigate the current financial worth of some of these companies.
- Discuss the growing problem of antibiotic resistance among the different species of bacteria responsible for causing diseases such as gonorrhea, typhoid, and meningitis.
- Trace the history of the development and production of interferon, insulin, or any other substance produced using techniques of genetic engineering.
- In the early days of genetic recombination research, fears of creating "monster" bacteria that could run amok in the human population were quite real. However, after careful evaluation of all laboratory procedures used in thousands of experiments, these fears seem exaggerated. Why do *you* feel this thinking has changed?
- It is known that the HIV virus that causes AIDS can delay its deadly effects for some time. Search the literature to find out if this is an instance of the virus entering a latent state before resuming its attack.
- Have students research the rapidly growing field of *proteomics*.

Possible Responses to *Critical Thinking* Questions

1. DNA bacteriophages are viruses that infect bacteria cells by injecting their DNA in host bacterial cells. Once the phage DNA enters the bacteria it can take over the host cell's machinery to produce more bacteriophages inside the bacterial cell. Once a large number of phage progeny are made inside the host cell, the cell bursts open and the phage progeny are free to infect other bacterial cells. Restriction enzymes protect the bacteria from bacteriophages by chopping up the phage DNA when it enters the host cell. The host cell's DNA is protected because bacterial DNA is methylated. Most restriction enzymes will not cut at its recognition sequence if that sequence is methylated.
2. If a talking chimp could be engineered, it is likely that the debate over using animals in research would intensify. While there are many protocols in place to ensure that research animals are not subjected to unnecessary pain and suffering, in many ways we are only able to speculate if the research is causing pain or suffering. In addition, the definition of unnecessary pain and suffering is not always clear. Currently there are committees that evaluate the use of animals in research and ensure that the research is conducted in a way that minimizes the risks to the animal subjects and maximizes the benefits of the research. If the chimps could vocally communicate their pain and suffering in our language, the protocols for animal research would likely be re-evaluated since the amount of pain and suffering to research animals would be more clearly understood. The issue is where do we draw the line? Where do the benefits of animal research (and there are many) outweigh the pain and suffering? If an animal can't communicate in our language, is it still ok to perform the research even after the talking chimps have communicated their pain and suffering? Or do we eliminate research on talking chimps but continue performing research on animals who can't talk?

3. Viruses are very complex and in many ways not well understood. It is known that most viruses naturally mutate very quickly. There is a possibility that modern influenza viruses could become more deadly on their own, as was demonstrated with the H1N1 strain in 2009. The benefits gained in the research performed on deadly viruses far outweigh the risks. There is plenty of data and many viruses available for terrorists to use for horrific purposes. Our best defense against bioterrorism attacks is to better understand how viruses function.

Possible Responses to *Data Analysis Exercise* Questions

1. A little over five days.
2. The modified mice; they learned the location in four days.
3. The modified mice; they learned the location in about two and one-half days.
4. Since the mice are using visual cues to help them remember where the platform was located in previous trials, and since the modified mice found the platform faster than the unmodified mice, the data indicate that the modified mice had the greatest improvement in memory.

16

EVIDENCE OF EVOLUTION

Chapter Outline

Objectives

1. Be able to cite what biologists generally accept as evidence that supports evolution.
2. Explain how observations from fossils, comparative morphology, patterns of development, and comparative biochemistry are used to reconstruct the past.
3. Explain the origin and eventual articulation of the views Darwin had on evolution.
4. Understand as well as you can the ideas and evidence that scientists have used to explain how life might have changed through time.
5. Explain how people came to believe that the populations of organisms that inhabit Earth have changed (evolved) through time.
6. Define natural selection.
7. Describe how Earth's history has affected biological change.

Key Terms

evidence
naturalists
confounding evidence
hypothesis
theory
species
biogeography
comparative morphology
fossils
evolution
catastrophism
mass extinction
inheritance of acquired characteristics
theory of uniformity
natural selection
artificial selection
fitness
heritable
gene
mutation
allele
adaptive trait
fossilization
fossil record
stratification
lineage
radiometric dating
half-life
geologic time scale
macroevolution
Proterozoic
Paleozoic
Mesozoic
Cenozoic
Archean eon
Pangea
continental drift
plate tectonics theory
Gondwana

Lecture Outline

16.1 Reflections of a Distant Past

A. The introduction introduces a central question when discussing the evidence of evolution: If no one was there, how do we know what happened? Multiple lines of evidence support evolution.
   1. Physical, chemical, and biological processes today can be used to analyze data from the past.
   2. Geological evidence can help date and describe past events (e.g., asteroid impacts).
   3. The fossil record can help place species into a timeframe.

B. Evidence points to a mass extinction that occurred 65.5 million years ago.

16.2 Early Beliefs, Confounding Discoveries

A. History of Early Beliefs
   1. As early as Aristotle, humans have been trying to categorize and organize living things.
   2. By the 14th century, a "great chain of being" was in place that organized life from lower forms to higher forms.
   3. European naturalists started to catalog new species in Asia, Africa, North and South America, and the Pacific Islands.
   4. By the 1800s, Alfred Wallace and other naturalists were moving beyond cataloging and trying to:
      a. Determine patterns in where species live and how they might be related.
      b. Start describing hypotheses about ecological and evolutionary forces driving change on Earth.

B. Questions From Biogeography
   1. Early naturalists cataloged diversity of plants and animals on expeditions to Asia, Africa, North and South America, and the Pacific Islands.
   2. When global voyages of the 16th century revealed unusual species not known in Europe, the students of biogeography began to question, "Where do all these species 'fit' in the great Chain?"
   3. Furthermore, if all species had been created at the same time and place, "Why were certain species found in only some parts of the world but not others, and how did so many species get from the center of creation to islands and isolated places?"

a. Flightless birds that run on long, muscular legs (Figure 16.2) live roughly equal distances from the equator in similar habitats on three separate continents. Wallace thought these birds may have all come from a common ancestor.

C. Questions From Comparative Morphology

1. Studies of the comparative morphology focused on revealing similarities and differences in body plan and structure of organisms. For example:

   a. Why do organisms look the same on the outside but not the inside? Plants and animal that look very similar outwardly but have very different reproductive structures or internal organ systems.

   b. Why do seemingly unrelated organisms look or develop similar structures? Organisms that have similar internal structures but don't seem related (e.g., the forearm of a human, a bat wing, and a porpoise fin).

   c. Why do certain organisms have unnecessary structures? Why do snakes have vestigial limbs? Why do humans have a vestigial tail?

D. Questions About Fossils

1. Studies of sedimentary beds have revealed that deposits were laid down slowly, one above the other.

   a. Why is there increasing complexity in fossils in more shallow layers?

   b. Why were there larger creatures existing at some later point in time that do not exist anymore?

E. This evidence, taken as a whole, did not fit with contemporary beliefs and suggested that species were not created in a perfect state, but, instead, changed over time.

16.3 A Flurry of New Theories

A. Squeezing New Evidence into Old Beliefs

1. Cuvier further suggested that the abrupt changes in the fossil record in different rock strata reflected the concept of catastrophism, dramatic geologic changes unlike what we see today.

   a. After each catastrophe, fewer species remained.

   b. The survivors were not new species; it was just that their ancestors' fossils had not been found.

2. Lamarck formulated a theory of inheritance of acquired characteristics—the idea that simple forms had changed into more complex ones by a built-in drive for perfection; for instance, a giraffe stretching its neck to reach higher branches would result in offspring with longer necks.

3. We know they are wrong, but these examples reflect a shift toward understanding new evidence.

B. Darwin and the HMS Beagle

1. As a child (early 1800s), Charles Darwin was curious about nature; but in college, he first pursued pre-medicine and finally received a degree in theology.

2. Botanist John Henslow arranged for Darwin (at age 22) to sail around the world as a ship's naturalist.

   a. Throughout the trip, Darwin studied and collected a variety of plants and animals.

   b. He was also reading Lyell's *Principles of Geology,* which proposed a theory of uniformity—the notion of a gradual, lengthy molding of Earth's geologic structure.

   c. Thus, Earth was not thousands, but possibly millions, of years old—was that enough time for species to evolve? How did species evolve?

16.4 Darwin, Wallace, and Natural Selection

A. A Key Insight—Variation in Traits

1. Darwin returned after five years at sea and began pondering the "species problem": What could explain the remarkable diversity among organisms?
2. In Argentina, Darwin had observed extinct glyptodonts that bore suspicious resemblance to living armadillos; Darwin wondered if the present species had evolved from the extinct one.
3. Thomas Malthus, an economist, had suggested that populations are limited in size by the resources available; if some resources were scarce there would be competition.
4. Darwin noted that individuals in a population were not always identical. While many traits were similar or common, other traits—like size or color—tended to vary.
5. Darwin felt that if some normally variant members of a population bore traits that increased their survival or reproduction, nature would select those same individuals to survive, reproduce, and possibly change future populations' traits.
   a. On the Galapagos Islands, the dozen or so species of finches all varied from one another to some extent but resembled the mainland finches to some degree also; perhaps they had descended from common ancestors.
   b. Darwin reasoned that a population is evolving when its *heritable* traits are changing through successive generations.

B. Natural Selection Defined
1. Nature would select the traits that were best suited to a certain environment.
2. The major points of Darwin's theory of natural selection as published in *On the Origin of Species* in 1859 are:
   a. *Observations about populations:*
      1) Populations have the reproductive capacity to increase in number over generations.
      2) As populations expand, resources will dwindle; individuals will run out of food, living space, and other resources.
      3) Individuals will end up competing for dwindling resources.
   b. *Observations about genetics:*
      1) Individuals of a certain species share certain traits (gene pool).
      2) Individuals of a natural population vary in the details of their shared traits (different alleles for a gene).
      3) Traits have a heritable basis, in genes. New variations arise from mutations.
   c. *Inferences:*
      1) Certain forms of a shared trait may make the bearer more competitive for scarce resources.
      2) Individuals better able to secure scarce resources tend to produce more offspring.
      3) Alleles associated with an adaptive trait become more frequent in a population.
3. Natural selection helps to describe not only the diversity of traits in a population, but also a mechanism for evolutionary change.

C. Great Minds Think Alike
1. Alfred Wallace was studying geographic distribution of species in the Amazon. He sent his work to Darwin for advice.
2. Darwin and Wallace had inferences that provided confounding support for natural selection.
3. *On the Origin of Species* was published in 1859. While many scientists readily accepted descent with modification—evolution—it took much more evidence (especially genetic evidence) for natural selection to gain wide acceptance in the scientific community.

16.5 Fossils—Evidence of Ancient Life

A. How Do Fossils Form?

1. Most fossils are skeletons, shells, leaves, seeds, imprints of leaves and tracks (trace fossils), and even fossilized feces (coprolites).
2. Fossilization is a slow process.
   a. Body parts or impressions must be covered by sediment or volcanic ash shortly after death.
   b. As water infiltrates the remains, metal ions and other sediments replace the mineral composition of the bones or harder tissues in the remains.
   c. External pressure from newly forming layers of sediment and mineralization lead to fossilization over time.
3. Preservation is favored when organisms are buried rapidly in the absence of oxygen, as oxygen leads to tissue decomposition.
4. Most fossilization occurs in the sedimentary rocks, with deeper layers of sediment containing older fossils than the layers on top.

B. The Fossil Record

1. Fossil records vary according to the type of organism (hard parts preserve well; soft parts do not), stability of the geographical region (sea floor versus eroding hill), and quality of the specimen.
2. The fossil record is far from complete, but some lineages are extensive; we have fossils for 250,000 known species, but many millions more would have existed.
3. Why are some species absent in the fossil record?
   a. The conditions for fossil formation do not always occur. Too much oxygen, scavengers at the death site, and other reasons could lead to lack of fossil formation.
   b. Some organisms lacked bones or hard parts, which meant that there was no material to fossilize.
   c. Some species existed for a short period of time or had small numbers of organisms in the population, decreasing the chances for fossilization.

16.6 Filling In Pieces of the Puzzle

A. Radiometric Dating

1. Radio isotopes decay at a constant rate into predictable products, daughter elements.
2. Because the decay of the isotopes is constant, the rate (half-life) can be determined, and the time since its formation can be calculated back in time.
3. Carbon-14 dating can be used to estimate fossils aged up to 60,000 years.
4. Older fossils are dated using volcanic rock in the layers above and below the fossil.

B. Finding a Missing Link

1. New fossil discoveries help to shape our understanding of evolutionary lineage.
   a. Scientists have long suspected certain natural relationships; for example, cetaceans (e.g., whales, dolphins, and porpoises) and artiodactyls (including hippopotamuses, camels, deer, pigs, sheep, and cows) shared some lower jaw similarities, and molecular comparisons showed similarity.
   b. A gradual change in whale lineage transitional states from land to see were missing as evidence until recently.
   c. Newly discovered fossils are starting to fill in the gaps. *Rodhocetus* and *Dorudon* both demonstrate whale-like skulls and sheep-like ankle bones in intact fossils.

16.7 Drifting Continents, Changing Seas

A. According to the theory of uniformity, mountain building and erosion has repeatedly changed the surface of the Earth in exactly the same ways through time.

B. An Outrageous Hypothesis
   1. A model was proposed in which there was a single world continent, named Pangea, which at one time extended from pole to pole, surrounded by a single huge ocean.
   2. The idea of continental drift explains the separation of the continents and the formation of great mountain ranges as the continents collided.
   3. Sea-floor spreading and plate tectonics theory show that the Earth's crust is moving.
   4. Continental drift and plate tectonics accounted for the discovery of similar fossils on different sides of the Atlantic Ocean.

C. A Big Connection
   1. Gondwana was an early continent that drifted southward from the tropics, across the south polar region northward, until it crunched into other land masses to form Pangea.
   2. These changes in the land, oceans, and atmosphere profoundly influenced the evolution of life.

16.8 Putting Time into Perspective

A. Layers of sedimentary rock act as a slice of geologic history.
   1. Radiometric layering and dating of the Earth hold clues about the sequence of organisms in Earth's history.

16.9 Reflections of a Distant Past

A. The K-T boundary consists of an unusual layer of clay that covers the entire Earth.
   1. The clay is high in iridium, not commonly found on Earth but rather asteroids.
   2. The K-T boundary is taken as evidence that an asteroid roughly 10 to 20 kilometers in diameter struck Earth about 65 million years ago, causing dramatic change.

Suggestions for Presenting the Material

- This chapter begins with a historical perspective. Present information with both a historical account and an emphasis on how emerging evidence has worked to change beliefs. Present as much evidence as you can. From this chapter, evidence from biogeography, comparative morphology, and geology (including fossil records, Earth history, and plate tectonics) are relevant.
- The National Science Education Center website (http://www.ncseweb.org/) has a variety of suggestions for presenting the evidence for evolution and links to other websites that have tutorials about evolution, fossil records, and more.
- The textbook authors enumerate three areas (biogeography, comparative anatomy, and fossils) that were puzzling to early scientists. Use a learning cycle approach (http://www.narst.org/publications/research/cycle.cfm) to introduce each topic. Learning cycles involve three steps: 1) Exploration, 2) Concept Invention, and 3) Concept Application. An example of how this might work with fossil evidence is as follows: 1) Students review pictures of potentially related fossils (or actual fossils) and get as much information about the fossils as possible. This could include radiometric or layering dates of fossils, locations of fossils, etc. 2) The students then try to draw conclusions about geological evidence as it relates to gradual change in the fossil record in order to define the concept of fossil evidence. 3) Finally, students work to apply that concept to other lines of, perhaps, less complete fossil lineages or multiple lineages in order to establish how fossil evidence supports evolutionary change.
- If you don't have time to investigate learning cycles, try to present the evidence first in order to allow your students to think about what the evidence means before they hear the synthesis about the evidence.

- If you need extra resources for geological information, there are two particularly informative websites:
  A. The American Geological Institute and the Paleontological Society published a short book entitled "Evolution and the Fossil Record" by John Pojeta and Dale Springer. An electronic version of the text is available online at: http://www.agiweb.org/news/evolution/index.html. This manuscript has good descriptions of how geological evidence is used to interpret evolution. There is a discussion of several different isotopes used for radioisotope dating. There is discussion of fossil lineages with special emphasis on mammals, humans, and whales.
  B. The University of California has an online paleontology museum: http://www.ucmp.berkeley.edu/. This is a very rich resource that has many other current external resource links. It also has sections that cover evidence for evolution from Earth's history.
- Before proceeding to the men who proposed a changing biological world, point out that the prevailing thought 200 years ago was "fixity of species." Because of the belief that species did not change, it was incumbent on humans to classify all living things. Although Linnaeus believed in this "fixity," his system is nevertheless still very valid and useful.
- One way to present the historical development of evolutionary thought is to chronicle the contributions of persons such as Lamarck, Lyell, Malthus, Wallace, and, of course, Darwin. Provide a spiraling narrative where you tell each individual's story concluding with their important evolutionary contribution. Finally, tie all of their work together by demonstrating how one individual influenced one or more of the others and how their cumulative work forms the basis for evolutionary theory. Set a historical timeframe; *On the Origin of Species* was originally published in 1859 at the time of the U.S. Civil War.
- Students rarely hear about Darwin's life other than his famous journey. Present his biography *before* his theory to spark interest. Perhaps the videotape listed in the Enrichment section could be used. You can then proceed to *natural selection* by first recalling *artificial selection* (maybe using dogs rather than pigeons as Darwin did in his book).
- Stress the tenuous conclusions that are in constant revision when scientists attempt to reconstruct the past. Just as a good medical diagnosis is not based on one examination or one lab test, a good analysis of past evolutionary history is not based on any one line of evidence, but rather several lines of corroborating evidence.
- You may wish to include a brief discussion of how radioisotopes are used to date fossils (section 16.6). Certainly, emphasis should be placed on *how* these calculations are used rather than the actual calculations.
- Provide examples from comparative morphology of vestigial anatomical structures that are retained by organisms (e.g., pelvic bones in snakes, the human appendix, etc.).

Classroom and Laboratory Enrichment

- Show a video describing Charles Darwin's voyage on the *HMS Beagle* and his thoughts as he traveled. The video series *Evolution* (2001, WGBH Educational Foundation) from PBS is excellent. Clips and other helpful material can be accessed at the following website: http://www.pbs.org/wgbh/evolution/
- Present fossil evidence (or 35 mm transparencies, filmstrips, or films of fossils) showing how a group of related organisms or a single genus (for example, *Equus*) has evolved and changed through time. The students will most likely be surprised at the size of the horse's early ancestors.

Pick a well-documented fossil lineage that shows many examples of gradual change or transitional states.

- If there is a museum of natural history near your campus, plan a field trip. The students would be able to view many relevant examples there to illustrate the concepts.
- Have a panel of other faculty from your campus come to class to serve as experts in the fields of: paleontology, geology, Earth history, fossilization, comparative anatomy, animal diversity, zoology, botany, radiometric dating, anthropology, paleontology, etc. Have these "experts" prepare a brief explanation of their field's evidence for evolution, and then the panel can field questions from students.
- Whales, like snakes, have pelvic girdles. Show an overhead diagram of this portion of the whale skeleton.
- Generate interest in Darwin's theory by bringing a copy of *On the Origin of Species* to class. Read selected chapter titles and portions of the text. Point out the lack of illustrations in the original edition.
- Discuss methods of fossil preservation. Examine actual fossils or films, videos, or slides of fossils. Visit collections of fossils in nearby museums. Discuss why there are so many gaps in the fossil record due to the conditions required for fossilization.
- Prepare a summary table of the tools used in "reconstructing the past." For each tool, list the procedure, reliability, advantages/disadvantages, accuracy, and so forth.
- Show actual fossils or photographs of fossils representing some of the life forms prevalent during the Paleozoic, Mesozoic, and Cenozoic eras.

Classroom Discussion Ideas

- This discussion may have started in Chapter 1, but have a discussion about how scientific knowledge is generated. What is the importance of evidence in generating a scientific theory? How is the use of the word theory different in the sciences than its use in other disciplines?
- What kinds of organisms are well represented in the fossil record? What types of organisms have left little or nothing in the fossil record? How does the process of fossil formation affect our knowledge of the history of organisms? Do the students feel there may be many species that are unknown, because they left no fossil record?
- How do worldwide distribution patterns of fossils suggest a common evolutionary origin for many organisms?
- What could fossils forming today tell scientists in the future?
- How real is the possibility of Earth being hit by an asteroid within your lifetime? If Earth were hit, how might that change life as we now know it?

Additional Ideas for Classroom Discussion

- What was Jean-Baptiste Lamarck's contribution to our modern understanding of evolutionary theory?
- What steps did Lamarck fail to perform before setting forth his hypothesis of inherited characteristics? It seems obvious to us today that acquired characteristics are not inherited. As an example, if you have your nose altered by plastic surgery, do your offspring have the ability to inherit your original nose or the revised one?

- How did the widespread discoveries of fossils in the 19th century help support Darwin's views on evolution?
- Does belief in the theory of evolution exclude belief in religion? Why or why not?
- Many other disciplines, like geology and anthropology, have discovered evidence for evolution. What is the importance of several different lines of confounding evidence all leading to the theory of evolution?
- This chapter focuses on many geological discoveries that are evidence for evolution. The American Geophysical Union and many other professional societies publish statements about the importance of evolution being a keystone theory in the sciences (http://www.agu.org/sci_soc/policy/positions/evolution.shtml). Why do professional societies make statements like this? Why is evolution so important when describing the current state of biological studies?
- Why was extensive travel a key ingredient in the development of Darwin's evolutionary thought? Do you think Darwin could have drawn the same conclusions if he had only studied the species in a single area?
- Can you think of any ideas commonly expressed today that are similar to Lamarck's understanding of evolution?
- How did the work of geologists such as Charles Lyell and others who were Darwin's contemporaries help Darwin create his principle of evolution?
- Those who wish to berate certain scientific principles sometimes say, "It's only a theory." This statement is used by those who oppose the theory of evolution. Does the use of "theory" in biology mean the concept is in doubt? Explain using examples.
- If you asked the following question in a sidewalk survey, what do you think the responses would be? "Darwin wrote a very famous book on the origin of ___________."
- Compare and contrast the principles of "uniformitarianism" and "catastrophism." Evaluate the physical evidence for each.
- What conditions favor fossil formation? What conditions are poor for fossil formation?
- What information about the structure and function of animals could be learned from an analysis of fossilized feces?
- Research articles on "recent" human evolution. Are there any current trends in human evolution? Are there any structures that appear to be disappearing in humans?
- Is evolution a static idea that was proposed by Darwin and has never been modified or challenged since? What is the importance of the emergence of evidence of evolution from biogeography, comparative morphology, and geological discovery?
- There have been many sci-fi movies based on the premise that an entire organism, like a dinosaur, could be produced from a small preserved sample. What are the fallacies of such a proposition? Do you think this endeavor will be possible in the future?

How Would You Vote? Classroom Discussion Ideas

- Monitor the voting for the online question. Although collecting evidence about past events is not ideal, it is the best we can do at the present time! Indirect evidence is not foolproof, but over time we may develop better technological skills to examine previous material. This can be compared to the advent of forensic investigations at a crime scene. Twenty years ago, it was only possible to determine blood type from a small sample. Now, of course, DNA fingerprinting is a much more precise diagnostic tool. Perhaps similar investigative instrumentation will tell us more about the evidence that has already been collected.

Term Paper Topics, Library Activities, and Special Projects

- Describe why evidence is crucial to understanding and defining scientific theories. Describe some of the early evidence that started to change people's views about Earth history and then led people to understand evolution.
- Describe how a trip through the Grand Canyon with a paleontologist would reinforce our modern understanding of evolution.
- How do today's biologists reconcile their personal faith in an organized religion with their belief in evolution? Research the viewpoints of some famous scientists on this issue (National Human Genome Research Institute Director Dr. Francis S. Collins has spoken on his views).
- Have one of your students design a Jeopardy-style quiz to test the knowledge of their classmates (http://jeopardylabs.com/).
- Can we see evolution actually happening? Find examples of natural occurrences in the wild or experimental situations in the laboratory in which we can observe evolution occurring.
- Learn more about the discovery of fossils of *Archaeopteryx* and the reactions of the scientific community to them. Describe other transitional fossils that have been discovered.
- Research a particular archaeological dig. What did the scientists discover there? What conclusions were drawn from the evidence they obtained?
- Describe how Darwin's development of his principle of evolution was an example of the scientific method in action.
- From time to time, Lamarck's hypothesis of "inheritance of acquired characteristics" is revived as an explanation for certain events. Is the idea totally without merit, or could this be the explanation for the inheritance patterns in certain microorganisms? (See *Scientific American,* Nov. 1988, p. 34.)
- The great "catastrophe" that dominated Cuvier's thinking was the flood of Noah as recorded in the Book of Genesis. This is still the cornerstone of creationist thinking. Investigate creationist writings to see how this event is critical to their theories.
- Darwin's emerging ideas on natural selection were not welcomed by the *Beagle* captain. Investigate how this challenge to his views strengthened Darwin's hypotheses.
- It is ironic that Darwin and Wallace would arrive independently at so important a concept as natural selection. Investigate the path each took.
- Describe famous fossil finds. You may wish to include famous fossils that were later found to be hoaxes, such as the Piltdown man discovered in England in 1912.
- Discover what fossil evidence has revealed about the past history of your region of the United States. You may be surprised about what you find. In one area in New Jersey, residents had been crossing a bridge over a creek for years. Eventually it was discovered that the "bridge" was actually a dinosaur's jawbone!
- Describe the process of radioactive dating. Discuss its accuracy in dating. What are its limitations?
- Trace the evolutionary history of one group of plants or animals throughout geologic time.
- Prepare a timeline tracing the geologic and biologic history of your section of the United States.
- Collect fossils, photographs, or descriptions of fossils from your region of the United States. What do they reveal about the past history of your area?

- Describe the process of fossilization. Describe what types of gaps exist in the fossil records, why they exist, and why their existence does not discount the processes of evolution.

Possible Responses to *Critical Thinking* Questions

1. There is a chance that all carbon dating performed on the rock sample is accurate. Perhaps part of the sample was unearthed from a previous era approximately 225,000 years ago. The carbon dating procedure assumes that the material being tested has remained undisturbed since it was placed there. Since those specimens are located together now, they would yield different carbon dating results. Also, the carbon dating procedure assumes that all organisms utilize carbon 14 as equally as they do carbon 12. This is not always the case. There was an incident off the coast of Hawaii recently where scientists performed carbon dating on the shells of living animals. The results stated that the shells were over 2,000 years old! It is results like these that help us realize that there can be obstacles to overcome when attempting to determine the age of carbon-dated substances.
2. When comparing human history, even your own history, in a time scale that represents the entirety of Earth's history, the time we have been around is very short. If the most recent epoch (the Holocene) started about 12,000 years ago and that represents 0.1 second, then an individual's time on Earth might be close to 0.001–0.0001 seconds on a 24-hour clock.

Possible Responses to *Data Analysis Exercise* Questions

The iridium level in an average rock on Earth is only about 0.4 parts per billion (ppb). The average meteorite would contain around 550 ppb. This enables scientists to determine if the origin of a rock is from Earth or another source.

1. The iridium content of the K-T boundary layer is 41.6 ppb.
2. The iridium content of the K-T layer was 41.24 ppb more than the level of iridium at 0.7 m above the layer.

17

PROCESSES OF EVOLUTION

Chapter Outline

Objectives

1. Explain how people came to believe that the populations of organisms that inhabit Earth have changed through time.
2. Understand the difference between microevolution and macroevolution.

3. Know the five assumptions of Hardy-Weinberg, and explain how the equation is used to make predictions about evolving populations.
4. Understand how variation occurs in populations and how changes in allele frequencies can be measured.
5. Describe how genetic drift leads to a loss in genetic diversity.
6. Know how mutations, gene flow, and population size can influence the rate and direction of population change.
7. Define natural selection in terms of differential survival and reproduction.
8. Describe the different kinds of selection mechanisms that help shape populations, and give examples of each type.
9. Describe the different isolating mechanisms that give rise to speciation.
10. Define an adaptation and explain the role adaptive traits play in an organism's survival.
11. Describe the patterns that may lead to macroevolution.

Key Terms

evolution
adaptation
population
morphological traits
physiological traits
behavioral traits
qualitative differences
quantitative differences
dimorphism
polymorphism
gene pool
alleles
gene mutation
lethal mutation
neutral mutation
allele frequencies
genetic equilibrium
microevolution
phenotype
Hardy-Weinberg equilibrium equation
directional selection
peppered moth
mark-release-recapture method
pest resurgence
antibiotic resistance
antibiotic
stabilizing selection
disruptive selection
sexual dimorphism
sexual selection
selecting agent
balanced polymorphism
sickle-cell anemia
malaria
genetic drift
probability
fixed
bottleneck
founder effect
inbreeding
emigration
immigration
gene flow
evolutionary adaptation
species
speciation
isolating mechanism
pre/post-zygotic
temporal isolation
reproduction isolation
mechanical isolation
behavioral isolation
ecological isolation
gamete incompatibility
hybrid inviability
hybrid sterility
allopatric speciation
sympatric speciation
parapatric speciation
polyploidy
macroevolution
coevolution
stasis
exaptation
adaptive radiation
extinction
evolutionary theory
key innovation

Lecture Outline

17.1 Rise of the Super Rats

A. Rats are one of the most effective human pests.
   1. Rats live easily off of human garbage and cause large amounts of damage to property and food spoilage.
   2. The rodenticide warfarin was very effective when it was first introduced in the 1950s.
   3. Within a few years, rats developed resistance; the chemical would no longer kill rats, through a mutation of the gene, the product of which was the target of warfarin.

B. The resistant rats happened to inherit a gene that made the chemical ineffective.
   1. The survivors passed on the gene to their offspring; soon resistant rats were the normal population.
   2. This is an example of evolution by natural selection.

17.2 Individuals Don't Evolve, Populations Do

A. Variation in Populations
1. Populations evolve, not individuals.
2. A population is a group of individuals belonging to the same species, occupying the same given area.
3. A population exhibits variation among the individual members, but they also hold certain morphological, physiological, and behavioral traits in common.

B. An Evolutionary View of Mutations
1. Mutations are heritable changes in DNA that can alter gene expression.
2. Mutations are random, and the phenotypic outcome may be neutral, beneficial, harmful, or even lethal to the individual depending on other interactions.
    a. A *lethal mutation* is an expression of a gene that results in death.
    b. *Neutral mutations*, whether or not they are expressed in phenotype, have no effect on survival and reproduction.
    c. *Beneficial mutations* are those that bestow survival advantages.
3. Mutations are the only source of new alleles—the genetic foundation for biological diversity.

C. Allele Frequencies
1. Individuals of the same population have the same number and kinds of genes.
    a. All of the genes in the entire population constitute the gene pool.
    b. Each gene exists in two or more slightly different molecular forms, called alleles.
2. Microevolution refers to changes in allele frequency of a population.

17.3 Genetic Equilibrium

A. Applying the rules of probability to sexual reproduction, mathematician Hardy and physician Weinberg independently came up with a baseline for non-evolving populations.
1. Evolution can be detected by a change in allele frequencies from the genetic equilibrium, as established by the Hardy-Weinberg rule.
2. These five conditions are necessary for a stable population:
    a. No mutations are occurring.
    b. The population is very, very large.
    c. The population is isolated from other populations of the same species.
    d. All members survive, mate, and reproduce (no selection).
    e. Mating is random.
3 Because these five conditions are rarely fulfilled in natural populations, any deviation from the reference point established by the "rule" will indicate evolution.

B. Applying the Hardy-Weinberg Law
1. Allele frequencies for any gene in the shared pool will remain stable unless the population is evolving.
    a. The formula used to track any deviation from the stable state is: $p^2 + 2pq + q^2 = 1$; $p + q = 1$, where p and q are allelic frequencies for A and a.
    b. This formula is known as the Hardy-Weinberg equilibrium equation.
    c. If traits show up in different proportions to the expected frequencies, given Hardy-Weinberg assumptions, it indicates that one or more of the five assumptions are not being met and some evolutionary force is affecting the population.

C. Real World Situations
1. Researchers use Hardy-Weinberg to estimate the frequency of carriers of alleles that cause genetic disorders and traits.
2. One example of this is the genetic disorder *hemochromatosis,* which affects people of Irish ancestry, causing them to absorb too much iron from their food.

17.4 Patterns of Natural Selection

A. Natural selection may be the most influential microevolutionary process.

B. An allele that ensures better survival or reproduction will influence the frequency of that allele.

C. Allele frequency can depend on the organisms involved and the selection pressure.

D. There are three major categories of selection: directional, stabilizing, and disruptive.

17.5 Directional Selection

A. Directional selection shifts allele frequencies in a consistent direction (selection in the direction of a particular range of phenotypes), which may be in response to environmental pressures or occur as a new mutation appears and is adaptive.

B. Examples of Directional Selection

1. The Peppered Moth

a. Populations of peppered moth show classic directional selection where the moth's coloration is in direct response to its environment; light moths are camouflaged on lichen-covered tree trunks, and dark moths are camouflaged on soot-covered tree trunks.

b. H. B. Kettlewell demonstrated experimentally that moths with a certain color phenotype would be most abundant depending on the pollution accumulating on the tree trunks; when pollution controls decreased the soot on trees, selection shifted to favor light-colored moths.

2. Pocket Mice

a. The larger population of rock pocket mice in the Arizona desert survives well because of its genetically-determined lighter fur color, which blends in with the granite; predator birds cannot spot them easily.

b. A smaller population of mice has a darker coat, which allows them to blend in with the dark basalt (from lava) and avoid being seen by predators.

c. Night-flying predatory birds are the selecting agents for the dark fur.

3. Antibiotic-Resistant Bacteria

a. Antibiotics are drugs that have proven very effective in treating bacterial-induced diseases. Some antibiotics, like streptomycin, affect the formation of bacterial cell walls.

b. Although bacteria do not reproduce sexually, some strains reproduce rapidly. Each generation has the potential to contain a beneficial mutation.

c. Overuse of antibiotics has led to the directional selection of resistant strains that are no longer susceptible to the drug.

17.6 Stabilizing and Disruptive Selection

A. Stabilizing Selection

1. Stabilizing selection favors the most common phenotype in the population.

2. Covas studied Weaver birds in the African savanna. The field studies suggest that bird body weight is a tradeoff between the risks of starvation and predation.

a. Leaner birds do not store enough fat.

b. Larger birds are more desirable for predators and less likely to escape.

B. Disruptive Selection

1. Disruptive selection favors forms at the extremes of the phenotypic range of variation and selects against the intermediate forms.

2. Thomas Smith discovered African finches for which bill size was either large or small, no in between.

a. Smaller-billed birds fed on soft seeds.

b. Larger-billed birds fed on harder seeds.

17.7 Fostering Diversity

A. Nonrandom Mating

1. Most species have distinctively male and female phenotypes—sexual dimorphism. Often males of a species are larger, more colorful, more aggressive, and/or present some special courtship behavior. Sometimes these traits are maladaptive.
2. Sexual selection is based on any trait that gives the individual a competitive edge in mating and producing offspring.
3. Usually it is the females that are the agents of selection when they pick their mates.

B. Balanced Polymorphism

1. In balancing selection, two alleles persist at high frequencies in a population.
2. Humans that are homozygous for sickle-cell anemia (Hb^S/Hb^S) develop the disease and may die at an early age.
3. However, individuals with alleles for both normal hemoglobin (Hb^A) and sickle-cell hemoglobin (Hb^S) have the greatest chance of surviving malaria. The sickle-cell allele persists in the population despite its relative disadvantage.

17.8 Genetic Drift and Gene Flow

A. Genetic Drift

1. Genetic drift is the random fluctuation in allele frequencies over time, due to chance occurrences alone.
   a. It is more significant in small populations because of the small numbers in the population.
   b. Genetic drift increases the chance of any given allele becoming more or less prevalent when the number of individuals in a population is small.
   c. Genetic drift may lead to a homozygous condition in most populations; the homozygosity occurs faster in smaller populations.
   d. Fixation means that one kind of allele remains at a specified locus in a population.
2. In *bottlenecks*, some stressful situation greatly reduces the size of a population, leaving a few (typical or atypical) individuals to reestablish the population. This bottleneck decreases the genetic diversity and can be a cause of genetic drift.
3. In the *founder effect*, a few individuals (carrying genes that may or may not be typical of the whole population) leave the original population to establish a new one. Because the gene pool of the population is provided for only by the founders, the diversity is limited, a random effect of drift.
4. Inbreeding refers to nonrandom mating among closely related individuals.
   a. It tends to increase the homozygous condition, thus leading to lower potential fitness and survival rates because of the lack of genetic diversity.

B. Gene Flow

1. Genes move with individuals when they move out of (emigration) or into (immigration) a population.
2. Gene flow is a microevolutionary process that reduces the effect of mutations, selection, and drift in a population.
3. Scientists are concerned that gene flow could lead to genetically modified genes entering wild populations.

17.9 Reproductive Isolation

A. Species are defined as interbreeding individuals that produce viable, fertile offspring and do not interbreed with other individuals.

B. Mechanisms of Reproductive Isolation

1. *Temporal Isolation*: Isolation due to the timing of an organism's reproductive cycle.
2. *Mechanical Isolation*: Isolation due to physical incompatibility between mates or pollinators.
3. *Ecological Isolation*: Isolation that occurs when related species become adapted to small changes in microenvironments within a similar home range.
4. *Behavioral Isolation*: Isolation that stops gene flow. For example, if female birds ignore mating dances of males from related species, no interbreeding will occur.
5. *Gamete Incompatibility*: A molecular difference between species that blocks physical fertilization of the egg.
6. *Hybrid Inviability*: Fertilization occurs, but a zygote fails to develop.
7. *Hybrid Sterility*: Fertilization produces a viable offspring that cannot produce.

17.10 Allopatric Speciation

A. Speciation

1. Speciation is not predictable, but certain principles underlie genetic change.
2. Genetic changes usually begin with some geographical isolation.
3. Allopatric speciation, perhaps the most common form of speciation, occurs when a species becomes separated by a physical barrier that leads to reproductive isolation.

B. Speciation in Archipelagos

1. An archipelago is an island formation that arises from the ocean due to volcanic activity.
2. Assuming there are no native species on the islands, wind and water currents bring seeds and small animals to the islands.
   a. Hawaii formed about one million years ago.
   b. Honeycreeper diversity on the island is the result of vacant habitat and low competition. As a result, rapid speciation occurred.

18.11 Other Speciation Models

A. Sympatric Speciation

1. Sympatric speciation is divergence within the same home range of a species.
   a. Polyploidy is a result of nondisjunction during cell division that can lead to a change in chromosome number.
   b. Polyploidy can occur in plants.
      1) Nondisjunction occurs in a shoot or flower.
      2) If self-fertilization occurs, this can lead to instant speciation.

B. Parapatric Speciation

1. Parapatric speciation occurs when one population extends across a large, diverse habitat. Distinct habitats exert selection pressures on parts of the population.
2. Divergence occurs on the opposite ends of the habitat, while a small hybrid zones exists where contact occurs in the midrange.

17.12 Macroevolution

A. Patterns of Macroevolution

1. *Exaptation*: The appearance of a trait that was originally used for something else. For example, feathers may have emerged in dinosaurs for insulation but serve as a pre-adaptation for flight in birds.
2. *Stasis*: A long-term lineage with relatively little evolutionary change.
3. *Mass Extinction*: The fossil record indicates more than 20 mass extinctions. Each extinction is followed by a period of adaptive radiation.

4. *Adaptive Radiation*: A dramatic increase in new species due to the presence of many new niches to fill in a habitat. This rapid adaptation may be in response to the development of a single novel trait (flight in birds) or as a result of loss of species previously filling the niches (extinction).
5. *Coevolution*: Process caused by ecological interactions like predator-prey, parasite-host, or flower-pollinator relationships.

B. Evolutionary Theory
1. Scientists still disagree on how macroevolution occurs.
2. Many scientists are working to discover how species are ultimately related.

17.13 Rise of the Super Rats (Revisited)

A. Rats that are resistant to warfarin require additional vitamin K.
1. When not exposed to warfarin, the gene is deleterious because it forces the rats to seek additional sources of vitamin K.

B. Since many rats are periodically exposed to warfarin, it serves as an example of balanced polymorphism.

Suggestions for Presenting the Material

- The main points concerning variability and evolution are as follows:

  Variation is the result of several factors.

  The Hardy–Weinberg equation provides the baseline for calculating gene frequencies under unrealistic conditions.

  Several factors yield change in the real world:

  - Mutation
  - Genetic drift (founder, bottleneck)
  - Gene flow
  - Natural selection (stabilizing, directional, disruptive)
- Ask students how they think natural selection worked in giraffe neck development. Many students are likely to describe that the giraffes extended their necks out of need. They see adaptations more as Lamarck saw them instead of how Darwin saw them. This is a good place to give students practice in correcting their mistaken conclusions about natural selection. For example, Lamarck: Giraffes developed long necks by continually reaching for food that was higher in trees; Darwin: Giraffes born with longer necks were more effective in winning male-male fights for mates, and thus were more reproductively successful in passing on those genes. Point out the importance of genetic variation in natural selection.
- Use artificial selection with domesticated dogs, for example, to introduce the concept of natural selection. Have the students research the incidence of certain conditions (e.g., hip dysplasia) in varying breeds of dogs. Can you see how these occur with more prevalence in particular breeds? Does this appear to be the result of inbreeding? Compare photos of various dog breeds to those of wolves. Can you see the huge variation in the appearance of different breeds even though they are derived from a common ancestor?
- Work with the students to develop a visual model that demonstrates how alleles will be selected for over time. Draw a picture with two rectangles representing a population's gene pool at two different times. Develop a model that uses the various microevolutionary processes (survival, sexual selection, gene drift, gene flow) to select for alleles in a population over time. Develop several scenarios that could be used to demonstrate the model. For example, one reason an allele is selected for is that it allows for better survival. Point out that giraffes with longer necks were

selected for because the longer neck ensured they would have a better food supply, despite the disadvantage that having a long neck is for drinking water. Peacocks provide a good example of sexual dimorphism caused by sexual selection.

- Natural selection is, in many scientists' views, the most important concept for biology students to understand. Therefore, it is vital that you clear up any student misconceptions by providing many clear examples of microevolutionary processes. Don't just explain examples, have students work through examples. Provide the students with examples of where selection might/should occur and have the students describe how selection would work in each scenario. As the students describe their scenarios for the class, use their misconceptions to point out more correct interpretations.
- Emphasize to students that evolution occurs in populations, not individuals, even if they can see the changes in an individual's phenotype. Stress that selection pressures result in the survival of some individuals in the population over others.
- Work several problems with the Hardy-Weinberg formula to demonstrate allele frequency.
- The different results of natural, stabilizing, directional, and disruptive selection are fairly easy to picture when looking at the butterfly graphs in the chapter. Try to help students conceptualize how each type of selection works using multiple examples from the text and from other sources. If you develop a model for microevolution as described above, have students apply scenarios with the model and provide enough information for natural selection examples that students should also be able to predict how selection will work in the sample scenarios. Several basic scenarios are presented as a starter below.

  Sample Scenario A – Stabilizing selection: Sharks are natural predators of seals. Seals have a variety of body size phenotypes. Sharks tend to attack smaller seals because they struggle less. Larger seals have a harder time escaping.

  Sample Scenario B – Directional selection: A new bird species migrates to a volcanic archipelago. Males of the species have several phenotypes for color ranging from a light brown, to a medium brown, to a dark brown. On the island, females show a preference for darker-brown males.

  Sample Scenario C – Disruptive selection: A finch species shows continuous variation in beak width. Birds with smaller beaks feed on smaller seeds, birds with medium beaks eat medium-size seeds, and birds with large beaks eat large seeds. A drought occurs that affects the plants that produce the medium-size seeds the most.
- Several of the topics in the chapter may not have sufficient visual material to meet your needs. Check genetics texts for photo examples of founder effects, bottlenecks, isolating mechanisms, etc.
- Pesticide resistance and antibiotic resistance are both fairly accessible and well-documented examples of natural selection that have occurred on observable time scales. Recent MRSA (methicillin-resistant staphylococcus aureus) outbreaks have propelled bacterial resistance into newspapers and magazines. Present a range of different scientific and popular articles that document MRSA. Spend time discussing why antibiotics and antibacterial soaps create the conditions that lead to selection in bacteria.
- Discuss the patterns for macroevolution. Show documented examples of coevolution and examples of adaptive radiation following migration to a new location or after mass extinctions.

Classroom and Laboratory Enrichment

- Choose an easy-to-see trait governed by one gene with two alleles, such as earlobe attachment (earlobes whose bases are not attached to the jawline) or tongue rolling (the ability to roll your tongue without holding it with the sides of your mouth), and ask students to determine their own phenotype. Determine the number of homozygous recessive individuals (*aa*) in the class. Use the

Hardy-Weinberg principle to calculate the frequencies of the dominant allele and the recessive allele. Examples: earlobe attachment (unattached – dominant, attached – recessive), hairline (widow's peaks – dominant, straight – recessive), freckles (freckles – dominant, no freckles – recessive), (tongue rolling – dominant, no tongue rollign – recessive)

- Demonstrate genetic drift by tracing changes in allele frequency through time. In small hypothetical populations, select a trait governed by two alleles and calculate the frequency of each allele. Different groups of students could be assigned populations of different sizes. Follow each population through several generations, as some of its members (selected by coin tosses) succumb to disease, predation, and other random causes of early death. How does population size affect genetic variation over time?
- Show slides or videos about endangered species that are threatened by sharp reductions in population size and subsequent loss of genetic variability due to genetic drift.
- What happens to the genetic variability of small, isolated populations of laboratory organisms after many generations without the introduction of new organisms? Design and implement an experiment using any organism with a short generation time and several easy-to-see traits that can be followed from one generation to the next.
- Find a good natural selection tutorial online (for example, http://www.biologycorner.com/worksheets/pepperedmoth.html has a good peppered moth example), and have students collect and analyze data using the simulation. This simulation could be used to generate numbers for the Hardy-Weinberg formula.
- How does artificial selection by humans affect gene frequencies of domestic plants and animals? Pursue this question with experiments or demonstrations.
- Prepare an overhead transparency on which you have written the solution to a Hardy-Weinberg problem (check a genetics or majors biology text). This method is more convenient than blackboard presentation, and you will feel more confident. Don't disclose the entire page at once. Instead, arrange the problem stems and solutions in such a way that one can be uncovered while the other is hidden. Or use PowerPoint slide to animate the steps of the calculations.
- Select a well-known example of the founder effect in a human population, such as the Amish population with Ellis-van Creveld syndrome. Using slides, show how a phenotypic characteristic (for example, polydactyly) "spreads" from one generation to the next. Are there any other human populations that illustrate the founder effect?
- Use a deck of cards to represent alleles in a gene pool, the black cards can be a dominant allele and the red cards can represent a recessive allele. Sort cards from the deck, two at a time, to represent genotypes in a population; show that when there is no selection pressure, the allele frequencies do not change. Then select for and against each allele to demonstrate what will happen to allele frequencies in each case.
- Explain the development of insect resistance to DDT as a modern-day example of natural selection. Point out that DDT was introduced to the world in the early 1940s, and in just 10 years, resistant strains were reported in many countries. By the time it was banned in the United States in 1973, virtually every housefly was resistant to its effects. How did DDT-use impact other organisms?

Classroom Discussion Ideas

- How could the results of various scientific experiments be influenced by using strains of laboratory mice that are continuously inbred?
- How might antibiotics and antibacterial soap affect bacterial populations, especially pathogenic populations?

- Since antibiotics only kill bacteria, they should not be used to treat viral infections. How might the widespread use of antibiotics for any type of infection lead to the development of antibiotic-resistant strains of bacteria?
- What is artificial selection? How does it differ from natural selection?
- How does sexual selection benefit a species? Would the introduction of alleles from a similar but different species introduce variety and thus help the species? Why or why not?
- What is speciation? How does speciation occur? When might you expect to see speciation?
- What is the difference between microevolution and macroevolution? What are the different types of evidence that support each of those concepts?

Additional Ideas for Classroom Discussion

- How does phenotypic variation arise? Ask students to list as many sources of phenotypic variation as they can. They should be able to remember how genetic variation comes about from their earlier study of genetics.
- What affect would phenotypes altered by environmental conditions have on future generations (e.g., plant color affected by soil ph)?
- How are new alleles created? Is the creation of new alleles an important source of genetic change? Why or why not?
- Why doesn't evolution lead to perfect organisms? Think of the tradeoff with giraffe necks, the benefit of being selected as a mate, food foraging at the risk of drinking, or sexual selection that leads to bright bird plumage that is detrimental to blending in with the environment.
- Although not a pleasant topic, many scientists predict that another mass extinction will take place. Review the arguments presented by these researchers.
- What are some phenotypic variations that might have assisted the success of *Homo sapiens*? Ask your students to think of some imaginative examples of variations that might be useful in the future evolution of our species.
- How representative of the human population is your class? Discuss the importance of sample size with reference to determining allele frequencies. Ask your students to think about gene-pool size and the founder effect, if they were stranded forever on an uninhabited island. Would certain alleles be overrepresented or underrepresented? What would happen to allele frequencies after many generations?
- Think of examples of human alleles whose frequencies vary from one global region to the next.
- What did Darwin's study of the different finch species among the Galápagos Islands tell him about speciation? What conclusions can you make about the evolutionary histories of the different species of Galápagos finches, given what you now know about the process of speciation?
- How does sexual selection benefit a species? Would the introduction of alleles from a similar but different species introduce variety and thus help the species? Why or why not?
- Which of the factors that cause changes in allelic frequencies could be under conscious human control?
- Some conservation groups are working to preserve the genetic material of endangered species (http://www.msnbc.msn.com/id/5526627/). Why might bringing these animals back from extinction using limited samples from the population be detrimental to rescuing those populations?

- Why is the statement "She has evolved into a fine pianist" *not* biologically accurate? Would a great tennis player, like Venus or Serena Williams, have children that are "naturally gifted" tennis players?
- Of the five sources of phenotypic variation, why is *mutation* the only one that *creates* new alleles? How do the others yield variation? What is the importance of the variation?
- How could the results of scientific experiments be influenced by using strains of laboratory mice that are continuously inbred?
- How might bacterial-resistant genes in non-pathogenic strains of bacteria affect us in the future? What might be the effect of releasing herbicide-resistant genes or genes that alter the ripening schedule of fruits into commercial plant crops?
- Research the coelacanth. Why was its rediscovery so important to scientists?
- Have your students research articles on drosophila from the Hawaiian Islands. Do they serve as an example of sympatric speciation?

How Would You Vote? Classroom Discussion Ideas

- Monitor the voting for the online question. The banning of antibiotics in animal feed has been discussed for some years, and there is progress. Perhaps the first effort should be a voluntary move to limit the use of antibiotics prescribed to humans on those animals most likely to pass it on to humans. This could be monitored to see if it is making a difference in the quantities transferred. If not, then an outright ban may be necessary.

Term Paper Topics, Library Activities, and Special Projects

- Read about research of the founder effect in human populations isolated by geography or custom.
- Douglas Adams and Zoologist Mark Carwardine authored a chapter on kakapos, a flightless bird in New Zealand (*Heartbeats in the Night*, pp 105-142 in Adams, D and Carwardine, M. (1990). Last "Chance To See." Ballantine Books: New York.). In the chapter, Adams discusses issues related to natural selection on islands (especially related to flightless birds), sexual selection (in regards to slowing down reproductive rates), and introduction of predators to the island. How does natural selection work on island populations? Why is this different from mainland areas? Why is the introduction of novel species so potentially damaging to indigenous species on the islands?
- Pick a species of interest. How might global warming be affecting selection in that population?
- What is the frequency of the allele for Tay-Sachs disease among Ashkenazi Jews? How do scientists explain the high frequency of this allele in this segment of the population?
- How has the loss of genetic diversity (possibly resulting from a population bottleneck at some time in the past) affected cheetahs? Report on recent research efforts in this area.
- Describe how artificial selection in the genus *Brassica* has resulted in several very different vegetable varieties.
- What is the frequency of the allele for cystic fibrosis in the United States? Does the frequency of this allele differ among different segments of the population? Is the allele frequency changing over time?
- How do commercial plant breeders and agricultural biologists maintain genetic variability among the plants they raise?
- Why is inbreeding harmful to a species? Select a species or a group of organisms (a dog breed, for example), and discuss the results of inbreeding.

- Prepare brief biographies of G. H. Hardy and W. Weinberg. How is it that they discovered their principle "independently"? Did they ever collaborate?
- Among invertebrates there are several hermaphroditic (both sexes in the same animal) species, such as the common earthworm. How is self-fertilization avoided when these animals reproduce? (Answer: anatomical features and differential timing of gamete maturation.)
- It is known that HbS/HbA (sickle-cell heterozygote) persons in Africa are more likely to survive a malarial infection. Is the percentage of heterozygous individuals in nonmalaria areas (such as the United States) different from that in malaria areas?
- Report on examples of reproductive isolation that occur in nature. Why does isolation lead to evolutionary change?
- If you were an evolutionary biologist, what are some of the criteria that should be included in defining what make a species? Why should those things count?
- Describe different mechanisms of speciation and describe how those mechanisms leads to speciation.
- Has speciation ever been demonstrated in living populations? How might a scientist define a speciation event?
- The giant panda is listed as an endangered species, since only approximately 1,000–2,000 exist in the wild in China today. How could man use selective mating to best preserve this species?
- Research the bearded vulture that lives in Europe, Asia, and Africa. How is the bottleneck effect threatening them?

Possible Responses to *Critical Thinking* Questions

1. Rama the camel has survived the prezygotic mechanisms for reproductive isolation insofar as a cross between a camel and a llama has produced a successful hybrid organism (for pictures check out http://www.taylorllamas.com/Camel-LamaCrossPhotos.html). Most hybrid organisms, however, are sterile. It is thought that llama and camel hybrids may be able to produce viable offspring because of the compatibility of their chromosome number (74).

   If Rama were able to successfully reproduce, it would be evidence that camels and llamas are the same species. Mayr's definition of a species included the need for interbreeding. This may be an artificial designation, as geographically separated species may still be able to reproduce; the physical barrier just prevents that from happening.

2. The scientific definition of a species specifies that the parents not only produce offspring, but that those offspring must be capable of successful reproduction themselves. Therefore, the two species of antelopes cannot be classified as a single species until they produce viable progeny.

3. If it is true that sexual selection is responsible for some uniquely human traits, then a simple experiment should be able to demonstrate a pattern of selection that favors these characteristics.

   If it is true that female selection has lead to the selection of "charming, witty" personalities in males, this preference should hold up in sample populations of females. For example, several men could be selected to be videotaped displaying social behaviors defined as "witty" and "charming." In the first experiment, the same male would portray a range of "male" behaviors including some deemed charming and witty. When asked which behaviors the females preferred, they should select the behaviors that are identified as charming and witty a majority of the time. In a similar experiment, two males would be videotaped, one who is more attractive, but less witty and charming, and another who is more charming and witty but less attractive. When video of these two archetypes are exhibited for females, females should choose witty and charming as a potential mate more frequently than physical features.

A similar experiment could be conducted in male populations. In males there should be a selection preference for less hair and softer features. Male subjects would be asked to rate photos of females that have been altered to show the same individuals with varying levels of hair and varying levels of "softness" in their features. The results should demonstrate a preference for the previously identified features.

Possible Responses to *Data Analysis Exercise* Questions

There is a constant battle between rodents and pesticides. Often rats that develop immunity to pesticides increase in the population.

1. The town with the most rats susceptible to warfarin was Ludwigshafen.
2. Stadtlohn had the highest percentage of poison-resistant wild rats.
3. In Olfen, 79 percent of the rats were warfarin-resistant.
4. It appears as though Stadtlohn had the most extensive applications of bromadiolone.

18

ORGANIZING INFORMATION ABOUT SPECIES

Chapter Outline

Objectives

1. Describe how cladistic systems are used to detail evolutionary lineages by the examination of similar characters.
2. Define morphological divergence and convergence and identify examples of evidence for each type of event.
3. Identify and describe differences in different cladistic approaches.
4. Describe the difference between homologous and analogous morphological structures.
5. Describe how mutations to genes that direct development could lead to morphological differences in adults of a species.
6. Describe how scientists describe biochemical differences between species, and identify examples of evidence for DNA and amino acid sequence conservation in species.
7. Identify how someone studying comparative genomics would conduct parsimony analysis.
8. Know how examining the incidence of mutations can help develop estimates of how long ago two lineages diverged.
9. Understand how knowing the relationships between species may help save endangered organisms, and learn about the transmission of viruses between species.

Key Terms

species
taxonomy
cladistics
taxon
genus
family
order
class
phylum
kingdom
domain
clade
cladistic analysis
cladistics
cladogram
phylogeny
character
derived trait
monophyletic group
comparative morphology
evolutionary tree
sister groups
morphological divergence
morphological convergence
homologous structure
analogous structure
molecular clock
development
master gene
mutation
homeotic gene
Hox/Dlx
biochemical traits
neutral mutation
DNA sequencing
DNA fingerprinting
comparative genomics
mitochondrial DNA
parsimony analysis

Lecture Outline

18.1 Bye Bye Birdie

A. Hawaiian honeycreepers were some of the first animals on the island of Kauai.
   1. Between 1.8 million and 400,000 years ago, the ancestors of the honeycreepers had great adaptive advantage on the newly forming islands because of the abundance of food and habitat and the lack of predators.
   2. Many species of honeycreepers emerged.

B. Humans arrived between 1000 and 1778 bringing with them dogs, cats, pigs, cows, goats, deer, and sheep.
   1. These animals also thrived in the new habitat and competed with or preyed on the honeycreepers.
   2. Today, many of the species have become extinct; only 71 species remain despite efforts to protect the birds. Twenty-six of those species are endangered.
   3. Invasive species force or threaten survival.

C. How do we know about the diversity? Evolutionary biologists use morphological and biochemical evidence to classify organisms.

18.2 Phylogeny

A. Phylogeny is the study of the evolutionary history of a species.
   1. Measurable, inherited characters are used to determine potential lineage relationships.
      a. Characters may be based on factors such as RNA analysis or by observing actual physical traits.
   2. A clade is a monophyletic group that consists of a single ancestor and all of its descendents.
      a. New findings may alter previously established clades.

B. Cladistics
   1. Cladistics is one phylogenic method that separates species into clades (branches) based on shared characteristics like physical, behavioral, physiological, or molecular features.
      a. Because organisms have many different characters, groupings will differ based on what type of character is used.
      b. The result of cladistic analysis is a cladogram, a diagram that shows a network of evolutionary analysis.

c. Cladograms represent data-based hypotheses about species relationships and are pliable based on new or emerging evidence.

18.3 Comparing Form and Function

A. Morphological Divergence

1. Populations of a species have diverged when gene flow between them has ceased.
2. Eventually common morphological traits will also diverge. However, the changes often represent some homology within a lineage.
3. Morphological divergence is a macroevolutionary pattern in which some morphological homology is retained. Vertebrate forelimbs are an example.
   a. Fossilized evidence shows all land vertebrates have a common ancestor that crouched low on the ground and walked on all four legs.
   b. This stem reptile had a five-toe limb that was adapted into many different land vertebrate lineages that include flight in bats and birds, fins in penguins and dolphins, and degeneration in snakes.
   c. Even though the vertebrate forelimbs are different in size, shape, and function, it is clear that they are alike in positioning and structure of the bony elements.
   d. Comparisons of early embryos show resemblance in the bony development. These similarities are evidence of shared ancestry.

B. Morphological Convergence

1. Similar body parts may emerge separately from different lineages. This is morphological convergence.
2. In this scenario, analogous structures emerge, and while the structures have the same features, they have different evolutionary lineages. Wings are an example of this convergent evolution.
   a. Wing use is governed by the same physical constraints that govern flight.
   b. Birds and bats have homologous forelimbs, but the wing is a thin membranous extension of the skin. Bird wings are lined with feathers that are extensions derived from skin.
   c. Insect wings develop differently. Instead of developing around a forelimb, insect wings develop as fused sacs that flatten and are strengthened with chitin.
3. Analogous structures (morphological convergence) are adaptations that emerge after the divergence of the species.

18.4 Comparing Biochemistry

A. Molecular Clocks

1. Mutations are random and can occur anywhere in the DNA.
2. Most mutations are neutral, that is they have little or no effect on an individual's reproduction or survival.
3. Neutral mutations help to identify when lineages diverge. More closely related species will have more similar mutations compared to lesser relationships.
4. Further evidence of common lineage can be found by correlating changes in the DNA with morphological changes in the fossil record.

B. DNA and Protein Sequence Comparisons

1. Comparisons of amino acid sequences can be used to determine species relationships.
2. The more identical the protein sequence, the more related the species.
3. Some essential genes have not changed much over time due to their utility. Take cytochrome *b* for example.
   a. Cytochrome *b* is essential for electron transfer chains to function properly.
   b. The structure of cytochrome *b* is fairly conserved over a large number of species (see Figure 18.6).

4. In amino acid sequences, single substitutions may have large or small effects based on the amino acid that is replaced and what it is replaced with.
5. Most mutations that affect phenotype are selected against, however some may prove adaptive.
6. Similarities in proteins do not always equal similarity in DNA sequence because of the redundancy in the genetic code.
7. Mitochondrial DNA can also be used in sequencing analysis. Mitochondria can be used to determine familiar relationships because the mitochondrial DNA is passed on intact without the effects of crossing over during meiosis or recombination during fertilization.

18.5 Comparing Patterns of Development

A. Embryo development is guided by a set of master genes.
   1. Some master genes called homeotic genes are responsible for shaping the developing embryo.
   2. Mutations in homeotic genes will have a dramatic effect on the final shape of the organism.

B. Similar Forms in Plants
   1. Mutations to a floral identity gene have a dramatic effect on plant morphology. Consider *Apetela1*.
      a. In wild cabbage, *Apetala1* mutations cause mutant flowers.
      b. In common wall cress, *Apetela1* leads to lack of flower petals.
      c. *Apetela1* mutations affect a wide range of plant lineages.

C. Developmental Comparisons in Animals
   1. Hox Genes
      a. All vertebrates go through similar stages in development. Changes in adult body plans can be attributed to mutations in onset, rate, or completion of early development.
      b. *Dlx* is a homeotic gene the causes limb bud formations. *Hox* is a master gene that suppresses *Dlx*.
      c. In pythons, *Hox* is expressed along the length of the embryo; limb buds form but do not develop into legs.
      d. *Dlx*/*Hox* regulation may be responsible for variations in number and position of limbs in mature animals.

D. Persistent Juvenile Features
   1. Skull development in humans and chimpanzees shows evidence of relationship.
      a. Juvenile skulls for humans and chimpanzees are identical in proportion.
      b. The skull morphology changes in later development, with human adult skulls more closely resembling a juvenile chimp skull.
   2. Axolotls salamanders retain larval traits into adulthood.

18.6 Applications of Phylogeny Research

A. Conservation Biology
   1. The Hawaiian honeycreepers provide a dramatic example of how evolution works.
      a. A period of adaptive radiation led to a series of new honeycreeper species emerging.
      b. However, now that many of these species are becoming extinct due to predation and competition, their genetic diversity is declining.
   2. Researchers are attempting to decide which species of honeycreepers are most different from the others. Attempts to save the honeycreepers that vary the most from the others will help to promote genetic diversity.

B. Medical Applications
  1. The genetic material of viruses changes frequently.
  2. The H5N1 is a flu virus that can infect birds and mammals.
     a. Humans can become infected with the virus from birds, but rarely from other humans.
     b. Pigs can become infected with the virus and transmit it to other pigs and man.
  3. Scientists can learn a lot about the infection ability of viruses by studying their evolution.

18.7 Bye Bye Birdie (Revisited)
A. In 2004, attempts were made to save the pooulis.
  1. A male was captured but died before a female could be found.
     a. Some cells were saved so clones may be produced; but scientists doubt the cloned birds would be viable without parents from whom to learn behavior.

Suggestions for Presenting the Material

- On page 296, there is a fairly simple example of how a parsimony analysis would work. Extend the example by providing your students with bags full of differently colored basic geometric shapes. Their task will be to separate the items in the bag with the goals of: a) creating the simplest possible relationships, and b) describing how their classification system works. As groups describe how they arrived at their outcome, use this as basis for describing how taxonomy works. Extend this activity by then asking your students to separate several familiar animals or plants. This process will demonstrate how many different ways there are to classify things and how difficult and variable the process of taxonomy can be depending on what characters you use for grouping.
- Provide historical perspectives on taxonomy. Start with Linnaeus and show how the same organisms can be grouped differently based on the characters used for analysis.
- Spend time making the distinction between divergence/homology and convergence/analogous structures.
- Provide other examples of convergence and divergence, homology and analogy. The book has several good examples, but there are others like mammal teeth patterns (divergence), or spines or thorns on plants (convergence).
- Page 301 has the comparative analysis of cytochrome *b*. Simplify that example and have your students compare the similarities.
- Modern photography of embryos at comparable stages does demonstrate developmental similarities. Use this photographic evidence to have a discussion about how small changes in development plans could lead to large morphological changes over time.
- Biochemical evidence of evolution is a current and expanding body of work. Use contemporary examples of how protein and DNA analysis is elucidating evolutionary lineages.
- Start with fairly straightforward examples of organisms that are easily classified and then work up to more difficult examples like dolphin/whale or platypus lineages.
- The website, http://biology.fullerton.edu/biol261/phylolab.html, presents an excellent tutorial on the interpretation of cladograms. Divide the class into small groups and have each discuss one of the cladogram questions on the website. Performing this type of practice exercise will help in the overall interpretation of the chapter.
- Use the example of the foot of varying mollusks to provide another example of homologous structures.

Classroom and Laboratory Enrichment

- The Tree of Life Project (http://tolweb.org/tree/phylogeny.html) has very detailed phylogeny trees and some good instructional tools for completing trees.
- The Indiana University website (http://www.indiana.edu/~ensiweb/lessons/psa.ball.html) has a project where students work through an example of gene deactivation as an example of common ancestry. This example uses the GULO gene, which is responsible for vitamin C synthesis in other mammals but is inactive in humans because of several mutations.
- Provide your students with other examples of DNA or protein sequences and have them analyze the data and determine how similar organisms are.
- *Hox* is a well documented gene in *drosophila* development and *drosophila* relationships. *HOM/Hox* expression has been studied in regards to segment formation in arthropods. Use comparisons in these lineages to demonstrate how master gene mutation can lead to dramatic morphologic change.
- This chapter comes after the chapters on genetics but before the chapters on development. Perhaps having a brief primer lesson on development patterns will help set a frame of reference for developmental changes.
- Have students construct evolutionary trees using one character at a time, then two, then more. Have students reflect on the changes that occur in their trees when including more characters. Have students compare their trees to those done by taxonomists.
- Recent genomic analysis of the platypus is shedding light on its common ancestry. Present and discus evidence used to determine where the platypus fits into the animal kingdom (http://www.nature.com/news/2008/080507/full/453138a.html, with video interview and podcast).
- Honeycreepers are also indigenous to Brazil. Are some of the species there also endangered? How are the Brazilian birds different from those in Hawaii?
- Research the literature for other examples of phylogeny based on character analysis. This website, http://www.pnas.org/content/97/21/11359.figures-only, shows some figures from a study comparing the mitochondrial DNA of flatworms. Look for other similar examples on the Internet.

Classroom Discussion Ideas

- What are some of the different methods you could use to classify the diversity of the honeycreeper species? What would be the best way to demonstrate evidence that the honeycreepers are descended from a single common ancestor?
- The platypus presents a variety of traits that we would consider novel for a variety of species that might not seem closely related. How could we work to classify the platypus? What will provide stronger clues, morphological status or genomic analysis?
- What are the different methods that phylogeneticists use to classify evolutionary change? How have these methods changed over time.
- For each of the following pairs of structures, have your class determine if they are analogous or homologous: moth wing and bird wing, shark fin and dolphin fin, and octopus eye and human eye.
- Show graphics of fetal and adult skulls of different mammals. Do they show the same proportional changes as the skulls of humans and chimpanzees?

Additional Ideas for Classroom Discussion

- How has taxonomy changed since Linnaeus' time?
- Why is evolutionary cladistics today so difficult in an evolutionary time-scale context? What type of evidence would be required to revise a cladogram?
- How does the human factor come into play when reconstructing evolutionary history?
- Discuss the benefits and problems associated with regional naming of organisms?
- How will biochemical analysis differ if the focus is on DNA or proteins? Which (DNA or protein) provides a more consistent basis for analysis? Which will be more conserved in related lineages?
- How does analysis of 20 species versions of cytochrome *b* provide evidence for common lineage? What does protein analysis tell us about common ancestry?
- What are some of the different methods of comparing proteins or comparing DNA, and how can the methods be used to demonstrate evolutionary change?
- The GULO gene (see above in the Enrichment section) allows other mammals to produce vitamin C. In humans, the GULO gene is called a pseudogene, a gene that exists in the genome but whose function has been deleted by mutation. What does this analysis tell us about evolutionary process? Why would humans have a gene that would be beneficial, but inactive?
- Comparative genetics has demonstrated that humans are roughly 1–2 percent different from chimpanzees, and that there is about 60 percent genetic conservation between human and fruit flies. Even more humbling is the comparison between humans and a banana! Why are these seemingly different organisms so genetically similar?
- What does the evidence from vertebrate forelimbs tell us about evolutionary history?
- How do the lineages of vertebrate forelimbs and the lineages of animals with wings tell us different evolutionary histories? How are the two patterns of development different?
- Why would species that look so different at an adult stage look so similar during embryonic development?
- Why would a master gene or a homeotic gene mutation be either so lethal or change the body plan outcome so drastically?
- What does the evidence obtained during *Hox/Dlx* experiments tell us about homeotic gene expression that may have played an important evolutionary role?
- What are the differences between lethal, neutral, and beneficial mutations? What would actually lead to a mutation being lethal, neutral, or beneficial?
- Why are most mutations neutral before becoming beneficial?
- What is a molecular clock and how are they calibrated?
- What is parsimony and how is it achieved?
- Give a detailed presentation of the axolotls salamander. What juvenile features can the students identify?

How Would You Vote? Classroom Discussion Ideas

- Monitor the online voting. There are several concepts to keep in mind that may help guide your discussion of captive breeding programs. Think about the problems associated with having such a limited gene pool. Look at the effect of captivity breeding programs versus programs that work to reestablish species in their natural habitat (perhaps African rhino species: http://www.msnbc.msn.com/id/22999778/).

- Many may argue that captive breeding is the only solution for the survival of severely endangered species. For example, if you were one of only three surviving poouli birds in the wild, the possibility of finding another of your species to mate with seems very improbable. In cases as disastrous as these, captive mating, although not always successful, may be the only viable option.
- Look into the literature to see if captive breeding is being attempted with other endangered species. Are there examples of captive breeding that have been successful? Which have been unsuccessful?
- The class is probably sympathetic to the fate of endangered species such as the brightly colored honeycreepers. Do your students feel as concerned about other endangered species, such as: the blackbelted crayfish or the duskytail darter? Do the students feel that all endangered species should receive the same level of attention, regardless of their appeal to humans? How about endangered plants and fungi?

Term Paper Topics, Library Activities, and Special Projects

- Describe how plants and animals were classified before Linnaeus.
- A new primate species is discovered. If you were a taxonomist, describe the steps you would take to classify the new species and determine its closest relative.
- Describe how bacteria are classified and how it is different from how other organisms might be classified.
- Prepare a report that helps a local zoo or botanical garden with their classification.
- Detail the adaptation of the horse hoof as an example of morphological divergence.
- Describe the difference between morphological divergence and convergence, including a discussion of homologous and analogous structures.
- Why does DNA and protein analysis provide a much more distinct evolutionary picture than morphology?
- Mitochondrial DNA provides some fairly clear evidence of human evolutionary lineage. Describe the benefit of studying mitochondrial DNA and detail the evidence provided by the genomic study of mitochondrial DNA.
- The Human Genome Project was an ambitious program to study the entire human genome. Several other genome projects have been completed and others are on the way. What can we learn about evolutionary lineage from these types of studies?
- What types of genes are highly conserved between species? Why does the conservation of those genes end up being important to survival?
- Compare and contrast the development of several closely related species. Where are the changes in their developmental plans? What leads to those changes?
- Recent work has elucidated a genomic comparison of the platypus. The platypus is an incredibly unique mammal that retains characteristics of birds and reptiles. It has venom and a reptilian gait, lays eggs, and has hair. The platypus bill is a sensory organ. While the platypus has mammary glands, it lacks teats like other mammals. How has genomic analysis led us to a better understanding of where the platypus fits into an evolutionary lineage?
- Research the early development of the idea of a "molecular clock."
- Compare the biochemical analysis of several seemingly unrelated species. Based on the data, which appear to be the most closely related?
- Look into other animal species that retain juvenile features as adults.

- Compare photographs of the embryos of many different species. Which have similar characteristics? Has the advent of the study of embryology influenced how scientists have reclassified different species?
- Look into the studies of viruses that appear to "jump" from infecting one species to another.
- Research the axolotls salamanders. Discuss how their juvenile features appear to be advantageous to the adults of the species.

Possible Responses to *Critical Thinking* Questions

1. The description of some modern species as primitive while others as more advanced is based on the false notion that evolution has some end goal and that humans are supposedly the most advanced organisms to have evolved. If these labels were to be applied, it would make more sense if they were applied to individual lineages. For example, if you were to examine the hominid lineage, they are perhaps more advanced than some of the other extinct branches of the lineage. Perhaps the more fitting description would be that modern humans are just better adapted to the current environment than all of the other members that have become extinct.
2. The phrase "ontogeny recapitulates phylogeny" sounds quite pretentious and may not immediately make sense. In a nutshell, the term refers to the fact that there are structures present on a human embryo that would have been present in our ancestors. For example, a human embryo has a yolk sac, gill slits, and a tail. Obviously, these features are not present in an adult human! They are evidence of traits that our ancestors possessed and, thus, show an insight into our evolution as a species.
3. Synpolydactyly is a disorder that leads to the development of webbed fingers. In order for this disorder to arise, a mutation would have to occur in the set of master genes that controls finger development. Scientists have discovered the precise Hox gene that, when mutated, results in synpolydactyly. Mutations at this site can also cause other limb abnormalities, such as brachydactyly (shortened fingers and toes).

Possible Responses to *Data Analysis Exercise* Questions

Related species may be identified using bone morphology and the analysis of DNA sequences. The honeycreeper clade was analyzed using these two criteria.

1. The two species that represent outgroups are the Nihoa and Laysan finches.
2. According to the cladogram, it appears that the akikiki and Maui alauahio appear to be most closely related to the poouli s.
3. According to the cladogram, there is no honeycreeper species more related to the outgroup species than the poouli s.
4. There are 17 nucleotide differences between the poouli s and *P. Montana*. Also there are 17 nucleotide differences between the *P. Montana* and *L. bailleui*.

19

LIFE'S ORIGIN AND EARLY EVOLUTION

Chapter Outline

Objectives

1. Identify the reasons astrobiologists feel that if life exists on other planets, it is likely underground.
2. Describe how life might have arisen on Earth approximately 3.8 billion years ago.
3. Describe the hypotheses for the formation of organic molecules.
4. Describe the factors that led to the divergence of the prokaryotic and eukaryotic lineages.
5. Describe the origins of cells and organelles.
6. Identify the key developments in the origin of metabolism leading to self-replicating systems.
7. Discuss the endosymbiotic theory and give evidence supporting it.

Key Terms

astrobiology
ozone layer
thermophile
hydrothermal vent
iron-sulfur world hypothesis
ribozymes
bioprospecting
nanobes
protocell
big bang
self-replicating systems
RNA world hypothesis
biomarkers
stromatolites
chemoautotrophs
Proterozoic
cyanobacteria
prokaryotic cells
eukaryotic cells
Rodinia
heterotrophs
autotrophs
endosymbiont hypothesis
glaucophytes

Lecture Outline

19.1 Looking for Life

A. Astrobiology involves the origin and distribution of life in the universe.
  1. Some organisms can live in extreme environments.
    a. Bacteria have been discovered in drastic environments (abnormal pHs, temperatures, pressures) and deep within the Earth's surface.

B. Scientists usually assume that water is necessary for life.
  1. Frozen water was discovered beneath the surface of Mars.

C. If life exists on other planets, it is likely underground.
  1. Other locations do not have ozone layers to shield an organism's DNA from damaging UV radiation.

19.2 The Early Earth

A. Origin of the Universe and the Earth
  1. The Big Bang Theory describes the instantaneous distribution of all matter and energy throughout the universe.
    a. Gaseous particles condensed into stars, where nuclear reactions began giving off light.
    b. Dying stars left behind clouds of dust and gas, which began to cool and form our solar system.
    c. As particles began clustering together and gaining mass, pre-planetary objects started to form increasing gravitational pull.
    d. About 4.6 billion years ago Earth and the other planets had formed.

B. Conditions on the Early Earth
  1. Formation of Earth did not lead to conditions we would recognize today.
    a. Debris fell from orbit as gravity increased, causing meteor impacts on a more molten Earth surface.
    b. Volcano eruptions led to formation of an early atmosphere of water vapor, carbon dioxide, nitrogen, and hydrogen.
    c. Free oxygen levels were low until about 2.2 billion years ago.
  2. When the Earth's crust cooled, water condensed, and rains began and carried minerals from rocks in runoff. This runoff carried nutrients into the seas where life began.

19.3 Formation of Organic Monomers

A. Organic Molecules From Inorganic Precursors
  1. Early experimentation demonstrated non-biological mechanisms for producing organic molecules.
    a. An amino acid was formed under laboratory conditions.

B. The Source of Life's First Building Blocks
   1. Lightning-Fueled Atmospheric Reactions
      a. Could large organic molecules have formed spontaneously and then evolved into the molecular systems of life?
      b. Stanley Miller used a lab apparatus to demonstrate synthesis of amino acids from hydrogen, methane, ammonia, and water under abiotic conditions.
   2. Reactions at Hydrothermal Vents
      a. Another theory states that the combination of heat from underwater hydrothermal vents, carbon dioxide, and potassium cyanide formed amino acids.
   3. Delivery From Space
      a. Other possibilities include the arrival of organic compounds from outer space and synthesis of biological molecules near hydrothermal vents in deep seas.
      b. The assembly of amino acids has been detected in carbon rich meteorites.

19.4 From Polymers to Protocells

A. Properties of Cells
   1. All cells have a plasma membrane, DNA, RNA, and ribosomes.
   2. Processes such as duplication and metabolism point to a common ancestor.
      a. Although no early cells exist, scientists use modern chemistry to try out various hypotheses.

B. Origin of Metabolism
   1. Metabolism can be described as a group of interacting molecules that copy themselves repeatedly and use different molecules to supply the reaction.
   2. Hypothesis #1: Proteins formed on clay tidal flats.
      a. Clay would have attracted amino acids with an electrical charge. Sunlight could have provided energy to form bonds.
   3. Hypothesis #2: Metabolic pathways evolved at hydrothermal vents.
      a. This hypothesis is called the iron-sulfur world hypothesis.
      b. Heat, minerals, and pressure combined at the vents to create conditions sufficient to induce organic compound synthesis.
   4. Experimental evidence supports part of each claim.

C. Origin of the Genome
   1. From accumulated organic compounds emerged replicating systems consisting of DNA, RNA, and proteins.
   2. An RNA world may have preceded DNA's dominance as the main informational molecule. Evidence of such has accumulated since the 1960s.
      a. RNA still serves as enzymes called ribozymes in cells.
      b. rRNA catalyzes protein formation.
      c. Self-replicating ribosomes have been synthesized in the lab.
   3. How DNA entered the picture is not yet clear. Perhaps DNA provided several advantages over RNA.

D. Origin of the Plasma Membranes
   1. The metabolism inside living cells cannot occur without a barrier against the chemical actions on the outside.
   2. Protocells were simple membrane-bound sacs that were capable of taking in substances and reproducing.
   3. Membrane-bound sacs can form spontaneously, incorporating proteins and fatty acids in conditions similar to the clay tidal flats.

19.5 Life's Early Evolution

A. Origin of Bacteria and Archaea

1. Molecular clock calculations indicate a common ancestor about 4.3 billion years ago. Primitive fossils date back approximately 3.5 billion years ago.
2. Genomic analysis of living prokaryotes indicate an important divergence 3.5 billion years ago that may have produced a branch leading to bacteria, and another lineage leading to archea and eukaryotes.
3. Evolution of the cyclic pathway of photosynthesis in bacteria tapped a renewable source of energy—sunlight; large accumulations of these cells are seen today as fossils (stromatolites).
4. By the dawn of the Proterozoic eon (2.5 billion years ago), the noncyclic pathway had evolved among cyanobacteria that were producing oxygen. This led to an oxygen-rich environment with three important consequences.
   a. An oxygen-rich atmosphere stopped the non-living synthesis of organic matter.
   b. Free oxygen permitted aerobic respiration, which now became the dominant energy-releasing pathway.
   c. Oxygen enriched the atmosphere and helped to screen UV rays, allowing life to move onto land.

B. The Rise of Eukaryotes

1. The oldest complete eukaryotic fossils are about 2.7 billion years old and had organelles.
   a. Biomarkers are lipids that are made by only one type of cell.
2. The earliest known organism is filamentous red algae.
   a. Sexual reproduction began in this early algae.
3. The earliest animal fossils date back around 570 million years.

19.6 How Did Eukaryotic Traits Evolve?

A. A Composite Ancestry

1. Eukaryote genes resemble those from both bacteria and archaea.

B. Origin of Internal Membranes

1. It is possible that the infoldings of the plasma membrane seen in prokaryotic cells could have led to the narrow channels that permit the separation of tasks and materials seen in the ER of eukaryotic cells.
2. Infolding is beneficial because it increases surface area for membrane-bound enzymatic/metabolic activity.
3. Infoldings could have surrounded the DNA to become the nuclear envelope that serves to protect the cell from invasions of foreign DNA. This would have protected cells from exposure to other DNA.
   a. Bacterial cells take up DNA from their surroundings and viruses.

C. Evolution of Mitochondria and Chloroplasts

1. According to the theory of endosymbiosis, one species becomes a resident inside another cell to the benefit of both.
2. Aerobic bacteria could have become the mitochondria; cyanobacteria could have become chloroplasts.

D. Evidence of Endosymbiosis in Living Cells

1. A laboratory culture of *Amoeba* became infected with a bacterium; some cells died but others thrived and became dependent on the invaders to make an essential enzyme for them.
2. Mitochondria are similar in size to bacteria, have their own DNA, and divide independent of the cell; and the mitochondrial inner membrane resembles a bacterial cell's plasma membrane.

3. Chloroplasts are believed to have originated by endosymbiosis too; they resemble cyanobacteria in metabolism and have DNA that is self-replicating.
4. Glaucophytes are protists with unique photosynthetic organelles resembling cyanobacteria with separate cell walls.

19.7 Looking for Life (Revisited)

A. Earth seems to be an appropriate size to sustain life.
   1. Mars is half the size of Earth.
B. Mars has a thinner atmosphere containing carbon dioxide, nitrogen, and a little oxygen.
   1. Most likely any organism on Mars would be anaerobic.

Suggestions for Presenting the Material

- This chapter continues the theme of evolution (Unit III) but "steps back" in time to look at the origin and early evolution of life in preparation for the survey of life-forms in Unit IV.
- Stress the tenuous conclusions that are in constant revision when scientists attempt to reconstruct the past. Just as a good medical diagnosis is not based on one examination or one lab test, a good analysis of past evolutionary history is not based on any one line of evidence, but rather several lines of corroborating evidence.
- Present the evidence. For example, the chapter talks about the Miller experiments that led to the formation of sugars and amino acids. Opponents of evolution often cite that scientists do not agree that Miller's conditions were accurate based on more contemporary analysis. However, many other studies have been done that replicate similar results under different conditions (http://www.ncseweb.org/icons/icon1millerurey.html for a summary). Present this evidence. Miller continued to work on this problem. There is a good web-based simulation of his technique (http://www.ucsd.tv/miller-urey/) with a video interview about his ideas and video that demonstrates the real experimental apparatus.
- Many current hypotheses about molecular origins focus on RNA as the important first molecule that could have led to DNA and proteins. Present evidence for many of the RNA-based hypotheses.
- Provide the students with data sets or simulations and help them make claims based on the empirical evidence.
- Because of the rather theoretical and speculative nature of the "origin of life" section, students' minds often wander because they don't have any concrete terms to write down. Use of visual material of any kind will help to retain focus.
- Note that The Timeline for Life's Origin and Evolution in section 19.6 presents an evolutionary tree of life using a time scale devoid of the usual era names.

Classroom and Laboratory Enrichment

- Prepare an overhead or slide summarizing the work of Redi, Spallanzani, and Pasteur in disproving spontaneous generation under "recent" conditions on Earth.
- Assemble a replica (without ingredients) of the apparatus Stanley Miller used in his famous experiment. Point out how really simple it was.
- Have students do reports on some of the different building block experiments since Urey/Miller. Have them summarize the outcomes and the likelihood of the scenario they study.

- Present evidence of current organisms that live in conditions on Earth that are extreme and how they have adapted to those conditions. Pick organisms that live in hot springs, thermal vents, or deep in the soil and Earth's crust.
- Describe some of the key cellular adaptations in a time scale relationship.
- Lay out the evidence that helps describe the endosymbiotic theory.
- Show actual fossils or photographs of fossils representing some of the life forms prevalent during the Paleozoic, Mesozoic, and Cenozoic eras.
- Discuss the locations of hydrothermal vents. There are distinct examples of food webs that exist in these unique habitats.
- Talk about the chemical composition of recovered meteorites. Has there been any indication that these meteorites contain the precursors for life?

Classroom Discussion Ideas

- Why do you think the Archeans are able to live in so many different extreme environments?
- Evolutionary biologists believe that life on Earth first evolved in the absence of oxygen. Where did the oxygen in our atmosphere come from?
- Would you consider nanobes to be living organisms? How are they like protocells?
- Can you think of any environment on Earth within which life cannot exist?
- Astrobiologists doubt the presence of life above ground on planets without an ozone layer. What are the ramifications for life on Earth if our ozone becomes damaged further?
- Discuss the function and appearance of some particular ribozymes, such as: hammerhead ribozyme, VS ribozyme, and hairpin ribozyme.

Additional Ideas for Classroom Discussion

- Diagram the apparatus used by Stanley Miller to study the synthesis of organic compounds in an atmosphere like that of early Earth. Ask students what they think of Miller's findings.
- On what evidence do scientists reconstruct the primordial Earth depicted in Figure 19.4?
- Why was no free oxygen (O_2) included in Miller's experiment? What did the electrical spark simulate?
- What distinguishes a nonliving lipid-bound sphere containing nucleic acids and amino acids from a living cell?
- Which came first, the chicken or the egg? That may not be a great evolutionary question; chickens were part of a group of animals that lay eggs. But here's one that you should actually take some time to ponder: Which came first: proteins, RNA, or DNA? What evidence is out there that supports any of those lines?
- Name some organisms living today that are virtually unchanged from their earliest appearances in the fossil record millions of years ago. Why do some organisms fail to change significantly throughout geologic time?
- In a hypothetical series of events leading from spontaneous formation of molecules to living cells, what do we know about how each step may have occurred?
- Why was aerobic respiration necessary for the evolution of eukaryotes?
- Describe the metabolic pathways used by the first living cells to obtain energy.

- What are some of the advantages of multicellularity? What are the advantages of a nucleus?
- Why do you think people believed as recently as 100 years ago that spontaneous generation still occurs on the Earth?
- The branching of prokaryotes during the Archean into archaebacteria, eubacteria, and eukaryotes is the basis for a new three-domain scheme of classification. Evaluate the merits of this scheme versus the more traditional five- (or six-) kingdom scheme.
- Look at the timeline scale in 19.6. Prokaryotes were around for a long time. What are some of the key adaptations that led to the radiations and origins of plants, animals, and fungi all around the same time?
- Why are extinctions important in the development of new species?
- Remember back to the last chapter where you read that some common ancestor diverged into bacteria and archea. Then the archea lineage diverged into eukaryotes. This chapter details how cyanobacteria, from the bacteria lineage, developed the early photosynthetic metabolic pathways. How is it possible that all plants, which are eukaryotes, are somehow related to bacteria that emerged about one billion years *after* the bacterial and eukaryotic lineages diverged?
- Show images of stromatolites and discuss their structure.
- What evidence exists that makes scientists conclude that the red algae was probably the fist eukaryote?

How Would You Vote? Classroom Discussion Ideas

- Monitor the voting for the online question. This is an interesting question considering the potential return of Mars probes. Perhaps this could lead to a good discussion of Andromeda strain scares in the 1950s and 1960s.
- This question could pose some interesting dilemmas. For example, could life on Mars be so different from our definition of life that we would not recognize it? Would we be transporting a potentially invasive form of life to our planet? Yet, by not searching for life on another planet are we passing up the potential to colonize another planet? A debate on this issue will undoubtedly result in a lively discussion!

Term Paper Topics, Library Activities, and Special Projects

- Discuss the history of the experiments by Stanley Miller.
- See if you can locate the original article by Miller and Urey in which they reported their famous experiment. Read it carefully to see what speculative application they made for their experiment.
- Although the idea of life originating on Earth from forms traveling from distant planets is highly speculative, there is evidence that exists that may support this hypothesis. Find the evidence and describe why it may be credible.
- In recent years, some people have questioned the significance of Stanley Miller's experiment. Prepare an evaluation of their criticisms.
- Discuss experiments that have been conducted since Miller in the 1950s and describe how they help to contextualize Miller's findings.
- Discuss recent controversial studies that use human mitochondrial DNA to draw conclusions about human evolution. Based on what you find about mitochondrial origins and reproduction and the endosymbiotic theory, describe the evidence that the mitochondria provides for early evolution.

- Research the laboratories that are currently investigating life on early Earth. What advances have they made from what has been presented in chapter 19?
- See if you can locate the research of the Australian team that is working with nanobes. What is the current status of their research? Are there any other research teams working with nanobes?
- The United States is working to incorporate future trips to Mars into its space program. Recent discovery of what may have been water on Mars is fueling the impetus for these trips. What would the significance of finding water or evidence of past water on Mars mean? What would it mean if we found evidence of life on other planets?
- Many researchers have investigated the effects of UV radiation on DNA. Read through several papers on the subject and make some generalizations.
- Research articles about life in the Atacama Desert (depicted in Figure 19.1). What are the drastic conditions there that seem almost incompatible with life?
- Read about the life of Stanley Miller. What research projects led to his monumental discoveries?
- Discuss the research by Jack Szostak that relates to the study of protocells. What conclusions were reached as a result of his experimentation?
- Section 19.4 discusses volcanic pools in Russia. What are the harsh conditions found there? What conclusions were drawn as a result of Deamer's experiments there?
- Make a poster-sized presentation of the timeline from section 19.6. Include photos obtained from the Internet to accompany your presentation.

Possible Responses to *Critical Thinking* Questions

1. There are two main reasons that fossils older than three billion years would not exist. First, there would not be much to fossilize and so the conditions would have to be absolutely perfect. Second, because of plate tectonics, the layers containing those organisms may not exist anymore. Not only would those fossils be at the deepest layers of sedimentation, but those layers may have been at the edge of where two plates meet. Those layers may have been destroyed by friction or returned to a deeper level and turned into molten magma.
2. There are several basic properties that a "minimal organism" would have to exhibit in order to be considered living: 1) The organism would need to have some method of providing itself with energy (metabolism). 2) It would have to be able to maintain a stable internal environment, providing materials needed for metabolism (homeostasis). 3) It would have to be capable of reproducing itself.

Possible Responses to *Data Analysis Exercise* Questions

Over many billions of years, asteroids have impacted the composition of the atmosphere.

1. A decline in asteroid impacts occurred before the atmospheric oxygen increased.
2. Since the first cells arose, the level of carbon dioxide has dropped and the level of oxygen has risen.
3. In today's world, oxygen is more abundant than carbon dioxide.
4. The rise in carbon dioxide at the far right of the graph is likely due to the burning of fossil fuels by cars and industry.

20

VIRUSES, BACTERIA, AND ARCHAEA

Chapter Outline

Objectives

1. Describe the two domains of "prokaryotes."
2. Know the structure and means of transmission of the HIV virus.
3. Describe the unique characteristics of "prokaryotes" and their metabolic diversity.
4. Be able to contrast the lytic and lysogenic pathways in a viral life cycle.
5. Discuss how "prokaryotes" reproduce.
6. Give examples of positive and negative impacts of bacteria on humans.
7. List characteristics of viruses in general.
8. Discuss the diversity present in bacteria and archaea.
9. Give specific examples of pathogens that cause human illness and how they do so.

Key Terms

pathogen
emerging disease
prokaryotes
bacteria
coccus
bacillus
spirillum
cell wall
Gram staining
Gram-positive bacteria
Gram-negative bacteria
glycocalyx
capsule
slime layer
bacterial flagella
pili
photoautotrophs
chemoautotrophs
photoheterotrophs
chemoheterotrophs
saprobes
bacterial chromosome
prokaryotic fission
plasmid
nucleoid
binary fission
horizontal gene transfer
transduction
transformation
conjugation
numerical taxonomy
strain
cyanobacteria
proteobacteria
nitrogen fixation
chlamydias
spirochaetes
endospore
magnetotactic
Archaea
methanogens
extreme halophiles
extreme thermophile
virus
viroids
protein coat
nucleic acid core
envelope
bacteriophages
lytic pathway
lysis
lysogenic pathway
latency
retrovirus
reverse transcriptase
vector
viral reassortment
metagenomics
infection
disease
epidemic
contagious diseases
pandemic
sporadic diseases
pathogen
AIDS
SARS
Ebola
antibiotic resistance
BSE
mad cow disease
prions
vCJD

Lecture Outline

20.1 Evolution of a Disease
- A. AIDS (Acquired Immune Deficiency Syndrome) is caused by HIV (Human Immunodeficiency Virus).
  1. Large numbers of people have contracted HIV, especially in sub-Saharan Africa.
- B. HIV was first isolated in the 1980s.
  1. Two strains exist, HIV-1 and HIV-2. Most people that are infected have HIV-1.
  2. HIV is similar to Simian Immunodeficiency Virus (SIV).
- C. Despite a global effort, a vaccine has yet to be developed.
- D. Pathogens can endanger human life, and many of them are viruses and prokaryotes.

20.2 Viruses and Viroids
- A. Viral Discovery
  1. In the late 1800s, scientists discovered a new plant pathogen that was able to pass through filters and was invisible under a light microscope.
  2. Viruses are non-cellular infectious agents that rely on a host for replication.
- B. Viral Structure
  1. Viruses consist of a protein coat containing a DNA or RNA core.
  2. Some viruses have a lipid coat.
     a. Polyhedral viruses have a coat that is many-sided.

b. Some animal viruses have a capsid on the top lipid coat.
3. For replication, a virus inserts its DNA or RNA into a host and uses the host's enzymes to replicate its proteins and nucleic acids. These components then reassemble.
    a. A bacteriophage is a virus that infects bacteria.

C. Ecological Role of Viruses
1. Some viruses are advantageous to humans.
    a. Baculoviruses kill organisms that destroy crops.
    b. Bacteriophages can destroy bacteria that could result in food poisoning.
2. Some viruses are disadvantageous to humans.
    a. Viruses can affect the health of crops, animals, and humans.

D. Viroids
1. Small RNAs that infect many crops.
2. Viroids are many times smaller than viruses and are comprised of a small circle of RNA.

20.3 Viral Replication

A. Overview of Viral Replication
1. There are five basic steps in the multiplication of viruses.
    a. *Attachment:* the virus recognizes and becomes attached to a host cell.
    b. *Penetration:* DNA or RNA, alone or whole virus, enters cytoplasm.
    c. *Replication and synthesis:* viral genes direct thr host cell into replicating viral nucleic acids, synthesizing viral enzymes and capsid proteins.
    d. *Assembly:* synthesized components are put together into new infectious particles.
    e. *Release:* new virus particles are released from the infected cell.

B. Bacteriophage Replication
1. Replication can proceed by way of two pathways.
    a. In the *lytic* pathway, the virus quickly accomplishes steps one through four listed above and causes the cell to rupture (lysis), spilling its contents and the viruses.
    b. In *lysogenic* pathways, the viral genes remain inactive inside the host cell (and its descendants); often the genes become integrated into the host DNA only to resume their destructive viral activity later.

C. Replication of HIV
1. In order to infect, HIV must attach to a white blood cell, the DNA must enter the nucleus, and reverse transcriptase then inserts the virus into the host's DNA.
2. When new virus is synthesized, it leaves the host cell with an envelope.
3. HIV drugs try to block some of the steps of an HIV infection, but they only prolong the inevitable.

20.4 Viruses as Human Pathogens

A. The Threat of Infectious Disease
1. Most infections from viruses, bacteria, or fungi are transmitted via blood or body fluids.
2. Some infections are spread via a vector (an animal that transmits the disease).

B. Common Viral Diseases
1. Some viral diseases are short-lived and cause respiratory or digestive problems.
2. Some viral diseases are more persistent.
    a. Examples are the HIV virus and herpes.
3. Some viral diseases can be prevented by administration of a vaccine.
    a. These include the childhood diseases measles, mumps, rubella, and chicken pox.

C. New Flus: Viral Mutation and Reassortment
1. Some viruses, such as those that cause the flu, mutate rapidly.
    a. Because those viruses change so frequently, researchers formulate new flu shots each year.

b. Even with a yearly flu shot, you can still get a strain of flu that was not included in the vaccine.

2. Flus are named for the structure of their proteins on the outside of the virus.
   a. For example, H stands for glycoprotein and N represents neuraminidase in the H1N1 virus.
3. Flu viruses have the ability to undergo reassortment where genes can be exchanged between viruses.
   a. For example, the H1N1 virus can be swine flu, avian flu, or a human strain.
4. The flu virus can affect one particular region (epidemic) or be a pandemic (worldwide).
5. The H5N1 virus originates in birds, but can infect humans who have contact with birds.

20.5 "Prokaryotes"—Enduring, Abundant, and Diverse

A. Two Lineages of "Prokaryotes"
1. The earliest cells were prokaryotes, cells with no nucleus.
2. Shortly after life began there was a branching between bacteria and archaea (which led to the eukaryotic lineage).

B. Identifying Species and Investigating Diversity
1. Bacteria have classically been classified based on shape, cell wall properties, metabolism, and other properties.
2. Automated gene sequencing, metagenomics, has elucidated prokaryotic diversity.

C. Metabolic Diversity
1. Autotroph or Heterotroph?
   a. Metabolic diversity is key to reproductive success in bacteria.
   b. Photoautotrophs are photosynthetic.
   c. Chemoautotrophs strip electrons from inorganic compounds and use that energy to build organic compounds from CO_2 and water.
   d. Photoheterotrophs use light energy and obtain carbon from organic compounds from their environment.
   e. Chemoautotrophs get both their carbon and their energy by breaking down organic compounds. This group includes many prokaryotes, some protests, and all animals and fungi.
2. Aerobe or Anaerobe?
   a. Almost all eukaryotes are aerobic (require oxygen).
   b. Bacteria and archaeans can be aerobic or anaerobic (in an environment lacking oxygen).

20.6 Structure and Function of "Prokaryotics"

A. Cell Size and Structure
1. Modern prokaryotes include bacteria and archaeans.
2. They are unicellular and do not enclose their DNA in a nucleus; instead it is in a nucleoid region of the cytoplasm.
3. All prokaryotic cells have ribosomes. Some have infoldings of their membrane.
4. Three basic shapes are common.
   a. Coccus—spherical.
   b. Bacillus (rod)—cylindrical.
   c. Spirillum—helical.
5. Nearly all bacteria have a cell wall, and some have an external slime coat that helps them adhere to surfaces.
6. Two kinds of filamentous structures may be attached to the cell wall.
   a. The *bacterial flagellum* rotates like a propeller to pull the cell along.

b. *Pili* help bacteria attach to one another in conjugation, or help them attach to surfaces.

B. Reproduction and Gene Transfer

1. Reproductive rates in prokaryotes are high; some species can reproduce every 20 minutes.
2. Some species reproduce using a budding mechanism.
3. More commonly, bacteria reproduce in a process called binary fission.
4. Some bacteria can also pass along genes without reproducing. During conjugation a plasmid—a small, self-replicating circle of DNA containing only a few genes—can be passed to another cell (horizontal gene transfer).

20.7 Bacterial Diversity

A. Representative Diversity

1. The Heat Lovers.
   a. Thermophiles exist in extreme environments. Members of the genus *Aquaticus* include bacteria that live in volcanic spring, thermal vents, and hot springs.
2. Oxygen-Producing Cyanobacteria.
   a. Cyanobacteria are good examples of chloroplast-containing bacteria.
   b. *Anabaena,* by means of heterocysts, can fix nitrogen.
   c. Some cyanobacteria have the ability to fix nitrogen.
3. Highly Diverse Proteobacteria
   a. Proteobacteria make up the largest, most diverse bacterial group (Gram negative).
   b. *Thiomargarita namibiensis* is a chemoautotroph that lives in marine environments and gets its energy from stripping electrons from sulfur.
   c. *Rhizobium* fixes nitrogen on the roots of legumes.
   d. *E. coli* and *H. Pylori* live in the human digestive system.
   e. Some free-living chemoautotrophic proteobacteria exhibit complex behavior. Magnetotactic bacteria are attracted by magnetic fields.
   f. Myxobacteria move as a group and feed on soil bacteria.
4. Thick-Walled, Gram-Positive Bacteria
   a. Gram positives are not a monophyletic group, and most are chemoheterotrophs with thick cell walls that retain the gram stain.
   b. *Lactobacillus* is used in dairy product conversions, such as yogurt.
   c. *L. acidophilus* lowers the pH of skin and vaginal linings.
   d. Some form resistant endospores that can survive harsh environmental conditions; for example, *Clostridium tetani* (tetanus).
5. Other Groups That Include Human Pathogens
   a. Spirochetes resemble a spring. A spirochete is responsible for causing Lyme disease.
   b. Chlamydias are intracellular parasites that affect animal cells.

20.8 The Archaea

A. Discovery of the Third Domain

1. Archaeans are prokaryotes that differ from other bacteria in their ribosomal RNA and cell walls; they also resemble eukaryotic cells by making histones and sharing the same start codon for transcription.
2. Some archaeans may resemble the first cells on Earth; the domain has been recently subdivided into three major groups.

B. Here, There, Everywhere

1. Extreme halophiles are "salt-lovers."

a. These species can tolerate high salt environments such as brackish ponds, salt lakes, volcanic vents on the seafloor, and the like.

b. Most are heterotrophic aerobes, but some can switch to a special photosynthesis, using bacteriorhodopsin to produce ATP.

2. Extreme thermophiles are "heat-lovers."

a. These bacteria live in hot springs and other very hot places, such as the thermal vents of the sea floor where temperatures exceed 250°C.

b. They use sulfur as a source of electrons for ATP formation.

3. Methanogens produce methane.

a. They inhabit swamps, mud, sewage, and the guts of animals.

b. They make ATP anaerobically by converting carbon dioxide and hydrogen to methane.

20.9 Evolution of a Disease (Revisited)

A. Most viral diseases do not kill the host quickly.

B. Some Europeans have a mutation that decreases the likelihood they will get AIDS.

C. An epidemic results if the disease spreads throughout the population.

Suggestions for Presenting the Material

- This chapter discusses two quite diverse groups: one that is living (bacteria) and one that is not (viruses). Emphasize the fact that these groups are together not because of any taxonomic relatedness but because they traditionally lie at the beginning of discussions of living things.
- Emerging diseases like West Nile virus and Avian Flu virus have the possibility of becoming epidemics or pandemics, and have been in the news frequently. Discuss these diseases with students including what might be needed for global precautions and preparations. Look for other viruses that are emerging and causing problems in your region.
- Present the organisms in this chapter not only in terms of evolutionary standing, but also in terms of the pathogenic capabilities.
- Show images of the different shapes of bacteria. Be sure to include some examples of species that will already be familiar to them.
- Most students are unfamiliar with the structure and function of the viruses and bacteria. Emphasize the nonliving nature of the viruses, a point that students often have trouble grasping. This may be a good time to review the requirements for a species to be considered as living. Look at each of these qualifications—which do viruses fail to meet?
- You may want to briefly review how taxonomists went from two kingdoms, to five kingdoms, to three domains.
- This chapter offers an excellent opportunity to discuss epidemiology and to show how scientists use the scientific method when attempting to find the causative agent of a disease. The widespread public awareness of AIDS also opens an avenue for discussion of the accuracy with which scientific stories are covered by the media.
- Use contemporary examples of bacteria. Use the recent bio-threat caused by anthrax, *E. coli* in the food supply, or an outbreak at a restaurant to demonstrate how epidemiologists might work to trace an outbreak.
- Discuss the role of the Center for Disease Control (CDC) in the control and eradication of diseases. What type of infections do the students feel warrant the most attention at the present time?

Classroom and Laboratory Enrichment

- Use the tip of a toothpick to collect bacteria from sources such as plaque from the surface of a tooth or yogurt with live cultures. Prepare a simple bacterial smear, stain with crystal violet, and observe at 1000x.
- Purchase a product known as "Glo Germ" that comes as a powder, gel, or oil. After the students apply the product to their hands, have them wash their hands as they normally would. Shine a UV light on their hands to draw attention to those areas that were not washed effectively enough to remove the presence of the "germ."
- Prepare Gram stains of bacterial species of varying morphology and from cultures obtained from biological supply houses.
- The *MythBusters* television show did an episode on "The Five-Second Rule." Get that episode and use it as a way to both discuss bacterial transfer, survival, and reproduction and practice the scientific method. Test the five-second rule to see how: different foods pick up bacteria at different rates, different areas have differing amounts of bacteria, and different colonies of bacteria grow at different rates. At the end of the experiment you will have data to analyze, and you will have many colonies of bacteria to use for further observation.
- Collect and examine cyanobacteria from stagnant ponds, tree trunks, and greenhouse flowerpots.
- Survey your environment for the presence of bacteria. This can be done with help from a microbiologist who can prepare media and plates. Then you and your students can: (a) take swabs of various surfaces in your institution—poll the students to think of areas to culture; (b) allow dust to settle on a plate; (c) allow insects to land; (d) apply samples of food; and so on.
- Remind students of the beneficial aspects of bacteria, including their usefulness in producing products through genetic engineering.
- Emphasize the importance of viruses and bacteria by showing a film or video of the misery these microscopic entities bring to humans and animals.
- Invite a microbiologist, physician, epidemiologist, and/or lab technician to you class to discuss how they interact with microorganisms.
- Discuss recent and fatal outbreaks of MRSA, antibiotic-resistant bacteria that affects populations of young people. What are the specific symptoms of a MRSA infection?
- Visit an electron microscope in a research laboratory where research on viruses is being done. Ask the technician to discuss preparation techniques for viral specimens and to demonstrate the operation of the microscope. If possible, allow students to prepare their own viral suspensions of a plant virus (such as tobacco mosaic virus) in the laboratory for subsequent examination under the electron microscope.
- Use overhead transparencies or videos to show the steps of a viral infectious cycle.
- Prepare an exhibit of living organisms or portions of organisms, such as leaves, affected by viruses.
- Gather information from local health authorities about any of the diseases caused by bacteria and viruses that are found in your area. Sexually transmitted diseases such as gonorrhea, syphilis, and AIDS would be good examples. What is the number of cases per month within your city or state? Is the number of new cases rising or falling?
- Create a matrix of common microorganisms. Have students work to fill in information about the different species including: type of microorganisms, pathogenicity, economic benefit and cost, how the organism is classified, and where the organism is likely to be found.
- Seek class members or faculty colleagues who may have traveled to a tropical area where diseases unknown in the United States are present. Ask them to report on any precautions taken before, during, and after their trip. Which inoculations were necessary?

- Invite someone from the local Board of Health or an epidemiologist from a nearby health facility to speak to the class. How do they identify an illness and track its origin? What steps are taken to stop the spread of disease?

Classroom Discussion Ideas

- How would you classify the viruses? Would you consider them to be nonliving? If the viruses are nonliving, why do you think they are covered in the study of biology?
- How does the human body respond to a sudden onslaught of viral invaders?
- Why do you think so many viruses are transmitted by infected birds?
- Why do antibiotics fail to work against viruses? Why are viruses so hard to target?
- If an attempt is made to treat viruses with antibiotics, what are the potential deleterious effects on the body?

Additional Ideas for Classroom Discussion

- In terms of pathogenicity, how can *E. coli* make us sick if it normally lives in our digestive system?
- Based on what you know about the life cycle of viruses, why are viruses used so frequently in genetic research or as a delivery vector in gene therapy?
- What might be the problem with letting genetically engineered viruses or bacteria into the environment?
- The smallpox virus has been nearly completely eradicated from the planet. The Center for Disease Control (CDC) still has small samples of the virus. Should we consider the smallpox virus an endangered species? Should the CDC destroy or maintain their viral culture of the smallpox virus? Why or why not?
- Normally, we would think of "autotrophic" as synonymous with "green" if we were considering members of the plant kingdom. What two sources of energy are available to *bacterial* autotrophs?
- What are different ways we could classify bacterial diversity?
- What are the differences in diagnosing and treating viral versus bacterial infections?
- Why are bacteria said to be "the most metabolically diverse" of all living groups? Why are organisms of such varied metabolism placed in the same group?
- Why are the methanogens, halophiles, and extreme thermophiles grouped as archaeans?
- What are viroids? How are they similar to and different from viruses?
- What is the role of disease in limiting the growth of human and animal populations? (Remember Malthus!)
- What is epidemiology? Discuss the roles played by the World Health Organization and the Centers for Disease Control and Prevention in the study and treatment of outbreaks of disease.
- What are the dangers of prescribing antibiotics to someone who does not have a bacterial infection?
- Why is it so important to take all the antibiotics your physician may prescribe for a bacterial infection, even if you start to feel better before you run out of pills?
- What could be the potential result of using antimicrobial soaps?
- What determines whether a species of bacteria is going to cause an illness?

- Recent evidence has emerged that demonstrates that not only are bacteria evolving resistance at an alarming rate, but some of the new resistant strains are actually using antibiotics for food. How could this scenario be possible?
- An antibacterial agent has been developed to add to the components of some children's toys. Does this sound like an effective measure?
- Discuss the disease tetanus. How is it transmitted? How is it prevented? Why is it a difficult disease to cure? Why do we not often hear of an individual that has the disease tetanus?

How Would You Vote? Classroom Discussion Ideas

- Monitor the voting for the online question. This question will definitely generate some good conversation. Show some video footage in class that demonstrates the AIDS epidemic in Africa in order to stimulate discussion on this topic.
- How would one live differently if they knew they were infected with the HIV virus? How would it alter their sexual practices? Would it influence their decision to have children?
- Would the results of this testing be confidential? What could be the repercussions of having others privy to your HIV status?
- Perhaps the ultimate question is: How would the government afford HIV tests for a large group of individuals? How could those with no health insurance afford the expensive regiment of medications to fight the HIV virus?

Term Paper Topics, Library Activities, and Special Projects

- The five-kingdom system of classification was proposed by Robert H. Whittaker in 1963. Locate the original article to see if his original version has changed much up to the present time.
- Are public swimming areas (pools, lakes, spring-fed ponds, and rivers) in your area required to routinely check for evidence of pollution from sewage effluent? Discover the maximum *E. coli* count allowed by law before the facility must be closed to public swimming. How is this figure determined? What does it mean? Why is it unsafe to swim in waters that have a relatively large number of *E. coli* bacteria?
- Detail the recent *E. coli* outbreaks that require recalls on beef, lettuce, green onions, spinach, and other foods in the United States. Have the authorities been able to trace these outbreaks back to a single farm or facility?
- Research some viral diseases that are not prevalent in the United States, such as the Ebola virus and Dengue fever. Why do these diseases normally occur outside of our country?
- Describe the safeguards the FDA has in place for our food supplies.
- Food radiation is a cheap and effective, yet controversial, way to reduce microbes in our food supply. Detail how the process works, and the benefits and drawbacks of radiation (ensure the use of quality references).
- Describe the role of certain species of bacteria in producing food products such as buttermilk, sour cream, yogurt, and sauerkraut.
- Describe the morphology and physiology of any one of the pathogenic genera of bacteria. Discuss the diseases caused by the members of the genus and their treatments.
- Where did viruses come from? Discover what scientists know about the evolutionary origin of the viruses. Who first discovered the presence of viruses and when?
- Research the swine flu scare in 1976. How did the government respond? Did the mass inoculations prevent a pandemic or simply serve as a waste of government funds?

- How are viruses destroyed? What kinds of chemicals and filters are used in the laboratory to ensure that an experimental liquid is virus-free?
- Research the history, mode of action, and treatment of several economically important viral diseases of crops.
- Discuss the role of the immune system in fighting viral outbreaks or bacterial infections. How does the immune system "recognize" viral strains or bacterial species that have caused disease within the individual on previous occasions?
- How are flu vaccines produced and why do they have varying effects from year to year? Why is there no vaccine developed to prevent the common cold?
- Collect stories about AIDS from magazines and newspapers. Analyze the stories for scientific accuracy and completeness. In what areas do such stories effectively cover AIDS? In what ways do they mislead or fail to inform the reader?
- Report on the latest scientific research in the treatment of any one of the diseases caused by viruses discussed in your text.
- It is known that flu epidemics (and pandemics) tend to occur in 10- to 40-year cycles. Check an epidemiology or medical textbook to locate possible explanations for this periodicity.
- How does a retrovirus differ from other viruses in its operation?
- Choose a disease caused by a microorganism described in this chapter and describe the following:
    1. Name of disease-causing organism. Use scientific name (*Genus species*) and common name.
    2. Name(s) of disease and symptoms. What organ system(s) does it primarily attack?
    3. Method of transmission and preventative measures. Is it contagious? Is there a vaccine? Is there a vector (an organism that transmits the disease)?
    4. Possible treatments for the disease.
    5. Anything else of interest about the disease. Does it primarily attack a certain group of people? Has it evolved or changed recently? Anything in the news about this disease lately?
- Research how scientists (virologists) study viruses. How can they perform experiments where they use replication of viruses?
- Recently researchers have discovered that childhood inoculations may not provide lifelong protection. For example, they have added a booster of pertussis to tetanus shots. How did this practice come about and why?
- Look into the polio epidemic in 1952. What symptoms result from infection with the polio virus? When was the vaccine developed? What steps are currently being taken to ensure that polio is eradicated worldwide?
- The scientist Edward Jenner noticed that milkmaids seldom developed smallpox. This was because they had previously been exposed to the related condition, cowpox. How did this discovery aid in Jenner's search for a vaccine?
- Have students prepare a poster or PowerPoint presentation contrasting the lytic and lysogenic pathways.

Possible Responses to *Critical Thinking* Questions

1. Plasmids can easily move from one bacterium to another during conjugation. During conjugation, the circular plasmid is broken by an enzyme. Now the thread-like plasma passes easily through the conjugation tube. After the conjugation process is complete and the cells are no longer connected, the plasmid once again becomes circular.

2. Non-enveloped viruses usually last longer outside of a host and can survive hand washing. This is most likely due to the adaptation that allows them to be non-enveloped. These viruses have adapted a different protein coat that would be resistant to environmental conditions that would destroy the contents of a protein coat. In enveloped viruses, their adaptation has rendered them helpless without the envelopment. If the host membrane dries up or becomes compromised it will affect the virus inside the membrane.
3. The crops that use nitrogen fixation via *Rhizobium* and those that use a commercial fertilizer both have access to available nitrogen. However, the use of fertilizers may cause water run-off to contain large amounts of nitrogen. This high concentration of nitrogen may cause eutrophication, which can severely limit the oxygen supply in bodies of water. This oxygen-poor environment can negatively impact the animal populations that reside there. Therefore, the use of *Rhizobium* bacteria is a more ecologically sound procedure.
4. The bacteria discovered far beneath the surface in Virginia would be classified as a chemoautotroph.

Possible Responses to *Data Analysis Exercise* Questions

Individuals' white blood cells contain HLA markers, which are used to identify self. The mutation HLA-B*52 allows HIV to go undetected in the infected individual.

1. The percentage of people with HLA-B*51 in Vancouver with HIV that has the escape mutation was 95 percent.
2. People with HLA-B*51 are more likely than those with other HLA types to have the virus with the mutation.
3. It appears as though the virus is adapting to host defenses.
4. In Japan overall, there is a fairly low prevalence of HIV infection, so the virus has not had as much opportunity to adapt to host defenses.

21

PROTISTS—THE SIMPLEST EUKARYOTES

Chapter Outline

Objectives

1. Describe the criteria to be classified as a protist.
2. Describe the origin of the various protistans.
3. Tell how protistans differ from bacteria.
4. Be able to compare protistans with other eukaryotes.
5. Distinguish the characteristics of each of the major protist groups, such as: flagellates, foraminiferans, radiolarians, ciliates, dinoflagellates, apicomplexans, stramenopiles, red algae, green algae, amoebozoans, and choanoflagellates.
6. Be able to discuss the positive and negative impacts of protists on other organisms.

Key Terms

protists
protozoa
primary endocytosis
secondary endocytosis
haploid
diploid
life cycle
alternation of generations
flagellated protozoans
trypanosomes
binary fission
parabasalids
diplomonads
hydrogenosome
cyst
kinetoplastid
euglenoids
pellicle
contractile vacuole
foraminifera
radiolarians
carbon cycle
plankton
ciliates
parasite
endosymbiont
micronucleus
macronucleus
conjugation
dinoflagellates
bioluminescence
algal blooms
red tide
Karenia brevis
neurotoxic shellfish poisoning
apicomplexans
alveolates
microtubule
malaria
sporozoites
merozoites
Plasmodium
gametocytes
artemisinin
vaccines
chrysophytes
golden algae
yellow-green algae
coccolithophores
diatoms
brown algae
Sargassum
kelps
stipes
blades
holdfasts
stramenopiles
oomycotes
water molds
downy mildews
white rusts
alginic acids
red algae
phycobilins
agar
carrageenan
green algae
Chlorophyta algae
Charophyta algae
Volvox
Chlamydomonas
Amoebozoans
amoebas
slime molds
fruiting body
pseudopod
plasmodial slime molds
cellular slime molds
plasmodium
cyclic-AMP

Lecture Outline

21.1 Malaria—From Tutankhamen to Today

A. Malaria is a leading cause of death worldwide, killing one child in Africa every 30 seconds.

1. Malaria is cause by *Plasmodium,* a single-celled protist that enters its host by means of mosquito bites.
   a. Individuals with one HbS gene have less risk of developing malaria.
   b. Mosquitoes infected with *plasmodium* are more apt to feed more often.
2. *Plasmodium* DNA has been found in the tomb of King Tutankhamen, so it appears to be over 3,500 years old.
3. *Plasmodium* concentrates in the liver and blood. Infection can lead to blindness, seizure, coma, and death.
4. Malaria has been controlled in the United States but remains a problem globally.

B. Although protists are sometimes considered simple eukaryotes, there is a vast diversity and complexity that can mark some of the different organisms in the protist kingdom.

21.2 The Many Protist Lineages

A. Classification and Phylogeny

1. Protists are eukaryotic organisms that are not fungi, plants, or animals.
2. There is no single trait that is unique to protists. They are a collection of lineages instead of a clade or monophyletic group.
3. Gene sequencing is elaborating group identities in the protist kingdom. Figure 22.2 displays the current groups including the lineages that lead to the plant, fungi, and animal kingdoms.

B. Cells, Colonies, and Multicellular Organisms
   1. Most protists are single-celled organisms.
   2. Some protists occur as colonies (many organisms living together, but capable of independent living).
   3. Other protists live as a multicellular organism where the cells may have individual specialized functions.

C. Autotrophs and Heterotrophs
   1. Some heterotrophic protists live in the soil and feed on decaying organic material or bacteria.
   2. Other heterotrophic protists live inside larger organisms as parasites or in some other form of symbiosis.
   3. Autotrophic protists have chloroplasts that developed through primary endocytosis (as described in Chapter 19) or secondary endocytosis.

D. Protists Life Cycles
   1. The protist life cycle is very diverse, as well.
   2. The haploid cell is the dominant form in many protists. Only the zygote is diploid (e.g., *Plasmodium*).
   3. Some protists demonstrate alternation of generations similar to plants between haploid and diploid states (e.g., algae).
   4. Finally, some protists are diploid as a dominant state (e.g., diatoms).
   5. Protists will reproduce asexually during times of favorable growth. Sexual reproduction occurs when conditions are less favorable.

21.3 Flagellated Protozoans

A. Group characteristics: single haploid cell, one or more flagella, heterotrophic, pellicle under the membrane, asexual reproduction (binary fission).

B. The Anaerobic Flagellates
   1. Diplomonads and parabasalids have multiple flagella and survive in low-oxygen water.
   2. Anaerobic flagellates lack mitochondria and produce ATP anaerobically with a hydrogenosome.
      a. Diplomonads include the infamous *Giardia lamblia,* which can enter the body in cyst form from drinking feces-contaminated water and result in severe diarrhea (giardiasis).
      b. A parabasalid called *Trichomonas vaginalis* can be transmitted during sexual intercourse and lead to damage of the urinary and reproductive tracts.

C. Trypanosomes and Other Kinetoplasts
   1. Kinetoplasts are flagellated protists with one flat mitochondrion. Some prey on bacteria in freshwater, but most are plant and animal parasites.
      a. *Trypanosoma brucei* is carried by the tsetse fly and causes African sleeping sickness.
      b. Chagas disease is caused by *T. cruzi,* a trypanosome carried by kissing bugs.

D. The Euglenoids
   1. Euglenoids are free-living, flagellated, photoautotrophic cells.
   2. They have the same chlorophyll as green algae and plants.
   3. An eyespot detects the sunlight necessary for photosynthetic activities.
   4. Contractile vacuoles collect excess water.

21.4 Foraminiferans and Radiolarians

A. Both of these protists are found in marine environments as part of the plankton. They are single-celled with an outer shell.

B. The Chalky-Shelled Foraminiferans
   1. Foraminiferans have a shell of calcium carbonate perforated by numerous holes through which the slender pseudopods extend.
   2. Foraminiferan shells have been accumulating since Cambrian times and lend clues through oxygen isotope ratios about past climate changes.
   3. Foraminiferans play a role in carbon cycling and balancing the acidity of the oceans.

C. The Glassy-Shelled Radiolarians
   1. Radiolarians have delicate, glasslike shells of silica through which stiffened, thin pseudopods extend.
   2. Their shells have two layers: the inner consists of organelles and the outer contains vacuoles filled with gas that act as floatation devices.

21.5 The Ciliates

A. Part of a monophyletic group called alveolates (ciliates, dinoflagellates, and apicomplexans). This group has alveoli sacs just under the cell membrane that may help stabilize the cell surface.

B. Ciliates are characterized by their numerous cilia that beat in synchrony on the cell surface; *Paramecium* is typical of the group.
   1. Other features include: a cell "mouth" for food entrance to waiting digestive vacuoles, contractile vacuoles to get rid of excess water, and trichocysts for defense.
   2. There are two types of nuclei: a small micronucleus and a larger macronucleus.
   3. Ciliates reproduce asexually by binary fission and may demonstrate a primitive form of sexual reproduction called conjugation in which genetic material is mutually exchanged.

21.6 Dinoflagellates

A. Dinoflagellates abound in fresh and marine habitats and are photoautotrophs or parasitic heterotrophs.

B. These marine cells display two flagella located in grooves of the cellulose covering.

C. Several dinoflagellates are bioluminescent and part of the ocean's plankton as major primary producers.

D. When population size increases dramatically it can cause algal blooms, leading to the infamous red tides, which can sicken and kill aquatic organisms from the metabolic wastes and oxygen depletion.

E. Some dinoflagellates produce a neurotoxin that causes neurotoxic shellfish poisoning when shellfish contaminated with the toxin of *K. brevis* are consumed.

F. Some dinoflagellates are bioluminescent, converting ATP energy into light energy.

21.7 The Cell-Dwelling Apicomplexans

A. Parasitic alveolates that must live part of the time inside specific cells of host species are called apicomplexans; they have a unique microtubular device to penetrate host cells.

B. Apicomplexans infect a variety of animals; their life cycle may involve multiple hosts.

C. Examples:
   1. Malaria, caused by *Plasmodium* and transmitted by mosquitoes, is a serious worldwide disease.
      a. The female *Anopheles* mosquito transmits the sporozoite to the human host during feeding.
      b. After multiplying first in the liver and then in the red blood cells, the merozoite stage breaks out into the bloodstream, causing terrific bouts of chills and fever.
      c. Malaria can be treated with drugs; vaccines are in development; and mosquito control is always an option.

2. Toxoplasmosis is caused by *Toxoplasma gondii.*
    a. Cysts can enter hosts through undercooked meat or contact with the feces of infected cats.
    b. *T. gondii* affects people who are immune compromised.

21.8 The Stramenopiles

A. This group is characterized by the presence of a flagellum that contains hair-like projections.
  1. Stramenopiles are autotrophs and contain chloroplasts that contain fucoxanthin, a brown pigment.
    a. The chloroplasts are thought to have evolved from a red alga by endosymbiosis.

B. Water Molds
  1. Oomycotes are important decomposers and nutrient recyclers in ecosystems.
  2. Oomycotes include water molds, downy mildews, and white rusts.
  3. Oomycotes have no chlorophyll and resemble fungi in their absorption of nutrients through filaments, but have cell walls of cellulose.
  4. *Phytophthora* is a major destroyer of crops and trees.

C. The Diatoms
  1. Diatoms have a silica "shell" composed of two perforated parts that overlap like a pillbox.
  2. Diatoms are single-celled or colonial, photosynthetic, and reproduce asexually and sexually.
  3. Diatom shells have a variety of commercial uses.

D. Brown Algae
  1. Brown algae are multicellular; they demonstrate an alternation of generation like plants, and range in size from microscopic filaments to large kelp 30 meters long.
  2. Brown algae include the large kelps of the intertidal zones and the *Sargassum* of the open ocean.
  3. Giant kelp beds are important ecosystems, supporting vast numbers of microorganisms, protists, and fishes along with other animals.

21.9 Red Algae

A. Red algae live in warm marine currents at great depths.
  1. Phycobilin pigments, perhaps from the endosymbiosis of cyanobacteria, can trap sunlight in deep marine waters.
  2. The modes of reproduction are diverse, with complex asexual and sexual phases, but the multicelled stages do not have tissues or organs.

B. Some forms can aid in reef building (stone-like cell walls); others yield agar; and carrageenan is used as a stabilizer in ice cream.

21.10 Green Algae

A. Green algae are photosynthetic (chlorophyll *a* and *b*), single and multicellular, store starch and deposit cellulose in a cell wall, and have chloroplasts that evolved by primary endocytosis.

B. This lineage evolved from cyanobacteria and is thought to be the sister group to land plants.

C. The Chlorophytes
  1. Single-celled algae that live in soil, on ice, or participate with fungi to form lichen.
  2. *Chlorella* and *Cladophora* was used to study photosynthesis.
  3. *Chlamydomonas* can reproduce sexually when conditions are not favorable.
  4. *Volvox* is a colonial Alga.
  5. Some green algae are more commonly called seaweed.

D. The Charophyte Algae

1. Many botanists consider land plants and charophyte algae to be a clade.
2. Most charophytes, like *Spirogyra*, live in freshwater. They range in size from single-celled species to filamental and multicelled disc shapes.

21.11 Amoebozoans and Choanoflagellates

A. Amoebozoans

1. Amoebas and slime molds are placed together in the group Amoebazoa.
2. Amoeboid protozoans have no permanent locomotor structures but form extensions of the cytoplasm and cell membrane in the form of pseudopods.
   a. Naked amoebas resemble tiny "blobs," as their plasma membranes constantly change the shape of the cell.
   b. *Entamoebas* live in the human intestine where they can cause a severe form of dysentery.
3. Slime molds are important in nutrient recycling and are common in leaf litter and soils of forests.
   a. They are heterotrophic, free-living, amoeba-like protistans.
   b. Plasmodial slime molds appear as a large multinucleate mass, creeping along the ground, engulfing food particles; at times they will produce spore-bearing fruiting bodies.
   c. Cellular slime molds spend most of their lives as an amoeboid mass, feeding and reproducing asexually; at times a stalk will arise from the mass to release spores.

21.12 Malaria: From Tutankhamen to Today

A. When female mosquitoes bite a human, they inject an anticoagulant called apyrase into the skin.
   1. Mosquitoes infected with *Plasmodium* have apyrase that is less effective.
      a. This forces infected mosquitoes to feed more often, which spreads the disease to more individuals.

B. *Toxoplasma gondii* reproduces asexually in rats.
   1. When the organism enters a cat, it can complete its life cycle.
      a. Infected rats prefer to reside in locations that are cat-scented.

Suggestions for Presenting the Material

- Because the protist lineage is not as clear cut as some other evolutionary groups, it is important to assure the students that water molds do, in fact, resemble fungi, and brown algae do have plant-like parts. Rather than dwelling on the imprecision of this situation, use it to emphasize the continuum of evolution.
- The text indicates the very uncertain nature of protistan classification today, but hints at solutions in the future based on molecular and genetic comparisons; emphasize that the "kingdom" Protista of old is probably on the way out, with all the various groups perhaps being considered as candidates for separate kingdoms.
- Try and use a historical perspective; present some older versions of protist classification schemes.
- Before presenting any of the phylogeny, present the students with several prime examples of protist species; try to have the students develop a classification scheme based on observable characteristics and given information about reproduction, size, or other characteristics that would help them start to identify the relationships.

- It is very difficult for students to get a sense of the relative size and shape of protists unless the instructor makes liberal use of photos, especially ones that give some comparison to objects of known size.
- Read more details about how *plasmodium* DNA was discovered in the tomb of King Tut. Do scientists feel that malaria was most likely the cause of death?
- Diseases offer a great way to make connections between protists and their impact on humans or plants, but make sure to stress that not all protists are pathogenic.
- It is difficult to discuss slime molds without having pictures, videos, or, even better, an actual slime mold present. These are not organisms most students are aware of and having visual aids helps.
- Figure 21.2 demonstrates current protist phylogeny that also includes suspected lineages for animals, plants, and fungi. Point out these lineages and ask students to describe why those lineages make sense (aside from genetic studies).

Classroom and Laboratory Enrichment

- Read a more expanded account of the Great Irish Potato Famine.
- Obtain samples of water from decorative fountains, flower pots, small ponds, and the like, and examine them for protistans.
- Kits for growing slime molds are available from biological supply houses.
- A great free website with spectacular microscopic images of protists (and other microorganisms) is http://www.mbl.edu/baypaul/microscope/general. It has been developed by the Astrobiology Institute at the Woods Hole Marine Biological Laboratories.
- The traditional lab exercise is to have some stock common protists (paramecium, euglena, amoeba, volvox, spirogyra, and red, green, and brown algae, for example) and observe them and detail their traits. Turn that into more of an investigation. Give students sets of characteristics and let them observe the specimens and try to match up the species they are observing with one the protist groups.
- Have the students use or create a dichotomous key or cladogram given several protists.
- Look for slime molds on moist logs and fallen trees in damp forest areas.
- Collect diatoms from the edges of quiet ponds and slow-moving streams.
- Gather information from local health authorities about any of the diseases caused by protists that are found in your area. Use this information to create a comparative analysis of the health costs of protists versus bacteria or viruses as pathogens.
- Work with students to create a comparative analysis of prokaryotes versus some common single-celled protists.
- Create a comparative analysis of plants, animals, and fungi to their protist lineages. This may be hard to do if you have not covered plants, animals, or fungi. Perhaps this would be a good starting point for creating these comparisons in order to keep those other kingdoms in an evolutionary framework.
- Many protists are highly mobile creatures and are amazing to watch. If you have a small class, secure some cultures and allow students to make their own preparations for microscopic observation. If your class is large, use a videotape (several biological supply houses offer these).
- Seek class members or faculty colleagues who may have traveled to a tropical area where diseases caused by parasitic protists unknown in the United States are present (even common!). Ask them to report on any precautions taken before, during, and after their trip.

- Revisit your discussion of sickle-cell anemia and the heterozygote advantage that carriers for this trait have in Africa and other areas prone to malaria. Include pictures of the sporozoan within the blood cells, if you can find some, as you are talking about the malaria parasite's life cycle. This is a good place to tie together concepts in an interesting fashion. Most students are interested in diseases they have little contact with.
- Show actual photos of the plasmodium organism inside red blood cells. Some Americans who have traveled to locations prone to malarial infections have developed the disease, including some soldiers that served in Vietnam.
- Make a chart and categorize protists into three categories. Are they more similar to plants, animals, or fungi? Can you see why the protists were previously placed in those three categories?
- Label a map with areas of the world where diseases such as malaria and sleeping sickness are common. How would you imagine these boundaries would change if global warming continues?
- Prepare a Jeopardy-type quiz for your students using the template found at http://jeopardylabs.com/
- Show pictures (not always for the weak stomached!) of various pathologies of individuals with parasitic protistan infections—again students become quite interested when seeing extreme cases and wish to learn more about the organism causing the disease and how to prevent it.
- Locate satellite photographs of the most recent red tide to show and discuss the consequences of such an algal bloom in the specific regions it occurs.
- Create a matrix that details the diversity of the protist kingdom. Compare the different groups based on physical, metabolic, reproductive, and evolutionary differences, but also include comparisons that take into account both the economic cost (think parasites and pathogens) and economic benefits that each group contributes.

Classroom Discussion Ideas

- What might happen if a natural disaster such as the Irish Potato Famine occurred today? What international conditions and attitudes have changed since that tragic event?
- What would be the consequences if protistans became obsolete?
- What causes red tides?
- What is the meaning of the root word of the organism volvox? How does this root word relate to the Volvo car company?
- Which of the types of algae are utilized as food sources for humans? What type of nutrients do they provide?
- Foraminiferans are important to the carbon cycle. Human impacts are changing that carbon balance by releasing more CO_2 into the atmosphere. What are some of the long-term effects of releasing more CO_2 into the atmosphere, both in general and in terms of the carbon cycle as it relates to the foraminiferans?

Additional Ideas for Classroom Discussion

- What are some of the key differences between prokaryotes and protists?
- What makes the water in a decorative fountain turn green?
- Why is it beneficial that some groups of protists have adapted to reproduce sexually only under conditions that are nutritionally poor?

- Algae occur in tremendous quantities in nature. To what extent have they been used for human or animal food? Are there any "algae farms"?
- Green algae are being touted as a potential solution in the field of biofuel and for lowering carbon emissions. What makes green algae such a versatile option in these areas?
- Why does the protist kingdom represent such a great diversity of traits compared to kingdoms that evolved from this group?
- Of what ecological value are the water molds and slime molds?
- What are some steps that tropical countries can take to reduce the rate of malaria? How effective is the addition of mosquito netting to reduce the incidence of malaria? Are prophylactic drugs readily available in countries where malaria is prevalent?
- Why did the effort to eradicate malaria fail? Which of Darwin's ideas was ignored in the eradication proposal?
- How is amoebic dysentery transmitted to humans?
- Why do sporozoans have such complicated life cycles? Does this complexity improve or hinder their survival chances?
- What features make *Euglena* seem like a "hybrid" of plant and animal?
- Why are chytrids and water molds more properly considered protists rather than fungi?
- Why are the red, brown, and green algae more properly considered protists rather than plants?
- What research is currently being done with the cellular slime mold *Dictyostelium*?
- What are some of the benefits of protists that humans have come to rely on? What are some of the economic and ecological effects of protists?
- Have one of the students prepare a poster highlighting the life cycle of *plasmodium*.

How Would You Vote? Classroom Discussion Ideas

- Monitor the voting for the online question. Try to strike a balance between being able to intervene to help a public health crisis like malaria and the overall effects of releasing DDT into the environment. Use the vote to create a discussion about the effect DDT may have as a selection agent.
- Research the ecological damage that resulted from previous DDT usage. Does the risk of damage to the environment seem like a reasonable trade-off?
- Do you think other methods, such as extensive use of mosquito netting in homes, would provide a better option?
- How effective are preventative medications in the fight against malaria? What is the expense? Are they readily available worldwide? Are there any dangerous side effects from the use of these medications?

Term Paper Topics, Library Activities, and Special Projects

- Investigate the nutritional value of kelp.
- Describe why genetic analysis is providing better information about relationships in the protist kingdom than other tactics have.
- Prepare a report on the Irish Potato Famine.
- Diagram the complete life cycle of *Plasmodium.*

- Chronicle the rise and fall of the campaign to eradicate malaria.
- Choose one disease caused by protists. What are the symptoms, treatments, and preventive measures that could be taken?
- What is chert? Which protist is responsible for its formation?
- Which protist's remains turn into limestone?
- Choose one protist and prepare an intricate drawing of its components. Be sure to mention factors such as its habitat, lifestyle, and mode of reproduction.
- Prepare a pamphlet that discusses the risk of toxoplasmosis from handling cat litter. Which populations should be the most concerned? What are the symptoms and deleterious effects of the disease? Can it be effectively treated?
- Compare the extent and severity of problems caused by viruses, bacteria, and protists.
- Survey the differences between the signs and symptoms you would find between viruses, bacteria, and protist pathogens. What signs and symptoms would be the same? What signs and symptoms would be different?
- Protists and prokaryotes can both act as pathogens. Describe the differences in how each of these groups actually acts to cause disease.
- Discuss the geographic distribution and economic impact of "red tides" in the United States.
- Write a report on any one of the diseases caused by protozoans. Discuss the historical roles played by these diseases in situations such as the colonization of new lands, wars, and the building of the Panama Canal.
- Prepare an analysis of why the chytrids and water molds are more properly considered protists rather than fungi.
- Research red tides—why are they dangerous to humans and other animals? Does this relate appropriately to the adage, "Never eat oysters in a month with no R in it"?
- Historically, the multicelled algae (red, brown, and green) were considered plants. Enumerate the reasons they are more properly considered protistans.
- Green algae may have a large impact in both the production of biofuel and in the reduction of CO_2 emissions from the burning of fossil fuels. Describe how these processes might work and detail the current state of research in these areas. How realistic is algae as a source of emission control and as a potential biofuel?

Possible Responses to *Critical Thinking* Questions

1. Certainly drinking the well or tap water from the local businesses or residences would not be safe in an underdeveloped country where sanitation is poor. Wherever we might be staying, we would need to avoid drinking water in restaurants or any iced drinks because our bodies would not be acclimated to the resident faunal microbes that the people native to the region would be used to. The only safe water to drink would be bottled water and water that has been boiled or purified. Raw fruits or vegetables would not be safe either, however tantalizing they may seem. If you must eat them, boil them before attempting to eat them, or better yet, do not order them in restaurants or buy them from open markets. Also avoid eating any lettuce or other greens at all to ensure your safety.
2. The protists that would be most likely to leave their imprint on the fossil record would be those with hard portions that would withstand fossilization. Diatoms, with their exterior shells, would be ideal for this process. Many other protists, such as amoebas, would be unsuitable for fossil formation. In addition, some foraminiferan shells have been viewed as fossil remains.

3. One of the main components of the diatom shell is silica. Diatom reproduction is an asexual process. One descendent cell gets half of the original diatom shell, but it must manufacture the other half of the shell. Without a sufficient supply of silica, this process would not be able to occur.
4. Recently there has been a lot of interest in the potential connection between toxoplasmosis infections and the risk of developing schizophrenia. At the present time, no definitive conclusions regarding this connection have been made. Researchers must be careful not to jump to conclusions too rapidly. Perhaps the symptoms of an extreme toxoplasmosis infection just mimic schizophrenia, but are actually caused by different agents. Also, one must keep in mind that individuals with a predisposition for schizophrenia may become infected with the *Toxoplasma gondii* organism more readily than the rest of the population. It is evident that more studies must be performed before concrete assumptions are made.

Possible Responses to *Data Analysis Exercise* Questions

Scientists wondered if individuals that were already infected with Plasmodium gametocytes were more attractive to mosquitoes.

1. Children with gametocytes were more attractive to mosquitoes in this study.
2. Both uninfected children and children infected with the asexual stage were the least attractive to mosquitoes.
3. The percentage of the total number of mosquitoes that were attracted to children with gametocytes was 10 percent.
4. This data appears to support Dr. Koella's hypothesis.

22

THE LAND PLANTS

Chapter Outline

Objectives

1. Outline the evolutionary advances that converted marine algal ancestors into plants that could live on land.
2. State the advances that converted primitive marsh plants into dry-land flowering plants.
3. Use a diagram to illustrate the evolutionary trends in plants with specific reference to sporophyte and gametophyte dominance.
4. Characterize the mosses, seedless vascular plants, gymnosperms, and angiosperms.
5. Discuss why the angiosperms are the most successful of all plants.
6. Understand the ecological effects of widespread deforestation.

Key Terms

charophytes
rhyniophytes
plants
embryophytes
root systems
shoot systems
lignin
vascular tissue
xylem
phloem
cuticle
stomata
gametophyte
sporophyte
spores
vascular plants
nonvascular
seedless
seed-bearing
homosporous
heterosporous
megaspores
microspores
pollen grains
seed plants
bryophytes
mosses
liverworts
hornworts
rhizoids
sporangium
gametangium
peat bogs
whisk ferns
rhizomes
lycophytes
club mosses
strobilus
horsetails
sphenophytes
ferns
frond
epiphytes
sorus, sori
coal
pollen sacs
microspores
pollination
megaspores
ovules
gymnosperms
conifers
cones
evergreen
deciduous
cycads
ginkgos
gnetophytes
angiosperms
flower
stamen
carpel
ovary
double fertilization
coevolution
pollinators
cotyledons
monocots
magnoliids
eudicots
endosperm
fruits
deforestation
shifting cultivation

Lecture Outline

22.1 Speaking for the Trees

A. Forests are an important ecological resource.
   1. Trees produce valuable organic compounds.
   2. Trees are an important supplier of oxygen and also remove carbon dioxide.
   3. Trees prevent erosion by holding soil in place.

B. Deforestation is an important ecological issue.
   1. British Columbia is one area that has been heavily deforested.

C. Wangari Maathai developed the Green Belt Movement, a plan to replace trees in Kenya.
   1. She distributed trees to women to plant and continue to nurture.
   2. Her organization was responsible for planting 40 million trees in Africa.

22.2 Plant Ancestry and Diversity

A. From Algal Ancestors to Embryophytes
   1. Plants share common characteristics: multicellularity, cellulose cell walls, and chloroplasts with chlorophyll *a* and *b*, and they store sugars as starch.
      a. Plants most resemble green algae.
   2. Land plants have embryophytes (an embryo that develops within the parent plant).

B. An Adaptive Radiation on Land
   1. Approximately 500 million years ago, the first plants arrived.
      a. By this time, enough oxygen had been produced by photosynthesis in the ocean to form the ozone layer, which was necessary to shield the plants from powerful UV radiation.
      b. The earliest plant fossils date back to 475 million years ago and most closely resemble bryophytes (mosses, liverworts, and hornworts).
   2. Plants have a life cycle that alternates between a diploid sporophyte and a haploid gametophyte.

3. Vascular plants (those that contain tubes for transportation of water and nutrients) arrived approximately 430 million years ago.
4. Seed plants were the first pollen producers and arrived approximately 385 years ago.
   a. Gymnosperms (conifers) were the earliest seed plants.
   b. Angiosperms (flowering plants) arrived last, around the late Jurassic or early Cretaceous period.

22.3 Evolutionary Trends Among Plants

A. From Haploid to Diploid Dominance
1. The life cycle of simple aquatic plants is dominated by the haploid *gametophyte* phase.
   a. Gametes of some green algae are all motile and of the same size; others are differentiated into motile sperm and immotile eggs.
   b. A watery environment was necessary for gametes to meet each other.
2. The life cycle of complex land plants is dominated by the large, diploid *sporophyte.*
   a. Cells within the sporophyte undergo meiosis to give rise to the haploid spores.
   b. The spore develops into the *gametophyte,* which produces the gametes.
3. Over time, the sporophytes, while developing extensive root and shoot systems, began holding onto their spores and gametophytes—protecting and nourishing them.

B. Structural Adaptations
1. Aboveground parts of plants became covered by a cuticle, and stomata became control points for controlling water balance.
2. Underground parts of plants developed into root systems, specialized for absorption of water and minerals through extensive cylindrical tubes.
3. Vascular tissue became increasingly extensive: xylem for conducting water and minerals, phloem for products of photosynthesis.
4. Extensive growth of stems and branches became possible due to the strengthening of cell walls afforded by deposits of lignin.

C. Pollen and Seeds
1. Bryophytes and some vascular plants reproduce by releasing spores.
2. Seed-bearing vascular plants produce seeds and pollen.
   a. The male gametophytes—pollen grains—are released from the parent plant to be carried by whatever means to the female gametophyte.
   b. Seeds are immature sporophytes with a waterproof covering. Many seeds are adapted with a means of dispersal.

22.4 Bryophytes

A. Bryophytes include the mosses, liverworts, and hornworts and contain no true vascular systems that are reinforced with lignin.

B. Mosses
1. Eggs and sperm develop in the *gametangia* at the shoot tips of the familiar moss plants.
2. After fertilization, the zygote develops into a mature sporophyte, which consists of a *sporangium* in which the spores develop.
3. Compressed layers of dead mosses form peat bogs.

C. Liverworts
1. Liverworts, like *Marchantia,* have root-like rhizoids that attach to the ground and can reproduce asexually or sexually.

D. Hornworts
1. Hornworts have a pointy sporophyte that can survive after the gametophyte dies.

22.5 Seedless Vascular Plants

A. Most of the seedless vascular plants that flourished in the past are extinct.
   1. Their present-day descendants (lycophytes, horsetails, and ferns) differ from bryophytes with respect to the sporophytes, which:
      a. Develop independently of the gametophytes.
      b. Have well-developed vascular tissues.
      c. Are the larger, longer-lived phase of the life cycle.
   2. Although the sporophytes of seedless vascular plants can live on land, their gametophytes cannot because they lack vascular tissues, and the male gametes must have water to reach the eggs.

B. Club Mosses
   1. Lycophytes (club mosses) were once tree-sized, but now are represented by small club mosses on the forest floor.
      a. The sporophyte has true roots, stems, and small leaves containing the vascular tissue.
      b. Strobili bear spores that germinate to form small, free-living gametophytes.
   2. This group is still closely tied to an aquatic environment because the sperm must swim to the eggs.

C. Whisk Ferns and Horsetails
   1. Whisk ferns are not true ferns, but they are shaped like whisk brooms with tiny reduced leaves.
   2. The sporophytes of whisk ferns have rhizomes that are short, branched, horizontal underground stems.
   3. The ancient relatives of horsetails were treelike; only the moderately sized *Equisetum* has survived; the plants are called sphenophytes and include scouring rushes.
      a. The sporophytes possess underground stems called rhizomes.
      b. The scalelike leaves are arranged in whorls around the hollow, photosynthetic stem.
   4. Spores are produced inside cone-shaped clusters of leaves at the shoot tip, called strobili.

D. Ferns
   1. Ferns are the largest, most diverse group of seedless vascular plants; they are mostly native to the tropics and are highly diverse in size.
   2. Ferns bear underground stems (rhizomes) and aerial leaves (fronds).
   3. Sori are clusters of sporangia that release spores that develop into small heart-shaped gametophytes.
   4. Some species of fern live as epiphytes, aerial plants growing attached to tree branches or trunks.

22.6 History of the Vascular Plants

A. From Tiny Branches of Coal Forests
   1. Vast forests of lycophyte trees and horsetail plants existed in the Carboniferous.
      a. As the sea levels rose and fell, forest trees were submerged in sediments protected from decomposers.
      b. First peat was formed, but increased pressure and heat produced coal.
   2. It has taken a remarkably short time for human technology to extract coal, one of the nonrenewable fossil fuels, from the ground.

B. Rise of the Seed Plants
   1. The most successful of the vascular plants are the seed-bearing species, which have escaped dependency on water for fertilization, relying instead on air currents and insects.

2. Seed ferns, gymnosperms, and angiosperms are the three main groups and differ from the seedless vascular plants in three ways.
   a. They produce microspores, which develop into pollen grains that carry the sperm to the female structures to accomplish pollination.
   b. They also produce megaspores, which develop into ovules and, at maturity, produce seeds; each seed is a mature ovule consisting of the embryo sporophyte (egg cell plus sperm) plus seed coats.
   c. Compared to seedless vascular plants, these plants have thicker cuticles, stomata recessed below the surface of the leaf, and other competitive traits.
   d. Some plants with seeds undergo secondary growth as wood.

22.7 Gymnosperms

A. Gymnosperms are vascular seed-bearing plants with a naked seed coat (no fruit around the seed).

B. Conifers

1. Seeds develop in a female cone while male cones develop pollen.
   a. Most are evergreens with needle- or scale-like leaves that have thick cuticles.
   b. They make up the most abundant (pines), tallest (redwoods), and oldest (bristlecone pine) trees.

C. Lesser-Known Lineages

1. Cycads are palm-like trees that flourished during the Mesozoic era.
   a. Only about 130 species still exist—confined to the tropics and subtropics.
   b. They bear massive cone-shaped strobili that produce either pollen (transferred by air currents or insects) or ovules.
2. Ginkgos have been reduced in diversity from the Mesozoic to only one surviving species today.
   a. They are unusual in being deciduous.
   b. They are remarkably hardy, showing resistance to insects, disease, and air pollutants.
3. Gnetophytes are the most unusual gymnosperms; they live in tropical and desert areas.

D. A Representative Life Cycle

1. The pine tree (sporophyte) produces two kinds of cones.
   a. Male cones produce sporangia that yield microspores that develop into pollen grains (male gametophyte).
   b. Female cones produce ovules that yield megaspores (female gametophyte).
2. Pollination is the arrival of a pollen grain on the female reproductive parts, after which a pollen tube grows toward the egg.
3. Fertilization, which is delayed for up to a year, results in a zygote that develops into an embryo within the conifer seed.

22.8 Angiosperms—The Flowering Plants

A. Angiosperms are vascular seed plants that make flowers and fruits. After fertilization, the ovule becomes the seed and the ovary becomes the fruit.

B. Angiosperms produce flowers and fruits

1 The male components of the flower are the stamens, which contain pollen.
2. The female components of the flower are the carpal with an ovary at its base.
3. The ovary eventually becomes the fruits.

C. The Angiosperm Life Cycle

1. The female gametophyte forms the ovary.
2. Pollen forms inside stamens.

3. Pollination leads to double fertilization: one sperm fertilizes the egg, the second sperm fertilizes a cell that becomes the endosperm.
4. Ovary tissue develops into the fruit that covers the seed.

D. Factors Contributing to Angiosperm Success
1. Accelerated Life Cycle
a. Most angiosperms develop rapidly and produce seeds quicker than gymnosperms.
2. Animal-Pollinated Flowers
b. The development of the flower leads to the attraction of insects, birds, and other animals that helped reproduction occur rapidly; this led to a great deal of coevolution in flower development and pollinators.
3. Enhanced Seed Dispersal
a. When buffeted by severe environmental challenges, the flowering plants did well thanks to their protected seeds and help from pollinators.

22.9 Angiosperm Diversity and Importance
A. Angiosperm Lineages
1. Magnoliids include magnolias, avocados, nutmeg, and black pepper plants.
2. Eudicots include familiar shrubs, trees (except conifers), and herbaceous plants.
a. Eudicots have two seed leaves and a branched network of leaf veins.
3. Monocots include grasses, lilies, and the major food-crop grains.
a. Monocots have one seed leaf and parallel arrangement of leaf veins.

B. Ecological and Economic Importance
1. Angiosperms are abundant and contribute to both environmental stability and economic factors.
a. They provide food and shelter for many animals.
b. They serve as the basis for the human diet (through either direct or indirect means).
c. The Quinoa plant is not only high in protein content, but is a complete source of amino acids.
d. Plant fibers are often used as the raw material in the manufacturing of clothing.
e. Plant oils are used as detergents, skincare products, lubricants, and fuels.
f. Woody plants are used as a fuel source and also for building materials.
g. Some plants produce secondary metabolites. which can be used as legal or illegal medications.

22.10 Speaking for the Trees (Revisited)
A. Trees hold about one and one-half times the carbon on Earth as air does.
1. Actively growing tropical forests hold more carbon than forests in areas with a shorter growing season.
2. If forests are replaced by crops, the carbon-storing capacity goes way down.
3. Also if forests are burned, the carbon is released into the air.

Suggestions for Presenting the Material

- When students think of plants, almost all of the examples that come to mind will be angiosperms. Counter this tendency by asking for examples of plants that do *not* have flowers.
- Spend time discussing the alternation of generations. This is a difficult concept for students. Try to compare it to the life cycle of an animal.
- Give the students flash cards with pictures of a plant and other relevant traits. Have the students try and classify plants based on their characteristics.

- Review the evolutionary trend from gametophyte dominance to sporophyte dominance (Figure 22.5). If students still find this confusing, they will have trouble comparing one plant life cycle to another. Highlight evolutionary hallmarks such as development of vascular tissue, dominant sporophyte, heterospory, nonmotile gametes, and seeds that distinguish simple plants from those that are more complex.
- Create a matrix that you and the students fill out to help clarify the evolutionary relationships in the plant kingdom based on several main traits: dominant generation, vascular tissue, roots, leaves, dispersal, reproduction, and size.
- Because of their natural geographic locations, many of the plants mentioned in the earlier sections of this chapter are not familiar to students. Transparencies of representative species, even made from photos in the book, will help remove the abstract quality of a ginkgo or cycad. When you can, however, bringing an actual sample or leaf from the tree will spark more interest.
- Emphasize that even though this chapter deals with land plants, many are still reliant on water for reproductive purposes. Be sure to explain this in detail.
- Discuss the massive deforestation in British Columbia and other areas of the world. What is being done at the present time to reclaim a natural environment?

Classroom and Laboratory Enrichment

- Look at fossils of ancient lycophytes, horsetails, ferns, and gymnosperms. Discuss how changing climates influenced the geographic distributions and sizes of these plants.
- Prepare a small display of portions of bryophytes, lycophytes, horsetails, ferns, and gymnosperms from local areas where plant collection is allowed. Prepared slides and live materials ordered from biological supply houses can supplement your collection.
- Go to a location where all of the representatives of the plant kingdom can be observed. Have students keep a journal of where they find each different type of plant, and then have them make inferences about what the plant's location says about the plant's characteristics and requirements.
- Research an area with drastic weather conditions, like Mt. Washington in New Hampshire. What plants are durable enough to withstand the drastic conditions near the top of the mountain? What adaptations allow them to survive in this unfavorable environment?
- Collect reproductive structures of gymnosperms (use photos, drawings, or models to represent those taxonomic divisions for which structures are unavailable). Compare them to the reproductive structures of angiosperms (students can dissect flowers).
- Use models, photos, drawings, or overhead transparencies to discuss the life cycle of pine (a good representative gymnosperm because it is familiar to students). Compare it to the life cycle of a typical angiosperm.
- Obtain different types of fruits (fleshy fruits, winged fruits, stick-tights, woody fruits, nuts, legumes, etc.). Have students study the seeds (potentially with a dichotomous key). Have the students try to describe how that fruit adaptation would have helped to increase the plants long-term survival.
- The chapter mentions coevolution of flowers and pollinators. Have the students study different pollination syndromes. Have them describe what a flower would have to look like to attract a certain type of pollinator. Show some photos of what common flowers would look like through the eyes of common pollinators. Often there is a pattern that is not evident to the human eye.
- Obtain a set of slides that will provide a survey of the plant world, including algae. Observe some of the components of plants microscopically, such as pollen grains and xylem.

- Which type of cone is most familiar to your students—the male or female one? Why?
- Choose a particular secondary metabolite. How does it serve as an adaption for that plant? How do humans use or abuse it?
- Redraw several of the lifecycle figures in this chapter, but omit several key labels. Photocopy these and distribute as a labeling exercise.
- Bring in representative leaves of a monocot (e.g., corn) and a eudicot (e.g., maple leaf). The different vein patterns will be evident to the students.

Classroom Discussion Ideas

- What happened to the treelike lycopods and horsetails that were dominant during the Carboniferous period? How did the Carboniferous period get its name?
- What features had to evolve in plants to enable survival on land?
- What adaptations were required for plants to come onto land?
- What adaptations led to the dominance of early vascular plants like ferns? What were key adaptations that led to gymnosperm and then angiosperm domination?
- Describe the life cycle of an unlabeled mystery plant. Are the students able to figure out a plant that reproduces via this method?

Additional Ideas for Classroom Discussion

- What are the only land plants with a dominant, independent gametophyte and a dependent sporophyte?
- What are some of the important adaptations that helped plants survive on land and why were they important?
- Why is pollen an important adaptation to living on land?
- How does the shape of a flower influence its potential pollinators?
- How is honeybee colony collapse syndrome impeding the pollination of some plants?
- Some monks consider ginkgo trees to have a religious significance. How has this helped the species survive? Why do we often find ginkgo trees in intercity habitats?
- What is the role of guard cells in the opening and closing of stomata?
- How are the "leaves" of conifers different that the leaves of deciduous trees? How do these differences help the conifers adapt to their environment?
- What major structural difference separates the bryophytes from the ferns?
- What are some differences and similarities between a pine cone and a fruit?
- Why is a gymnosperm considered to have a naked seed?
- Which type of pollination is more efficient—wind pollination, as seen among conifers, or insect pollination, as seen among some of the angiosperms?
- Discuss the various kinds of coevolutionary adaptations seen among plants and their pollinators.
- What adaptive advantage(s) might gymnosperms have had over the other plants living at that time?
- What are several factors that have led to the dominance of angiosperms?

How Would You Vote? Classroom Discussion Ideas

- Monitor the voting for the online question. Certainly it would be environmentally wise to refurbish tropical forests, but there are some definite obstacles to overcome in such a project. First of all, I doubt that American voters would care to fund such a project. Secondly, the governments of the land that was reforested would have to guarantee that deforestation would not be allowed in those areas. If it were not properly monitored, we would simply be supplying a new area for deforestation and monetary gain.

Term Paper Topics, Library Activities, and Special Projects

- Prepare a list of the vascular plant flora on your campus or some other local area.
- Find vegetation maps showing the worldwide distribution of major vegetation associations of gymnosperms and angiosperms (for example, grasslands, temperate forests, coniferous forests, and so on).
- Investigate the extent of removal of trees and small plants in your vicinity that has occurred in the past few years in preparation for commercial property development.
- Examine and document the relationship between plants and either protist, bacterial, or viral pathogens in your region. Have there even been any outbreaks in your area? What are the lasting effects?
- Assess the balance between producing healthy, oxygen-yielding lawn plants and the fertilizers and pesticides used to keep them that way.
- Read about the "balanced terrarium" concept. Set up one and attempt to prove if the theory is workable. Do some experimentation with your small ecosystem terrarium. Can you see changes that benefit the ecology of your small biome? Which factors are helpful?
- Evaluate the effects of possible global warming on the world's grain-producing regions. Will all areas be affected negatively? Will some be affected positively?
- Estimate the number of acres of land that is not available for food production because it is part of the right-of-way of the U.S. interstate highway system.
- Describe the example of coevolution as it pertains to pollination syndromes. Give some examples of how these adaptations would occur.
- What are some of the economic impacts of plants on human daily life? In what ways are humans affecting the plant kingdom in a negative manner that could have big impacts on ecosystems and on humans?
- Have each student in the class choose a plant species out of a hat. Have them develop a poster that lists the important characteristics, geographic constraints, and life cycle of their particular species. In addition, make sure each student can place their plant in one of the main categories studied in this chapter.
- Prepare a Jeopardy-type quiz (http://jeopardylabs.com/) using this premade format. Use the main categories of plants as the topics for the questions.
- Research the life of Wangari Maathai of Kenya. Her plan for reforestation was quite simple, yet very effective. Why do you think her plans were successful?

Possible Responses to *Critical Thinking* Questions

1. The note would have to indicate that there is no pollen source in fern species. Instead, the spores that develop from the "seeds" underneath the fronds develop into the gametophyte generation.

When this gametophyte is formed it has two distinct regions where eggs and sperm are produced. The addition of water allows the sperm to swim to the eggs, and fertilization can occur. In this case, there are no true seeds and the sperm are flagellated, unlike pollen that you would find in gymnosperms and angiosperms.

2. The diploid stage may be more advantageous to genetic diversity. This can be seen in the example of a slightly disadvantageous mutation of a recessive allele that becomes advantageous in the future. Because the allele is disadvantageous, it would be selected against in the population. However, because the allele is recessive, it is only expressed when paired with another recessive allele. If paired with a dominant allele, the recessive allele will have no effect. Because some of the recessive alleles will end up in heterozygous plants, the recessive alleles will remain in the population until a time when they might become more advantageous.
3. Pollen in angiosperms travels via several methods. One important mode of pollen transportation is by the action of specific pollinators. The flowers of angiosperms attract pollinators by looking and smelling attractive. Certain specific signals tend to attract pollinators of the same species, so pollen from the flower of one species is apt to travel to another flower of the same species. This allows for little wasted pollen. Also, some seeds travel through the digestive system of birds or animals, so that the seed coat is broken down and deposited with its own fertilizer. The major method of pollen dispersal for conifers, such as the pine tree, is wind. This method is highly inefficient, because much of the pollen does not contact another tree of the same species.
4. Since bryophytes such as mosses absorb most of their water from the air, they also have the secondary effect of obtaining harmful gases from the air. Gaseous pollutants such as sulfur dioxide easily dissolve in water. Because of this unique characteristic of mosses obtaining water (along with dissolved pollutants) directly from the air, scientists often examine mosses for deleterious signs of air pollution.
5. Mosses do not have lignin to give them support and they do not have xylem to transport water. With no vascular system, there is no organized way to move water around the plant. A moss is somewhat like a sponge, since it just soaks up water from the air. Therefore, a moss cannot become large without a system of ductwork to transport water and nutrients around the plant. A tall plant would have an advantage, because it has easy access to sunlight. Lower plants have to absorb whatever sunlight passes through the upper canopy of trees.

Possible Responses to *Data Analysis Exercise* Questions

The United Nations Food and Agriculture Organization (UNFAO) is tracking the abundance of forests worldwide.

1. In 2000, there were 677 million hectares of forested land in North America.
2. Between 1990 and 2010, Asia, Europe, and North America all increased their amount of forested land.
3. The area that lost the most forested land between 1990 and 2000 was South America, and the area that lost the most forested land between 2000 and 2010 was Africa.
4. The tree-planting initiative in China appears to be successful since the amount of forested land is increasing.

23

FUNGI

Chapter Outline

HIGH-FLYING FUNGI
FUNGAL TRAITS AND CLASSIFICATION
- Structure and Function
- Life Cycles

THE FLAGELLATED FUNGI
ZYGOSPORE FUNGI AND RELATIVES
- Zygote Fungi
- Microsporidia—Intracellular Parasites
- Glomeromycetes—Partners of Plants

SAC FUNGI—ASCOMYCETES
- Life Cycle
- Human Uses of Sac Fungi

CLUB FUNGI—BASIDIOMYCETES
- Life Cycle
- Ecology and Diversity

FUNGAL PARTNERS AND PATHOGENS
- Fungal Partnerships
- Lichens
- Mycorrhizae
- Fungus-Farming Insects
- Fungal Pathogens
- Plant Pathogens
- Human Pathogens

HIGH-FLYING FUNGI (REVISITED)
SUMMARY
DATA ANALYSIS EXERCISE
SELF-QUIZ
CRITICAL THINKING

Objectives

1. Describe the various types of fungal body plans, patterns of reproduction, and natural history.
2. Discuss the economic impact of fungi on humans.
3. Describe the general characteristics and life style of fungi representatives from the following categories: chytrids, zygote fungi, sac fungi, and club fungi.
4. Provide two examples of symbiotic relationships with fungi and the specific role of each participant.

Key Terms

mutualism
lichen
fungi
saprobes
parasites
extracellular digestion and absorption
mycelium, mycelia
hypha, hyphae
spores
chytrids
mycosis
microsporidia
glomeromycetes
zygomycetes
sac fungi
budding
club fungi
zygomycosis
zygote fungi
zygospore
sporangium, sporangia
mushrooms
gills
basidiospores
dikaryotic
ascospores
asci
truffles
yeasts
decomposers
histoplasmosis
alkaloids
ergotism
symbiosis
endophytic fungi
photobiont
mycobiont
mycorrhiza -izae

Lecture Outline

23.1 High-Flying Fungi

A. Although not known for their mobility, fungi can travel great distances in the form of spores that travel on articles carried by wind.
   1. Increasing drought in Africa has increased dust particles in the air, which has increased the potential for fungal spores to be carried to the Caribbean.
   2. On days when the trans-Atlantic wind currents increase, cases of asthma increase.
   3. It is thought that increased fungal spores in the Caribbean have contributed to the loss of reef in the area.

B. Wheat stem rust, a fungus, caused great crop destruction until the 1960s.
   1. Norman Borlaug developed a breeding program to develop wheat that was resistant to the fungus.
   2. In 1999 a new strain of wheat rust (Ug^{99}) was discovered.
      a. This new strain of fungus is spreading worldwide.
      b. Scientists are working to develop a resistant strain of wheat.

23.2 Fungal Traits and Classification

A. Structure and Function
   1. Fungi are spore-producing heterotrophs with chitin cell walls that utilize organic matter.
      a. Most are saprobes; they get their nutrients from nonliving matter and cause its decay.
      b. Others are parasites; they thrive on tissues in living hosts.
      c. All fungi rely on extracellular enzymatic digestion and absorption.
      d. Fungi are valuable decomposers in all environments.
   2. Most fungi are multicellular.
   3. The food-absorbing part of the fungus is a mesh of branching filaments called the *mycelium.*
      a. Each tubular filament is a *hypha* with chitinous walls.
      b. Interconnections and perforations allow cytoplasmic flow necessary for transport to nonabsorptive parts of the body.

B. Life Cycles
   1. Like most protists, either a haploid or dikaryotic (two haploid nuclei in one cell) stage dominates the fungal life cycle.

2. Fungi disperse by means of spores.
    a. Asexual reproduction is mostly by spores produced in sporangia.
    b. Sexual reproduction proceeds through the formation of gametes in gametangia as well as by spores.

23.3 Flagellated Fungi

A. Chytrids are an ancient fungal lineage with flagellated spores.
   1. They have gametes that swim in water, wet soil, and exist in some animal digestive systems.

B. Most chytrids feed on organic wastes and remains, helping to recycle nutrients.
   1. Some aid herbivores in the digestion of cellulose.
   2. Some chytrids are pathogens.
      a. A parasitic chytrid is damaging frog populations worldwide.

23.4 Zygote Fungi and Related Groups

A. Zygote Fungi
   1. Zygomycetes form a zygospore during reproduction.
      a. They have haploid mycelium with no dikaryotic hyphae.
      b. Most are saprobes, some are parasites, and a few have mutual relationships with plant roots.
   2. In the zygomycetes group of fungi, sexual reproduction begins when two hyphae (different mating strains) grow toward each other and fuse.
      a. Gametangia form and make haploid nuclei, which later fuse to form a diploid zygospore.
      b. The zygospores later release haploid spores, which form in sacs at the tips of the hyphae.
   3. *Pilobolus* passes through an animal's digestive tract and, when deposited on feces, throws sporangium up to two meters.

B. Microsporidians—Intracellular Parasites
   1. Microsporidians are single-celled intracellular parasites of animals (e.g., fish, insects).
   2. Microsporidians cause honeybee colony collapse.
   3. A microsporidian spore has a long polar tube that it uses to connect with a host cell and inject the contents of the spore into the host.

C. Glomeromycetes—Partners of Plants
   1. Glomeromycetes and plant roots from a mycorrhiza.
   2. Their association with the plant-cell walls helps nutrients enter plant-cell roots.

23.5 Sac Fungi—Ascomycetes

A. Sac fungi form sexual spores called ascospores inside sac-shaped cells called asci, which are enclosed in reproductive structures of interwoven hyphae.
   1. Multicelled sac fungi include edible morels and truffles; most of the food-spoiling molds are also sac fungi.
   2. Single-celled yeasts are sac fungi.
   3. Septa in the ascomycete hyphae prevent damage by preventing the organism from drying out.

B. Life Cycle
   1. Some ascomycetes can reproduce asexually by the process of budding or by producing haploid spores called condidia.
   2. Sexual reproduction involves formation of spores inside a saclike cell (ascus).
      a. Sexual reproduction starts when two compatible hyphae meet and form a dikaryotic hyphae.

C. Human Uses of Sac Fungi

1. Humans use sac fungi for a variety of purposes.
    a. Food: truffles and morels.
    b. Fermentation: *Saccharomyces cerevisiae* helps bread rise and produces beer and wine, an *Aspergillus* makes soy sauce and citric acid for soda, and *Penicillium roquefortii* helps produce blue cheese.
    c. Medicine: *Penicillium chrysogenum* is used for antibiotics, an *Aspergillus* lowers cholesterol, and *Trichoderma* prevents organ rejection.
    d. Agriculture: a sac fungi species may help control roundworm populations in agricultural settings.

23.6 Club Fungi—Basidiomycetes

A. Life Cycle

1. In the club fungi, club-shaped sexual spores form on the gills of mushrooms, which are the spore-producing structures of this group.
2. The aboveground part of the fungal body is the common mushroom consisting of a stalk and a cap.
    a. Basidiospores are produced in club-shaped structures on the outer surface of the cap.
    b. When spores land on a suitable site, they germinate to produce extensive underground mycelia that then reproduce sexually, resulting in a dikaryotic stage.
3. Sexual reproduction is accomplished when two compatible mating strains make contact.
    a. Cytoplasmic fusion results in a dikaryotic mycelium.
    b. Eventually, the nuclei will fuse to form a zygote, which undergoes meiosis to form haploid spores dispersed by the wind.

B. Ecology and Diversity

1. Many club fungi are decomposers.
    a. They are among the only organisms that can break down the lignin in wood.
    b. Shelf fungi and the honey mushroom are common pathogens in forests.
    c. Jelly fungi feed on other fungi that destroy trees.
2. Chanterelles are oddly shaped, edible mushrooms.
3. Stinkhorns have an unpleasant odor to attract insects so that they aid in spore dispersal.
4. Many mushrooms are poisonous (e.g., death cap mushroom).

23.7 Fungal Partners and Pathogens

A. Fungal Partnerships

1. Lichens
    a. Lichens are mutualistic associations between fungi and cyanobacteria, green algae, or both.
    b. The fungus receives a long-term source of nutrients, which it absorbs from the photosynthetic cells.
    c. The lichen helps shelter the photosynthetic portion and anchor it to the substrate.
    d. Lichens live in inhospitable places such as bare rock and tree trunks.
2. Mycorrhizae
    a. A mycorrhiza is a symbiotic relationship in which fungi hyphae surround roots of shrubs and trees.
    b. Because of its extensive surface area, the fungus can absorb mineral ions and facilitate their entry into the plant.

3. Fungus-Farming Insects
    a. Some insect species nurture fungus crops so they can consume the matter that the fungus decomposes.

B. Fungal Pathogens
  1. Plant Pathogens
    a. The majority of fungi are decomposers, but some feed on live plants.
    b. Examples of fungi that harm plants are powder mildew and wheat stem rust.
    c. Ergotism is a type of food poisoning from consuming *Claviceps purpurea* fungus.
    d. A fungus has destroyed many American chestnut trees.
  2. Human Pathogens
    a. Fungal infections occur on the skin as athlete's foot, "ringworm," and vaginitis.
    b. System-wide fungal infections occur in AIDS patients and other immunocompromised individuals.

23.8 High-Flying Fungi (Revisited)

A. Researchers have sent model planes on a mission to collect fungal spores.
  a. Over a dozen species of Fusarium (a plant pathogen) spores were collected

Suggestions for Presenting the Material

- Ask students to name examples of fungi, and use these examples when discussing fungal diversity. Students will be surprised at the variety of organisms found in this kingdom.
- A general discussion of fungi is best shown with examples of living fungi. These can be obtained or prepared with little effort. The following are some examples of resources for the living fungi you can use in your classroom.
  1. The grocery store has mushrooms of Basidiomycetes; you can find many varieties. Choose mushrooms with large caps and easily seen gills, like portabella mushrooms.
  2. You may find morels of the Ascomycetes in a gourmet food store. While they are expensive by the pound, you can purchase just a few for examples.
  3. Bring in some wild mushrooms if you can find any. You can cut the stipe from the mushroom and place the cap gill side-down on white paper for several days to make a spore print (cover it with a jar to prevent the spores from blowing away). You can view the spores under a microscope.
  4. Lichens are abundant and easy to collect. Try to find a variety of types for students to observe such as lichens on rocks, tree bark, and branches.
  5. You can readily purchase some yeast at the grocery store and place it in sugar water for a few hours. Students can look at the yeast under a microscope to observe budding.
- Discuss with your students the characteristics of the fungi that place them as closer relatives of animals than plants. Students will have a hard time understanding why something that seems so plant-like actually has more in common with them. Make sure they understand why fungi are placed where they are in the tree of life.
- The non-scientist might assume that a fungus is a plant. Name the few key characteristics that immediately separate a fungus from a plant.
- Give the students several key examples of fungal groups with their descriptions and have the students construct cladograms representing fungal diversity.

- Create a matrix of fungal diversity that details not only the fungal characteristics of group membership (size, shape, reproduction), but also both the pathogenic potential and economic benefit of each fungal group.
- Create a matrix that compares the group traits of Bacteria, Archaea, Protists, Plants, and Fungi. Have students use this matrix to try toplace examples of organisms into each kingdom to see how effective their classification scheme is.
- Discuss the white nose disease that is destroying many bat populations in the United States. Which fungus is responsible for the condition? What are scientists doing to protect these populations?
- Discuss the variety present in the size of fungus. Be sure to mention the spectrum from single-celled yeast to an example of *Armillaria solidipes* that covers 3.4 square miles!

Classroom and Laboratory Enrichment

- Use overhead transparencies to show life cycles of species of protists, fungi, and plants. If the life cycle is unlabeled, you can ask your students to find the points at which meiosis and fertilization occur. Ask them which part of the life cycle is haploid and which part is diploid.
- Demonstrate variety within the kingdom Fungi by growing cultures of representative fungal species or ordering them from a biological supply house. Use 35 mm slides to survey the fungi. Use prepared microscope slides to look at vegetative hyphae and reproductive structures of representative fungi.
- Collect samples of plant tissues exhibiting signs of pathogenic fungi. Some examples include leaves infected with powdery mildew, rusts, or black spots; young seedlings killed by "damping off" (caused by the fungus *Pythium*); and citrus fruits covered with blue-green *Penicillium.*
- Ask the produce manager of a local supermarket to save rotting or damaged fruit for one or two days (or bring your own!). Place the fruits on display in lab and allow students to look at fungi with a dissecting scope or to make wet mounts and view them under the compound scope.
- Bring in a panel of people in your area that deal with fungi on a regular basis to start a discussion of the economic and ecological impact of different local fungal species. Panelists could include: brew masters from local wineries or breweries, mycologists, farmers or agricultural outreach specialists, physicians that treat fungal infections, pharmacologists, mold-removal specialists, etc.
- Prepare a collection of photographs of the effects of fungal infections in humans. Discuss how fungal infections are controlled.
- Start a culture of bread mold *(Rhizopus)* by wiping a small piece of preservative-free bread across a dusty floor or cabinet top, misting with water, and placing in a covered Petri dish for several days.
- Grow *Pilobolus* on extremely fresh horse manure that has been placed on filter paper in a culture dish, covered with an upside-down beaker. Soon after *Pilobolus* has started to appear, sporangia ejected by *Pilobolus* stalks will appear on the inside of the beaker.
- Collect fungi from forests and fields after cool, damp weather conditions. Lichens can be collected from a wide variety of locations regardless of weather conditions.
- Prepare a yeast culture in lab by dissolving an envelope of baker's yeast and a small amount of sugar in a beaker of warm water. Keep the beaker warm. Make a wet mount and observe budding yeast cells under the microscope.
- Demonstrate the ability of yeast to perform fermentation by making beer or wine in the laboratory.
- Use fresh grocery store mushrooms *(Agaricus)* as an example of club fungi. Pass them around the classroom or lab, and ask students to observe the stalk, cap, and gills.

- Redraw several of the life cycle figures in this chapter, but omit several key labels. Photocopy these and distribute as a labeling exercise.
- Have a mycologist from your State Department of Agriculture address your class. Ask him/her to bring in preserved specimens to pass around the class. Have him/her describe the telltale appearance of poisonous mushrooms indigenous to your area. If time and weather allow, take the class on a hike to view fungi in their natural habitat.
- Describe the conditions under which mushrooms are farmed.

Classroom Discussion Ideas

- Why are lichens considered early indicators of the impact that pollution may have in an area?
- Fungi play several important roles in many ecosystems. What are these roles and what would be the impact of losing fungal diversity in an ecosystem?
- Speculate about what might happen if the global environment deteriorates to a degree where no more lichen species are surviving (consider the old-growth forests in your answer).
- Divide the class in half and have one portion research fungi that infect plants and the other group look into fungi that affect animals. Which would have a more significant economic impact in our country?
- What is a fairy ring? How does it obtain its characteristic shape?
- If there is someone in the class with a fish aquarium at home, ask them to discuss the common fungi that invade the tank. Are these fungi as common under natural conditions?
- Discuss honeybee colony collapse disorder. How prevalent is it in your area? Can you envision how this could adversely affect the ecology of a region?
- Prepare a Jeopardy-type quiz (http://jeopardylabs.com/) for the students. Each general type of fungus could serve as a category.
- Does anyone in the class have a fungal allergy? If so, how is it treated?

Additional Ideas for Classroom Discussion

- Describe the similarities and differences between fungal spores and spores found among members of the plant kingdom.
- Mention the work of Norman Borlaug in combating the wheat stem rust type of fungi. How did he go about creating a rust-resistant form of wheat? What would you estimate to be the economic savings worldwide as a result of his research?
- Fungi are often compared to plants. Why is that comparison incorrect? Why have people historically compared fungi and plants? What are fungi more closely related to and, aside from DNA evidence, why is that relation more correct?
- What are some reasons biologists study fungi?
- What feature is the basis for classification of the fungi?
- What are the ecological roles that fungi play?
- Why are club and sac fungi more successful (evolutionarily) than other fungal species like chytrids, zygomycetes, and glomeromycetes?
- What does it mean to say that a fungal cell is dikaryotic and why is that beneficial to fungal species?
- What is the advantage of using spores to disperse fungal species?

- Wildlife biologists have occasionally observed wild bears that appear to stagger and walk unsteadily after consuming large quantities of fallen fruit in late summer and early autumn. What has happened to them?
- The relationship between the algae and fungi that compose lichen is mutualism. What is the symbiotic relationship of the entire *lichen* to the *tree* to which it is attached?
- Is it true that lichens grow only on the north side of trees? What is the basis for this? Is this also true of lichens in the Southern Hemisphere?
- Why would a fungus make and secrete an antibiotic? (Answer: Possibly to protect the food it is feeding on from bacterial competitors.)
- Why do you think something like ergot (a sac fungi that poisons grains) would produce animal toxins?
- How can the bread in your home or apartment suddenly sprout the characteristic black knobs of *Rhizopus* bread mold when there is no other moldy bread in your clean house?
- Where are you likely to find fungal infections on humans and why?
- *Candida albicans* is a common cause of oral and genital forms of yeast infections. A common home remedy for these infections is consumption of yogurt with *L. acidophilus* in it. Why might this work, along with other treatment, to help fight off a yeast infection?
- Research fungi that target primarily only one type of crop. For example, anyone who runs a vineyard would be well informed about the anthracnose fungi, which attacks grape vines. Likewise, someone who monitors an apple orchard would look out for the signs of apple scab, another fungal disease.
- Look into athlete's foot and toenail fungus. Why are the feet prime targets for this type of fungal infection?

How Would You Vote? Classroom Discussion Ideas

- Monitor the voting for the online question. This topic will no doubt stir some emotional debate as the opium and heroin trade in Afghanistan fuels both drug trade and, in turn, has ties to terrorist organizations. Help students analyze the issue beyond just killing the opium poppies, and have them examine the other ecological effects that could be caused by introducing the fungal spores.
- One of the important issues with spraying a fungus over widespread areas would be the long-term effects on the flora and fauna of that location. Also, the fungus can enter water supplies and be consumed by humans. In addition, since many of the poppy fields are located in foreign countries, it might be difficult to obtain permission for the process of spraying a sample of fungi on their countryside.

Term Paper Topics, Library Activities, and Special Projects

- Discuss the economic importance of fungi, both as agents of decay and disease and as organisms important in research and industry.
- Discuss the diagnosis and treatment of fungi that grow on the human skin and mucous membranes.
- Describe the role of yeasts in the making of beer and wine.
- Compile a list of wild mushrooms found in your area.
- Consult a textbook on insect control methods to investigate the use of fungi as biocontrol agents for insects.

- Obtain a listing of the active ingredients in an antifungal medication for athlete's foot. Consult the Merck Index to learn how these chemicals inhibit fungal growth.
- Obtain a field guide to the edible mushrooms. What easily seen features warn us of poisonous varieties?
- Write a report about the use of lichen species as indicators of pollution.
- Detail the common types of fungi that create problems around the house. Detail methods that are used to remediate mold and fungus problems or prevent future issues.
- Investigate some fungal lung disease, such as histoplasmosis. Are particular populations at risk for this condition? What are the symptoms and treatments for this disease?
- What is thrush? When is an individual particularly prone to thrush? Which parts of the body are typically affected? What are the symptoms, treatments, and preventative efforts?
- When was "ringworm" discovered? What is its official name? How is the present name misleading for the layperson?
- Do some background research on fungi in your local ecosystem. Describe the impacts that the loss of fungal species has in your area because of global warming or pollution.

Possible Responses to *Critical Thinking* Questions

1. Most likely, various species of fungi that have the bioluminescent ability are successful because they attract insects that will help with spore dispersal. In addition, the glowing fungi may discourage other animals from consuming it.
2. Skin-based fungal infections are often harder to treat than bacterial infections for several reasons. First, bacterial infections tend to reside in the blood stream or body fluids, and drugs can be delivered through the digestive system and introduced into the bloodstream to fight bacteria. Fungi, however, live in the dermis and epidermis. These layers are not blood rich, so taking a pill to be delivered by the blood stream will probably not reach the fungi. Additionally, the fungi may be too deep for a topical cream to reach, or a person may stop using the cream when the symptoms subside.
3. Since bacteria reproduce asexually, the offspring are identical to the parent. Sexual reproduction is designed to increase genetic variability. Therefore, the offspring that are the product of sexual reproduction are not identical to the parent fungi. When variation occurs, it makes the organism have varying characteristics and, thus, harder to destroy.

Possible Responses to *Data Analysis Exercise* Questions

The honey mushroom is a parasite of both living and dead trees. Canadian foresters performed a study to see if stump removal helped prevent further damage by the mushrooms to the forest.

1. The larch trees were most often killed by *A. ostoyae* in control forests, and birch trees were the least affected in that control group.
2. In larch trees, 27 percent of the control group were killed and 3 percent of the experimental forest were destroyed.
3. The data supports the hypothesis that removal of stumps infected with the honey mushroom helps to decrease the spread of the fungus through the forests.

24

ANIMAL EVOLUTION—THE INVERTEBRATES

Chapter Outline

Objectives

1. Describe the major advances in body structure and function that made invertebrates and vertebrates increasingly large and complex.
2. Discuss the relationship between segmentation and the development of paired organs and paired appendages.
3. List the functions of a coelom, and describe the role coelomic development played in animal evolution.
4. For each major invertebrate phylum, list the name, the distinguishing characteristic(s), and common examples.
5. Trace the development of symmetry, body cavity, cephalization, and segmentation in the invertebrates.

Key Terms

GGC gene
animals
invertebrates
heterotrophs
ectoderm
endoderm
epithelium
extracellular matrix
integrins
cadherins
connective tissue
mesoderm
microvilli
choanoflagellates
colonial theory
signaling molecules
radial symmetry
bilateral symmetry
cephalization
anterior
posterior
ventral
dorsal
gut
incomplete digestive system
complete digestive system
blastopore
protostomes
deuterostomes
coelom, coelomate
peritoneum
pseudocoelom
sponges
sessile animal
spicules
collar cells
larva, larvae
budding
gemmules
placozoans
Ediacarans
Cnidarians
cnidocyte
nematocysts
gastrovascular cavity
medusa
polyp
epithelium
gastrodermis
epidermis
nerve net
mesoglea
hydrostatic skeleton
gonads
planula
organs
organ systems
flatworms
hermaphrodites
parasites
definitive host
intermediate host
turbellarians
flukes
pharynx
ganglia
protonephridia
flame cells
transverse fission
tapeworms
scolex
proglottids
annelids
earthworms
leeches
seta, setae
oligochaetes
polychaetes
detritus
parapods
cuticle
brain
nerve cords
ganglion
nephridium, -dia
trochophore larva
rotifers
tardigrade
mastax
mollusks
radula
mantle
gastropods
gills
chitons
bivalves
torsion
cephalopods
closed circulation
jet propulsion
roundworms
nematodes
trichinosis
elephantiasis
pinworms
hookworms
arthropods
antenna
open circulation
trilobites
crustaceans
chelicerates
insects
myriapods
centipedes
millipedes
exoskeleton
chitin
molting
jointed appendages
tracheas
metamorphosis
chelicerates
horseshoe crabs
arachnids
chelicerates
myriapod
book lungs
pedipalps
crustaceans
barnacles
copepods
insect

millipedes	foregut, midgut, hindgut	larvae, nymphs, pupae	sea lilies
centipedes	Malpighian tubules	Lyme disease	sea stars
insect head	uric acid	echinoderm	water-vascular system
insect thorax		tube feet	sea cucumbers
insect abdomen			

Lecture Outline

24.1 Old Genes, New Drugs

A. Cone snails are valuable.

1. To some people, they are tasty treats or prized jewelry.
2. All 500 species of these predatory mollusks secrete paralyzing toxins that can kill humans.
3. These conotoxins may be the source of new drugs because each species of cone snail targets specific molecular targets with its conotoxins.
   a. One species secretes a conotoxin that is more potent than morphine, but not addicting.
   b. Another species secretes a toxin that one day might help epileptics.

B. A gene that codes for an enzyme in the conotoxin pathway, GGC (gamma-glutamyl carboxylase), has been conserved through evolutionary time, showing up today not only in the cone snail, but also in humans and fruit flies.

24.2 Animal Traits and Body Plans

A. What Is an Animal?

1. Animals are multicellular heterotrophs with tissues arranged into organs and organ systems that ingest other organisms, or parts of them.
2. Most are motile at some stage of their life cycle, and they reproduce sexually, and in some cases asexually, or both; their embryos develop through a series of stages.

B. Variation in Animal Body Plans

1. Organization
   a. All animals are multicellular and show an internal division of labor.
   b. A key innovation for animals was development of tissues. Tissue development starts in the embryo.
      1) The outer ectoderm is the tissue, giving rise to the epithelium that lines body surfaces and forms other organs, and in some species, serves as an external skeleton (e.g., insect cuticle).
      2) Endoderm develops into the gut lining and connective tissues, serving as the structural material for an internal skeleton.
      3) A third tissue layer forms between the other two, the mesoderm, which is the source of muscles and other organs in all animals more complex than jellyfishes.

C. Body Symmetry

1. Animals show either radial (round) or bilateral (right and left sides) symmetry; bilateral animals also show anterior (head end), posterior (tail end), dorsal (back), and ventral (belly) orientations.
2. Cephalization means having a definite head end with a concentration of feeding and sensory features; bilateral animals evolved more complex brains and sensory organs.

D. Gut and Body Cavity

1. The place where food is digested is the gut; some are saclike, with one opening—a mouth—where food enters and waste exits; others are tube-like, with two openings.

a. A saclike gut is an incomplete digestive system, which evolved first.
b. "Complete" digestive tracts have a tubular gut (mouth and anus) for continuous food processing, often through specialized regions.
1) In protostomes (mollusks, annelids, and arthropods), the blastopore becomes the mouth.
2) In deuterostomes (echinoderms and chordates), the blastopore becomes the anus.
2. The coelom is the body cavity between the gut and the body wall, lined with peritoneum from the mesoderm.
a. Some animals (flatworms) do not have a coelom but instead are packed solidly with tissue between the gut and body wall.
b. Most bilateral animals have a coelom (lined with peritoneum), a space between the gut and body wall that allows internal organs to expand and operate freely.
c. Others, such as roundworms, have a "false" coelom (pseudocoelom), partly lined with peritoneum.

E. Circulation
1. A large-bodied animal requires a circulatory system that can move substances faster than diffusion alone.
a. With larger animals comes a division of labor with a compartmentalization of tasks in the body.
b. As new levels of organization evolved, so did the means of integrating different cell activities.

F.Segmentation
1. A segmented animal is composed of repeating body units (for example, the earthworm).
2. The segments may be grouped and modified for specialized tasks, like in insects.

24.3 Animal Origins and Adaptive Radiation

A. Colonial Origins
1. Colonial theory states that the first animals evolved from a tiny colony of flagellated, amoeba-like cells.
2. Choanoflagellates with flagellated collar cells may be the evolutionary ancestors to the animal lineage.
a. They make signaling molecules and adhesion proteins found in multicelled animals.
b. Sponges are at the base of the animal family tree, and they have flagellated collar cells, which supports the view that they share a common ancestor with the choanoflagellates.

B. Early Signs of Animal Life
1. Fossils found in Oman were 635 million years old.
a. These ancient animals had molecular markers similar to sponges.
2. Ediacarans were discovered to be 570 million years old.
a. Ediacarans may be descendents of sponges, arthropods, and other invertebrates.

C. The Cambrian Explosion
1. A dramatic adaptive radiation occurred during the Cambrian period, probably because continental drift caused mass allopatric speciation.
a. New habitats were created by global warming and an increase in the level of oxygen.
2. Once predators arose, hard body plans would have been selected for.
3. Mutations helped produce adaptive traits.

24.4 Sponges

A. Characteristics and Ecology
1. Sponges (phylum Porifera) have an asymmetric body with no true tissues, no organs.

2. Between two layers of body cells there is a semifluid matrix with needlelike spicules for support.
3. Collar cells line the interior chambers.
   a. By means of their beating flagella, these cells move large volumes of water in through body pores and out through the large opening at the top of the body.
   b. They also trap suspended food particles in their collars and transfer the food to amoeba-like cells in the matrix.
4. Skeletal spicules and chemical secretions are used to deter predators.

B. Sponge Reproduction and Dispersal
1. Sponges reproduce sexually or asexually.
   a. Sperm are released into the surrounding water to be picked up by a nearby sponge and directed to the egg within the matrix; the zygote develops into a free-swimming larva.
   b. Sponges can produce buds or fragments.
   c. Some freshwater sponges can survive unfavorable conditions by producing a gemmule, a small cluster of cells enclosed in a hard coat.
   d. Most sponges are hermaphrodites.

24.5 Cnidarians—Predators with Stinging Cells

A. Body Plans
1. Cnidarians are tentacled, radial animals.
2. This group includes jellyfishes, sea anemones, and hydrozoans *(Hydra)*.
3. The phylum name comes from their ability to sting by discharging nematocysts.
4. Cnidarians have simple body plans.
   a. The medusa resembles an umbrella and floats like a tentacle-fringed bell in the water; oral arms surround the central mouth.
   b. The polyp is tube-like and is usually attached to some substrate; it may be solitary or part of a colony.
   c. The digestive cavity is saclike (only a mouth) and can accommodate prey larger than the cnidarian itself.
   d. An outer epidermis covers the body, and an inner gastrodermis lines the digestive cavity.
      1) A nerve net running through both layers coordinates the animal's response to stimuli.
      2) Some jellyfishes also have sensory cells and contractile cells.
   e. A jellylike mesoglea lies between the outer and inner body layers.
      1) Jellyfishes have abundant mesoglea, helpful in providing buoyancy and in swimming.
      2) Polyps have little mesoglea but use the water in their guts as a hydrostatic skeleton.

B. Diversity and Life Cycles
1. The life cycle of a cnidarian may have a polyp and medusa stage, or it may have just the polyp.
   a. The medusa is usually the sexual form with gonads.
   b. The zygote develops into a swimming larva called a planula.
2. There are four main cnidarian classes.
   a. Hydrozoans: *Obelia* and *Hydra.*
   b. Anthozoans: coral and sea anemone.
   c. Cubozoans: box jellies.
   d. Scyphozoans: true jellyfish.

24.6 Flatworms—Simple Organ Systems

A. Flatworms have a flat, bilateral, cephalized body with no coelom. Organs and organ systems are present.

   1. One hypothesis is that the ancestor of flatworms was segmented and had coelom, but that flatworms lost those traits.

B. Structure of a Free-Living Flatworm

   1. Turbellarians (planarians) are free-living and aquatic.
   2. The gut is saclike with a single (mouth) opening through which a pharynx extends for food gathering.
   3. The organism has a pair of nerve cords and clusters of nerve cell bodies.
   4. Branching tubules, with flame cells, regulate body fluid volume and composition.
   5. Asexual reproduction is by transverse fission of the body.

C. Flukes and Tapeworms—The Parasites

   1. Flukes are internal parasites that require a primary host (such as a human) for sexual reproduction and an intermediate host (such as a snail) for development.
   2. Tapeworms are intestinal parasites of vertebrates.
      a. They absorb predigested nutrients from the host because they have no digestive tract.
      b. The body consists of an anterior scolex solely for attachment to the host's gut and a string of proglottids, each of which possesses both male and female organs.

24.7 Annelids—Segmented Worms

A. Annelids are bilateral worms with a coelom and segmentation. Nearly all segments bear chaetae, chitin-reinforced bristles.

B. The Marine Polychaetes

   1. *Nereis* (sandworms) are active predators with reinforced jaws.
   2. Fan worms and feather duster worms live in a secreted tube.

C. Leeches—Bloodsuckers and Others

   1. Leeches live in water, lack bristles, and have suckers at both ends.
   2. Most leeches are scavengers or predators of small invertebrates. A few will pierce the skin of larger animals.
      a. Leeches inject an anticoagulant into the host to prevent clotting while it feeds on blood.

D. The Earthworm—An Oligochaete

   1. Oligochaetes, like earthworms, have a segmented body plan with a fluid-filled coelom.
   2. Gas exchange occurs at the skin and a closed circulatory system, powered by five hearts, circulates oxygen.
   3. Earthworms have a complete digestive system, regulate their body fluids with nephridia in each segment, and have a crude nervous system controlled by a rudimentary brain.
   4. The brain controls muscles that allow the worm-movement to occur.
   5. Earthworms are hermaphrodites; two will swap sperm.

24.8 Mollusks—Animals with a Mantle

A. General Characteristics

   1. Mollusks have a fleshy, soft bilateral body with a small coelom.
   2. Some have a head with eyes and tentacles.
   3. All have a mantle, a skirt-like tissue covering the body that is responsible for the secretion of a shell in many mollusks.
   4. Some have a tongue-like organ called the radial, which rasps at food.

B. Mollusk Diversity

1. Mollusks are second only to arthropods in diversity. There are four main classes: chitons, gastropods, bivalves, and cephalopods.
2. Chitons are marine animals with a dorsal shell with eight plates. They scrape algae off of rocks with their radula.
3. Gastropods (snails, slugs) are named for a single muscular foot that makes up most of their lower mass.
   a. They have a distinct head and an inhalant siphon.
   b. They undergo torsion during development that moves body parts out of normal position.
   c. Gastropods that live on land secrete a mucous to prevent the organism from drying out.
4. Bivalves (mussels, clams, scallops) have a hinged, two-part shell and powerful retractor muscles.
   a. They have a reduced head, but eyes around the mantle serve to alert the organism to danger.
   b. They have a triangular foot for digging.
   c. They lack a radula, instead they trap food in mucous on their gills while siphoning water.
5. Cephalopods (squids, octopi) are faster, smarter and have a closed circulatory system.
   a. The body of a squid is modified for a highly active predatory lifestyle; it has tentacles and beaklike jaws.
   b. They move by a type of jet propulsion caused by mantle contractions.
   c. To support greater activity, the circulatory system is a closed one; the nervous system is well developed with a large brain; the eyes form images; and learning and memory are possible.
   d. Cephalopods became the fastest, largest, and smartest of all the invertebrates with the most complex behavior of all mollusks.

24.9 Rotifers and Tardigrades—Tiny and Tough

A. Rotifers share a common ancestry with flatworms since they are bilateral, cephalized, and also have a false coelom.
   1. Structurally they are remarkably complex, possessing a crown of cilia, jaws, digestive tract, protonephridia, nerve cells, eyespots, and muscles.
   2. Most are aquatic, and all prey on bacteria and microscopic algae with a unique jaw-like mastax that grinds up their food.
   3. Most rotifers reproduce via parthenogenesis (the development of unfertilized egg into an offspring).

B. Tardigrades are slow walkers with a complete digestive system, no circulatory or respiratory systems, and a reduced coelom.
   1. Tardigrades are tough—they can withstand drastic temperatures and may remain dormant for long periods.

24.10 Roundworms—Unsegmented Worms That Molt

A. Roundworms are also known as nematodes.
   1. They are bilateral and possess a slender, tapered body.
      a. The digestive tract is complete—mouth and anus for continuous food processing.
      b. Reproductive organs lie in a false coelom filled with fluid.
      c. A tough cuticle covers and protects the body.
   2. *Caenorhabditis elegans* is a rather famous nematode because its simplicity of body plan and small genome make it an excellent organism for research studies.

B. Most roundworms are small and free-living, but some are parasitic on plants and animals.
   1. In trichinosis, undercooked pork is the source of a roundworm that moves from the digestive tract of the host to encyst in the muscles.
   2. Elephantiasis is a severe swelling of the legs due to blockage of lymph flow by small roundworms deposited by a mosquito during feeding.
   3. Pinworms are common parasites of young children; hookworm adults live in the small intestine of their host.

24.11 Arthropods—Molting Animals with Jointed Legs

A. Arthropods are bilateral with a reduced coelom. They have hard, jointed external skeletons, complete digestive systems, open circulatory systems, and respiratory and excretory systems.
   1. Arthropods are evolutionarily successful. Success is measured by having the most species, producing the greatest number of offspring, occupying the most habitats, possessing terrific defenses, and being able to exploit new resources.
   2. The four main lineages are trilobites (now extinct), chelicerates, crustaceans, insects, and myriapods (centipedes, millipedes).

B. Key Arthropod Adaptations
   1. Hardened Exoskeleton
      a. It is a combination of protein and chitin (plus calcium in some) that is flexible, lightweight, yet protective.
      b. It is a barrier to water loss and can support a body deprived of water's buoyancy.
      c. Exoskeletons restrict growth and so must be shed periodically (molting process).
   2. Jointed Appendages
      a. Arthropod appendages are jointed at membranous areas where body parts abut.
      b. Appendages became specialized for feeding, sensing, locomotion, sperm transfer, and spinning silk.
   3. Highly Modified Segments
      a. Body segments became more specialized, reduced in number, and grouped together.
      b. In some lineages, this has resulted in head, thorax, and abdomen regions.
   4. Sensory Specializations
      a. The compound eye provides a wide angle of vision.
      b. Many individual units allow motion perception.
      c. Most arthropods have paired antennae to detect chemicals and the sense of touch.
   5. Specialized Developmental Stages
      a. Metamorphosis transforms insects from immature larval stages, through a pupal stage, to adult.
      b. Larval stages concentrate on feeding and growth, whereas the adults specialize in dispersal and reproduction.

24.12 Chelicerates—Spiders and Their Relatives

A. Chelicerates include some marine species such as horseshoe crabs and the more familiar arachnids.

B. Arachnids include spiders, scorpions, ticks, and mites.
   1. Spiders are keen predators that trap insects in their webs, produced as silk strands from the abdomen; some are poisonous such as the brown recluse and black widow.
   2. The chelicerate body bears eight legs plus a pair of chelicerae to pierce prey and a pair of pedipalps to manipulate the food (or transfer sperm!).

3. Unique respiratory organs called book lungs reside in an invagination of the abdominal wall; they greatly increase the surface area available for gas exchange in an open circulatory system.
4. Some mites are free-living; others are serious pests of plants and animals.

25.13 Myriapods

A. Millipedes and centipedes have long, segmented bodies with many legs.
B. Millipedes are cylindrical, slow-moving vegetarians.
C. Centipedes have a more flattened body, move rapidly, and prey on small invertebrates using their fangs and venom glands.

24.14 Crustaceans

A. Crustaceans include shrimps, lobsters, crayfishes, crabs, barnacles, and pillbugs.
   1. The name is derived from the crusty exoskeleton.
   2. Most are important components of food webs, and several serve as human food also.
B. The crustacean body is divided into many segments.
   1. Like other arthropods, they repeatedly molt and shed the exoskeleton.
   2. Appendages on the body include two pairs of antennae, a pair each of mandibles and maxillae, and five pairs of legs.
C. Unusual crustaceans include the tiny copepods, which are integral to marine food webs, and the shell-encased barnacles, which cause problems when they attach to piers, rocks, and even other animals.

24.15 Insects—Diverse and Abundant

A. Characteristic Features
   1. The body is divided into three regions: head (sensory and feeding), thorax (locomotion: by six legs, usually two pairs of wings), and abdomen.
   2. The complete digestive tract is divided into three regions: foregut, midgut (digestion and absorption), and hindgut (water reabsorption).
   3. Unique small tubes (Malpighian tubules) attached to the gut and lying free in the abdominal cavity process metabolic waste (uric acid) and aid in water retention.
   4. Three pairs of legs extend from the thorax.
   5. Insects have an open circulatory system.
   6. Insects have a complete digestive system.
B. Insect Origins
   1. It was previously thought that insects were closely related to myriapods.
   2. The current hypothesis is that insects descended from crustaceans.
C. The Importance of Insects
   1. Ecological Services
      a. The vast diversity of insects and flowering plants is believed to have arisen from coevolution of pollination syndromes.
      b. Loss of habitat, pesticides, and disease are threatening some insects.
      c. Insects are important foods for other animals.
      d. Insects, like flies, help dispose of wastes and remains.
   2. Competition for Crops
      a. Insects are our main competitors for food; we lose between one-third and one-fourth of our crops to insects.
   3. Parasites and Vectors for Disease
      a. Mosquitoes are considered the deadliest animals because of their ability to act as a vector for pathogens.

b. One of the most dangerous threats to humans is mosquitoes.
   1) Mosquito-borne disease kills about three million people annually; malaria and West Nile virus are two of the biggest concerns.
   2) Females target any warm-blooded animal nearby, drawing blood to enable her to produce her eggs; eggs must be laid in standing water.
   3) The warmer the weather, the more active the mosquitoes, which does not bode well with a warming climate.

24.16 The Spiny—Skinned Echinoderms

A. The Protostome—Deuterostome Split
   1. The echinoderms are the first animal that has a three-layer embryo that is also a deuterostome.

B. Echinoderm Characteristics and Body Plan
   1. Echinoderm means spiny skinned, referring to their outer skin made of calcium carbonate.
   2. Larvae are bilateral but adults are radial in symmetry.
   3. The nervous system is decentralized; there is no brain.
   4. The unique water-vascular system operates the tube feet, which have suction disks that can be used in locomotion and prey capture.
   5. Sea stars can evert their stomachs when feeding.
   6. Gas exchange occurs across their feet and projections on their body surface.
   7. There are separate sexes and the reproductive parts are in their arms.
   8. Sea stars and other echinoderms have the ability to regenerate appendages.

C. Echinoderm Diversity
   1. Brittle stars are the most diverse species. Most are sea floor scavengers with a central disk and snakelike arms.
   2. Urchins have brittle, spiny projections for protection. Many graze on algae.
   3. Sea cucumbers have a hardened outer covering and many of their parts are reduced. They feed by eating their way through decaying organic matter.

24.7 Old Genes, New Drugs (Revisited)

A. Marine animals provide a host of commercial uses, from food to medicine. However, marine species are on the decline due to habitat destruction and overharvesting.

Suggestions for Presenting the Material

- This diverse chapter begins with definitions of some basic terms used in describing animals. Then the "march through the phyla" begins. This can be a tedious and overwhelming experience.
- This is a long chapter, decide what your goals for student learning are and then decide how you will approach the content. For example, in an introductory course for non-majors you may choose to focus on how animals are separated into their individual phyla. If this is the case, you should start by defining characteristics that are used to classify animals into each phylum. Then, instead of focusing on every example in each phylum, focus on identifying traits and key examples of membership in each phylum. Then use the individual example species as a way to practice classification.
- Work with students to develop a matrix that defines traits that compare and contrast the animal phyla.
- The present chapter begins with true multicellular animals—the sponges and placozoans.

- The beginning of this chapter contains a very useful figure (Figure 24.2). It is a concise listing of the phyla that are to be covered in this chapter.
- In a survey that reduces volumes of information to about 30 pages, there must be a brevity that will certainly shortchange someone's favorite animal group. However, the authors have been fair in presenting the chief characteristics for which each phylum is noted. Even so, the few features may be too many, and further reduction may need to be made by the individual instructor.
- If the instructor has a good grasp of animal diversity, especially invertebrates, the chapter may seem oversimplified, but to a botanist it may be quite the opposite. No matter where you find yourself in this spectrum, remember the naive student, and have compassion.
- One way to enliven your presentation is to relate the members of each phylum to the students' daily lives. This may be more difficult for sponges than arthropods, but with a little forethought, it can be done. See samples in the Enrichment section.
- Have students or groups of students prepare summaries of each phylum that they present to the class. Make sure to structure the presentations so that each student/group has to give a minimum listing of information.
- Discuss how the science of embryology has influenced the classification of animals. Do you think future experimentation will cause reassessment of our current classification criteria?

Classroom and Laboratory Enrichment

- There is no scarcity of visual material depicting the diversity of animal life. It ranges from professionally made 2 x 2 transparencies, to single-phylum videos, to full-length video surveys of the animal kingdom, such as David Attenborough's *Life on Earth* (available at retail outlets). It is important to show the students video of certain species to demonstrate the similarities in animal behavior. For example, starfish are eager predators, but unless you see them attack in time-lapse it is hard to understand their timeframe.
- If you are fortunate to live in or near a large city with a zoo, arrange a field trip, but this time with a difference. Prepare the students for note taking on various topics such as classification, body symmetry and cavities, body system development, ecological niche, and so on. Comment on the lack of animal representatives from the invertebrate phyla (at least ones that are plainly visible).
- If you do not live near a zoo, take your class outside and look for evidence of invertebrates on campus.
- Most, or perhaps all, of your students should have an accompanying laboratory experience where they can see, touch, and dissect representatives of the various phyla. If not, it will be even more crucial that you present adequate visual material—use slides or photographs from the Internet available for educational use.
- The common laboratory activity that accompanies a chapter like this usually involves a process where the students follow directions and make simple observations while looking at preserved materials. For a more authentic and hands-on experience, take the lab book away. Most biology suppliers have survey of invertebrate diversity kits with six or eight animals; Wards sells an eight-species kit with a roundworm, an earthworm, a starfish, a grassfrog, a crayfish, a grasshopper, a perch, and a clam. Save the perch and the frog for the later discussion of vertebrates.
    A. Start the activity by giving a brief presentation on the physical characteristics of animals.
    B. Next, have the students clarify the traits of each animal in the kit without a manual or text. Try not to directly answer student questions; instead, have them write their questions down and then research them briefly in the text or in a lab manual.

C. When the students have clearly identified the traits of each animal in the survey, challenge them to use those traits to construct a cladogram that represents invertebrate diversity, based on the traits they have identified.

D. Next, after the students have a cladogram that represents their survey animals, give them unknown animals that are close relatives to the animals in the survey kit. Have the students test their cladograms by using them to identify unknown animals.

- As mentioned in the Presentation section, relating animals to daily life will enhance your lectures. Below is a sampling that you can build on.

  PORIFERA: Natural *sponges* (expensive) are still the best for cleaning purposes. Try to have one to show students as you are talking about them. If possible, an example or picture of each type of sponge might be interesting for comparison—glass sponges, calcium carbonate sponges, sponges with spongin.

  CNIDARIA: We wouldn't want to tangle with a *jellyfish,* but a piece of *coral* on display is okay. There are lots of good examples of coral that students can view.

  PLATYHELMINTHES: The *tapeworms* and *flukes* have disgusting parasitic habits but are all a part of nature's balance. Students are interested in parasitic diseases and love it if you have photographs (warn those with delicate stomachs!).

  NEMATODA: Everyone is familiar with *roundworms* as parasites of pets, but do you know that humans can get them too?

  ANNELIDA: The familiar *earthworm* is a very beneficial tiller of the soil, but is its relative the *leech* so well respected?

  ARTHROPODA: The largest phylum contains pesky *insects* as well as tasty *lobsters.*

  MOLLUSCA: *Snails* and *clams* are quite familiar—we even eat them! But what about *squid* and *octopus?*

  ECHINODERMATA: *Sea stars* seem exotic because they and their relatives are found only in the sea.

  CHORDATA: Finally, "familiar" animals, but they constitute less than 5 percent of all the animals on the Earth (Chapter 25).

- Invertebrates are often taken for granted because of how common it is to eat shellfish or destroy insect populations. In a non-majors class, you may want to spend time trying to relate this chapter to the ecological disadvantages of destroying the habitats of these organisms or overharvesting certain species.
- Work with your students to complete a matrix that compares all of the major kingdoms by comparing and contrasting different characteristics.
- If your budget allows, purchase some live planaria and some food to maintain the animals. As you know, *planaria* are free-living flatworms. Because they have two nerve cords that run down their body, they can be dissected in some interesting ways. You will need a dissecting microscope and a sharp scalpel for this experiment. Make an incision from the front of the organism, between its eyes, and almost to the middle of the specimen. This "surgery" will not damage the nervous system of your *planaria* and in a short time; he will actually form two distinct heads! This can also be done from the tail end of the organism, and it will develop two tails. You can continue these surgeries and the animal will continue to produce additional heads and tails and will survive until it becomes too cumbersome to move toward the food source.
- The dissection of an earthworm is often surprising for the beginning biology students. They envision the earthworm as such a simple animal with no specialization of tissues. Surprise them by illustrating segmentation and the representation of the different organ systems. The earthworm will undoubtedly earn your students' respect after they view the internal structures during the dissection!

Classroom Discussion Ideas

- What makes cone snails more fascinating than other snails?
- Prepare a Jeopardy-style game for the class using the following template: http://jeopardylabs.com/. The categories can be the phyla discussed in this chapter.
- How can a toxin like conotoxin, which kills, be the potential source of new drugs?
- What selection pressures might you speculate led to the evolution of such potent toxins?
- What is the explanation for the finding of similar DNA (e.g., GGC) in *very* different organisms?
- What have scientists learned from studying the anticoagulant from leeches, hirudin? We tend to think of leeches as an undesirable animal. Are there any medicinal uses for leeches today?
- Students may have trouble envisioning a sponge as a living animal. Because the adult is sessile (non-moving), many would classify it as a plant. What animal characteristics does it possess?
- What are the key ways we define animals? How do we classify the diversity in the animal kingdom?
- Show the class the diversity that exists in what we call coral. The non-scientist would probably classify coral as a plantlike organism. Why? What characteristics does it have that clearly make it an animal?

Additional Ideas for Classroom Discussion

- How would you define something as an animal?
- Why are protozoans no longer included in the kingdom Animalia?
- Even if you cannot remember all the details concerning the members of each phylum, can you list the major niches that each phylum seems to fill?
- Describe the differences between radial and bilateral symmetry. What are the differences between protostomes and deuterostomes?
- What is the importance of the rise of layers in the developing embryo?
- When a pet owner says, "My animal has worms," what worm is most likely present? How could you distinguish between a flatworm and a roundworm, other than by shape? How would the veterinary technician test for the presence of worms? Is this the same method that would detect worms in humans?
- Some people don't consider an organism a true animal unless it bleeds red when injured. Do any of the animals presented in this chapter fit this "definition"?
- The blood fluke, *Schistosoma,* is an important human parasite. What role do parasites play in nature? Are they always the "villains"? *Schistosoma* affects many people worldwide each year. Why do you think we have not discovered a drug to prevent these infections? Do you think conditions that affect patients in underdeveloped countries get less attention from researchers?
- Why is the word "primitive" not accurate in describing early groups like sponges and cnidarians?
- Arthropods as a group have more unique features than perhaps any other group. Name as many of these features as you can.
- Insect populations, particularly *Drosophila melanogaster,* are often used for genetic experimentation. What features make the fruit fly ideal for this function?
- What characteristics make insects develop resistance to insecticides?
- Why do people normally refuse to eat insects when insects' close relatives such as crayfish and lobsters, and near relatives such as snails and oysters, are gourmet items?

- Let's face it, no one likes having unexpected insects dropping in, but what would be the effect of losing insect species from habitats? Why are flies important?
- The television show *Deadliest Catch* is an exciting show, but overfishing of crab species can take a toll on an ecosystem. What could be a possible outcome of taking only the largest crabs that are caught? The weakest part of a crab shell is the underside, which is exposed when the smallest crabs are thrown back into the water. How could throwing back crabs that are caught affect the crab populations?
- Initiate a discussion about cubomedusa, the box jellyfish. Do you think it deserves the title of "the world's most venomous creature"? How many human deaths result from encounters with this species annually?
- The organs of snails exhibit torsion to fit into their spiral shells. Slugs also show this type of torsion. What does this tell you about the origin of slugs?

How Would You Vote? Classroom Discussion Ideas

- Monitor the voting for the online question. Bottom trawling is when fishing boats drag nets on the sea floor. The UN recently has tried to block these actions. This is part of the bigger question: What would happen if we were to lose these species from their natural habitats? Shrimp, lobster, and other seafood tastes good, but at what ecological cost?
- In addition, the majority of the species obtained from this type of non-discriminate method will not be edible species or will simply be too small to eat. The students need to weigh the cost to the ocean floor ecology versus the easier, cheaper way to collect dinner!

Term Paper Topics, Library Activities, and Special Projects

- Describe how recent genetic analysis is changing how we view invertebrate classification.
- Seafood includes many invertebrates: clams, scallops, crabs, lobster, shrimp, etc. Over-fishing these species puts a strain on their natural ecosystems. An alternative is farming these species. How does the impact of farming these species affect ecosystems compared to fishing in the natural environments? What regulations are attempting to preserve these species?
- In the early days of biological investigation, sponges and even some cnidarians were classified as plants. Search some older textbooks to see when and why scientists changed their minds.
- Prepare a report on the extent of flatworm parasitic infestations in humans. List the condition, number of cases, and economic loss to society.
- The phylum Echinodermata is unique in not possessing any freshwater representatives. The reasons for this should be found in an invertebrate biology textbook; see if you can locate the details.
- Often fisherman place seine nets across a body of water to obtain fish. The fisherman perceives starfish as a nuisance since they become entangled easily in the nets. Sometimes the fisherman reacts angrily and chops the starfish into pieces and throws them back in the sea. Why is this not an intelligent decision?
- Research coral bleaching. How does the destruction of coral reefs dramatically impact the habitat of other ocean species? Are there current efforts to save the coral reefs? What are these efforts?
- Are there any freshwater cnidarians? If so, what are they and how do you think they came to occupy the freshwater niche?
- Research the history of the use of natural sponges including harvesting methods, present demand, and current supply conditions.

- Mosquitoes are vectors for many blood-borne diseases. Many times localities will spray DDT to control mosquito populations to stop the spread of outbreaks. What are the ecological and evolutionary problems that this type of spraying could lead to?
- Aside from their role as a vector of disease, we dislike mosquitoes since they bite and produce itchy marks on the skin. Do all mosquitoes bite? Why do they need blood? What are other food sources for mosquitoes?
- How is the Portuguese man-of-war unlike jellyfish? How is it like jellyfish? Discover the facts about jellyfish stings, including the man-of-war, and report on the number of humans affected yearly.
- In the oceans we see an incredible diversity of invertebrate species. Detail how that diversity changes at different depths in the oceans.
- What are the risks in eating mollusks? How can the risk be reduced? Amont which mollusks is the risk highest?
- Research the extent to which insects are used as human food in countries around the world.
- Investigate the reports of intelligence in cephalopods, especially octopods, including examples of their performances. Investigate the eye of the octopus? How is it like our eyes? Could this be why the octopus is considered the smartest invertebrate?
- Chordates dominate our thinking when the word *animal* is used. But they constitute about 5 percent of the total species. Relate this fact to the concept of pyramids (energy, biomass, numbers) as presented in Unit VII.
- An interesting animal to research is the giant squid. It has a structure like that of smaller squids, but its size is amazing. One of his eyes is the size of a car's headlight! Giant squid are reclusive, so the only specimens that scientists can study are primarily the dead ones that wash up on the shore.

Possible Responses to *Critical Thinking* Questions

1. Sponges, cnidarians, mollusks, and echinoderms probably are not parasites of mammals because of the lack of environmental interaction or overlap of niches. That is, these four groups of invertebrates are aquatic, many marine, while mammals for the most part are terrestrial. In addition, the animals from these invertebrate phyla are filter feeders. Their method of eating involves taking in large amounts of water and through filtration, separating food sources from the water. This is most definitely not compatible with a parasitic lifestyle.
2. If lobsters are being killed at a higher rate following increased usage of insecticides, it is reasonable to suspect the pesticides. Most of these chemicals attack the nervous system of the pest. Even though insects and lobsters are very different in size and live in different habitats, their nervous systems work by the same mechanisms. Therefore, we would expect any nerve poison to work the same in both. While sprayed on land to combat mosquito populations in standing water, the pesticides would be included in any runoff into the Long Island Sound, which would directly affect lobster populations.
3. It is advantageous for a tapeworm to be able to self-fertilize, because its lifestyle does not involve contact with other tapeworms. The typical scenario is that a tapeworm attaches via its scolex to the intestine of its human host. Therefore, self-fertilization is really the only option, since there is not another tapeworm present!

Possible Responses to *Data Analysis Exercise* Questions

The blood of horseshoe crabs can be used to test the safety of injectable drugs. Scientists performed experiments to see if withdrawing blood from horseshoe crabs impacted their survival.

1. The most control crabs and the most bled crabs died in trial number 5.
2. The bled crabs had a higher mortality rate than the control group in this study.
3. It appears as though bleeding the horseshoe crabs harms the specimens more than just capture alone.

25

ANIMAL EVOLUTION—THE CHORDATES

Chapter Outline

Objectives

1. Describe the four characteristics that are distinctive of chordates.
2. Distinguish between invertebrates in general, invertebrate chordates, and vertebrate chordates.
3. Trace the trends in vertebrate evolution from fishes to mammals.
4. Understand the adaptations that were necessary for organisms to move onto land.
5. Give an example of each of the major classes of vertebrates, and tell how that class differs from the others.

Key Terms

Archaeopteryx
chordates
notochord
nerve cord
endoskeleton
cartilage
gill slits
pharynx
tail
vertebrates
urochordates
tunicates
filter feeders
lancelets
cephalochordates
fish
hagfish
craniates
ostracoderms
jaws
placoderms
bone tissue
vertebrae
fins
gills
scales
lungs
swim bladder
bony fishes
cartilaginous fishes
ray-finned fishes
lobe-finned fishes
swim bladder
coelacanths
lungfishes
tetrapods
amphibians
amniotes
amniote egg
synapsids
sauropsids
reptiles
dinosaurs
K-T asteroid impact theory
global broiling hypothesis
cloaca
turtles
lizards
tuataras
snakes
crocodilians
endotherms
birds
feathers
migration
mammals
placental mammals
behavioral flexibility
therapsids
monotremes
marsupials
eutherians
placenta
primate
prosimians
arboreal
anthropoids
hominoids
hominids
bipedalism
culture
foramen magnum
prehensile
opposable
Sahelanthropus tchadensis
australopiths
humans
Homo
Homo habilis
Homo erectus
Homo sapiens
multiregional model
African emergence model

Lecture Outline

25.1 Transitions Written in Stone
- A. The absence of transitional forms was an early obstacle to Darwin's theory of evolution.
  1. The discovery of *Archaeopteryx* specimens, which display both reptilian (clawed forelimbs, teeth, and bony tail) and bird features (feathers), was significant.
  2. *Archaeopteryx* (ancient winged one) lived about 150 million years ago.
- B. Such fossils are witness to the history of life.

25.2 Chordate Traits and Evolutionary Trends
- A. Chordate Characteristics
  1. Chordates are coelomate, bilateral animals.
  2. All chordates, at some time in their lives, have four distinctive features.

a. A *notochord* is a long rod of stiffened tissue that supports the body; later it changes to bony units in vertebrates.
b. A *dorsal, tubular nerve cord* lies above the notochord and gut.
c. A muscular *pharynx with gill slits* is positioned at the entrance to the digestive tract.
d. A *tail*, or rudiment thereof, exists near the anus.

B. Invertebrate Chordates
1. Cephalochordates or lancelets are small fishlike animals with tapered bodies.
a. They lie buried in the sand, filtering food from the stream of water passing through the pharynx.
b. Muscles are arranged in a segmented pattern on both sides of the notochord; circulation is closed (but no red cells); and respiration is directly across the body wall.
c. Lancelets display all four of the vertebrate characteristics throughout their lives.
2. Urochordates (tunicates, or sea squirts) are marine organisms covered with a gelatinous tunic.
a. The larval stage resembles a tadpole and has a notochord in the tail.
b. The adult is sessile, maintaining a constant flow of water entering through the gill slits, bringing in food particles (filter feeding) and oxygen and carrying away wastes.
c. Metamorphosis to adulthood results in a loss of the notochord and tail, a regression of the nerve cord, and an expansion of the pharynx for filter feeding.

C. Overview of Chordate Evolution
1. Vertebrates have an internal skeleton, which encloses and protects internal organs and works with muscles to produce movement. Internal skeletons have several advantages over external skeletons.
a. The cells are living, so the skeleton does not have to be molted.
b. It allows for greater flexibility.
c. It is lightweight.
2. The vertebrate notochord develops into the vertebral column, which encloses and protects the spinal cord.
3. Vertebrates have large brains with paired eyes and paired ears.
4. With the exception of lampreys, vertebrates have jaws.
5. Fins with bony supports led to tetrapods.
6. Vertebrates developed amniotic eggs suitable for life on land.

25.3 Jawless Fishes

A. Fishes are ectoderms (their body temperature depends on their environment).
1. Early fossils show cartilaginous fishes with no jaws about 530 million years ago.

B. The jawless fishes today are lampreys and hagfish.

C. Lampreys
1. They have no jaws or fins, but they do have a backbone.
2. Lampreys undergo a metamorphosis, so the larval form and the adult form are dissimilar.
3. Parasitic lamprey use their oral disk to attach to other fish, and they use a tooth-covered tongue to scrape away at their host.

D. Hagfishes
1. They detect worms or animal carcasses via sensory tentacles and use toothlike plates to pull apart the food.
2. Hagfish are often used to create "eelskin" products for humans.

25.4 Evolution of Jawed Fishes

A. The first jawed fishes evolved around 410 million years ago.
   1. Gill arches became jaws over time.
   2. Scales and paired fins (pectoral and pelvic) also became present.

B. The "age of fishes" was approximately 416–369 million years ago
   1. Placoderms and over 200 other species have appeared in fossils.
      a. Placoderms had large jaws and bony armor.
      b. Placoderms were probably extinct at the end of the Devonian Period.
   2. Acanthodians and sharks were also seen in the fossil record.

25.5 Modern Jawed Fishes

A. Cartilaginous Fishes
   1. All possess a streamlined body with a cartilaginous endoskeleton, gill slits, and fins.
   2. The group Chondrichthyes includes the sharks, skates, rays, and chimaeras.
      a. Sharks are formidable predators, with their powerful jaws and replaceable teeth.
      b. Skates and rays live on the ocean bottom where they feed on invertebrates; some can jolt prey with electricity or sting with a venomous tail spine.
   3. Most cartilaginous fishes have a cloaca, which emits digestive wastes and also egg cases in females.

B. Bony Fishes
   1. Bony fishes have a bony skeleton and covers that protect their gills. They also have a swim bladder to regulate their depth.
   2. Ray-Finned Fishes
      a. The ray-finned fishes are highly maneuverable thanks to their fins, which are supported by rays that originate from the dermis.
      b. Almost all ray-finned fishes belong to a group called the teleosts.
   3. Lobe-Finned Fishes
      a. The lobe-finned fishes bear fleshy extensions on the body.
      b. Lungfishes have gills and one, or a pair of, "lungs" that are modified gut wall outpouchings.
      c. Coelacanths, lobe-finned fishes, were thought to be extinct until they were rediscovered in 1938.
      d. Lobe-finned fish are most closely related to amphibians.

25.6 Amphibians—First Tetrapods on Land

A. Adapting to Life on Land
   1. Amphibians are land-dwelling vertebrates that have a three-chambered heart and require water for reproduction.
   2. Other adaptations include reliance on lungs, changes to the inner ear to hear better in air, and eyes protected from drying out.
   3. The selective advantage to living on land is survival in areas where water supply changes seasonally.
      a. Amphibians are still tied to the water, since their eggs would dry out quickly on land.

B. Modern Amphibians
   1. All amphibians are carnivores as adults.
   2. They release eggs into the water, which hatch into larvae that have gills.
   3. Hormones prompt a metamorphosis into adulthood; most adults lose their gills and develop lungs. Some aid this process by breathing across their skin.
   4. Salamanders have an elongated body with a tail that persists into adulthood.

a. When they walk, the body bends from side to side, much like a fish moving through water.

b. Adults may retain larval features including gills and a tail.

c. Some larvae may become sexually mature but not reach a true adult stage.

5. Caecilians have lost their limbs and vision.

a. These unusual creatures live burrowed in the forest floor where they hunt for invertebrate prey.

b. They have no limbs but do have small scales embedded in the skin.

6. Frogs and toads are the best known.

a. These animals possess long hind limbs capable of responding to powerful muscles.

b. Their success on land is due, in part, to the excellent prey-grasping capability of the tongue attached at the front of the mouth.

C. An Ongoing Decline

1. Amphibians are in trouble.

a. Six species of frog, four species of toad, and eleven species of salamander in the United States and Puerto Rico are currently listed as threatened or endangered.

b. Many declines correlate with shrinking and deteriorating habitats; amphibians must have pools of standing water to breed and these are being filled.

2. Long-term changes in climate, increases in ultraviolet radiation, spread of fungal and parasitic diseases, as well as introduction of new species into the amphibian habitats are also causing numbers to decline.

3. Pollution and chemical contamination of their aquatic habitats is a contributing factor.

25.7 The Amniotes

A. Amphibians gave rise to amniotes, who are characterized with three features critical to their escape from water dependency.

1. They produce amniote eggs with covering membranes and a shell, which allow the eggs to be laid in dry habitats.

2. They have a toughened skin due to keratin, which is resistant to drying.

3. Their kidneys are good at conserving water.

B. The two major groups of amniotes are mammals and reptiles.

1. Dinosaurs are thought to be related to reptiles.

a. Now birds are felt to be descended from dinosaurs.

b. It is thought that an asteroid hit the Earth by the end of the Cretaceous period and caused the extinction of dinosaurs.

c. The impact crater for the asteroid that hit Earth during the Cretaceous-Tertiary boundary was found in the Gulf of Mexico.

24.8 Non-Bird Reptiles

A. General Characteristics

1. All species of turtles, lizards, tuataras, snakes, and crocodilians are cold blooded and have internal fertilization and a cloacal opening for reproduction and excretion.

B. Major Groups

1. Turtles

a. Turtles possess a distinctive shell that offers protection while conserving water and body heat.

b. Instead of teeth, turtles have horny plates that are used to grip and chew food.

c. Turtle eggs are vulnerable to predators, resulting in declining numbers.

2. Lizards and Snakes

a. Lizards are the most diverse reptiles.

b. Most lizards are small-bodied insect eaters, although the marine iguanas of the Galápagos are herbivores; their most usual habitats are deserts and tropical forests.
c. Some, such as the monitor lizard, can subdue deer, while many are prey for other animals.
d. Snakes are descended from short-legged, long-bodied lizards.
e. All are carnivores, many with flexible jaws that permit swallowing quite large, whole prey.
f. Snakes are limbless but retain vestiges of hind limbs.
g. Many are venomous and may bite humans, especially when provoked.

3. Crocodilians
   a. Crocodiles and alligators all live in or near water.
   b. The body plan includes a long snout; body temperature is regulated behaviorally (ectothermic).
   c. They show complex behavior, as when the parents guard nests and assist hatchlings into the water.

25.9 Birds—The Feathered Ones

A. General Characteristics
1. Birds produce eggs with internal membranes that harden when calcium forms around the outer membrane.
2. Birds lack teeth; instead they have a jaw bone covered with layers of keratin.
3. Birds are endothermic and their feathers serve as insulation.
4. Feathers are derived from organs in the skin, and in covering the wings make a good flight surface and conserve metabolic heat in the body.
5. Bones in the bird body are lightweight because of air cavities within them.
6. To keep air constantly flowing for respiration, birds have adapted a series of air sacs that continually keeps air moving to the lungs.
7. The heart is four-chambered, and the lungs are highly efficient because of their "flow-through" design.

B. Avian Diversity
1. There are 10,000 named species of birds ranging from tiny hummingbirds to large, flightless ostriches.
2. Birds exhibit migratory behavior.
   a. Seasonal day length is a triggering factor.
   b. Most of the travel, sometimes very long distances, is from breeding grounds and wintering places.

25.10 The Rise of Mammals

A. Mammalian Traits
1. Hair covers at least part of the body (whales are an exception).
2. Milk-secreting glands nourish the young.
3. Dentition (incisors, canines, premolars, and molars) is extensive and specialized to meet dietary habits.
4. Brain capacity is increased, allowing more capacity for memory, learning, and conscious thought.
5. Mammals show *behavioral flexibility*: the ability to expand on the basics with novel forms of behavior.

B. Mammalian Evolution
1. Monotremes are egg-laying mammals.
   a. Examples are the spiny anteater and the platypus.

2. Marsupials are pouched mammals.
    a. Examples are kangaroos and aardvarks.
3. After continental movements, marsupials and monotremes were isolated in Australia.
4. Placental mammals evolved after Pangea separated.
    a. Placental mammals are more fully developed at birth and more likely to survive predation.
    b. In many instances, placental mammals thrived while populations of monotremes and marsupials declined.

25.11 Modern Mammalian Diversity

A. Egg-Laying Monotremes
1. Monotremes are represented today only by the duck-billed platypus and the spiny anteater in Australia and Papua New Guinea.
2. Anteaters have protective spines, burrow, and eat ants.
3. Monotremes lay eggs but suckle their young.

B. Pouched Marsupials
1. The marsupials give birth to tiny, blind, hairless young that find their way to the mother's pouch, where they are suckled and finish their development.
2. Marsupials living today are: kangaroos, koalas, Tasmanian devils, and opossums.

C. Placental Mammals
1. Placental mammals nourish their young within the mother's uterus by the placenta—a composite of maternal and fetal tissue.
    a. The placenta is the organ of exchange of nutrients and wastes between the maternal blood and the fetal blood.
2. Placental nourishment is more efficient than nourishment of the pouched animals.
3. Representatives of this group are found in virtually every aquatic and terrestrial environment.
4. Orders of placental mammals are:
    a. Rodentia – rats, mice, hamsters, squirrels, beavers, porcupines, guinea pigs.
    b. Chiroptera – bats.
    c. Soricomorpha – moles, shrews.
    d. Carnivora – dogs, cats, wolves, bears, foxes, weasels, seals, sea lions, walruses.
    e. Cetacea – whales, dolphins.
    f. Artiodactyl – cattle, deer, goats, pigs, hippos.
    g. Perissodactyla – horses, zebras, rhinos.
    h. Primates – lemurs, monkeys, apes, humans.

12.12 Transitions Written in Stone (Revisited)

A. Private collectors hold some rare fossils in private collections.

B. Many scientists argue that private ownership undermines research efforts.

Suggestions for Presenting the Material

- In contrast to the information given in the text on invertebrates, students should be more familiar with the vertebrates. In fact, they may be overly confident and not listen as attentively as they should. Challenge student assertions; the group that is described as reptiles may be a good place to challenge conceptions.
- Interest can be sparked by use of slides and videos to show exotic vertebrate animals in their natural habitat.

- Additional interest can be generated by allowing any students that have cared for, or studied, vertebrates to share their experiences.
- This chapter, just like the invertebrate chapter, contains a great deal of diversity of species. Decide what your goals are for student learning and let that guide how you present the information. What is most important: an understanding of how vertebrates are classified, how vertebrate evolution progressed, or all of the examples in the text equally? If you are teaching an introductory course, especially to non-majors, it may be more appropriate to focus on understanding classification and how the lineages progressed.
- The authors have gone to special lengths to present the vertebrates based on their evolution. This should be emphasized in lecture.
- Work with students to develop a matrix that defines the characteristics of several groups within the vertebrate group.
- Have each student in the class choose a representative animal from this chapter. Every student should explain how their animal fits the criteria to be considered a chordate. Are the necessary characteristics present in the adult animal? Also mention at least one adaptation for each animal that makes it well-suited for its environment.
- Discuss the advantages of having a placenta. Most individuals see the placenta as merely an avenue for nutrition from the mom. It also serves an immune function—it prevents the mom from detecting something foreign in her body and expelling her offspring before it is fully developed. Show a photo of a newborn kangaroo. This organism is expelled from the mother kangaroo's body prematurely, due to the lack of a placental barrier. Therefore, it is necessary for the newborn kangaroo to complete its development in the mother's pouch.
- Show images of lancelets and tunicates to the class. What phylum do they initially appear to represent? Name the requirements to be classified as a chordate. Are these characteristics present in the adult organism?
- Note that all vertebrates contain an endoskeleton. Compare and contrast this endoskeleton with the exoskeleton of insects, for example. Which appears to be the more successful model and why?

Classroom and Laboratory Enrichment

- If you are fortunate to live in or near a large city with a zoo, arrange a field trip, but this time with a difference. Using the matrix described above, have the students view the vertebrates and try to fit them into their classification schemes.
- If you cannot physically go to a zoo, have the zoo come to you. Try to arrange a visit from a zookeeper or zoo outreach official; they may have prepared presentations that they are available to give to schools.
- If any students have vertebrate pets suitable for showing in the laboratory, allow them to show the animals and describe any unusual aspects of their lives or habits.
- If you are fortunate to have an animal-rearing facility on your campus, arrange a visit to dispel the notion that animals are just warehoused in these places.
- Instead of lecturing on the vertebrate groups, have students prepare presentations that detail each group. Give the students minimum requirements they have to define and then let them choose how to present examples of their group.
- Arrange a visit from a local Department of Conservation or Department of Fish and Wildlife to come into your class and discuss the types of invertebrates that live in your area and the issues that affect them. Ask them about conservation efforts that occur in your biome to conserve the variety of species.

- Nearly every campus has some kind of vertebrate collection. Bring some of the specimens to the classroom or arrange for a tour of the museum.
- There is no scarcity of visual material depicting the diversity of animal life. It ranges from professionally made 2 x 2 transparencies, to single-phylum films, to full-length video surveys of the animal kingdom, such as David Attenborough's *Life on Earth* (available at retail outlets).
- If your budget allows, purchase some representative chordates to dissect. You may want to just exhibit previously dissected animals at the front of the lab. Make sure the students can see the traits that help to categorize these specimens.
- Discuss the features present in an amniote egg. What is its primary advantage?
- Describe a typical example of both an ectothermic and an endothermic model. How does their lifestyle impact their feeding pattern? Note how an endothermic animal, such as a mouse, must derive heat from the breakdown of frequent meals, whereas an ectothermic animal, such as a snake, can subsist on less-frequent meals since it derives its heat from the environment.
- Research the difference between a cartilage- and a bony-skeleton. Which is better for flexibility? Which is better suited for weight bearing?

Classroom Discussion Ideas

- Is the general public more concerned about the extinction of a vertebrate or an invertebrate? Why do you think there might be a difference in the level of concern?
- Dating of fossil remains is critical to understanding human evolutionary sequence. How is the age of fossils determined?
- Why was *Archaeopteryx* such a hard fossil to characterize? Why did some people not believe it was possible for such an animal to exist?
- List some vestigial organs present in animal species today. Can you envision their past significance?
- Have a student report on the discovery of fossils from *Dunkleosteus*, a prehistoric jawed fish. Where was it discovered? Do scientists have a theory as to why it is extinct?
- Discuss the structure of a swim bladder in fish. What does it enable an organism to accomplish?
- Relate the story of the "rediscovery" of the coelacanth in 1938.
- Discuss what changes in the sensory organs of amphibians took place to allow them to survive on land. Be sure to include the changes to the inner ear and the development of eyelids. Even though amphibians can live on land, how are they forever dependent on a watery environment?

Additional Ideas for Classroom Discussion

- Rarely are entire fossil skeletons found in one geographical site. Rather, a skeleton is a composite of many "finds." How do scientists know which bones to group together?
- Organize a debate on the use of vertebrate animals as subjects of medical and scientific research. Are there alternatives to their use? Are these alternatives practical? Why might it be important to use more closely related species, like simian species, for medical research than more distantly related ancestors like amphibians?
- Are all chordates vertebrates? Are all vertebrates chordates? Explain.

- Evaluate the extent to which humans should go when breeding unusual animals simply for "show." Are there any breeds that you know of that suffer anatomical or physiological anomalies just for the sake of a good show animal?
- What kinds of animals are the animal-rights movements concerned about? Which ones do they not see as worthy of their protests?
- What role do hunters and fishermen play in the ecological balance of nature? Is their contribution to game management significant?
- Why do you think it is that the unusual reptiles and mammals are found on islands and island continents?
- Recent genetic studies are shining a light on where monotremes like the platypus fit in relation to other mammals. What characteristics do monotremes have in common with more recent mammals? What traits does the platypus have that indicate its divergence from other mammals?
- What role did the K-T extinction play in the mammalian radiation? What allowed mammals to radiate successfully?
- Have each student select an extinct chordate species and investigate the structure of their animal. Do they think the extinction of this animal was due to man's actions or a natural phenomenon? Is there any way this could have been prevented? What can we learn to prevent future extinctions?
- Why is it necessary for amphibians to produce very large amounts of eggs?
- Which modern-day snakes show x-ray evidence of remnants of hind limbs? What does that indicate about their past ancestors?
- Debate the question, "Were dinosaurs more similar to birds or reptiles?"
- Most individuals consider bats to be dangerous animals due to their adverse presentation in literature. What is the diet of most species of bat? Are rabid bats common? Also research the fungal disease that is endangering the lives of many bats today.
- How do rodents serve as a vector for transmission of the hantavirus to humans? How prevalent are cases of hantavirus infection?

How Would You Vote? Classroom Discussion Ideas

- Monitor the voting for the online question. The topic of private ownership of fossils should generate some interesting discussion. Other questions to consider might be: Should scientists sell fossils to individuals or corporations to fund their work? Should there be rules about owners of such important parts of Earth's history. It was Indiana Jones, albeit in a movie, who had a famous quote: "These belong in a museum!"
- Take a poll in your classroom: If any of your students found a rare fossil, would they consider it to be their own personal property? Would they sell it to a private investor or donate it to scientists for research purposes?

Term Paper Topics, Library Activities, and Special Projects

- Chordates dominate our thinking when the word *animal* is used. But they constitute about 3 percent of the total species (based on the numbers in Table 26.1). Relate this fact to the concept of pyramids (energy, biomass, numbers) as presented in Unit VII.
- What is the relative extent of extinction of vertebrates compared with that of invertebrates?
- Evaluate the literature of the animal rights movement. Is it scientifically sound? Does it place emotion above the public good?

- Research the ethical basis (if there is any) of how we should treat animals. If you come to any conclusions about treatment of vertebrates, can you formulate as strong an argument for invertebrates?
- Research the evolution of an animal that is common today. How has it changed throughout the ages? The horse is a good animal to examine for this question.
- Prepare an analysis of the contribution that hunters and fishermen make to the management of animals.
- There are some chordates that serve as parasites, such as the lamprey. Research the prevalence of lampreys in Lake Erie in the 1970s. How have human efforts restored the ecological balance in this ecosystem?
- Amphibians represent a transition between water living and land living. Detail how the combination of traits in amphibians allows them to live on land, but still ties them to water.
- Reptile is an outdated concept based on what we now know about the species that make up that group. Prepare an argument about why it is that reptiles are not a monophyletic group.
- Movies like *Jurassic Park* feed our imagination with wonderful images of what dinosaurs may have been like. More recent analysis of *Tyrannosaurus rex* demonstrates that it would have been a very slow animal. Detail the reality of what it would have meant to be a dinosaur that was as big as a house or small building.
- Many species of amphibian are in jeopardy of extinction. What environmental factors are thought to be the problem? Are these issues due to the intervention of man? What could we do to prevent the disappearance of these organisms?
- Compare and contrast crocodiles and alligators. Be sure to include their native habitats and the physical distinctions between the two groups.
- Nearly everyone is fascinated by venomous snakes. Make a list of the 10 most venomous snakes in the world and their locations. These may not be the same as a list of the most dangerous snakes in the world. The snakes that should be the most feared are not only venomous, but short-tempered as well.
- List and discuss the adaptations that allow birds to fly. Which of these traits are missing in flightless birds?
- Make a poster discussing the structure of the various teeth types present in mammals. From looking at the complement of teeth from an organism, can you make some assumptions about its diet?

Possible Responses to *Critical Thinking* Questions

1. It is easier for modern biologists to accept the idea that a mammal can have reptile-like traits, because we have a lot more evidence of the links between reptiles, birds, and mammals. This would include more fossils and specimens as well as molecular data. In 1798, the idea of evolution by natural selection had not been considered—Darwin published *Origins* in 1859. Therefore, each individual organism was created complete and unchanging according to the science in 1798. Who would blame scientists that thought the carcass of the platypus was an elaborate hoax, since they have such unique characteristics?
2. Flightless birds lay very large eggs. The kiwi bird of New Zealand lays an egg that can weigh up to 25 percent of the bird's weight! You do not see this in birds that are capable of flight, because the additional weight would severely hinder their ability to get off the ground.

3. One way to determine the sex of a bird relies on the coloration of its feathers. However, if the bird is monomorphic (males and females look alike), you may not be able to distinguish the sex of your bird by external examination. Most bird experts recommend that, if you are really eager to determine the sex of your bird, it will either require surgery to examine internal structures or a DNA analysis. The sex of a puppy can easily be determined by an external examination.
4. Many large species, such as those of whales and sharks, are filter feeders. The ocean is filled with small organisms and plankton that serve as a readily available food source. The animal moves water into their mouth and retains the food while expelling the water. An animal of a great size might otherwise have difficulty locating a constant source of large animals to feed on.

Possible Responses to *Data Analysis Exercise* Questions

Australian crested pigeons make a louder-than-normal noise when they take off in an alarmed state. Researchers wanted to see if this noise was produced to warn other pigeons of a dangerous situation.

1. The pigeons did respond differently to non-alarmed-flight whistles than alarmed-flight whistles.
2. Lowering the amplitude of the alarmed-flight noise made fewer birds respond to its message.
3. This experiment clearly demonstrates that birds responded to a distress whistle from other birds by the huge differences in the percentages of the various experimental groups.

26

HUMAN EVOLUTION

Objectives

1. Understand the general physical features and behavioral patterns attributed to early primates, and know primates' relationship to other mammals.
2. Trace primate evolutionary development through the Cenozoic era.
3. Contrast Neanderthals with *Homo sapiens*.
4. Learn the distinctions between the primate species discussed in the chapter.
5. Understand the distinction between hominoids and hominins, and distinguish between *Australopithecus* and *Homo.*
6. List the advantages of bipedalism.
7. Learn the features of the multiregional and replacement models of the dispersal of *Homo sapiens*.

Key Terms

primates
Australopiths
Hominoids
Homo
Homo habilis
Hominids
bipedalism
culture
foramen magnum
prehensile
opposable
Homo erectus
Homo sapiens
prosimians
arboreal
Sahelanthropus tchadensis
Anthropoids
Humans
Neanderthal
Hominins
Culture
multiregional model
replacement model
paleoanthropology

Lecture Outline

26.1 A Bit of a Neanderthal

A. Paleoanthropology is the study of prehistoric humans.

B. *Homo neanderthalensis* remains were first discovered in Germany and are estimated to be 40,000 years old.

1. Other fossilized Neanderthal skeletons have been found that confirm that it was a real population, not just an example of a deformed skeleton.
2. Neanderthal features: pronounced forehead, wide-set nose, stocky stature.
3. Neanderthals were widespread and often coexisted with *Homo sapiens*.
4. DNA shows that some Neanderthals mated with *Homo sapiens* in the Middle East.

26.2 Primates: Our Order

A. Primate Characteristics

1. Primates have increased mobility with arms and feet.
2. Eyes are present on the front of the head and the brain generates a 3D image.
3. The primate brain is large, with increased areas for interpretation of senses (other than smell).
4. The variation of teeth types in a primate indicates a varied diet.
5. Primates thrive on social interactions, and usually only one or two offspring are produced at a time.

B. Origins and Early Branches

1. Primates arrived on the scene approximately 85 million years ago.
2. About 50 million years ago, the primates branched into two new suborders: the wet-nosed primates (Strepsirrhini) and the dry-nosed primates (Haplorhini).
   a. Lemurs, with their characteristic cleft nose, are representatives of the wet-nosed suborder.
   b. Humans and most other primates are in the dry-nosed suborder.
   c. Tarsiers are the oldest dry-nosed animals still present on Earth.
3. Arthropods include: monkeys, apes, and humans.
   a. Arthropods originated in Africa or Asia.

26.3 The Apes

A. Hominoid Origins and Divergences

1. Hominoids probably branched off from a common ancestor with Old World monkeys about 30 million years ago.
   a. Hominoids were characterized by large brains and an upright posture.

2. Members of the species *Proconsul* lived in Africa 20 million years ago.
   a. Proconsuls had flattened molars, but no tail.
3. There are different theories on the relationship between apes of the Miocene period and modern-day apes.
   a. One theory states that modern apes in Africa are derived from an ape lineage from Europe.
   b. Another theory says that African apes evolved in Africa and that European apes have no current descendants.

B Modern Apes
1. Gibbons
   a. Gibbons live in groups in Southeast Asia.
   b. They are sometimes called "lesser apes" and typically weigh between 15 and 30 lbs
2. Orangutans
   a. Orangutans live alone in either Sumatra or Borneo
   b. They are typically 175–200 lbs.
3. Gorillas, Chimpanzees, Bonobos
   a. All are classified as African great apes.
   b. They walk on their knuckles and live alone.
   c. Chimpanzees and bonobos are our closest living relatives.
   d. Chimpanzees show a more aggressive temperament, and bonobos prefer sexual acts not related to reproduction.

C. A Human-Ape Comparison
1. Humans are hairless as compared to apes.
2. Humans have skeletal adaptations that allow them to be bipedal (walk upright).
   a. Skeletal changes include: curves of the backbone, arched feet, a spinal cord that enters the center of the skull, and a non-opposable big toe.
   b. Human hands are capable of grasping objects with a precision type of grip.
   c. A human brain is much larger than that of a chimpanzee.

26.4 Rise of the Hominins

A. Early Proposed Hominins
1. Hominins are the lineage that is most related to humans.
2. Skeletal evidence indicates that they walked upright.
   a. Skulls have been found with openings for the spinal cord that are much like that of humans.
   b. Femurs similar to those of modern humans have also been viewed in the fossil record.
3. Complete skeletons of *Ardipithecus* have been located.
   a. Ardipithecus is probably a hominin that both walked upright and swung through the trees in an apelike fashion.

B. Australopiths
1. *Australopithecus afarensis* skeletons have been found in eastern Africa.
   a. Australopiths were small, upright-walking organisms that retained the ability to climb readily.
   b. They had small bones and teeth.
2. *Paranthropus* descended from *Australopithecus*, but aer not thought to be ancestors of humans.

a. They had strong teeth and jaws, which enabled them to eat a rough diet when more desirable foods were unavailable.

C. Factors Favoring Bipedalism

1. Bipedalism is energy efficient, keeps the body cooler, allows for a better view of the surroundings, and frees the upper extremities for other purposes.

26.5 Early Humans

A. Classifying Fossils—Lumpers and Splitters

1. Lumpers tend to group fossils together despite their differences.
2. Splitters tend to highlight the differences between fossils and to call them separate species.

B. *Homo habilis*

1. Fossils from *H. habilis* ("handy man," due to the use of tools) appear to be 2.3 million yearsold.
2. Scientists cannot decide if *H. habilis* should be classified as a species of *Australopithecus* or in the genus *Homo.*

C. *Homo erectus*

1. *Homo erectus* (upright man) was about 1.5 meters tall and had a larger brain than *H. habilis*.
   a. Turkana boy lead scientists to believe that *H. erectus* were long-distance runners, but future fossil finds implied that *H. erectus* had a shorter stature.
2. *Homo erectus* traveled long distances from Africa to Dmanisi, Georgia, and ultimately to Indonesia and China.

D. Early Culture

1. Tool-making was an early cultural event.
   a. Approximately 3.4 million years ago, stones were used to remove meat from bones.
   b. Later, around 1.4 million years ago, more sophisticated tools were made in a variety of shapes.
2. Scientists feel that a meat-eating lifestyle brought about the need for the use of tools.
3. Both *H. habilis* and *H. erectus* are not thought to be able to speak, since they do not show the necessary anatomical features.

26.6 Recent Human Lineages

A. Origin and Dispersal of *Homo sapiens*

1. *Homo sapiens* appears, according to the fossil record, to be 195,000 years old.
2. There are two models that attempt to explain the dispersal of *Homo sapiens.*
   a. In the multiregional model, *Homo sapiens* evolved from subpopulations of *H. erectus* in the various parts of the world to which they had migrated many years before.
   b. In the replacement model, *H. sapiens* originated in Africa and migrated out to replace the *H. erectus* populations already there.
3. Fossil evidence and strong data from the DNA sequencing of mitochondria, X and Y chromosomes, and autosomes support the replacement model.
   a. The oldest *H. sapiens* fossils are from Africa.

B. Pre-Modern Homo Species

1. Scientists discovered 18,000-year-old hominin fossils.
   a. This hominin would have lived at the same time as modern humans.
   b. Scientists are unsure whether to categorize the remains as belonging to *Homo floresiensis, Homo erectus, Homo sapiens,* or *Australopithecus.*

26.7 A Bit of a Neanderthal (Revisited)

A. Neanderthals were not as primitive as previously thought.

1. They appear to be capable of speech and had a social structure.
2. Neanderthals were short in stature, stocky, and did not have a protruding chin.
3. There is evidence that Neanderthals mated with modern-day humans approximately 60,000 years ago.
4. The cause of the demise of Neanderthals is unknown, but may be due to competition, climate changes, or disease.

Suggestions for Presenting the Material

- Depending on the region of the country and your particular institution, the discussion of human origins may, or may not, spark some controversy in your class. Whether we acknowledge it or not, this is an area where religious beliefs and scientific explanations conflict. Carefully craft your discussions to present the maximum amount of scientific evidence without deliberately being offensive one way or the other. Remember that science is an epistemology where evidence and methodology trumps personal beliefs. Present evidence and evaluate the evidence. This is also a good opportunity to reiterate several topical concepts that have already come up during your semester, including: the nature of science, the meaning of a theory, and how confounding evidence supports evolution.
- The origins of primates and the evolutionary trends that resulted in certain key characteristics are quite universally accepted.
- Invite anthropologists that document human evolution into your class to present their findings and spark a discussion.
- Emphasize the fact that *Australopithecus* and *Homo* species were contemporaries.
- Because there are several genus and species names associated with primate evolution, each with distinguishing characteristics, perhaps you could construct a table on an overhead transparency (or printed handout) summarizing this data.

Classroom and Laboratory Enrichment

- Because of the interest in human origins, numerous videotapes and slide sets are available (check supply catalogs in your A/V center). Some may be more technical; others may be for the general public.
- If you are fortunate to have an expert in human evolution available, by all means arrange for an illustrated lecture on this complex subject.
- View museum displays depicting early human evolution and life.
- Contrast the structure and function of the hands and feet of apes and humans. How does the structure of human hands make them better adapted for tool making?
- Design a Jeopardy-style quiz for the students. The categories could be different species of primates including human ancestors. A template is available at: http://jeopardylabs.com/
- Where are the majority of the fossils of the human lineage found? What environmental conditions must be met for successful fossilization to occur?

- Look into the criteria to become a paleoanthropologist. What are the courses that one must take in college to pursue that career pathway? Is a master's degree necessary? What are the standard salary ranges for this position?

Classroom Discussion Ideas

- What biological characteristics define what it means to be human? How is that different than what we know of our closer relatives?
- Review the advantages of bipedalism. Are there any disadvantages that you can imagine? Some potential thoughts are: varicose veins, back problems, and problems with childbirth.
- Contrast the traits of a tarsier with a lemur. Name similar and dissimilar characteristics.
- How does "Ardi" compare to "Lucy"? Where was each discovered? How complete was each specimen? Which one is representative of an earlier specimen?
- What can fossilized footprints tell about the organism that produced them? How would one determine the stride of that species by examination of the foot imprint?

Additional Ideas for Classroom Discussion

- What characteristics define a "primate"? What additional traits separate primates from other mammals?
- What characteristics distinguish *Australopithecus* from *Homo*?
- Based on the information presented in this chapter, do most students consider themselves a "lumper" or a "splitter"?
- Divide the class into two sections. Have one side present an argument for the multiregional model and the other discuss the replacement model of human lineage. Which side appears more plausible to the majority of the class?
- Compare and contrast the features and lifestyles of *Homo habilis* and *Homo erectus*.
- Show the locations of major fossil finds on a map of the world.

How Would You Vote? Classroom Discussion Ideas

- Monitor the voting for the online question. This is a particularly fascinating question that is sure to illicit strong responses from the class. Many individuals will have a problem with experimentation on a species like the chimpanzee, which possesses human-like characteristics. On the other hand, experimentation on chimpanzees would provide valuable information due to their many similarities to humans. There may be some individuals that suggest experimentation on human populations instead. How would these participants be compensated? Is it ethical to perform potentially dangerous experimentation on humans?

Term Paper Topics, Library Activities, and Special Projects

- Prepare a report on the methods illustrators use to reconstruct fossilized humans. Assess the degree of freedom individual artists use in their work (check the Readings list at the end of this chapter).
- Pick a human trait and find evidence for its evolution. For example, what do we know about the evolution of speech, or intelligence, or the use of tools?
- There are more examples of the hominid lineage; detail what we know about other hominids and how they may be related to our lineage.
- Investigate the controversy surrounding the skeleton called "Lucy."
- Research the recent discovery of the relationship between human and chimpanzee DNA.
- Examine the characteristics that are present in Neanderthals. Make a chart comparing these traits to those of modern man. What are the major differences? What have DNA analyses revealed? Read more about the work of Svante Paabo and report to the class.
- Modern man is still evolving. What are some potential changes that might be expected to eventually occur? As an example, do you think humans are evolving taller?
- Design a poster-sized timeline that contains the appearance of the major primates discussed in this chapter.
- Compare the cranial capacity of *Austalopithecus* and *Homo sapiens*.
- What do you feel was *Austrlopithecus*' most improved trait over its predecessors?

Possible Responses to *Critical Thinking* Questions

1. It is true that bonobos and chimpanzees have different "personality" traits. Studies have described bonobos as sensitive and lively, whereas chimps are characterized as being coarse and hot-tempered. Although we might like to align ourselves with the more flattering personality profile, according to DNA evidence, we are equally related to both species. Researchers report that we have approximately 98 percent of our DNA in common with both bonobos and chimpanzees.
2. A tree that represents the relationship between chimpanzees, Neanderthals, the finger's DNA, and a modern human based on DNA evidence is shown below:

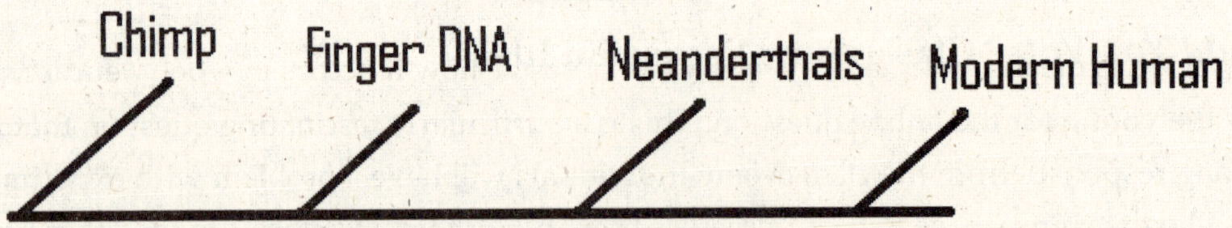

Possible Responses to *Data Analysis Exercise* Questions

Scientists have found a mutated MC1R allele in Neanderthal fossils. They performed experimentation to see if the allele impacted skin and hair color.

1. The MC1R activity was much greater in the monkeys with the normal allele.
2. It appears that the mutation probably produced reddish hair and pale skin in Neanderthals.
3. The green fluorescent protein serves as a control.

27

PLANT TISSUES

Chapter Outline

SEQUESTERING CARBON
THE PLANT BODY
- Basic Body Plan
- Overview of Tissues
- Meristems

SIMPLE AND COMPLEX TISSUES
PRIMARY SHOOT STRUCTURE
A CLOSER LOOK AT LEAVES
- Leaf Similarities and Differences
- Leaf Fine Structure

PRIMARY STRUCTURE OF ROOTS
SECONDARY GROWTH
TREE RINGS AND OLD SECRETS
MODIFIED STEMS
SUMMARY
DATA ANALYSIS EXERCISE
SELF-QUIZ
CRITICAL THINKING

Objectives

1. Understand how plants can reduce the amount of carbon in the atmosphere.
2. Describe the generalized body plan of a flowering plant.
3. Define and distinguish among the various types of ground tissues, vascular tissues, and dermal tissues.
4. Understand the primary shoot and root structure.
5. Explain how plant tissues develop from meristems.
6. Know the functions of stems, leaves, and roots.
7. Explain what is meant by *secondary growth,* and describe how it occurs in woody eudicot roots and stems.
8. Understand the relationship between tree rings and the environment.
9. Understand how some stems are modified and function in storage and reproduction.

Key Terms

shoots	apical meristems	cotyledons	xylem
roots	lateral meristems	parenchyma	vessel members
ground tissue system	primary growth	mesophyll	tracheids
vascular tissue system	secondary growth	collenchyma	phloem
dermal tissue system	eudicot	sclerenchyma	sieve-tube members
meristems	monocot	lignin	companion cells

epidermis
periderm
terminal buds
lateral buds
node
internode
vascular bundles
cortex
pith
blade
petiole
simple leaves
compound leaves
palisade mesophyll
spongy mesophyll
veins
primary root
lateral roots
root cap
root hairs
vascular cylinder
pericycle
endodermis
taproot system
adventitious roots
fibrous root system
herbaceous plants
woody plants
vascular cambium
cork cambium
secondary xylem and phloem
wood
bark
cork
heartwood
sapwood
sap
early wood
late wood
stele

Lecture Outline

27.1 Sequestering Carbon

A. Plant Tissue Systems and Their Function

1. Humans release a large amount of carbon dioxide into the atmosphere by burning fossil fuels.
   a. Excess atmospheric greenhouse gases traps heat in the Earth's atmosphere.
   b. Greenhouse gases may cause changes in the Earth's climate.
2. Carbon sequestration is the removal of carbon dioxide from the atmosphere.
3. Plants have a natural ability to sequester carbon.
   a. Photosynthesis uses the energy from the sun to build sugars from absorbed carbon dioxide and water.
   b. Cellulose and lignin, materials that strengthen plants, contain large amounts of carbon-containing compounds.
   c. When the plant dies, the carbon is slowly returned to the atmosphere; since plant materials decay slowly, it takes years for the carbon to re-enter the atmosphere.
4. Currently, forests worldwide hold more than twice as much carbon as the atmosphere; the forests absorb about three billion tons of carbon dioxide each year, about one-third of the amount released by humans.

27.2 Components of the Plant Body

A. Eudicots versus Monocots

1. Seed leaves: monocots—one; dicots—two.
2. Flower parts: monocots—multiples of threes; dicots—multiples of fours or fives.
3. Leaf veins: monocots—parallel; dicots—netlike array.
4. Pollen grains: monocots—one pore or furrow; dicots—three pores or furrows.
5. Vascular bundles: monocots—arranged throughout stem; dicots—arranged in a ring.

B. Plant Tissue Systems and Their Function

1. The aboveground system—shoots—consists of stems, leaves, and flowers.
   a. Stems provide support for upright growth, increasing the likelihood that leaves will be able to collect the sunlight needed for photosynthesis.
   b. The photosynthetic cells in leaves use the light energy to make sugars.
   c. Flowers attract pollinators, which are often required for seed production.
2. The belowground system—roots.
   a. They absorb water and minerals from soil and conduct them to the shoot.
   b. They store food; they also anchor and support the plant.

3. Plant systems contain three different tissues.
   a. The dermal-tissue system covers and protects the plant's surfaces.
   b. The ground tissue makes up the bulk of the plant body.
   c. The vascular-tissue system contains two kinds of conducting tissues that distribute water and solutes through the plant body.
4. Plant tissues originate from meristems—localized regions of self-perpetuating embryonic cells.
   a. Apical meristem at the tips of roots and stems is responsible for growth and elongation.
      1. Descendants of some of these cells will develop into the specialized tissues of the elongating root and stem.
      2. Growth originating at root and shoot tips is labeled primary growth.
   b. Lateral meristem tissues are responsible for the increase in diameter of older roots and stems.

27.3 Two Categories of Plant Tissues

A. Simple Tissues
   1. Parenchyma makes up most of the soft, moist primary growth of plants.
      a. These thin-walled, pliable cells are alive at maturity and retain the capacity to divide.
      b. Parenchyma participates in photosynthesis (mesophyll), storage, secretion, and wound healing.
   2. Collenchyma cells function to structurally strengthen the plant (for example, "strings" in celery).
      a. Collenchyma cells are alive at maturity and are commonly arranged as strands or cylinders beneath the dermal tissue of stems.
      b. The primary cell walls of collenchyma become thickened with cellulose and pectin at maturity.
   3. Sclerenchyma cells provide mechanical support and protection in mature plants.
      a. The secondary walls are thick and often impregnated with lignin, which strengthens and waterproofs cell walls.
      b. Sclerenchyma cells form *fibers* such as in cloth, rope, and paper; others called *sclereids* form strong coats around seeds, as in a peach pit.

B. Complex Tissues
   1. A dermal tissue system called epidermis is a single layer of cells that covers all primary plant parts.
      a. Waxy secretions from the epidermis form the cuticle, which covers the external surfaces of the plant to restrict water loss and resist microbial attack.
      b. Specialized openings in the epidermis called stomata regulate water and gaseous exchange with the air.
      c. The periderm replaces the epidermis when roots and stems increase in diameter and become woody.
   2. Vascular tissues function in the distribution of water, minerals, and sugars throughout the plant.
      a. Xylem consists of two kinds of cells, both dead at maturity, to conduct water and minerals absorbed from the soil.
         1) *Vessel members* are short cells joined end to end to form a vessel with perforation plates at the ends of each member.
         2) *Tracheids* are long cells with tapered, overlapping ends.
         3) Both vessels and tracheids are waterproofed with lignin and can transport water upward and laterally in the plant.

b. Phloem transports sugars and other solutes throughout the plant.
   1) Phloem contains living cells called *sieve tube members* that are connected end to end at the sieve plate to form sieve tubes.
   2) *Companion cells,* a type of parenchyma, are located adjacent to the sieve tube members, and function to load and unload sugars from the phloem.

27.4 Primary Structure of Shoots
- A. Internal Structure of Primary Shoots
  1. A vascular bundle is a multi-stranded cord of primary xylem and phloem running lengthwise through the ground tissue of shoots.
  2. The arrangement of vascular bundles differs between eudicots and monocots.
     a. Eudicots have vascular bundles arranged as a ring underneath the epidermis that divides the ground tissue into the outer cortex and inner pith.
     b. In monocots, the vascular bundles are scattered throughout the ground tissue.
- B. Primary Growth
  1. Terminal buds are a shoot's main zone of primary growth.
     a. Underneath the terminal bud surface is a shoot apical meristem, which constantly produces more cells during the growing season.
     b. The cells that divide from the shoot apical meristem differentiate into specialized tissues.
  2. Lateral buds form in the leaf axil, a region between the upward growing stem and outward growing leaf.
     a. Each axillary bud is a dormant shoot of mostly meristematic tissue.
     b. Hormones secreted by the terminal bud keep the lateral buds dormant.

27.5 A Closer Look at Leaves
- A. Leaf Structure and Function
  1. Most leaves are thin with a high surface-to-volume ratio.
  2. In some environments, leaves may reorient themselves during the day to maximize exposure to sunlight.
  3. In other environments, leaves may reorient themselves to reduce water loss.
- B. Variation in Leaf Type
  1. Monocot versus Eudicot
     a. Eudicot leaves are simple or compound and have a thin, flat blade, which is attached to the stem by means of a stalk, or petiole.
     b. Monocot leaves have flat blades, the base of which forms a sheath around the stem.
- C. Compound versus Simple Leaves
  1. Compound leaves have blades divided into leaflets.
  2. Simple leaves are undivided but may be lobed.
- D. Leaf Fine Structure
  1. Epidermis covers all leaf surfaces.
     a. It may be smooth or covered with a variety of hairs, scales, or other specializations.
     b. The epidermis has small openings, or stomata, which allow for gas exchange.
     c. The waxy cuticle covers the epidermis to minimize water loss.
  2. Mesophyll is a photosynthetic parenchyma.
     a. Photosynthetic parenchyma cells (in the mesophyll layer) are located between the extensive surface areas of the upper and lower epidermis.
     b. CO_2 enters through the stomata and diffuses through air spaces into the photosynthetic tissue; the O_2 byproduct is released from the plant.

c. Dicots have two layers of mesophyll, the columnar and spongy parenchyma, while monocots do not have a single layer of mesophyll.

3. Veins are the leaf's vascular bundles.
   a. Veins (vascular bundles) form a network for water, solutes, and photosynthetic products.
   b. In eudicots, large veins branch into smaller ones embedded in the mesophyll; in monocots, veins are quite similar in length and run parallel with the leaf's long axis.

27.6 Primary Structure of Roots

A. The Root System
   1. The root system is at least as extensive as the shoot system.
   2. Taproot and Fibrous Root Systems
      a. Most eudicots have a taproot system consisting of the primary root and its lateral branchings.
      b. Most monocots have a fibrous root system where the primary root is replaced by adventitious roots with lateral branches.

B. Internal Structure of Roots
   1. The root's structural organization is laid out in a seed; the primary root pokes through the seed coat first.
   2. Cells in the apical meristem divide and then differentiate into the root cap, epidermis, ground tissues, and vascular tissues of the root.
   3. The root cap protects the apical meristem of the soft, actively growing root as it pushes through the soil.
   4. The root epidermis, with its extensions called root hairs, increases the root's surface area available for absorption of water and solutes.

C. Primary Growth
   1. Growth originates in the apical meristem located in the root tip.
   2. Cell division in the root apical meristem gives rise to the protoderm, ground meristem, and procambium; these differentiate into the dermal, ground, and vascular tissues, respectively.
   3. The pericycle surrounds the vascular cylinder and consists of parenchyma cells that actively divide perpendicular to the root axis, giving rise to lateral roots.

27.7 Secondary Growth

A. Secondary growth increases the circumference of woody plants.
   1. Lateral meristems are cylindrical, meristematic tissue that runs lengthwise through the stems and roots.
      a. The vascular cambium of woody plants such as eudicots and gymnosperms consists of two types of cells: long, narrow cells increase the height of the stem and small, rounded cells produce rays that increase the stem's circumference; these cells expand and cause secondary growth by producing secondary xylem and phloem.
      b. The cork cambium gives rise to the periderm, a dermal tissue that consists of parenchyma and cork; bark consists of the periderm and secondary phloem.
   2. Secondary growth is influenced by seasons; during the wetter spring months, early wood is produced with large xylem vessels; in the dryer summer months, late wood is produced with small xylem vessels; each band of early and late growth comprises a growth ring.

B. Heartwood and Sapwood
   1. Heartwood lies at the center of older stems and roots.
      a. It is a depository for resins, oils, gums, and tannins.

   b. It is clogged and no longer functions in transport.
2. Sapwood is secondary growth located between heartwood and the vascular cambium.
   a. It is wet, pale in color, and not as strong.
   b. It is rich in a sugary fluid transported from the roots and is used in the production of maple syrup.

27.8 Tree Rings and Old Secrets

A. The production of yearly tree rings is influenced by environmental conditions such as fires, droughts, floods, landslides, and glacier movements.

B. Analysis of trees growing during early English settlements on the East Coast provides evidence that these colonies were impacted by severe drought.

27.9 Modified Stems

A. Stolons are modified stems that branch from the main stem; adventitious roots and shoots sprout from the node and form new plants; strawberry plants have stolons.

B. Rhizomes are the fleshy, scaly underground portion of the main stem that grow parallel to the soil surface and function as the main storage tissue; ginger root is a rhizome.

C. Bulbs are underground sections of stems encased in layers of overlapping scales that function primarily to store starch for use when environmental conditions are unfavorable; a basal plate separates the roots from the scales; onions are bulbs.

D. Corms are similar to bulbs except they are solid instead of layered.

E. Tubers are similar to corms, but they do not have a basal plate; potatoes are an example.

F. Cladodes are aboveground stem modifications that function to store water; cacti have cladodes.

Suggestions for Presenting the Material

- Emphasize the fact that this chapter concentrates primarily on *angiosperms.*
- The information in this chapter is very visual in nature, so use color slides, models, and diagrams whenever possible. Even if students are seeing many of these structures in lab while they are covering this chapter in lecture, they will gain much reinforcement by seeing diagrams and photos of plant cells, tissues, and systems in lecture.
- Emphasize the link between structure and function in plants.
- Stress the differences between plants and animals, particularly in regard to growth. The concept of growth only at plant meristems, which is different from the way in which animals grow, is initially puzzling to many students.
- Distinguish between the terms *herbaceous* and *woody, apical* and *lateral, primary* and *secondary.*
- Remind students that the structures discussed in this chapter are vegetative structures (define this term); structures used for sexual reproduction will be covered in Chapter 29.
- Introduce useful and familiar plant examples as you go through this chapter. Students are aware, of course, of the importance of plants in our day-to-day existence, but many forget the role plants play in our lives. Use "grocery store" examples; students will be intrigued to hear more about the plants and plant parts they have taken for granted. Bring in plants and fruits and vegetables whenever possible to demonstrate plant structures.
- Wood is another area that is familiar to some students, particularly those who have done woodworking. You can use many examples in this area to introduce points on plant structure and growth.

Classroom and Laboratory Enrichment

- Distribute unusual types of plant tissues around the lecture classroom or lab room. Some possible examples include a fresh celery stalk cut in two (notice strands of collenchyma running along the "ribs" of the stalk), hemp used in making rope (fibers), cotton bolls (fibers), and nutshells (sclereids).
- Whenever possible, visit a greenhouse or park. Have the students find different plants and identify the structures discussed in the chapter. For example, the students could explore differences between monocots and eudicots, woody and herbaceous plants, and/or differences between compound and simple leaves.
- Obtain information about wood from lumber and paper companies. Several companies can supply posters and other materials about trees used for lumber and paper.
- In the lecture classroom, project a figure of a woody twig, and ask students to point out structures such as nodes, internodes, apical meristem, terminal bud, axillary bud primordia, and terminal bud scale scars.
- Demonstrate dendrochronology. Using an overhead projection (or in small groups of students, an actual portion of a tree cross-section), discuss how interpretation of growth rings can reveal drought, fire, disease, windfall, harvesting, and periods of normal growth. Show students a tree-boring device; let them interpret trunk samples obtained with it.
- Pass varied samples of leaves around the room. Ask students how leaf morphology varies with climate.
- At various times of the year, bulbs, corms, tubers, and rhizomes are readily available to bring into the classroom. Discuss the differences between them.
- If the number of students in the class permits it and the physical environment is suitable, take a short field trip to examine the plants and trees on your campus.
- Make ample use of plant structure models that will emphasize the 3D quality lacking in flat photos. This is especially true of conducting tissue.
- Desert plants must balance the need for carbon dioxide against the threat of desiccation. What are some adaptations of desert plants that allow them to open their stomata often enough to get the carbon dioxide sufficient for photosynthesis? Discuss how alternative photosynthetic pathways such as C4 and CAM photosynthesis (Chapter 7) have evolved in response to environmental pressures.
- What happens to transpiration rates on hot days? Dry days? Humid days? Breezy days?

Classroom Discussion Ideas

- Compare the lifestyles of plants and animals. In what ways does the nonmobility of plants influence their structure?
- Reports of topsoil erosion and mineral leaching are numerous. Are there finite amounts of soil and soil nutrients? Will we ever completely exhaust our sources of plant sustenance?
- In what ways are animals dependent on plants for survival?
- How did companion cells acquire their name?
- How does growth in plants differ from growth in animals? What would humans look like if they grew like plants?

- What is the difference between primary growth and secondary growth? What kind(s) of growth occur(s) in a maple tree? Where would you look in the maple tree to find primary growth? Secondary growth? What is the difference between an apical meristem and a lateral meristem?
- What causes "growth rings" in wood? Does one ring always represent one growing season? Does some wood lack growth rings? Why or why not?
- What is girdling? Ask students to think of some examples of girdling that they might have seen (damage done to the bark of small trees by electric or gas-powered weed trimmers is one example). Ask how girdling might occur in nature (nibbling of bark by deer or porcupines is one possibility).
- What is the purpose of the root cap? Is there such a thing as a "shoot cap"? Why or why not? Is there any structure on the shoot tip that is analogous to the root cap?
- What plants have root systems and shoot systems that can be used as food? Many of these plants have modified structures such as roots (for example, carrot), stems (for example, ginger), or leaves (for example, celery, an enlarged petiole) that are eaten.
- Present some familiar examples of common and/or economically important plants such as corn, tomatoes, lettuce, rice, and wheat, and ask students to classify them as monocots or eudicots.
- How useful are plant parts such as leaves, stems, and roots when one is attempting to identify a plant? Are such plant parts a reliable indicator of species?
- Ask your students if pines, firs, and spruces are monocots or eudicots. (The answer, of course, is that conifers are gymnosperms and hence are not classified as either monocots or eudicots.) The ensuing discussion will help students learn the differences, not yet covered in the text, between gymnosperms and flowering plants.
- When you eat an apple, what ground tissue are you eating?
- What is the biggest monocot you can think of? (Some possible answers might be bamboo or palm.)
- What is cork? Where does the cork used in wine bottles come from?
- Plants are the source of many useful products including some insecticides. Do you know the source of pyrethrum? (Answer: mum flowers) Of nicotine? (Answer: tobacco leaves) Of rotenone? (Answer: *Derris* root)
- Why are plants "taken for granted" in our culture?
- Which type of wood, heartwood or sapwood, would be preferable for construction. Why? (Heartwood no longer conducts water and minerals and is dry; heartwood is denser and stronger.)

How Would You Vote? Classroom Discussion Ideas

- Monitor the voting for the online question. Most people (and companies) likely do not want to invest in a significant enough change to truly reduce their carbon dioxide emissions. Thus, carbon offset programs are largely an excuse to continue living our current lifestyle. Currently many carbon offset programs are under fire due to lack of regulation. Many critics point out that the majority of these offset programs fund tree planting efforts, and the calculations these programs use to determine the amount of carbon sequestered in a tree are based on growth in tropical regions. In addition, most of these programs do not consider how much carbon dioxide will return to the atmosphere after the tree dies. There are some programs that use the money from purchased offsets to fund projects that reduce carbon dioxide emissions. Such projects fund green energy, energy conservation initiatives, and methane recovery and destruction. However, these projects also have little regulation, and despite the fact that most carbon offset programs are certified, many experts also question the certification process.

Term Paper Topics, Library Activities, and Special Projects

- What are some of the woody plant species used for lumber? Find the names of as many as you can; you may be surprised at the number! Describe some of these species and discuss their uses.
- Many plant parts provide dyes that can be used to color fabrics. Prepare a demonstration or an exhibit of plant species used as sources for dyes.
- Learn more about the history of paper making, and discuss how modern papers are made.
- Describe some of the morphological adaptations found among plants of extreme climates (e.g., tundra, deserts, and bogs).
- Bamboo and cork flooring are often sold as an eco-friendly flooring option. Why are these products considered eco-friendly and what evidence supports this claim?
- Describe some of the plant species whose leaves, stems, and/or roots can be used as sources for drugs. Just a few of the many examples to include in your research are coca, marijuana, *Ephedra*, foxglove, and opium poppy.
- Describe the morphology, habitat, and geographic range of the insectivorous plant species found in the United States.
- Can plant parts such as leaves, roots, and stems be used to grow new plants? Discuss techniques of vegetative propagation; describe its role in commercial greenhouses and nurseries.
- Investigate the effects on plants that the gypsy moth has had in the northeastern United States.
- What factors make the vast majority of the United States suitable for intensive agriculture?
- Trace the pathway water would follow from the soil solution to the exterior of the leaf. Include movement through the cells, tissues, and systems of the plant.
- How would the morphology of a tree trunk growing in a tropical rain forest compare to one growing in a temperate forest?

Possible Responses to *Critical Thinking* Questions

1. The plant with the yellow flower is a eudicot while the plant with the purple flower is a monocot. A typical eudicot has flower parts in fours or fives (or multiples of fours and fives). Note that the yellow flower has five petals. A typical monocot has flower parts in threes (or multiples of three). Note that the purple flower has three petals.
2. The initials that Oscar carved on the tree will still be at the same height when he returns 10 years later. This is because apical meristems are located at the tips of shoots. In other words, trees grow from their tips not their base. If Oscar were to cut down the tree he would see a growth ring corresponding to each year that the tree had been alive. Each growth would consist of early wood, produced in the spring, and late wood, produced in the fall. Oscar might also gain some insight into what the environmental conditions were like in the rainforest during the lifetime of the tree. This is because environmental conditions such as drought, fire, and floods can influence the appearance of growth rings.
3. This is a eudicot stem. Note that the vascular bundles are arranged in a ring. If this were a monocot stem, the vascular bundles would be scattered throughout the stem (see Figure 27.6). If this were a dicot root, the xylem would be centrally located in the shape of a star, with phloem located between the points of the star (see Figure 27.13).
4. The waxy cuticle on the aboveground tissues prevents water loss. The root tissues are specialized to absorb water. A waxy cuticle on the belowground tissue would inhibit water absorption.

5. Trees grow in height because cell divisions occur in the apical meristems located in the tips of branches. Once a branch has lengthened, it then expands only in diameter. The increase in diameter is due to the activity at the lateral meristems. Trees are larger at the base because, in that region, the apical meristems have been inactive and the lateral meristems have been active for a longer period of time, as compared to the branches located at the top of the tree.

Possible Responses to *Data Analysis Exercise* Questions

1. At approximately 770 A.D., there is a point that extends to about -1.5 PDSI. This indicates a severe drought. As a comparison, the "dust bowl" (indicated by the * on the graph) didn't quite register a -1 PDSI on the graph. Thus, the drought in 770 A.D. was more severe than the "dust bowl."
2. The most severe drought occurred from approximately 1550 A.D. to 1600 A.D. At the height of this drought, the PDSI was -1.5.

28

PLANT NUTRITION AND TRANSPORT

Chapter Outline

Objectives

1. Know which elements are essential to plant health.
2. Explain how water is absorbed, transported, used, conserved, and lost by a plant.
3. Describe how the intake of CO_2 is connected with water loss.
4. Know how translocation of organic substances occurs, according to the pressure flow theory.
5. Understand how plants can help clean up the environment through phytoremediation.

Key Terms

phytoremediation
macronutrients
micronutrients
soil
humus
loams
topsoil
leaching
soil erosion
root hairs
mycorrhizae
mutualism
nitrogen fixation
root nodules
vascular cylinder
endodermis
Casparian strip
epidermis
transpiration
xylem
tracheids
vessel members
cohesion-tension theory
negative pressure
turgor pressure
cuticle
waxes
pectin
cellulose fibers
cutin
stoma, stomata
guard cells
CAM plants
abscisic acid, ABA
phloem
sieve-tubes
companion cells
translocation
source regions
sink regions
pressure flow theory
sieve plate

Lecture Outline

28.1 Leafy Clean-Up

A. The process of phytoremediation involves the use of plants to take up, accumulate, or degrade environmental contaminants.

1. Hybrid poplar trees have been used to absorb organic solvents and degrade them.
2. Alpine pennycress accumulates and stores toxins inside specialized organelles; the contaminated plants can then be harvested and destroyed.

B. Only a few plant species are naturally able to tolerate environmental toxins; however, genetically engineering plants that can't tolerate the toxins may increase the number of species that can be used for phytoremediation.

28.2 Plant Nutrients and Availability in Soil

A. The Required Nutrients

1. Sixteen essential elements are required for plant growth and survival.
   a. Nine elements are called macronutrients (used in significant quantities): C, H, O, N, K, Ca, Mg, P, and S.
   b. Seven are used only in trace quantities (micronutrients): Cl, Fe, B, Mn, Z, Cu, and Mb.
2. Deficiencies in any nutrient can visibly impact a plant's health.

B. Properties of Soil

1. Soil consists of particles of minerals mixed with humus (dead organisms and their litter).
   a. Particles come in three sizes: sand, silt, and clay.
   b. Clay, the smallest, holds onto nutrients as water percolates through the soil.
   c. Plants do best in loams, soils with nearly equal proportions of the three particle types.
2. Layers of soil can be classified by profile properties; topsoil, the uppermost, is the most essential layer for plant growth.

C. Leaching and Erosion

1. Leaching refers to the removal of some of the nutrients from soil as water percolates through it.
2. Erosion is the movement of land under the force of wind, running water, and ice.
3. The loss of topsoil can have a huge economic impact due to inability to grow crops.

28.3 How Do Roots Absorb Water and Mineral Ions?

A. Specialized Absorptive Structures

1. Root hairs are extensions of the root epidermal cells that constantly form just behind the root tip; they greatly increase the absorptive surface.
2. Mycorrhizae (fungi growing around plant roots) aid in absorbing minerals that are supplied to the plant in exchange for sugars. This symbiotic relationship is beneficial to both.
3. Root nodules of legumes harbor bacteria that convert gaseous nitrogen to ammonia and are useful in the growth of plants in the process called nitrogen fixation; this is a form of mutualism.

B. How Roots Control Water Uptake

1. Water and solutes move from the soil across the root epidermis and seep through and around the root ground tissue until reaching the vascular cylinder.
   a. A sheetlike layer of cells, the endodermis, surrounds the vascular cylinder, a column of vascular tissue in the center of the root.
   b. Waxy secretions from the endodermal cells form the water-repellent Casparian strip, forcing water to move into the cells of the endodermis.
   c. Membrane transport proteins in the endodermal cells help control the type and amount of absorbed solutes and water that will be distributed throughout the plant.
2. Most flowering plants also have an exodermis, a layer of cells just inside the root epidermis, which also has a Casparian strip that functions just like the one next to the root vascular cylinder.

28.4 Water Movement Inside of Plants

A. Water Flow through Xylem

1. Water moves from roots to stems and then to leaves though xylem pipelines, which consist of vessel members and tracheids.
2. The xylem pipelines are formed when vessel member cells die.
   a. When individual vessel member cells die, the secondary walls remain, forming the pipeline.
   b. The vessel members are stacked on top of each other and are connected by large openings at the ends, known as the perforation plate.
   c. Xylem vessel members evolved more recently than tracheids and are the main water-conducting tubes in angiosperms.
3. Tracheids are shorter and thinner than vessel members; they contain no perforation plates; water moves through pits in the walls, which are the remnants of plasmodesmata.

B. Cohesion-Tension Theory

1. Water moves through xylem from the roots to the leaves; in tall trees this can be a distance of more than 100 meters.
2. The cohesion-tension theory of water transport explains water movement in plants.
   a. Water lost from the leaves due to transpiration is replaced from the roots by osmosis; this creates a continuous negative pressure (tension) in the plant.
   b. Due to cohesion, unbroken columns of water in the xylem resist rupturing as tension pulls them upward.
   c. The constant loss of water by transpiration causes tension inside the xylem, allowing more water and solutes to be pulled into the roots from the soil before moving up to the leaves.

28.5 Water-Conserving Adaptations of Stems and Leaves

A. Most of the water (more than 90 percent) absorbed by a plant is lost due to evaporation from the leaves; only a small amount of water is available to maintain the plant's metabolism.

B. The Water-Conserving Cuticle
   1. The cuticle is a translucent, water-impermeable layer of waxes, pectin, and cellulose fibers embedded in cutin; it is secreted from epidermal cells that cover the outer surfaces of the plant.
   2. The cuticle does not prevent sunlight from entering the plant but does restrict water loss, the inward diffusion of CO_2, and the outward diffusion of oxygen.

C. Controlled Water Loss at Stomata
   1. Stomata are tiny, collapsible openings of the plant epidermis that regulate the passage of water, carbon dioxide, and oxygen; a pair of guard cells controls the opening and closing of the stomata.
   2. Stomata open and close in response to environmental cues; open stomata allow carbon dioxide to enter (a benefit), but also allow water to be lost (a detriment).
      a. When plants are exposed to sunlight, potassium and water move into the guard cells, causing them to swell (turgor pressure); the stomata of most plants are open during the day and closed at night.
      b. When water becomes scarce, abscisic acid (a hormone) is released by the root cells; abscisic acid causes a burst of nitric oxide, which allows calcium ions to enter the guard cells; in response to the calcium ions, malate, chloride ions, and water exit the guard cells; all of these changes cause the stomata to close and the plant to minimize water loss.

28.6 Movement of Organic Compounds in Plants

A. Conducting Tubes in Phloem
   1. Phloem is a living vascular tissue with organized arrays of conducting tubes, fibers, and parenchyma cells.
   2. Sieve tube cells are alive at maturity and are interconnected side by side and end to end from the roots to the leaves.
   3. Companion cells are located next to the sieve tubes and function to actively transport the products of photosynthesis into the sieve tubes.
   4. Carbohydrates are mainly stored as insoluble starch molecules that must be converted to more soluble carbohydrates, such as sucrose, before being transported throughout the plant.

B. Translocation
   1. The term *translocation* is the technical name for the transport of sucrose and other compounds through phloem.
   2. Movement of molecules through phloem is from sources (mostly leaves) to sinks (flowers and fruits).
   3. Observations of plant-sucking insects demonstrate that the sugary fluid in the phloem is under high pressure.
   4. According to the pressure flow theory, translocation depends on pressure gradients.
      a. Solutes are loaded by active transport into the phloem from a source (e.g., leaves); water also enters by osmosis due to the increase in solutes.
      b. Pressure builds in the sieve tubes, pushing the sucrose-laden fluid out of the source, into the stem, and on to the sink (e.g., fruit).

Suggestions for Presenting the Material

- Students should be able to make an easy transition to this material if the role of function in determining plant morphology was stressed in presenting the previous chapter. Emphasize that plants are supported by a "skeleton" formed by a continuous column of water inside sturdy xylem tubes.
- Students have a difficult time understanding how water moves. Review some of the terms learned earlier that relate to water movement, such as osmosis and turgor pressure. Simple demonstrations such as using a wet paper towel versus a dry paper towel to absorb a puddle of water can be used to demonstrate that water moves toward decreasing water potential.
- To help students understand the large surface area of a plant's root system, provide data on the surface areas of some typical plant root systems. Ask them to guess the ratio of *shoot* surface area to *root* surface area of a typical plant.
- This chapter provides many good opportunities to discuss the selective role of the environment in shaping such features as stomata and root systems.

Classroom and Laboratory Enrichment

- Demonstrate the abundance and fragile nature of root hairs. Germinate radish seedlings in a Petri dish lined with paper towels. Pass the dish around the classroom and allow each student to take a seedling and examine the root hairs. What happens to the root hairs minutes after the seedling is removed from the dish? Why?
- Demonstrate how species adapt to their surroundings by discussing the number, size, location, and distribution patterns of stomata in leaves of different species. Include some unusual examples, such as aquatic plants with stomata on upper leaf epidermis, conifers with sunken stomata, and plants with pubescent leaves.
- Examine tomato seedlings suffering from a deficiency of one of the macronutrients. This can be prepared as a lab experiment of several-weeks duration, or a demonstration (slides) of the results can be shown instead.
- Use a simple soil-testing kit in lab to test samples of several different local soils. What are some steps that could be taken to improve each of the soils tested, if necessary?
- Set up demonstrations of root pressure or transpiration in lecture or lab. For example, grow some corn seedlings for 1–2 weeks. Cut the plant, leaving only 2–3 cm of the stem. The root pressure will cause a drop of water to form at the cut.
- To measure transpiration, place a plant (sunflower seedlings work well) in approximately 30 cm of clear tubing that just fits around the roots and stem of the plant. Shape the tubing into a "U" and add water to the tubing. Record the change in water height over time as a measure of transpiration. Environmental conditions can be altered to see the effect on plant transpiration. For example, repeat the experiment with a fan blowing on the plant, or place a plant in the sun and compare the results with a plant placed in the dark.
- Show slides of chloroplasts containing starch grains. Where did the starch come from? Would you be more likely to see such grains in the morning or in the afternoon? What will happen to the starch grains?
- In lab, provide prepared microscope slides of the undersides of plant species from different environments. In lecture, show slides or diagrams of the lower leaf epidermis.
- Compare the rates of recovery after the wilting of three tomato seedlings that have each been cut off at the base of the main stem (as described below) and then placed in a beaker of water: (1) seedling is cut; (2) seedling is cut while plant is briefly submerged under water; and

(3) seedling is cut, then allowed to sit on the desktop for 15 minutes before being placed in water. Which seedling exhibits the least amount of wilting at the end of the lab period? The most? Why?

- Test slices of various fruits and vegetables for starch content by applying an iodine solution (should turn blue-black).
- Coat the leaves of various plants with clear nail polish and allow to dry 5–10 minutes (you may need to experiment with the drying time). Carefully peel the nail polish and observe the peels under a dissecting scope. Epidermal cells and stomata will be visible. This could be used to demonstrate stomata of plants adapted to different environments, or to perform the peels on the top and bottom of the leaves in order to observe the different densities of stomata.
- Demonstrate negative pressure in plants by sandwiching two dry microscope slides together. Fill the slide sandwich with plain water using a small pipette or needle. Make a puddle of water with food coloring added. Place one of the short edges of the slide sandwich just so it touches the colored water. Place a tissue at the other end of the sandwich to create a constant negative pressure within the slide sandwich. Watch the colored water as it is pulled toward the tissue.
- Grow plants hydroponically and place different concentrations of fertilizer in the water. How much fertilizer is too much? What happens to the plant when too much fertilizer is added?
- After a heavy rain, visit a construction site where the land has been cleared of plants. Use this as an opportunity to discuss the role of plants in preventing erosion. At some construction sites you may be able to discuss the different layers of soil as well.
- Place a stalk of celery in water with food coloring. Over time, slice cross sections from the stem and observe the plant's vascular tissue.
- Obtain a chart showing color photos of the symptoms of mineral deficiencies as listed in Table 28.1. Perhaps a plant nursery or fertilizer supplier can help you. If you cannot obtain a copy of a chart you would like, ask permission to photograph it for a slide.

Classroom Discussion Ideas

- How could responsible government agencies allow such an ecological disaster as the Aberdeen Proving Grounds contamination to happen?
- What is so bad about having lead, arsenic, mercury, and other metals in drinking water?
- What types of home water filters (purifiers) will or will not remove metals from drinking water?
- Are consumers of individual well water necessarily at more risk than consumers of municipal supplies?
- What happens to plants after they have accumulated toxic compounds?
- Genetic manipulation of plants to make more species with the genes required for bioremediation sounds like a good thing. Could it ever be a detriment?
- Is it possible that the scenario described in section 28.1 could result in exchanging contaminated *water* for contaminated *plants*?
- At what kinds of sites might bioremediation be required? Mines? What types of industries?
- How does the cost of bioremediation compare to the cost of mechanical removal of contaminated sites? This information is readily available on the Internet.
- How do the tracheids and vessel members found in xylem conduct water even though they are dead at maturity? In contrast, why must phloem cells remain alive to perform their function?
- Desert plants must balance the need for carbon dioxide against the threat of desiccation. What are some adaptations of desert plants that allow them to open their stomata often enough to get the

carbon dioxide sufficient for photosynthesis? Discuss how alternative photosynthetic pathways such as C4 and CAM photosynthesis have evolved in response to environmental pressures.

- What are some of the endangered plant species in your state? Discuss possible reasons why these plants are endangered. For example, do the endangered species primarily grow on beaches that are now experiencing tremendous overdevelopment? Or are the plants' habitats becoming lost to farmland or erosion?
- What are the invasive species of plants that are a problem where you live? Track the origin of these species and discuss how they traveled to the area.
- Research the history of your state flower and/or tree. Why were they chosen?
- What happens to transpiration rates on hot days? Dry days? Humid days? Breezy days?
- Ask students who have raised tomatoes or other garden plants if they have ever observed "midday wilt," a phenomenon in which even well-watered plants temporarily wilt during the late afternoon. Ask them why this happens. (Midday wilt occurs when transpiration exceeds the rate of water uptake.)
- What are some crop plants that are particularly adept at storing sugars or starches?
- In what ways are animals dependent on plants for survival?
- Reports of topsoil erosion and mineral leaching are numerous. Are there finite amounts of soil and soil nutrients? Will we ever completely exhaust our sources of plant sustenance?
- How do plants combat insect pests in nature? How do we help plants resist insect attack?

How Would You Vote? Classroom Discussion Ideas

- Monitor the voting for the online question. The general idea of genetic engineering is usually not as debatable as more specific uses of this technique. It is the idea of the unknown that concerns many people. What will happen if genetically engineered plants "run amok"? In the case discussed here, the plants are engineered to uptake and store toxins, which is quite helpful to our environment and personal lives. Which is worse: the risk of a GM (genetically modified) organism free in the environment or the toxins in the contaminated site making their way into groundwater systems, wells, streams, or even bays or oceans?

Term Paper Topics, Library Activities, and Special Projects

- Discuss the role of each of the macronutrients in plant metabolism and growth.
- What role has the fibrous root system of grasses played in the establishment and maintenance of prairies in the United States? What happens to the species composition of prairies if such areas are interrupted by roads, farming, or railroads? Discuss the history of the American prairies.
- Describe the role of mycorrhizae in successful seedling growth among species of gymnosperms. How do commercial lumber companies ensure that the proper mycorrhizal fungi will be present on the roots of their tree seedlings?
- Learn more about soil testing. Describe how a typical soil-testing kit works.
- Visit a nursery or garden center where lawn and garden fertilizers are sold. List the N-P-K ratio for each of the different fertilizers. Explain differences among N-P-K ratios of fertilizers for lawns, vegetables, and flowers. Why do fertilizers for different purposes have such different N-P-K ratios? Summarize the roles of nitrogen, phosphorus, and potassium in plant functioning and development.
- What are the effects of acid rain on plant functioning?

- Discuss the effects of extremely cold climates, such as Arctic tundra, on the ratio of shoot systems to root systems. Why is so much of the plant underground in such climates?
- Locate a report (check USDA documents) showing the decline in soil fertility in the United States in the past 100 years.
- Research the tradeoff between applying fertilizer to crops to improve yield and preventing too much buildup of fertilizer in streams.
- Insects such as aphids can be controlled by insecticides introduced into the plant via uptake by the roots. They are called "systemic" insecticides. How do these chemicals accomplish their control? Give an example.

Possible Responses to *Critical Thinking* Questions

1. The three micrographs are all from the vascular tissue known as xylem. Micrograph A is a close-up of a perforation plate located at the ends of the vessel members. Micrograph B shows three vessel members stacked on top of each other; note that at the junction of each vessel member is a perforation plate. Micrograph C shows tracheids. Notice that tracheids are thinner and more pointed than vessel members. Tracheids are connected by pits.
2. Insufficient nitrogen in a plant will have a negative impact on the synthesis of amino acids and the proteins from which they are assembled. This will, in turn, affect the structure of the plant, which is incorporating proteins, plus it will curtail the synthesis of enzymes needed for metabolic activities. Lack of nitrogen will also adversely affect the synthesis of nucleic acids needed for information storage (DNA) and decoding (RNA).
3. Water is important for almost all cellular functions. When water is abundant, plants store water in vacuoles, which increases the turgor pressure of cells, causing them to be plump. In addition, when water is in abundance the stomata open during the day, allowing photosynthesis to take place, but close at night in order to conserve water. During your vacation as the soil became dry, the root cells released abscisic acid, which in turn released nitric oxide. This caused an increase in calcium ions in the guard cells, which pumped potassium and chloride ions, malate, and water out of the guard cells, causing them to collapse. The collapsed guard cells closed the stomata in an effort to conserve the plant's water. As the plant remained in the dry soil, the only water available to maintain cellular functions was in the plant's vacuoles. As water was removed from the vacuoles, the turgor pressure decreased and the cells became less plump, causing the plant to wilt. Plants can survive wilting to a degree; however, at some point the plant will have lost too much water and will not recover even if abundant water is applied.
4. When moving a plant from one location to another, it is a good idea to take as much soil as practicable with the root mass. This will ensure that the mycorrhizae are substantially intact and can continue functioning in the new location, and that the fragile root hairs so essential for water/mineral absorption are not stripped off.
5. Stomata allow carbon dioxide, used during photosynthesis to make sugar, to flow into the plant. The byproduct of photosynthesis is oxygen, which must be released from the plant. Stomata also allow the plant to regulate water loss. If the stomata remain open, too much water could be lost and the plant will wilt and die. If the stomata remain closed, no gas exchange will occur and no photosynthesis will take place.
6. Transpiration is a process of evaporation of water from the leaves of plants. The rate would be affected by environmental factors, somewhat like sweating from human skin. If the surrounding air is dry, more moisture can leave the surface and be taken up by the air. Conversely, humid air already contains large amounts of moisture and cannot take on much more. Additionally, a breeze moving over the surface will take any moisture-laden air away and replace it with drier air, capable of absorbing moisture.

Possible Responses to *Data Analysis Exercise* Questions

1. Five. Four were planted and one was not planted in the soil (unplanted).
2. The unplanted transgenic control shows very little, or no, uptake in the first three days of the experiment; in that experiment the TCE concentration remains at 15,000 μ g/m^3 for the first three days. The planted transgenics remove TCE from the air the fastest. This is seen as a decrease of TCE from ~15,000 μ g/m^3 to less than 10,000 μ g/m^3 in less than two days.
3. The air around the transgenic plants contained less than 5,000 μ g/m^3 The air around the vector control plants contained more than 15,000 μ g/m^3.
4. One explanation is that the transgenic plants are removing the TCE from the air and incorporating it into the plant tissue. Alternatively, the transgenic plants could be releasing a volatile compound that converts the TCE to another compound. If the air was measured for TCE content and the presence of other compounds, the researchers might be able to distinguish between these two possibilities. Alternatively they could harvest the plant material from the plants and determine if the transgenic plants contained more TCE incorporated into their plant tissue.

29

LIFE CYCLES OF FLOWERING PLANTS

Chapter Outline

PLIGHT OF THE HONEYBEE

REPRODUCTIVE STRUCTURES OF FLOWERING PLANTS

- Anatomy of a Flower
- Diversity of Flower Structure

FLOWERS AND THEIR POLLINATORS

A NEW GENERATION BEGINS

FLOWER SEX

SEED FORMATION

FRUITS

EARLY DEVELOPMENT

ASEXUAL REPRODUCTION OF FLOWERING PLANTS

SENESCENCE

SUMMARY

DATA ANALYSIS EXERCISE

SELF-QUIZ

CRITICAL THINKING

Objectives

1. Describe the typical patterns of life cycles in flowering plants.
2. Draw and label the parts of a perfect flower. Explain where gamete formation occurs in the male and female structures.
3. Understand the events that lead to the production of gametes in plants.
4. Define and distinguish between *pollination* and *fertilization.*
5. Understand how seeds form and why they are an important food source.
6. Discuss the coevolution of flowers and their pollinators.
7. Trace embryonic development from zygote to seedling.
8. Discuss the importance of fruits to flowering plants; include a description of dispersal methods.
9. Describe the various styles presented by asexual reproduction in flowering plants.
10. Understand how plants undergo senescence and abscission in response to seasonal cues.

Key Terms

sporophyte
gametophyte
whorls
receptacle
floral shoot
calyx
corolla
sepals
petals
stamen
filament
anther
pollen sacs
pistil
pollen grains
carpels
stigma
ovary
ovules
seed
perfect flowers
imperfect flowers
pollination vectors
pollinators
nectar
microspores
megaspores
pollination
double fertilization
endosperm
cotyledons
dormancy
germination
coleoptiles
hypocotyls
plumule
radical
abscission
senescence
fruit
simple fruits
aggregate fruits
multiple fruits
true fruits
accessory fruits
dehiscent
indehiscent
drupes
berries
pomes
vegetative reproduction
tissue culture
propagation

Lecture Outline

29.1 Plight of the Honeybee

A. Honeybees are important pollinators.

1. They pollinate a variety of crop species.
2. Honeybees are unique because they can survive in man-made hives and be transported wherever they are needed, making them a pollinator invaluable to farmers.
3. Colony collapse disorder is jeopardizing the honeybee population; the cause of this disorder is not clear.

B. Other pollinators are also at risk.

1. Plants and pollinators have coevolved and depend on each other for survival.
2. When pollinator populations decline, fruit production also declines and the animals that depend on these fruits for food (including humans) will also suffer.

29.2 Reproductive Structures of Flowering Plants

A. Floral Structure and Function

1. Flowers form on a modified branch of the sporophyte when master genes in the apical meristem are turned on.
2. Flower parts are arranged in whorls of modified leaves on the end of the receptacle.
   a. Sepals are the outermost green, leaflike parts arranged in a ring called the calyx.
   b. Petals are the colored parts located between the reproductive structures and the sepals, arranged in a ring called the corolla.
   c. Male parts consist of the stamens—a slender stalk (filament) capped with an anther, inside which pollen sacs enclose pollen grains.
   d. The female floral reproductive parts are the carpels, vessel-shaped structures with an expanded lower ovary (with ovules), a slender column (style), and an upper surface (stigma) for pollen landing.
3. Meiosis of cells within flowers produces the haploid spores (microspores in the anther, megaspores in the ovule), which then undergo mitosis to produce the haploid gametophytes and ultimately become the egg or sperm.
   a. The egg and sperm fuse to form the diploid zygote.
   b. As the zygote develops into a plant, the seed is formed.

B. Diversity in Flower Structure
   1. Complete flowers have all four whorls (sepals, petals, stamens, and carpels); incomplete flowers are missing one or more whorls.
   2. Perfect flowers have both stamens and carpels (both sexes on one flower); imperfect flowers produce either stamens or carpels and are known as either "male" or "female" flowers.
   3. Imperfect flowers must be cross-pollinated; the offspring produced by cross-pollination are generally more genetically diverse, and are more vigorous than those produced by self-pollination.
   4. While self-pollination may be advantageous when plants are widely spaced apart, even perfect flowers often have adaptations that force or encourage cross-pollination.

29.3 A Closer Look at Flowers and Their Pollinators

A. Pollination vectors, such as wind currents, insects, birds, or other animals, are agents that bring pollen grains to female floral parts.
   1. Many plants are pollinated by wind, which randomly distributes pollen from plant to plant.
   2. Other Plants Attract Living Pollinators

B. Attraction of pollinators to flowers.
   1. Bright colors (carotenoids and anthocyanins) with strong patterns attract birds, butterflies, and bees.
   2. Sensory receptors in some animal pollinators are exploited by flowers with fragrant oils that produce intense fruity or musky odors.
   3. Sugar-rich nectar and pollen are encouraging rewards for some pollinators and reinforce their return visits.
      a. Nectar feeds butterflies, bees, and hummingbirds with a tasty reward.
      b. Pollen is an abundant source of vitamins and minerals.
      c. Flowers have coevolved to fit precisely with a specific pollinator.

29.4 A New Generation Begins

A. Microspore and Megaspore Formation
   1. Egg Formation
      a. In the carpel, a mass of tissue forms ovules (potential seeds) enclosed by integuments (protective tissue).
      b. A diploid "megaspore mother" cell divides by meiosis to produce four haploid megaspores, three of which disintegrate.
      c. The surviving megaspore undergoes three rounds of mitosis with no cytoplasmic division, generating a single cell with eight haploid nuclei.
      d. Ultimately the cytoplasm divides unevenly to produce seven cells: one haploid egg cell, one endosperm mother cell with two haploid nuclei, and five cells that support the process of fertilization.
   2. Pollen Formation
      a. In anthers, large numbers of diploid "microspore mother" cells divide by meiosis to form four haploid *microspores.*
      b. Each microspore will divide by mitosis and differentiate to form pollen grains.
      c. Each pollen grain consists of an inner cell located in the cytoplasm of the outer cell; both cells are surrounded by a protective coat.

B. Pollination and Fertilization
   1. When a pollen grain lands on a stigma, pollination has occurred.

2. After a pollen grain lands on a stigma, one of the two pollen cells forms a pollen tube; the other cell divides by mitosis to produce two sperm cells.
3. Guided by chemical cues, the pollen tube grows through the tissues of the ovary to an ovule.
4. When the pollen tube penetrates the embryo sac, the two sperm cells travel down the pollen tube and complete the double-fertilization event.
    a. One sperm fuses with the egg nucleus to form a diploid zygote.
    b. The other sperm nucleus fuses with the two endosperm nuclei in the endosperm mother cell to yield a triploid endosperm, which will nourish the young, developing plant.

29.5 Special Features of Plant Sex

A. The Pollen Coat
1. Protects the two cells inside the pollen grain as it is carried by wind or pollinators.
2. This tough outer coat is so resistant to degradation that pollen grains are often found in fossils.

B. Interaction Between Pollen and Stigma
1. When a pollen grain lands on the stigma, nutrient-rich fluids from the stigma penetrate the tough pollen coat, allowing the pollen grain to resume metabolic functions such as pollen tube formation.
2. The female gametophyte secretes species-specific chemical signals that guide the pollen tube growth to the ovule.

29.6 Seed Formation

A. Embryo and Endosperm Development
1. A diploid zygote is produced when one sperm cell fuses with the egg cell; the zygote divides and differentiates into the embryonic sporophyte.
2. A triploid endosperm is produced when one sperm cell fuses with the diploid endosperm mother cell; nutrients accumulate in the endosperm.
3. As the embryo matures the integuments harden to form the protective seed coat.
4. The mature embryo, endosperm, and seed coat constitute a seed.

B. Seeds are also an important food source for humans.
1. In eudicots, the nutrients of the endosperm are transferred to two large leaves known as the cotyledons; in monocots, the nutrients remain in the endosperm.
2. Rice, wheat, rye, barley, and oats are grown for their nutritious seeds.
    a. The germ (embryo) contains proteins and vitamins.
    b. The bran (seed coat) contains minerals and fiber.
    c. Milling is a process that removes the bran and the germ, leaving only the starch-filled endosperm.
3. Corn is the most widely used seed. Among its many uses, popcorn results when the endosperm bursts upon heating.

29.7 The Formation and Function of Fruits

A. A fruit is a mature ovary with seeds (ovules) inside.

B. Classification of Fruits
1. Fruits may be classified as simple, aggregate, or multiple based on the arrangement and type of carpels present.
2. Fruits can be categorized based on the type of tissue from which they form. True fruits come from the ovarian wall and its contents, while accessory fruits come from the floral parts along with the ovary.

3. Fruits are known as dry or juicy (fleshy).
   a. Dry dehiscent fruits split along definite seams in the fruit wall to release seeds (acorns, peas, and strawberry "seeds" on the surface of the red fleshy part are examples). Dry indehiscent fruits have walls that do not pop open, and seeds are dispersed inside the intact fruit (maple seeds, sunflower seeds, and corn are examples).
   b. Three major categories of fleshy fruits are drupes with pits (cherries, olives, apricots), berries with one or many seeds (grapes, tomatoes), and pomes with seeds in a core tissue (apples, pears).

C. Fruits Function in Protection and Dispersal of Seed
1. Dispersal increases reproductive success by limiting competition between parent and offspring.
2. Dispersal also allows the species to colonize new areas.

D. Fruits Are Adapted to Certain Dispersal Vectors
1. Water-dispersed seeds have fruits that provide floatation.
2. Wind-dispersed seeds have fruits that resemble wings.
3. Animal-dispersed seeds may have hooks or spines that cling to animal fur or clothing.
4. Some fruits will dry and break open, propelling seeds away from their parents.
5. Animals are attracted to and eat some fruits, facilitating germination as the seeds pass through the digestive track. They are then dispersed in the animal feces.

29.8 Early Development

A. Breaking Dormancy
1. In many climates, seeds enter a period of dormancy; the seeds remain dormant until environmental conditions are favorable for seedling survival.
2. Environmental factors break dormancy.
   a. All species require water to swell and rupture the seed coat.
   b. The seeds of some species must be abraded (often by chewing) before water can enter.
   c. Seeds adapted to cooler climates must be exposed to freezing temperatures before germination.
   d. Other seeds must be exposed to bright light.
   e. Seeds from plants adapted to regions that experience periodic wildfires must be exposed to fire or smoke before germination.
3. Germination Events
   a. Seasonal rains provide the water amounts necessary to swell and rupture the seed coat; water also activates the enzymes necessary to hydrolyze the stored starches.
   b. The starches are converted to sugar, which provides the energy for the meristems to initiate cell division; oxygen is also required.
   c. Repeated cell divisions produce a seedling with a primary root; when the primary root breaks through the seed coat, germination is complete.

B. Patterns of Early Growth
1. Growth is defined as an increase in the number, size, and volume of cells.
2. Development is the emergence of specialized, morphologically different body parts.
3. In monocots, a single, rigid shoot (coleoptiles) grows up through the soil; the coleoptile protects the delicate primary shoot that has formed in the seed.
4. Early growth in dicots.
   a. The radical emerges from the seed first, then the hook-bent hypocotyls.
   b. The bent hypocotyls pulls the delicate cotyledons through the soil.
   c. Once the cotyledons emerge from the soil, light causes the hypocotyls to straighten.
   d. On exposure to light, the cotyledons begin photosynthesis.

e. As other leaves emerge, the cotyledons are eventually no longer needed and they shrivel and fall off the stem.

29.9 Asexual Reproduction of Flowering Plants

A. Asexual Reproduction in Nature

1. Many plants can reproduce asexually by vegetative growth, including shoots and runners.
   a. In this mode of reproduction, all of the plants produced are genetically identical clones.
   b. Examples of this form of growth include quaking aspen in Colorado, which stretch across hundreds of acres, and the 43,600-year-old King's holly plant in Tasmania.
2. Some plants must propagate clonally because they are triploid; their chromosomes cannot be divided equally in meiosis and, therefore, meiosis fails.

B. Induced Propagation

1. Vegetative propagation (cuttings) can result in new plants produced from leaves that form roots.
2. In grafting, the stem of one plant is fused to the roots of another, hardier plant; many apple trees are actually grafts; seeds from a well-producing apple tree do not necessarily generate offspring that are as productive as the parent trees; therefore, a well-producing apple tree is grafted onto a hardy stem; the grafted trees are as productive as the parent clone.
3. Tissue culture propagation can result in whole plants produced from a group of cells.
4. In some species, fruits form in the absence of fertilization.

29.10 Senescence

A. Plants adapted to regions with periods that are too cold or too dry for plant growth often enter a stage of dormancy where the plant is still alive but not undergoing growth.

B. As plants prepare for their dormant stage, they undergo senescence, a period when fruits and leaves drop from the plant.

1. The dropping of leaves, flowers, fruits, and other parts is called abscission; abscission may be caused by stress or in response to seasonal changes.
2. Senescence is aging; it is the sum total of the processes leading to the death of the whole plant or the abscission of plant parts.
   a. The recurring cue is a decrease in day length, which signals a plant that the growing season is ending.
   b. Ethylene, a plant hormone, is produced causing the plant's leaves and fruits to mature.
   c. The ethylene signals the cells located in the petioles and fruit stalks to produce enzymes that digest their own cell walls.
   d. As cell walls deteriorate, the extracellular matrix that holds cells together breaks down, causing the fruit or leaf to fall from the plant.
   e. This process often leaves a scar on the plant.

Suggestions for Presenting the Material

- Students frequently have trouble understanding the plant life cycle because it is so different from animal life cycles. Be sure to emphasize the importance of alternation of generations; spend plenty of time going over a diagram of the plant life cycle. Compare it to a drawing or diagram of the human life cycle to give students a familiar reference point.

- Give examples of a sporophyte and a gametophyte in the life cycles of some common plants. Explain the difference between a spore and a gamete. It may be necessary to briefly review meiosis I and II and terms such as *haploid* and *diploid,* especially if it has been some time since the students studied mitosis and meiosis.
- Students will find it easier to comprehend the development of male and female gametophytes if they have dissected a flower before discussion. If students wonder why the events of gamete formation and fertilization are so complicated, remind them that these are very advanced plants; plant evolution and diversity will be discussed later.
- Have the students draw and label different parts of the plant as it undergoes development.
- Time-lapse videos are easy to find and are an excellent way to present plant growth and development.

Classroom and Laboratory Enrichment

- Bring in flowering plants if possible, or at least show color photos of angiosperms in flowers. Ask students to point out the gametophyte and sporophyte portions of the plant.
- For a demonstration of growth at apical meristems, mark the root tips or shoot apical meristems of sturdy just-sprouted seedlings (beans or peas are fine) at measured intervals with India ink. Keep the seeds moist in a Petri dish lined with paper towels. Measure the rates of growth after one week. Exactly where along the root or shoot is the increase in length occurring?
- Use models, photos, and diagrams to present floral structure. Then dissect at least one type of flower, preferably one with large parts, in lab or lecture. Lilies or gladiolas work well.
- Determine if the food stored in sprouting seeds is starch or sugar by treating the seeds with tetrazolium solution and Lugol's solution. Alternatively, there are several virtual labs that allow students to explore this topic.
- Show time-lapse films of flower and fruit formation.
- In species with hard seed coats, examine the effects of seed scarification (the removal or breakage of seed coats) on germination rate. Students can use a seed scarifier, if available, or gently rub seeds between blocks covered with a fine grade of sandpaper. Compare germination rates between seeds that have been scarified and those left unscarified.
- How does soaking seeds in water overnight before sowing affect germination rate? Compare germination rates between presoaked seeds and unsoaked seeds.
- Compare the cotyledons of monocots and eudicots by examining recently sprouted corn and bean seedlings.
- Display some inflorescences of grasses (if available) in the lab or lecture classroom. Use diagrams or photos of corn inflorescences as examples of imperfect flowers; corn is a good choice because of the large "tassels" (staminate flowers) and because students are familiar with the ear of corn (the end product of many fertilization events).
- Learn the parts of a seed by dissecting bean and corn seeds after they have been softened in water for several hours.
- Use microscope slides and/or projected slides of a lily to discuss microspore and megaspore development.
- View germinating pollen grains under the microscope in lab or with a microprojector in lecture. Most pollen grains will germinate on a microscope slide in a drop of water.

- Prepare a demonstration of different kinds of fruits, or ask students to bring fruits to class or lab. Students will be fascinated to see the relationship between the parts of the flower before fertilization and the subsequent fruit parts.
- Use techniques of vegetative propagation or tissue culture to grow new plants. This can be done by the students in lab or can be prepared ahead of time, ideally with different stages of growth represented as a demonstration.
- Show scanning electron micrographs of the pollen grains of some familiar plants.
- Find pictures of pollen fossils and compare them to living pollen.
- Show close-up photos of bees and the pollen-carrying devices on their legs. Alternatively, if your group is small, observe specimens of these insects under stereomicroscopes.
- Locate photos of flowers that are formed in various ways to lure insects to a light and feed.
- Compare the cotyledons of monocots and eudicots by examining recently sprouted corn and bean seedlings.

Classroom Discussion Ideas

- Compare and contrast the advantages and disadvantages of sexual reproduction in flowering plants.
- How does growth in plants differ from growth in humans? Why can growth in plants be seen as a counterpart to movement in animals?
- Why do so many species of flowering plants reproduce both sexually and asexually?
- What is the adaptive value of seed dormancy?
- Why do grasses keep growing even after being repeatedly trimmed by lawn mowers or grazing animals? Where is the meristem located in shoots of grasses?
- Discuss how pollinators and their flower species might have coevolved.
- Recently, several food corporations have offered money to researchers working on colony collapse disorder. Discuss what products these companies might produce.
- Look up and discuss the latest ideas on what is causing colony collapse disorder.
- Speculate as to what might happen to certain plant species if their pollinators become extinct.
- Why do botanists use flowers rather than leaves or stems as indicators of species identity?
- Can you tell by a flower's appearance if it is wind-pollinated or insect-pollinated? What are some clues suggesting that a flower is wind-pollinated? What are some floral features suggestive of insect pollination?
- What are some of the advantages and disadvantages of asexual reproduction among flowering plants?
- What is the difference between pollination and fertilization?
- Distinguish between megaspores and microspores.
- What is included in an ovule of a flowering plant? What events take place inside the ovule? What are some of the changes that take place inside an ovule after fertilization has occurred?
- Is a pollen grain analogous to a human sperm cell? Why or why not?
- Discuss floral diversity. Ask students to name different kinds of flowers, and then discuss the shapes, types of parts, and pollination of each.
- What is double fertilization?

- Cut open apples, pears, green beans, strawberries, oranges, pineapples, and any other fruits or vegetables you have on hand in class or lab. Identify the floral origin of as many parts as you can. For example, which part of the fruit was the ovary wall? The carpel? The integument? The sepal? The stigma and style?
- Define the terms *fruit* and *vegetable*. What is the difference between these two terms? Why do we use the term *fruit* when we are talking about tomatoes and green beans? Ask students for examples of fruits, and use the textbook to help classify each one.
- Why do many fruits change from green to red, yellow, or orange as they ripen? Of what adaptive value is the sweet smell produced by most fruits?
- Is there any truth to the allegation that honey is actually "bee vomit"?
- Why do you think there are poisonous seeds, berries, leaves, and stems in the plant kingdom?
- After studying this chapter, do you see flowers as providing beauty to enhance the human experience, or do you perceive them as more functional? Explain.

How Would You Vote? Classroom Discussion Ideas

- Monitor the voting for the online question. What a dilemma. Here is a new, safer way to deliver pesticides that are needed to protect our crops, but it imperils the pollinators we need to ensure the development of our crops. Obviously, much research needs to be done before we place such a load of these chemicals in the environment that we wipe out the bees and other vital pollinators.

Term Paper Topics, Library Activities, and Special Projects

- Examine diversity among flowers. Describe the coevolution of flowering plants and insects.
- Describe the different uses of each part of the wheat grain. What is wheat germ? Wheat bran? How does white flour differ from whole wheat flour?
- Why are commercial bananas and many commercial varieties of grapes seedless? How are seedless varieties of normally "seedy" fruits such as watermelons created?
- Recently the "doomsday vault" containing a collection of seeds from around the world opened in Norway. The vault is located deep inside a frozen mountain. Discuss why the seeds must be kept at such extreme temperatures. How long do you think the seeds might last? What seeds should be placed in the vault?
- How long can most seeds remain viable? Learn more about documented cases of extreme seed longevity. What steps can be taken to increase seed viability? What are some of the actions taken by seed companies to ensure maximum seed viability?
- What are some species whose seeds require stratification (cold, moist conditions for several weeks prior to sowing) for successful germination? What is the survival value of such a requirement?
- Look up and report on what factors limit growth of plants above certain altitudes and how these factors specifically affect plant growth and development.
- Identify as many of the flowering plants on campus as you can. If flowers are available, collect them, identify them, and bring them back to class or lab. One group of students could prepare a map of campus trees and plants and lead other groups in a campus plant walk.
- Select a well-known flowering plant species, and prepare a timetable showing when the reproductive events leading up to seed formation occurs.
- Learn more about some of the reproductive isolating mechanisms that discourage self-pollination among many flowering plant species.

- Describe commercial uses of asexual reproduction in flowering plants.
- Describe the different uses of each part of the wheat grain. What is wheat germ? Wheat bran? How does white flour differ from whole wheat flour?
- Why are commercial bananas and many commercial varieties of grapes seedless? How are seedless varieties of normally "seedy" fruits such as watermelons created?
- Discuss the role of evolution in floral diversity. What is an example of a primitive flower? An advanced flower?
- Learn more about the role of pollen in human allergy. Collect daily and monthly information on the types and amounts of pollen found in your area. What species have the most pollen? What months of the year have the highest pollen counts? Should we regulate the planting of nonnative ornamental vegetation in cities and towns in states such as Arizona, where people have moved seeking low pollen counts?
- Discuss the use of pollen grains as indicators of the past vegetation history of an area.
- Describe different seed dispersal mechanisms used by flowering plants. Make a list of dispersal mechanisms found among local plants or plants on campus.
- Research the corpse flower. What are its pollinators and lifecycle?
- Research the process by which bees make and store honey.
- Document the role of animals in seed dispersal and the extent to which this helps plants.

Possible Responses to *Critical Thinking* Questions

1.

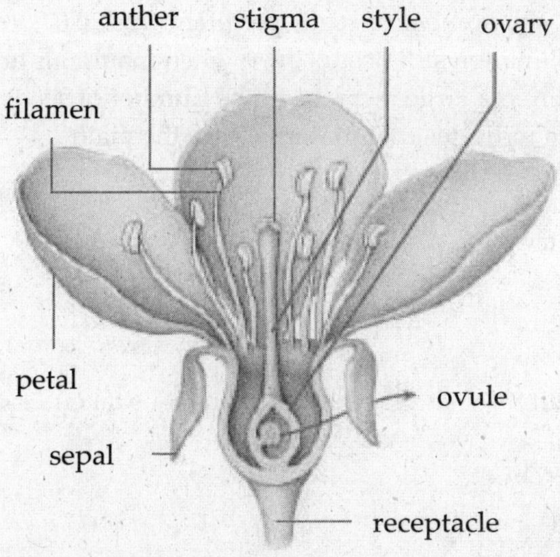

2. Dull-colored flowers with no scent are most likely pollinated by the wind. If you review Table 29.1, you will see that bees, bats, butterflies, and moths are attracted to some type of odor. Thus, these animals will not be attracted to flowers with no scent. Birds are attracted to flowers with no scent, and they are attracted to flowers that are brightly colored. Since wind is an indiscriminate pollinator, there is no selective advantage for plants that are wind pollinated to devote resources to producing brightly colored, scented flowers.
3. The seedling shown is an example of a monocot. Monocots have a single coleoptile that emerges from the seed. The coleoptile encases and protects the more delicate leaves as the seedling

emerges from the soil. If the seedling were a dicot, the bent hypocotyl would emerge from the seed and pull the two cotyledons through the soil. Once the seedling emerges from the soil, the hypocotyl will straighten and the cotyledons will begin photosynthesis.

4. In the case of the kereru birds and their job as dispersing agents for seeds of the Puriri tree, things look grim. We can imagine that long ago there were several species of birds that could carry the large seeds far and wide, but predators and/or competitors, declining habitat, and other human impacts have thwarted nature and reduced the dispersal agents to only one. If the one species of kereru is the sole dispersal agent, it is likely that the native trees it continues to feed from will not be the Puriri trees. Since the Puriri tree is valued for its hardwood, we can assume it is being harvested regularly, which would not increase its population numbers in New Zealand. Both factors combine to make it unlikely that the Puriri tree will be able to thrive without the kereru's continual presence. If the dispersal agent's populations are not large enough to disperse the seeds in sufficient number, and the tree is being harvested for wood, the Puriri tree will dwindle in number to a point of no recovery.

Possible Responses to *Data Analysis Exercise* Questions

1. Seven of the thirteen rodents had pollen on their snout, which is an indication that the rodents were pushing their heads past the stamens of the flowers to get to the nectar.
2. The data shown in part A of Figure 29.23 would not be enough to show that the rodents were the main pollinators of *M. depressa*. First, thirteen is not a large enough sample to establish that the rodents are the main pollinators. Second, even if more rodents were collected that had evidence of pollen, it would not exclude the possibility that other species were the main pollinators.
3. When mammals were excluded from the plants by placing the plants in cages, the number of seeds per plant was 1.95. When mammals had access to the plants, the number of seeds per plant was 20.0.
4. Mammals are not required for pollination since some pollination still occurs even when mammals are prohibited from accessing the plants. However, since there is a large increase in the number of seeds when mammals are allowed access to the plants, the data indicates that mammals are the main pollinators.

30

COMMUNICATION STRATEGIES IN PLANTS

Chapter Outline

Objectives

1. Understand how hormones regulate development throughout a plant's lifetime.
2. Know what role the five major hormones (auxin, cytokinin, gibberellin, abscisic acid, and ethylene) play in the regulation of growth and metabolism in plants.
3. Understand that the five major hormones typically work together, either synergistically or in opposition.
4. Understand how hormones play a role in tropisms.
5. Know how circadian rhythms are driven by the cyclic expression of transcription factors.
6. Understand how hormones initiate responses to abiotic and biotic stresses.

Key Terms

plant hormones
gibberellins
auxins
apical dominance
indoleacetic acid, IAA
cytokinins
flavonoid
ethylene
abscisic acid, ABA
brassinosteroids
jasmonates
salicylic acid
systemin
nitric oxide
aleurone
amylase
polar transport
tropisms
gravitropism
statoliths
phototropism
thigmotropism
heliotropism
tendrils
circadian rhythm
photoperiodism
biological clock
phytochrome, *Pfr and Pr*
short-day plants
long-day plants
day-neutral plants
vernalization
solar tracking
systemic acquired resistance (SAR)

Lecture Outline

30.1 Prescription: Chocolate

A. How Cocoa Benefits Humans

1. A flavonoid known as epicatechin is found in cocoa.
2. Epicatechin performs a variety of functions in humans.
   a. It protects against oxidative tissue damage that occurs after a heart attack or stroke.
   b. It enhances memory.
   c. It kills cancer cells.

B. How Cocoa Benefits Plants

1. Epicatechin is a secondary metabolite made in plants; it is not required for the immediate survival of the *Theobroma cacao* tree.
2. Epicatechin benefits the cacao tree because it functions in plant immunity.

30.2 Introduction to Plant Hormones

A. Plants are organisms, and the individual specialized cells within a plant must communicate with each other.

B. Chemical Signaling.

1. Plant hormones are extracellular signaling molecules that function at very low concentrations and can influence cellular processes in cells located far away from where the hormone originates.
2. Plant hormones influence a variety of plant processes including: plant growth and development, immunity and defense responses, and seed germination.
3. Hormones are typically released by one type of cell and detected by cells that have a receptor; the cell with the hormone receptor may be located far away from the cell releasing the hormone.
4. Cells typically respond to a hormone in a concentration-dependent manner; the response may include a change in gene expression, enzyme activity, or solute concentration.
5. There are several different plant hormones; a cell's response depends on the integration of signals received from several different hormones.
6. All cells in a plant are capable of making hormones, hormones move throughout the plant by diffusion and by transport through xylem or phloem.

30.3 Auxin: The Master Growth Hormone

A. The most abundant naturally occurring auxin is indole-3-acetic acid (IAA).

B. *Auxins* play a critical role in all aspects of growth and development.

1. Auxins influence cell division and elongation either positively or negatively depending on the tissue.
2. Auxins are produced at apical meristems for roots and shoots and coleoptile of monocots.
3. Auxins produced at shoot tips prevent lateral bud growth—apical dominance.
4. Auxins help prevent abscission where leaves, flowers, or fruits drop from plants.

C. Polar Transport of Auxin

1. Auxins are in highest concentration at the apical meristem or coleoptile and move down toward the shoot's base through the parenchyma cells.
2. As auxin moves through the plant, it enters the top of a cell and leaves through the bottom of a cell, generating an unequal distribution of auxin (polar transport).
3. Auxin exerts its effect on plants by changing the pH of the cell walls.
   a. At low pH the cell wall is more flexible.
   b. Turgor pressure can irreversibly expand the softened cell wall.

D. Auxin coordinates the actions of other hormones, including gibberellins, cytokinins, and ethylene.

30.4 Cytokinin

A. Cytokinin stimulates cell division in root and shoot meristems.

B. Cytokinin is mostly made in the roots and transported to the shoots.

C. The effects of cytokinin are antagonistic to the effects of auxin.

1. For example, in a growing plant tip, high levels of auxin suppress the lateral buds (apical dominance); high levels of auxin in the shoot suppress cytokinin.
2. If the growing tip is removed, auxin decreases, cytokinin increases, and the lateral buds begin to grow and produce auxin.

30.5 Gibberellin

A. Gibberellin promotes stem elongation, germination, and starch hydrolysis.

B. Plants with defective gibberellin receptors exhibit a dwarf phenotype.

C. Gibberellin increases transcription of genes by releasing transcriptional repressors.

30.6 Abscisic Acid

A. Abscisic acid (ABA) inhibits cell growth, helps prevent water loss (by promoting stomata closure), and promotes seed and bud dormancy.

1. ABA accumulates in seeds as they mature.
2. Seeds cannot germinate until ABA levels decline; what triggers ABA to decline is unknown.

B. Abscisic acid synthesis begins in the chloroplasts; therefore, the concentration of ABA is highest in the leaves.

C. Binding of ABA to receptors on the nuclear membrane initiates a cascade of phosphorylation events that ultimately activates hundreds of transcription factors.

1. Genes activated by ABA are involved in metabolism, stress response, and embryonic development.
2. Genes repressed by ABA are involved in growth.

D. NADPH oxidase is a plasma membrane protein activated by ABA.

1. NADPH oxidase transfers electrons from NADPH inside the cell, producing oxygen radicals and hydrogen peroxide.
2. The oxygen radicals and hydrogen peroxide interact with nitrate reductase, releasing a burst of nitric oxide.
3. Nitric oxide breaks down ABA and thus completes a feedback loop that regulates ABA.

30.7 Ethylene

A. Ethylene is a gas and easily passes through the lipid membranes of cells.

B. Ethylene is involved in germination, growth, abscission, ripening, and stress responses.

C. All cells can produce ethylene from methionine and ATP.

1. Negative feedback regulates ethylene and ensures that a proper amount of ethylene is maintained for growth and development; low levels of ethylene help regulate auxin levels.
2. Positive feedback loops cause a large amount of ethylene to be produced; high levels of ethylene regulate fruit ripening and abscission.

D. Synthetic ethylene is used commercially to ripen fruits; unripe fruits are picked, transported, and sprayed with ethylene to induce ripening prior to being sold.

E. Disrupting the ethylene biosynthesis pathway has led to the creation of genetically modified tomatoes that have a longer storage life.

30.8 Tropisms

A. Responses to Gravity

1. Gravitropism is the growth response to gravity—shoots grow up, roots grow down.
2. Auxin, together with a growth-inhibiting hormone, may play a role in promoting or inhibiting growth in various regions of the plant.
3. Statoliths, which are unbound starch grains in the plastids, respond to gravity and may trigger the redistribution of auxin.

B. Responses to Light

1. Phototropism is a growth response to light.
2. Bending toward the light is caused by elongation of cells (auxin stimulation) on the side of the plant *not* exposed to light.
3. Phototropins are pigments that absorb blue wavelengths of light and signal the redistribution of auxin that initiates the elongation of cells.

C. Responses to Contact

1. Thigmotropism is a shift in growth triggered by physical contact with surrounding objects.
2. This response to auxin and ethylene is prevalent in climbing vines and in the tendrils that support some plants.

30.9 Sensing Recurring Environmental Changes

A. A circadian cycle is completed in a 24-hour period.

1. Many plants adjust their leaves such that the leaves are horizontal during the day but folded toward the stem at night; even plants put in constant darkness will respond for a few days after being removed from the day/night cycle.
2. Photoreceptor molecules regulate the circadian rhythms by allowing the plant to sense light.
   a. Phytochrome, a blue-green pigment, is the alarm button for some biological clocks in plants.
   b. Phytochrome can absorb both red and far-red wavelengths with different results.
      1) The pigment is converted to an active form (Pfr) at sunrise and to an inactive form (Pr) at sunset.
      2) Its activation induces cells to take up free calcium ions, which combine with proteins to initiate responses.

B. Length of Darkness and Flowering

1. The flowering process is keyed to changes in day length throughout the year.
   a. "Short-day plants" flower in late summer or early autumn when day length becomes *shorter* (e.g., poinsettias).
   b. "Long-day plants" flower in the spring as day length becomes *longer* (e.g., spinach).
   c. "Day-neutral plants" flower when they are mature enough to do so.
2. Phytochrome is the trigger for flowering.
3. In some plants, flowering only occurs after vernalization or exposure to low temperatures (winter).

30.10 Responses to Stress

A. Water Shortage

1. Abscisic acid is synthesized.
2. ABA synthesis causes a burst of nitric oxide to be made; this causes calcium ions to move in and water to move out of the guard cells, thus closing the stomata.

B. Biotic Stress Response

1. Cell surface receptors bind microbial pathogens, causing ethylene to be synthesized.

2. Ethylene promotes the transcription of defense response genes.
3. If enough pathogen receptors are activated, a burst of nitric oxide closes the stomata to prevent any further pathogen entry; the only other entry point for a pathogen is through a wound.
4. Pathogens that enter through a wound cause a surge of hydrogen peroxide and nitric oxide (hypersensitive response).
5. The hypersensitive response often kills the pathogen and the infected plant tissue.
6. Plants also have a long-term defensesystem that is initiated by a signal from infected tissues; in response salicylic acid is produced and hundreds of genes involved in pathogen resistance are transcribed.

Suggestions for Presenting the Material

- You can ask students to think about the common gardening practices presented below that involve concepts presented in this chapter to give them familiar reference for the more detailed information in the sections. Ask them to explain why (and how) the following strategies work:
  1. Keeping fruit from ripening: Fruit should be kept in a space with a constant flow of oxygen.
  2. Growing vegetables from seeds: Seeds need to be planted in soil that can drain well and the seed must be watered thoroughly.
  3. Pruning: Cutting the tip off the shoot of a plant will make the plant grow bushier.
  4. Forcing bulbs: Bulbs must be kept cool for at least 12 weeks before they will bloom inside.
  5. Growing a tree from a seed: Seeds should be dried until the seed coat cracks before they are planted.
- Discuss with your students once again how growth in plants differs from growth in animals.

Classroom and Laboratory Enrichment

- Introduce the term *hormone* and discuss the need for growth-regulating hormones. There are many lab experiments designed to investigate the role of hormones in plant growth and development; many of them are available from biological supply houses in the form of kits. These can be prepared ahead of time and used as demonstrations or performed by the students. These kits can be used to examine the effects of auxins, gibberellins, and cytokinins on plant growth and development.
- Design and implement experiments involving seed germination. Vary conditions such as temperature or light, and examine the effects on germination rate.
- How does complete darkness affect seedling growth? Compare the lengths and weights of bean or pea seedlings raised in light with those raised in complete darkness.
- Investigate the role of the intact shoot tip in inhibiting lateral bud development in *Coleus*. What happens to lateral buds if the shoot tip is removed? Design an experiment in which applications of IAA dissolved in a paste of lanolin mimic the effects of the intact shoot tip.
- Discover the effects of different wavelengths of light on phototropism. Different colored films can be used to filter out certain wavelengths of light. For example, a red theatrical filter will absorb blue and transmit red.
- Dwarf varieties of plants can be purchased from biological supply companies. The dwarf phenotype can be rescued (in some varieties) by applying gibberellin. You could determine if the amount of gibberellin applied correlates to the amount of rescue.

- Examine the effects of ethylene on fruit ripening or abscission. For example, place bananas in a bag with or without apples and observe the difference in ripening. How does "one bad apple spoil the bunch"?

Classroom Discussion Ideas

- Why do many fruits change from green to red, yellow, or orange as they ripen?
- The first transgenic plants sold for human consumption were tomatoes that had been modified such that no ethylene was produced. What are the benefits of these tomatoes? Potential risks?
- How do hormone production and activity differ in plants and animals? What are some similarities shared by plants and animals? What are some differences?
- What is "pinching back"? Why does it make plants bushier?
- What is "bolting"? Ask any of your students who have raised spinach or lettuce if they are familiar with this term. What can gardeners do to inhibit bolting?
- How could a sap-feeding insect actually stimulate plant growth? (Answer: The plant works harder to replace lost sap.)
- How could a foliage-feeding insect increase growth of understory plants? (Answer: increased light penetration.)
- How could irrigation of cotton plants increase insect damage? (Answer: More green leaves support more larvae.)
- Discuss the role plant movement plays in flowering plants. What is the adaptive purpose(s) of this movement?

How Would You Vote? Classroom Discussion Ideas

- Monitor the voting for the online question. Herbal remedies have been around for many years. In fact, one of the problems with taking an herbal remedy nowadays is that in the past herbal remedies were used *instead* of prescription medications. People taking prescription medications should understand that not only are they taking an herbal remedy that likely has not been subjected to rigorous safety tests, but even if it has been deemed safe it is unlikely that the herbal remedy has been tested for drug interactions. In addition, consumers should be aware that the supplement market is currently a booming business. In addition to forgoing safety tests, companies eager to sell their herbal product often exaggerate the product's effectiveness.

Term Paper Topics, Library Activities, and Special Projects

- Would gibberellins ever be used as applications to commercial plantings? Would you ever want to use them for your house plants? Why or why not?
- Is it safe to treat crop plants with plant hormones? What impact might the hormones have on humans? What impact might the hormones have on weeds that might be growing near the crop plants?
- How are plant hormones similar to animal hormones? How are they different?
- What might be an evolutionary advantage to having more than 80 different forms of gibberellins in flowering plants and fungi?
- Describe how insect infestations or plant diseases can affect plant growth.

- Why are seedlings raised in complete darkness white or yellow instead of green? Describe the role played by sunlight in chlorophyll synthesis.
- How are auxins, gibberellins, cytokinins, and abscisic acid used by commercial growers? How is ethylene used to hasten fruit ripening?
- Look up the geographic distributions of several long-day plants, short-day plants, and day-neutral plants. How is the effect of day length on flowering related to the geographic range of a particular plant species?
- Describe synthetic auxins used as herbicides. How do these compounds actually work? Why does 2,4-D kill dicot weeds but not grasses? How are these compounds manufactured? What is their impact on the environment?
- Discuss the use of Agent Orange during the Vietnam War. What are its side effects? Was its use justified?
- What effect(s) would petroleum-solvent insecticides have on plants if they were used instead of insecticides formulated in water?

Possible Responses to *Critical Thinking* Questions

1. During the normal germination process, abscisic acid (ABA) levels must first decline. Since the presence of ABA represses expression of genes that are involved in growth, when ABA levels decline these genes are now expressed. One of the genes expressed as ABA levels decline is the gene that encodes NADPH, an enzyme that produces hydrogen peroxide in the cell. Hydrogen peroxide enhances the expression of genes involved in gibberellin synthesis. Since gibberellin promotes growth, hydrogen peroxide promotes germination and seedling growth by increasing the amount of gibberellin in the seed. Professional gardeners who soak seeds in hydrogen peroxide are promoting gibberellin synthesis.
2. Plants grow tall and spindly when they do not receive enough light, since light inhibits stem elongation. Phytochrome receptors of blue light cause the cessation of straight growth in seedlings when they are exposed to light. Flavoproteins absorb the blue light wavelengths, which results in a redistribution of auxins. Seedlings germinated in darkness are experiencing greater amounts of hormones. These could be varying amounts of gibberellins, ethylenes, and auxin.
3. A mutated gene in the wall cress plant would have increased hypocotyl elongation in the light, increased apical dominance, and severe downward leaf growth. Further effects from the excess auxin could include dramatic developmental defects including embryo and emerging leaf symmetry anomalies, premature inflorescence development, altered leaf arrangements along the stem, reduced petal size, abnormal stamens, sterility, and root-growth defects.
4. There are major differences between how plant and animal hormones function; and it is unlikely that a plant hormone would influence growth and development in humans. Human cells do not have the same hormone receptors and signaling pathways that a plant does; therefore the plant hormone would not be able to initiate a signaling pathway in humans. An exception may be phytoestrogens, which are plant hormones that are chemically similar to estrogens. Phytoestrogens are weaker than human estrogens but they do cause hormonal effects in humans. Some studies have shown that phytoestrogens positively influence human health by protecting against cancer; however, other studies have shown that high levels of phytoestrogens can cause reproductive problems.
5. In the tip of a coleoptile are light-sensing pigments called phototropins. When the phototropins absorb light, auxin efflux carriers accumulate on the side of the plant that receives the least

amount of light. This causes more growth on the shaded side of the plant; thus the plant bends toward the light. If you remove or cover the light-sensing tip, as in A and C, the plant cannot detect light and no bending will occur. Both B and D will bend toward the light because the tip is able to sense the light and the efflux carriers can accumulate on the shaded side of the plant.

Possible Responses to *Data Analysis Exercise* Questions

1. Plants attacked by budworms and thrips (HVT) produced a total of 11 different volatiles in an amount of 13,563 ng/day. If the statistical data from the original article is included in the analysis, this amount is not significantly different from the amount of volatiles produced by exposure to just budworms (HV).
2. When plants were exposed to budworms and thrips (HVT), 6,166 ng/day of β-caryophyllene was produced. In the original article this number is not statistically different from the amount of β-caryophyllene produced when exposed to just budworms (HV).
3. The original article includes the statistical significance of the numbers in this table. From the table shown in Figure 30.21, β-ocimene and β-caryophyllene are both produced when the plants are attacked by thrips and by budworms. Β-caryophyllene is also produced during mechanical wounding (40 ng/day); however, in the original article the amount produced during mechanical wounding compared to exposure to thrips is not statistically different; therefore the production of β-caryophyllene may be due to physical injury of the plant and not just predation. The amount of β-ocimene produced by mechanical wounding shown in Figure 30.21 is 15 ng/day; however, in the original article this number is not statistically different from the amount produced in the control (0 ng/day). Thus, β-ocimene is not produced in response to wounding but is produced in response to predation by thrips or budworms (non-specific response to predation).
4. There are several chemicals that are produced in response to predation by budworms, but not thrips. They include: myrcene, linalool, indole, nicotine, β-elemene, α-humulene, and caryophyllene oxide. As shown in Figure 30.21, these chemicals are not produced in response to predation by thrips but are produced in response to predation by budworms. If the statistical numbers from the original article are included in the analysis, sesquiterpene and α-farnesene can be added to the list because they are not produced in quantities significantly different from the control (0 ng/day) when exposed to thrips.

31

ANIMAL TISSUES AND ORGAN SYSTEMS

Chapter Outline

Objectives

1. Describe the various levels of animal organization (cells, tissues, organs, and organ systems), and be familiar with the anatomical terms provided.
2. Know the characteristics of the four main tissues, noting their structure and function.
3. Know the types of cells that compose each tissue type, and cite some examples of organs that contain significant amounts of each tissue type.
4. Characterize each of the major organ systems of the human body.
5. Describe how the four principal tissue types are organized into an organ such as the skin.
6. Know the structure and functions of human skin.
7. Understand negative feedback mechanisms and be able to describe an example.

Key Terms

stem cells
embryonic stem cells
adult stem cells
extracellular fluid
interstitial fluid
tissue
organ
organ systems
homeostasis
epithelium, -lia
basement membrane
squamous
cuboidal
columnar
simple epithelium
stratified epithelium
microvilli
glands
exocrine glands
endocrine glands
tight junctions
adhering junctions
gap junctions
connective tissue
fibroblasts
collagen
elastin
loose connective tissue
dense, irregular connective tissue
dense, regular connective tissue
tendons
ligaments
cartilage
bone tissue
adipose tissue
blood
plasma
red blood cells
white blood cells
platelets
skeletal muscle tissue
sarcomere
cardiac muscle tissue
smooth muscle tissue
nervous tissue
neuroglial cells
neurons
sensory neurons
interneurons
motor neurons
germ layers
ectoderm
mesoderm
endoderm
skin
epidermis
dermis
sweat glands
keratinocytes
keratin
melanin
negative feedback
sensory receptor

Lecture Outline

31.1 Stem Cells—It's All About Potential

A. Stem cells form when a zygote first begins to divide.
   1. Stem cells can divide indefinitely without differentiating.
   2. They can be coaxed into forming many cell types.
   3. A fertilized egg that has gone through less than four divisions is totipotent (it can turn into a fetus if implanted).
      a. Cells that have undergone further divisions are pluripotent (cannot become a fetus, but can still form any cell types in the body).

B. The most pliable of stem cells comes from human embryos, which may be able to repair damaged nervous tissue.
   1. Ethical issues have been raised because of the source of the embryonic tissue.
   2. Adult stem cells may be useful as an alternative to some cell development.

31.2 Organization of Animal Bodies

A. Levels of Organization
   1. A *tissue* is a group of cells that performs a common task.
      a. Epithelial tissue covers the outside of the body and lines many internal areas.
      b. Connective tissue has many functions, including binding things together and support.
      c. Muscle tissue moves body parts.
      d. Nervous tissue reacts to stimuli.
   2. Each *organ* consists of different tissues working together for a common goal.
   3. *Organ systems* consist of two or more organs interacting for a common task.

B. The Internal Environment
   1. Animals are primarily made of water with dissolved solutes.
      a. Most of the fluids of the body are intracellular (inside cells).
      b. The remaining fluids in an animal are extracellular.

c. Interstitial fluids (fluids between cells) make up the bulk of the extracellular fluid.

C. Evolution of Animal Structure

1. An animal's structure evolves over generations to adapt to their environment.
   a. Animals have developed circulatory systems to move substances around the body since diffusion would not be sufficient in a large organism.
   b. Lungs develop from outpouching of the gut to replace gills in animals living on land.

31.3 Epithelial Tissue

A. General Characteristics

1. In this epithelium tissue, one surface is free and the other adheres to a basement membrane.
2. Many types of epithelial tissue, such as feathers, nails, hooves, beaks, and hair, contain keratin.

B. Variations in Structure and Function

1. *Simple* epithelium is one-cell thick and may have flat (squamous), cuboidal, or columnar cells.
   a. Simple squamous epithelium allows substances to diffuse through readily in areas such as the lungs.
   b. Simple cubical and simple columnar epithelium may contain cilia to move substances along, as in the oviducts.
   c. Microvilli may be present to increase surface area for absorption.
2. *Stratified* epithelium has many layers and is found in regions that get much wear and tear—as in human skin.
3. In epithelium, cells are linked tightly together with specialized junctions, providing both structural and functional links between individual cells.
   a. Tight junctions fuse the plasma membranes from adjacent cells to provide a waterproof barrier.

C. Epithelial Secretions

1. Glands are secretory organs derived from epithelium.
2. *Exocrine* glands often secrete through ducts to free surfaces; they secrete mucus, saliva, wax, milk, and so on.
3. *Endocrine* glands secrete hormones directly into intercellular fluid for distribution by the blood.

D. Carcinomas—Epithelial Cell Cancers

1. Frequent divisions that occur in epithelial tissue provide lots of opportunity for errors that can lead to cancer.
   a. Carcinomas (cancer originating from epithelial cells) account for 95 percent of all cancers.

31.4 Connective Tissues

A. Most connective tissue contains cells and fibers (collagen and/or elastin) secreted by fibroblasts, all scattered in a ground substance.

B. Soft Connective Tissues

1. *Loose connective tissue* supports epithelia and organs, and surrounds blood vessels and nerves; it contains fibroblast cells and fibers plus macrophages.
2. *Dense, irregular connective tissue* has thicker fibers and more of them, but fewer cells; it forms protective capsules around organs.
3. *Dense, regular connective tissue* has its fibers in parallel; this is the arrangement found in tendons (muscle to bone) and ligaments (bone to bone).

C. Specialized Connective Tissues

1. *Cartilage* contains a dense array of fibers in a jellylike ground substance.
   a. It cushions and maintains the shape of body parts; it resists compression and is resilient.
   b. Locations include the ends of bones, parts of the nose, external ear, and disks between vertebrae.
2. *Adipose tissue* cells are specialized for the storage of fat, which can be used as an energy reserve and as cushions to pad organs
3. *Bone tissue* stores mineral salts, produces blood cells, and provides spaces for its own living osteocytes.
   a. Organized as flat plates and cylinders, bones support and protect body tissues and organs; some have sites for blood cell production.
   b. Bones work with muscles to perform movement.
4. *Blood* transports (in plasma) oxygen (red blood cells), wastes, hormones, and enzymes; it also contains clotting factors (platelets) to protect against bleeding and components to protect against disease-causing agents (white blood cells).

31.5 Muscle Tissues

A. Muscle tissue contracts in response to stimulation and lengthens.

B. Skeletal Muscle Tissue

1. *Skeletal* muscle tissue attaches to bones for voluntary movement; it contains striated, multinucleated, long cells.
2. Each unit, called a sarcomere, is contractile; muscle makes up 40 percent of the weight of average humans.

C. Cardiac Muscle Tissue

1. *Cardiac* (heart) muscle is composed of short, striated, branching cells that can function in units.
2. Contraction signals pass quickly at gap junctions, and the tissue is packed with mitochondria to supply ATP for the continual beating; no oxygen equals heart attack.

D. Smooth Muscle Tissue

1. *Smooth* muscle tissue contains spindle-shaped cells; it lines the gut, blood vessels, and glands; its operation is involuntary like cardiac.
2. This tissue is not striated, hence the name, and its contractions are slower than skeletal but can be prolonged.

31.6 Nervous Tissue

A. Nervous tissue exerts the greatest control over the body's responsiveness to changing conditions.

1. Neurons are excitable cells, organized as lines of communication throughout the body.
   a. Sensory neurons receive stimuli and send messages to the brain.
   b. Interneurons store information and coordinate responses.
   c. Motor neurons send signals to muscles or glands.
2. Neuroglia are diverse cells that protect and metabolically support the neurons.
   a. Some neuroglia cells provide insulation and speed up reactions.

31.7 Organ Systems

A. Organs in Body Cavities

1. Vertebrates have a large body cavity known as a coelom.
   a. The diaphragm divides the coelom into the thoracic cavity (containing lungs, heart) and the abdominal cavity (housing the digestive organs).
2. Also, the cranial cavity houses the brain and the spinal cavity contains the spinal cord.

B. Vertebrate Organ Systems
   1. Figure 31.12 briefly describes the eleven organ systems (integumentary, muscular, skeletal, nervous, endocrine, circulatory, lymphatic, respiratory, digestive, urinary, and reproductive) that contribute to the survival of the living cells of the vertebrate body.
   2. The formation and function of the organs are outcomes of a long-term program of growth and development.
   3. The organ systems work together to maintain homeostasis in the body.

31.8 Human Integumentary System
A. The outer covering of animal bodies is called the integument.
   1. In vertebrates, the integument consists of skin and the structures derived from epidermal cells such as scales, feathers, hair, beaks, horns, nails, and so forth in an outer epidermis and underlying dermis.
   2. The skin covers and protects the body from abrasion, bacterial attack, ultraviolet radiation, and dehydration; it helps control internal temperature and helps make vitamin D; its sensory receptors help the brain detect environmental stimuli.
B. Structure of Human Skin
   1. Epidermis is a stratified epithelium, with an outermost layer consisting of flattened, dead cells filled with keratin, a tough, water-insoluble protein that accumulates in the cells.
      a. Melanocytes in the epidermis produce skin pigments and protect the skin from UV radiation.
   2. The dermis is beneath the epidermis and is composed of dense connective tissue that contains many fibers.
      a. Epidermally derived gland cells also lie in the dermis.
      b. Sweat glands produce a fluid that is released in response to stress (overheating and fright, for example).
      c. Oil glands (sebaceous) lubricate and soften the skin, plus they produce secretions that reduce bacterial populations on the skin.
C. Evolution of Human Skin
   1. Chimpanzees and bonobos have pink skin covered with hair.
   2. When humans lost their hair, they developed dark skin to protect them from sunlight.
      a. Scientists believe that dark skin color was present around 1.2 million years ago.

31.9 Negative Feedback in Homeostasis
A. Sensory receptors detect changes in the body and send messages to the brain.
B. Negative feedback mechanisms are active in the body to maintain homeostasis.
   1. An example of a negative feedback mechanism involves the maintenance of body temperature.
      a. If you are hot you excrete sweat, which cools down the body as it evaporates.
      b. If you are cold you shiver to produce body heat.

31.10 Stem Cells—It's All About Potential
A. Skin substitutes can be made from human foreskins, since they are a good supply of keratinocytes and fibroblasts.
B. Scientists are hoping that fibroblasts can act like embryonic stem cells.
   1. These altered fibroblasts are called induced pluripotent stem cells (IPSCs).
   2. Inserting genes into fibroblasts via viruses made them unsuitable for use.
   3. Researchers at Harvard are successfully making fibroblast to serve as IPSCs by the use of modified RNA.

Suggestions for Presenting the Material

- Although this chapter includes brief discussions of cell functions, embryonic tissues, and human organ systems, the main topic is *tissues*.
- The presentation of tissues will be more meaningful if slides are shown during your lecture. Observe the location of the basement membranes and also the orientation of the fibers. Notice how the fibers are positioned differently in both dense irregular and dense regular connective tissue.
- Even though the structure of bone and the types of muscles are introduced here, the skeletal system and muscle physiology are topics discussed more fully in subsequent chapters.
- It is difficult for students to think of bone as a living tissue. Mention to the class that your bones undergo a process known as remodeling. This means that approximately 10 percent of your bones are broken down and rebuilt annually. This explains why we have a lifelong need for calcium in our bones. This may help the students think of bones as a work in progress, instead of a piece of plaster.
- There is really no need for details of body systems listed in this chapter because each will be discussed in later chapters.
- Skin structure and function is best presented by using an overhead transparency. This will allow the instructor to relate the layers of the integumentary system to the function of the structures in each layer.
- Use one of the videos on CengageNOW or the Multimedia Manager to introduce this chapter. These are helpful in grabbing the interest of students.
- Name a function or an organ of the body and see if the students can name the appropriate organ system.
- List some sources of extracellular fluid in the body (other than interstitial fluid).

Classroom and Laboratory Enrichment

- Select slides of various types of tissues for projection onto a large screen. Ask the students to identify the type of tissue and where it is found in the body. Show the location of the basement membrane in each slide, if visible. Make sure to show examples of epithelial tissue. Can the students identify the cell shape and the thickness of the tissue?
- Invite an athlete who has suffered a knee injury and has had corrective surgery to describe the damage and reconstructive process. How is the prognosis different if an athlete damages bone or cartilage?
- During the discussion of bone, pass a cleaned bone (from a meat market) around the classroom. Comment on the nonliving and living composition of the bone.
- To show that bone is hard but not indestructible, treat bone fragments with a variety of common laboratory acids and alkalis.
- Have prepared microscope slides of each tissue type available for student viewing.
- Use a model of the various organs and organ systems to illustrate their structure and function.
- Borrow an anatomical model from an anatomy lab. Have the students discover which organs are located in the body cavities covered in this chapter.
- Exhibit a vertebrate embryonic or fetal skeleton that is specially stained to show the cartilage.
- Demonstrate that bone has both organic and mineral components by soaking one chicken bone in acetic acid (to remove minerals) and by heating another in an oven at a high temperature (to remove organic material).

- Take the opportunity to educate this young audience on skin cancer—causes, prevention, and the statistics of the disease. Several companies offer comprehensive posters on skin cancer. What are the risk factors for skin cancer? Show the ABCDs of skin cancer (refer to the American Melanoma Foundation website) so that the students might recognize the appearance of a cancerous growth on the skin.
- Have each student or lab group select an organ and report on the organ system it belongs to and the various tissue and types that make up that organ. Organs such as the stomach or heart serve as good examples.

Classroom Discussion Ideas

- Why are stem cells so valuable and sought after in embryological research?
- Why do some groups label stem cell research as unethical?
- Discuss where embryonic stem cells come from and the controversies surrounding this matter.
- Have the class make a list of diseases that could possibly benefit from stem cell research.
- What are the minimal tasks that a living cell and organism must perform to remain alive?
- Research government rulings on stem cell research. Are there examples of the government funding such experimentation? If so, is the source of the cells an embryo or an adult?
- Almost every summer, football players expire due to hear exhaustion. Why are they unable to maintain homeostasis? Is the heavy equipment preventing the evaporation of sweat from the skin? Is the problem more prevalent in a humid environment?

Additional Ideas for Classroom Discussion

- Why is blood—a liquid—considered a *connective* tissue? Perhaps it is easier to envision blood as a tissue if you realize that a transfusion reaction is much like an organ rejection.
- Is there any validity to the cynic's observation that "beauty queens are just exposing a lot of well-placed dead cells"?
- Discuss how the pancreas serves as both an exocrine and an endocrine gland.
- Rising blood-sugar levels after a meal normally trigger insulin secretion, which in turn causes glucose to be converted to glycogen for storage. How is this similar to the response of an air conditioner thermostat to rising room temperature? Is this an example of a negative feedback mechanism? Can you think of any other examples of negative feedback systems in the body?
- What is liposuction? Does it permanently remove adipose tissue from the treated areas? Why is there a limit to the amount of adipose tissue that can be safely removed from the body at one time? Are there any risks to this procedure?
- Astronauts who orbited the Earth early in the space program experienced considerable loss of bone mass under gravity-free conditions. How was this remedied in subsequent flights? Would individuals that are bed-bound for long periods of time experience the same issue?
- Probably some of your students have been hospitalized at some time in their lives. They might have received an IV of saline (salt water). How do the physicians know what concentration of saline should be infused? Since they do not want water to move in or out of your blood cells, they give a saline concentration that is the same as the concentration of saline in the intracellular fluid. It is in this way that homeostasis is maintained.

How Would You Vote? Classroom Discussion Ideas

- Monitor the voting for the online question. This question of what source can, or cannot, be used for stem cell research is unfortunately clouded by political and religious stances. From a purely biological research standpoint, the value of these cells to the advancement of science outweighs the question of their source.
- How would your students feel about stem cell research if the cells were from an adult as opposed to an embryonic source?
- The students may want to discuss the plight of the famous "octomom." Her doctor produced many fertilized eggs in the laboratory. Eventually, she was given three choices for her stored embryos: implant them in her, donate them to another family, or give them to scientific research for stem cell studies. A situation was created that had many ethical implications. How would your students react to this dilemma?
- Have students complete classroom polling using the JoinIn clickers.

Term Paper Topics, Library Activities, and Special Projects

- Osteoporosis is a topic of current interest, especially to women. Can calcium supplements prevent, or do they simply delay, the stooped posture so prevalent in elderly women?
- What roles, if any, do estrogen replacement therapy and exercise play in the prevention of osteoporosis?
- Consider the pros and cons of stem cell research. With your research, state a definitive position on your support or rejection of stem cell research.
- Choose a skin disease to research. Some examples are vitiligo, psoriasis, alopecia, Kaposi's sarcoma, and scleroderma.
- Albinos produce little or no melanin. How does this affect their lifestyle? Can you see how albinism is more than just a cosmetic condition?
- Make a list of cancers that originate from epithelial tissue. What are the risk factors for each of these cancers? Are there lifestyle changes that could reduce these risks?
- Make a poster-sized chart comparing and contrasting the three types of muscle. Be sure to mention differences in appearance and function.
- Research some additional functions of neuroglial cells. You will soon be sure to realize their importance in the nervous system.

Possible Responses to *Critical Thinking* Questions

1. When deciding whether to test the safety of cosmetic products on laboratory grown tissues (LGTs) or on living animals, perhaps a two-phase approach should be envisioned. Why not *begin* with testing on LGTs? We know that these tissues are fairly close to the "real thing," or they would be rejected by the bodies onto which they are grafted. To some critics of testing on living animals, this might be sufficient. But can we always be sure that the LGTs are going to react in *exactly* the same way as tissues in the living animal will? Certainly it would be a tragedy to have to admit to a person suffering harm from a cosmetic, "Well, we never tested it on a *real human*." Perhaps the second phase of testing on live animals would require fewer animals based on the testing on LGTs, but I believe such trials will probably be necessary just to be sure.
2. As stated, chemotherapy and radiation treatments target rapidly dividing cells. Other cells that reproduce frequently are also affected by these treatment methods. Hair cells undergo rapid cell division, so a patient undergoing these medical procedures usually loses their hair as well. In an

ideal situation, the medical treatments would target only the cancerous cells and leave all other cells in the body unscathed.

3. A definition of emerging properties mentions that these characteristics are only seen in collections of cells (tissues), not in individual cells. An emerging property of epithelial tissue is to form a waterproof barrier. Cartilage, a type of connective tissue, has the emerging property of forming flexible structures in the body. Smooth muscle has the emerging property of forming sphincters that control the movement of the food from one structure to the next in the digestive system. Lastly, we can see that nervous tissue develops the ability to form a communication network throughout the body.
4. The tissue in the diagram is ciliated columnar epithelium. You can see the rectangular shape of the cells, and the cilia serve the function of sweeping material out of the respiratory tract.

Possible Responses to *Data Analysis Exercise* Questions

Because diabetics often have decreased circulation to the lower extremities, wounds in those areas are frequent and difficult to heal. Experiments have been devised to test the effectiveness of cultured skin products.

1. Approximately 45 percent of the wounds treated with cultured skin were healed at eight weeks versus 24 percent of those undergoing standard treatment.
2. At 12 weeks, 40 percent of the wounds treated with the standard method were healed as opposed to 55 percent of the wounds treated by the newer method.
3. The healing difference between the group that received cultured skin and those that had standard treatment was evident at four weeks.

32

NEURAL CONTROL

Chapter Outline

Objectives

1. Contrast invertebrate and vertebrate nervous systems.

2. Describe the visible structure of neurons, neuroglia, nerves, and ganglia, both separately and together as a system.
3. Describe the distribution of the invisible array of proteins, ions, and other molecules in a neuron, both at rest and as a neuron experiences a change in potential.
4. Understand how a nerve impulse is received by a neuron, conducted along a neuron, and transmitted across a synapse to a neighboring neuron, muscle, or gland.
5. Outline some of the ways by which information flow is regulated and integrated in the human body.
6. Describe the organization of peripheral versus central nervous systems.
7. Identify the parts of primitive brains, and explain how the human brain is more advanced.
8. Be able to describe neurological diseases, such as multiple sclerosis, Guillain-Barre syndrome, Alzheimer's disease, depression, and brain tumors.
9. Understand the effects of many categories of drugs, such as stimulants, narcotics, and hallucinogens.
10. Describe the functioning of the limbic system and how memories are made.

Key Terms

neuron
neuroglia
nerve
sensory neurons
interneurons
motor neurons
nerve net
nerve cord
cephalization
ganglion
central nervous system
peripheral nervous system
dendrites
axons
membrane potential
input zones
trigger zone
conducting zone
output zones
resting membrane potential
action potential
sodium–potassium pumps
threshold potential
action potential
positive feedback
synapse
synaptic integration
neuromuscular junction
neurotransmitter
neuromodulators
acetylcholine, ACh
norepinephrine
epinephrine
dopamine
serotonin
GABA
drug addiction
stimulants
hallucinogens
analgesics
myelin sheath
somatic nervous system
autonomic nervous system
viscera
sympathetic neurons
parasympathetic neurons
fight-flight response
spinal cord
meninges
white matter
gray matter
reflex
brainstem
medulla oblongata
cerebellum
pons
cerebrum
thalamus
hypothalamus
cerebrospinal fluid
blood-brain barrier
forebrain
cerebral hemispheres
pineal gland
corpus callosum
cerebral cortex
primary motor cortex
primary somatosensory cortex
limbic system
motor areas
sensory areas
association areas
frontal lobe
occipital lobe
temporal lobe
parietal lobe
premotor cortex
Broca's area
primary visual cortex
prefrontal cortex
cingulate gyrus
hippocampus
amygdala
reticular formation
neuroglial cells
oligodendrocytes
microglia
astrocytes
ependymal cells
myelin
Schwann cells

Lecture Outline

32.1 In Pursuit of Ecstasy

A. Ecstasy is a psychoactive drug that makes the user feel accepted, relaxed, and good.

1. The active ingredient is MDMA, which disrupts controls over serotonin in the brain, causing neurons to release too much.
2. Excess serotonin can overstimulate cells, causing feelings of empathy, energy, and euphoria and can cause the body's internal temperature controls to break down.
3. Lower serotonin levels contribute to a loss of concentration, memory problems, and depression.

B. Danish researchers have shown that brain scans become altered in those that have used Ecstasy.

32.2 Evolution of Nervous Systems

A. Nerve Nets
1. Nearly all animals have a nervous system, forming communication lines for detecting stimuli and responding in suitable ways.
2. The nerve net in the cnidarians and echinoderms reflects their radial symmetry.
3. The nerve net extends through the body but does not focus information.
4. Instead, it allows for simple, stereotyped movements that provide the basic operating machinery of nervous systems.

B. Bilateral, Cephalized Invertebrates
1. The neuron, or nerve cell, is the basic unit of communication in all nervous systems.
   a. *Sensory* neurons are receptors for specific sensory stimuli.
   b. *Interneurons* in the brain and spinal cord integrate input and output signals.
   c. *Motor* neurons send information from integrator to muscle or gland cells (effectors).
2. Flatworms are the simplest animals with bilateral symmetry, which is reflected in their arrangement of muscles and nerves; apparently genes for bilateral body plans arose even before radial animals and their expression is suppressed in cnidarians.
   a. The ladderlike nervous system includes two longitudinal nerve cords, associated ganglia, and nerves.
   b. Some flatworms have a small brainlike clump of nerve cell bodies (ganglia) at the head end of the nerve cords (an example of cephalization).
3. *Cephalization* (formation of a head) evolved in concert with bilateral nervous systems in nearly all animal groups.

C. The Vertebrate Nervous System
1. The *central nervous system* of vertebrates includes the brain and spinal cord.
2. The *peripheral nervous system* includes all of the nerves carrying signals to and from the brain and spinal cord.
   a. The autonomic nervous system monitors and controls involuntary actions.
   b. The somatic nervous system monitors and controls voluntary activities.
   c. The peripheral nervous system contains 12 cranial nerves and 31 spinal nerves.

32.3 Neurons—The Great Communicators

A. Functional Zones of a Neuron
1. Each neuron consists of three main parts.
   a. The *cell body* contains the nucleus and metabolic machinery for protein synthesis.
   b. *Dendrites* are numerous, usually short extensions that receive stimuli (input zones).
   c. An *axon* is usually a single, rather long extension (conducting zone) that transmits impulses to other cells at its branched endings (output zones); signals actually arise in trigger zones.
2. The neuron is organized into an input zone, trigger zone, conducting zone, and output zone.

B. Properties of the Neuron Plasma Membrane

1. A resting neuron maintains a steady voltage difference across its plasma membrane.
   a. The inside is more negatively charged than the outside.
   b. This is called the *resting membrane potential.*
2. Two properties of the neuron membrane permit a resting potential.
   a. The lipid bilayer bars the free passage of potassium ions and sodium ions.
   b. Ions can flow from one side to the other through channels in transport proteins.
3. There are more potassium ions inside and more sodium ions outside the resting neuron membrane.
   a. Potassium ions have a tendency to leak out by facilitated diffusion through channel proteins.
   b. Most of the sodium channels are "gated" and remain closed most of the time, keeping the concentration outside high.
   c. However, small amounts of sodium do leak in and must be pumped out (and potassium pumped in) by the *sodium-potassium pump.*

32.4 The Action Potential

A. Grade Potential and Reaching Threshold
   1. "Local" means the signal does not usually spread beyond the input zone; however, if the stimulation is strong enough, an adjacent trigger zone may respond.
   2. "Graded" means that the signals at the input zone vary in magnitude depending on the intensity and duration of the stimulus.
   3. When a stimulus reaches a certain minimum—a threshold—gated channels open and sodium rushes in.
      a. In an accelerating way, more and more gates open (example of positive feedback).
      b. At threshold, the opening of more gates no longer depends on the stimulus but is self-propagating.

B. An All-Or-Nothing Spike
   1. Action potentials are *all-or-nothing* events—at any given time, a neuron is either resting or excited.
   2. When depolarization in one region is ended, the sodium gates close and potassium gates open.
   3. The sodium-potassium membrane pumps also become operational to fully restore the resting potential.

C. Propagation of an Action Potential
   1. The action potential is self-propagating and moves away from the stimulation site to adjacent regions of the membrane undiminished.
   2. A brief (refractory) period follows at each depolarization site—sodium gates shut, potassium gates open—during which the membrane is insensitive to stimulation.

32.5 How Neurons Send Messages to Other Cells

A. Chemical Synapses
   1. A chemical synapse is a junction between a neuron and an adjacent cell, separated by a synaptic cleft into which a neurotransmitter substance is released.
      a. The neuron that releases the neurotransmitter molecules into the cleft is called the *pre*synaptic cell.
         1) First, gated protein channels open to allow calcium ions to enter the neuron.
         2) Calcium causes the vesicles to fuse with the membrane and release the transmitter substance into the cleft.
      b. The neurotransmitter binds to receptors on the membrane of the *post*synaptic cell.

1) Neurotransmitters may have excitatory effects if they drive a cell's membrane to the threshold of an action potential.
2) Neurotransmitters may have inhibitory effects if they help drive the membrane away from threshold.

2. Neurotransmitters may have an excitatory effect, driving the membrane toward the threshold of an action potential.
3. In other cases, it will have an inhibitory effect and pull the membrane away from the threshold.
4. There are several kinds of neurotransmitters.
   a. Acetylcholine (ACh) is the transmitter released at neuromuscular junctions, which are a type of chemical synapse between a motor neuron and a skeletal muscle fiber.
   b. ACh diffuses across the cleft and binds to membrane receptors on muscle fiber, having an excitatory effect and stimulating muscle contraction.

B. Cleaning Up the Cleft
1. Neurotransmitter molecules must be removed promptly from the synaptic cleft.
2. Some molecules diffuse out; acetylcholinesterase degrades many; others are actively pumped back into the presynaptic cells by membrane transport proteins.

C. Synaptic Integration
1. Excitatory and inhibitory signals compete at the input zone.
   a. An excitatory postsynaptic potential (EPSP) is a summation of signals that brings the membrane closer to threshold (depolarizing effect).
   b. An inhibitory postsynaptic potential (IPSP) drives the membrane away from threshold by a hyperpolarizing effect.
2. In *synaptic integration,* competing signals that reach the input zone are reinforced or dampened, sent on or suppressed; signals can also be integrated when they arrive one after another.

32.6 A Smorgasbord of Signals

A. Neurotransmitter Discovery and Diversity
1. Early experiments by Otto Loewi revealed how the neurotransmitter ACh works.
   a. ACh works on skeletal muscle, smooth muscle, the heart, glands, and the brain.
   b. It stimulates contractions when it binds to skeletal muscle fibers; it slows contraction in heart muscle.
2. Both norepinephrine and epinephrine (adrenaline) are neurotransmitters that prime the body to respond to stress.
3. Dopamine affects fine motor control and pleasure-seeking behaviors.
   a. When dopamine-secreting neurons are destroyed in the brain it causes Parkinson's disease.
   b. Learning occurs through dopamine-based pathways.
   c. Variations in dopamine levels may affect mood, motivation, and attention spans.
4. Serotonin is a small neurotransmitter derived from the amino acid tryptophan, which affects mood and memory; low levels are related to depression.
5. GABA (gamma amino butyric acid) is the most common inhibitory signal in the brain and is derived from glutamate.
6. Neuromodulators are neuropeptides that enhance or reduce the effects of a neurotransmitter on target neurons.
   a. One neuromodulator that enhances pain perception is called substance P.
   b. Enkephalins and endorphins are natural painkillers that inhibit the release of substance P and are secreted in response to strenuous activity or injury.

B. Disrupted Signaling

1. Neurological Disorders
    a. Alzheimer's disease is a form of dementia that damages neurons in the brain and involves lower levels of Ach.
    b. Parkinson's disease results in tremors caused by a dopamine shortage.
    c. Individuals with ADHD have lower levels of dopamine, which results in inattentiveness.
    d. Depression may be the result of lower levels of serotonin, dopamine, or norepinephrine.
2. Psychoactive Drugs
    a. Psychoactive drugs, both legal and illegal, are often taken to mediate pain, mental illness, or stress.
    b. Tolerance to a drug means users must take larger and larger doses to obtain the same effect.
    c. Habituation and tolerance can lead to drug addiction.
    d. Addictive drugs stimulate the release of dopamine, a neurotransmitter involved in the sense of pleasure.
    e. Stimulants increase alertness and anxiousness.
        1) Nicotine and caffeine block Ach receptors.
        2) Cocaine increases the sense of pleasure by blocking reabsorption of norepinephrine, dopamine, and serotonin.
        3) Amphetamines increase dopamine, serotonin, and norepinephrine, reducing appetite and energizing users.
        4) MDMA (Ecstasy) and crystal meth are amphetamines.
    f. Depressants slow motor responses by inhibiting Ach output.
        1) Alcohol and barbiturates are depressants.
        2) Alcohol stimulates the release of endorphins and GABA, so users experience a brief euphoria followed by depression.
    g. Analgesics
        1) Analgesics mimic endorphins and enkephalins, the natural pain killers secreted by the brain.
        2) Morphine, codeine, oxycodone, and heroin are common addictive pain killers.
    h. Hallucinogens
        1) These drugs skew sensory perception by interfering with acetylcholine, norepinephrine, and serotonin.
        2) Marijuana acts like a mild depressant and gives mild euphoria, but it can also cause disorientation, anxiety, and hallucinations.
        3) LSD, mescaline, and psilocybin are also examples of hallucinogens.

32.7 The Peripheral Nervous System

A. Axons Bundled as Nerves

1. The human peripheral system has two types of nerves based on location.
    a. Spinal nerves (31 pairs) connect with the spinal cord and innervate most areas of the body.
    b. Cranial nerves (12 pairs) connect vital organs directly to the brain.
2. Signals between brain or spinal cord and body regions travel by nerves.
    a. Axons of motor neurons, dendrites of sensory neurons, or both are bundled together in a nerve.
    b. Peripheral nerve axons are covered by a myelin sheath derived in part from neuroglial Schwann cells.

3. The sheath acts as an electronic insulator that greatly speeds the propagation of action potentials.
    a. Each section of the sheath is separated from adjacent ones by a node where the axon membrane (plentiful in gated sodium channels) is exposed.
    b. The action potentials jump from node to node, which is fast and efficient.

B. Functional Subdivisions
1. Somatic and Autonomic Systems
    a. The *somatic* nerves relay sensory information from receptors in the skin and muscles and motor commands to skeletal muscles (voluntary control).
    b. The *autonomic* nerves send signals to and from smooth muscles, cardiac muscle, and glands (involuntary control).
2. Sympathetic and Parasympathetic Nerves
    a. *Sympathetic* nerves increase overall body activity during times of stress, excitement, or danger; they also call on the hormone epinephrine to increase the "fight-flight" response.
    b. *Parasympathetic* nerves tend to slow down body activity when the body is not under stress.
    c. Opposing sympathetic and parasympathetic signals control most organs.

32.8 The Spinal Cord

A. An Information Highway
1. The spinal cord is a pathway for signal travel between the peripheral nervous system and the brain.
    a. The cord is also the center for controlling some reflex actions.
    b. The spinal cord (and also the brain) is covered with tough membranes—the meninges—and resides within the protection of the stacked vertebrae.
    c. Gray matter contains the cell bodies, dendrites, unsheathed axons, and neuroglia.
    d. White matter contains myelin sheathed axons and neuroglia.
2. Signals move up and down the spinal cord in bundles of sheathed axons.

B. Reflex Pathways
1. Reflexes are simple, stereotyped movements made in response to sensory stimuli, and considered to be the most ancient pathways of information flow.
2. In the simplest reflex, the reflex arc, sensory neurons directly synapse on motor neurons.
    a. In the stretch reflex, receptors of sensory neurons (muscle spindles) transmit impulses to the spinal cord, where direct synapses with motor neurons occur.
    b. The rate of signal transmission along the axons of sensory receptors depends on the extent to which the muscle is stretched.
    c. The familiar knee-jerk response is another simple reflex.

32.9 The Vertebrate Brain

A. Brain Development and Evolution
1. In embryonic development, the neural tube forms the brain and spinal cord.
2. The brain is divided into a forebrain, midbrain, and hindbrain in vertebrates.
    a. The hindbrain is the region where spinal cord and brain join.
    b. The midbrain is large in fishes and amphibians and reduced in birds and mammals.
    c. In mammals and birds, the forebrain has taken over some midbrain activities.

B. Ventricles and the Blood-Brain Barrier
1. The brain and spinal cord are bathed with cerebrospinal fluid that exists within a system of cavities and canals.
2. The fluid cushions vital nervous tissue from sudden, jarring movements.

3. The blood-brain barrier operates at the plasma membranes of cells, forming the capillaries that service the brain.
   a. Tight junctions fuse the capillary cells together, forcing substances to move through the cells to reach the brain.
   b. Membrane transport proteins allow essential nutrients (glucose) to move through but bar wastes (urea) and certain toxins.

C. The Human Brain
1. An average-sized human brain weighs about 3 pounds and has about 100 billion interneurons.
2. The medulla oblongata has influence over respiration, sleep/waking cycles, and swallowing.
3. The *pons* ("bridge") possesses bands of axons that pass between brain centers.
4. The *cerebellum* acts as reflex center for maintaining posture and coordinating limbs.
5. The *cerebrum* integrates sensory input and selected motor responses.
   a. The human cerebrum is divided into left and right cerebral hemispheres, which communicate by means of tracts called the corpus callosum.
6. The *thalamus* (below cerebrum) relays and coordinates sensory signals.
7. The *hypothalamus* monitors internal organs and influences responses to thirst, hunger, and sex.

32.10 A Closer Look at the Human Cerebrum

A. Functional Areas of the Cortex
1. The left hemisphere deals with speech, math, and analytical skills; the right half interprets music, judges spatial relations, and assesses visual input.
2. The body is spatially mapped out in the primary motor cortex of the frontal lobes.
   a. Each *frontal* lobe includes the motor cortex, which coordinates instructions for skeletal muscles.
   b. The frontal lobe also includes the premotor cortex (learned patterns of motor skills) and Broca's area, which helps translate thoughts into speech, creating complex sentences.
3. Sensory areas in the cerebral cortex assist in perceptions of the meaning of particular sensations.
   a. The *parietal* lobe contains the primary somatosensory cortex—the main receiving area for signals from the skin and joints.
   b. The *occipital* lobe, which is located in the rear, has centers for vision.
   c. The *temporal* lobe, near each temple, is a processing center for hearing and houses centers for influencing emotional behavior.
4. Association areas—occupying all parts of the cortex except primary and sensory areas—integrate, analyze, and respond to many inputs.

32.11 Emotion and Memory

A. The Limbic System
1. The limbic system, located at the middle of the cerebral hemispheres, governs our emotions and has roles in memory.
2. It is distantly related to olfactory lobes and still deals with the sense of smell, especially as it relates to memory.
3. Connections from the cerebral cortex pass through the limbic system, allowing us to correlate organ activities with self-gratifying behavior, such as eating and sex.

B. Making Memories
1. "Memory" is the storage and retrieval of information about previous experiences.

2. Information becomes stored in "memory traces"—chemical and structural changes in brain regions.
    a. Short-term memory lasts from seconds to hours and is limited to small bits of information.
    b. Long-term memory is more permanent and seems to be limitless.
    c. Declarative memory stores facts and impressions of events.
3. Emotions influence memory retention.

32.12 Neuroglia—The Neuron' Support Staff

A. Types and Functions of Neuroglia
1. Neuroglia cells outnumber neurons in the human brain 10 to 1. They act as a framework holding neurons in place.
2. Oligodendrocytes make myelin in the brain and Schwann cells make myelin in the peripheral nerves.
3. Astrocytes, the most abundant cells in the brain, control local concentrations of ion and neurotransmitters and they function in immunity. They also make lactate and synthesize nerve growth factor to support neurons.
4. Ependymal cells line the brain's cavities and the spinal cord's central canal. The action of their cilia keeps the cerebrospinal fluid flowing in a consistent direction through the system of cavities and canals.

B. Neuroglia in Disease
1. Multiple sclerosis (MS) is an autoimmune disease by which the myelin sheaths are being destroyed.
    a. MS is believed to have both a genetic and an environmental basis.
2. Guillain-Barre syndrome involves the destruction of myelin sheaths in the peripheral nervous system.
    a. This disease is usually reversible.
3. An excess amount of beta-amyloid in the brain is indicative of Alzheimer's disease.

C. Brain Tumors
1. Unlike neurons, neuroglial cells continue to divide in adults.
2. Sometimes neuroglia cells divide uncontrollably and result in a glioma—the most common form of brain cancer.
3. Brain tumors can also arise from uncontrolled division in cells in meninges or as a result of metastasis.
4. Researchers are still unsure about the impact of heavy cell phone use on the development of brain tumors.

32.13 In Pursuit of Ecstasy (Revisited)

A. MDMA (the active ingredient in Ecstasy) affects the amount of serotonin that remains in the synaptic cleft.
1. This results in a temporary pleasurable effect.
2. After a time period, there is less serotonin and depression may occur.
3. Memory may also be impaired by the low serotonin levels
4. Dopamine and norepinephrine levels may also be lowered.
5. The blood-brain barrier may be altered up to 10 weeks after taking Ecstasy.

Suggestions for Presenting the Material

- To grab the students' attention, start the lecture with any of the ABC videos available from the Multimedia Manager and CengageNOW.

- One of the most effective comparisons of the nervous system is to the worldwide telephone network. Although the analogy is not perfect, it does convey the truth that billions of individual phone sets can send impulses (communicate) with any other phone, or several phones at one time, via a connecting wire or microwave signal. This analogy particularly is relevant to the study of the spinal cord. Tracts of nerves that are traveling in a similar direction in the spinal cord are bundled together. This seems similar to the organization of phone lines that may be bundled together when they are on the way to a particular location.
- Students ranging in scientific expertise from that of beginning freshman to third-year medical student all agree that the nervous system is one of the most difficult to comprehend at any level. Therefore, extra time and thorough explanations are especially needed in this chapter.
- The function of the neuron membrane in permitting passage of Na^+ and K^+ ions is confusing. Initially, you may wish to focus on sodium only, and then expand to the role of potassium.
- The changes in the neuron membrane can be conveniently demonstrated using Figure 32.8 (a–d) and the words *polarized, depolarized,* and *repolarized,* which are conventional terms but are not used in this edition of the text. The Multimedia and CengageNOW provide an animation as well.
- The concept of "all-or-nothing events" and "thresholds" can be illustrated by describing the use of a firearm. When the trigger is pulled and reaches the critical point (threshold) at which the hammer is released, the bullet leaves the barrel and travels the expected distance. Of course, the bullet either goes or stays (all or nothing), and the manner in which the trigger is activated (slowly or quickly) should not influence the speed of bullet travel. Keep in mind that, at any given time, a gun is either firing or not firing—just like a neuron is either resting or excited. Appropriately enough, scientists even describe a nerve impulse as "firing"!
- Equally effective in illustrating the "all-or-nothing" concept is the use of a device present in every classroom—light switches.
- There are tests to check the functioning of each cranial nerve. Have your students perform these tests. For example, if they can identify the smell of coffee, it appears their olfactory nerve is functioning normally.
- Emphasize the temporary nature of the acetylcholine bridge across the synapse by comparing it to a pontoon bridge used by the military to cross small streams and rivers.
- If the students can recite the sequence of structures through which an impulse passes during a *reflex arc,* such as in Figure 32.17, they have a good grasp of the nerve conduction pathways. Add the ion flow across the membranes, and the story is pretty well complete!
- Emphasize the difference between a *neuron* and a *nerve*. Students often have difficulty distinguishing between them because the words sound so much alike.
- Some terms used to describe the divisions are not parallel. For example, *autonomic* (not a misspelling of "automatic" as some students think) is used to designate nerves *not* under voluntary control, and *somatic* is used to designate nerves under voluntary control.
- You might be surprised at the number of students who cannot distinguish the backbone (vertebral, or spinal, column) from the spinal cord. Give them some assistance by referring to Figure 32.15.
- Emphasize the continuity of fiber tracts between the brain and spinal cord. Stress the primary functions of the spinal cord as a reflex center versus the brain as a sense-interpretation and directed-response center.
- The extent to which each instructor requires the students to delve into brain regions and functions will vary. Some instructors may want to select the major brain regions (cerebrum, hypothalamus/pituitary, cerebellum, and medulla) for special emphasis.
- Students generally find it easier to distinguish between the sympathetic and parasympathetic divisions of the autonomic nervous system if they are told that the sympathetic division is involved in

mobilizing "fight-or-flight" reaction, while the parasympathetic division produces a general "slowing-down" and "business as usual" response. Use an example of the functioning of each system that students will relate to easily. For example, if you see a white car by the side of the road that you perceive to be a police car, your sympathetic nervous system may respond by speeding up your heart rate. As you get closer and realize that it is simply a disabled car, your parasympathetic system returns your heart rate to normal.

Classroom and Laboratory Enrichment

- The concept of thresholds and all-or-nothing events can be demonstrated by using dominoes (or for large classes, several audiocassette cases). Line up about 20 dominoes placed on end and spaced about one inch apart. Ask a student to gently touch one end domino to begin the progressive fall. Emphasize that the student's touch (threshold stimulus) caused a standing row (polarized) to begin falling (depolarization) at a constant speed (all-or-nothing event). Pose the following question (and demonstrate the answer): Would a greater and faster stimulus cause more rapid falling? To demonstrate *repolarization,* a second student could begin resetting the dominoes even before the falling is complete.
- Have your students perform some simple reflexes, such as the papillary reflex. Everyone is familiar with the response when a flashlight shines in your eye. As you are performing this and other reflexes, have your students name the specific parts of a reflex arc.
- Arrange with a physics student or instructor for a demonstration of an action potential as recorded on an oscilloscope screen.
- Permit students to demonstrate the knee-jerk reflex arc by using percussion hammers. It is important to ask the subjects to close their eyes to prevent "cheating."
- Show a film or video of an animation of nerve impulse transmission.
- Exhibit models of neurons and neuroglial cells.
- Provide microscope slides of longitudinal sections and cross-sections of nerves for student viewing.
- Have microscope slides of neurons available for laboratory demonstration. Be sure to point out the long cytoplasmic extensions—dendrites and axons.
- Many laboratories have preserved specimens of the human or other vertebrate brain, which are valuable aids to comprehending the size and arrangement of brain parts.
- Using live *Hydra* and *Dugesia* (planaria), test for nervous response to touch; vibration; light; mild, acid, or alkali; and heat. Are there differences between the two species with respect to degree and speed of response?
- Use a dissectible model of the neurons, neuroglial cells, the brain, and brain tumors to illustrate the important concepts.
- Exhibit a vertebral column/spinal cord/herniated disc model to demonstrate why so much pain and functional loss are associated with herniated discs. Note how the inner nucleus pulposus of a disc leaks out of the outer annulus fibrosus. The pain results when the nucleus pulposus leans on nearby nerves.
- Show a film or video on brain function.
- Use a spinal cord/vertebral column cross-sectional model to illustrate the relation between the two structures.
- Some students may be familiar with the children's game called "whisper down the lane." This game can be used to illustrate the transmission of a nerve impulse. First, line up a row of students

from one side of the room to another. Each student should pass a message along, one by one, through the line until the message gets to the end. This process illustrates the transmission of a nerve impulse when it does not contain a myelin sheath. To mimic the transmission in a myelinated neuron, a student would lean over and give the message to a student several places away. The message will get to the end faster, because the impulse skips major portions. This is similar to the transmission of a nerve impulse when the axon is myelinated.

Classroom Discussion Ideas

- Why are teenagers and young adults so susceptible to taking recreational drugs such as Ecstasy?
- Do you think persons at a "rave" even know what drugs they might be taking?
- Borrow brain models from an anatomy lab. Can you identify the major portions listed in this chapter? Refresh your memory of the functions of each of these parts.
- Would an education campaign about the dangers of Ecstasy have any deterrent effect on young "ravers"?
- The information on the psychoactive drugs and their deleterious effects on the body may discourage the informed biology student from this type of drug experimentation.
- Investigate neural tube defects, such as spina bifida. How does this disability damage the spinal cord? This disease has been shown to be caused by both genetic and environmental factors. There are studies attempting to isolate the genetic imperfection, and they have determined the environmental cause—the folic acid level in the mother. Since the neural tube forms very early in fetal development (4–6-week gestation), it is probably not effective to put folic acid in prenatal vitamins. By the time a woman realizes she is pregnant, it may be beyond the sixth week of gestation. Now they are putting folic acid in commonly consumed food such as flour in the hopes of decreasing the incidence of the disease.
- Do your students understand that many reflexes do not involve the brain? They are just directly wired through the spinal cord. You can prove that all reflexes do not require communication with the brain by probing an animal that contains only a nerve net. The organism will recoil from pain as a reflex even though it does not even have a brain!
- Some scientists describe the formation of memories as locating a footpath in the woods. The more times you travel the same pathway, the more grasses get trampled down and the path becomes easy to locate. The same holds true for memories. The more you retrace the neural pathways, the easier a memory is formed. So, the underlying message to your students is to go over their notes daily!

Additional Ideas for Classroom Discussion

- What would be the result of demyelination of axons, such as occurs in multiple sclerosis? On first thought, you may think the destruction of myelin sheaths would not be that problematic for the patient. After all, there are neurons in the body that are never wrapped in myelin sheaths and they work perfectly. The problem that results from MS is that the destruction of the myelin sheaths leaves behind scarring, which may impede the conduction of the nerve impulse.
- On hearing that salt was not good for him, a freshman college student began a fanatical program to eliminate all sodium chloride from his diet. By cooking his own meals, he was able to eliminate virtually all sodium. What complications could he expect as a result of his rash action?

- If neurons operate under the all-or-nothing principle, how are we able to distinguish soft sounds from loud sounds, or a gentle touch from a crushing blow?
- To most amateur musicians, the playing of sixteenth notes is a challenge, but to trumpet virtuoso Wynton Marsalis, thirty-second and sixty-fourth notes are a breeze. Describe the action of nerves and tongue muscles that regulate the air flow through the mouthpiece.
- Why does a physician's tapping of the knee or elbow reveal the status of the nervous system *in general,* not just the condition of those two joints?
- Why does "jumping" conduction afford the best possible conduction speed with the least metabolic effort by the cell?
- How do medications such as Novocain block the nerve impulse so that you do not feel pain?
- Do you see why the neurotransmitter must be removed after a nerve impulse? If not, the neuron would be confused—is that the last impulse or do you want me to contract again?
- Talk about the fight-flight response. Note how it is designed to give the individual a little extra speed or strength in an emergency. Often we feel this response in a perceived emergency. Ask someone in the class to get up and sing a song or give a speech. Often the heart rate increases due to the fight-flight response. Some individuals with adrenal tumors have a constant feeling as though they were in a dangerous situation. Can you imagine how stressful that would be?
- Why does drinking a large amount of coffee or other caffeine-containing beverage tend to make a person "nervous" or "jittery"?
- Do invertebrates, such as the cockroach, feel pain?
- The central nervous system (and closely associated ganglia) houses the cell bodies of neurons. As opposed to the peripheral axons and dendrites, the cell bodies are not regenerated after traumatic injury. What advantages and disadvantages does this structural arrangement pose for humans?
- Why does a small speck of food stuck between your teeth feel like a large chunk when rubbed with your tongue?
- The exact mode of action of the famous, and now banned, insecticide DDT has never been elucidated (after nearly 50 years of research). However, textbooks describe it as a "central nervous system" poison. What does this imply?
- Explain why elderly people may be unable to remember what they ate for breakfast but can relate the details of a teenage romance.
- Discuss the characteristics of brain disorders such as Parkinson's disease and Alzheimer's disease. Investigate potential causes of these diseases by looking into recent research.
- Investigate the structure of the vertebral column. Note how it protects the spinal cord, yet it also provides areas for major nerves to access the cord.
- Read about Phinneas Gage, a survivor of a traumatic brain injury. From observing the changes in his personality after his accident, do you think the limbic system was damaged?
- What is "hangman's fracture"? With this injury the brainstem is damaged. Why is that so dangerous?
- Research experiments in which the corpus callosum of epileptic patients was severed. Was this treatment effective? Were there any adverse effects from the surgery?

How Would You Vote? Classroom Discussion Ideas

- Monitor the voting for the online question. Scientific research has shown that MDMA, the active ingredient in Ecstasy, makes individuals feel more socially comfortable. Then the question arises—could thies drug have a clinical use for those suffering from extreme cases of social anxiety? One would have to carefully weigh the pros and cons of this type of treatment. On the plus side, we know that there can be social benefits from the use of this category of drug. On the downside, researchers see long-lasting deleterious effects from the use of Ecstasy. Much more research should be performed concerning the disadvantages of extensive drug use before they are licensed for clinical purposes. How to the students feel on this issue?

- Have students complete polling using the JoinIn clickers.

Term Paper Topics, Library Activities, and Special Projects

- The neurons of the human body can communicate one with the other much the same as telephones in your city can intercommunicate. In the telephone system, wires touch wires to pass the impulse, but neurons are not directly "wired." Investigate the effects on the body of the elimination of synapse function such as would be caused by organophosphate pesticides, which inhibit acetylcholinesterase.
- One of the most effective antidotes for the organophosphate (OP) poisoning referred to above is *atropine.* Investigate its mechanism of action. Based on what you find, could administration of atropine be harmful if OP poisoning *has not* occurred?
- Prepare a list of neurological disorders in which you focus on the specific cause of the difficulty in each case. Multiple sclerosis is an interesting disease to investigate. Some researchers have noticed that there appear to be "hot spots" for the disease. These are areas or neighborhoods where the incidence of MS is considerably higher than in other areas. Can you find any evidence in research to support this theory?
- Ask a resource person to explain the consequences of central nervous system damage as opposed to peripheral damage.
- Investigate some of the factors that determine the speed at which an impulse is conducted in a neuron.
- Why are injuries to the central nervous system, such as gunshot wounds, more permanently debilitating than those to the peripheral system?
- Using the mode of action of organophosphate insecticides as a tool, delve into the similarities and differences between the physiology of insect and human nerve function.
- Prepare an argument for the suppression of a presently readily available drug, say, alcohol, or prepare an argument for the legalization of marijuana.
- Explore the research relating dreams to actual events—past and future. What do dreams tell us about ourselves?
- Discuss the basis for the use of acupuncture for relieving pain or providing anesthesia.
- Research the "gate theory" of pain transmission.
- Investigate the use of biofeedback for controlling pain, heart rate, and other autonomic functions.
- Research and report on any neurotoxin, disorder, or drug and report on its effects on the nervous system.
- Botox is a neurotoxin used to make skin look younger. Investigate where Botox comes from and how it works, and formulate an opinion on how you feel regarding this cosmetic procedure.
- Investigate the vagus nerve. Is it a cranial nerve? What areas of the body does it affect?
- What is the sodium-potassium pump? What is its function in a resting neuron? Does this imply that it is work to be a resting neuron? How about we rename it a "ready" neuron?

Possible Responses to *Critical Thinking* Questions

1. The length of the giraffe primary afferent axon (from toe to neck) is 15 feet. In nature, animals must grow at a regulated pace, which allows for constant feedback and conditioning of the body structures. Axons initially grow out from neurons and follow a chemical stimulus to connect with another neuron. However, once the axon has reached its target, a process of stretch-growth must ensue as the animal grows. Mechanical changes in the growing brain, spine, and other bones are the starting point for natural stretch-growth in axons. In an intriguing experiment, researchers at the University of Pennsylvania School of Medicine have induced nerve fibers—or axons—to grow at rates and lengths far exceeding what has been previously observed. To mimic extreme examples in nature like the giraffe, and to learn more about neuronal physiology, they have mechanically stretched axons at rates of eight millimeters per day, reaching lengths of up to 10 centimeters without breaking. In the present study, the team led by Douglas H. Smith, MD, Professor of Neurosurgery and Director of the Center for Brain Injury and Repair, placed neurons from rat dorsal root ganglia (clusters of nerves just outside the spinal cord) on nutrient-filled plastic plates. Axons sprouted from the neurons on each plate and connected with neurons on the other plate. The plates were then slowly pulled apart over a series of days, aided by a precise computer-controlled motor system. One particular challenge of neurons with very long axons is that they have a very large area of membrane to maintain. In addition, needed nutrients must travel long distances to service the entire cell.
2. PTSD is known to affect the hippocampus and the amygdale, which are both components of the limbic system. The limbic system works with the cerebral cortex, affecting emotion and contributing to memory. Other components of the limbic system and the cerebral cortex may also be disrupted in PTSD. Also, since it is known that the hippocampus and amygdale are affected, other internal homeostatic controls may be out of balance in patients. For instance, anxiety, depression, and social phobias are also common in PTSD victims.
3. All too often we think of babies as miniature adults, but they are not. The undeveloped blood-brain barrier is one good example. The adult body can process perfectly normal hormones, amino acids, ions, etc. even if their concentrations vary somewhat to the high side. Even alcohol, caffeine, and nicotine can be detoxified. But to the susceptible fetus and newborn, any of these substances could enter the brain in concentrations capable of causing damage. Thus, in addition to paying careful attention to her newborn's diet, a conscientious nursing mother would limit her indulgences for the health of her newborn baby. Both parents should continue to be careful in the foods they provide to their baby as he or she develops.

Possible Responses to *Data Analysis Exercise* Questions

Studies have been performed to see the effect on the offspring of pregnant rats that were exposed to MDMA (the active ingredient in Ecstasy).

1. During the first gibr minutes, the rats that were prenatally exposed to saline moved around more than those exposed to MDMA.
2. The rats exposed to MDMA prenatally showed 76 photobeam breaks during their second five minutes in a new cage.
3. The rats exposed to MDMA moved around the most in the last minutes, when compared to rats exposed only to saline.
4. This study appears to show some differences in the brains of those rats exposed prenatally to MDMA and those exposed just to saline.

33

SENSORY PERCEPTION

Chapter Outline

Objectives

1. Describe and note examples of each of the six general categories of sensory receptors.
2. Contrast the mechanism by which the somatic and visceral senses work.
3. Understand how the senses of smell, taste, balance, and hearing function.
4. Identify and describe the function of each of the parts of the human ear.
5. Describe how the sense of vision has evolved through time.
6. Identify and describe the function of each of the parts of the human eye.
7. Understand how noise pollution affects humans and other animals.

Key Terms

echolocation
sensory systems
stimulus
perception
mechanoreceptors
pain receptors (nociceptors)
thermoreceptors
chemoreceptors
osmoreceptors
photoreceptors
sensory adaptation
sensory perception
somatosensory cortex
somatic sensations
visceral sensations
pain
referred pain
olfaction
olfactory receptors
pheromones
vomeronasal organ
taste receptors
sweet
sour
salty
bitter
umami
organs of equilibrium
vestibular apparatus
utricle
saccule
semicircular canals
hearing
outer ear
pinna
middle ear
eardrum
inner ear
cochlea
scala vestibuli
scala tympani
basilar membrane
organ of Corti
hair cells
tectorial membrane
vision
eyes
photoreceptors
lens
ciliary photoreceptors
simple eyes
compound eyes
conjunctiva
cornea
camera eyes
retina
choroid
iris
pupil
ciliary body
sclera
aqueous humor
vitreous body
visual accommodation
ciliary muscle
fovea
rod cells
cone cells
rhodopsin
optic nerve
blind spot
colorblindness
astigmatism
nearsightedness
farsightedness
macular degeneration
glaucoma
cataract
trachoma

Lecture Outline

33.1 A Whale of a Dilemma

A. Whales move using acoustical cues.
   1. Sound moves five times faster in water than air.
   2. Whales have more neurons to collect auditory information.
   3. Jaws pick up the vibrations, which travel through a layer of fat to the middle ear.

B. Whales use echolocation.
   1. They emit high-pitched sounds that bounce off objects.
   2. Noise from human endeavors, like new military sonar systems, may be raising havoc with whale acoustical systems.

33.2 Overview of Sensory Pathways

A. Sensory neurons are classified based on the type of stimulus to which they respond.

B. Sensory Receptor Diversity
   1. *Mechanoreceptors* detect forms of mechanical energy (pressure, position, and acceleration).
   2. *Pain receptors* detect tissue damage.
   3. *Thermoreceptors* detect heat energy.
   4. *Chemoreceptors* detect chemical energy in specific substances dissolved in fluid.
   5. *Osmoreceptors* detect changes in solute concentration (water volume).
   6. *Photoreceptors* detect visible and UV light.

C. From Sensing to Sensation
   1. The somatic sensations arise from sensory receptors located in tissues throughout the body; special senses rely on receptors that are restricted to certain body parts.

2. Sensory receptors transduce stimulus energy into action potentials, which are assessed by the brain using three factors.
   a. Genetically determined *pathways* of neurons in the brain can interpret incoming action potentials only in specific ways; for example, receptors from eyes "see" only light.
   b. Strong stimulation of a receptor causes a greater *frequency* of action potentials.
   c. Strong stimulation causes a greater *number* of neurons to fire.
3. In sensory adaptation the frequency of action potentials decreases or stops even when the stimulus is maintained; for example, clothing is no longer felt once it is put on for the day.

D. Sensory Perception
1. The brain assigns meanings to sensory signals.

33.3 Somatic and Visceral Sensations

A. Somatic sensations are easily localized, whereas visceral sensations are more difficult to define.

B. The Somatosensory Cortex
1. Sensory nerve pathways from different receptors lead to different parts of the somatosensory cortex of the brain.
2. Cells in this region are laid out like a map, with different regions corresponding to the functional importance of the different body parts.

C. Receptors near the Body Surface
1. Free nerve endings are simply branched endings of sensory neurons in the skin that function as mechanoreceptors, thermoreceptors, and pain receptors.
2. Encapsulated receptors are of several types.
   a. Meissner's corpuscles adapt slowly to vibrations of low frequencies.
   b. The bulb of Krause is a thermoreceptor that is sensitive to temperatures below 10°C.
   c. Ruffini endings are sensitive to steady touching and pressure, and to temperatures above 45°C.
   d. Pacinian corpuscles are located both in the dermis and near joints; they are able to detect rapid pressure changes associated with touch and vibrations.

D. Muscle Sense
1. Mechanoreceptors in muscle joints, tendons, ligaments, and skin detect limb motions and the body's position in space.
2. Examples include the stretch receptors of muscle spindles.

E. Pain
1. Sensations of somatic pain come from receptors in the skin, skeletal muscles, joints, and tendons.
2. Sensations of visceral pain, which are associated with internal organs, are related to excessive chemical stimulation, muscle spasms and fatigue, and inadequate blood flow.
3. Both somatic and visceral pain can be superficial or deep.
4. Injured cells release chemicals, like bradykinins, that activate nearby pain receptors.
   a. Those signals enter the spinal cord, causing release of substance P, a neuromodulator, which activates neurons to signal the sensory cortex.
   b. Different signals result in emotional responses and release of natural opiates to lower pain perception.
5. When the brain projects pain from the internal organs to the skin it is referred pain.
   a. Heart attacks are often perceived as radiating pain from the left shoulder and arm, neck, and chest wall.

b. Since the skin encounters more painful stimuli than internal organs, the brain may interpret most sensory input as coming from the most frequent source—the skin.

33.4 Chemical Senses

A. Sense of Smell

1. The sensory pathways of olfaction and taste begin with chemoreceptors.
2. Olfactory receptors detect water-soluble or volatile substances.
   a. The message is sent from olfactory cells to the limbic system and the cerebral cortex.
   b. Due to the decreased number of receptors in humans and their location, some animals (e.g., dogs) can detect and identify many more odors.

B. Sense of Taste

1. Taste receptors are chemoreceptors that enable animals to distinguish nutritious from noxious substances.
   a. Receptors of some animals are located on antennae, legs, tentacles, or fins.
   b. In humans, taste receptors are often components of taste buds, distributed mostly on the tongue.
   c. The five main tastes include sweet, sour, salty, bitter, and umami.

C. Pheromones—Chemical Messages

1. Some receptors respond to pheromones, which are molecules released outside the body to elicit a social response in a member of the same species.
   a. Reptiles and most mammals have a vomeronasal organ that responds to pheromones.

33.5 Diversity of Visual Systems

A. Requirements for Vision

1. Vision requires eyes (photoreceptors) and a neural program in the brain that can interpret the patterns of action potentials.
2. Photoreceptors contain pigment molecules that absorb photon energy, which can be converted to excitation energy in the sensory neuron.
3. A visual field is the part of the outside world that an animal sees, made easier with a lens.
4. Invertebrate eyes are less complex.
   a. Some animals do not have concentrations of photoreceptors in any particular location (e.g., earthworms).
   b. Many invertebrates have photoreceptor cells that detect changes in light intensity but do not form images (e.g., scallops).
   c. Insects and crustaceans have compound eyes with numerous photosensitive units, each capable of sampling a portion of the visual field to assemble a visual mosaic.
   d. Squids and octopuses have camera eyes, each with a lens, cornea, and retina.
   e. Convergent evolution may have led to similarities between cephalopod and vertebrate eyes.
5. The position of eyes varies—animals with two forward-facing eyes have depth perception.
6. Nocturnal animals have large eyes and a reflective layer that helps collect light.

33.6 A Closer Look at the Human Eye

A. Anatomy of the Eye

1. The outer layer consists of a sclera ("white" of the eye), which covers most of the eye; the cornea covers the front.
2. The middle layer consists of a choroid, ciliary body, iris, and pupil.

a. The choroid absorbs light that photoreceptors do not.
b. Light enters the eyeball's chamber through a lens with a pupil opening, which is bathed with jellylike substances (aqueous humor on the lens and vitreous body behind the lens).

3. The pigmented iris controls the amount of light entering through the pupil.
4. The cornea and lens bend the light rays so that the image is in focus on the retina.

B. Focusing Mechanisms

1. The lens position or shape are adjusted in ways that focus all incoming rays onto the retina.
   a. In fish and reptiles, the lens is moved forward and back (like a camera lens) to focus.
   b. In birds and mammals, the ciliary muscle changes the shape of the lens to focus.
2. When the ciliary muscle encircling the lens relaxes, the lens flattens and moves the focal point further back; when the muscle contracts, the lens bulges and moves the focal point forward.
3. When the eye's accommodation does not work, eyeglasses are needed.

33.7 Light Reception and Visual Processing

A. Structure of the Retina

1. A pigmented epithelium packed with arrays of ciliary photoreceptors known as rod cells and cone cells lies between the retina and the choroid.
2. Rods are sensitive to dim light and detect changes in light intensity.
   a. Rod cells are most abundant outside of the fovea.
   b. Rod cells are the basis for coarse perception of movement and for peripheral vision.
3. Cones respond to high-intensity light, contribute to sharp daytime vision, and detect colors.
   a. The fovea has the greatest number of cone cells.
   b. Cone cells are the basis for sharp vision and for color perception.

B. How Photoreceptors Work

1. Photoreceptors, linked to neurons, are located in the retina.
2. Each rod cell contains molecules of rhodopsin that can be altered by light, resulting in voltage changes in membranes.
3. Cone cells each carry a different pigment for red, green, and blue colors; cone cells at the fovea (center of retina) provide the greatest visual acuity.

C. Visual Processing

1. The sense of vision is the result of processing the information through levels of synapsing neurons.
2. Stimulation begins in the rods and cones, moves to bipolar sensory neurons, and then moves to ganglion cells, whose axons form the optic nerves that lead to the brain's visual cortex.
3. Before leaving the retina, signals flow among horizontal cells and amacrine cells, which dampen or enhance the signals.
4. Ganglion cells form restricted areas of the retinal surface called "receptive fields," which respond best to small spots of light.
5. Axons of the two optic nerves end in the lateral geniculate nucleus of the brain, where the positions of the receptive fields correspond to those of the retina; final interpretation of sight occurs in the visual cortex.

33.8 Visual Disorders

A. Color Blindness

1. Red-green colorblindness is an X-linked, recessive abnormality.

2. Some or all of the cone cells that detect red or green wavelengths are missing.

B. Lack of Focus
   1. Astigmatism results from unevenly curved corneas that affect the focusing of light in an inherited manner.
   2. In nearsightedness, the eyeball is too long or the ciliary muscle contracts too strongly; the object focuses in front of the retina.
   3. In farsightedness, the eyeball is not long enough or the lens is lazy; the object focuses behind the retina.
   4. As people age, a normal eye lens loses some of its natural flexibility and glasses or surgery are needed to correct focusing problems.

C. Age-Related Disorders
   1. *Age-related macular degeneration* (AMD) is a loss of the photoreceptor cells in the macula and fovea, the areas of most precise image focus.
   2. *Glaucoma* results from too much aqueous humor inside the eyeball, causing damage to the blood vessels and ganglion cells, affecting vision.
   3. A *cataract* is a gradual clouding of the lens, reducing the amount of light entering the eye.

33.9 Sense of Hearing

A. Properties of Sound
   1. Hearing is the perception of sound.
   2. Sounds are traveling vibrations of mechanical energy.
   3. These wavelike forms of mechanical energy show amplitude (loudness) and frequency (pitch).

B. The Vertebrate Ear
   1. The external ear in mammals has a pinna for collecting sounds.
   2. The middle ear picks up vibrations from the eardrum and passes them to three small bones (hammer, anvil, and stirrup), which amplify sounds before transmittal to the inner ear.
   3. In the cochlea of the inner ear, acoustical receptors in the form of hair cells respond to pressure waves transmitted through the surrounding fluid.
      a. Impulses are sent along the auditory nerve to the brain for interpretation.
      b. The hair cells in the organ of Corti of the human ear can be permanently damaged by prolonged exposure to intense sounds.

33.10 Organs of Equilibrium

A. The sense of balance depends on the organs of equilibrium located in the inner ear.
   1. The vestibular apparatus (utricle, saccule, and semicircular canals) is a closed system of fluid-filled sacs and canals inside the ear, loaded with mechanoreceptors.
      a. An organ located in the *semicircular canals* detects changing movements (dynamic equilibrium) when fluid bends hair cells attached to sensory neurons.
      b. An organ of static equilibrium is inside each utricle and saccule, which detects linear movements of the head relative to the ground (static equilibrium).
   2. The brain evaluates input from all receptors and integrates the information to maintain awareness of body position.

B. Stroke, inner ear infection, or loose particles in the semicircular canals cause vertigo, a sensation that the world is spinning; vertigo also comes from conflicting sensory inputs.

C. Overstimulation of the hair cells of the vestibular apparatus can result in motion sickness.

33.11 A Whale of a Dilemma (Revisited)

A. Noise pollution is a man-made problem.

1. Excessive noise caused by humans is a threat to animals and humans.
2. Hearing loss may be caused by damaged hair cells resulting from exposure to excessive noise.
3. Studies are being performed that indicate noise pollution is deleterious to animals.
   a. Whales appear stressed when they have to "shout' to communicate with other whales.
   b. Birds may have trouble obtaining a mate if their auditory signals are not heard by others.

Suggestions for Presenting the Material

- The information on sensory systems may be more familiar to your students because of previous exposure to the material. Most junior and senior high school health and biology classes provide a fair introduction to the sensory organs.
- Assuming your students *do* possess basic knowledge of the senses, it remains for you to emphasize two areas. The first is to relate the sense receptor and its interpretation within the brain. This is the subject of the initial portion of the chapter. The second is to provide some depth to the students' understanding of sensory receptor mechanisms.
- Two of the more difficult questions beginning students pose are: "How do I distinguish, say, sight from sound?" and "How do I perceive varying intensities of a stimulus?" Emphasize the role of the brain as an interpreter of impulses directed to specific regions by specialized receptors. Also point out that the frequency of action potentials and the number of axons that "fire" provide the quality we call "intensity" of stimulus.
- Each of the senses provides unique input. Try to draw distinctions between those that operate rather independently (for example, sight) and cooperatively (for example, taste and smell).
- As you describe each sense, you should describe the structure of the sense organ, the mechanism of stimulus reception, and the interpretation of that stimulus. For example, the eye perceives light by reaction with chemicals on the retina to give the sensation of degrees of light and color.
- Be sure to point out to the students that incoming light must pass through several neuronal layers before it reaches the rods and cones. This seems backward, but it works! Refer them to Figure 33.18 and its animation.
- When covering the nervous system and the structure of our brains, we have an opportunity to brag about the superiority of humans. This discussion of the senses can be rather humbling for the human race! Discuss how some animals surpass our detection of sensory stimuli. Also, be sure to mention how the sense organs of animals are adapted to suit their particular lifestyle and environment.

Classroom and Laboratory Enrichment

- The simple detection of taste by a blindfolded person is still a favorite activity. Ask volunteers to hold their nose and close their eyes while drops of various liquids (vinegar, onion juice, lemon juice, and so on) are placed on the tongue. Ask them to identify the substances, but not respond, until you have repeated the experiment with the students using *both* smell and taste receptors.
- If your lecture room or laboratory can be sufficiently darkened, you can demonstrate the abilities of rods and cones by a simple demonstration. Pull the shades and turn out the lights, quickly pull

a red cloth from your pocket, and ask students to identify the color. Substitute other colors, change the light intensity, and wait for iris accommodation as variations in the protocol.

- One of the usual practices in optometrists' offices is to take instant photos of the retina. Ask for permission to make 2 x 2 transparencies or slides of several photos, perhaps some exhibiting defects, and show them to the class. If the doctor will speak to the class, even better!
- A model of a cross-section through the organ of Corti is an excellent aid to comprehending this rather complex structure.
- Use dissectible models of the ear and eye to illustrate their structure.
- Use a Snellen chart to demonstrate the visual acuity test.
- If available, have the students use the Ishihara color charts for color blindness. They enjoy this.
- Demonstrate the use of the ophthalmoscope for viewing the retina.
- Demonstrate the use of the otoscope for viewing the tympanic membrane.
- Make up several animals that live in extreme environments. Have students brainstorm what sensory adaptations these animals may have to survive in their environment.
- Have the students perform the Weber and Rinne hearing tests. Challenge the students to decide whether sound waves travel better when conducted through bone or air?
- Position a student in the front of the room. Ask them to stand still for two minutes. This should be an easily accomplished task. Now ask them to again stand still for two minutes but, this time, make them close their eyes. You will probably note that the participant will sway a little side to side. This proves that we use visual input to maintain equilibrium. Individuals such as ice skaters may also focus on certain spots as they spin around to keep their balance.
- If your budget allows, do a demonstration of a cow-eye dissection. Have the students handle the lens, so they can envision its shape being altered by the ciliary muscles.
- Pass samples of PTC paper around the classroom. Some will detect a bitter flavor, while others will taste nothing. It is a great example of how our senses can differ.
- Poll the class—do any of the students have myopia, an astigmatism, presbyopia, or hyperopia? Define these terms before your poll.
- Ask the students if they can design a better external ear. Anyone who creates a larger funnel with cardboard will conquer the challenge.

Classroom Discussion Ideas

- If neurons operate under the all-or-nothing principle, how are we able to distinguish soft sounds from loud sounds, or a gentle touch from a crushing blow?
- What action should government take to ensure the preservation of a particular sense, say hearing? What responsibility rests on the individual?
- Is the defense of the nation more important than at-risk whales? Can a compromise be reached?
- Some animals appear to have a varied combination of rods and cones that suits their lifestyle. It is postulated that birds have a high percentage of cones, since they have excellent resolution of detail (e.g., a hawk swooping down to get a mouse) and the males have brightly colored feathers to attract the females. On the other hand, to our eyes a zebra may not look like it has suitable coloration, since it is easily seen in the wild. When you consider that the main predators of the zebra see only muted colors, he blends better into his environment.
- What is tinnitus? Do physicians know what causes ringing in the ear? What are some potential treatments?
- We know that pheromones play a large role in the selection of mates in many species. Do they play a role in the selection of partners in humans? Are there any studies on this topic?

- Why does a cold influence our sense of taste? Actually, a head cold only interferes with our sense of smell. Do you see how we incorporate our senses of smell and taste together?
- Some science stores sell a lens where you can see the world as an insect does. Pass it around the class, so they can visualize the world as an insect does by utilizing a compound eye.

Additional Ideas for Classroom Discussion

- Do invertebrates, such as the cockroach, feel pain?
- It's trivia quiz time; name the sense that:
  a. Is most easily fatigued (thank goodness!).
  b. Can be dulled by smoking.
  c. Cannot be shut out easily.
  d. Has more receptors in more places than any other.
  e. Uses small bones.
  f. Operates like a camera.
- Sometimes musicians are said to have a "trained ear." What does this expression really mean?
- What is the advantage to an insect of having a compound eye?
- Why do many persons in their mid-forties need to use bifocal lenses?
- How is the exposure to intense, unwanted sound different from, say, exposure to unwanted light or smells?
- Is there any scientific basis to that "carrots are good for your eyes" slogan? Do carrots contain any of the substances that are necessary for the production of rhodopsin?
- What is "motion sickness"? How can it be controlled?
- In our "civilized" world, many people experience hearing loss as a result of aging, a condition called presbycusis. A study revealed that this condition did not exist in a primitive Sudanese tribe, the Mebans. This study suggests that some environmental factor of the civilized world is responsible for this type of deafness. What is that factor?
- Discuss how pheromones can be used for insect control as an alternative to the use of pesticides.
- Play a recording of the calls of a humpback whale to get the students into the mood to hear about the effects of noise pollution on aquatic animals.
- Discuss olfactory adaptation. This shows why you may not notice the odor from the sewage treatment next door. You have become adapted to the awful smell, but a visitor will definitely notice it!

How Would You Vote? Classroom Discussion Ideas

- Monitor the voting for the online question. It would be highly desirable to limit the underwater noise that large ships make, but is it reasonable? Could we expect all government officials to deny citizens the oil and other goods these ships carry in exchange for whale safety? First of all, to do this in the United States would take a lot of persuasive legislation to convince the citizenry to forego some shipped goods. To be able to extend this to other nations is highly doubtful.
- Have students complete classroom polling using the JoinIn clickers.

Term Paper Topics, Library Activities, and Special Projects

- Investigate the use of biofeedback for controlling pain, heart rate, and other autonomic functions.
- Scientists are gathering increasing amounts of evidence from laboratory studies and human testing that shows gradual hearing loss caused by exposure to highly amplified music. Report on the dangers—are they real or imagined?
- One of the most intriguing subjects is the phenomenon of "phantom" pain. Explore its manifestations.
- Based on your library research, prepare an "awards" list for the animal group that exhibits the keenest of each of the five major senses (sight, hearing, smell, taste, and touch).
- How do local anesthetics block the sensation of pain?
- Describe the various problems associated with vision that are correctable with lenses, surgery, drugs, or other means.
- How can animals such as fly larvae (maggots) respond to and move away from light when they have no eyes of any kind?
- How does a detector device that checks blood vessel patterns in the eye and compares them to known records provide a better security system for military installations than do fingerprints?
- Radial keratotomy, a surgical procedure for correcting myopia, is controversial. What does this procedure involve, and what are the pros and cons of its use?
- Investigate the differences between sensorineural deafness and conductive deafness.
- Have students explore some of the websites referenced in CengageNow to better appreciate and understand the complexity of the senses.
- Research the LASIK eye surgery procedure. How does it improve vision? What individuals are not candidates for this procedure and why?
- Scientists consider the octopus the most intelligent invertebrate. Do you think this may be due to the fact that they have a camera eye, like we do?
- What is a detached retina? How could it occur? What are the treatment options?
- Research the phenomenon called lazy eye. How is this treated by putting a patch over the good eye? What can happen if it is not treated in childhood?
- How does a cochlear implant treat some cases of deafness?

Possible Responses to *Critical Thinking* Questions

1. Nocturnal animals have a structure called the *tapetum lucidum,* which is located in or behind the retina. This structure, which produces the "eye shine" effect, serves the purpose of reflecting light back to the retina. This enables the animal to see better in low-light situations. The drawback of this structure is that the reflected light may result in a somewhat blurry image.
2. Our organs of taste, taste buds, are located on papillae on the tongue. Each taste receptor is capable of detecting one of the taste categories (sour, sweet, salty, bitter, and umami). Therefore, receptors for both sweet and bitter could be simultaneously stimulated. When combinations of the different taste receptors are stimulated, it enables us to identify a great many specific tastes.
3. While it is unlikely that humans have a true magnetic sense, if we consider all the people who have gotten lost in the woods and have not been able to determine which direction to proceed, there remain those people who seem to have an uncanny sense of direction even in new environments. In 1995, magnetic particles (magnetite) were discovered in human brains, which suggested that humans may be sensitive to magnetic fields. To test this theory, an experiment

was performed (before the discovery of the magnetite) on third-year zoology students at the University of Manchester in 1976. The students were driven away from the university by way of an unfamiliar and winding route while blindfolded, and then asked to point in the direction of the university while still blindfolded and then without their blindfolds. To the surprise of all, students did consistently better while blindfolded following their instincts than following their logic and memory, unblindfolded. These results prompted further experiments in which the experiment was repeated but with the students all wearing little bars of metal on their heads—half were magnets, the others were controls of brass (non-magnetic). The students wearing the magnets lost their sense of direction. But the students wearing the non-magnetic brass could still point to the university. Somehow the magnets interfered with their sense of direction. Source: Baker, R. Robin. 1989. *Human Navigation and Magnetoreception*. Manchester: Manchester University Press, ISBN: 0719018102.

4. No, this experiment is not sufficient to attribute pain to insects. In addition to observing behavioral changes, you would want to measure physiological and biochemical responses of the insect. Remember pain is a reaction to tissue damage. Since insects have brains and a nervous system, they can potentially feel pain.

Possible Responses to *Data Analysis Exercise* Questions

In this exercise, studies were performed to look at the long-term effects of exposure to loud noises.

1. The sound frequency of approximately 600 hertz was most easily detected by all three individuals.
2. The 1,000 hertz sound had to be 10 decibels to be heard by the 50-year-old carpenter.
3. The 25-year-old carpenter had the best hearing at the 4,000–6,000 hertz range, and the 50-year-old carpenter had the worst hearing in that same range.
4. From this study, it appears as though both age and noise exposure contributed to the hearing decline in the 50-year-old carpenter. However, a study with many more participants would have to be performed to provide a thorough study.

34

ENDOCRINE CONTROL

Chapter Outline

Objectives

1. Know the general mechanisms by which molecules integrate and control the various metabolic activities in both vertebrate and invertebrate animals.
2. Understand how water-soluble and lipid-soluble hormones produce an effect on target cells.
3. Understand how the neuroendocrine center controls secretion rates of other endocrine glands and responses in nerves and muscles.

4. Know the major endocrine glands and their secretions.
5. Be familiar with other endocrine glands and their role in the body.
6. Know how sugar levels are regulated by hormones and the associated diseases.
7. Differentiate the modes of action of steroid and nonsteroid hormones.
8. Be familiar with the hormonal disruptions of some herbicides and pesticides.

Key Terms

endocrine disrupters
local signaling molecules
animal hormones
neurotransmitters
pheromones
endocrine system
steroid hormones
amine hormones
peptide hormones
protein hormones
second messenger
hypothalamus
pituitary gland
antidiuretic hormone, ADH
oxytocin
releasers
inhibiting hormones
releasing hormones
adrenocorticotropin, ACTH
thyrotropin, TSH
follicle-stimulating hormone, FSH
luteinizing hormone, LH
prolactin, PRL
somatotropin, STH
growth hormone, GH
thyroid gland
thyroid hormone
negative feedback loops
goiter
hypothyroidism
hyperthyroidism
parathyroid glands
parathyroid hormone, PTH
pancreas
exocrine cells
endocrine cells
pancreatic islets
glucagon
insulin
diabetes mellitus
type 1 diabetes
type 2 diabetes
hypoglycemia
adrenal glands
adrenal cortex
adrenal medulla
aldosterone
cortisol
corticotropin releasing hormone, CRH
Cushing's syndrome or hypercortisolism
gonads
testosterone
estrogens
progesterone
puberty
secondary sexual traits
sex hormone
pineal gland
circadian rhythm
melatonin
molting
ecdysone
thymus
thymosins

Lecture Outline

34.1 Hormones in the Balance

A. Pesticides and herbicides may be endocrine disrupters.

1. In lab experiments, the herbicide atrazine caused tadpoles to develop both male and female reproductive organs.
2. Zebra fish exhibit additional female characteristics when exposed to atrazine.

B. It is very controversial, but some investigators believe that chemicals in the environment are contributing to earlier onset of puberty and low sperm counts in humans.

34.2 The Vertebrate Endocrine System

A. Mechanisms of Intercellular Signaling

1. Signaling molecules are hormones and secretions that can bind to target cells and elicit a response.
2. There are four main types of signaling molecules.
   a. *Animal hormones* are secreted from endocrine sources and some neurons, and are then transported by the blood to remote targets.
   b. *Neurotransmitters* are secreted from neurons and act on immediately adjacent target cells for a short time.
   c. *Local signaling molecules* are secreted from cells of many different tissues; they alter chemical conditions in local tissues and are swiftly degraded.

B. Discovery of Hormones
   1. In the early 1900s, Bayliss and Starling first demonstrated that a hormone (later named secretin) released into the blood triggers secretion of pancreatic juices.
      a. They discovered that an extract that was secreted from pancreatic cells exposed to acids could stimulate the pancreatic cells of another animal to secrete bicarbonate.
      b. This hormone was called secretin.
      c. Starling named these chemicals that direct activities of the body "hormones."
   2. The sources of hormones may be collectively called the "endocrine system," which is intricately connected with the nervous system.

C. Neuroendocrine Interactions
   1. The nervous system and endocrine system are closely linked.
   2. Most organs receive and respond to both nervous signals and hormones.
   3. Hormones influence brain development and other nervous processes, and the nervous system affects hormone secretion.

34.3 The Nature of Hormone Action

A. From Signal Reception to Response
   1. In the three steps of cell-to-cell communication: 1) hormones and other signaling molecules interact with protein receptors of target cells; 2) the signal becomes transduced to a molecular form, which acts within the receiving cell; and 3) the cell may make a functional response.
   2. Different classes of hormones trigger these steps.
   3. Intracellular Receptors
      a. *Steroid* hormones are assembled from cholesterol and stimulate or inhibit protein (especially enzyme) synthesis by switching certain genes on or off.
      b. They easily diffuse through the lipid bilayer of the plasma membrane, bind to chromosomal proteins in the nucleus, and then activate transcription.
      c. They form a hormone-receptor complex by binding to a receptor in the cytoplasm or nucleus.
      d. Most often, it binds to a promoter near a hormonally regulated gene.
      e. Transcription and translation result in a protein product that carries out the target cell's response to the signal.
   4. Receptors at the Plasma Membrane
      a. Peptide and protein hormones and other water-soluble signaling molecules cannot cross the plasma membrane of target cells, so they must first bind to a receptor on the plasma membrane.
      b. The hormone-receptor complex activates transport proteins or triggers the opening of gated channel proteins that span the membrane.
      c. The hormone-receptor complex may stimulate the production of cyclic AMP, a *second messenger*, which amplifies the signal by activating numerous enzymes.

B. Receptor Function and Diversity
   1. Not all cells are responsive to hormone molecules and switch on or off an activity due to the hormone.
   2. Cells will not respond at all to a hormone unless they have functional receptors for it.
   3. Variations in receptor structure also affect responses.

34.4 The Hypothalamus and Pituitary Gland

A. The hypothalamus and pituitary gland work jointly as the neural-endocrine control center.
   1. The hypothalamus is a portion of the brain that monitors internal conditions and emotional states.

2. The pituitary is a pea-sized gland connected to the hypothalamus by a stalk.
   a. The posterior lobe of the pituitary consists of nervous tissue and releases two neurohormones made in the hypothalamus.
   b. The anterior lobe consists of glandular tissue, and secretes six hormones and controls the release of others.
   c. An intermediate lobe (not in humans) produces secretions that induce color changes in fur color of vertebrates.

B. Posterior Pituitary Function
1. The axons of neuron cell bodies in the hypothalamus extend down into the posterior lobe of the pituitary.
2. Two hormones are released into the capillary bed.
   a. Antidiuretic hormone (ADH) acts on the walls of kidney tubules to control the body's water and solute levels.
   b. Oxytocin triggers uterine muscle contractions to expel the fetus and acts on mammary glands to release milk.

C. Anterior Pituitary Function
1. The hypothalamus produces releasing and inhibiting hormones that target the anterior pituitary.
2. The anterior lobe releases six hormones that stimulate other endocrine glands.
   a. *Adrenocorticotropin* (ACTH) stimulates the adrenal cortex.
   b. *Thyroid stimulating hormone* (TSH) stimulates the thyroid gland.
   c. *Follicle-stimulating hormone* (FSH) stimulates egg formation in females and sperm formation in males.
   d. *Luteinizing hormone* (LH) also acts on the ovaries to release an egg and on the testes to release sperm.
   e. *Prolactin* acts on the mammary glands to sustain milk production.
   f. Growth hormone (GH) acts on body cells in general to promote growth.

D. Feedback Controls of Hormone Secretion
1. In positive feedback mechanisms a stimulus causes a response that increases the intensity of the stimulus (e.g., the release of oxytocin during childbirth).
2. Negative feedback mechanisms are more common. In these cases a stimulus elicits a response that decreases the stimulus (e.g., thyroid hormone secretion).

34.5 Growth Hormone Functions and Disorders
1. The body does not produce large quantities of each hormone.
2. But experience has shown that the amount, no matter how tiny, is critical to normal body functioning.
   a. In childhood, too little GH can cause pituitary dwarfism, while too much causes gigantism.
   b. Over-secretion of GH in adulthood causes a thickening of skin and bones called acromegaly.

34.6 Sources and Effects of Other Vertebrate Hormones
1. In addition to major endocrine glands, vertebrates have hormone-secreting cells in some organs.
2. Cells in most tissues have receptors for more than one hormone, and the response of one hormone may oppose or reinforce that of another.

34.7 Thyroid and Parathyroid Glands
A. Feedback Control of Thyroid Function

1. The human thyroid gland lies at the base of the neck in front of the trachea.
2. It secretes thyroid hormone (two amines, *thyroxine* and *triiodothyronine*), which influences metabolic rates, growth, and development.
3. Secretions of thyroid hormone are controlled by negative feedback loops to the anterior pituitary and hypothalamus.
   a. Secretion of thyroid hormone is inhibited when excess amounts of hormone are in the blood.
   b. Synthesis of thyroid hormone requires iodine, which we obtain from food.

B. Thyroid Disorders
1. If the blood levels of iodine are too low, the pituitary responds with too much TSH (thyroid stimulating hormone), causing the thyroid gland to enlarge abnormally in what we call a goiter.
2. Hypothyroidism in adults results in lethargy and weight gain, and results from a low blood level of thyroid hormone; it stunts growth in children and delays sexual maturation, while iodine deficiencies in pregnant mothers causes preventable mental impairment.
3. Hyperthyroidism increases heart rate and blood pressure, causing weight loss and bulging eyes, and results in Graves' disorder and goiters.

C. Thyroid Disruptors
1. When the pollutant perchlorate is in drinking water, the water is unfit for human consumption.
   a. It decreases the production of thyroid hormone.
2. Perchlorate in amphibians inhibits metamorphosis.

D. The Parathyroid Glands
1. Four parathyroid glands are embedded in the thyroid gland and respond to the changing levels of calcium in the blood by releasing parathyroid hormone (PTH).
   a. Certain bones and kidney cells are the hormone's targets.
   b. A drop in calcium level causes PTH levels to rise, resulting in removal of calcium from bone and an activation of vitamin D (to help in calcium absorption from the gut).
   c. When calcium levels rise, the PTH levels are reduced.
2. Young children who do not get enough vitamin D are at risk for bone problems; when the calcium level is low, PTH secretion leads to breakdown of existing bone, causing rickets.

34.8 Pancreatic Hormones

A. Regulation of Blood Sugar
1. The pancreas is a dual-function gland; its exocrine function is to secrete digestive enzymes.
2. Certain cells within the pancreas have an endocrine function.
   a. Alpha cells secrete *glucagon,* which causes glycogen stored in the liver to be converted to glucose, raising its levels in the blood.
   b. Beta cells secrete *insulin,* which stimulates the uptake of glucose by liver, muscle, and adipose to reduce glucose levels in the blood, especially after a meal.

B. Diabetes
1. Diabetes mellitus is a metabolic disorder in which cells do not take up glucose as they should.
   a. As a result, sugar accumulates in blood and in urine.
   b. Complications develop throughout the body.
   c. Uncontrolled diabetes damages blood vessels and nerves, especially in the arms, hands, legs, and feet.
2. Type 1 Diabetes
   a. In type 1 diabetes, insulin is no longer produced because the beta cells have been destroyed by an autoimmune response; treatment is by insulin injection.

b. Type 1 diabetes accounts for only 5 to 10 percent of all reported cases, but it is the most dangerous.

3. Type 2 Diabetes
   a. In type 2 diabetes, the insulin levels are near normal but the target cells cannot respond to the hormone; controlling diet is an effective treatment.
   b. Worldwide, this type of diabetes is soaring; there is an association with western eating habits and sedentary lifestyles.

34.9 The Adrenal Glands

A. The Adrenal Cortex

1. One adrenal gland is located on top of each kidney.
2. Among the secretions of the outer portion are the glucocorticoids such as cortisol, which helps control blood glucose levels.
   a. Cortisol secretion is an example of a homeostatic feedback loop.
   b. When blood levels of glucose fall (as in hypoglycemia), the hypothalamus releases CRH → anterior pituitary → ACTH → adrenal cortex → cortisol, which prevents muscle cells from withdrawing glucose from the blood.
   c. When the body is stressed, as in painful injury, the nervous system provides an override mechanism in which the levels of cortisol remain high to promote healing.

B. The Adrenal Medulla

1. This inner portion of the adrenal glands secretes *epinephrine* and *norepinephrine* under direction from sympathetic nerves from the hypothalamus via a negative feedback mechanism.
2. Its secretions mobilize the body during times of excitement or stress ("fight-or-flight" response).

C. Stress, Elevated Cortisol, and Health

1. Researchers have been studying how chronic social stress affects a troop of olive baboons for over 20 years.
2. Physiological responses to chronic stress interfere with growth, the immune system, sexual function, cardiovascular function, memory, and learning.
3. In humans, the impact of long-term elevated cortisol levels can result in a rare metabolic disorder called Cushing's syndrome or hypercortisolism.
   a. Symptoms include a puffy, rounded face, fat deposition around the trunk of the body, high levels of blood sugar and high blood pressure, high infection rates, weakened muscles, impotence or loss of menstruation, and thinning skin.
   b. In addition to the physical symptoms, research has shown that the hippocampus shrinks in patients with the highest cortisol levels, resulting in memory impairment.
   c. Studies of stressed individuals indicate that repetitive stress may destroy the body's ability to mediate the stress response.
   d. The link between human socioeconomic status and stress-related heath issues is being probed by researchers.

D. Cortisol Deficiency

1. Damage to adrenal glands can cause slow or no secretion of cortisol, resulting in hypocortisolism (Addison's disease).
2. Symptoms include fatigue, weakness, depression, weight loss, and darkening of the skin and can be treated with synthetic cortisone.

34.10 The Gonads

A. Homeostatic feedback loops govern reproductive function by the sex hormones estrogens, progesterone, and testosterone.

1. Puberty occurs when the reproductive organs and structures mature.
   a. Female ovaries increase estrogen production, causing secondary sexual traits to develop.
   b. Male testes respond to the increase in testosterone by producing sperm and developing secondary sexual traits.
2. Females make a small amount of testosterone, which influences the desire for sex.

34.11 The Pineal Gland

A. Located in the brain, this gland is sensitive to light and seasonal influences; its secretion, melatonin, is part of the biological clock.

B. Circadian Rhythms
1. Melatonin is secreted based on the length of day according to one's biological clock.
   a. More melatonin is secreted at night, so it helps regulate our sleeping/waking cycles.
   b. Jet lag and irregular work schedules may interrupt normal melatonin secretion.
2. There are theories about melatonin secretion inhibiting cancer.

C. Seasonal Effects
1. In the absence of light melatonin is secreted; thus, in winter, high levels of the hormone are instrumental in suppressing reproductive activity in hibernating animals.
2. In winter, seasonal affective disorder ("winter blues") causes some people to be depressed, crave sleep, and binge on carbohydrates; exposure to light causes the pineal gland to shut down and brings about mood improvement.

34.12 The Thymus

1. The thymus gland lies beneath the breastbone and secretes thymosins and thymulin.
   a. These hormones help infection-fighting white blood cells, called T cells, to mature.
2. The thymus grows until a person reaches puberty, following which it shrinks in size.

34.13 Invertebrate Hormones

A. Evolution of Hormone Diversity
1. Molecular evidence points to gene duplication and subsequent divergences as a source for the diverse hormones and hormone receptors in vertebrates.
2. Studies of sea anemones have shown similar receptor and other signaling molecules in the plasma membrane, helping to trace evolutionary history of some vertebrate hormones and receptors to signaling molecules in invertebrates.

B. Hormones and Molting
1. Molting, the period of shedding body coverings, in arthropods is controlled by hormones unique to invertebrates.
2. Ecdysone promotes molting in insects; juvenile hormone retards the same process.
3. Chemicals that mimic or interfere with ecdysone and other hormones can be used as insecticides.

34.14 Hormones in the Balance (Revisited)

A. When human cells encounter atrazine they increase production of aromatase.
1. Aromatase encourages testosterone to convert to estrogen.

B. Phthalate, produced primarily in the production of plastics, impacts the production of sex hormones.
1. Phthalate produces early breast development in females and lowered sperm development in males.
2. It is recommended that phthalate exposure be minimized to pregnant women and young children.

Suggestions for Presenting the Material

- The "core" of this chapter is the section describing the various endocrine glands, their secretions and functions; Figure 34.2 and its animation are excellent aids.
- Other important topics include signaling molecules and feedback loops.
- When discussing signaling molecules (Animation/Figure 34.3), emphasize the chemical nature of steroids (lipid-bilayer soluble) versus proteins (not lipid soluble) and the need for a second messenger, cyclic AMP. Playing this animation will go a long way to providing visual context for the array of new terms.
- Because the chapter contains excellent figures (for example, 34.2 and 34.5) and tables (34.1, 34.3, and 34.4), these can be used to great advantage. You can request for students to bring their texts to class and invite them to follow along. You can also prepare your own overhead transparencies or slides of the figures and tables to help everyone keep up the pace.
- This chapter presents a maddening array of new words—hormone names that are long and unfamiliar. As an aid to learning, subdivide the name and give the literal meaning of each portion, for example, adreno (adrenals), cortico (cortex), and tropic (stimulate).

  Emphasize the necessity of learning both the hormone name and its abbreviation, which is often more commonly used than the name itself.
- Take this opportunity to point out antagonistic hormone pairs: calcitonin/parathyroid hormone, insulin/glucagon.
- Notice that even though the gonadal hormones are included in Table 34.3, they are not discussed thoroughly until later chapters.
- Emphasize that the posterior pituitary gland does not synthesize the hormones it secretes.
- Point out that some organs function as both endocrine and exocrine glands.
- Discuss the impact of diabetes on humans and the role our diet and lifestyle play in the perpetuation of this disease.
- The students may be amazed that males and females produce some of the same reproductive hormones. Note that the hormone names were based on their functions in females.

Classroom and Laboratory Enrichment

- Human nature is such that students are very interested in the abnormalities that hyper- and hyposecretion of human hormones cause. You can stimulate interest in the overall area of hormone control by showing slides or transparencies of the physical manifestations of such imbalances.
- Ask a local health scientist or practitioner to report on his/her experiences with hormone therapy.
- If a member of the class is willing to share his/her experiences as a diabetic, arrange for such a presentation before class begins and allow time for questions.
- Seek evidence of a class member who has experienced or witnessed an epinephrine-mediated "emergency response." Ask him/her to report. Is anyone in the class required to carry an "EpiPen"?
- Survey local grocery stores to determine the relative stocks of iodized and non-iodized salt. Are there implications for the unwary consumer?
- Use a dissectible mannequin or a dissected fetal pig to show the locations of the various endocrine glands.

Classroom Discussion Ideas

- Once you have shown the video, open a line of discussion that causes students to think critically about the tradeoff between the use of chemicals to increase food production and the negative impacts on animals and humans.

- Discuss the possibility that the current high incidences of cancer and other diseases or malformations are the result of chemicals that are pervasive in our lives.
- If atrazine is found to be harmful to amphibians after further ongoing research, how might farmers who have depended on atrazine react if it is proposed that it be removed from the market?
- As humans of today are dying of cancer and heart disease, what were the major diseases of 100 years ago?
- Compare the average age of longevity in the United States today with that of one hundred years ago.
- Discuss the impact hormones in our environment and food are having on changing the onset of puberty and sex traits in animals.
- Look into the use and eventual ban of other chemicals that have deleterious effects on animals, such as DDT and PCBs. How long did it take for scientists to convince lawmakers to restrict their use?
- Why is the pituitary often called the master gland? Do you think that this title is well-deserved since the hypothalamus directs many pituitary activities?
- Be sure to stress to the students that both the nervous system and the endocrine system control activities of the body. The difference is in the way that the control is administered—the nervous system does so via nerve impulses and the endocrine system utilizes hormones.
- Once a student learns the function of a hormone, it may be easy for them to visualize situations where hypo- or hyper-secretion takes place. The secretion of human growth hormone is an ideal example. Hyposecretion results in pituitary dwarfism, and hypersecretion is called gigantism. What is the treatment for pituitary dwarfism?
- Mention to the students that if a patient takes too many medicinal steroids, he may exhibit symptoms similar to Cushing's syndrome. This makes sense since the adrenal hormones involved in Cushing's syndrome are categorized as steroids.

Additional Ideas for Classroom Discussion

- Beverage alcohol inhibits the action of ADH. How is this unseen physiological event evidenced during a night of bar-hopping? Can you think of other substances that inhibit the action of ADH?
- Do hormones occur only in vertebrates? What is the function of arthropod hormones?
- The exoskeleton of an insect seems like a terrific adaptation since it roughly serves as a suit of armor for the organism. The disadvantage of an exoskeleton occurs during molting, when the insect is extremely vulnerable. Discuss the overall advantages and disadvantages of this body style with the class.
- Have a student bring in an early ultrasound of a fetus. Note that it may be too early to tell if it is a boy or a girl, because the ovaries and testes are in similar positions in an early fetus. They both descend into their proper positions later in the pregnancy, and then one is able to determine the baby's sex.
- Discuss the research regarding pancreatic cell transplants.
- Why does insulin have to be administered by injection rather than orally?
- Using knowledge gained in a freshman biology class, an athlete decided he might be able to raise his blood sugar quickly by injecting glucagon. This attempt is doomed for what reasons?
- What is the possible connection between the pineal gland and puberty?
- What is the connection between the pineal gland and sunlight?
- Some hormones seem to be doing another's duties, for example: sex hormones from the adrenals, blood sugar control by epinephrine, and thyroxine regulation of growth. Why is this so?

- What are anabolic steroids? Why do some athletes use them? What are the dangers associated with their use?
- Oxytocin is commonly used to induce labor. How does it work?
- Why do certain hypoglycemics, who regularly ingest excessive amounts of sugar, frequently develop diabetes later in life?
- Untreated diabetes mellitus victims tend to be very thirsty and yet produce large volumes of urine. Why is this so?
- Women may experience some mild uterine contractions while nursing their babies. Why is this beneficial to a woman's post-pregnancy health?

How Would You Vote? Classroom Discussion Ideas

- Use CengageNOW for additional details.
- Monitor the voting for the online question. The question of whether to continue to use agricultural pesticides that are questionable in their effects is a huge one both economically and environmentally. The regulation of chemicals used in food production that may disrupt hormone function in untargeted species can have devastating impacts on populations locally and regionally. While it is difficult to wait for scientific studies to fully investigate all aspects of potential chemical interactions, it may prove ecologically judicious to seek answers before such chemicals are released into our ecosystems. While awaiting the results of research on the effects of certain pesticides, would farmers be able to control pests and weeds at a cost that would still allow a profit to be made on their crops? Would increased prices for this control be passed on to the consumer? Would there be alternative pest and weed controls available for use that are not harmful to nontarget organisms? Should the use of insect pheromones be considered as a viable alternative to pesticides?
- Have students complete class polling using the JoinIn clickers.

Term Paper Topics, Library Activities, and Special Projects

- Discuss the ethical issues of administering somatotropin to persons of normal stature who wish to become "super athletes."
- Investigate and report on the fascinating discovery of the role of insulin by researchers Banting and Best.
- Select a major hormone and prepare an in-depth report on the abnormalities that may result from hypo- and hyper-secretion.
- The role of hormones in insect development has been elucidated in only the past 40 years. Check an insect physiology text, and prepare a chronology of this research.
- Report on current research designed to correct type 1 diabetes, which is the result of autoimmune responses.
- Investigate which human hormones are now being produced using genetic engineering methods.
- Research the differences between diabetes mellitus and diabetes insipidus. Note the derivations of the names: diabetes mellitus = honey overflow, and diabetes insipidus = tasteless overflow. Believe it or not, the names are based on the fact that laboratory technicians used to taste urine samples as one of their duties! The urine from a diabetic may contain excess sugar and taste sweet, whereas the urine from a patient with diabetes insipidus will be highly diluted, and therefore tasteless. How would a physician distinguish between the two diseases since they both show increased thirst and urine production?
- When was cAMP discovered? When did scientists realize its function as a second messenger?

- Look into the position of the pituitary gland in the *sella turcica* of the sphenoid bone. This provides a very protective environment for this important gland. How do surgeons access the pituitary to remove a tumor?
- There is a seventh hormone secreted from the anterior lobe of the pituitary, called melanocyte stimulating hormone. It has minimal functions in humans, but what does it do in some animals?
- How is an overactive thyroid treated? Is there a possibility that the treatment will now make the patient's thyroid underactive?
- Research studies have involved removing the pineal glands of birds. What does this do to their internal time clock?
- Since the thymus is involved with the maturation of T cells, do you think that if the thymus could remain vital throughout life it would help HIV patients?
- As children, many of us were told that "sleeping makes you grow." Is there any scientific basis for this statement?
- Find out why wastewater treatments are unable to remove estrogens from the water. Research other hormones that might remain in the water after passing through treatment plants that could be of concern to us.
- Using INFOTRAC, have students research new findings in diabetes treatment or control. Assign students a one-page summary of an article of interest.
- Have individual students or small groups work on a position paper related to the "How would you vote" topic on the release of chemicals that disrupt hormone actions in animals but increase human food supplies.

Possible Responses to *Critical Thinking* Questions

1. If a woman had a tumor in the anterior lobe of her pituitary gland, she might produce milk even if she were not pregnant. It would affect prolactin, which is the hormone that stimulates lactation.
2. The ovary is intimately involved in the feedback loop. Without the ovary, the loop is disrupted and the anterior pituitary will produce high levels of LH and FSH.
3. If a diabetic injects too much insulin, it may lower the blood glucose to a dangerously low level. The brain requires glucose as fuel to perform basic functions. If glucagon is administered, it will raise the blood sugar again—hopefully to a normal level. This example illustrates how important it is that the proper amount of insulin be administered to diabetics.

Possible Responses to *Data Analysis Exercise* Questions

In previous studies, agricultural chemicals were known to decrease the sperm count in some animals. This data was collected to see if it has a similar effect on humans.

1. The highest sperm count was in NYC and the lowest was in Columbia, Missouri.
2. The highest sperm motility was in NYC and the lowest was in Missouri.
3. Aging and the presence of STDs do not seem to be a factor to explain the low sperm count in Missouri. However, those groups with the low sperm count did have a slightly higher percentage of smokers, so that factor cannot be totally discounted.
4. These studies strongly suggest that living in a farmland area can result in lower sperm counts.

35

STRUCTURAL SUPPORT AND MOVEMENT

Chapter Outline

Objectives

1. Compare invertebrate and vertebrate motor systems in terms of skeletal and muscular components and their interactions.
2. Describe the details of bone construction.
3. Explain in detail the structure of muscles, from the molecular level to the organ-systems level.
4. Explain how biochemical events occur in muscle contractions and how antagonistic muscle action refines movements.
5. Describe the impact of exercise, disease, and aging on bone and muscles.
6. Study the effects of myostatin on muscle development, and its potential implications.

Key Terms

androstenedione, androcreatine
hydrostatic skeleton
exoskeleton
endoskeleton
vertebral column
vertebrae
intervertebral disks
axial skeleton
appendicular skeleton
foramen magnum
osteoblasts
osteocytes
osteoclasts
compact bone
spongy bone
red marrow
yellow marrow
bone remodeling
osteoporosis
joint
ligament
cartilage
sprain
arthritis
bursa
bursitis
skeletal muscle
muscle fiber
tendon
myofibrils
sarcomeres
Z band
actin
myosin
sliding-filament model
sarcoplasmic reticulum
cross-bridge formation
creatine phosphate
motor unit
myoglobin
muscle twitch
tetanus
muscle tension
muscle fatigue
muscular dystrophies
botulism
tetanus

Lecture Outline

35.1 Muscles and Myostatin

- A. An adult individual has all the muscle cells they will ever have.
  1. Muscle cells can increase in size as a result of proper nutrition and exercise.
  2. Some hormones such as human growth hormone and testosterone also increase muscle size.
- B. Myostatin is a protein that slows down the enlargement of muscles by restricting the development of certain proteins.
  1. If someone does not have the ability to respond to myostatin, they may develop larger muscles and increased strength.
     - a. Some whippets are born with the inability to produce myostatin and have abnormally large musculature for the breed.
- C. Scientists are attempting to develop medications that inhibit myostatin production to use as a treatment for diseases that involve the destruction of muscles.
  1. It is probable that some athletes would abuse these medications to achieve their fitness goals.

35.2 Invertebrate Skeletons

- A. Hydrostatic Skeletons
  1. Many soft-bodied animals have a hydrostatic skeleton and tubular body.
  2. One example is the earthworm, which applies contractile force against a fluid-filled coelomic chamber for movement.
- B. Exoskeletons
  1. In addition to hydraulic pressure, arthropods have a hinged exoskeleton with simple attachment sites for sets of muscles that move their parts like levers.
  2. Hydraulic pressure works in a spider when the cephalothorax muscle contracts, causing blood to fill the hind legs, which helps the spider jump high.
- C. Endoskeletons
  1. Echinoderms and vertebrates have endoskeletons.
  2. An endoskeleton is an internal framework in which muscles attach.

35.3 The Vertebrate Endoskeleton

- A. Features of the Vertebrate Skeleton

1. All vertebrates have an endoskeleton of either cartilage or bone.
2. Vertebrate skeletons are divided into two major portions.
    a. The *appendicular skeleton* consists of the pectoral girdle with attached upper limbs, and the pelvic girdle with lower limbs.
    b. The *axial skeleton* includes the skull, vertebral column (individual bones separated by cartilaginous intervertebral disks), ribs, and sternum.

B. The Human Skeleton
1. The human skeleton has many features.
    a. The skull bones are flattened and protect the brain and sensory organs.
    b. The ribs and breastbone form a protective cage around the heart and lungs.
    c. The vertebral column protects and houses the spinal cord, supports the skull and other extremities, and provides an attachment site for muscles.
    d. The pectoral and pelvic girdles allow movement and provide further protection of various organs.
2. In humans, natural selection favored an ability to walk upright and led to a modification of the backbone to have an S-shaped curve.

35.4 Bone Structure and Function

A. Bone Anatomy
1. Bones have several roles.
    a. Bones interact with muscles to maintain or change the position of body parts.
    b. Bones support the skin and soft organs.
    c. Bones form compartments that enclose and protect soft internal organs.
    d. Bone tissue acts as a depository for calcium, phosphorus, and other ions.
    e. Parts of some bones are sites of blood cell production.
2. Bone is a connective tissue with living cells (osteocytes) and collagen fibers distributed throughout a ground substance that is hardened by calcium salts.
    a. Osteoblasts are the cells that form bone based on cartilage models.
    b. In bone, remodeling minerals are deposited and withdrawn (by osteoclasts) during the growth and development processes.
3. Compact bone tissue forms the bone's shaft and the outer portion of its two ends.
    a. Concentric layers form around canals that contain blood vessels and nerves (Haversian systems).
    b. The living bone cells reside in the ground substance.
4. Spongy bone tissue has areas of red marrow that produce blood cells.
5. Yellow marrow contains fat as a reserve energy source, and it is located in the central cavity of many long bones.

B. Bone Formation and Remodeling
1. The embryo of a vertebrate is made of cartilage, but converts to bone before birth.
    a. Sharks and other members of chondrichthyes retain a cartilage skeleton.
2. The bones of a vertebrate are constantly being remodeled.
    a. Osteoblasts are the bone-forming cells that secrete organic substances that become mineralized.
    b. Osteoclast cells digest the organic matrix of bone during the process of bone remodeling.
3. Bone turnover helps to maintain calcium levels for the entire body; enzymes from bone cells dissolve bone tissue and release calcium to the interstitial fluid and blood.
    a. Calcitonin from the thyroid causes levels to decline by storing the excess calcium in bones.

b. Parathyroid hormone detects low levels of calcium and pulls sufficient quantities out of storage.

4. Osteoporosis (decreased bone density) is associated with decreases in osteoblast activity, sex hormone production, exercise, and calcium uptake.
   a. To reduce the risk of osteoporosis, ensure proper dietary intake of calcium and vitamin D; avoid smoking, excessive alcohol, and soft drink intake; and get regular exercise.

35.5 Skeletal Joints—Where Bones Meet

A. Types and Functions of Joints
   1. Joints are areas of contact or near-contact between bones.
      a. Fibrous joints are fixed in place, like the skull bones.
      b. Cartilaginous joints, such as between the ribs, permit slight movement.
      c. Synovial joints are freely-movable joints stabilized by ligaments—straps of dense connective tissue that attach bone to bone. These joints are found in places like your knee, ankle, and elbow.

B. Joint Health
   1. Common Joint Injuries
      a. Stretching or twisting a joint may result in a strain; tearing ligaments or tendons is a sprain.
      b. Common knee injuries include torn cruciate ligaments and torn meniscus cartilage, both of which may require surgery to heal properly.
      c. If a dislocation occurs, the bones must be placed in their proper position and immobilized.
   2. Arthritis and Bursitis
      a. Arthritis is the inflammation of a joint.
      b. In osteoarthritis, the cartilage at the end of the bone has worn away.
      c. In rheumatoid arthritis, the membranes in the joints become inflamed, the cartilage degenerates, and bone is deposited into the joint.
      d. Bursitis is the inflammation of a bursa or fluid-filled sac that cushions the joint.

35.6 Skeletal-Muscular Systems

A. Skeletal muscles are functional partners of bones.
   1. Each skeletal muscle contains several bundles of perhaps hundreds or thousands of muscle cells (fibers).
      a. Tendons, cordlike straps of dense connective tissue, attach muscle to bone.
      b. Skeletal muscles, often arranged in antagonistic pairs, interact with one another and with bones.
      c. Some skeletal muscles provide movement not associated with bone, such as facial muscles, movements of the tongue, and eyeball movement.
      d. Skeletal muscles also produce heat necessary to maintain a normal body temperature.
   2. Because most muscle attachments are located close to joints, only a small contraction is needed to produce considerable movement of some body parts.

B. There are three types of muscle in the human body.
   1. Only skeletal muscle is the functional partner of bone.
   2. Cardiac muscle is found only in the heart wall.
   3. Smooth muscle is found in soft internal organs such as the digestive tract.

35.7 How Does Skeletal Muscle Contract?

A. Structure of Skeletal Muscle

1. Muscle cells (fibers) are composed of myofibrils, which are composed of two kinds of parallel filaments.
2. The striated appearance of skeletal muscle corresponds to sarcomere units repeated along a myofibril.
   a. Actin is a thin filament composed of two beaded strands twisted together.
   b. Myosin is thicker; each molecule has a bulbous head and long tail, making it resemble a golf club.
3. The actin filaments are anchored at each end by the Z band (or disk), surrounded by the myosin filaments.
4. All of the sarcomeres and their component myofibrils contract in parallel.

B. Sliding-Filament Model

1. Muscles shorten because the sarcomeres shorten within each cell by the sliding-filament model.
2. The mechanism "pulls" the Z disks of each sarcomere toward each other.
   a. By forming cross-bridges, the myosin filaments slide along and pull the actin filaments toward the center of the sarcomere.
   b. The cross-bridges are formed when the local concentration of calcium exposes binding sites.
   c. ATP supplies the energy for both attachment and detachment.

35.8 Nervous Control of Muscle Contraction

A. Nervous Control of Contraction

1. Muscle cells exhibit an action potential when the voltage difference across the plasma membrane reverses abruptly and briefly in response to a stimulus.
2. The sarcoplasmic reticulum is a system of membranous chambers that wraps around the myofibrils—taking up, storing, and releasing calcium ions.
3. When the action potential arrives, calcium ions flow out of the chambers and diffuse into the myofibrils, where they reach actin filaments.
4. Calcium allows actin and myosin to interact by affecting the release of troponin and tropomyosin.
5. When a muscle is at rest, calcium levels are low and tropomyosin wraps around actin, covering myosin binding sites.
6. Troponin, a globular protein attached to tropomyosin, has a site that can reversibly bind calcium ions.
7. When the calcium level is low, proteins on the cross-bridge binding sites are joined tightly, forcing out tropomyosin and blocking the binding site.
8. When calcium flows into the sarcomere, it binds with the troponin, changing its shape and allowing the tropomyosin filament to return to the groove at the actin filament; the binding site is now exposed.

B. Motor Units and Muscle Tension

1. A motor unit consists of a motor neuron and all of its synapsing muscle fibers.
2. Muscle tension depends on the number of muscle fibers contracting.

C. Disrupted Control of Skeletal Muscle

1. Muscular Dystrophies
   a. Muscular dystrophies are a class of genetic disorders in which muscles progressively weaken and degenerate.

b. A mutation on the X chromosome disrupts the normal action of dystrophin, one of the proteins in the plasma membrane of muscle fibers. This mutant form allows foreign material to enter a muscle fiber, and the fiber deteriorates.

2. Motor Neuron Disorders
   a. When motor neurons cannot signal muscles to contract or signaling is impaired, skeletal muscles weaken or become paralyzed.
   b. Polio and amyotrophic lateral sclerosis (ALS) are motor neuron disorders.
3. Botulism and Tetanus
   a. *Clostridium botulinum* is an anaerobic soil bacterium that can cause botulism.
      1) The toxin enters motor neurons and stops the production of acetylcholine.
      2) Affected persons must be treated immediately to prevent cessation of heart beating and breathing.
   b. *C. tetani* endospores can live in the soil for years.
      1) After entering the body through deep wounds, the spores germinate and release atoxin that travels to the spinal cord and brain.
      2) In the spinal cord, the toxin blocks release of GABA from neurons, allowing muscles to continually contract with no controls, thus gradually weakening over several days.
      3) Prolonged contraction results in clenching the jaws (lockjaw) and curving the backbone.
      4) When the paralysis reaches the cardiac and respiratory muscles, death follows.
      5) Vaccines have virtually eradicated tetanus in the United States.

35.9 Muscle Metabolism

A. Energy-Releasing Pathways
   1. During brief periods of intense muscle activity, creatine phosphate is the source of phosphate to remake ATP.
   2. When muscle action is moderate, most of the ATP is provided by aerobic electron transport phosphorylation, which is dependent on oxygen supply and the number of mitochondria present.
   3. During intense and prolonged muscle action, anaerobic glycolysis produces low amounts of ATP, but this also results in an oxygen debt.
   4. The lactate produced during anaerobic respiration leaves skeletal muscle to be transported by the blood to be used as fuel by other cells.

B. Types of Muscle Fibers
   1. Red fibers contain large amounts of myoglobin, giving them a darker color.
      a. These fibers have better endurance and can be called slow fibers, since they are slow to react.
   2. Therefore, white fibers have no myoglobin, they are lighter in color.
      a. These fibers are quick to react, but fatigue easily.
   3. The mixture of skeletal muscle types varies in individuals and may make some athletes better suited for different sports.

C. Effects of Exercise
   1. When a muscle is kept in a state of tetanic contraction, there is a decline in the muscle's capacity to generate force—muscle fatigue.
      a. Muscles trained by a pattern of brief, intense exercise fatigue and recover quickly (weight lifting).
      b. Muscles used in prolonged, moderate exercise fatigue slowly.
   2. Muscle tension decreases as adult humans age, but exercise remains beneficial in improving blood circulation and preventing loss of muscle tissue.

3. With regular exercise, muscle cells do not increase in number; however, they do increase in size and metabolic activity and become resistant to fatigue.
    a. Aerobic exercise, not intense but long in duration, increases the number of mitochondria and blood capillaries.
    b. Strength training affects fast-acting muscle cells by forming more myofibrils and more enzymes of glycolysis.
4. An enzyme called lipoprotein lipase (LPL) helps muscles absorb fatty acids and triglycerides from blood.
    a. Heavy exercisers have high LPL levels, which puts them in a low cardiovascular risk category.
    b. Sitting is a hazardous activity because it lowers levels of LPL, so movement should occur on a regular basis for optimum heart health.

35.10 Muscles and Myostatin (Revisited)

A. Duchenne muscular dystrophy is due to a mutation on the X chromosome.
1. These patients manufacture an abnormal protein that ultimately destroys the muscle fibers.
2. Patients are almost always boys, since the females would probably possess another normal X to take over normal functioning.
3. Researchers are looking into medications that inhibit myostatin production.
    a. This would increase muscle development.
    b. One drawback of the inhibition of the myostatin production would be a tendency for fragile tendons.

Suggestions for Presenting the Material

- Although this chapter's title may imply that the content will be about muscles only, remind the students that muscles can move the body *only* in conjunction with the bones.
- Students, especially non-science majors, may question the value of learning the names of bones. However, with today's emphasis on the human body, the use of the anatomical names for body parts, including bones, is becoming more common.
- The formation, development, and replacement of bone are more meaningfully presented by referring briefly to the previous material on tissues.
- It is nearly impossible to present the ultrastructure of muscle without a visual similar to Figure 35.14, and on a microscopic level Figure 35.17. Using the analogy of a rope (see the Enrichment section below) is very helpful.
- Don't miss the opportunity when discussing the sliding-filament model to emphasize the molecular explanation for the fact that individual muscles can only pull, not push. Again, the rope analogy is helpful.
- The dual role of calcium as the provider of bone hardness and as muscle facilitator should be made clear.
- Emphasize that ATP is required for *both* muscle contraction and relaxation as well as for the active transport of calcium back into the sarcoplasmic reticulum.
- When discussing both the skeletal and muscular systems, it is helpful to access an articulated skeleton. Be sure to show the students how the bones are held together via wire on the skeleton. Many people have the misconception that bone-to-bone interaction is what holds our skeleton together. Emphasize that it is the musculature over the top of the bones that keeps the bones in place. Show the class the sternoclavicular joint, which is the only point of connection between and arm and the torso. Once we have observed this joint, it is inconceivable that we could pick up a

heavy load and not have our arm fall off! Another way to emphasize this point is to examine a weightlifter. If he wants to lift more weight, he does not alter his bones; instead he strengthens the associated muscles.

- Discuss the advantages and disadvantages of an exoskeleton (e.g., more protective, but leaves the animal in a vulnerable state during molting). An endoskeleton, like our own, grows along with us, so it doesn't need replacement. However, our skeleton leaves some areas rather unprotected, such as our abdominopelvic area. Note that the victims of violent attacks often have defensive wounds on their hands as they try to cover that vulnerable belly area.

Classroom and Laboratory Enrichment

- Ask a forensic pathologist to tell the class about the wealth of information that skeletal remains can reveal about one's health and medical history at the time of death.
- Demonstrate the action of muscle by using a "muscle contraction kit," available from biological supply houses.
- If you have one available, the use of a real human skeleton rather than a transparency will better stimulate student interest and present add a three-dimensional aspect to your lecture.
- Arrange for a body builder to appear before the class (more effective if unannounced). Describe the origin, insertion, and function of some major muscles as they are flexed.
- Students can visualize the ultrastructure of muscles more readily if the comparison to a large rope is made. The best is one used for boat anchorage because it is made of many subunits.
- If you can locate a ratchet mechanism (preferably not enclosed), your explanation of the actin/myosin cross-bridges (Figure 35.17) will be more comprehensible.
- Show a video of arthroscopic surgery. Many orthopedic surgeons routinely produce such videos and give them to their patients.
- Use models of freely-movable joints to illustrate their structure.
- Obtain a fresh cow knee joint to demonstrate the structure and tissues of that joint. Also show a model of the knee joint. When one observes the various tendons and ligaments of the joint, it is easy to see that it is an area of the body that is frequently injured.
- If available, use a model of a sarcomere to facilitate the students' comprehension of that microscopic structure.
- If possible, bring a living earthworm into the laboratory. If the students have an opportunity to see it move, they may have a better understanding of the mechanics of a hydroskeleton.
- Show a starfish or brittle star to the class. On first look, it may appear that the organism possesses an exoskeleton. Emphasize that it has an endoskeleton with strong plates of calcium-carbonate embedded in it.
- Show a video representation of the sliding-filament theory. If one is not readily available, one can be found on the website "How Stuff Works."

Classroom Discussion Ideas

- Discuss the negative aspects of "self-medication" with supplements designed to enhance muscle performance.
- What motivates young athletes to take enhancing drugs?
- What could be bad about taking a chemical such as creatine, which is produced by the body normally?
- Examine various advertisements for supplements to determine scientific validity.

- In the first section of this chapter, we are introduced to Liam, a toddler whose muscles do not respond to myostatin. We see that he can lift weights as though he were an adult. He is an unusual child; is it wise to have a normal child lift weights at a young age?

Additional Ideas for Classroom Discussion

- Distinguish between hydrostatic skeleton, endoskeleton, and exoskeleton.
- In reference to a hydrostatic skeleton, mention that of a jellyfish. When the organism washes up on the shore, he appears as a blob with no real structure. Of course, this is because without sufficient water, his hydroskeleton is not functional.
- The exoskeleton and muscle arrangement of ants allow them to accomplish extraordinary feats for their small size. Why are there not larger animals with similar motor system arrangements?
- Consider the present evolutionary state of the human knee. Is it sufficient for the punishment modern athletic activity places on it?
- Why is bone considered "nonliving" by those unfamiliar with its structure?
- What technological and research developments allowed the sliding-filament *theory* of the 1960s to become the sliding-filament *model* of the 1980s?
- Evaluate this statement: Muscles only pull. If this is true, how can you *push* a door open?
- Which muscles are collectively called the "hamstrings"? In which sports are they most likely to be injured and why?
- What is a "slipped" or herniated disk? What are its most common causes?
- Discuss the four curves (i.e, cervical, thoracic, lumbar, and sacral) of the human backbone. Which of these are present at birth? Which curves form when the baby develops the proper musculature?
- Since the students know something about the features of both bones and cartilage, have them examine the attachment of the ribs to the sternum via cartilage. If the rib cage was entirely bone, it would be a fairly brittle arrangement. The cartilage attachment makes us able to perform CPR on a patient without breaking their ribs.
- Most individuals do not envision that bones contain blood vessels. Now that the students know that blood cells are made in the red marrow, they can see that blood vessels are necessary in bone to get the newly made cells into the general circulation.
- Have each student in the class choose a muscle from Figure 35.15. Then they should demonstrate the location, origin(s), insertion(s), and action(s) of that muscle.
- Divide the class into two teams. Give each team slips of paper representing the steps of a muscle contraction. See which team can put the steps in the proper order first.
- In the earlier chapter on cellular components, the students learned that the function of smooth endoplasmic reticulum varies depending on where it is found in the body. Now they know that the function of sarcoplasmic reticulum, a type of smooth endoplasmic reticulum, is to store and release calcium ions.

How Would You Vote? Classroom Discussion Ideas

- Monitor the voting for the online question. It is very unfortunate for the American consumer that dietary supplements are *not* regulated by the FDA. This "loophole" allows anyone to sell anything for any reason with no guarantee (by testing results) that the product is: 1) *effective* for the purposes listed on the label, and 2) safe taken as directed. There is little doubt that this oversight will have far-reaching negative health repercussions in future years.

- Ask the class if any of its members have taken supplements to improve their muscle development. If possible, ask those that have why they began this practice. Athletes tend to rely readily on the advice of someone at the gym without researching the consequences or consulting a doctor.
- Have students complete classroom polling with JoinIN clickers.

Term Paper Topics, Library Activities, and Special Projects

- A challenging task is the assembly of a disarticulated skeleton. If your department has one, attempt to lay the bones out on a lab table in their approximate position and articulation. This is a good group project.
- Investigate the difference(s) in the development of muscles for power (weight) lifting versus development for body sculpting and exhibition.
- Document the development of the sliding-filament theory of muscle contraction and the research evidence that supports it.
- Report on the technique of arthroscopic surgery.
- Research the following spinal disorders: spina bifida, scoliosis, lordosis, and kyphosis.
- Investigate the use of electrical stimulation to accelerate the healing of bone fractures.
- Discuss the muscle disease called *myasthenia gravis*, its suspected cause, and the type of treatment currently used.
- Research osteoporosis. Report on the disease and several ways to prevent it. Be sure to include lifestyle changes (e.g., exercise and diet) as well as medicinal treatments and preventions.
- Contrast the difference between muscular dystrophies and multiple sclerosis.
- Investigate the use of Botox as a cosmetic procedure. How does it work? Where does the toxin come from? Is it something you would get? What are some actual clinical applications for the use of Botox?
- The clavicle is the most commonly broken bone in the body, because it takes only 5–20 lbs of pressure to break it. Examine the structure and position of the collarbone to determine why it is so vulnerable to breakage.
- Examine the skeletal elements of both a male and female pelvis. What criteria would an archeologist use to determine the sex of a skeleton?
- The text mentions that an embryo has a skeleton made of cartilage. Why is this advantageous? What is the advantage for the child of replacing cartilage with bone prior to birth?
- Research the outbreak and subsequent discovery of an effective vaccine for polio.
- Although osteoporosis is usually considered a disease affecting the elderly, what can one do in younger years to prevent it? What populations are particularly prone to osteoporosis?
- Investigate the different causes of arthritis. What are the different treatment options?

Possible Responses to *Critical Thinking* Questions

1. It seems as though there is a constant debate among athletes and scientists about the benefits of taking creatine supplements. Some individuals recommend its short-term use for activities that involve quick bursts of energy, such as weight lifting and sprinting. Most sources insist that it does not improve performance in activities that involve endurance, such as marathon running. In fact, the use of creatine in the days leading up to a marathon may bring about weight gain due to water retention. Other reports list incidences of muscle cramping and potential kidney

damage, especially while dehydrated. Lastly, creatine supplements are not licensed by the FDA, so I would be concerned about their overall safety. I would recommend that my friend not take creatine prior to her marathon, but most importantly, she should remain properly hydrated during the race!

2. After death, calcium diffuses out of the sarcoplasmic reticulum and binds to the troponin of the muscle. This allows for the formation of cross-bridges, and the muscle will contract. These actions utilized the remaining ATP in the muscle fiber. Therefore, there is no more available ATP to initiate the actions to return the muscle to the relaxed state. The muscle will remain in a state of contraction until the muscle begins to deteriorate.

3. Duchenne muscular dystrophy is caused by a single mutant gene on the X chromosome. It is an X-linked recessive condition. Therefore, if a male has Duchenne muscular dystrophy, he has inherited the X with the mutation from his mother. Since there is no incidence of the disease in his wife's family, Mike need not worry about his children being affected by the disease.

Possible Responses to *Data Analysis Exercise* Questions

In this study, the vertebral surface area was studied for both individuals with osteogenesis imperfect (OI) and for an untreated group of OI patients. This data was collected to judge the effectiveness of a treatment for OI.

1. All of the treated children showed an increase in vertebral area after a year.
2. None of the untreated subjects illustrated an increase in vertebral area in the same time period.
3. The rate of fracture was significantly higher in the control group.
4. According to this study, it appears that the experimental drug can slow bone breakdown and reduce fractures in young patients with OI.

36

CIRCULATION

Chapter Outline

A SHOCKING SAVE
THE NATURE OF BLOOD CIRCULATION
- Open and Closed Circulatory Systems
  - Evolution of Vertebrate Circulation

HUMAN CARDIOVASCULAR SYSTEM
- The Pulmonary Circuit
- The Systemic Circuit

COMPONENTS AND FUNCTIONS OF BLOOD
- Functions of Blood
- Blood Volume and Composition
  - Plasma
  - Red Blood Cells
  - White Blood Cells
  - Platelets

HEMOSTASIS
BLOOD TYPING
- ABO Blood Typing
- Rh Blood Typing

THE HUMAN HEART
- The Cardiac Cycle
- Setting the Pace for Contraction

BLOOD VESSEL STRUCTURE AND FUNCTION
BLOOD PRESSURE
MECHANISMS OF CAPILLARY EXCHANGE
VENOUS FUNCTION
BLOOD AND CARDIOVASCULAR DISORDERS
- Altered Blood Cell Count
- Cardiovascular Disease
  - Atherosclerosis
  - Hypertension
  - Rhythms and Arrhythmias

INTERACTIONS WITH THE LYMPHATIC SYSTEM
- Lymphoid Organs and Tissues

A SHOCKING SAVE (REVISITED)
SUMMARY
DATA ANALYSIS EXERCISE
SELF-QUIZ
CRITICAL THINKING

Objectives

1. Explain how the cardiovascular systems of vertebrates differ from those of invertebrates.
2. Describe the function and composition of blood.
3. Trace the routes of blood flow in the human cardiovascular system, including pulmonary and systemic circuits.
4. Explain what is happening during each portion of the cardiac cycle.
5. Understand the locations and characteristics of the various types of blood vessels.
6. Discuss the factors that cause blood to exist under different pressures.
7. Describe the composition and function of the lymphatic system.

Key Terms

sudden cardiac arrest
cardiopulmonary resuscitation, CPR
defibrillator
automated external defibrillator, AED
circulatory system
blood
hemolymph
heart
interstitial fluid
open circulatory system
closed circulatory system
capillaries
pulmonary circuit
systemic circuit
plasma
red blood cells (erythrocytes)
hemoglobin
cell count
white blood cells (leukocytes)
platelets
hemostasis
agglutination
ABO blood typing
Rh blood typing
cardiovascular
aorta
pericardium
myocardium
atrium, atria
atrioventricular (AV) node
ventricle
inferior vena cava
superior vena cava
coronary arteries
atrioventricular (AV) valve
semilunar valve
cardiac cycle
diastole
systole
cardiac muscle
sinoatrial (SA) node
arteries
arterioles
capillaries
venules
veins
blood pressure
systolic pressure
diastolic pressure
pulse
vasodilation
vasoconstriction
ultrafiltration
capillary reabsorption
anemia
leukemia
thrombus
embolus
blood clot
atherosclerosis
low-density lipoproteins (LDL)
high-density lipoproteins (HDL)
atherosclerotic plaque
hypertension
arrhythmias
electrocardiogram
lymph vascular system
lymph
lymphoid organs and tissues
lymph nodes
spleen
thymus gland

Lecture Outline

36.1 A Shocking Save

A. An electrical signal generated by a natural pacemaker in the heart wall causes the heart muscle to contract, creating the heart beat.
   1. Sudden cardiac arrest is the cessation of the beat, which halts the flow of the blood.
   2. CPR and defibrillation can restore the heart beat.

B. Matt Nader, a high school football player, went into cardiac arrest during a high school game.
   1. CPR and defibrillation using an automated external defibrillator (AED) saved his life.
   2. Through his testimony, Texas legislators passed a law requiring high school athletic events to have AEDs readily available.

36.2 The Nature of Blood Circulation

A. Open and Closed Circulatory Systems
   1. A circulatory system is an internal transport system with three components.
      a. Blood is a fluid tissue composed of water, solutes, and formed elements.
      b. Blood vessels are tubes of various diameters through which the blood is transported.
      c. The heart is a muscular pump that generates pressure to keep the blood flowing.
   2. Interstitial fluid "bathes" the cells of the body.
      a. The volume, composition, and temperature of this fluid must be carefully maintained.
      b. Exchanges between interstitial fluid and blood keep the internal environment tolerable.
   3. Arthropods and most mollusks have an open system.

a. Hemolymph is pumped from a heart into large tissue spaces where organs are "bathed."
b. The hemolymph mixes with interstitial fluid, and after accessing cells, returns to the heart via pores.
4. Vertebrates have a closed system.
a. All the vessels and the heart are connected so that blood remains enclosed.
b. Blood volume is constant and is equal to the heart's output at any time.
c. Flow rate slows as blood moves through the fine capillaries of the capillary beds.

B. Evolution of Vertebrate Circulation
1. In fishes, blood flows in a single circuit, passing through a heart of two chambers.
2. In amphibians the three-chambered heart is partially partitioned into right and left halves, permitting a partial separation into two circuits.
3. Birds and mammals have two separate circuits of blood flow.
a. The right half of the heart receives deoxygenated blood and pumps it to the lungs of the pulmonary circuit.
b. The left half receives blood from the lungs and pumps the oxygen-rich blood to all of the tissues and organs in the systemic circuit.

36.3 Human Cardiovascular System

A. The general route of blood circulation is: heart → arteries → arterioles → capillaries → venules → veins → heart.

B. The Pulmonary Circuit
1. In the *pulmonary circuit*, oxygen-poor blood is pumped to the lungs from the right side of the heart, and oxygen-rich blood is returned from the lungs to the left side.

C. The Systemic Circuit
1. In the *systemic circuit*, oxygen-rich blood is pumped from the left side of the heart to all the body.
2. Usually a given volume of blood in either circuit passes through only one capillary bed; an exception is blood from the digestive tract, which passes through the liver before entering the general circulation.

36.4 Components and Functions of Blood

A. Functions of Blood
1. It carries oxygen and nutrients to cells, and it carries secretions and wastes away from them.
2. It helps stabilize internal pH.
3. It contains phagocytic cells that fight infection.
4. It equalizes body temperature in birds and mammals.

B. Blood Volume and Composition
1. In humans, body size and the concentrations of water and solutes dictate blood volume.
a. On average, humans have about 5 liters (10 pints).
b. In vertebrates, blood is a viscous fluid, thicker than water and slower flowing.
c. Blood's fluid portion is called plasma; the cellular portion consists of blood cells and platelets.
d. Stem cells are unspecialized cells that retain the capacity for mitotic cell division.
2. Plasma
a. About 50–60 percent of blood volume is plasma, which is composed mostly of water.
b. Some plasma proteins transport lipids and vitamins; others function in immune responses and blood clotting.

c. Plasma also contains ions, glucose, lipids, amino acids, vitamins, hormones, and dissolved gases. It also acts as a solvent for hundreds of different plasma proteins.

3. Red Blood Cells (Erythrocytes)
   a. In mammals, red blood cells are biconcave disks that transport oxygen.
   b. Red blood cells contain hemoglobin—an iron-containing protein that binds with oxygen.
   c. They form from stem cells in bone marrow, lose their nuclei, and live about 120 days.
   d. The number of cells per microliter (about five million) is called the cell count.
4. White Blood Cells
   a. White blood cells, or leukocytes, remove dead or worn-out cells and protect us against invading microbes and foreign agents.
   b. There are several types of white blood cells.
      1) Granulocytes, named for their visible granules in the cytoplasm, are neutrophils, basophils, and eosinophils.
      2) Neutrophils undergo phagocytosis to capture bacteria.
      3) Eosinophils can combat parasitic worms and are prevalent during allergy season.
         c. Basophils are active in the inflammatory response.
      4) Agranulocytes, white blood cells that lack granules in the cytoplasm, are lymphocytes and monocytes.
      5) Lymphocytes, the "B" and "T" cells, are involved in the immune responses.
      6) Monocytes become macrophages that destroy foreign particles via phagocytosis.
5. Platelets
   a. These are fragments of megakaryocytes produced by bone marrow stem cells.
   b. They function in blood clotting and last only 5–9 days.

36.5 Hemostasis

A. Hemostasis is the process that stops blood loss when a vessel is damaged and constructs a framework for repairs.
B. There are three sequential steps.
   1. Spasm of the smooth muscle in the damaged blood vessel stops blood flow for a few minutes.
   2. Platelets clump to plug the rupture.
   3. The blood coagulates with help of fibrinogens and forms a clot; the clot then retracts into a compact mass, which is the blood clot.
C. Clot formation involves a cascade of enzymatic reactions.
   1. Patients with hemophilia lack a particular clotting factor and have difficulty forming clots.

36.6 Blood Typing

A. Each kind of cell bears "self" markers, or recognition proteins, at its surface that provide its unique identify.
   1. When certain markers on red blood cells of a blood donor and a recipient differ, the recipient's immune system attacks the donated cells.
   2. The defense response called agglutination occurs when proteins called antibodies bind to foreign cells and make them form clumps that attract phagocytes.
   3. Blood typing—the analysis of the surface markers on red blood cells.
B. ABO Blood Typing
   1. ABO blood typing is based on surface markers on red blood cells.
   2 Type A has A markers; type B has B markers; type AB has both markers; type O has neither marker.

C. Rh Blood Typing

1. Rh blood typing is based on the presence or absence of the Rh marker.
2. An Rh^- person (lacking this marker) transfused with Rh^+ blood (with this marker) will produce antibodies to the Rh marker.
3. There are risks in childbirth or pregnancy (*erythroblastosis fetalis*) if an Rh^- woman bears a second Rh^+ child.
    a. If an Rh^- mom is exposed to a first pregnancy with an Rh+ baby, she will develop the anti-Rh antibody.
    b. If the mom's second baby is Rh+, the mom's anti-Rh antibody will cross the placenta and destroy the baby's blood cells in utero.

36.7 The Human Heart

A. Heart Structure and Function

1. The heart tissue is layered.
    a. The outer covering of the heart is the pericardium, which is partially a fluid-filled sac and the outer part of the heart wall.
    b. The bulk of the heart wall is the heart muscle—myocardium—serviced by coronary circulation.
    c. The heart is lined with a smooth endothelium.
2. Nutrients and oxygen are delivered to the heart tissues by the coronary arteries.
3. The heart has four chambers and four valves.
    a. Each half of the heart consists of an atrium (receiving) and a ventricle (pumping) separated by an atrioventricular valve.
    b. Blood exits each ventricle through a semilunar valve.

B. The Cardiac Cycle

1. The cardiac cycle consists of a sequence of contraction (systole) and relaxation (diastole).
    a. As the atria fill, the ventricles are relaxed.
    b. Pressure of the blood in the atria forces the atrioventricular valves to open; the ventricles continue to fill as the atria contract.
    c. The ventricles contract, the atrioventricular valves close, and blood flows out through the semilunar valves.
    d. The heart sound "lub" is made by the closing of the AV valves; the "dup" sound is the closure of the semilunar valves.

C. Setting the Pace for Contraction

1. Cardiac muscle has orderly arrays of sarcomeres, which contract by a sliding-filament mechanism.
2. Because of the close junctions of cardiac muscle cells, they contract in unison.
3. Excitation for a heartbeat is initiated in the sinoatrial (SA) node (also known as the cardiac pacemaker) then passes to the atrioventricular (AV) node for ventricular contraction; this is the cardiac conduction system.
4. The nervous system adjusts rate and strength.

36.8 Blood Vessel Structure and Function

A. Blood is distributed by means of arteries, arterioles, capillaries, venules, and veins.

1. Blood pressure is fluid pressure of the blood due to ventricular contractions.
    a. The flow rate is directly proportional to the pressure gradient between the start and end of the vessel; it is high in contracting ventricles and in the beginning of the arteries, and low in relaxed atria.
2. The flow rate is inversely proportional to the vessel's size or resistance to flow.

B. Rapid Transport in Arteries
   1. Arteries are large-diameter vessels that present low resistance to flow as they conduct blood *away from* the heart.
   2. Because of their elastic walls, arteries tend to "smooth out" the pulsations associated with the discontinuous pumping cycle of the heart.

C. Flow Distribution at Arterioles
   1. Blood flow to organs, except the brain, is a function of activity.
      a. The brain gets a constant supply.
      b. When you exercise, blood flow to the kidneys and gut slows.
   2. Neural and endocrine signals cause changes in arteriole diameter by stimulating the muscle cells in the walls.
      a. If the blood pressure increases, the arterioles are instructed to relax (vasodilation).
      b. If the pressure decreases, the diameter of the arterioles decreases (vasoconstriction).
   3. Arterioles serve as control points where adjustments can be made in blood volume distribution.

D. Following arterioles, the blood enters capillary networks.
   1. The oxygen is given up to the tissues in the capillary network.
   2. The blood from several capillaries flows into a venule.
   3. After the venules, the blood enters veins and travels back to the heart.

36.9 Blood Pressure

A. A special instrument with a cuff surrounding the upper arm is connected to a pressure-measuring device.
   1. The peak pressure (systolic) is recorded when the ventricles are contracting—120mm is typical.
   2. The lowest pressure (diastolic) is reached when the ventricles are relaxing—80mm.

B. Blood pressure is related to blood volume, constriction of the arterioles.
   1. Receptors on the aorta and in carotid arteries of the neck alert a control center in the brain when blood pressure drops or increases.
   2. In response the brain calls for changes in cardiac output and arteriole diameter.

36.10 Mechanisms of Capillary Exchange

A. Capillary Function
   1. Capillaries are diffusion zones for *exchanges* between blood and interstitial fluid.
      a. A capillary is the smallest tube (red blood cells travel single-file) in the path of circulation.
      b. Total resistance is less than in arterioles, so the drop in blood pressure is not as great.
      c. Its wall consists of a single layer of endothelial cells, which facilitates diffusion to and from the interstitial fluid.
   2. Movement across the capillary is by several modes: diffusion (of oxygen and carbon dioxide), endocytosis and exocytosis (of proteins), between the cells (of ions), and bulk flow (of water).
      a. At the beginning of a capillary bed, there is a movement of plasma out into the interstitial fluid in a process known as ultrafiltration.
      b. Further on, some tissue fluid moves into the capillary through clefts between its endothelial walls in a process known as reabsorption.

36.11 Venous Function

A. Capillaries merge into venules then into veins.
   1. Blood pressure and resistance to flow are both low; valves prevent backflow.

a. When valves become damaged, varicose veins (in the legs) or hemorrhoids (in the anus) form.
b. Clots may develop in a leg vein from valve damage or inactivity.
1) A clot may dislodge from the leg and travel to the heart or lungs.
2. Veins are blood volume reservoirs (50–60 percent of blood volume) because their walls can distend or contract.
3. The movement of skeletal muscles squeezes the veins and pushes the blood along against the forces of gravity.

36.12 Blood and Cardiovascular Disorders
A. Altered Blood Cell Count
1. Anemias are conditions in which there are too few, or deformed, RBCs.
a. Hemorrhagic (sudden) and chronic (slow) anemias follow blood loss.
b. Certain bacteria and protozoans replicate in RBCs and cause hemolytic anemias.
c. Insufficient iron causes iron deficiency anemia.
d. Sickle-cell anemia and thalassemias arise from mutations that either alter the hemoglobin or stop its synthesis altogether.
2. Polycythemias (far too few RBCs) and blood doping make blood flow sluggish.
3. Infectious mononucleosis is a viral disease in which too many monocytes and lymphocytes form; it may last several weeks with a gradual recovery.
4. Leukemias are cancers of the bone marrow, which impair WBC formation.
5. Lymphomas are cancers that originate from B or T lymphocytes, producing tumors in lymph nodes and the lymphatic system.
B. Cardiovascular Disease
1. Major risk factors for cardiovascular disease are genetics, smoking, obesity, lack of exercise, hypertension, high cholesterol level, and diabetes mellitus.
2. Atherosclerosis
a. In this condition, lipids such as cholesterol build up in the arterial wall.
b. Low-density lipoproteins (LDLs) infiltrate the walls, causing an atherosclerotic plaque to form.
c. High-density lipoproteins (HDLs) also bind cholesterol, but are more desirable since the liver is able to metabolize them.
d. Platelets gather at the site and initiate clot formation.
e. Enlarging plaques and blood clots narrow or block arteries.
f. With coronary bypass surgery, doctors stitch a section of blood vessel from another part of the body to the aorta and coronary artery below a clogged area.
g. Laser angioplasty uses lasers to vaporize the plaques.
h. During balloon angioplasty, a small balloon is inflated inside a blocked artery to flatten the plaques.
3. Hypertension
a. Hypertension refers to chronically high blood pressure, even at rest.
b. It is referred to as the silent killer because people are often unaware they have it.
c. Hypertension tends to run in families.
d. Diet, lack of exercise, and salt intake increase risk.
e. The heart may enlarge enough to pump less efficiently and interfere with the delivery of oxygen to the brain, heart, and other vital organs.
4. Rhythms and Arrhythmias
a. Electrocardiograms (ECGs) can reveal arrhythmias, an abnormal heartbeat.
1) Bradycardia is a below-average resting cardiac rate, which may be the result of ongoing exercise.

2) Tachycardia, fast heartbeat, is caused by exercise or stress.

b. Atrial and ventricular fibrillation are repeated contractions that disrupt the normal cardiac cycle.

36.13 Interactions with the Lymphatic System

A. Lymph Vascular System

1. The lymph vascular system includes lymph capillaries and lymph vessels.
2. It returns excess water and proteins (lymph) to the bloodstream, transports fats, and brings foreign materials to the lymph nodes for disposal.
3. Lymph capillaries begin blindly in the tissues of the body; they lead to lymph vessels, which in turn lead to ducts that return the fluid to the bloodstream.

B. Lymphoid Organs and Tissues

1. Lymph nodes are strategically located at intervals along lymph vessels.
   a. Before entering blood, lymph trickles through at least one node and gets filtered.
   b. Masses of white blood cells are located inside the nodes and attack nonself items.
2. The organs and functions include:
   a. The lymph nodes (with resident cells) located along the lymph vessels help remove bacteria and cellular debris.
   b. The spleen is the largest lymphoid organ and it removes spent RBCs, holds macrophages, and produces red blood cells in human embryos.
   c. The thymus secretes hormones that regulate the activity of lymphocytes and is a site where they multiply and mature.

36.14 A Shocking Save (Revisited)

A. Most cardiac arrest cases are not attended to before health professionals arrive.

B. CPR has been replaced with CCR (cardiocerebral resuscitation).

1. CCR involves only chest compressions—enough air moves into the lungs via this method.

C. Automated External Defibrillators (AEDs) are more readily available in public places.

Suggestions for Presenting the Material

- This chapter includes a discussion of closed and open circulatory systems. Students will be familiar with a closed system because that is the type in the human body; but the open concept implies a great deal of "hemorrhaging," which sounds *terminal,* but in this context is *normal.*
- One of the strengths of the Starr and Taggart text is the inclusion of excellent summaries. Use the figures and animations to help the students with these topics. See CengageNOW for additional information and sources.
- When discussing the functions of blood, it may be helpful to refer to other lectures that will expand on the topic. Such instances include: white blood cells and immunity, red blood cells and respiration, and nutrient transport.
- Because of the complexity of the entire cardiovascular system, the simplified scheme in Figure 36.5 is useful for introducing the concepts of pulmonary and systemic circuits. The concept of oxygen-rich and oxygen-poor blood can be emphasized here. This can be followed by the heart pathways and contraction sequence.
- The heartbeat, pulse, and blood pressure are measurable quantities of interest to students; therefore, these deserve as much lecture time as is feasible.

- Capillary exchange is a topic that allows you to review previous lectures on diffusion and active transport.
- The mechanism of clotting, and the somewhat confusing term hemostasis (*not homeostasis)* used to describe it, may need special attention and/or simplification.
- Blood typing is confusing to students. This is especially true because most believe that the ABO markers and the Rh markers are intimately connected, since blood type is nearly always expressed that way—O^+, for example. Stress the independent nature of these two sets of markers. It is also helpful to mention that the ABO and Rh factors are only a few of the antigens that are located on red blood cells. There are over 400 more!
- Usually students feel they have a fair grasp of circulation until the lymphatic system is introduced. Then it is a "what's this for?" expression. Stress the necessity for such a system and the *one-way return* of fluid to the general blood supply.
- Make sure that the students understand the difference in pressure between an artery and a vein. The artery has a great deal of pressure, since it is the first type of vessel the blood encounters after leaving the heart. Since veins are located at the end of the trip back to the heart, they are exposed to much-reduced pressure. Explain to the students that if you cut an artery and a vein, there would be very different results. (Do not try this at home!)
- Typically arteries contain oxygenated blood and veins contain deoxygenated blood. How are the pulmonary veins and arteries different?
- Mention that the heart exhibits autorhythmicity—it is self stimulating. This is unlike other muscles of the body. -How does this influence the idea of clinical death?

Classroom and Laboratory Enrichment

- Ask a physician to demonstrate an artificial pacemaker; include comments on the limitations and usefulness of such an artificial device versus the natural SA node.
- Borrow a sphygmomanometer and ask a person skilled in its use to explain how blood pressure is determined, using members of the class as volunteers.
- Create or acquire a blood cell model with both ABO antigens and Rh factors. Purchase a simulated blood-typing kit (available from Ward's). This kit utilizes plastic-coated particles, so there is no risk of disease transmission. Have the students type the four patients provided. At the end of the activity, ask questions about who could transfuse to which other patient safely.
- Request a cow heart(s) from a local meat processor (be sure to ask them to leave the aorta on it) to use in a lab setting. Students are amazed at the size of the heart! Dissect both the atria and ventricles to show students the similarity in mammal heart structure and function. Show the students the SA node and other key features of the exterior of the heart. If the major vessels are not present, you can poke a glass rod down through each hole to help determine which vessel was originally there.
- Determine the resting and active pulse rates for a variety of body types in the class. Can you make any generalizations from your data?
- Obtain a recording of heart sounds as they would be heard through a stethoscope. Relate sounds to events of the normal and abnormal cardiac cycle. Pass a stethoscope around the room so everyone can hear their own heart sounds.
- To illustrate cardiovascular disorders, show a video of a heart bypass operation. Using a model, illustrate for students what is "bypassed" in the procedure.
- Discuss the role of cholesterol and its contribution to heart disease.

- Do a demonstration of the dissection of an earthworm. Typically, the students think the earthworm is a primitive organism. They may be surprised to learn that the earthworm has a closed circulatory system and more than one heart.
- When you examine diagrams of the hearts of various animals, which ones do not mix oxygenated blood with deoxygenated blood? Why is this an important adaptation?
- Examine prepared slides of blood smears. Try to identify each of the five types of white blood cells. Notice that mature red blood cells do not have a nucleus. How is this explained by their function?
- A machine that performs cell counts does so based on cell size. When observing red blood cells, white blood cells, and platelets list them in order from largest to smallest.
- Examine a cutaway view of the heart, such as seen in Figure 36.11c. Can you tell which of the four chambers of the heart work the hardest by examining the thickness of the chamber walls?
- If you are feeling brave, take a live goldfish and spread its tail under a dissecting microscope. You will be able to see red blood cells traveling single-file through the capillaries.
- Explain why they call skeletal muscle action "milking a vein." How does the movement of skeletal muscles and valve action prevent clot formation?
- Have everyone in the class choose an artery or a vein from Figure 36.4. Then have each student tell where each vessel supplies blood to or collects blood from, and whether the blood is oxygenated or deoxygenated.
- If possible, obtain a speaker from the local chapter of the American Red Cross. This representative can discuss the conditions each blood product would treat, expiration dates, and storage requirements.
- Look up the symptoms of a transfusion reaction. Many of these symptoms resemble those of a tissue rejection. This may make the students more comfortable thinking of blood as a tissue.
- Have anyone who knows their blood type in the class announce what other blood types they could safely receive and for whom they could serve as a suitable donor.
- Each student should record their own pulse rate or that of a lab partner. Note: do not use your thumb to measure someone's pulse, since your thumb has a pulse. What could it mean if the pulse in your leg is different than the pulse in your wrist?

Classroom Discussion Ideas

- How can you explain the fact that persons who die of heart attack (lack of oxygen to heart muscle) have perfectly adequate amounts of oxygenated blood in their heart chambers?
- Should CCR training be a required skill taught and learned in high school or college?
- Evaluate the risk to the public of administering first aid (CCR or AED defibrillator) when so many people are "sue happy."
- Would you want to own an AED? Should most public places be required to have one available?
- The textbook mentions that bystanders are hesitant to perform CPR on a heart attack victim. How will this change with the advent of CCR, where no mouth-to-mouth resuscitation is necessary?

Additional Ideas for Classroom Discussion

- How can a worker in a police crime lab determine if the blood found at a crime scene is human?
- The heart is really a "double pump." It is also, of course, divided into four chambers. Does this mean that one pump consists of atria, the other of ventricles, *or* does it mean the left and right sides are pumping to separate circulations? Explain your reasoning.
- Why is the lymph system such a "highway" for the spread of certain metastatic cancers?

- Why is hemophilia in *females* almost never seen?
- Evaluate the truthfulness of the statement "I'm a blood relative." Is there a more accurate expression that could replace this one?
- Have students reflect on and discuss the ceaseless activity of their own heart. Have them complete the simple calculations for how many times per hour, day, month, and year their own heart beats.
- In small groups, have students compile a list of common activities of college-age students that are considered risk factors for heart disease.
- Think about the differences in the composition of hemolymph and blood.
- In today's world, there are often severe blood shortages. Occasionally, scientists try to develop artificial blood and ways to utilize animal blood for human use. Look into some of these methods. How are they successful or unsuccessful?
- Stress to the students that clot formation requires both a series of clotting factors and an adequate platelet count.
- The Rh factor's involvement in pregnancy is often a difficult concept for the beginning biologist. Be sure to re-explain it in detail. Now there is a product called RhoGAM® to eliminate this problem —explain its mechanism. Give the students this problem: a mother had 12 pregnancies in the early 1900s. Only one child survived. Which child lived and why?
- Be sure to stress that valves in the heart and in veins have the same function—to prevent the backflow of blood.

How Would You Vote? Classroom Discussion Ideas

- Monitor the voting for the online question. There are many good topics that high schools should add to their curricula, including lifestyle education (smoking, birth control, etc.). Most of these topics are concerned with maintaining one's health and wellbeing. Learning CPR is preparation for helping someone else. It is proven that it does save lives. It seems it would be a worthwhile addition to a required health curriculum.
- Have students complete class polling using the JoinIn clickers.

Term Paper Topics, Library Activities, and Special Projects

- Evaluate the reported links between lipids and cardiovascular diseases.
- Survey the various corrective surgical procedures that are routinely performed on the heart and its vessels. Select one or two for an in-depth report.
- It is often said that "the heart never rests." True, it does beat continuously from before birth until death, usually at old age. However, it does rest for 0.3 seconds after each beat. Assuming a steady pulse of 70 beats per minute, calculate the *total* amount of time the heart has rested in a person 75 years old.
- The Rh factor is named for the Rhesus monkey. Trace the historical discovery of this protein marker in primates and humans.
- Death of newborn babies from *erythroblastosis fetalis* (Rh factor related) have been virtually eliminated since the 1950s. How has this been accomplished?
- Have students use Thomson's INFOTRAC to research one type of cardiovascular disorder of interest. Have them report on their results in a short paper.
- Have students complete a position paper taking a pro or con position on the trend toward further regulation of activities and foods that are considered prime contributors to cardiovascular disease in the U.S.

- Have students consult their medical records and create a short description of their blood type. What would their red blood cells look like? What ABO or Rh elements are present?
- Look up arteriosclerosis, which is commonly known as hardening of the arteries. How is it related to atherosclerosis?
- Research the disease malaria. Obtain a photograph of a red blood cell containing the deleterious organism.
- What is the chemical composition of lymph? How does it differ from plasma? How is it transported around the body?
- Lymphoid organs such as tonsils and the spleen have definite functions. How do we compensate if those organs are removed?
- Borrow an AED (automated external defibrillator) from the public safety department at your campus. Show the class the necessary steps for its operation.
- What is RhoGAM? How and when was it developed? How does it save the lives of many babies?

Possible Responses to *Critical Thinking* Questions

1. Moving the leg muscles during a long airplane flight or during any other time of prolonged inactivity is a good idea. Why? Because blood in the veins of the legs is under practically zero pressure and can be moved upward in the body toward the heart only by the squeezing pressure of the skeletal muscle on the vessels. Moving about the cabin would be a good idea, but in today's smaller jets, this may be impractical (especially with the beverage cart blocking the way!). Nevertheless, if you are unable to move in the cabin, you can move your legs while seated and attempt to exercise the muscles at least a little bit. In addition, people who have taken recent long airplane trips should see a physician if they see any hot, red areas on a leg where there has been no injury.
2. Mitochondria provide energy for the cell to perform all its functions. The cardiac muscle cells produce 70–90 beats per minute over the individual's entire lifetime. This easily explains the large amount of mitochondria in cardiac muscle. Skeletal muscle cells, on the other hand, do have more periods of rest where ATP provided by the mitochondria is not needed.
3. Since the valve is not properly closing, blood backwashes into the atrium, creating turbulence. This turbulent flow can be heard as a murmur (the *whoosh*) with a stethoscope.

Possible Responses to *Data Analysis Exercise* Questions

The states in the southeastern U.S. are known as the "stroke belt," since they have an increased incidence of stroke deaths. This study compares stroke deaths in the Southeast to those in New York state.

1. More black people in the "stroke belt" die from strokes than white people in that same area.
2. The white population in New York has a slightly higher death rate than the black population in the same state.
3. White people living in the "stroke belt" have a higher death rate than black people living in New York.
4. This data show evidence that illustrates that there are more deaths from stroke in the southeastern U.S. than in New York state. It does not definitely prove that this difference in survival rate is due to the proximity of healthcare facilities. Many more factors would need to be explored, such as diet and whether the participants were smokers.

37

IMMUNITY

Chapter Outline

Objectives

1. Describe typical external barriers that organisms present to invading organisms.
2. Understand the process involved in the nonspecific inflammatory response.
3. Understand how vertebrates (especially mammals) recognize and discriminate between self and nonself tissues.
4. Distinguish between antibody-mediated and cell-mediated patterns of defense.
5. Explain the mechanisms of immunological self/nonself recognition, specificity, diversity, and memory.
6. Explain the basis for immunization.
7. Describe some examples of immune failures, and identify as specifically as you can which weapons in the immunity arsenal failed in each case.
8. Understand the symptoms, diagnostic testing, treatments, and potential for vaccines for AIDS.

Key Terms

human papillomavirus (HPV)	dendritic cells	MHC markers	membrane bound antibodies
immunity	basophils	T cell receptors, TCRs	immunoglobulins
complement	mast cells	specificity	helper T cells
antigen	eosinophils	diversity	cytotoxic T cells
innate immunity	B cell	memory	allergen
pathogen-associated molecular pattern (PAMP)	cytotoxic T cell	memory cells	allergy
adaptive immunity	T cell	effector cells	antihistamines
cytokines	natural killer cells, NK	antibody-mediated immune response	anaphylactic shock
interleukins	normal flora	cell-mediated immune response	immunization
interferons	lysozyme	antibodies	vaccine
neutrophils	plaque	B cell receptor	autoimmune response
macrophages	chemotaxis	secreted antibodies	AIDS
	inflammation		HIV
	fever		
	self/nonself recognition		

Lecture Outline

37.1 Frankie's Last Wish

A. About 3,600 women die of cervical cancer a year in the United States.
   1. Cervical cancer is caused by the human papillomavirus (HPV).
   2. Routine gynecological exams and pap smears are effective at screening for pre-cancerous cells resulting from HPV.

B. In 2006, Gardasil, a vaccine against four strains of genital HPV, was approved by the FDA.

37.2 Integrated Responses to Threats

A. Evolution of the Body's Defenses
   1. Immunity is the body's ability to resist and combat infections with a multitude of infectious invaders, most of which have coevolved with humans and every other animal.

2. Discriminating between self and nonself was a key innovation in the evolutionary history of animals, giving them the ability to detect antigens on viruses, bacteria, and other foreign cells, as well as tumor cells, toxins, and allergens.
3. Pattern receptors of early animals were functionally connected to chemical responses, causing the release of complement (circulating proteins that can tag or kill microbes) when anything was bound to the receptors.
   a. Innate immunity offers general and immediate response against infection.
   b. Adaptive immunity evolved later and is triggered by an antigen creating a defense response to a diversity of threats.

B. Three Lines of Defense
   1. The first line of defense includes physical, chemical, and mechanical barriers against invading pathogens.
   2. Second, innate immunity starts immediately after a pathogen has been detected or after internal tissue damage; phagocytic white blood cells, complement, and acute inflammation and fever can counter many threats.
   3. Third, adaptive immunity is set in motion where white blood cells defend the body against the pathogen by targeting specific antigens.

C. The Defenders
   1. White blood cells (WBCs) circulate in blood and the lymph. They also reside in lymph nodes, spleen, liver, kidneys, etc. where they stand ready to defend; some are phagocytic, all are secretory.
      a. WBCs secrete cytokines, which are cell-to-cell signaling molecules that control every aspect of immunity;
      b. Examples of cytokines include interleukins, interferons, and tumor necrosis factors.
   2. Different types of WBCs have specialized tasks.
      a. *Neutrophils* are the most abundant and rapidly phagocytized bacteria.
      b. *Macrophages* are mature monocytes that patrol the tissue fluids and the blood.
      c. *Dendritic cells* alert the immune system to the presence of antigen.
      d. *Eosinophils* target parasites too large for phagocytosis.
      e. *Basophils* and *mast cells* secrete histamine, which sustains inflammation.
   3. *B and T lymphocytes* (B and T cells) are central to adaptive immunity, shuffling information in antigen-receptor genes into diverse combinations to defeat a limitless number of specific pathogens.
   4. *Natural killer cells* destroy infected or cancerous body cells that are undetected by cytotoxic T cells.

37.3 Surface Barriers

A. The skin is in constant contact with the external environment so it picks up many microorganisms.

B. Microorganisms that typically live on human surfaces, including the interior tubes and cavities of the digestive and respiratory tracts, are called normal flora.

C. Our surfaces provide a stable environment and nutrients for flora, and in return the flora deter more aggressive species from colonizing body surfaces, help us digest food, and make nutrients (B_{12}) that we depend on.

D. Normal flora can cause serious illness if they invade tissues.

E. The mouth harbors huge populations of different types of bacteria including *staphylococcus*, *streptococcus*, and *lactobacillus*.
   1. A few species of the 400 or so that live in the mouth cause dental plaque.
   2. Dental plaque is a biofilm that sticks to teeth. These bacteria break down carbohydrates and secrete organic acids, which etch away enamel and make cavities.

3. Tight junctions between the gum epithelium and the teeth form a barrier, preventing these bacteria from entering the body.
4. Periodontitis is caused by the secretions of anaerobic microbes that cause inflammation of gum tissues.
5. Atherosclerosis, a disease of inflammation, is associated with one of these anaerobic species, *Porphyromonas gingivalis*.

F. MRSA (methicillin-resistant *Staphylococcus aureus*) is a formidable enemy since it is resistant to many antibiotics.

G. Barriers to Infection

1. Physical, chemical, and mechanical barriers keep microorganisms on the outside of body tissues.
2. Healthy, intact skin is an effective physical barrier.
3. Mucus provides a mechanical barrier by coating epithelial linings and trapping bacteria.
   a. Ciliated mucous membranes in the respiratory tract sweep out bacteria and particles.
   b. Lysozymes in the mucus act as a chemical barrier and degrade bacterial cell walls.
   c. Stomach and intestinal secretions can kill bacteria.
   d. Urine's flushing action keeps pathogens from the urinary tract.

37.4 Triggering Innate Defenses

A. Complement

1. Macrophages patrolling interstitial fluid are the first to encounter a threat, engulfing and digesting almost anything other than undamaged body cells; if their pattern receptors bind to a pathogen, they begin to secrete cytokines, which signal for more aid.
2. Complement immediately binds to the antigen at a phagocyte's surface or to circulating microbes.
   a. These proteins are activated in a cascading fashion, yielding large concentrations of activated complement molecules in a localized tissue region.
   b. Activated complement proteins have several effects.
      i. Some attract phagocytic cells.
      ii. Some attach directly to pathogens.
      iii. They help guide maturation of immune cells and mediate their interactions.

B. Phagocytic Leukocytes

1. Neutrophils
   a. Neutrophils are abundant and often first on the scene in an infection.
   b. They undergo phagocytosis or eject intercellular substances to form a net that traps foreign particles.
2. Macrophages and Dendritic Cells
   a. Macrophages engulf foreign material and secrete cytokines that alert other body cells of the presence of an invader.
   b. Dendritic cells undergo phagocytosis, especially in the respiratory pathways.
   c. Dendritic cells also present foreign antigens to T cells.

37.5 Inflammation and Fever

A. Inflammation

1. Cytokine secretions from macrophages and activated complement cause inflammation.
   a. First, mast cells in connective tissue respond to complement or to the antigen by secreting histamine and cytokines into the interstitial fluid.
      1) Histamine causes the blood vessels to dilate and increases blood flow to hasten the arrival of circulating phagocytes attracted by cytokines.
      2) Localized warming and redness occur at the site of damage or invasion.

b. Second, fluid seeps from blood vessels, causing swelling and delivery of infection-fighting proteins to the tissues.

B. Fever

1. Fever occurs when the body's core temperature exceeds the hypothalamus' normal set point.
2. Fevers of around 100°F can enhance immune functions.

37.6 Antigen Receptors

A. Antibody Structure and Function

1. B cells make antibodies.
   a. An antibody molecule has four polypeptide chains—two identical "light" chains and two identical "heavy" chains.
   b. Each antibody has a variable region that is specific to an antigen.
2. There are five classes of antibodies, each serving different functions.
   a. IgM and IgD, the first to be secreted during immune response, trigger the complement cascade.
   b. IgG antibodies activate complement proteins and neutralize many toxins; they are long-lasting and can cross the placenta to protect the fetus.
   c. IgE antibodies stimulate basophils and mast cells to secrete histamine.
   d. IgA, present in saliva, tears, and mucus, helps repel invaders at the start of the respiratory system.
3. Each B cell is bristling with antibodies that all have the same kind of binding site for a specific antigen.

B. The Making of Antigen Receptors

1. Before a B cell leaves bone marrow, it is synthesizing up to 100,000 unique antigen receptors; until it encounters its antigen, it is called a "naive" B cell.
2. T cells also form in the bone marrow, but are not mature until they have traveled through the thymus gland and become exposed to thymosin.
   a. T cells get receptors for MHC markers.
   b. They also get TCRs—their unique antigen receptors—by random gene combinations.
3. To ensure that a T cell will not attack its own body, thymus cells make small peptides that are derived from many of the body's own proteins and attach them to MHC markers as built-in quality controls for "bad" TCRs.
4. By the time naive T cells leave the thymus, their surfaces are full of functional TCRs.

37.7 Overview of Adaptive Immunity

A. Characteristics of Adaptive Immune Responses

1. In vertebrates, the adaptive immune system "adapts" to different antigens encountered during an individual's lifetime.
2. Self/Nonself Recognition
   a. Cells can distinguish self from nonself with self-recognition markers (MHC markers and TCRs).
   b. Lymphocytes will ignore the *self* markers on the body's own cells but will respond to *nonself* markers (antigens) on foreign cells.
3. Specificity
   a. Specificity means that defenses target specific antigens.
4. Diversity
   a. B and T cells bear *tremendously diverse receptors,* which have the potential to trigger responses to a billion different kinds of threats.
5. Memory

a. The immune system shows *memory,* wherein a portion of the B and T cells are set aside for future battles against the same threat.

B. The Two Arms of Adaptive Immunity

1. Adaptive immunity has two separate arms for defense that work together to eliminate diverse threats.

a. *B cells* and their progeny (effector cells) produce antibodies, which are specific substances that tag targets for destruction; this is called the *antibody-mediated* response.

b. *Cytotoxic T cells* and *natural killer cells (NK)* destroy infected body cells and tumor cells (with viruses, for example) in what is referred to as *cell-mediated* immune responses.

C. Antigen Processing

1. Initially a macrophage, B cell, or dendritic cell engulfs a foreign object.

2. Next a vesicle is formed and fuses with a lysosome.

3. The enzymes in the lysosome digest the invader.

a. The lysosome also contains MHC markers that attach to the pieces that remain following phagocytosis.

4. The antigen-MHC complexes fuse with the plasma membrane at the border of the cell.

a. This serves to initiate additional immune responses.

D. Intercepting and Clearing Out Antigen

1. T cells recognize antigen only if a macrophage, dendritic cell, or B cell presents it and then enters a lymph node after engulfing it; there the T cells are alerted to the threat.

2. Daily, about 25 billion lymphocytes pass through each lymph node; lymph nodes trap most of free antigen that might be circulating.

3. When effector cells have reduced the antigen-bearing agents in the body, the immune response slows and then stops.

37.8 The Antibody-Mediated Immune Response

A. When the pathogen enters the body, it is coated with complement and shunted to a lymph node where naive B cells await.

B. The antigen binds with the antibody and is taken into the B cell only to reemerge as an MHC-antigen complex to be displayed on the cell surface.

C. According to the theory of clonal selection, antigen "chooses" specific T cells because they bear a receptor that can bind to them.

1. After an encounter with a helper T cell, the B cell undergoes mitosis to produce many B effector cells and memory cells.

2. Effector cells produce enormous quantities of antibodies (primary immune response), which will seek out antigens (freely circulating in extracellular fluid) and mark them for destruction by phagocytes and complement proteins.

37.9 The Cell-Mediated Immune Response

A. An antibody-mediated response is not effective against intracellular pathogens; the cell-mediated response targets sick or infected body cells.

B. Cytotoxic T Cells: Activation and Action

1. Cytotoxic T cells are stimulated by interleukins and interferons.

2. The clones of cytotoxic T cells recognize the antigen-MHC complexes on infected cells and kill them by punching holes in their cell membranes with proteins called perforins; they also can induce apoptosis.

3. The main targets of cell-mediated responses are cells infected with intracellular pathogens, tumor cells, and cells of transplanted organs.

C. The Role of Natural Killer (NK) Cells

1. Natural killer cells are not activated by antigen-MHC complexes.
2. NK cells appear to be lymphocytes (but not B or T) produced in the bone marrow.
3. NK cells kill tumor cells and virus-infected cells spontaneously, without the presence of antibodies.

37.10 When Immunity Goes Wrong

A. Allergies

1. An allergy is a secondary immune response (hypersensitivity) to a normally harmless substance, called an allergen; examples of allergens include drugs, food, pollen, spores, and venom from insects.
2. Exposure triggers production of IgE antibodies, which cause the release of histamines and prostaglandins.
3. A local inflammatory response results; death can even occur due to anaphylactic shock, a condition in which blood pressure drops and tissues swell, blocking airways.

B. Overly Vigorous Responses

1. Ideally the immune system should destroy invading cells, but leave the body's cells unscathed.
2. Severe allergic reactions can lead to anaphylactic shock.
   a. Anaphylactic shock can involve constriction of airways and shock.
3. Sometimes a "cytokine storm" occurs that can lead to organ failure and potential death.

C. Autoimmune Disorders

1. In autoimmune disorders, lymphocytes turn against the body's own cells.
2. Rheumatoid arthritis is an inflammation of the joints caused by antibody that treats the body's own IgG molecules as if they were antigens.
3. Graves' disease (thyrotoxicosis) is an overproduction of thyroid hormones, which cause elevated metabolic rates, heart fibrillations, nervousness, and weight loss.
4. Multiple sclerosis arises when autoreactive T cells trigger inflammation of myelin sheaths, disrupting nerve transmission.

D. Immunodeficiency

1. When cell-mediated immunity is weakened, infections that would normally not be serious become life-threatening.
2. Primary immune deficiencies are present at birth and result from altered genes or abnormal development; severe combined immunodeficiency (SCID) and adenosine deaminase deficiency (ADA) are examples.
3. Secondary immune deficiencies are losses of immune function after exposure to some outside agent, like a virus such as AIDS.

37.11 HIV and AIDS

A. Symptoms of HIV Infection

1. Initially an individual may feel fine and think they have a flu-type illness.
2. Then opportunistic infections are seen: yeast, *pneumocystis jiroveci*, Kaposi's sarcoma, and a general feeling of malaise accompanied by fever, night sweats, and weight loss.

B. HIV Revisited

1. AIDS is a group of disorders that follow infection by HIV.
2. The virus cripples the immune system and makes the body highly susceptible to usually harmless infections.
3. There is no cure for those already infected.
4. A Titanic Struggle
   a. HIV is a retrovirus that only infects macrophages, dendritic cells, and helper T cells.

b. The virus takes over the cell's machinery to produce massive quantities of new HIV particles.
c. The first stage is mostly cleared by the body's adaptive response, but HIV particles continue to multiply in the lymph nodes and shed viral envelope proteins, which enter the blood; years or decades may pass with normal immune functioning.
d. Glycoproteins shed from HIV envelopes bind to IgE, causing an inflammatory response and prompting more production of IgE instead of the needed IgG in a continuing cycle.
e. Eventually, as the adaptive immunity mechanisms become less and less effective, the number of T cells destroyed exceeds the new T cells made, and the battle tilts in favor of the virus.

C. Transmission
1. The most common mode of transmission is by unprotected sex with an infected partner.
2. Infected mothers can pass it to a newborn during pregnancy, birth, or breastfeeding.
3. Small amounts of blood on shared needles can be passed among drug abusers.

D. Testing
1. Most AIDS tests check blood, saliva, or urine for antibodies that bind to HIV antigens.
2. Currently reliable tests are only available at clinical laboratories. Home tests may give false-negative results.

E. Treatments
1. Current drugs cannot cure HIV, but some can slow down its progression by interfering with viral replication.
2. Vaccines have not been effective because the virus replicates in the immune system and mutates quickly.
3. Researchers are working to develop an effective vaccine using an engineered virus with enough HIV components to provoke an immune response but not pose a threat.
4. Education and prevention are key to slowing the spread of HIV.

37.12 Vaccines

A. A primary vaccine mimics an infection; a booster brings about a secondary response and potentially a lifelong immunity.

B. The first vaccine was developed in the 1700s to the disease smallpox.
1. Edward Jenner injected liquid from a cowpox lesion into a patient.
a. Later, when exposed to the smallpox virus, the test subject was immune.
2. The smallpox virus was eradicated in 1977 due to the effective use of the vaccine.

C. Progress on an HIV Vaccine
1. Since the HIV virus mutates frequently, it is difficult to develop a vaccine that would be effective against all variants.
2. More than 25 models of HIV vaccines are currently being tested.
a. One promising vaccine involves the injection of three antibodies that come from a man who has survived AIDS for more than two decades.
b. It is thought that these antibodies may be able to be delivered to a patient via gene therapy.

37.13 Frankie's Last Wish (Revisited)

A. The Gardasil® vaccine is made of viral capsid proteins that develop into virus-like particles (VLP).
1. The proteins are produced by a genetically engineered yeast.
2. The vaccine does not transmit the virus, but protects against the four strains of the HPV virus.

Suggestions for Presenting the Material

- A quick glance at the figures in this chapter should convince anyone that the subject of body defense mechanisms is a difficult one both to teach and to learn. However, with patience and explicit use of those same figures, the topics can be mastered.
- The understanding of defense against foreign organisms by the human body is complicated by the fact that so many mechanisms and factors are operating at the same time. Remind students to use summary tables and animations provided in CengageNow to help with this information.
- You may wish to compare the "lines of defense" mentioned in the chapter to the military defense of a country. There are many analogies such as "general barriers" (moats aren't very useful anymore) and "scorched earth" (thank you, General Sherman). Nowadays, missiles (third line?) are very specific and fairly accurate.
- Students sometimes have difficulty distinguishing "antibody" from "antigen." This may help: Antigen is short for ***anti***body ***gen***erator. An antigen is something that encourages the body to make an antibody against it.
- The function of the thymus gland is expanded here in more detail from its introduction in the discussion of the endocrine system; remind students of the interconnection between endocrine control and immunity in addition to circulation and neural control.
- The topics of *immunization* and *immune diseases* are always of interest to students and should be given sufficient time to allow for student discussion.
- Remind the students that they have all had experiences with lymph nodes. When a patient complains of "swollen glands," they are actually mentioning the fact that lymph nodes in the neck area are undergoing an immune battle due to a foreign invader.
- Remind the students that phagocytosis is a non-specific process—the macrophage engulfs something that it determines is nonself. On the other hand, antibody production is a specific approach. The B cells make antibodies to a specific enemy, such as the measles virus.

Classroom and Laboratory Enrichment

- The dramatization of the suffering and death of a victim of AIDS (or a similar disease) will serve as an attention-getter for this topic.
- Tracking down the cause of an annoying allergy can involve some real detective work. Survey the class for such an experience, and ask for a brief oral report if the person is willing to share his/her experience.
- Ask an allergist to address the class, if available. How can an individual decrease their reaction to an allergen via a series of injections? Are there some allergies that are so strong and capable of eliciting an anaphylactic reaction, they cannot be lessened by allergy shots? Are some allergies life-threatening?
- With the assistance of a microbiology student, prepare Petri dishes onto which smears from the human mouth, nose, hands, head, as well as commonly touched surfaces are made. Identify the microorganisms present in each location.
- Does an insect's body carry many germs? Attempt to answer this by letting different insects including a cockroach, house fly, and cricket crawl over the surface of an agar-filled Petri dish.
- Interview a hospital epidemiologist to find out how a hospital environment fights the spread of infections, particularly MRSA.

- When discussing fevers, mention that the increased temperature disrupts the homeostasis in the body. The individual with a high fever will begin to sweat in an attempt to restore a normal temperature and resume homeostasis.
- In literature, milkmaids are always described as pretty. This is probably because they were immune to smallpox because of their exposure to cowpox. Therefore, they would not have the disfiguring scars of a smallpox victim.

Classroom Discussion Ideas

- How is AIDS perceived as a disease in differing countries of the world (homosexual, heterosexual, prostitutes, etc)?
- Could AIDS be the "grimmest" of the grim reapers Malthus wrote about in his essay (see bullet 3 in the section below)?
- What could be done to stem the epidemic of AIDS in African countries?
- Why hasn't anyone found a vaccine for AIDS yet?
- Why was the AIDS epidemic ignored for such a long time? Was the blood bank community slow in responding to protect the blood supply?
- Since advent of the AIDS epidemic, universal precautions have been instituted in medical settings. Under these conditions, everyone is considered dangerous, so you would not expose yourself to the blood or body fluids of any patient.
- The thymus is involved in the maturation of T cells. Unfortunately the thymus shrivels up and becomes less active in adulthood. If researchers could develop a way to keep the thymus very active throughout life, do you think this could be used as a treatment for AIDS?

Additional Ideas for Classroom Discussion

- Where does our term *vaccination* derive its meaning?
- Every year a small number of children die from diseases that develop as a result of vaccines received to protect them. It seems to be an inherent hazard associated with mass preventative inoculation. Is it worth the risk? Can you debate both sides of the issue?
- Thomas Malthus proposed three "grim reapers" that would restrain human population growth. One of these was "pestilence," or disease. How effective is disease as a population-limiting factor in the developed countries versus the underdeveloped countries?
- If there are so many infectious people as patients in hospitals, why aren't doctors and nurses continuously ill?
- What happens when parents refuse to inoculate their babies as mandated by various state and federal agencies? What are the inoculations for?
- Cancer of the thymus gland is called a thymoma, and is not common. If one of the treatments of this cancer is to remove the thymus gland, what might happen to a 30-year-old patient? What if the patient is two years old?
- Fever and inflammation are natural responses of our immune system. Is it wise to take over-the-counter medications to reduce these responses?
- Show a slide of a stained blood smear. Review the descriptions of the five types of white blood cells. After identifying each type of white blood cell, discuss its function in the immune system.
- Make sure the students understand the difference between the functions of T cells and B cells. B cells make an antibody after the T cells present the foreign object to them.

- There are some areas of the human body that maintain an acidic pH, such as the stomach and the vagina How does this help prevent the development of bacterial infections in those areas?
- A newborn is born with some immunity from its mother. In addition, some maternal antibodies are transmitted through the ingestion of colostrum (the thin yellow milk that the baby receives from mom in the first few days of life). How long does this immune protection from the mother last?

How Would You Vote? Classroom Discussion Ideas

- Monitor the voting for the online question. There is a certain segment of the population that feels that vaccinations are responsible for instilling illnesses, such as autism, in the population. Look into research that attempts to connect autism and other conditions to vaccination practices. Does this research sound feasible to the class? What other types of studies could be performed to settle this debate? Sometimes vaccination is no longer necessary, if the virus has been eradicated. This was the case with the smallpox virus, so individuals no longer receive that vaccine. There are other viruses, such as the polio virus, that are still prevalent, and if vaccinations were discontinued another epidemic could erupt. Poll the class to determine if they think the government has the right to mandate vaccinations.
- Have students complete final polling using JoinIN clickers.

Term Paper Topics, Library Activities, and Special Projects

- Controversy still surrounds the polio vaccines—Salk and Sabin. Explore the details of how each of these vaccines is made and used. Include the advantages and disadvantages of each.
- Research on the cause and treatment of AIDS has been rapid and continues to progress. Report on the latest strategies.
- Although vaccines are available throughout the world for the prevention of measles, diphtheria, and polio, there are about 20 other infectious diseases for which vaccines could be developed, but there seems to be little incentive to do so. Report on the reasons this is so.
- Polio and smallpox have been conquered by effective vaccination programs. Prepare a report on the development of the vaccine for either of these diseases; be sure to include the chronology of events leading up to the marketing of the vaccine.
- In the 1970s, the world was mesmerized by the "bubble boy," David Vetter, who had SCID and who lived for 12 years in a sterile plastic bubble. Research the history of David Vetter's treatment. What current treatments are available for children born with SCID? Would gene therapy work in this case?
- Report on the avian flu virus. Is there a vaccine for this virus?
- Research and report on human papillomavirus (HPV) and the vaccine available for the virus. What do you think of administering this virus to young children? Should this series of vaccinations be added to those of children shortly after birth?
- Based on the administration of Gardasil to females up to the age of 26 today, what decrease in the incidence of cervical cancer would we expect to find in 20 years? Recently Gardasil is recommended for administration to boys. Why do you think boys are included in this vaccination protocol even though they cannot get cervical cancer?
- Look into the connection between periodontal infections and cardiovascular health in recent literature.

- We tend to think of the childhood diseases (measles, mumps, chicken pox, rubella) as simply a nuisance. We forget that some individuals die from these illnesses each year. Which of these diseases may be detrimental for a pregnant woman to develop?
- Name bodily fluids that contain lysozymes. What is their purpose?
- When an individual receives a transfusion of incompatible blood, how does the immune system address this problem?
- Research which categories of antibodies can cross the placenta and affect the child in utero.
- Choose a particular autoimmune disease and learn the symptoms and potential treatments.

Possible Responses to *Critical Thinking* Questions

1. Many of us get a flu shot each year to protect us from infection with certain viruses. It is quite possible that you could get the flu, regardless of having the injection. Virologists estimate which viruses will come around each season. This is not just a guess on their part, because they study worldwide trends before drawing any conclusions. There is always the likelihood that you could become infected with an influenza virus that was not included in that year's vaccine. Also there is the possibility that you don't develop antibodies properly against those viruses. This explains why some individuals contract the common childhood diseases more than once. Lastly, there is the slim chance that the virus used to make the vaccine was not totally inactivated. So, the yearly flu shot is certainly not a guarantee that you will avoid contracting an influenza virus during that season, but it is one of the best defenses we have at this time.

2 Using monoclonal antibodies for immunization is passive immunity. Passive immunity is sometimes referred to as temporarily induced immunity. The body does not develop memory monoclonal antibodies since these are mouse antibodies. Thus the monoclonal antibodies are recognized as foreign and removed from circulation. Therefore, they are not kept around long. Since the body recognizes IgG from one's own immune system as *self,* these are not destroyed and the response to these antibodies is longer-term.

Possible Responses to *Data Analysis Exercise* Questions

In this study, researchers attempted to make a connection between the presence of various HPV viral infections and the incidence of cervical cancer.

1. At 110 months, approximately 1 percent of the women who had no cancer-causing HPV infections developed cervical cancer. In this same time interval, 17 percent of the women who tested positive for HPV16 had cervical cancer.
2. Those individuals that test positive for both HPV16 and HPV18 would probably be best represented by the line showing the incidence of HPV16-positive participants.
3. This study does not show the overall risk of cervical cancer in all types of HPV-positive individuals, because the one line represented all other cancer-causing HPV types combined. The incidence of cervical cancer would have to be investigated individually for each of the other HPV types as well.

38

RESPIRATION

Chapter Outline

Objectives

1. Understand the behavior of gases and the types of respiratory surfaces that participate in gas exchange.
2. Compare the mechanisms used in invertebrate and vertebrate respiration.
3. Be able to trace the route of air into and out of the human lungs.

4. Understand how the human respiratory system is related to the circulatory system, to cellular respiration, and to the nervous system.
5. Understand how respiration can be disrupted by damage to respiratory centers in the brain, physical obstructions, infectious disease, and pollutants.
6. Explain how humans and other animals adapt to deal with high altitude and deep water conditions.
7. Understand the risk of carbon monoxide exposure and its consequences.
8. Learn the health conditions associated with cigarette smoking.

Key Terms

nicotine
respiration
partial pressure
respiratory surface
surface-to-volume ratio
ventilation
respiratory proteins
hemoglobin
myoglobin
integumentary exchange
gills
lungs
tracheal system
spiracles
book lungs
countercurrent exchange
pharynx
larynx
glottis
epiglottis
trachea
bronchus, bronchi
bronchioles
alveolus, alveoli
diaphragm
intercostal muscles
respiratory cycle
inhalation
exhalation
Heimlich maneuver
vital capacity
tidal volume
respiratory membrane
oxyhemoglobin, HbO_2
bicarbonate, HCO_3^-
carbonic acid, HCO_3
carbonic anhydrase
carbon monoxide
bronchitis
emphysema
secondhand smoke
hypoxia
altitude sickness
acclimatization
erythropoietin

Lecture Outline

38.1 Carbon Monoxide—A Stealthy Poison
- A. Carbon Monoxide is a colorless, odorless poison.
  1. Hemoglobin binds more readily to carbon monoxide than it does to oxygen.
  2. Symptoms at around 15 percent exposure include nausea, dizziness, chest pain, and confusion.
  3. Smokers of a pack of cigarettes per day have a carbon monoxide exposure of around 5 percent.

38.2 The Nature of Respiration
- A. Gas Exchanges
  1. Respiratory systems rely on the diffusion of gases (oxygen and carbon dioxide) down pressure gradients.
  2. Gases enter and leave the internal environment by crossing moist respiratory surfaces.
     - a. The initial gas exchange occurs between the capillaries and the alveoli in the lungs.
     - b. The next gas exchange is between the capillaries and the tissues of the body.
- B. Factors Affecting Diffusion Rates
  1. Surface Area
     - a. As an animal grows, its surface area increases at a lesser rate than its volume, making diffusion of gases into the interior a problem.
     - b. Therefore, animals either must have a small, flattened body that keeps internal cells close to the surface or they must have specialized respiratory organs to move the gases inward.

2. Ventilation
    a. Moving air or water past a respiratory surface keeps the pressure gradient across the surface high and thus increases the rate of gas exchange.
    b. Humans and frogs breathe in and out to move air in and out of the lungs.
    c. Fish and other animals that live in the water have mechanisms that move water across their respiratory surface.
3. Respiratory Proteins
    a. The main transport pigment is hemoglobin, each molecule of which binds four molecules of oxygen in the lungs (high concentration) and releases them in the tissues where oxygen is low.
    b. Some invertebrates utilize hemerythrin or hemocyanin for oxygen transport.
    c. Myoglobin is another iron-containing respiratory pigment, which is a good storage molecule of oxygen because it has a higher affinity for oxygen.

C. Respiratory Medium—Air or Water?
1. The atmosphere contains 21 percent oxygen.
    a. Obtaining oxygen from the air is easier than procuring oxygen from water.
2. The dissolved oxygen (DO) content of water is crucial for aquatic animals.
    a. Water that flows freely with a lower temperature has a higher DO.
    b. Pollution and an excess of bacteria, algae, or protist growth can severely lower the DO.
    c. As the DO lowers, insects and fish species disappear.
    d. When the oxygen level is lower than 4 parts per million, only some annelids can survive.

38.3 Invertebrate Respiration

A. Respiration in Damp or Aquatic Habitats
1. Integumentary exchange occurs when gases diffuse directly across a moist body surface.
    a. This method of gas exchange is only adequate for small animals such as sponges, cnidarians, and flatworms.
2. Gills are highly folded, thin-walled projections that may be internal or external.
    a. They enhance exchange rates between the blood of aquatic animals and their watery environment.

B. Respiratory Adaptations to Life on Land
1. Snails and slugs live on land and in water, and have lungs in addition to gills.
2. Insects and spiders use a tracheal system that consists of repeatedly branching, air-filled tubes reinforced with chitin.
3. Some spiders and scorpions have book lungs in addition to tracheal tubes to enhance respiration.

38.4 Vertebrate Respiration

A. Respiration of Fishes
1. Gills contain filaments that hold many capillary beds where gases are exchanged with blood.
2. In all fishes, respiration occurs when water flows into the mouth, enters the pharynx, and then moves out of the body through the gill slits.
3. Water flows *over* the gills and blood circulates *through* them in opposing directions.
4. This mechanism, called countercurrent flow, is highly efficient in extracting oxygen from water, whose oxygen content is lower than air.

B. Evolution of Paired Lungs
1. Lungs became increasingly important as aquatic tetrapods spent more time on land.

2. Various animals use different mechanisms for respiration.
   a. Frogs in the larvae stage utilize gills and skin; as adults they use paired lungs and skin for respiration.
   b. Amniotes have waterproof skin and no gills; they use well-developed lungs for respiration.
      1) Birds have additional air sacs that move air in a one-way flow.

38.5 Human Respiratory System

A. The System's Many Functions
   1. The lungs accomplish gas exchange via alveoli.
   2. The respiratory system assists in sense of smell and in speech.
   3. It also helps return venous blood to the heart, and rid the body of excess heat and water.
   4. Controls over breathing adjust the body's acid-base balance as well as the body's temperature.

B. From Airways to Alveoli
   1. The Respiratory Passageways
      a. Air enters or leaves the respiratory system through nasal cavities where hair and cilia filter dust and particles, blood vessels warm the air, and mucus moistens the air.
      b. Air moves via this route: pharynx → larynx (route blocked by epiglottis during swallowing) → vocal cords (space between is glottis) → trachea → bronchi → bronchioles → alveoli.
         1) The vocal cords lie at the entrance to the larynx.
         2) When air is exhaled through the glottis, the folds of the cords vibrate to produce sounds, which are under regulation by nerve commands connecting them to the elastic ligaments that regulate the glottal opening.
   2. The Paired Lungs
      a. Human lungs are located in the thoracic cavity, one on each side of the heart; the rib cage encloses and protects the lungs.
      b. Each lung is covered with a pleural membrane, which covers the lung's outer surface and lines the inside of the thoracic cavity.
      c. Inside the lungs, respiratory bronchioles bear outpouchings of their walls called alveoli, which are usually clustered as alveolar sacs.
      d. Alveoli provide a tremendous surface area for gaseous exchange with the blood located in the dense capillary network surrounding each alveolar sac.
   3. Muscles and Respiration
      a. The diaphragm is a sheet of smooth muscle beneath the lungs; intercostal muscles are skeletal muscles between the ribs.
      b. The diaphragm and the intercostal muscles interact and exchange the volume of the thoracic cavity during breathing.

38.6 Cyclic Reversals in Air Pressure Gradients

A. The Respiratory Cycle
   1. In inhalation, the diaphragm contracts and flattens, muscles lift the rib cage upward and outward, the chest cavity volume increases, internal pressure decreases, and air rushes in.
   2. In exhalation, the actions listed above are reversed; the elastic lung tissue recoils passively.
   3. Pressure gradients between air inside and outside the respiratory tract change in each respiratory cycle of inhalation and exhalation.

4. Exhalation is passive when you are quietly breathing; it is active and energy-requiring when exercising with the need to expel more air.
5. The Heimlich maneuver forces air out of the lungs into the trachea and can dislodge the food, allowing the victim to resume breathing.

B. Respiratory Volumes
1. The maximum volume the lungs can hold is the total lung volume, which is 5.7 liters in males and 4.2 liters in females.
2. The tidal volume, about 0.5 liters, is the volume of air that moves into and out of the lungs in one respiratory cycle.

C. Control of Breathing
1. Respiratory centers in the brain control the rate and depth of breathing.
2. When activity levels increase, chemoreceptors sense changes in the blood pH and signal the respiratory center to alter breathing levels.
3. Reflexes, such as swallowing or coughing, and commands from the sympathetic nerves alter breathing patterns.

38.7 Gas Exchange and Transport

A. The Respiratory Membrane
1. The alveolar epithelium, the capillary epithelium, and their basement membranes form a respiratory membrane.
2. Oxygen and carbon dioxide passively diffuse across the membrane in response to partial pressure gradients.

B. Oxygen Transport
1. Blood cannot carry sufficient oxygen and carbon dioxide in *dissolved form* to satisfy the body's demands; hemoglobin helps enhance its capacity.
2. Oxygen diffuses down a pressure gradient into the blood plasma → red blood cells → binds to hemoglobin (four molecules per hemoglobin to form oxyhemoglobin).
3. Hemoglobin gives up its oxygen in tissues where partial pressure of oxygen is low, blood is warmer, partial pressure of carbon dioxide is higher, and pH is lower; all four conditions occur in tissues with high metabolism.
4. Myoglobin is found in cardiac muscle, and some skeleton muscles helps to store oxygen.

C. Carbon Dioxide Transport
1. Because carbon dioxide is higher in the body tissues, it diffuses into the blood.
2. Ten percent is dissolved in plasma, 30 percent binds with hemoglobin to form carbaminohemoglobin, and 60 percent is in bicarbonate form.
3. Bicarbonate and carbonic acid formation is enhanced by the enzyme carbonic anhydrase, which is located in the red blood cells.
4. Hemoglobin buffers these reactions, keeping the blood from becoming too acidic.

38.8 Respiration in Extreme Environments

A. High Climbers
1. At high altitudes, the partial pressure of oxygen is lower than at sea level.
2. The lungs of permanent residents of high mountains have more alveoli and blood vessels plus larger ventricles in the heart and more mitochondria in muscle tissue.
3. Acclimatization allows newcomers to high altitudes to adjust.
    a. The kidney cells release erythropoietin, which induces production of more red blood cells.
    b. Increased blood cell number creates more resistance to flow, which in turn makes the heart work harder to pump the blood.

B. Deep-Sea Divers

1. Since human divers use tanks of compressed air, they risk *nitrogen narcosis*, since water pressure increases with depth.
    a. Fluid pressure causes more gaseous nitrogen than usual to dissolve in the body's interstitial fluid, causing the gas to dissolve into the cell membrane's lipid bilayer.
    b. Signal propagation in neural membranes becomes disrupted, leading to diver euphoria and drowsiness, like being tipsy.
    c. At deeper depths, below 106 to 122 meters, divers can become comatose.
2. If a diver ascends too rapidly, the change in pressures will force the nitrogen to leave the tissues of the body and pass into the blood, often as bubbles, causing pain in the joints known as "the bends" or decompression sickness.
3. The respiratory system of the leatherback turtles, sperm whales, and other marine animals are modified to collect and store oxygen by several mechanisms including the use of myoglobin, deep breathing, and gliding.

38.9 Respiratory Diseases and Disorders

A. Interrupted Breathing
1. Sleep apnea and sudden infant death syndrome (SIDS) are caused by a stop in breathing.
    a. To decrease the risk of SIDS, have the baby sleep on their back or side.
2. Damage to the respiratory control center and weak signals (fewer serotonin receptors) may lead to these respiratory stresses.

B. Tuberculosis and Pneumonia
1. About one-third of the human population carries the bacteria that cause tuberculosis.
    a. Approximately 10 percent of these carriers will develop the disease, which can be cured with long treatment courses of antibiotics.
2. Other viruses and bacteria can infect the lungs.
    a. Pneumonia is a general term for inflammation caused by an infectious organism.

C. Bronchitis, Asthma, and Emphysema
1. Chronic irritation of the lining of the bronchioles leads to bronchitis, in which there is an excess of mucus that may promote bacterial growth.
2. Asthma is constriction of the airways often caused by a trigger, such as allergies, exercise, or irritants.
3. In emphysema, the walls of the alveoli become fibrous and inefficient in exchange of gases.

D. Smoking's Impact
1. Tobacco use kills millions and in the U.S. drains over $22 billion a year from the economy.
    a. Smoking kills about half of its users.
2. Secondhand smoke is a real danger to innocents who do not participate in the life-threatening habit themselves.
3. Smoking marijuana may also lead to chronic throat problems, bronchitis, and emphysema.

38.10 Carbon Monoxide—A Stealthy Poison (Revisited)

A. Carbon monoxide exposure is reversible.
1. In a normal environment, half of the carbon monoxide will be replaced with oxygen in 4–5 hours.
2. This process can be accelerated by exposing the patient to 100 percent oxygen in a hyperbaric chamber.

B. Carbon monoxide exposure should be limited.
1. Don't smoke or expose yourself to second-hand smoke.

2. Annually check any heaters that use fossil fuels.
3. Monitor wood burning stoves and fireplaces carefully.
4. Install carbon monoxide detectors.

Suggestions for Presenting the Material

- The presentation of respiration can be effectively accomplished by following the sequence of the text. The outline begins with a survey of respiratory surfaces, then focuses on human respiratory organs and function, and concludes with mention of respiratory problems.
- When describing various respiratory surfaces, emphasize the one common feature they all share—moisture.
- Distinguish the arthropod *tracheas* from other respiratory surfaces by emphasizing their independence from the circulatory system.
- A convenient way to present the human respiratory system is to display Figure 39.12 (or its animation) and follow the pathway of an inhaled and exhaled breath.
- As you describe the *glottis* and *epiglottis,* be sure to include a note on the *Heimlich maneuver* (Figure 38.16). Mention that a variation on the Heimlich maneuver can be performed if an individual is alone while choking.
- Emphasize the correct pronunciation of *larynx* (lair-inks) and *pharynx* (fair-inks).
- Be sure to stress the passivity of the lungs (compare to balloon) during respiration, and emphasize the role of the diaphragm and rib muscles.
- Highlight the differences between the ways oxygen and carbon dioxide are transported in the blood.
- *Respiratory control* is a fitting capstone to previous discussions.
- Emphasize that the respiratory organs have some non-respiratory functions such as coughing, sneezing, speech, yawning, regulation of pH, and sense of smell.
- Be sure to clarify the difference between breathing and respiration. Breathing or ventilation refers to the act of air moving in and out of the lungs. Respiration refers to the actual gas exchange involving oxygen and carbon dioxide.
- Now that you know the connection between respiratory surfaces and the need for moisture, can you see why earthworms are often seen on wet sidewalks?
- Discuss the large surface area of the alveoli. Some sources say it is over 70 m^2!
- Much of the ductwork in the human respiratory system contains cartilage to prevent its collapse. Demonstrate how this distribution of cartilage minimizes and disappears by the time the air gets to the alveoli, so that gas exchange can occur.

Classroom and Laboratory Enrichment

- Show how the measurement of oxygen consumption can be used to determine rate of metabolism by use of a simple respirometer (see a biological supply catalog). Alternatively, a computer simulation of the experiment may suffice.
- Use a spirometer (either the hand-held or water-displacement models) to measure the tidal volumes of members of the class. It is best to measure the tidal volume three times on each individual in the class and then average the three values. Are there any significant differences between different populations in the class? Males versus females? Smokers versus non-smokers? Regular exercisers versus couch potatoes?

- Ask for volunteers to debate non-smoker versus smoker rights. Ask them to provide data rather than emotional attacks.
- Have a person who has visited a high-altitude location report on the breathing discomforts he/she experienced.
- Construct or purchase a working model of the lungs, chest cavity, and diaphragm. If your university has an animal or meat lab you may be able to get unpreserved sheep's lungs to demonstrate how they expand by using a flexible pipe as a trachea and blowing into the lungs. Alternatively, display a freeze-dried preparation of a sheep's lungs.
- Demonstrate the Heimlich maneuver on a class volunteer; then ask classmates to demonstrate (gently!) on one another.
- Invite a scuba diver to discuss the special gas composition and gas exchange problems associated with deep dives. Have the diver explain the preventative steps that are taken to avoid the "bends."
- Use a chart or dissectible mannequin to locate major organs of the human respiratory system.
- Exhibit a model of a human larynx and trachea.
- Display a freeze-dried preparation of a sheep's lungs or obtain a sheep pluck (a lung and heart combination) from a butcher shop.
- Obtain preserved lung tissues of a smoker and non-smoker. Create a display of these lungs presenting statistics on the effects of smoking on the body.
- Everyone has experienced a time where something went down the "wrong pipe." Show a model of the respiratory system to illustrate the positions of both the trachea and the esophagus. Describe how the epiglottis helps prevent this from happening.
- Show slides of the alveoli to illustrate how the membranes are very thin, to facilitate diffusion.
- Demonstrate ventilation using a Boyle's law apparatus. If one is not available, you can build your own by using a water bottle, two balloons, a straw, a rubber band, and some duct tape. Cut the bottom off of the water bottle and stretch one of the balloons across the entire bottom of the bottle. Secure the balloon tightly with duct tape. Now attach the balloon to one end of the straw with the rubber band. Insert the straw-balloon apparatus into the water bottle. Cover the remaining area at the top of the bottle with duct tape. Now you can see how altering the position of the balloon at the bottom (representing the diaphragm) alters the inflation of the inner balloon (representing a lung).

Classroom Discussion Ideas

- Why hasn't the message concerning the dangers of smoking reached teenagers and altered their taking up of the habit? How might education efforts be focused to "get through" to them?
- Should smokers be subject to higher insurance rates (medical and automobile) due to the higher costs they incur, to avoid forcing the insurance companies to pass on the costs to everyone else?
- Should pregnant women who smoke be fined, or treated as mothers accused of child abuse are treated?
- Cigarette packs now display graphic photos depicting individuals that have developed lung disease as a result of smoking. Do you think these pictures will serve as an effective deterrent?
- Obtain slides of diseased lungs from a local hospital pathology lab to show the actual result of exposure to cigarette smoke.
- How do cigarette ads target certain populations, such as children and women? Do you think any of these ad campaigns should be discontinued?
- Highlight a student who is now an ex-smoker. What method did they use to break the habit? How would they advise others who are interested in quitting?

- Present the class with appropriate hotlines to call if they desire to break the smoking habit. One of these numbers is 1-800-QUITNOW.

Additional Ideas for Classroom Discussion

- Which of the following *respiratory surfaces* does not require participation of the blood for delivery of oxygen to the tissues: (a) integument, (b) gills, (c) tracheas, or (d) lungs?
- What is the singular advantage of the one-way flow of air in the *parabronchi* of the bird lung?
- What is happening in the condition we call "hiccups"? What causes it? What are the best short-term remedies? On what physiological principles (if any) are they based?
- Why is the best body position for public speaking and singing, a standing or "sitting tall" position?
- The air at high altitudes is sometimes described in everyday language as "thin." How does this translate in technical terms?
- Can you die from holding your breath? Explain the neural mechanisms that are operating here.
- What are the functions of the sinuses?
- "Respiratory distress syndrome" (hyaline membrane disease) is the primary cause of respiratory difficulty in immature newborns. What are its symptoms and cause? How is it treated? How does it help to determine the earliest gestational age that is survivable?
- How might a change in water temperature affect the rate of oxygen uptake from the environment for a marine fish? Would the change also affect carbon dioxide elimination?
- Make a list of organisms that respire entirely via integumentary exchange. What characteristics do these animals share?
- How does the flapping of wings help in the ventilation of insects and birds?
- Draw a diagram or use a prepared graphic to illustrate countercurrent exchange in fishes.
- Stress the importance of the diaphragm, the primary muscle involved in breathing.

How Would You Vote? Classroom Discussion Ideas

- Monitor the voting for the online question. As the text states, carbon monoxide exposure is a particularly dangerous poison, because it is odorless and colorless. In addition, a victim of carbon monoxide exposure may become headachy and tired, so the symptoms may go unnoticed. So the answer to eliminating carbon monoxide poisoning lies with prevention. Have a student in the class look up the average numbers of carbon monoxide deaths per year. In addition, another student could determine the cost of a carbon monoxide detector. Do the students think that hotels would be willing to absorb the additional cost? Can you put a price on a human life? Do most of the members of your class have carbon monoxide detectors in their homes?
- Have students complete polling using JoinIN clickers.

Term Paper Topics, Library Activities, and Special Projects

- Vertebrate muscular activity is dependent on an oxygen supply carried by the blood (specifically, red cells). When demand exceeds supply, an *oxygen debt* is incurred and activity slows or stops. Such is not the case with insects, with their indefatigable flight muscles. Investigate why this difference exists.

- Certain woodwind musicians have perfected a breathing technique that allows the production of continuous sound from the instrument. Investigate reports of this technique, and interview a practitioner. Arrange a demonstration, if possible.
- The length of the vocal cords that stretch across the glottis help to determine the pitch of your voice. Longer vocal cords produce a lower pitch. Relate this information to the stringed instruments of an orchestra. Can you see why a cello has a much deeper pitch than a violin?
- What is happening in the condition we call "hiccups"? What causes it? What are the best short-term remedies? On what physiological principles (if any) are they based?
- Research how many people in the United States die of simple choking each year. What age is most affected? What is the most commonly lodged object? Are there other demographics in this group or is it a random event.
- Using cigarette ads gathered from magazines published during the past 40 years, show the change in public attitude toward smoking.
- How might the anatomy and physiology of persons who were born and raised at very high altitudes be different from those who were born and raised in the lowlands and who have only recently become acclimated to high elevations?
- How do nicotine patches work? How effective are they? Research the statistics available for their success rates.
- Investigate the effects of air pollution on respiratory functions. Look into the air quality ratings for your area. How many were unsuitable over the last year?
- Look up the Tubifex sludge worms. What adaptations do they have that allow them to survive in water with a low oxygen content?
- Choose one of the gas laws (Boyle's, Charles', Dalton's, or Henry's) and discuss how it relates to either respiration or ventilation.
- Discuss three methods of transport for carbon dioxide in the bloodstream.
- How do athletes take advantage of the function of erythropoietin when performing blood doping?
- Choose a lung disease to present to the class. Possible conditions are: emphysema, black lung disease, asthma, and COPD.

Possible Responses to *Critical Thinking* Questions

1. A zinc deficiency alters the structure, and thus the function, of carbonic anhydrase. Carbonic anhydrase is a critical enzyme that catalyzes the reaction of carbon dioxide and water to carbonic acid, which is later converted to bicarbonate. Without zinc, this reaction is impaired and the removal of carbon dioxide is reduced.
2. The human heart is a two-pump system where oxygenated blood and deoxygenated blood are clearly separated. When studying Figure 38.21, it is not surprising that some of the vessels have similar partial pressures of oxygen and carbon dioxide. For example, the pulmonary veins are returning oxygenated blood to the heart. Therefore, it is logical that the same levels of oxygen and carbon dioxide would be present at the start of the systemic capillaries prior to the gas exchange that occurs in the capillary network. On the same note, the vessels at the start of the systemic veins carry deoxygenated blood back to the heart. Once this blood passes through the right side of the heart, it enters the pulmonary arteries on the way to the lungs. Thus, again the partial pressures of oxygen and carbon dioxide would be the same in those two vessels.
3. Oxygen is an important component of aerobic respiration because it serves as an electron acceptor in the electron transport chain.

4. It is in the best interest of the fetus that fetal hemoglobin has a greater affinity for oxygen than adult hemoglobin. This allows the fetus better access to oxygen from the placental system even though the maternal oxygen level is rather low there. By approximately 3–6 months of age, the infant will have entirely converted their fetal hemoglobin to the adult form.

Possible Responses to *Data Analysis Exercise* Questions

Radon, like carbon monoxide, is another stealthy poison, since it is both odorless and colorless. The difference between the two substances, however, is that radon is released from rocks and soil. Studies are performed to assess the danger of radon exposure.

1. Approximately 20 smokers would expire from radon-induced lung cancer over a lifetime of 1.3 pCi/L exposure.
2. The radon level would have to be approximately 12 pCi/L in order to have the same amount of non-smokers expire as smokers in the previous question.
3. For a smoker who is living in a home with a normal radon level, the risk of expiring from radon exposure is almost three times greater than dying of an auto accident.

39

DIGESTION AND NUTRITION

Chapter Outline

Objectives

1. Know the various ways in which a digestive system can be structured. Realize the behavioral limitations of organisms with incomplete digestive systems.
2. Understand the structure and function of the various regions of the human digestive system.
3. Summarize the daily nutritional requirement of a 25-year-old man who works at a desk job and exercises very little. State what he needs in energy, carbohydrates, proteins, and lipids, and name at least six vitamins and six minerals that he needs to include in his diet every day.

4. Explain how the human body manages to meet the energy and nutritional needs of the various body parts even though the person may be feasting sometimes and fasting at other times.
5. Know the requirements of vitamins, minerals, and phytochemicals that are needed daily.
6. Understand the importance of microbes in the digestive tract.
7. Know the ill effects from eating disorders that involve either too much or too little nutrition.

Key Terms

adipose tissue
probiotic
leptin
obesity
ghrelin
gastric bypass surgery
nutrition
digestive system
incomplete digestive system
complete digestive system
motility
secretion
digestion
absorption
elimination
food-intake
food-processing
crop
gizzard
cloaca
ruminants
gut
lumen
tongue
pharynx
esophagus
trachea
epiglottis
sphincter
stomach
large intestine, colon
gastrointestinal tract
peristalsis
rectum
anus
tooth
enamel
dentin
pulpy matrix
incisors
canines
premolars
molars
salivary glands
saliva
salivary amylase
bicarbonate (HCO_3^-)
mucins
hydrochloric acid
gastric fluid
pepsinogen
chyme
gastrin
pepsins
peptic ulcers
pyloric sphincter
small intestine
duodenum
jejunum
ileum
mucosa
trypsin
chymotrypsin
pancreas
lipases
bile
liver
gallbladder
emulsification
triglycerides
segmentation
cholecystokinin, CCK
gastric inhibitory peptide, GIP
secretin
microvilli
villi, (villus)
brush border cells
cotransporters
micelle formation
chylomicrons
cecum
bulk
constipation
feces
appendix
appendicitis
colon polyps
colonoscopy
virtual colonoscopy
organic metabolism
food pyramid
complex carbohydrates
high glycemic index
essential fatty acids
cholesterol
complete proteins
incomplete proteins
essential amino acids
Mediterranean diet
antioxidant
low-carb diets
ketones
vitamins
minerals
phytochemical
ideal weight
body mass index (BMI)
kilocalorie
PYY3-36

Lecture Outline

39.1 Your Microbial "Organ"

A. Before 1980, physicians thought that ulcers were caused by stress or diet.

B. Later, researchers discovered that *Helicobacter pylori*, a bacterium, was largely responsible.

1. Not everyone that has *H. pylori* develops ulcers.
2. *H. pylori* can be destroyed by antibiotics.
   a. Individuals without *H. pylori* are more apt to have GERD.
3. Infection with *H. pylori* increases one's risk of stomach cancer.

C. Scientists feel that a decline in *Bifidobacterium* may be a factor in irritable bowel syndrome (IBS).

1. Many patients with IBS get relief by administration of a probiotic dose of *Bifidobacterium.*

D. Physicians are realizing that the microbial balance in our digestive system is important for good health.

39.2 The Nature of Digestive Systems

A. A digestive system mechanically and chemically reduces food to particles and molecules small enough to be absorbed into the internal environment.

B. Incomplete and Complete Systems

1. An incomplete digestive system (for example, in a flatworm) has one opening.
    a. Food enters and waste leaves through the same opening.
    b. Digestive products are absorbed directly to the needy tissues.
2. A complete digestive system is a tube with two openings, allowing food to move in one direction through the lumen; it performs five tasks.
    a. *Mechanical processing and motility* is the breaking up, mixing, and transporting of food material.
    b. *Secretion* is the release of needed enzymes and other substances into the lumen.
    c. *Digestion* is the chemical breakdown of food matter to molecules small enough to cross the gut lining.
    d. *Absorption* is the passage of digested nutrients into the blood and lymph.
    e. *Elimination* is the expulsion of undigested and unabsorbed residues at the end of the gut.

C. Diet-Related Structural Adaptations

1. Beaks and Bites
    a. Birds have a beak that is designed to accommodate its diet.
        1) The pigeon has a short beak to pick up seeds off the ground.
    b. Mammals have different numbers and types of teeth appropriate for their food intake.
        1) Carnivores have prominent canine teeth for ripping meat.
        2) Herbivores do not have canines, but use incisors for functions such as pulling up grasses.
        3) Humans and some other mammals have broad molars, which are used for grinding.
2. Gut Specialization
    a. Birds have a crop that fills with food, a gizzard that grinds up food, and a stomach with keratin plates for grinding.
    b. Ruminants have many chambers classified as stomachs.
        1) The first few chambers contain microbes to digest cellulose.
        2) Over time the animal regurgitates its food to perform additional mechanical digestion.
    c. Herbivores typically have longer digestive tracts than carnivores, with expandable stomachs to accept a lot of food in a single sitting.

39.3 Overview of the Human Digestive System

A. The human digestive system is a tube with two openings and many specialized regions.

1. The mouth is designed to break the food into smaller pieces and begin digestion via exposure to saliva.
2. The pharynx (throat) is a shared structure that leads to the esophagus.
3. The stomach churns the food and exposes it to gastric juices.
4. The small intestine is an area of much digestion due to the accessory structures.
5. The large intestine serves to absorb water and remove wastes from the body via the anus.

B. The digestive system also contains accessory organs that contribute to digestion.
   1. The salivary glands secrete saliva, which begins the digestion of starches in the mouth.
   2. The liver produces bile, which emulsifies fats.
   3. The gallbladder stores and concentrates bile.
   4. The pancreas secretes pancreatic juice, which is rich in digestive enzymes.

39.4 Digestion in the Mouth

A. Thirty-two teeth in humans interact with saliva to mechanically and chemically prepare food in the mouth.
   1. Teeth are hardened jaw appendages with an enamel coat over dentin and calcium with a pulpy matrix.
      a. Incisors bite off chunks, canines tear, and premolars and molars grind food.
   2. Saliva (from salivary glands) contains salivary amylase to begin carbohydrate digestion, bicarbonate to neutralize acids, and mucins to lubricate.

39.5 Food Storage and Digestion in the Stomach

A. The stomach is a muscular sac that stores and mixes food, secretes substances that dissolve and degrade food, and controls the rate at which food enters the small intestine.
   1. Gastric fluid includes hydrochloric acid, pepsinogens, and mucus.
      a. HCl dissolves bits of food to form a soupy chyme; it also converts pepsinogen (inactive) to pepsin (active).
      b. Pepsin begins the digestion of proteins.
      c. Normally, mucus and bicarbonate ions protect the stomach lining; but if these are blocked, hydrogen ions stimulate the release of histamine, which in turn stimulates release of more HCl, which may result in a peptic ulcer.
   2. Peristaltic contractions churn the chyme and keep the sphincter of the stomach's exit closed, but small amounts are released at regular intervals into the small intestine.

39.6 Structure of the Small Intestine

A. The three regions are the duodenum, jejunum, and ileum.
   1. These regions form a total of 16–23 feet of coiled intestine.

B. The inner lining of the small intestine has several adaptations.
   1. There are villi, fingerlike projections, lining the small intestine.
      a. Each villus is covered in microvilli, sometimes referred to as a brush border.
   2. The villi and microvilli increase the internal surface area for more effective absorption.

39.7 Digestion and Absorption in the Small Intestine

A. Secretions from the liver, gallbladder, and pancreas enter via a common duct to make the small intestine the site of the most digestion in the body.

B. Carbohydrate Digestion and Absorption
   1. The digestion of carbohydrate begins in the mouth with salivary amylase breaking polysaccharides into disaccharides.
   2. In the small intestine, pancreatic juice performs this same function.
   3. In the brush border regions, disaccharides are further broken down into monosaccharides.
      a. The monosaccharides enter the brush border cells and enter a villus on their way to the bloodstream.

C. Protein Digestion and Absorption
   1. The digestion of proteins begins in the stomach, with pepsin breaking proteins into polypeptides.

2. When polypeptides or fats enter the small intestine, cholecystokinin (CCK) is released into the bloodstream.
    a. This causes the pancreas to release pancreatic enzymes, trypsin and chymotrypsin, into the small intestine to produce peptide fragments.
3. Brush border enzymes break the fragments into amino acids, which enter brush border cells and eventually the bloodstream.

D. Fat Digestion and Absorption
1. Fat digestion begins and ends in the small intestine.
    a. Bile from the liver and/or gallbladder emulsifies the fats.
        1) Emulsification involves taking a big fat globule and breaking it into smaller globules, which facilitates the enzymatic breakdown of fats.
2. Lipase from pancreatic juice begins to digest the small globules of fats.
3. The digested fats enter a villus via diffusion in the brush border cells.
4. Inside the villi, triglycerides develop protein coats so that as lipoproteins they can move into interstitial fluid.
5. The triglycerides travel from interstitial fluid, to lymph vessels, and to the bloodstream.

E. Fluid Absorption
1. The small intestine absorbs approximately 80 percent of the water that is in the small intestine.

39.8 The Large Intestine

A. Structure and Function
1. The large intestine stores and concentrates feces—undigested and unabsorbed material, water, and bacteria.
2. The large intestine begins as a cup-shaped pouch at its junction with the small intestine (appendix attached here).
3. The main portion of the large intestine, the colon, contains *E. coli* bacteria that make vitamin B12.
4. It is draped across the lower abdomen and ends in a rectum (feces storage), which opens to the outside through the anus.

B. Disorders
1. Several factors, including stress and a low-bulk diet, can delay defecation, resulting in constipation.
2. Fecal material lodged in the appendix can lead to the complications of appendicitis.
3. Some people are genetically predisposed to develop colon polyps, which start as benign growths, but may later become cancerous.
    a. Colon cancer is highly curable when detected early enough.
    b. Diagnosis can come from a colonoscopy and a virtual colonoscopy, which uses x-rays and a computer to generate an image of the colon.

39.9 Metabolism of Absorbed Organic Compounds

A. Nutrient molecules are shuffled and reshuffled once they have been absorbed.
1. All cells continually recycle some carbohydrates, lipids, and proteins by breaking them apart.
2. Cells use the products as energy sources and building blocks.

B. When you eat, excess carbohydrates and other organic compounds are converted to fat for storage in adipose tissue or converted to glycogen in the liver and muscle tissue.

C. Between meals, glucose levels are maintained by breakdown of glycogen reserves in the liver, and amino acids are converted to glucose; adipose cells degrade fats to glycerol and fatty acids, all which enter the blood.

D. The liver stores, converts, and maintains the concentrations of required organic compounds in the blood; it inactivates most hormones, sending them to the kidneys for excretion, and it removes worn-out red blood cells and detoxifies chemicals.

39.10 Human Nutritional Requirements

A. USDA Dietary Recommendations

1. The USDA has recently issued a set of nutritional guidelines to replace its earlier "food pyramid," based on extensive nutritional research.
2. The diet recommends lowering the intake of refined grains, saturated fats, *trans*-fatty acids, and added sugars or caloric sweeteners, and no more than one teaspoon of salt daily.
3. More fruits and vegetables with high potassium and fiber content are encouraged, with fat-free or low-fat milk products and whole grains; 55 percent of daily caloric intake is to come from carbohydrates.

B. Energy-Rich Carbohydrates

1. Complex carbohydrates provide the body with glucose, fiber, and vitamins.
   a. Soluble fiber present in many fruits and vegetables helps move food through the digestive tract.
   b. Soluble fiber also helps lower cholesterol and lower your heart disease risk.
2. Highly processed carbohydrates such as refined sugar and high fructose corn syrup are empty calories since they have little nutritional value.
3. Approximately 1 percent of the population has celiac disease, where the villa in the intestines is inflamed due to ingestion of gluten.
   a. A diet devoid of gluten solves the problem.

C. Good Fat, Bad Fat

1. Phospholipids and cholesterol are important components of membranes; fats are energy reserves and provide insulation and cushioning.
2. The body needs very little polyunsaturated fat to supply the essential fatty acids, those not made by the body itself.
   a. Polyunsaturated fats include omega-3 fatty acids and omega-6 fatty acids.
      1) Omega-3 fatty acids can reduce inflammation associated with cardiovascular disease and arthritis.
      2) These same fatty acids help to keep a diabetic's glucose level more consistent.
3. Oleic acid from olive oil can help prevent heart disease.
4. A diet that is laden with lots of meat and dairy products could cause an increased incidence of heart disease and cancer.
5. *Trans* fats have been shown to be even more deleterious to one's heart health.

D. Body-Building Proteins

1. Of the 20 different amino acids in proteins, eight are essential (that is, must be supplied in the diet).
2. Most proteins in animal tissues are complete; their amino acid ratios match human nutritional needs.
3. Nearly all plant proteins are incomplete, in that they lack one or more amino acids that are essential for humans.
   a. A vegetarian diet can supply all essential nutrients if they are eaten in adequate combinations.

39.11 Vitamins, Minerals, and Phytochemicals

A. Humans need small amounts of at least 13 organic molecules, called vitamins, to assist in cellular metabolism.

1. Some studies suggest that supplementing vitamins A, C, and E may counter the effects of aging, protecting the immune system by inactivating free radicals.

B. Inorganic substances, called minerals (Ca, Mg, K, and Fe, for example), are also needed.

C. A balanced diet will normally meet all requirements for these substances for people who are in good health; excessive intake is at the least wasteful and at the worst harmful.

D. Phytochemicals, supplied by plants, are also essential to reduce the risk of certain diseases.

39.12 Maintaining a Healthy Weight

A. What Is a Healthy Weight?

1. Body mass index (BMI), a ratio of weight and height, is a good way to measure ideal or overweight conditions.
   a. A score of 25 to 29.9 are considered overweight; a score of 30 or more indicates obesity.

B. Why Is Obesity Unhealthy?

1. Obesity is an overabundance of fat in adipose tissue that may lead to health problems.
   a. Type II diabetes, heart disease, cancer, etc. are only some of the potential health issues associated with obesity.
2. Obese individuals have additional triglycerides in their fat cells, which interferes with their functioning.
   a. These damaged cells encourage inflammation in the body that can increase cancer risks or interfere with the functioning of insulin.

C. Genetics of Obesity

1. Genes may have an influence on whether or not we gain weight.
2. A study of twins found that genetic differences affected the response each set had to overfeeding or to losing weight.
3. Scientists have discovered the ob gene, which produces leptin, an appetite suppressor.
   a. Experiments performed on mice show that those without the ob gene become obese.
   b. Few individuals have a leptin deficiency.
4. Another more common gene called flo has been isolated in humans and also leads to obesity.
5. In most individuals, the secret to dieting is not genetic—just move more and eat less.

D. Eating Too Little

1. Anorexia nervosa is a condition where an individual is not within 15 percent of their normal weight.
   a. Anorexia may have a genetic basis, but is also largely due to social pressures.
   b. Anorexia can have disastrous effects on bone and heart health.
2. Bulimia nervosa is a condition where an individual binges and then purges by vomiting.
   a. This condition may damage both esophageal cells and teeth.
   b. It can also lead to an improper pH, which upsets the body's homeostasis.

39.13 Your Microbial "Organ" (Revisited)

A. It is difficult to instill live cultures of microbes into the body and have them survive.

1. Some are given as pills or in foods such as yogurt.

B. Some scientists suggest a procedure called a fecal transplant.

1. This involves the transmission of feces from a healthy individual into the colon of a person whose colon is microbe-depleted.

Suggestions for Presenting the Material

- After a brief discussion of incomplete versus complete digestive systems, this chapter focuses on two main topics: (a) human digestive organs and function, and (b) human nutritional needs and metabolism.
- The traditional and most logical method of presentation is to follow a mouthful of food as it passes from mouth to anus. Along the way, you can be as detailed as your course requires. For example, you may ask students to know structures, general secretions, and main functions as presented in Figure 39.5 but add only a few, all, or none of the enzymes in Table 39.1
- Similarly, you will need to inform students as to the amounts of material from Tables 39.3 (vitamins) and 39.4 (minerals) you require them to learn. Certainly, the authors of the text did not intend for these tables to be memorized entirely but provided them for reference and completeness.
- As each digestive organ is discussed, reference to an overhead transparency of Figure 39.5 (human digestive system) should be made. Students can also follow along using the summary material provided in Table 39.1.
- At some point in your discussion, be sure to emphasize that *digestion* and *absorption* are inseparable in the total function of providing nutrition to body cells.
- Students will enjoy your lectures more if you include brief notes on the various "problems along the way" that cause us minor, and occasionally major, distress.
- Nutrition is receiving increasingly more emphasis in our lives. You may wish to devote an entire lecture to this timely topic. This is also an excellent opportunity to review the contents of Chapter 3 (carbon compounds in cells).
- This is an ideal time to discuss some of the fad weight-loss diets as well as the more legitimate ones. Students are extremely interested in this topic, and it is a beneficial one for them to discuss.
- When discussing obesity, introduce the concept of body mass index (BMI) as an indicator of the degree of obesity. Consult a nutrition text for details.
- The pancreas is both an exocrine and an endocrine gland. Show a histology slide of the pancreas and point out both acini cells (produce pancreatic juice) and islets of Langerhans (produce insulin and glucagon). It is interesting to see the distinct clusters of cells with different functions.
- Mention the time that food is spent in each digestive structure—from several seconds in the esophagus to maybe days in the large intestine.
- Has anyone in the class had their gallbladder removed? Have them describe their symptoms of gallbladder disease. Did they have a large incision or the latest laparoscopic procedure?
- For each structure in the human digestive tract, name the mechanical and chemical (enzymatic) digestion that occurs.
- If the students are overwhelmed with all the digestive enzymes, stick to the main ones:
    - Saliva – amylase
    - Gastric juice – pepsin
    - Pancreatic juice – trypsin, lipase, and amylase
    - Liver, gallbladder – bile
    - Small intestine – localized hormones

Classroom and Laboratory Enrichment

- Because the digestive organs lie cramped in a small space, one upon the other, drawings such as Figure 39.5 are not as useful as showing life-size models. If your department has one, use it throughout your journey through the G-I tract.
- Demonstrate peristalsis by placing a ball of suitable size inside a flexible tube (such as a section of old bicycle tire inner tube) and squeezing to move it along.
- Show a film depicting the consequences of vitamin and mineral deficiencies in the human diet.
- Ask if any volunteers from within the class, or outside, would be willing to tell the class about his/her digestive or eating disorder.
- Use molecular models to demonstrate the process of digestion.
- Mix oil and water together in a flask to show their immiscibility. Then add soap to the mixture to illustrate emulsification.
- Demonstrate the action of amylase on carbohydrates. Chew crackers for a few minutes. Remove some of the cracker mixture from your mouth and test it with iodine. (A positive test for the presence of starch is that iodine turns starch a blue-black color.) Now continue chewing the rest of the cracker for quite a while. Eventually the cracker will begin to taste sweet, indicating that the starch has been broken down into sugars. You can confirm this with the iodine test (it should not turn a darker color). This shows why the digestion of starches must be revisited later in the digestive tract. I highly doubt that any of us take a two-hour lunch to complete starch digestion in the mouth!
- Have each student journal their food intake for three days. Dissect each meal to determine if it looks like minimum daily requirements are met. Are there any deficiencies? Are there too many "empty" calories? Have other students critique your diet with suggestions for improvement.
- Obtain a tooth model from an anatomy lab. Illustrate the parts of a typical tooth. Pay special attention to the periodontal ligaments that hold the tooth securely in its socket.
- Does anyone in the class have the full complement of 32 teeth? Many will not, because it appears as though our mouths are evolving smaller and have inadequate room for wisdom teeth.

Classroom Discussion Ideas

- Millions of people around the world suffer from deficiencies in amount and nutritional composition of food. Surprisingly, dietary disorders of persons in affluent countries result from "too much of good things." What are the consequences of the American diet?
- Diet plans for weight reduction are numerous and proliferating daily. How can the wary consumer recognize a plan that could be dangerous?
- With the discovery of hormones that are influential in appetite, is it possible that overweight persons will dismiss their problem with "My hormones made me do it"? How can thyroid hormones influence your weight?
- Ask the class to describe different diets they have tried. Do these diets sound like they provide the minimum daily requirements of nutrients? Which diets have been successful over time?

Additional Ideas for Classroom Discussion

- What is meant by "heartburn"? Is its use in television antacid advertising misleading, especially for young viewers? What would you propose as a better term?

- How is the stomach of a cow like the gut of a termite? How could antibiotics given to a ruminant animal for a blood infection interfere with digestive function?
- What do you think of the programs that call for regimes of fasting and "purification of body fluids"? Are they biologically sound?
- Give some of the reasons dietary fiber, such as bran, is so important in our diet.
- Why do some adults, who could drink milk as infants without difficulty, experience intestinal pain (due to gas) and/or dehydrating diarrhea when they drink milk?
- In an incomplete digestive system, what types of foods would be avoided due to elimination difficulties? What is an obvious problem with an incomplete digestive system?
- Show photos of the beaks of a number of birds. From these photos can you imagine their food sources? The photos of Darwin's finches would be great examples.
- Look up the fascinating story of how Marshall and Warren discovered that *H. Pylori* caused the majority of ulcers—their research resulting with these scientists winning a Nobel Prize in 2005.

How Would You Vote? Classroom Discussion Ideas

- Monitor the voting for the online question. The idea of a fecal transplant sounds like a distasteful undertaking! In the past there have been incidences where improperly sterilized colonoscopy tools have transmitted diseases, such as hepatitis, from one patient to another. This raises questions about the safety of a procedure like fecal transplants. On the other hand, if such a procedure could remedy a painful lifelong condition, maybe it should be considered. This should produce a lively debate among your students!
- Try to determine which diseases could be transmitted via feces. Are there adequate tests to screen donors for these diseases?
- Poll your class.

Term Paper Topics, Library Activities, and Special Projects

- Survey your class to collect data on height and weight and calculate their BMIs. Do your classmates fall within the ranges given here?
- From the library, obtain a "calorie chart." Monitor and record your caloric intake for a week. Prepare a report.
- Ulcers are regarded by some people as a badge of success for bank presidents and young stockbrokers. Investigate the serious nature of this medical problem, including the ages of the sufferers and what treatments are prescribed.
- *Anorexia* and *bulimia* seem to have appeared only recently as eating disorders. Trace the history of what is known about these conditions.
- The role of vitamins in human health is a fascinating story. Select one or two vitamins and report on the history of discovery surrounding each.
- Investigate how the drug cimetidine (Zantac) suppresses the secretion of acid by the parietal cells of the stomach.
- Investigate recent findings concerning the cause of ulcers, namely the bacterium *Helicobacter pylori.*
- Find out why drinking coffee or other caffeine-containing beverages increases the sensation of hunger.
- Have genetic researchers found the "gene" for hunger? Research this possibility and then discuss what that might mean for the "obese" United States.

- Research exactly what is done during a gastric bypass surgery. How much of the stomach remains functional? How does this differ from a lapband procedure?
- Look up the symptoms of appendicitis. From what you know now about the large intestine, why is it not a good idea to delay treatment for the condition?
- How is hydrochloric acid from the stomach neutralized in the small intestine?
- Design a vegetarian diet that includes all of the necessary components.
- Prepare a paper on one of the vitamin or mineral deficiencies. Which are the most deleterious?
- It's interesting to discover why British sailors were previously called "Limies." It is because they were always sucking on limes to avoid scurvy!
- Look into the studies involving leptin. Do you think scientists will invent a way to supplement our supply of leptin as a remedy to weight gain?
- Which do you suppose it more treatable, obesity or anorexia? Why?

Possible Responses to *Critical Thinking* Questions

1. There is no doubt that the incidence of anorexia has increased over the last 20 years. This could not be enough time for such a significant change in allelic frequency to occur. Instead, the increase can most likely be blamed on the media's obsession with thinness. This pressure would exert its strongest influence on young women who are captivated with current celebrities and view them as role models.
2. Significant changes occur in the digestive system of a python when it ingests its infrequent meals. The pH would drop drastically to activate pepsin to initiate the digestion of proteins. In addition, the acidic pH would also serve to destroy some bacteria that may be present in the dead animal. The microvilli increase in size to increase the internal surface area for effective absorption of the nutrients that result from the digestive process.
3. It is a true statement that not all vegetables are equally calorie dense. The main difference between sweet potatoes and kale is that sweet potatoes are a source of soluble fiber. The presence of soluble fiber changes how nutrients are absorbed. Most sources say that soluble fiber adds approximately 2–4 calories per gram of soluble fiber. The fiber present in kale is insoluble, so it passes through the body and adds no additional calories.
4. In Figure 5.13, one can see that the optimum pH for pepsin activity is around 1.5. The hydrochloric acid in the stomach serves not only to activate the pepsin, but also destroys some pathogens that may have entered the gastrointestinal tract.
5. Lactose intolerance is a dietary concern for many people. When one consumes yogurt that contains active bacterial cultures, the bacteria break the lactose down into lactic acid. Therefore, the lactose level would be much lower and yogurt may be more easily tolerated by some individuals with lactose intolerance.

Possible Responses to *Data Analysis Exercise* Questions

Scientists were interested to see if the number of AMY-1 alleles in different populations correlated with their dietary starch intake.

1. It appears as though approximately 30 percent of the Hadza population had fewer than 5 copies of the AMY-1 gene.
2. Yes, some European Americans did have more than 10 copies of the AMY-1 gene.
3. This study seems to establish a link between number of copies of the AMY-1 gene and a diet that is high in starches.

40

MAINTAINING THE INTERNAL ENVIRONMENT

Chapter Outline

TRUTH IN A TEST TUBE

REGULATING FLUID VOLUME AND COMPOSTION

- Fluid Regulation in Invertebrates
- Fluid Regulation in Vertebrates

THE HUMAN URINARY SYSTEM

- Organs of the System
- Nephron Structure

HOW URINE FORMS

- Glomerular Filtration
- Tubular Reabsorption
- Tubular Secretion
- Concentrating the Urine

REGULATING THIRST AND URINE CONCENTRATION

ACID-BASE BALANCE

WHEN KIDNEYS FAIL

- Causes of Kidney Failure
- Treating Kidney Failure

HEAT GAINS AND LOSSES

- How the Core Temperature Can Change
- Endotherms, Ectotherms, and Heterotherms

RESPONSES TO HEAT OR COLD

- Responses to Heat Stress
- Responses to Cold Stress
- Seasonal Dormancy

TRUTH IN A TEST TUBE (REVISITED)

SUMMARY

DATA ANAYLYSIS EXERCISE

SELF-QUIZ

CRITICAL THINKING

Objectives

1. Explain how the chemical composition of extracellular fluid is maintained by mammals.
2. Compare how invertebrates and vertebrates maintain fluid balance.
3. Describe the components of the human urinary system.
4. Understand the processes of urine formation and excretion, and the hormonal controls involved in these processes.
5. Understand the degrees to which ectotherms, endotherms, and heterotherms can control their body temperatures.
6. Know how the kidneys help maintain a proper pH in the body.
7. Explain how heat gain and loss occur in birds and mammals and how these animals maintain a steady body temperature.
8. Understand what factors can be measured by a urinalysis.

Key Terms

interstitial fluid
extracellular fluid
osmosis
contractile vacuoles
flame cells
nephridia
uric acid
Malpighian tubules
urinary system
kidneys
urine
urinary excretion
urea
uric acid
ammonia
ureter
urinary bladder
urethra
renal cortex
renal medulla
nephrons
Bowman's capsule
proximal tubule
loop of Henle
distal tubule
collecting tubule
glomerulus
peritubular capillaries
glomerular filtration
tubular reabsorption
tubular secretion
thirst center
antidiuretic hormone (ADH)
aquaporins
renin
aldosterone
atrial natriuretic peptide (ANP)
acid-base balance
buffer system
bicarbonate-carbon dioxide buffer system
kidney stones
kidney dialysis
hemodialysis
peritoneal dialysis
kidney transplant
core temperature
thermal radiation
conduction
convection
evaporation
ectotherms
endotherms
heterotherms
fever
shivering response
non-shivering heat production
hypothermia
estivation
hibernation

Lecture Outline

40.1 Truth in a Test Tube

A. Analysis of urine is a routine medical procedure.
   1. The sugar level, pH, protein content, and concentration are checked.
   2. Home pregnancy kits test for hormones in the urine; declining hormone levels in urine can indicate menopause in older women.

B. Athletes also have to undergo urine tests as a condition of their eligibility to perform.

C. Urine is a remarkable indicator of health, hormonal status, and drug use.

40.2 Regulating Fluid Volume and Composition

A. The volume and composition of extracellular fluid (interstitial plus blood) must be maintained within tolerable ranges.
   1. Water and solute gains must be balanced by water and solute losses.
   2. Animals can lose water and solutes in feces and urine, exhalations and secretions.
   3. Animals gain water by eating and drinking, and in aquatic animals through osmosis across the body surface.
   4. In most animals, excretory organs rid the body of unwanted solutes and excess water.

B. Fluid Regulation in Invertebrates
   1. Sponges excrete metabolic wastes at the cellular level using diffusion, and they combat excess water by using contractile vacuoles.
   2. Planarians use pairs of highly branched tubules with flame cells to adjust water and solute levels in the body.
   3. Segmented worms, such as earthworms, have pairs of nephridia in each body segment that serve as excretory organs.
   4. Insects and spiders use Malpighian tubules and convert ammonia to uric acid to conserve water.

C. Fluid Regulation in Vertebrates
   1. Freshwater fishes and amphibians gain water by osmosis and lose it in a dilute urine.
   2. Marine bony fishes have less salt than their surroundings; they lose water and make up for it by drinking seawater and pumping out excess solutes through gills.
   3. Waterproof skin and efficient kidneys are two key adaptations that allowed amniotes to live on land.
   4. Reptiles and birds convert ammonia to uric acid while mammals convert it to urea.

40.3 The Human Urinary System
   A. Organ of the System
      1. The human urinary system consists of two kidneys, each with a ureter leading to a urinary bladder (for storage), with an open channel (urethra) leading to the body surface.
      2. Each kidney is a bean-shaped structure about the size of a fist, with cortex and medulla regions covered by a tough coat of connective tissue.
         a. Kidneys filter a variety of substances from the blood.
         b. Most of the filtrate is returned to the blood; about 1 percent ends up as urine.
         c. The kidneys regulate the volume and solute concentrations of extracellular fluid.
      3. Urine flows from each kidney through a ureter to a urinary bladder (for storage) and then out of the body through the urethra.
      4. Urination is a reflex response but can be controlled by nervous and muscular actions.
   B. Nephron Structure
      1. Overview of Nephron Structure
         a. Nephrons filter and retain water and solutes, leaving concentrated urine to be collected in the central renal pelvis.
         b. Filtration occurs in the glomerulus—a ball of capillaries nestled in the Bowman's capsule.
         c. The Bowman's capsule collects the filtrate and directs it through the continuous nephron tubules: proximal → loop of Henle → distal → collecting duct.
         d. Blood Vessels around Nephrons
            i. The peritubular capillaries exit the glomerulus, converge, and then branch again around the nephron tubules, where they participate in reclaiming water and essential solutes.

40.4 How Urine Forms
   A. Glomerular Filtration
      1. Blood pressure forces filtrate (water and small solutes) out of the glomerular capillaries.
         a. Blood enters the glomerulus under high pressure; arterioles here have wider diameters than most.
         b. Glomerular capillaries are highly "leaky" to water and small solutes.
            1) Blood cells, proteins, and other large solutes cannot pass the capillary wall into the capsule.
            2) Filtrate is collected by the Bowman's capsule and funneled into the proximal tubule.
   B. Tubular Reabsorption
      1. *Tubular reabsorption* takes place in the small tubules of the nephron, where water and solutes move across the tubular wall, out of the nephron, and into the surrounding capillaries.
      2. About 99 percent of the filtrate's water (all the glucose and amino acids), almost all the sodium ions, and 50 percent of the urea are returned to the blood.

3. The tubule wall and the capillary wall each have a certain number of transporters that can bind a specific substance, such as glucose or amino acids; the substance is excreted in the urine only when all transporters are saturated.

C. Tubular Secretion
1. *Tubular secretion* moves substances from the capillaries into the nephron walls.
2. Capillaries surrounding the nephrons secrete excess amounts of hydrogen ions and potassium ions into the nephron tubules, where they will be excreted in urine.

D. Concentrating the Urine
1. A concentrating mechanism in the kidney makes even the most dilute urine contain more solutes than plasma or most interstitial fluid.
   a. Filtrate and interstitial fluid are isotonic in the kidney cortex, so there is no net movement of water from one to the other.
   b. Interstitial fluid is hypertonic in the kidney medulla, so water is drawn out of the filtrate.
   c. In the descending limb of the loop of Henle, water moves out by osmosis, but in the ascending portion sodium is pumped out by transporters.
2. This interaction of the limbs of the loop produces a very high solute concentration in the deeper parts of the kidney medulla and delivers a rather dilute urine to the distal tubule.

40.5 Regulating Thirst and Urine Concentration

A. Thirst Regulation
1. The thirst center in the hypothalamus is alerted by nerve signals from a dry mouth; water intake reduces urine output.
2. Osmoreceptors of sensory neurons in the brain detect the rise in sodium levels and signal the hypothalamic thirst center that you are thirsty.

B. Effect of Antidiuretic Hormone
1. When signaled by osmoreceptors, the hypothalamus stimulates the pituitary gland to secrete ADH.
   a. ADH (antidiuretic hormone) promotes water conservation.
      1) ADH makes the walls of distal tubules and collecting ducts more permeable to water, and thus the urine becomes more concentrated.
      2) As the volume of extracellular fluid rises and solute concentration declines, ADH secretion slows.
   b. Loss of blood pressure or nausea and vomiting can also trigger ADH secretions.
2. Aquaporins selectively allow water to diffuse rapidly across the plasma membrane; ADH alters reabsorption in target cells by affecting these passive transporters.

C. Effect of Aldosterone
1. Cells in the arterioles release the enzyme renin in response to a decline in the volume of extracellular fluid.
2. Renin starts a chain of reactions that results in the secretion of aldosterone by the adrenal glands, located above each kidney.
3. Aldosterone stimulates the production and placement of sodium-potassium pumps into the plasma membrane of cells in the collecting duct wall; the urine becomes more concentrated.
4. Atrial natriuretic peptide (ANP) makes urine more dilute by inhibiting the secretion of aldosterone and also by indirectly inhibiting the rennin secretion.

40.6 Acid-Base Balance

A. Acid-base balance is maintained by controlling hydrogen ions through buffer systems, respiration, and excretion by the kidneys.

B. Buffers can neutralize hydrogen ions by the bicarbonate-carbon dioxide buffer system; the lungs can eliminate carbon dioxide.

C. Only the urinary system can eliminate excess hydrogen ions.

1. The HCO_3^- that forms in the nephron cells is moved to the capillaries where it neutralizes excess acid.
2. The H^+ that forms in the cells is secreted into the tubular fluid, where it combines with bicarbonate ions to form carbon dioxide (which is returned to the blood and excreted by the lungs) and water (which is excreted in the urine).
3. Thus, hydrogen ions are permanently removed from extracellular fluid.
4. Life-threatening metabolic acidosis develops when kidneys cannot excrete enough of the H+ released during metabolism.

40.7 When Kidneys Fail

A. Causes of Kidney Failure

1. Most kidney problems in the United States are outcomes of diabetes mellitus and high blood pressure.
2. While some people are genetically predisposed to kidney problems, toxins such as lead, arsenic, and pesticides may accumulate in kidney tissue, causing them to fail.
3. High protein diets increase the risk for kidney stones and cause the kidneys to work hard to dispose of nitrogen-rich breakdown products.
4. Renal failure occurs when the rate of filtration through glomerular capillaries drops by half.

B. Kidney Dialysis

1. A kidney dialysis machine is used to restore proper solute balances after renal failure.
2. Hemodialysis connects the machine to a vein or artery and pumps blood through semi-permeable tubes soaked in solutes; as a patient's blood flows through the tube, the wastes diffuse out and solute concentrations are restored as the cleansed, balanced blood flows back into the patient.
3. Peritoneal dialysis pumps a fluid of a specific composition into a patient's abdominal cavity, allowing the peritoneum (lining of abdominal cavity) to function as the membrane for dialysis.
4. About 12,000 people are recipients of kidney transplants annually in the United States.
   a. There is a shortage of suitable donors; 40,000 remain on the waiting list.
   b. Most are available after donors' deaths or from relatives or friends.
   c. Kidneys from living donors have a higher success rate in transplants than a kidney from a dead person.

40.8 Heat Gains and Losses

A. How the Core Temperature Can Change

1. The core temperature of an animal body rises when heat from the surroundings or metabolism builds up.
2. Four processes drive the exchanges of heat.
   a. *Thermal radiation* is the gain of heat from some source, or the loss of heat from the body to the surroundings, depending on the temperatures of the environment.
   b. *Conduction* is the transfer of heat from one object to another when they are in direct contact, as when a human sits on cold (or hot!) concrete.
   c. *Convection* is the transfer of heat by way of a moving fluid such as air or water.
   d. *Evaporation* is a process whereby a heated substance changes from a liquid to a gaseous state with a loss of heat to the surroundings.

B. Endotherms, Ectotherms, and Heterotherms

1. Ectotherms (such as lizards) have low metabolic rates; therefore, they must gain their heat from the environment in what we call behavioral temperature regulation.
2. Endotherms, such as birds and mammals, generate heat from metabolic activity and exercise controls over heat conservation and dissipation by means of adaptations that reduce heat loss, such as feathers, fur, or fat.
3. Heterotherms, such as the hummingbird, generate body heat during their active periods but resemble ectotherms during inactive times.

40.9 Responses to Heat or Cold

A. Responses to Heat Stress

1. When mammals become too hot the hypothalamus sends signals to widen the diameter of blood vessels to allow greater volumes of blood to reach the skin and dissipate the heat.
2. Evaporative heat loss by sweating is a common cooling mechanism.
   a. Sweating to dissipate heat can only be effective when the external temperatures are high enough to cause evaporation.
   b. Nearly all mammals (except marine species) sweat; many pant or lick their fur to assist evaporative cooling.
3. Hyperthermia is a rise in core temperature, with devastating effects.
4. Fever is a defensive response against pathogens that occurs with a rise in the core temperature above the normal set point.

B. Responses to Cold Stress

1. Mammals respond to cold by redistributing blood flow, fluffing hair and fur, and shivering.
2. In some responses hairs or feathers become more erect to create a layer of still air that reduces convective and radiative heat losses.
3. Shivering responses are common responses to cold, but are not effective for very long and come at high metabolic cost.
4. Non-shivering responses include the release of thyroid hormones that bind to brown adipose tissue, increasing metabolism.
5. Hypothermia is a condition in which the core temperature drops below normal; it may lead to brain damage and death.

C. Seasonal Dormancy

1. Hibernation is a time during the cold season when the animal slows down its respiratory and metabolic rates.
   a. Some animals awaken to feed and others rely on previously stored energy.
   b. Examples of some hibernating animals are: bears, bats, rodents, and some reptiles and amphibians.
2. Estivation occurs when desert animals become dormant in the hot season by burrowing underground.

40.10 Truth in a Test Tube (Revisited)

A. The kidneys reabsorb nutrients, but water-soluble drugs and metabolites remain in the urine.

1. Younger individuals have more efficient kidneys that clear drugs from the body more quickly.

Suggestions for Presenting the Material

- Reference Figures 40.9 and 40.10 and their animations to help students understand nephron structure.
- To help prevent student confusions, in the various figures distinguish between structures carrying *blood* and those carrying *filtrate.*
- An analogy to the common drip-type coffee brewing machine is helpful (see the Enrichment section).
- Review of ADH and aldosterone functions should be made during your presentation of kidney function.
- In your lecture, include some examples of larger desert mammals, such as the eland, and the special adaptations they have for conserving water and for regulating their body temperature.
- Take advantage of the animations and videos available on CengageNOW and the multimedia manager to help student's grasp this difficult subject matter.
- If you use the word *excretion* in your lectures, clearly distinguish it from the word *elimination,* which is the voiding of undigested waste via the anus.
- Be sure to explain the inadequacy of the layman's terms *warmblooded* and *coldblooded.*
- For the three processes that are involved in urine production, create a flow chart (no pun intended) that shows the direction of the flow and also whether the process is specific or nonspecific, as follows:

Bloodstream Nephron

Glomerular filtration (non-specific) -------→

←---- Tubular reabsorption (specific)

Tubular secretion (specific) -------→

- Discuss the different eating habits of endotherms and ectotherms. How can an animal like a snake survive with quite infrequent meals? Why does a shrew have to consume several times its own body weight to survive?

Classroom and Laboratory Enrichment

- To aid the students' conceptualization of the nephron function, the following comparison to a drip-type coffee maker is made:

Nephron Part	*Coffee Brewer Part*
a. Afferent arteriole carrying blood in	a. Hot water
b. Blood with wastes	b. Coffee grounds
c. Glomerulus	c. Filter paper
d. Bowman's capsule	d. Filter holder
e. Proximal and distal ducts, Henle's loop, collecting ducts	e. Carafe

- The storeroom-cleaning analogy reveals a possible explanation for why the kidney removes from the blood much more than it will eventually excrete. Pose this question based on the two scenarios that follow. Which of the following, (a) or (b), results in a more efficient cleaning of the storeroom?
  a. Carefully removing and disposing of only those few selected items that are in plain view and identifiable as "no longer needed."

b. Removing *all* items from the storeroom; then sweeping, dusting, and mopping; and finally replacing only those items selected as "still worth keeping."

- The complete analysis of urine can reveal a wealth of information concerning the status of body metabolism. Ask a clinical lab technician to speak on modern analysis techniques.
- If possible, invite a kidney transplant or dialysis patient to discuss his or her condition with the class. Some kidney centers have a speaker's bureau for just this purpose. They may also provide dialysis equipment for observation.
- Use a mannequin to show the locations of the urinary organs.
- Exhibit a model of a kidney to illustrate its parts and the blood vessels associated with it.
- Display a model of a nephron.
- Use a model of a renal corpuscle to illustrate its structure.
- Provide microscope slides of the kidney for student viewing.
- If your school policy does not prohibit working with body fluids, have students do a dipstick urine test on themselves. This simple test can provide you with some valuable information, such as the pH of the urine. The range for a normal urine's pH is 4.8–8. This is quite a large range. Note that most of the normal values are somewhat acidic to discourage bacterial growth.
- If you cannot test real urine, Ward's Natural Science sells artificial urine samples that show both normal and abnormal conditions without any risk of disease transmission.
- Contrast the appearance of Malpighian tubules and nephridia. Which features do they share? In what way do they resemble nephrons?

Classroom Discussion Ideas

- What possible argument could be made for drinking your own urine? What are the arguments against it? Would it be prudent if you were on a deserted desert island? What are the consequences of drinking salt water?
- Name several conditions of the body that can be determined from the composition of one's urine.
- Should athletes be singled out over the general public for drug screening tests? What other groups should be tested? How many in the class have been drug screened as a prerequisite to employment?
- Can the urine of individuals be tested for human growth hormone (HGH)? This seems to be the focus of many investigations into the habits of athletes. The question results, "Should the athletic feats of athletes on performance-enhancing drugs be compared with the sports records set by athletes who did not take any drugs?"

Additional Ideas for Classroom Discussion

- Of these three processes—filtration, reabsorption, and secretion—which is (are) accomplished by a kidney dialysis machine? Explain any limitations of the device.
- Why do high-protein diet supplements for increasing muscle mass or losing weight include warnings saying that water intake must be increased when consuming the product?
- In the storeroom-cleaning analogy (see the Enrichment section), which scenario do you think results in a better cleaning of the storeroom? Do you think the same would apply to kidney function?

- When asked what the kidney does, most people would probably respond that it filters the blood. Why is this answer not a complete statement of kidney function?
- Obviously, humans can survive using only one kidney. Why then do we have two?
- Is it possible to overload our kidneys' capacity by excessive intake of water?
- Why does eating salty food make you thirsty?
- Why does eating salty food make you temporarily gain weight?
- Why do bars frequently put out salty foods as snacks, such as peanuts or pretzels, while serving alcohol?
- Contrast the difference as to how saltwater fish and freshwater fish handle excretion.
- What are the pressures involved that regulate glomerular filtration?
- Every summer, several football players expire from heat exhaustion. Why do you think their bodies cannot handle the heat stress?
- The text mentioned that lab technicians once had to taste urine as part of their testing. The urine of a patient with diabetes mellitus might taste sweet due to the excess sugar that did not all get reabsorbed during tubular reabsorption. The disease diabetes insipidus involves a shortage of antidiuretic hormone (ADH). These two diseases might get confused by some, because the symptoms—excessive thirst and frequent urination—are the same. The name diabetes insipidus means "tasteless overflow," because that patient's urine would be extremely dilute. We normally urinate 1½–2 liters a day. Experts say that without ADH, we would urinate 12 liters a day!

How Would You Vote? Classroom Discussion Ideas

- Monitor the voting for the online question. Certainly an argument could be made that drug testing of employees is an invasion of privacy. But the argument could also be made that not screening could be more problematic to more people. The reasoning would be bolstered by noting that one employee's reckless use of drugs could endanger many hundreds of lives, as in a bus driver or airline pilot. Employers may feel that illicit drug use may result in more sick days or inefficiency on the job.
- Have students complete polling by using JoinIN clickers.

Term Paper Topics, Library Activities, and Special Projects

- Investigate the workings of a kidney dialysis machine. Include historical perspectives and recent technological advances.
- Although Western cultures find the practice bizarre, the consumption of one's own urine is practiced in Eastern cultures (India, for example). Report on the supposed benefit of such actions and the possible dangers.
- What are "kidney stones"? What are some of the factors responsible for their formation?
- Investigate the reasons humans cannot meet their water needs by drinking seawater exclusively.
- Popular wisdom reasons that because incidence of colds and flu increases in fall and winter, it is the drop in temperature and human exposure to it that are to blame. Find out if this is really true. Are there more compelling causes?
- What is "gout"? Research the past history of gout. Is this condition still around today?
- Investigate deaths by water intoxication. What is it? Who is at risk? How often does someone die from water intoxication?

- The textbook shows a painting of a seventeenth-century physician examining a urine sample. When did this practice begin? What tests were the first to be performed on urine? How do these tests differ today?
- Why do some sources suggest consuming cranberry juice to prevent bladder infections? Is this a valid suggestion and why?
- What information is gained by a physician performing a cystoscopy? A cystometrogram?
- Research the hibernation of an animal, like a bear. How long does their hibernation last? Are there any studies measuring their respiratory and metabolic rates while hibernating?

Possible Responses to *Critical Thinking* Questions

1. Kangaroo rats are able to survive in the desert with virtually no drinking water. The majority of water reabsorption in the kidneys occurs in the loop of Henle. The kangaroo rats' longer loop of Henle enables them to conserve water in their habitat by maximizing the concentration of urine and minimizing water loss from their system. The higher urine concentration allows them to use much less water than most other mammals in order to excrete waste. The longer loop of Henle provides for a longer distance over which the concentration gradients of the ions can be developed, and thus provides for more reabsorption of water from the tubules into the peritubular capillaries.
2. Polar bears are a good example of this relationship between body size and environment. They have large, compact bodies with relatively small surface areas from which they can lose their internally produced heat—an important asset in cold climates. The larger the animals, the more heat they will produce via metabolism. The amount of heat loss increases as the proportion of exposed surface area to body mass increases. Since that proportion is greater in small animals, they lose heat more quickly. An animal with long legs, ears, or a tail has more surface area than an animal of the same size that has shorter appendages. In extremely cold environments, a smaller body shape with short appendages would be more efficient at maintaining body heat because it would have relatively less surface area compared to body mass.

Possible Responses to *Data Analysis Exercise* Questions

Scientists have often questioned the necessity for organic foods (those not produced with pesticides). This experiment was designed to answer that question by monitoring the urine of children exposed to both organic and conventional foods.

1. The urine during phase two, when ingesting an organic diet, contained the lowest level of metabolite.
2. The maximum level of chlorpyrifos was detected in phase one of the study, where a conventional diet was consumed.
3. It appears from this study that switching to an organic diet lowered the levels of malathion and chlorpyrifos in the urine excreted by the children in the study.
4. The study shows that organic foods expose the participant to fewer harmful substances than conventional foods. However, it is up to the consumer to weigh the benefits of organic foods against the increased costs of an organic diet.

41

ANIMAL REPRODUCTIVE SYSTEMS

Chapter Outline

Objectives

1. Understand how asexual reproduction differs from sexual reproduction. Know the advantages and problems associated with having separate sexes.
2. Describe the structure and function of the human male and female reproductive systems.
3. Understand conditions that may impact the male and female reproductive tracts.
4. Know the principal means of controlling human fertility.
5. Know the various STDs presented in this chapter and the various modes of transmission.

Key Terms

asexual reproduction
sexual reproduction
intersex condition
hermaphrodite
external fertilization
internal fertilization
placenta
gonads
testes, testis
testosterone
scrotum
seminiferous tubules
sperm
secondary sexual traits
puberty
epididymis
vas deferens
ejaculatory ducts
urethra
penis
semen
seminal vesicles
prostate gland
prostaglandins
bulbourethral glands
prostate cancer
testicular cancer
spermatogonia
primary spermatocytes
Sertoli cells
secondary spermatocytes
spermatids
testosterone
luteinizing hormone, LH
follicle-stimulating hormone, FSH
gonadotropin releasing hormone, GnRH
Leydig cells
ovaries
oocyte
oviduct
uterus
endometrium
cervix
vagina
labia majora
labia minora
clitoris
estrous cycle
menstrual cycle
follicular phase
ovulation
luteal phase
corpus luteum
estrogens
progesterone
menopause
primary oocytes
ovarian follicle
zona pellucida
secondary oocyte
polar body
erection
ejaculation
orgasm
ovum
abstinence
rhythm method
withdrawal
douching
vasectomy
tubal ligation
spermicidal foam
spermicidal jelly
diaphragm
condoms
birth control pill
birth control patch
morning after pills
abortion
in vitro fertilization
sexually transmitted diseases, STDs
human papillo-mavirus, HPV
genital warts
trichomoniasis
chlamydial infection
genital herpes
gonorrhea
syphilis
HIV
AIDS

Lecture Outline

41.1 Intersex Conditions

A. The International Olympic Committee (IOC) began gender testing in 1968.
   1. A test that detects the *SRY* gene on the Y chromosome is used to determine sex.
   2. The *SRY* gene triggers testes development in a normal XY individual.
   3. The testing program has not unveiled men pretending to be women, but it has turned up people brought up and believing to be women but carrying a Y chromosome.

B. Individuals with androgen insensitivity syndrome (AIS) have female reproductive organs, but also testes within the body cavity.
   1. These AIS individuals are usually raised as females, but should have the testes removed to reduce cancer risks.
   2. Some babies are born with partial AIS, which gives them abnormal genitalia for either sex and often requires corrective surgery.

C. Intersex conditions challenge our thinking about what is a female and what is a male.

41.2 Modes of Animal Reproduction

A. Asexual Reproduction
   1. Asexual reproduction is a useful strategy in stable environments.

2. Asexual reproduction by fragmentation, budding (for example, sponge), or parthenogenesis results in offspring identical to the parents.
   a. In fragmentation, a portion of the parent becomes the offspring.
   b. Budding is the condition in which a small offspring grows off of the parent and then separates.
   c. In parthenogenesis an unfertilized egg becomes the offspring.

B. Sexual Reproduction
1. In sexual reproduction, the male and female gametes combine at fertilization.
2. Sexual reproduction permits adaptation through variation but is biologically costly because the sexes are separate.
   a. Animals must produce gametes and must find each other (usually) for fertilization to occur.
3. Through sexual reproduction, the offspring are more likely to have a gene combination that is suitable to their new environment.

C. Gamete Formation and Fertilization
1. Some animals, such as tapeworms and roundworms, are hermaphrodites, producing both eggs and sperm at the same time.
2. More typically, vertebrates have separate sexes that are fixed for life—they are either male or female.
3. Most land animals have internal fertilization, while most marine animals use external fertilization.
4. Offspring may develop inside the mother or outside of the maternal body.

D. Nourishing Developing Young
1. Most animals are nourished by yolk inside of the amniote egg.
2. Placental mammals utilize the placenta as a means for the developing offspring to obtain nutrients.

41.3 Reproductive System of Human Males

A. The Male Gonads
1. Human males have two testes located in the scrotum.
   a. This is the site of sperm development, and the testes must be several degrees cooler than body temperature.
   b. Testosterone, a sex hormone, is also produced in the testes.
   c. The male reproductive system includes accessory organs, glands, and ducts.
2. Sperm production begins during puberty, the stage when secondary sexual characteristics emerge.

B. Reproductive Ducts and Accessory Glands
1. Each testis contains many seminiferous tubules where sperm are continuously formed.
2. Sperm move from a testis → epididymis (for maturation and storage) → vas deferens → ejaculatory ducts → urethra (located inside the penis).
3. The sperm-bearing fluid (semen) is formed by secretions from the seminal vesicles (fructose and prostaglandins) and the prostate (buffers against acidic vagina).
4. The bulbourethral glands secrete a mucus-rich fluid into the vagina during sexual arousal.

C. Disorders of the Male Reproductive Tract
1. The prostate gland can enlarge due to cancer or inflammation.
   a. Prostate cancer is the second most common type of cancer causing death in males.
2. There are about 7,000 cases of testicular cancer each year in the United States.
3. Routine examination and blood tests are necessary to detect these subtle cancers.

41.4 Sperm Formation

A. Germ Cells to Mature Sperm

1. Sperm form in the walls of the seminiferous tubules of the testes.
2. Diploid spermatogonia undergo mitosis → primary spermatocytes, which undergo meiosis I → haploid secondary spermatocytes, which undergo meiosis II → haploid spermatids → mature sperm.
3. Sertoli cells in the tubule provide nourishment and chemical signals to the developing sperm.
4. Each sperm has a head (nucleus and cap), midpiece (mitochondria), and tail (flagellum).

B. Hormonal Control of Sperm Formation

1. Testosterone, produced by Leydig cells located between the lobes in the testes, stimulates spermatogenesis.
   a. Testosterone also initiates the secondary sexual characteristics and helps to develop normal sexual behavior.
2. Luteinizing hormone (LH) is released from the anterior pituitary (under prodding by GnRH from the hypothalamus) and stimulates testosterone production.
3. GnRH also causes the pituitary to release FSH, which stimulates the production of sperm, beginning at puberty.

41.5 Reproductive System of Human Females

A. Female Gonads

1. The ovaries are responsible for maturation of oocytes.
   a. Ovaries also produce the hormones estrogen and progesterone.

B. Reproductive Ducts and Accessory Glands

1. The egg is released from the ovary → oviduct → uterus (zygote will implant in its lining, the endometrium).
2. The lower part of the uterus is the cervix, which extends into the vagina, which in turn leads to the outer genitalia: labia majora, labia minora, and clitoris.

C. The Menstrual Cycle

1. Humans and other primates have a menstrual cycle.
2. During each cycle an oocyte matures and escapes from the ovary.
   a. If it is fertilized, the egg may implant in the endometrium.
   b. If there is no implantation, the uterine lining is sloughed at the end of each cycle of (approximately) 28 days.
3. A decline in hormone secretions correlates with the onset of menopause, the cessation of a female's reproductive capacity.

D. Disorders of the Female Reproductive Tract

1. Many women have fibroid tumors that cause additional bleeding and pain.
2. Uterine cancer may cause additional bleeding between periods and can be diagnosed by Pap smears.
3. Ovarian cancer is more difficult to detect, so it is more deadly than uterine cancer.

41.6 Preparations for Pregnancy

A. The Ovarian Cycle

1. At birth about two million immature eggs (primary oocytes) are already present and arrested in meiosis I.
2. Of the approximately 300,000 oocytes still present at age seven, only about 400–500 will mature in a lifetime.
3. The follicle consists of a layer of cells (granulosa) surrounding the primary oocyte; the granulosa cells gradually deposit a layer of material around the follicle.

4. During the menstrual cycle, one oocyte resumes meiosis I to form a secondary oocyte and a polar body (both haploid).
5. At about mid-cycle, there is a surge of LH that causes ovulation—the release of the secondary oocyte.
6. Following ovulation, the remaining follicle becomes a corpus luteum, which secretes estrogen and progesterone.
   a. If there is no fertilization of an egg, the corpus luteum disintegrates.
   b. If a pregnancy occurs, the corpus luteum remains functional until the placenta is fully formed.

B. The Uterine Cycle
   1. During the first five days of the menstrual cycle, the innermost lining of the uterus sloughs off.
   2. During the next phase, the uterine lining is rebuilt.
   3. During the first half of the cycle, the hypothalamus signals the anterior pituitary to release LH and FSH, which in turn stimulate the ovary to secrete estrogen.
   4. The corpus luteum persists for about 12 days, secreting progesterone that inhibits further FSH and LH secretion.
   5. If fertilization does not occur, the corpus luteum degenerates, progesterone and estrogen levels fall, and FSH and LH are again secreted to begin another cycle.

41.7 PMS to Hot Flashes

A. PMS, premenstrual syndrome, is related to discomfort a week or two before menstruation.
   1. Hormones cause milk ducts to enlarge, making the breasts swell and become tender.
   2. Cycle-induced changes also cause depression, irritability, anxiety, headaches, and sleeping disorders.

B. Menstrual pain can be caused by prostaglandins secreted during menstruation that stimulate contractions of smooth muscle in the uterine wall.
   1. Many women do not even notice these contractions.
   2. Others may experience a dull ache or sharp pain.

C. Menopause occurs when the eggs are no longer maturing and the hormone levels drop.
   1. Three-fourths of women in menopause get hot flashes and night sweats.
   2. Hormone replacement, diet, alcohol, and exercise can lessen hot flashes and night sweats.

41.8 When Gametes Meet

A. Sexual Intercourse
   1. In male sexual arousal, the spongy tissue spaces inside the penis become filled with blood to cause an erection.
   2. During coitus, mechanical stimulation of the penis causes involuntary contractions that force semen out and into the vagina.
   3. Ejaculation in the male and similar contractions in the female are termed orgasm.
   4. Viagra® medication is prescribed to counter erectile dysfunction in men.

B. Fertilization
   1. Of the 150 million to 350 million sperm deposited in the vagina during intercourse, only a few hundred ever reach the upper region of the oviduct where fertilization occurs.
      a. Sperm may live for about three days following ejaculation.
      b. About 30 minutes after being deposited in the vagina the sperm may reach the oviducts, the entry to the fallopian tubes.
   2. Only one sperm will successfully enter the cytoplasm of the secondary oocyte after digesting its way through the zona pellucida.

a. The arrival of that sperm stimulates the completion of meiosis II, which yields a mature ovum.
b. The sperm nucleus fuses with the egg nucleus to restore the diploid chromosome number.

41.9 Preventing or Seeking Pregnancy

A. Birth Control Options

1. Abstinence is most effective, but may be unrealistic.
2. In the rhythm method, there is no intercourse during the days when an egg is capable of being fertilized.
3. Withdrawal before ejaculation would seem to be effective, but is not.
4. Douching is similarly ineffective due to the speed with which sperm enter the uterus.
5. Surgery to cut and tie the oviducts (tubal ligation) or vas deferens (vasectomy) is effective and generally considered an irreversible method to prevent sperm and egg union.
6. Spermicidal foam and jelly are toxic to sperm but not reliable unless used in combination with a barrier device like a diaphragm.
7. A diaphragm fits over the cervix and prevents entry of sperm into the uterus.
8. Condoms prevent sperm deposition in the vagina but must be used with care.
9. The birth control pill (and birth control patch) contains synthetic female hormones and prevents ovulation when taken faithfully according to directions; the patch delivers the same hormones as the pill but is applied to the skin.
10. Progestin injections (Depo-Provera®) or implants (Norplant®) inhibit ovulation over several months.
11. "Morning-after pills" intercept pregnancy by blocking fertilization or preventing implantation.

B. Infertility

1. About two-thirds of the causes for infertility are due to a problem with the female.
   a. A problem with hormone levels may prevent ovulation.
   b. Polycystic ovarian syndrome allows the follicles to mature, but ovulation does not occur.
   c. Endometriosis or scarring from STDs can cause discomfort and may result in a tubal pregnancy.
      i. A tubal pregnancy cannot survive, because there is not enough space or nutrition for the developing fetus.
2. Some reasons for infertility relate to the male reproductive system.
   a. Some males have either a low sperm count or a high number of abnormal sperm.
   b. Problems with scarring or ejaculation can also impact fertility.

41.10 Sexually Transmitted Diseases

A. Consequences of Infection

1. Sexually transmitted diseases (STDs) infect millions of Americans each year.
   a. The social consequences are enormous; women develop more complications than men.
   b. Pelvic inflammatory disease may cause pain and lead to infertility.
   c. STDs can harm the unborn child.

B. Major Agents of Sexually Transmitted Disease

1. *Trichomonas vaginalis*, a protozoan, causes soreness and discharge from the vagina; males are usually symptom-free.
   a. Untreated infections can lead to infertility.

2. *Chlamydia trachomatis* causes the most common STD, chlamydia.
   a. It shows few symptoms but can lead to pelvic inflammatory disease.
   b. Chlamydia may cause pneumonia and eye infections in the offspring of an infected mom.
3. *Neisseria gonorrhoeae*, a bacterium, enters the body through mucous membranes during sexual intercourse and causes gonorrhea.
   a. Because the initial symptoms are mild, treatment is often delayed, allowing the bacterium to multiply out of control.
4. The spirochete *Treponema pallidum* enters the body from an infected sexual partner and causes syphilis.
   a. Initially the spirochetes produce a localized ulcer that heals, but the organisms continue to multiply in the spinal cord, brain, eyes, bones, joints, and mucous membranes with serious consequences.
5. Human papillomavirus (HPV) is becoming widespread in the United States.
   a. Some strains cause genital warts; others can cause cervical cancer.
   b. There is now a vaccine to protect against HPV infection in both males and females.
6. The STD herpes is caused by the *Herpes simplex* virus, which can invade the mucous membranes of the mouth or genitals by direct contact.
   b. Blisters may form, disappear, and then reappear under stressful conditions.
   c. If a mom has an active infection at the time of delivery, it can have drastic effects on the infant.
7. Infection by the human immunodeficiency virus (HIV) leads to AIDS, an incurable STD that leads to a complete breakdown of the immune system.
   a. Opportunistic infections are the eventual cause of death.
   b. HIV spreads by anal, vaginal, and oral intercourse as well as by intravenous drug use.
   c. The use of a condom and lubricant can prevent the spread of HIV.

41.11 Intersex Conditions (Revisited)

A. In the past, XY individuals born with a micropenis had surgery to make them a female.
   1. Studies have shown that the majority of these individuals were unhappy with their sexual reassignment.

Suggestions for Presenting the Material

- Most students approach the topic of reproduction with a sigh of relief and an attitude that says "finally, something I know *everything* about." The intuitive instructor will build upon what *accurate* information the students already know and will gently, but authoritatively, correct misinformation. This also prohibits any belittling of incomplete, or inaccurate, "folklore." Tell them that they will definitely learn some facts that they did not previously know about reproduction.
- The sequence of topics is logically presented in the chapter: male and female structures, menstrual cycle, sexual union, fertility control, and prenatal development.
- There are numerous excellent animated figures available to help you present this material. The animated figures provide excellent visual context for your students.
- When comparing the male and female systems, it is helpful to note that the male produces and delivers sperm, much as the female produces and delivers eggs. However, the female also provides: (a) a site for fertilization, and (b) a site for embryonic and fetal development. This provides a convenient lead into the discussion of the menstrual cycle.

- The details of the menstrual cycle are of interest to both sexes but especially to females, of course. Because events are happening simultaneously in the pituitary, ovary, and uterus, it is virtually a necessity to keep Figure 41.10 and 41.11 in constant view. The critical feature of this figure is the timeline along the bottom, which puts all events into perspective.
- These points need emphasis in your lecture on female reproduction:
  a. Females are born with a finite number of eggs, which means eggs grow old (implications for causing genetic defects in offspring).
  b. Menstrual cycle can be defined as "the monthly release of an egg and all the preparations for it."
  c. Retention or sloughing of endometrium is determined by progesterone levels at the end of the menstrual cycle.
- You may be able to surprise your students with the fact that only a few days of each month comprise the "fertile period." But hasten to inform them that the fertile days can "move around" depending on a variety of nutritional, psychological, and health factors.
- The most practical aspect of the chapter is Section 41.9 "Preventing or Seeking Pregnancy." Students are eager for this information, especially when it can be presented with special reference to the mode of action of each device. Be sure to emphasize the effectiveness of each method as shown in Table 41.2.
- The topic of sexual diseases is presented in this chapter in Section 41.10. Individual instructors may, or may not, wish to present this. But certainly some reference, even without details, should be made to the toll these diseases exact on society.
- Older students in your class may be less informed than some of the younger ones about reproduction due to the revamping of sex education in school. Undoubtedly your older female students had a quick movie on their menstrual cycle while the boys were in gym class. Today's youth see movies about the sexual development of both sexes. This way they are much more informed about the entire subject of reproduction. Do your students agree with this newer method of sexual education?
- What are the advantages and disadvantages of asexual and sexual reproduction? Why is it advantageous for an animal like a snail to be a hermaphrodite? (This way, when it finally catches up with another snail—mating can always occur!)
- When discussing male and female reproduction, it is useful to mention their similarities. First of all, some of the same hormones play an integral role in both systems. Be sure to point out the following pairs of homologous structures:
  - Penis – clitoris
  - Scrotum – labia majora
  - Testes – ovaries

  Can you find other homologous structures in the male and female systems?
- Another amazing thing is the sheer numbers involved with reproduction. A female has several million eggs and the average ejaculation contains somewhere between 50–500 million sperm!

Classroom and Laboratory Enrichment

- Because you probably teach students with a great range of sexual knowledge and experience, adjust your enrichment activities accordingly. For example, many students will appreciate observing birth control devices or slide photos of them.

- If you decide to present details of the physical manifestations of sexually transmitted diseases, use discretion in which slides you show and give warning before showing them so students may choose to look away.
- Students enjoy bragging about their sexual knowledge. Perhaps you can bring some perspective to this by preparing a true/false quiz of common facts and fallacies associated with human reproduction. Allowing the students to remain anonymous, administer the quiz prior to your lecture. Tabulate the results and report them to the class as you give the accurate information.
- Show purchased slides of the various stages of oocyte development. In addition, show a prepared slide of sperm. Can the students identify the three main portions: the head, the midpiece, and the tail? To ensure that your students understand the huge difference in size between an egg and a sperm, be sure to show a photo of sperm surrounding an egg. An excellent micrograph can be found at the following web address: http://news.bbc.co.uk/nol/shared/spl/hi/pop_ups/03/health_ivf_step_by_step/img/1.jpg
- Create a Jeopardy-style quiz by using the format at the following website: http://jeopardylabs.com/
- It is important to stress to the class that both sexes have FSH and LH, but they were named for their female functions.
- Note that in the different phases of the menstrual cycle, events take place both in the ovaries and the uterus.

Classroom Discussion Ideas

- These issues and decisions are emotional, and professionals can help make sound decisions. How much should professional input play a role in these decisions?
- List pros and cons of delaying the surgery and also performing the surgery as soon as possible.
- At what age to you think a child is qualified to determine his/her sexual orientation?
- What are the most important criteria, genetic testing or the determination by a surgeon of which procedure would be a safer alternative?
- What methods or combinations of methods do you think sports officials should use to determine the sex of athletes?

Additional Ideas for Classroom Discussion

- All animals reproduce at rates sufficient to maintain their population. Humans are the only ones whose proliferation seems to be under very few limiting factors. Is this so? Why?
- Using anatomical terms, explain why men who have had a vasectomy operation are still able to expel normal amounts of semen but no sperm.
- Explain the events that result in the production of identical and fraternal twins.
- What propels sperm from their point of origin to the opening where they exit the body?
- What mechanisms prevent the entry of more than a single sperm into the egg?
- Many communities, and even states, restrict the teaching of human reproduction. Why do you think this body system is singled-out over, say, digestion or respiration for such a prohibition?
- Non-disjunction occurs more often in older eggs. What diseases increase their incidences with advanced maternal age? Are there tests to detect these abnormalities? At what age do physicians recommend amniocentesis?
- When mentioning birth control methods, it should be addressed that a vasectomy is a less-invasive procedure than a tubal ligation. With a tubal ligation, it is necessary to enter the abdominopelvic body cavity, whereas, a vasectomy can be performed by making an incision in the scrotum.

How Would You Vote? Classroom Discussion Ideas

- Monitor the voting for the online questions. This issue is a tough one. These decisions are very personal. Families need to consider input from the medical professional community before making the decision to perform surgery or not. It is almost impossible to measure the effects of having the surgery or delaying it. Research the issue more using CengageNow.
- Undoubtedly the surgeon will suggest reassignment based on which procedure is less invasive. Should this be the sole criteria?
- If genetic testing is performed, should the reassignment be based on those results?
- How would you raise the child until they are old enough to decide? Do you tell others that your child is a boy or a girl?
- Would having no sexual identity until the gender assignment is made be just as deleterious as assigning the inappropriate sex?
- Have students complete class polling using the JoinIn clickers.

Term Paper Topics, Library Activities, and Special Projects

- It is a curious, but real, fact that most sex crimes are committed by males. Investigate what psychologists and physicians say about the underlying cause(s) for this behavior.
- Sexual dysfunction is a frustrating situation for those involved, whether male or female. Prepare a list, based on your reading, of the most prevalent disorders and their treatment.
- We hear about "sperm banks" now and then. Do such repositories actually exist? Where are they? How do they function?
- Any interruption in the menstrual cycle, whether temporary or permanent, is cause for concern. Report on the causes and effects of the cessation of menstruation in females who drastically reduce their body weight (anorexia) or body fat (as in body building).
- Search for the physiological explanation for the cessation of menstruation (menopause)—usually when a woman is between the ages of 40 and 50. Is there any comparable phenomenon in men?
- It is known that overcrowding and stressful conditions reduce reproductive behavior in rodents. Is there any published evidence of such a phenomenon in humans?
- Research the family planning practices of China. Find out the current practice of child restriction and the effects this is having on China's demography. There have been articles written about the rewards given to families who have daughters; is this a valid or regular practice in the country?
- Examine the eggs (or photographs) of different species. Which have more yolk? Which have only small amounts of yolk? What is the function of the yolk sac in humans?
- Research the details of "female circumcisions." In what countries is this procedure performed? Why is this performed? Is there any medical benefit from this procedure?
- Make a chart that compares spermatogenesis (sperm formation) with oogenesis (egg formation).
- Research the development of the Gardasil injection to prevent HPV infection.
- When were birth control pills invented? How do they "fool" the body so that you avoid a pregnancy? What are the health risks from taking the pill?
- How does an ovulation test kit work? What hormone does it measure?
- Choose an STD to report on. Make sure to include the symptoms and potential treatments in your document.

Possible Responses to *Critical Thinking* Questions

1. Hypertension (high blood pressure) causes the blood vessels to constrict; drugs work to keep the blood flowing through the vessels. High blood pressure drugs interfere with sexual behavior by opening the blood outflow from the penis during stimulation. The drugs block the vascular receptors on the smooth muscle as blood fills a penis that would normally stay erect. Instead of keeping the blood in until ejaculation, as normal, channels are opened as the blood flows in and the penis cannot stay erect. This leads to erectile dysfunction, loss of sex drive, and ejaculatory failure.
2. An analysis of shared derived characteristics would help to answer these questions. Essentially, you need to gather information to establish relationships to the common ancestor Did the common reptilian ancestor fly or not? More information regarding bone structure would help to answer this question. The ancestors tracing further back most likely would not have a penis, but those diverging later on the evolutionary timeline might have a penis.
3. Follicle stimulating hormone (FSH), as the name implies, stimulates follicles to mature. If a woman had additional FSH, she may have more than one follicle that reaches maturity and is released during ovulation. If two eggs become fertilized at the same time, fraternal twins will result.
4. Lysosomes are organelles in animal cells that contain enzymes that degrade and recycle organelles. The lysosome digests the sperm mitochondria.

Possible Responses to *Data Analysis Exercise* Questions

Some females are born with genitals that appear to have varying degrees of masculinity. Scientists have discovered that females that have a 21-hydroxylase deficiency also have higher testosterone levels. This study was performed to see if administration of dexamethasone would prevent formation of these intersex variations.

1. In this study, four daughters that were born from moms given dexamethasone had normal female genitals.
2. According to the data provided, none of the untreated women had earlier phenotypically normal daughters.
3. All of the women that previously had daughters with level 4 or 5 masculinization had daughters that showed improvement.
4. In this experiment, it shows that administration of dexamethasone to pregnant women can reduce the effects of her developing daughter's 21-hydroxylase deficiency.

42

ANIMAL DEVELOPMENT

Chapter Outline

Objectives

1. Describe early embryonic development and distinguish each of the following: oogenesis, fertilization, cleavage, gastrulation, organ formation, and tissue specialization.
2. Outline the principal events of prenatal development.
3. Understand the importance of the placenta and extraembryonic membranes to the developing embryo.
4. Describe the evolutionary constraints on development.
5. Understand the effects of nutrition, infectious agents, alcohol, caffeine, smoking, and prescription drugs on embryonic development.
6. Know the process of labor and delivery, as well as nursing the baby post-delivery.
7. Understand the *in vitro* fertilization procedure and other methods of artificial fertilization.

Key Terms

cleavage
blastula
gastrulation
germ layers
gastrula
in vitro fertilization
cytoplasmic localization
blastomere
vegetal pole
animal pole
gray crescent
blastocyst
ectoderm
endoderm
mesoderm
embryonic induction
cell differentiation
morphogens
morphogenesis
apoptosis
differentiation
embryonic induction
pattern formation
master genes
homeotic genes
somites
fetus
morula
implantation
extraembryonic membranes
amnion
yolk sac
chorion
allantois
placenta
human chorionic gonadotropin, HCG
neural tube
teratogen
fetal alcohol syndrome, FAS
labor
oxytocin
lactation
prolactin

Lecture Outline

42.1 Mind-Boggling Births

A. In 1978 the first "test tube baby" was born by the reproductive technology, *in vitro* fertilization (IVF).
   1. This procedure involves injecting the mom with hormones to mature many eggs, injecting the sperm into the egg in the laboratory, and inserting the fertilized egg in the uterus.
   2. Over three million children have been conceived using IVF.

B. Multiple births are becoming more common.
   1. Fertility drugs and IVF are driving the increase in higher-order multiple births.
   2. Children born as multiple births have a higher risk of miscarriage and birth defects.
   3. Multiple newborns usually have lower birth weights and higher mortality rates.

C. The "octomom" had twelve embryos implanted and gave birth to eight infants.
   1. Fertility doctors are advised to limit the amount of embryos implanted at one time.

42.2 Stages of Reproduction and Development

A. Gamete formation: eggs or sperm form and mature within the parents.

B. Fertilization begins when a sperm penetrates an egg and is completed when the sperm nucleus fuses with the egg nucleus, resulting in formation of the zygote.

C. Repeated mitotic divisions—cleavage—convert the zygote to a blastula; cell numbers increase but not cell size.

D. Gastrulation results in three germ layers, or tissues.
   1. *Ectoderm* is the outer layer; it gives rise to the nervous system and the outer layers of the integument.
   2. *Endoderm* is the inner layer; it gives rise to the gut and organs derived from it.
   3. *Mesoderm* is the middle layer; muscle, organs of circulation, reproduction, excretion, and skeleton are derived from it.

E. Organ formation begins as germ layers subdivide into populations of cells destined to become unique in structure and function.

F. During growth and tissue specialization, organs acquire specialized chemical and physical properties.

42.3 From Zygote to Gastrula

A. Components of Eggs and Sperm

1. The sperm contributes little more than the paternal DNA.
2. The oocyte contains the majority of materials that will affect early development.
3. Penetration of the egg by the sperm triggers a structural reorganization in the egg cytoplasm.
   a. In a frog egg, microtubules move granules from the animal pole to form a *gray crescent* near the equator opposite the penetration site.
   b. Near the crescent, the body axis of the frog embryo will become established and gastrulation will begin.
   c. Experiments by Hans Spemann have shown that the substances needed for proper development are in the gray crescent.

B. Cleavage—The Start of Multicellularity

1. After fertilization, the zygote begins a series of divisions in which each cell is pinched into two cells (blastomeres).
2. This process is not random and different blastomeres will end up with different genetic messages in a process known as cytoplasmic localization.
3. Radial cleavage starts with cuts perpendicular to the mitotic spindle, producing cells of similar size but with different parts of the cytoplasm.
4. In other cells (frog, for instance), the cuts do not go all the way through, so the cells produced are smaller at the animal pole.
5. In mammals, rotational cleavage results in an inner cell mass (future embryo), which forms on the inside of a hollow sphere.
6. The amount of yolk stored inside the egg also affects cleavage patterns.
   a. Cleavage is incomplete when an abundance of yolk impedes the cytoplasmic division, like in the insects, reptiles, birds, and most fishes.
   b. When little yolk is present, the first cut divides all the cytoplasm in complete cleavage (amphibians and mammals).

C. Gastrulation

1. Experiments by Hilde Marigold proved that the cells in the dorsal lip of an opening are descended from the gray crescent.
   a. Cells from the dorsal lip of a salamander were implanted in a different salamander.
   b. A salamander with two joined bodies developed.
   c. If no cytoplasm from the gray crescent is present, development will not progress normally.

42.4 How Specialized Tissues and Organs Form

A. Cell Differentiation

1. From gastrulation onward, cell lineages also engage in selective gene expression, which is the start of cell differentiation.
2. Morphogens are signaling molecules produced by master genes.
   a. They diffuse out and form a concentration gradient in the embryo.
   b. A morphogen's effect on target cells is proportional to its concentration.

B. Responses to Morphogens

1. Morphogenesis is the progression of differentiated cells into tissues and organs; it is the result of several events.
2. There are proteins that serve as maternal effect genes.
   a. These genes are expressed during egg production and they influence development.
   b. In fruit flies, a gene called the bicoid gene influences the development of separate anterior and posterior ends.

C. Embryonic Induction
   1. Embryonic induction indicates that on embryonic tissue influences the development of neighboring cells.
   2. Sheets of cells expand and fold as cells change shape, forming organs such as the neural tube.
      a. Signals from the notochord direct the formation of the neural tube.
      b. The formation of the neural tube begins by the thickening of the neural plate near the notochord.
      c. Microtubules form and the edges of the plate fold inward to form a neural groove.
      d. The edges of the neural plate are drawn together to form the completed neural tube.

D. Cell Migrations
   1. Cells move from one location to another due to either hormonal or chemical signals.
      a. This process occurs in the formation of the neural crest.
   2. During cell migrations, the cells move like an amoeba via the action of actin microfilaments until adhesion proteins hold it in place.

E. Apoptosis
   1. Apoptosis is programmed cell death, which helps sculpt body parts.
   2. Apoptosis is the genetically programmed elimination of tissues and cells that are used for only short periods in the embryo or adult.
      a. Enzymes from lysosomes digest away portions of cells, so that those cells die.
      b. Apoptosis helps remove the webbing between human fingers and also disposes of the tadpole's tail.

42.5 An Evolutionary View of Development

A. A General Model of Animal Development
   1. Through studies of roundworms, fruit flies, fish, and mice, researchers have come up with a general model of animal development.
   2. A key point of this model is that where and when particular genes are expressed determines how an animal body develops.
      a. Molecules confined to different areas of an unfertilized egg induce localized expression of master genes in the zygote, and products of these genes diffuse outward forming a concentration gradient that forms along the head-to-tail and dorsal-to-ventral axes.
      b. Depending on where they fall within these concentration gradients, cells in the embryo activate or suppress other master genes.
      c. This positional information affects expression of *homeotic genes*, genes that regulate development of specific body parts.

B. Developmental Constraints and Modifications
   1. The basic body plans of the major animal groups have not changed due to a limited number of master genes.
   2. These genes have imposed phyletic constraints in addition to the more well-known physical and architectural constraints.
      a. An example of a physical constraint is the surface-area-to-volume ratio.
      b. Architectural constraints are imposed by body axes.
      c. Phyletic constraints are those imposed by interactions among genes that regulate development in a lineage.

42.6 Overview of Human Development

A. Pregnancy lasts an average of 38 weeks.
   1. Embryo formation takes about two weeks.
   2. The embryonic period lasts from the third to the end of the eighth week.
   3. The fetal period extends from the eighth week until birth.

B. The first cleavage starts 12–24 hours after fertilization.
C. It takes one week for the blastocyst to form and then it embeds in the mother's uterus.
D. The prenatal period is divided into three trimesters.
E. After birth, the body continues to grow and continues to change proportions.

42.7 Early Human Development

A. Cleavage and Implantation
   1. During the first few days after fertilization, the zygote undergoes repeated cleavages as it travels down the oviduct.
   2. By the time it reaches the uterus, it is a solid ball of cells (morula), which is transformed into a blastocyst.
      a. Implantation begins about six days after fertilization.
      b. The inner cell mass of the blastocyst is transformed into an embryonic disk that will develop into the embryo proper within the next week.

B. Extraembryonic Membranes
   1. Membranes start forming outside the embryo and have several functions.
      a. The *amnion* is a fluid-filled sac that keeps the embryo from drying out and acts as a shock absorber.
      b. The *yolk sac* becomes a site for blood cell formation.
      c. The *chorion,* a protective membrane around the embryo, forms a portion of the placenta and secretes a hormone (human chorionic gonadotropin) that maintains the uterine lining after implantation.
      d. The *allantois* does not function in waste storage (as it does in birds) but is active in blood formation and formation of the urinary bladder.

C. Early Hormone Production
   1. Cells of the blastocyst secrete the hormone HCG, which stimulates the corpus luteum to continue the secretion of estrogen and progesterone, preventing menstruation.
   2. HCG is also detected in home pregnancy tests as early as the third week of pregnancy.

42.8 Emergence of the Vertebrate Body Plan

A. By two weeks after fertilization, a two-layered embryonic disk consisting of ectoderm and endoderm has formed.
   1. The primitive streak, a forerunner of the neural tube from which the brain and spinal cord will form, has appeared.
   2. Some cells also form the notochord, from which the vertebrae will form.
B. Toward the end of the third week, mesoderm has developed and is giving rise to somites—segments of bones and skeletal muscles.
C. Pharyngeal arches start to form that will contribute to the face, neck, mouth, nose, larynx, and pharynx; spaces in the mesoderm will become the coelomic cavity.

42.9 The Function of the Placenta

A. The placenta is a combination of uterine lining and extraembryonic membranes.
   1. At full term, the placenta will cover approximately one-fourth of the inner surface of the uterus.
   2. The placenta forms early in pregnancy.
B. Materials are exchanged from blood capillaries of mother to fetus, and vice versa, by diffusion.
   1. The maternal blood and fetal blood do not mix!
   2. After the third month, the placenta produces large amounts of HCG, progesterone, and estrogen to maintain the uterine lining.

42.10 Emergence of Distinctly Human Features

A. By the end of the fourth week, the embryo is 500 times larger than when it started but still smaller than a centimeter in length.

B. It has embarked on an intricate program of cell differentiation and morphogenesis, including development of limbs, circulation, and umbilical cord.

C. The second trimester encompasses months four, five, and six; the individual is now called a fetus; the heart is beating; fuzzy hair covers the body.

D. The third trimester extends from month seven until birth; the earliest delivery in which survival on its own is possible is the middle of this trimester.

42.11 Miscarriages, Stillbirths, and Birth Defects

A. What Can Go Wrong

1. A miscarriage is the loss of a pregnancy before 20 weeks—after that time, a loss is called a stillbirth.
   a. The risk of a miscarriage is about 12–15 percent, and only 1.5 percent chance if a normal embryo is seen via ultrasound at 8–11 weeks.
2. Birth defects occur in approximately 3 percent of births.
   a. Common birth defects involve the heart, neural tube, and cleft lip anomalies.

B. Risk Factors

1. Chromosome abnormalities are responsible for 5–10 percent of still births and 50 percent of miscarriages.
   a. These risk factors increase as the parents' ages increase.
2. Women who are happy and are of a normal weight are less apt to miscarry.
3. Teratogens are substances that interfere with proper fetal development.
4. A mother requires a well-balanced diet to fuel fetal development.
   a. Deficiencies in iodine and folic acid can lead to specific defect in the offspring.
5. There are some infectious diseases that cause the mom's unborn child to have serious issues.
   a. Rubella (German measles) can cause developmental problems if the mom was not previously vaccinated.
   b. Toxoplasmosis, which can be transmitted via contact with cat litter, can cause serious problems with the child or cause a miscarriage.
6. Fetal alcohol syndrome results in physical and mental abnormalities caused by alcohol consumption by the mother.
7. Pregnant women should avoid caffeine, cigarette smoke, and hot tub use to avoid a miscarriage.
8. Certain medications (e.g., Paxil and Accutane) can cause heart abnormalities in the developing infants.

C. Morning Sickness

1. Two-thirds of women experience morning sickness from weeks 6–12 of pregnancy.
2. Morning sickness may have an adaptive function, providing protection against teratogens and other harmful substance.
   a. Some of the substances that seem the most distasteful to pregnant women are those that would be most likely to contain dangerous microbes.

42.12 Birth and Lactation

A. Labor and Delivery

1. The birth process (labor) begins with contractions of the uterine muscles; the cervical canal dilates and the amniotic sac ruptures.

    a. The hormone relaxin softens the cervical connective tissues and makes the bridges between the pelvic bones looser.
    b. The hormone oxytocin induces powerful uterine contractions.
  2. The fetus is expelled, accompanied by fluid and blood; the umbilical cord is severed, and finally the placenta is expelled.
  3. Corticotropin-releasing hormone affects the timing of labor, and it may contribute to post-partum depression.

B. Surgical Delivery
  1. A cesarean section (C-section) involves surgically opening the uterus to remove the baby.
    a. Reasons for performing a C-section are: abnormal positioning of the baby or placenta, a kinked umbilical cord, or to avoid the transmission of sexually transmitted diseases.

C. Nourishing the Newborn
  1. The mammary glands first produce a special fluid for the newborn; then, under the influence of prolactin, they produce milk.
  2. Oxytocin is released in response to suckling and further increases the milk supply.
  3. Besides providing nourishment, human breast milk contains antibodies that protect a newborn from some viruses and bacteria.

42.13 Mind-Boggling Births (Revisited)

A. New techniques have expanded on the idea of *in vitro* fertilization.
  1. Intracytoplasmic sperm injection actually propels the sperm into the egg to be later implanted in the uterus.
  2. A blastocyst developed from another woman's egg can also be implanted in the uterus.
  3. A woman's egg could be fertilized in the lab and then implanted in a surrogate.

B. Some screening can be performed prior to implantation to rule out birth defects.

Suggestions for Presenting the Material

- There are numerous excellent animated figures available to help you present this material. The animated figures provide excellent visual context for your students.
- Table 42.2 presents a good overview of human development, and Figure 42.18 presents a good depiction of human embryo development. The specifics of each development in each time interval can lead to a "cataloging" approach, which can be alleviated by using the videotape referred to in the Enrichment section.
- Although it is not always convenient to do so, the demonstration of live chick embryos is a real attention-arresting sight. Don't neglect to place an embryo under a stereomicroscope to see the heartbeat and blood flow.
- The early development of sea urchin embryos is not as difficult to demonstrate as that of the chick. Biological supply houses sell demonstration kits. Timing is a critical factor for viewing all the stages, so you should plan to videotape the sequence.
- When discussing the placenta, be sure to mention that it not only supplies nutrients and oxygen to the offspring, but it also forms an immune barrier. If humans did not have a placenta, the mother's immune system would eventually detect something "foreign" in her body and the fetus would be rejected. The presence of a placenta prevents this from occurring. Notice that animals like the kangaroo have no placenta. Therefore, the offspring is expelled from the mom at an immature stage and must complete development in the pouch.

- Set up a Jeopardy-type quiz for your students, which may help them distinguish between similar terms, such as blastula, gastrula, etc. A template that contains the setup can be found at: **http://jeopardylabs.com/**

Classroom and Laboratory Enrichment

- If at all possible, show a videotape or film depicting development of some animal. Because of the dynamic nature of this process and the rapid changes, static photographs are woefully inadequate.
- The topic of prenatal development will be greatly enhanced by the use of a videotape such as *The Miracle of Life,* distributed by Crown Video through retail outlets.
- Discussion of the tadpole's tail change into a tailless frog gives students a familiar visual image of how apoptosis in development works.
- If your budget allows, purchase some prepared slides of the various stages of embryonic development. Slides of a whitefish blastula are often available for this purpose.
- Name a number of species that undergo metamorphoses as part of their development.

Classroom Discussion Ideas

- Why do think the number of multiple births has increased so dramatically in the past 20 years? Part of the reason involves reproductive technology, but also women that have children at older ages are more prone to multiple births. Present the multiple-birth statistics from earlier generations with that of the current multiple-birth trends.
- What are the risks of mothers in their 40s and even 50s giving birth? Evaluate both the risk to the mother and the fetus/child. There are even examples of women giving birth to their own grandchildren via the use of their daughters' donor eggs!
- List ways in which the increased number of multiple births results in increased costs to society.
- Will Americans ever agree to controls over fertility and reproduction as some other countries have? Do you think there should be legislation to prohibit the amount of eggs fertility doctors could implant at once? Should physicians that disobey these laws face serious ramifications?

Additional Ideas for Classroom Discussion

- The incidence of Down syndrome is said to increase with maternal age, especially for mothers over age 40. Based on the information in the present chapter, can you explain why?
- The placenta supplements, or completely replaces, the activity of three organ systems in the fetus. What are they?
- Many communities, and even states, restrict the teaching of human reproduction. Why do you think this body system is singled out over, say, digestion or respiration for such a prohibition?
- When an insect is in the pupal stage, there is seemingly no activity. Some people have even called it the "resting stage"—erroneously! Biochemically and histologically, what is happening during the pupal stage?
- Explain this quote by Lewis Wolpert (1986): "It is not birth, marriage, or death, but gastrulation which is truly the most important time of your life."
- Make a chart detailing the three germ layers and the tissues they become.
- Emphasize the importance of the gray crescent tissue.
- Discuss how the study of embryology has changed scientists' views on classification.

How Would You Vote? Classroom Discussion Ideas

- Monitor the voting for the online question. The tradeoff between concerns over high-risk pregnancies and assisting couples in enhancing their fertility is a difficult question to consider. Have your students break into small groups and present both the pro and con arguments. On the board or overhead projector, summarize the primary arguments and categorize them as: personal, social, economic, etc.
- Were any of the students in the class created by the use of reproductive technology? They would be certain to have strong feelings on the issue!
- How does the selling of eggs differ from organ donation? Does it damage the donor in any way? Does it impact their future fertility in any way? Are the drugs used to bring about the maturation of many eggs harmful?
- Do you think fertility records should be available to the offspring? Should a child be able to find out anything about their egg or sperm donor?
- What characteristics would someone look for in a sperm or egg donor? Intelligence? Good health? An attractive appearance?
- Have students complete class polling using the JoinIn clickers.

Term Paper Topics, Library Activities, and Special Projects

- We hear about "sperm banks" now and then. Do such repositories actually exist? Where are they? How do they function?
- Any interruption in the menstrual cycle, whether temporary or permanent, is cause for concern. Report on the causes and effects of the cessation of menstruation in females who drastically reduce their body weight (anorexia) or body fat (as in body building).
- Search for the physiological explanation for the cessation of menstruation (menopause)—usually when a woman is between the ages of 40 and 50. Is there any comparable phenomenon in men?
- It is known that overcrowding and stressful conditions reduce reproductive behavior in rodents. Is there any published evidence of such a phenomenon in humans?
- Research the family planning practices of China. Find out the current practice of child restriction and the effects this is having on China's demography. There have been articles written about the rewards given to families who have daughters; is this a valid or regular practice in the country?
- Investigate the use of juvenile hormone-mimicking chemicals to control insects. What are the successes, failures, limitations, advantages, and prognoses for the future?
- Embryologists can transplant imaginal discs (invaginated epidermal sacs programmed to produce adult structures at metamorphosis) of insect larvae to produce very unusual adults (for example, legs where antennae should be). Investigate the procedures used and the results produced. Could this be done in vertebrates?
- Research the discovery of the homeotic box or homeotic genes in vertebrates. How similar are they across groups? How do they compare to human gene sequences? What does the discovery suggest about the evolutionary phylogeny of animals?
- How is *in vitro* fertilization performed? What are the chances of success? What additional procedures have been developed based on IVF technology? What are their chances for success?
- Read the original research performed by Hans Spemann in the early 1900s concerning the importance of the gray crescent in animal development. Was this study innovative for its time?
- As you have seen from the text, the neural tube closure occurs very early in fetal development. Researchers have discovered that the incidence of neural tube abnormalities can be decreased by

taking folic acid supplements. Their subsequent idea was to include folic acid in prenatal vitamins. Now folic acid is included in everyday food items, such as flour, to help reduce the occurrence of these conditions. Do you see a problem with this solution? After first discovering she is pregnant, when does a mom visit the doctor for prenatal vitamins?

- Look into the research relating to the bicoid protein. Have experiments been performed on organisms other than fruit flies?
- What happens to the tail that humans have during fetal development?
- What is the mechanism of the "morning-after" pill? How does it impede implantation?
- What do pharyngeal arches later become?
- Choose one of the extraembryonic membranes. How does it function in humans? Does its function differ in other organisms?
- Research a specific teratogen. How does it impede normal development?
- What is thalidomide? What was its original use? What abnormalities did it produce? When was its use restricted for pregnant women?

Possible Responses to *Critical Thinking* Questions

1. There is good reason rubella would cause so many of its effects on the fetus during the first trimester. It is during this time that the organs are developing; limbs form, and toes and fingers are sculpted. Growth of the head surpasses that of other body regions. By eight weeks, all major organs and systems have been formed, which is why the first three months of development (first trimester) is when the infection of the rubella virus has the most effect.
2. Germ cells have an important property that somatic cells (body cells) do not. This characteristic is that germ cells have the potential to differentiate into many different kinds of cells in various tissues. This ability becomes evident in the many different types of structures that can be found in a teratoma. Most teratomas are benign (non-cancerous), but they can contain many unusual collections of tissue. It is thought that most teratomas are present from birth, although they may be discovered much later in life.
3. Oxytocin has a two-fold effect in the mother's body. One of its functions is to produce the uterine contractions that result in the baby's birth. The other function relates to the milk let-down reflex while the baby is nursing. If alcohol reduces oxytocin production, the baby will not get as much milk during the nursing process as it normally would.

Possible Responses to *Data Analysis Exercise* Questions

Evidence has indicated that there may be a possible correlation between multiple births and the incidence of birth defects. This study in Florida, 1996–2000, set out to gather data to test that hypothesis.

1. The most common type of birth defect in the single-birth group was heart defects.
2. Heart defects were more common in multiple births than among single births.
3. Multiples have more than twice the risk of developing central nervous system defects as compared to single births.
4. According to this study, a multiple pregnancy does not increase the relative risk of a chromosomal defect in offspring.

43

ANIMAL BEHAVIOR

Chapter Outline

Objectives

1. Understand how scientists have proven that some behavioral traits are genetic.
2. Learn about the concepts of instinctive behavior, learned behavior, imprinting, and conditioning.
3. Understand how behavior is influenced by environment, as in behavioral plasticity and epigenetic behavior.
4. Know the instinctual responses to stimuli, such as kinesis and taxis.
5. Be able to describe how adaptive behaviors develop.
6. Study the various forms of communication between individuals of a species.
7. Know the basis for sexual selection and parental care in various animal populations.
8. Compare the pros and cons of animals living in groups.
9. Understand why some animals exhibit subservient behavior for the wellbeing of the population.

Key Terms

stimulus
instinctive behavior
fixed action pattern
learned behavior
imprinting
classical conditioning
operant conditioning
habituation
observational learning
communication signals
behavioral plasticity
pheromone
kinesis
migration
taxis
tactile display
lek
territory
dominant hierarchy
sexual selection
selfish herd
altruistic behavior
eusocial behavior
theory of inclusive fitness

Lecture Outline

43.1 Alarming Bee Behavior

A. Africanized "killer bees" have arrived in the United States.
   1. This type of bee resulted from African bees that mated with European varieties.
   2. These bees are no more venomous than regular honeybees, but they are much more aggressive.
      a. There have been rare fatalities, particularly in those that are allergic to bee stings.
   3. They have a heightened sensitivity to the alarm pheromones released from a fellow bee.
      a. When threatened, a bee releases a warning pheromone that brings other bees to the area.

43.2 Behavioral Genetics

A. Genetic Variation within a Species
   1. Animals react to different stimuli in a way that is genetic in nature.
      a. Experiments performed by mating two different types of garter snakes with different food preferences helped to prove this.
      b. Fruit flies show an identified genetic marker to indicate whether they are "rovers" or "sitters"
         1) Rovers move around as they feed and sitters remain in one spot.
         2) These two distinct groups of flies show different amounts of an enzyme responsible for foraging.

B. Genetic Variation among Species
   1. Hormone production, which is genetic, influences animal behavior.
      a. Studies were performed on voles relating to oxytocin levels and the animal's preference for monogamy.
      b. Additional studies indicated a link between arginine vasopressin hormone and promiscuity in voles.

C. Human Behavior Genetics
   1. It is thought that most human traits are based on several genes and environmental influences.
   2. Experiments are being performed to see if autistic children either produce less oxytocin or have fewer oxytocin receptors.
      a. Trials are underway to determine if oxytocin could be a treatment for autism.

43.3 Instinct and Learning

A. Instinctive Behavior
   1. Animals are born with some instinctive behaviors.
      a. An example is the procedure by which cuckoo birds discard other eggs in the foster parent's nest.

2. The cuckoo birds' actions are considered an example of a fixed action pattern.
    b. A fixed action plan means that once the action is initiated, the rest of the actions automatically follow without the need for additional cues.

B. Time-Sensitive Learning
  1. Imprinting is when a particular behavior is learned during a certain time period.
     a. The standard example of imprinting shows baby geese following any maternal figure when exposed at an early age.
     b. There appears to be a window of opportunity for birds to learn a species-specific song.

C. Conditioned Responses
  1. Animals can learn throughout life based on a positive and negative reward system.
     a. Classical conditioning can be defined as an animal connecting two stimuli together when presented at the same time.
        i. The typical example of classical conditioning is Pavlov's dogs salivating due to the anticipation of food.
  2. Operant conditioning occurs when an animal changes his behavior based on a positive-negative reward system.

D. Other Types of Learned Behavior
  1. Habituation is when an animal learns a behavior even though it has not been exposed to a reward system.
     a. Lobsters learn to recognize other lobsters they have battled.
  2. Observational learning occurs when an animal learns to mimic an activity performed by another animal.

43.4 Environmental Effects on Behavioral Traits

A. Behavioral Plasticity
  1. Behavioral plasticity is when behavioral traits are changed by environmental factors.
     a. An example occurs when caterpillars infested with parasites consume harmful alkaloids to rid themselves of the parasites.
     b. Under normal circumstances, the caterpillars would shun the harmful alkaloids.
  2. Male cichlid fish can be dominant or subordinate depending on the social environment.

B. Epigenetic Effects
  1. Heritable changes occur in behavior without changing the DNA sequence.
     a. A female rat who doesn't get much grooming from her mother does not groom her offspring.
        1) Researchers have observed demethylation of the DNA of those rats not receiving the tactile stimulation early in life.
        2) This demethylation is passed on to their offspring.

43.5 Movements and Navigation

A. Taxis and Kinesis
  1. An innate directional response is called taxis.
     a. Planarians automatically move away from light and toward gravity.
  2. Kinesis is defined by an animal speeding up or slowing down its rate with no regard for direction.
     a. Planaria move more in light than darkness.

B. Migration
  1. Migration is when an animal makes a determined effort to arrive at a new habitat.

a. Animals, like birds, often winter in a warmer environment and then return to the original location.
b. Other animals return to its hatching site to breed and die.

2. Some animals use an innate compass that enables them to detect the variations in the Earth's magnetic field.
3. Some animals use the location of the moon and stars to find their direction.

43.6 Communication Signals

A. Evolution of Animal Communication
1. Animals use various means of communication to relay information to another of their species.
   a. The communication persists only if it is of benefit to both parties involved.

B. Types of Signals
1. Pheromones are chemical signals and often active in mate selection.
2. Animals emit auditory signals to signal prospective mates or to warn others of danger.
3. Visual displays are often used to attract a mate.
4. A tactile display involves one individual transmitting a message by touching another.
   a. The bees' waggle dance relates the distance and location of a food source to other bees.

C. Eavesdroppers and Counterfeiters
1. Some predators listen to communication between organisms to locate prey.
   a. Bats use this method to located frogs.
2. Other animals mimic the signals of other species to attract a meal.
   b. Other predator insects imitate the flashes of fireflies to lure them closer.

43.7 Mates, Offspring, and Reproductive Success

A. Mating Systems
1. Individuals often compete in various ways for mating privileges known as sexual selection.
   a. Male hangingflies must bring large gifts of food to win over females.
   b. Females observe the male fiddler crabs waving their large claw.
   c. Male birds put on a colorful display to impress females.
   d. A lek is an area where birds exhibit their mating displays.
   e. A territory refers to an area where males fight off others for domination.

B. Parental Care
1. Many species involve parental care duties.
   a. Many birds and some mammals are cared for by both parents.
   b. Young reptiles, with the exception of crocodiles, do not require parental care.
   c. Most mammals are cared for by the mother animal.

432.8 Living in Groups

A. Defense against predators.
1. Often groups of animals deter predators.
   a. Examples include sawfish caterpillars and other animals such as prairie dogs, who give a warning call.
   b. A selfish herd is when the members of a group of animals tend to hide behind one another.

B. Improved Feeding Opportunities
1. Animals in groups may have advantageous feeding opportunities.
   a. Group hunting may not actually provide more food, but may be better for protection.

b. Animals in groups may learn behaviors from each other, like the utilization of tools in primates.

C. Dominance Hierarchies

1. Some animals establish hierarchies in their group structure.

a. Wolves develop packs and only the dominant members can mate.

D. Regarding the Costs

1. In some circumstances, living in groups is disadvantageous.

a. Groups may attract predators and spread diseases more readily.

b. Animals in a group must compete for food and space.

43.9 Why Sacrifice Yourself?

A. Social Insects

1. Eusocial animals have developed a system where there are only a few breeding individuals.

a. Insects that have this system are ants, termites, and bees.

b. Other insects have auxiliary functions to support the queen.

B. Social Mole-Rats

1. African mole-rats are the only mammals with this organizational structure.

C. Evolution of Altruism

1. Workers in a eusocial society show altruistic behavior, which means working toward the good of the group.

a. The theory of inclusive fitness explains that this behavior helps promote reproductive success of relatives.

b. Since relatives share the same gene pool, this behavior helps promote reproductive success of their own genes.

43.10 Alarming Bee Behavior (Revisited)

A. Honeybee females sting, but it sacrifices their life.

B. While the stinger is in the skin, additional venom can enter the skin.

1. Remove the stinger to prevent more venom from pumping into the skin.

2. The stinging sensation results from the injection of mellitin.

a. Mellatin results in the flow of ions that translate into the sensation of pain in the brain.

Suggestions for Presenting the Material

- It might be interesting to start out your discussion of animal behaviors by talking about particular animal actions and see if the students can make a guess as to how they are derived. Start out with some easy ones; for example, a monkey learns which lever to press to get a reward. As your discussion continues, get into some more confusing behaviors, such as why a dog circles around before it sits. This will enable the students to see that it is not always so easy to determine the cause or method by which a behavior originates. This may spark their interests in learning more about animal behaviors.
- If possible, show some slides illustrating animal behavior. Many of our students are primarily visual learners and they may understand the actions better by actually viewing them.
- Be sure to stress the specific definitions of classical and operant conditioning so that the students are clear on the differences.
- Utilize a "Jeopardy" of "Who Wants To Be a Millionaire" format to learn key terms. Templates can be found at the following website: http://teach.fcps.net/trt2/links/powerpointgames.htm

- There may be students in the class that have taken their dog to obedience class. Have them describe the process and what type of learning it utilized.

Classroom and Laboratory Enrichment

- For those students in the class with some animal experiences, have them name behavior that seems based on instinct. Does there seem to be any advantage to this behavior at one time? Is there any advantage to this behavior now? If not, why does the behavior persist?
- When training animals to learn a behavior, what method works best? If you provide positive reinforcement, how do you determine the most effective reward?
- Humans record habit memory in an area of the brain known as the *corpus striatum*. Is this area of the brain present in other animals that exhibit the habituation type of learned behavior?
- Can you think of other specific courtship displays in other animals? In some species of lizards, for example, the female releases hormones that prepare her for reproduction only after she is stimulated by the male's visual display.
- Has anyone viewed the television program "Meerkat Manor"? Have the meerkats on the program displayed any of the behaviors discussed in the chapter?
- The text shows that groups of animals, such as lions, are not more effective hunters in a group. Why do you suppose they often continue this behavior in spite of its lack of success?
- Place an ant farm in the classroom. They are inexpensive and fairly easy to maintain. Observe the functions of the different groups of ants in their eusocial community.

Classroom Discussion Ideas

- Discuss the role of pheromones in insect management. Traps can be devised containing female pheromones and a sticky surface. When the males enter, expecting to find females of their species, they are trapped. Some farmers also use pheromones to simply encourage damaging insects away from their crops by placing pheromones in a distant location. Why are pheromones not used more often by commercial exterminators or regular homeowners?
- Could the pheromones of Africanized honeybees be different enough from those of regular bees that they could be used to capture them?
- Do you envision Africanized honeybees spreading further into additional states? Why or why not?
- Recently there has been a decline in the number of populations of normal honeybees. Do you have any ideas why this may be occurring?
- Which traits of the Africanized honeybee make it more adaptive than the European honeybee?
- Why would any Africanized honeybees sting so rapidly when they can sting only once? Does this seem like an adaptive behavior?
- With the advent of global warming, do you envision the Africanized honeybee colonies to spread northward?
- Should drastic methods be undertaken to destroy Africanized honeybees in the U.S.? Even at the expense of destroying indigenous populations of bees that are important for fertilization?
- How have other induced species proved detrimental to their new environments? How were these non-native populations addressed? Could this provide valuable information as far as how the Africanized honeybee situation could be handled?

Additional Ideas for Classroom Discussion

- We have seen that animals respond to different stimuli. Often animals respond to stimuli that we cannot even detect. For example, it is said that a shark can smell a few drops of blood in an area the size of a swimming pool. For each of our special senses (vision, smell, taste, hearing), name an animal whose ability to detect stimuli may be more acute than ours. How is this ability adaptive?
- From the studies performed on birds, it seems as though they have a window of opportunity to learn to sing a species-specific song. Do humans have this same time period during which they must learn language? This may be hard to prove or disprove since there are few examples of humans developing without early exposure to language. Do you think this could affect an individual's ability to learn a second language more easily early in life?
- Can you think of other examples of a fixed-action behavior of instinctive behavior like that of the cuckoo and the foster parent? Do humans exhibit any behaviors that seem similar?
- Does your household pet exhibit any of the behaviors noted in this chapter? Which of their behaviors appear instinctive? Which ones are learned behaviors? Do they initiate any communication signals to you or other animals? Can you easily interpret what some of these signals mean?
- From the bright coloration of many male birds' feathers, we can assume that birds can discern colors and that they are used as a visual display for prospective mates. Research some additional specific courting behaviors in different species of birds.
- The chapter mentions the fact that chimpanzees use sticks to extract termites from their mound. Can you think of other similar primate behaviors utilizing primitive tools?
- Discuss the different levels of prenatal care given to various animal species.
- Often the alpha male of a wolf pack is the largest individual. Can you see a genetic advantage to passing those genes along? Do humans keep some of these same characteristics in mind when they select a mate?
- Investigate the study involving the natives in Papua New Guinea and infanticide. Can you find other cultures with a similar practice? Can you see any increase in this type of behavior in ghetto areas where the daily stress is high?
- Oxytocin is sometimes called the "cuddle hormone." Do you think this nickname is accurate, considering that it may involve the monogamous practices of voles?
- Mention examples of migration that occurs over long distances. The gray whale is an excellent example, since they travel approximately 5,000–6,800 miles!
- How do insects make sounds by rubbing their legs together? What is the purpose of these sounds?

How Would You Vote? Classroom Discussion Idea

- Monitor the voting for the online question. Obviously there is something in the genetics of the Africanized bees that gives them a heightened response to the alarm hormone.
- These bees would be especially dangerous for the many individuals who react adversely to insect bites. These highly allergic individuals may experience dangerous anaphylactic shock as a result of a single bee sting and may require an emergency-department visit.
- If genetic engineering were successfully performed on the Africanized bees, they might be able to convert their aggressive nature to that of normal honeybees.

- The question really involves how you want to spend your genetic-research money. I think most individuals would rank eradication of diseases like cancer and AIDS as a much more important use of their research funds.

Term Paper Topics, Library Activities, and Special Projects

- In the studies examining behavioral genetics, fruit flies were utilized to isolate a particular gene that determines if flies are rovers or sitters. Why is Drosophila used so often for genetic studies? When did researchers begin using fruit flies in the study of genetics? What features do they possess that make them well adapted to this kind of study?
- Research information regarding the functions of oxytocin and antidiuretic hormone in humans. Both of these hormones are made in the hypothalamus and stored in the posterior lobe of the pituitary gland. Since the oxytocin level appears to be associated with autism-like disorders, have any studies compared the hypothalamus from normal individuals with that of autistic patients?
- Perform additional research into Lorenz's studies on imprinting in geese. Can you find any studies with other species where imprinting occurs?
- Look into Koko's World, a project where humans taught sign language to gorillas. There is evidence as part of this study that other gorillas began imitating Koko's use of sign language appropriately. What type of learned behavior does this represent?
- How did researchers go about translating the motions of the honeybee waggle dance? Can humans actually locate the source of the food by interpretation of the dance alone?
- Human pheromones are for sale on the Internet. Can you find any studies that indicate their role in human mate selection?
- Read Ivan Pavlov's original paper on classical conditioning from the 1890s. He originally set out to study the digestive enzymes of dogs from an anatomical standpoint. His research changed focus when he noticed a "psychic secretion" in the dogs' mouths. Do you think you could have derived his theory of classical conditioning if presented with the same laboratory results?
- Read more about Stevan Arnold's research involving the feeding behavior of garter snakes. Do you think this same genetic alteration that affects feeding preferences exists in other animals? Other similar studies involve the feeding practices of rats—what did they conclude?
- Can you locate any research that attempts to connect oxytocin levels or number of oxytocin receptors and autism?
- Ludwig Huber and Bernhard Voelkl performed experiments in which marmosets learned certain behaviors by observing the actions of other marmosets. Are there any similar studies utilizing other species?
- This chapter mentions the experiment that illustrated that rats that received little grooming behavior as infants often do not provide this kind of behavior to their offspring. Scientists have proven that their DNA actually changed and this change was passed on to their offspring. Do humans that receive little nurturing during infancy often fail to provide this practice to their offspring? Do you think epigenetic effects of this type occur in humans or is it strictly learned behavior?
- Devise an experiment that would test the internal compass of birds.
- An interesting phenomenon occurs with sea turtles called arribada. Masses of sea turtles migrate to the same beach to lay eggs. How far do they travel? How do you think they locate the same location each year?

Possible Responses to *Critical Thinking* Questions

1. The act of moths flying toward the light seems to be an instinctual behavior. These types of actions can remain in a species even though they no longer serve a purpose, or in this case are actually disadvantageous. I would equate this behavior to that of a dog who spins around in several circles before lying down. Both of these behaviors are based on instinct and persist long beyond their usefulness.
2. Since the non-breeding Damaraland mole-rats are not related to those that breed, the purpose of their behavior cannot be genetic in nature. The researchers feel that the actions of the non-breeding mole-rats are ecological, meaning that it enables the mole-rats to survive more successfully long term in their current environment.

Possible Responses to *Data Analysis Exercise* Questions

African honeybees appear to be quite dominant in their newly adopted environment. This study traces their entry into the United States.

1. The Africanized bees first became established in Texas.
2. It appears as though Florida, Arkansas, and Louisiana first developed colonies of Africanized bees in 2005.
3. It is likely that Africanized bees were transported to Florida via humans, because there are no established colonies in Mississippi or Alabama, which are located between Florida and other infested states.

44

POPULATION ECOLOGY

Chapter Outline

Objectives

1. Know the different types of population distributions and their characteristics.
2. Learn how population sizes are estimated.
3. Describe what is meant by zero population growth and exponential growth, and their effects on the overall population size.
4. Characterize the density-dependent and density-independent factors that affect a population's growth.
5. Be able to describe what is meant by a life table and know the three types of survivorship curves.
6. Understand how natural selection influences population growth.
7. Learn the stages of growth in human populations over the years.
8. Observe how the total fertility rates differ in countries and understand the reasons they differ.
9. Characterize the demographic transition model, which illustrates human population growth rates.
10. Explain how the pre-reproductive population will impact population growth.

Key Terms

demographics
population
population size
age structure
reproductive base
population density
population distribution
quadrats
mark-recapture sampling
plot sampling
immigration
emigration
migration
zero population growth
per capita growth rate
exponential growth
doubling time
biotic potential
limiting factor
carrying capacity
logistic growth
density-dependent factor
density-independent factor
life history pattern
cohort
life table
type I survivorship curve
type II survivorship curve
type III survivorship curve
r-selected species
K-selected species
total fertility rate
demographic transition model
ecological footprint
replacement fertility rate

Lecture Outline

44.1 A Honking Mess

A. The Canadian geese population in the U.S. is increasing.
   1. These geese are often distasteful to humans because their feces contaminate lakes and grassy areas.
   2. Geese have been known to cause airplane accidents by causing engine failure.

B. Many Canadian geese still migrate to Canada, but non-migratory birds are becoming more prevalent.
   1. The non-migratory birds save energy by not traveling and can devote more energy to reproduction.
   2. Researchers are looking for ways to limit the non-migratory geese populations without harming the migratory birds.

44.2 Population Demographics

A. Population Size
   1. Population size is defined by the number of individuals in a population.
   2. Since it is difficult to count all individuals in a population, different methods are used.
      a. Plot sampling involves dividing an area into a grid, sampling the animals in several plots on the grid, and multiplying to determine the approximate number in the population.
      b. The mark-recapture method begins by having some representatives of the population tagged.
         1) The portion of marked animals in the second sample is taken to be representative of those marked in the whole population.

B. Population Density and Distribution
   1. Population density is the number of individuals per unit area or volume.
   2. Population distribution describes the location of individuals relative to one another.
      a. In clumped distribution, the density of the animals is arranged in clumps, possibly because of patchy resources.
      b. In near-uniform distribution, the organisms are fairly evenly placed in the environment.
      c. A random distribution pattern is one in which the individuals have no uniformity in their placement.

C. Age Structure
   1. An age structure lists the number of individuals in each age category.

a. Those in the pre-reproductive category are considered the reproductive base.

D. Effects of Scale and Timing

1. Factors such as the scale of the sampling area and the timing of the study may impact the information concerning a population's size.

44.3 Population Size and Exponential Growth

A. Gains and Losses in Population Size

1. Members of a population may leave (emigration) or enter a new population (immigration).

B. From Zero to Exponential Growth

1. When zero population growth occurs, it means that the number of individuals born is equal to the number dying.

2. The per-capita growth rate equals the birth rate minus the death rate.

a. If the per-capita growth rate is more than zero, the population is exhibiting exponential growth.

b. A J-shaped curve represents a population undergoing exponential growth.

C. The term biotic potential indicates the largest amount of increase that can occur in that particular population.

44.4 Limits on Population Growth

A. Environmental Limits on Growth

1. Limiting factors are components that are not plentiful and may restrict population growth.

B. Carrying Capacity and Logistic Growth

1. The carrying capacity is the largest number of individuals that a certain environment can support.

a. An S-shaped curve, representing logistic growth, is indicative of how a population naturally changes.

C. Two Categories of Limiting Factors

1. Density-dependent factors are those that become more critical as the population increases.

a. Examples of density-dependent factors are food, water, and incidence of disease.

2. Density-independent factors are those that are not influenced by the size of the population.

a. Examples of density-independent factors are floods, fires, and earthquakes.

44.5 Life History Patterns

A. Life Tables and Survivorship Curves

1. Life tables illustrate the number of individuals that survive in various age categories.

a. This involves the focusing on a cohort, a group of individuals born during the same interval.

2. A survivorship curve is a visual representation of the age-specific survival of a population.

a. A type I curve shows that the individuals usually survive until old age.

1) Animals exhibiting a type I curve produce a small amount of offspring that require much care, e.g., humans.

b. A type II curve illustrates that the survival rate does not relate to age, e.g., squirrels.

c. A type III curve shows that the majority of the individuals do not survive to maturity.

1) Animals exhibiting a type III curve produce many offspring that do not require much care, e.g., sea urchins.

B. Life History Strategies

1. A life history pattern is defined as how an organism allocates its resources between growth, maintenance, and reproduction in its lifetime.
   a. An r-selected species is one with many offspring needing little care.
      1) These animals tend to be small, have a short lifespan, and may be killed off due to density-independent factors.
   b. K-selected species produce few offspring that need much care.
      1) These animals are usually larger and populations, controlled by density-dependent factors, can approach the carrying factor.

44.6 Evidence of Evolving Life History Patterns

A. A Long-Term Study of Guppies

1. Life history traits can change as a response to an alteration in the types of predators.
   a. An example of this was shown by two isolated populations of guppies where there were different predators.
      1) As a result of the studies, it was concluded that differences between guppies preyed upon by different predators was genetic.

B. Overfishing of Atlantic Cod

1. The life history of the cod population in the North Atlantic changed due to over-fishing.
   a. Because of the overfishing, the cod population began to reproduce earlier.

44.7 Human Population Growth

A. The human population's rate of increase is largely due to migration into new climate zones, new technologies that increased the carrying capacity, and the elimination of some limiting factors.

B. Early Innovations and Expansions

1. This rate of growth is due to the fact that humans can spread easily into new habitat.
   a. Man has developed fire and tool-making abilities that are passed on from one generation to the next.
2. Humans have developed new technologies to increase the carrying capacity of the environment.
   a. Man learned how to cultivate crops, raise livestock.

C. From the Industrial Revolution Onward

1. Since the 1800s, the human population has increased dramatically.
2. The human population has learned how to overcome some limiting factors.
   a. Man learned how to combat many diseases and use fossil fuels for energy production.
   b. Fertilizers and pesticides improved agriculture.
   c. Improvements in nutrition, sanitation, and medicine also had a large impact.
3. It is estimated that the population on Earth will reach nine billion by 2050.

44..8 Anticipated Growth and Consumption

A. Fertility and Age Structure

1. The average number of children born to each woman of reproductive age is the total fertility rate.
   a. The fertility rate worldwide has decreased from 6.5 to 2.6 in the last 50 years.
   b. This decrease still puts the worldwide fertility rate above the number that keeps the population at a constant level.
   c. The replacement fertility rate is the average number of children a woman has before she replaces herself with a daughter who reaches reproductive age successfully.
   d. Approximately 1.9 billion people are approaching reproductive age.

B. The demographic transition model connects industrial development and changes in population growth rates.
   1. In countries where industrialization has not yet occurred, the birth rate is high.
      a. Children are needed to perform duties on a farm, e.g., many African countries.
   2. In industrialized nations, the birth rate declines, e.g., United States.
      a. Industrialized nations use a larger percentage of resources of the world.
   3. In post-industrialized nations, the population size may decrease.

C. Resource Consumption
   1. The term ecological footprint refers to the amount of the Earth's surface that is needed to support a level of development and consumption in a sustainable fashion.
      a. The U.S.'s ecological footprint is three times higher than other world residents and nine times higher than a typical Indian citizen.
      b. As other less-developed nations progress, we may not have enough land to sustain the Earth's population.

44.9 A Honking Mess (Revisited)

A. In 2009, a plane landed successfully on the Hudson River after the engines were damaged by geese.
   1. The DNA from the geese remnants obtained from the engines proved that they were from Canada, not New York.

Suggestions for Presenting the Material

- After presenting a population concept, mention the studies from the text that serve as environmental evidence. Have the students predict the outcome of the study. This will require that they fully understand the meaning of the concept and will encourage participation. If the class does not agree on a single outcome, take a vote before revealing the experimental results.
- Ask students if they can think of another environmental study that relates to the population definitions studied in this chapter.
- Name some various organisms and ask the class to determine whether they best represent a type I, type II, or type III survivorship curve.
- The website http://www.peterrussell.com/Odds/WorldClock.php provides a current census of the world's population on a running counter. You can even illustrate how much the U.S. and world populations have increased during your lecture!
- Students will perhaps be most interested in studies of population as they affect human population growth. Examination of the changes in worldwide patterns of population growth since the turn of the century will highlight the overwhelming need for humans to find ways to control the global population growth rate. The inclusion of human population growth studies in this chapter allows students to see that we are not exempt from the rules and limitations that govern all populations.
- Exploration of population ecology also sets the stage for interesting discussions of the socioeconomic impacts of population growth and the ethical questions related to regulating population growth.
- Use a "Jeopardy" or "Who Wants To Be a Millionaire" format to quiz students on key terms. A template for both types of questions can be found at: http://teach.fcps.net/trt2/links/powerpointgames.htm

Classroom and Laboratory Enrichment

- Divide the area surrounding your campus into quadrats for population studies. Examine the distribution of species on each plot of land. Determine the population density of an organism in your quadrat. Can you identify if the population distribution is clumped, uniform, or random? Identify factors that you believe might influence species distribution (some examples might be nutrient availability, amount of sunlight, moisture, and manmade disturbances). What changes could you initiate to influence the speciation in your quadrat?
- Have the students represent the individuals in a population. Designate part of the room as a river, a mountain, etc. Initiate artificial changes in the environment, such as a drought, a flood, introduction of new predators, new food sources, etc. How would this impact both the distribution and the size of your imaginary population?
- Graph the rates of population growth for several of the nations of the world. Discuss reasons for the differences between nations.
- Show examples of age-structure diagrams for human populations of different nations. What conclusions can be drawn about these nations' economies by examining the diagrams? Are the students able to predict which age-structure diagrams came from which countries?
- Show a copy of a life table as published in an entomology text book. These are especially good examples because they show differential death rates in the various stages of metamorphosis.
- Using the equations for expressing population dynamics, work through examples of problems taken from an ecology textbook.
- Have several students do a plot sampling in a forest or field. It may be difficult to count organisms, but they could easily tally the plants in that specific area. In addition, they could determine if the distribution of plant is random, clumped, or near-uniform.

Classroom Discussion Ideas

Research the events that occurred on Easter Island and discuss the following points:

- Research a more in-depth look at the events that occurred on Easter Island.
- What were the factors that determined the extinction of the human population on Easter Island? Were these factors density-dependent or density-independent?
- What changes could have been initiated to prevent the population destruction at Easter Island?
- Can you name any other populations that are similar to that of Easter Island?
- Examine the situation on Roanoke Island. How does this differ from the events on Easter Island?

Additional Ideas for Classroom Discussion

- Pick a species of animal that is prevalent in your area. Have the class discuss the best and most accurate method for determining its population size. Would a capture-recapture method be practical for this population?
- The class members could discuss the advantages and disadvantages of both r-selection and K-selection reproduction methods. Name examples of organisms that fall into both categories.
- Some organisms (bamboo, cicadas) reproduce only a single, brief interlude during their life span but produce a large number of seeds or offspring during this short period of time. Some other plants have seeds that have the ability to remain dormant prior to germination. How do these patterns benefit a species?
- How has modern medical care changed the survivorship curve for humans since the turn of the century? How might the AIDS epidemic alter these curves particularly in some African nations?

- What factors should determine the carrying capacity of the planet for humans? Do these actually operate? Do others operate instead?
- List several resources humans depend on in our daily living. How many of these resources are unlimited? For those that are not, what should be done to ensure ?
- Name several well-known species whose population numbers are in a decline. Are the factors that determine this population density-dependent or density-independent? Are they an example of an r-selected or a K-selected reproductive method? Have manmade disturbances influenced this population? What could man do to reverse this trend?
- Give the class some imaginary data obtained from a capture-recapture method. Have the students calculate the approximate population size using the information presented on page 792.
- Obtain some data on specific growth rates of bacteria from a microbiology class. Calculate the doubling time for that specific species.
- What are the ethical complications with limiting family size? Do you think nations with high rates of population growth should set a legal limit on the number of children a family may have? Do you feel that birth control can be mandated?
- How do you expect the population of China to be impacted by the government's incentives to control family size? What problems can you foresee for the future since they now produce such an inordinate number of male offspring?
- What environmental factors might influence various human phenotypes (skin color, size, rate of maturity, etc.)?
- How might the current trend toward delayed childbearing change the population growth in the United States? Why would an increase in parental age change the population structure?
- What density-independent factors influence the size of insect populations? Could we use this knowledge to devise non-chemical methods of insect control?
- What is the relationship between the size of the offspring and their number per reproductive event?
- Some mammal populations often breed in the springtime and larger males seem to be the desired mates. What are the advantages of these practices to the population? Do humans show any of these same biases?
- Why will the human growth rate of a country like Mexico continue to soar for many years to come even if stringent birth control measures are started immediately?
- Can you envision any solutions to the economic crisis that will result when the baby boomers reach old age?
- Which type of population distribution would you be likely to find in plants? How does this differ in animals?
- Think of some examples of introduced species in an area (e.g., the kudzu plant, zebra mussels, rabbits, etc). Did the introduction of these species upset the native populations? How did man's intervention cause the problem? Could human actions help solve the problem of the invasive species?
- Examine U.S. census data for your county or state at http://www.census.gov. See if you can calculate the per-capita growth rate from this data. If pertinent figures are not available, make up some sample examples for the calculations.
- As an example of exponential growth, examine the following facts concerning reproduction in rabbits:
    - o Rabbits sexually mature at five months.
    - o Their gestational period is 31 days.

- o The average litter size it six rabbits.
- o A female can have eight litters per year.
- o For this study, we are assuming the following: start with one female, there are no deaths, and the population is 50 pecent female and 50 percent male.
- o The end result after one year is 1850 rabbits!
- o Graph the figures to see if this data demonstrates exponential growth.
- o Can you see why rabbits became an invasive organism when they were introduced in Australia?

How Would You Vote? Classroom Discussion Ideas

- The question relates to possible methods to control the increasing deer population in the eastern United States.
- How have manmade influences altered the deer populations through the destruction of their native habitat and the elimination of many of their predators? Is man capable of repairing the damage to this ecosystem?
- What density-dependent and density-independent factors affect the deer populations?
- Divide the class into three groups and have each group present arguments in favor of different methods of deer population control: increase hunting, use artificial birth control methods, or let nature take its course.
- Can anyone in the class suggest an alternative solution to the three already mentioned?
- Some businesses, such as golf courses, employ herder dogs to chase geese off of the property. Does this ultimately solve the problem?
- Can you suggest the implementation of any way to prevent geese from being sucked into airplane engines?

Term Paper Topics, Library Activities, and Special Projects

- Have a student choose a country and examine its population figures over different centuries. Can the changes in population be explained by the demographic transition model?
- Assume a per capita rate of 0.65 per animal per month in a prairie dog population. Project out what the population would be in two months, four months, six months, and one year. When you graph your figures, does a J-shaped curve result?
- Examine one well-studied natural disaster, such as the tsunami in 2004 or the western wildfires in 2008. Can you find any documentation of population changes that have resulted?
- Look at the effects of events like the potato blight in Ireland or the Black Plague on the subsequent size and growth of the human population in Europe.
- Investigate the current United States policy on immigration. What effect does this have on its population? Would you suggest any changes?
- Look up information on population densities of several rural areas and also some urban areas in the United States. Do you see any correlation between population density and crime rates?
- Research information about organizations concerned with world overpopulation.
- Locate current data on human population growth in several countries around the world. Which countries are growing faster than the world average? Which ones are slower? Are any countries experiencing a negative population growth?

- A study in the 1980s showed that there were few young sturgeons in the Delaware River although there was a thriving adult population. Research this study and see if you develop similar conclusions.
- Read several essays on human populations to learn the relationship between number of people and rate of consumption of nonrenewable resources. Which countries waste the most? The least?
- Investigate the population growth or decline for a particular species. Then discuss the specific dependent and independent factors that affect these populations.
- Choose one species and describe its reproductive habits. Could it be clearly classified as an r-selected or a K-selected species? Why?
- Read studies concerning the fate of the sturgeon population in the Delaware River. Report on the findings to the class. Does it simply involve overfishing (as in the Atlantic cod in the chapter) or are there other factors?
- Examine an age structure map for a particular country. What information can you derive from studying this map?

Possible Responses to *Critical Thinking* Questions

1. The selection pressure for survival from a predator like the cichlids may have influenced a duller appearance with the male guppies. Flashier males might attract more unwanted attention from the predators. When released from the predation pressure, the males may have been selected for "gaudiness" because the females prefer that appearance. Sexual selection could now be operating in the male guppy populations after they have been released from predation pressure.
2. The age structure diagram on the left appears to be from a pre-industrialized nation with a rapid growth rate. Individuals are more likely to have many children if they are needed to help with agriculture. Therefore, the largest groups of individuals are the younger ones. The death rate is quite high from birth on, which may be the result of poverty and malnutrition. It also looks as though this population does not have many medical advances since only a very few live until old age. With this type of rapid growth rate, density-dependent limitations, such as food and water, may be a great factor in the future.
3. The age structure diagram on the right shows a very different picture. In this population there are almost an equal amount of individuals at each age, and it represents a zero growth rate. One could speculate that this is a country that is in some way limiting its birth rate. This population appears to be from an educated country and the current status is probably quite good economically and socially.

Possible Responses to *Data Analysis Exercise* Questions

Researchers decided to study the populations of marine iguanas in the Galapagos Islands. Select iguanas were marked and their health, survival, and habits were studied over time.

1. There were greater numbers of marked marine iguanas on Santa Fe Island at the time of the first census.
2. There was no change in the population size on Genovesa Island between the first and second census. The population on Santa Fe Island dropped dramatically between the first and second census.
3. If an adverse event had affected both islands, the populations of marine iguanas would have plummeted on both islands. Since the population on Santa Fe Island was the only one that decreased dramatically, it appears as though the oil spill caused the decline.

45

COMMUNITY ECOLOGY

Chapter Outline

FIGHTING FOREIGN FIRE ANTS
WHICH FACTORS SHAPE COMMUNITY STRUCTURE?
MUTUALISM
COMPETITIVE INTERACTIONS
- Effects of Competition
- Resource Partitioning

PREDATOR-PREY INTERACTIONS
- Models for Predator-Prey Interactions
- Cyclid Changes in Abundance

AN EVOLUTIONARY ARMS RACE
- Coevolution of Predators and Prey
- Coevolution of Herbivores and Plants

PARASITES AND PARASITOIDS
- Parasitism: Strangers in the Nest
- Parasitoids
- Biological Pest Controls

ECOLOGICAL SUCCESSION
- Successional Change
- Factors That Influence Succession

SPECIES INTRODUCTION, LOSS, AND OTHER DISTURBANCES
- The Role of Keystone Species
- Adapting to Disturbance
- Species Introductions

BIOGEOGRAPHIC PATTERNS IN COMMUNITY STRUCTURE
- Latitudinal Patterns
- Island Patterns

FIGHTING FOREIGN FIRE ANTS (REVISITED)
SUMMARY
DATA ANALYSIS EXERCISE
SELF-QUIZ
CRITICAL THINKING

Objectives

1. Learn some basic ecological terms: habitat, niche, commensalisms, mutualism, and symbiosis.
2. Know how mutualism can be beneficial to both species involved.
3. Understand the complex relationships between competitive species.
4. Describe the different types of predator responses to increases in prey densities.
5. Know how predators and prey adapt to be more successful.
6. Learn the lifestyle of parasites and parasitoids.
7. Know how cowbirds have adapted to changes over time.
8. Be able to characterize the steps of both primary and secondary succession.
9. Learn what is meant by a keystone species and how species introduction can change a community.
10. Through the use of examples, see how an introduced species may devastate a community.
11. Know which factors play a role in where species are located worldwide.

Key Terms

habitat
community
niche
commensalism
mutualism
interspecific competition
predation
prey
parasitism
symbiosis
character displacement
ecological niche
competitive exclusion
resource partitioning
camouflage
herbivory
warning coloration
mimicry
parasitoids
brood parasitism
social parasites
pioneer species
primary succession
secondary succession
intermediate disturbance hypothesis
keystone species
jump dispersal
exotic species
indicator species
biogeography
area effect
distance effect
equilibrium model of island biogeography

Lecture Outline

45.1 Fighting Foreign Fire Ants

A. The accidental introduction of fire ants in the United States disrupted the natural community.
   1. Invasive species, such as the fire ant, are finding new habitats due to increased global trading.
   2. The introduction of fire ants proves detrimental to the native ant populations.
   3. The fire ants have even impacted the number of some bird species, because they devour their eggs.
   4. In addition, the fire ants can disrupt normal pollination activities, and therefore damage plant species.

B. A community is defined as all of the species that live in a region.
   1. The introduction of fire ants to regions of the U.S. has dramatically influenced the communities that have been invaded.

45.2 Which Factors Shape Community Structure?

A. Where a species resides is its habitat, whereas a niche is its role in the community.
   1. Factors influencing the niche of a plant would be soil, water, light, etc.

B. There are many types of relationships that exist between species.
   1. Commensalism is when one species in the relationship is benefited and the other is unaffected.
   2. Symbiosis refers to the close relationship between two species that benefits at least one of them.
      a. Commensalism, mutualism, and parasitism can be symbiotic relationships.

45.3 Mutualism

A. Mutualistic relationships are those in which both organisms are benefited.
   1. Insects serve as pollinators, while plants provide nectar for the insect.
      a. Scientists designed a plant that made little nectar.
      b. The plant eventually disappeared, because insect pollinators avoided it.
   2. Legumes change nitrogen into a usable form and the plants provide nutrition.
   3. In a lichen, the fungi serves to soak up water while the plant again provides nutrition.

4. The *E. coli* in your digestive tract provide the host with vitamin K, while the bacteria benefits from the food in the host's colon.
5. The anemone fish protects the anemone, and the anemone provide defense for the fish in the form of nematocysts.

45.4 Competitive Interactions

A. Competition between species is usually not as intense as competition within a species.
   1. Each species must establish its own ecological niche.
      a. The niche of each species includes both biotic and abiotic factors.

B. Interference competition is when one species prevents another from accessing a resource.
   1. For example, a scavenger may chase another animal away from the prey.
   2. Also, some plants release substances that prevent other plants from establishing near them.

C. In exploitative competition, each species reduces the amount of a resource by consuming it.
   1. For example, deer and blue jays both feed on acorns, so they both decrease the amount of available food for the other.

D. Effects of Competition
   1. Competitive exclusion is when one species out-competes the other and drives it to extinction.
      a. When two species of paramecium were in the same environment, one thrived and one died.

E. Resource Partitioning
   1. Species may be able to survive together if they partition the resources.
      a. When two species of salamander coexist, they partition the resources unequally and one species becomes larger than the other.

45.5 Predator-Prey Interactions

A. Models for Predator-Prey Interactions
   1. The number of prey can influence the quantity and type of predators.
      a. In a type I response, a fairly constant number of prey are killed.
         1) The amount of prey killed depends on their density.
         2) Examples include spiders and filter feeders.
      b. In a type II response, the number of prey killed depends on the skill level of the predator.
         1) Initially, there are many more kills, but eventually it slows down since predators can only eat so much.
         2) Examples include large animals like tigers, wolves, etc.
      c. In a type III response, the number of prey killed increases at a slow rate, and then quickly and finally levels off.
         1) This could be due to the predator switching to a different type of prey.
         2) The predator could be learning more effective ways of hunting prey.
         3) The rapid rise in kills could involve the prey running out of hiding places.

B. Cyclic Changes in Abundance
   1. Often there are situations in which an increase or decrease in number of prey organisms is followed by a similar change in the amount of predator organisms.
      a. This cycle of change occurs approximately every 10 years in the Canadian lynx and snowshoe rabbit populations.
         1) When rabbit populations flourished, so did the lynx populations.
         2) When the rabbit population decreased due to predation, so did the lynx population.

b. Researchers discovered that the one-predator-one-prey model was not entirely accurate.
    1) Other factors that contribute to the cyclic changes in the rabbit population are multiple predators and the availability of different food sources.
2. It is important that scientists understand the cyclical nature of predator-prey relationships so that endangered animal species can be saved.

45.6 An Evolutionary Arms Race

A. Coevolution of Predators and Prey
1. Prey develop various defenses for survival.
    a. Some have a natural camouflage to hide them from predators.
        1) Examples include bittern birds, caterpillars, and lithop plants.
    b. Some have warning coloration to alert a predator to a bad taste or possible sting.
        1) An example is the yellow jacket.
    c. Some illustrate mimicry, where an organism appears like another organism that is dangerous or distasteful.
        1) Examples include the viceroy butterfly mimicking the monarch and other insects resembling yellow jackets.
2. Predators develop various adaptations.
    a. Some develop better hunting methods.
        1) An example is the swift cheetah.
    b. Some utilize camouflage to ambush prey.
        1) Examples include the undetectable scorpion fish and the polar bear.

B. Coevolution of Herbivores and Plants
1. Plants have developed two types of defenses to deter herbivory (animals eating plants).
    a. Some plants can re-grow quickly after being eaten.
    b. Other plants have defense mechanisms like spines and ill-tasting substances.

45.7 Parasites and Parasitoids

A. Parasitism
1. A parasitic lifestyle benefits the parasite and usually harms the host.
    a. Parasites may weaken the host or cause sterility.
    b. A successful parasite should not destroy the host.
    c. Often parasites utilize a vector to deliver the parasite to a suitable host organism.
        1) Vectors include insects and other arthropods.
2. Hosts can minimize the effects of parasites.
    a. Carriers of the sickle-cell trait are resistant to malaria.
    b. Other hosts perform grooming activities that enable them to discover and remove parasites.
    c. Some hosts produce chemicals to repel parasites.

B. Strangers in the Nest
1. Social parasites are those that take advantage of another animal's behavior.
    a. An example is the cowbird who lays its eggs in another bird's nest so that the other bird serves as a foster parent.
    b. This practice is known as brood parasitism.

C. Parasitoids
1. A parasitoid is a parasite that lays eggs in an insect's body and destroys it.

D. Biological Pest Controls
1. Parasites and parasitoids can be used as biological controls in an attempt to eliminate an undesirable organism.

a. These biological controls should not harm other non-harmful species.

45.8 Ecological Succession

A. Successional Change

1. A pioneer species is one that settles in a vacant habitat.
2. A primary succession is when an area lacking soil is originally colonized.
    a. Lichens and mosses settle first because they can inhabit an area with little or no soil.
    b. Soil is developed from plant litter and other species settle.
3. A secondary succession relates to an area's recovery from a fire or natural disaster.

B. Factors that Influence Succession

1. The factors that relate to the organisms that occur during succession are sometimes unpredictable.
    a. Factors that determine the species populations during succession are soil composition, climate, and often chance events.
2. The intermediate disturbance hypothesis states that the number of species inhabiting an area is highest when the disturbances are less drastic.

45.9 Species Introduction, Loss, and Other Disturbances

A. The Role of a Keystone Species

1. A keystone species is one that has an overwhelming effect on the environment.
    a. Examples include periwinkle snails and beavers.

B. Adapting to Disturbance

1. Some species have a selective advantage because they can withstand or benefit from a disturbance.
    a. For example, some plants can germinate only after a fire has occurred.
2. Indicator species are those that are particularly sensitive to environmental changes.
    a. When the trout population in a stream declines rapidly, it may indicate a low oxygen level.

C. Species Introductions

1. An exotic species is one that is dispersed from its home habitat.
2. Some exotic imported species may upset the natural balance in the new environment.
    a. A common algae present in fish tanks can dominate natural waterways.
    b. The kudzu plant from Japan is extremely fast-growing and difficult to control in the United States.
    c. Australia attempts to control a rabbit infestation.
    d. Hearty gray squirrels introduced into Europe out-survive the native red squirrels.

45.10 Biogeographic Patterns in Community Structure

A. Latitudinal Patterns

1. Biogeography studies the natural locations of species.
2. The greatest number of species settles close to the equator.
    a. This is due to the amount of rainfall, temperature, and the fact that tropical environments are well-established communities.

B. Island Patterns

1. Newly formed islands are an excellent habitat for studying speciation.
    a. The equilibrium model of island biogeography attempts to predict the amount of speciation on an island.
    b. The distance effect says that the amount of speciation can be estimated by its distance from the mainland.

c. The area effect indicates that islands with a greater area will support more species, and these populations are usually large and less likely to become extinct.

45.11 Fighting Foreign Fire Ants (Revisited)

A. Phorid flies, parasitoids, have been imported from Brazil to try to reduce the fire ant populations.
   1. The female fly lays her eggs in the ant and the larva becomes larger and eventually causes the fire ant's head to fall off.

B. Other organisms, such as fungi and protists, are being investigated to see if they can help control the number of invasive fire ants.

Suggestions for Presenting the Material

- Explain the philosophy behind each of the types of species interactions. For example, how does a parasite derive the maximum amount of benefit from the host without causing its death? How can it maintain its lifestyle without being detected by the host?
- The elaborate species interactions described in the chapter offer an opportunity to discuss coevolution. Examples such as the array of yucca species in Colorado, each pollinated exclusively by one kind of yucca moth species, emphasize the point that individuals don't evolve, populations do. Students will be able to see many good examples of adaptive traits in this chapter.
- The coevolution of predator and prey is another good example of the impact of one species on the evolution of another. After reading and discussing this chapter, students should understand that communities are shaped by a complex web of many different factors.
- Show some slides of animals in nature exhibiting camouflage, mimicry, and warning coloration. Can the students always spot the organism in the photo?
- Use a "Jeopardy" or "Who Wants To Be a Millionaire" format to quiz students on key terms. The templates for both of these quiz formats can be found at: http://teach.fcps.net/trt2/links/powerpointgames.htm
- Discuss the introduction of Japanese beetles into the U.S. How did they enter the country? What control methods have been initiated? Some beetle traps utilize pheromones, but some researchers worry that many crops are destroyed by insects traveling to these traps. How can the use of pheromones be used effectively? Is this a safer method of insect control than the use of pesticides?

Classroom and Laboratory Enrichment

- Look into the chemical relationship between the nodules on legumes and their ability to alter nitrogen. When was this discovered? What particular chemical reactions are involved? Can you envision any way to artificially induce these changes in atmospheric nitrogen?
- Look at some preserved samples of human parasites. How do they enter the host's body? What can be done to prevent their introduction into the body?
- Choose a community, list its species, and categorize them as producers, consumers, decomposers, of detritivores.
- Examine construction sites, flooded river banks, plowed fields, and other places that have been recently disturbed. Can you find several plant species that you would describe as pioneer species?

- Look at any natural setting. Describe the habitat and niche for every organism observed.
- Show the graphs (Figure 45.6) of the classic experiments of Paramecium growth that Gause performed. Why did Paramecium caudatum decrease to near extinction in the containers but thrive in nature?
- Have the students name other examples of camouflage in nature. After they name a few, show examples such as the phasmids (walking sticks).
- Select any environment and take a look at the predator-prey relationships within it. Draw a Venn diagram to see what food sources may overlap between two predators. How does this overlapping affect those particular prey populations?
- Examine a vegetated area on campus or in an area nearby. How are the plants in the area competing for resources? Suggest some ways in which competition has shaped the plant community.
- Describe patterns of succession at edges of stream beds, rivers, or coastlines.
- Look in your own backyard or in areas that surround your school for examples of resource partitioning.
- Using the observation that grass quickly establishes itself in cracks in the pavement of a highway on which traffic has been blocked for some time, describe what is happening using terms from the chapter.
- Refer to Table 45.1 on page 810. Go around the room and see how many examples of the various types of two-species interactions the students can name.
- Discuss the biological control system that is used to combat infestation by gypsy moths.

Classroom Discussion Ideas

- Have the class voice their opinions on the ideas of instilling parasitoids in the environment to eliminate fire ants. What else should be considered when introducing a species such as the Phorid flies?
- Do the Phorid flies have a deleterious effect on native ant populations or any other naturally occurring insects?
- Why do insects introduced into the United States become such pests when they were not so in their native country?
- Do the Phorid flies serve as a vector for any diseases in other species such as man or livestock?
- Do the students have any alternative suggestions for controlling the fire ant population? How would one go about creating a pesticide that would only affect the fire ant population?
- Is there any possibility that insect pheromones could be used to remove the harmful fire ants from the environment? Why are biological controls not used more commonly by the average homeowner?
- Have there been any previous examples of foreign insect infestation that could be studied? Were there any methods that proved effective against the invading insects?

Additional Ideas for Classroom Discussion

- Are certain plants "born" to be weeds? Or do they achieve that status by human condemnation?
- Investigate some of the adaptations that parasites have undergone to survive in the caustic environment of the host's digestive tract.

- What is the difference between true parasitism and social parasitism? Can the students give examples of both types of lifestyles?
- Re-examine the graph on page 821. Would you expect a major disturbance such as tsunami to result in a rapid variety of speciation? Why or why not?
- Why is resource partitioning essential for groups of functionally similar species living together?
- In some areas of the country, wildfires are a natural phenomenon. Should they be allowed to proceed without human intervention?
- Relating to environmental issues, voters tend to vote with their wallets rather than with scientific concerns. How can we stop this dangerous trend?
- What characteristics distinguish a pioneer species? Are pioneer species good competitors against later successional species? Why are pioneer species dependent on the frequent advent of open, disturbed places?
- Discuss predator-prey interactions. Why are the cycles of predator and prey abundance, shown in Figure 45.10, described as idealized? What do you think a predator would do if deprived of its primary prey item? Examine the actual diets of several predatory species; how do these diets change from one month to the next throughout the year? How can environmental disturbances such as fires, floods, climate fluctuations, and insect outbreaks influence the predator-prey cycle? What are some of the other variables that may be overlooked in predator-prey interactions?
- Would you expect competition between two finches of different species to be less intense or more intense than competition between two finches of the same species? Explain your answer.
- The monarch butterfly is orange and black and tastes bad (birds eating them spit them out immediately); viceroy butterflies are almost indistinguishable from monarchs but taste good. Which of these is the model and which is the mimic?
- Why should so-called "good ideas" like kudzu get more scrutiny before being released into a habitat?
- According to your text, "In primary succession changes begin when pioneer species colonize a barren habitat." Are there any uninhabited places left on Earth for pioneer plants and animals to colonize? What would create such a setting?
- There are different types of mutualism. Investigate each of these types and the following examples:
    - Trophic mutualism (derive benefit from resources) – zooanthellae algae and coral polyps
    - Dispersive mutualism (help in distribution of pollen) – plant and insect pollinator
    - Defensive pollinator (protective advantage) – acacia tree and ants
- Review the three types of responses seen in predator-prey interactions. Can the students name examples for each of these models?
- Discuss the methods that plants utilize to deter herbivory. How many examples can the students name?

How Would You Vote? Classroom Discussion Ideas

- Monitor the voting for the online question. Students may become most engaged in a discussion if they break off into groups to discuss their opinions on a question. If the class is divided into two groups, they could discuss the effectiveness of the process of inspecting imported goods. They should examine the possible effectiveness of the process and also its financial implications. For example, is it more economical to undertake the tedious process of inspecting foreign goods or to attempt to eradicate a species once they are established? Most individuals would probably vote for the most economical choice (unless they are ecologists!).

- Investigate foreign species that have entered our country accidentally via imported goods. Are they still a big problem or were attempts to eradicate them successful?

Term Paper Topics, Library Activities, and Special Projects

- A student could pick an organism and investigate how that particular introduced species disrupted the natural environment. What effect did it have on other native species? What steps are being initiated to control the population of the foreign species? Do you have any alternative methods to reduce the influence of that species?
- Examine several articles that discuss the method by which a bacterial form of mitochondria became incorporated into cells as an organelle. When did scientists develop this theory? Are there any other potential explanations for this feature?
- Look into the excellent example of mimicry between the scarlet king snake and coral snake. They both exhibit the same coloration, but only the coral snake is poisonous. The old adage says, "Red next to yellow can kill a fellow, red next to black—venom lack." Do you think most predators take the time to look at the order of the colors? Therefore, the scarlet king snake's coloration is effective to deter predators.
- Research the parasite Schistosoma. Even though this organism infests millions of people annually, most people have not even heard its name. Why do you think this organism is not well-known? How does the parasite get into a human's body?
- Study the specific changes in the finch population on the Galapagos Islands in additional detail. Why did Darwin decide to study speciation in that particular location? Was his research very unique at that point in time?
- Research Kettlewell's study of the peppered moth in industrialized England. Although this study is primarily studied to discuss evolution, it can also be used in reference to camouflaged animals and their adaptability.
- Find other examples of insect parasitoids. Do they infect their hosts in the same manner as the Phorid flies? Does this appear to be a successful lifestyle?
- Write a report on the effects of interspecific competition on a native species whose populations have been adversely affected by an introduced species.
- How did disturbance by human intervention help initiate secondary succession in American prairies?
- Report on the successful control of the cottony-cushion scale by ladybugs in California.
- When one thinks of a parasite-host interaction, one usually thinks of relationships between two animal species. Research the strangleweed mentioned on page 818. What species usually serve as its hosts?
- The water hyacinth has become a severe problem in some waterways. How was it introduced into this country? How could it be controlled?
- Describe succession as it has occurred following a specific major disaster such as a flood, mudslide, fire, or volcanic eruption.
- The Pine Barrens are a unique habitat in New Jersey. The soil is quite acidic and fires are a normal occurrence. Research this environment and list the pioneer species that it supports during its frequent succession.

- At what point will the growing number of plant species in a previously disturbed area stop increasing? What factors will halt the rise in species composition? Examine studies of island ecology that seek to answer this question.
- One of the most recent U.S. invasive species is the northern snakehead fish. How was it introduced? Mark its current territory on a map. Why has it been so successful?
- Select a group of related species for which distribution data are available and construct a graph of patterns of species diversity corresponding to latitude.
- Discuss examples of mutualism among plants and animals.
  - Zebra mussels are a species that was introduced in the Great Lakes. What problems are the zebra mussels causing? What is being done to eradicate them?
  - Examine the relationship between whales and barnacles that attach to their side. What type of relationship does this depict?
  - Pick one of the pairs of animals listed below and describe their symbiotic relationship.
    - o Zebra and ostrich
    - o Ratal (African mammal) and African honeyguide
    - o Hornbill and guenon monkeys
    - o Southern Rufous woodpecker and black tree ants
  - Refer to the website http://invasivespeciesinfo.gov, which was mentioned in the chapter. Compile a report for the class on one of these introduced species and what efforts are being made to decrease its impact on the environment.
  - Investigate the relationship between termites and intestinal flagellates. What type of species interaction does this represent?
  - Perhaps one of the animals most adept at camouflage is the octopus. It is said that an octopus can even mimic the pattern of a checkerboard in an effort to be unseen. Scientists are uncertain whether the changes in coloration are controlled by hormones or by the nervous system. Look into the research—which theory do you support?

Possible Responses to *Critical Thinking* Questions

1. The principal of competitive exclusion best explains the situation when cows are instilled with an increase of naturally occurring bacteria to discourage the growth of an undesirable strain. Since both species would inhabit the same niche, it is reasonable that the well-established species would not allow the other to effectively colonize. This seems much more desirable that feeding the cows antibiotic-laced food for several reasons. First, the antibiotics may destroy the natural flora of the cow's digestive tract along with the harmful strain. This may make the digestive process in the cows more difficult. Secondly, the consumers of the milk or meat from the cow may ingest small amounts of antibiotics. Therefore, we may be creating an atmosphere for antibiotic-resistant organisms to develop in the consumer.
2. If flightless birds have existed for many generations in an island environment, it is not surprising that none develop the ability to fly. There would be no adult birds of that species to encourage that skill. Also, the current structure of the flightless birds is not designed for flight.

Possible Responses to *Data Analysis Exercise* Questions

Fire ants are an introduced species that causes discomfort in many southern states. This study was designed to test the effectiveness of ant-decapitating phorid flies and the microsporidian *Thelohania solenopsae.*

1. The population size of the control fire ants increased over the first four months of the study.
2. The fire ants in the two types of treated plots decreased over the same time period.
3. If the study ended after one year, one would conclude that the biological controls had a major effect.
4. At the end of the study at 28 months, one could still conclude that the efforts to eradicate the fire ants were somewhat successful. It appears, however, that some of the ants had become resistant to the pesticide by the study's end.

46

ECOSYSTEMS

Chapter Outline

Objectives

1. Understand the trophic levels in an ecosystem.
2. Learn the highly interactive relationships of a food web.
3. Know the way energy flows through an ecosystem through the study of biomass and energy pyramids.
4. Realize the way that toxic substances become highly concentrated in the top carnivores of a food web.
5. Be able to explain how elements are cycled through living organisms and the environment.
6. Explain how water goes through the cyclical process of traveling between bodies of water, land, and the atmosphere.
7. Understand how carbon is cycled between the ocean and the atmosphere.
8. Be able to explain how greenhouse gases have an adverse effect by helping to create global warming.
9. Know how nitrogen changes form and travels between the atmosphere and the land.
10. Understand the impact of excessive nitrogen.
11. Explain the phosphorus cycle and how it passes between the ocean and the land.

Key Terms

ecosystem
primary producers
consumers
detritivores
decomposers
trophic levels
food chain
food web
grazing food chain
detrital food chain
detrital food web
primary production
biomass pyramid
energy pyramid
biological magnification
biogeochemical cycle
water cycle
watershed
aquifer
groundwater
runoff
soil water
salinization
desalinization
atmospheric cycle
global climate change
greenhouse gas
carbon cycle
greenhouse effect
global warming
nitrogen cycle
nitrogen fixation
ammonification
denitrification
nitrification
phosphorus cycle
sedimentary cycle
eutrophication

Lecture Outline

46.1 Too Much of a Good Thing

A. Phosphorus is a substance that is necessary for life.
   1. Plants obtain phosphorus from the soil and animals get their supply from consuming plants or other animals.
   2. If the soil is depleted of phosphorus, fertilizers may be added to supplement the soil.

B. When fertilizers enter the runoff, it can cause problems in water supplies.
   1. In the water of lakes and rivers, eutrophication may occur.
      a. Algae blooms cause the water to become polluted and make it inhabitable for many other organisms.

C. Now scientists are aware of the problems man has created by disrupting the nitrogen cycle.

46.2 The Nature of Ecosystems

A. Overview of the Participants
   1. An ecosystem is the sum of the organisms residing there and the environment.
      a. A primary producer is the plant that serves as an autotroph by harnessing the sun's energy.
      b. A consumer is the animal or heterotroph that derives energy from consuming the plant or other animals.
      c. A detritivore is an animal that consumes debris and small bits of organic matter.
      d. A decomposer eats wastes and remains of plants and animals.
      e. Minerals increase and decrease in natural cycles.

B. Trophic Structure of Ecosystems
   1. The organisms of an ecosystem develop trophic levels or feeding relationships.
      a. A food chain represents the passage of energy from one trophic level to the next.
      b. Plants are the primary producers, and they represent the first trophic level.
      c. The second trophic level is represented by animals that eat plants, which are called primary consumers.
      d. Secondary producers (third trophic level) consume animals at the second trophic level.
      e. Finally, the fourth trophic level (third-level consumers) consume animals from the third trophic level.

46.3 The Nature of Food Webs

A. A food web is a complex interaction among many species of the ecosystem.
   1. In a grazing food chain, the energy goes from producers to consumers.
   2. In a detrital food chain, the energy goes from producers to detritivores and decomposers.

B. How Many Transfers?
   1. An alteration in one species of a food web may affect many different organisms.
      a. Scientists have discovered how complicated food webs are, "Everything is linked to everything else."

46.4 Energy Flow

A. Primary Production
   1. Primary production is the rate at which plants harness the sun's energy.
   2. This depends on the availability of water and nutrients.
   3. Primary production is higher on land than in water.

B. Ecological Pyramids
   1. A biomass pyramid is used as a tool to represent the dry weight of the organisms at each trophic level.
      a. The plants or producers make up the base of the pyramid.
      b. Consumers make up the upper portion of the pyramid, with the largest carnivores at the very top.
   2. An energy pyramid helps show how energy is lost when transferred to each trophic level.

C. Ecological Efficiency
   1. Only about 5–30 percent of the energy in the tissues of an organism ends up in the tissues of the next trophic level.
      a. Energy is lost because some is lost as heat, and many parts of an animal cannot be digested.
   2. The energy transfer in watery ecosystems is usually more efficient than those on land.

46.5 Biogeochemical Cycles

A. In biogeochemical cycles, nutrients move through environmental stores and living organisms.
   1. The elements enter the living portion of the cycle by becoming incorporated into plants.
   2. Examples of biogeochemical cycles are the water, carbon, nitrogen, and phosphorus cycles.

46.6 The Water Cycle

A. How and Where Water Moves
   1. The water cycle begins when water evaporates from bodies of water and transpiration occurs in plants.
   2. Next, water condenses in clouds and rains down.
   3. Water collects in watersheds, aquifers, and groundwater.
      a. Most individuals get water supply from groundwater.
      b. Groundwater can be easily polluted and difficult to correct.

B. Limited Fresh Water
   1. Groundwater is the major water supply for about half of the U.S.
      a. Salt water is replacing many coastal aquifers.
      b. Other areas, especially in the southwest, have depleted groundwater.
   2. A future water supply may be the ocean through utilization of a desalinization process to remove the salts.

46.7 Carbon Cycle

A. Terrestrial Carbon Cycle

1. Soil, consisting of humus and soil organisms, contains much more carbon than the atmosphere.
   a. In tropical areas more carbon is in living plants, whereas in the temperate zone the majority of the carbon is in the soil.
2. Tilling the soil increases the amount of carbon in the atmosphere.

B. Marine Carbon Cycle

1. Most of the carbon is in seawater.
   a. The carbon in the ocean is formed from the shells of small organisms.
   b. The crust lifts up and becomes part of the land mass.
   c. Eventually erosion breaks down the rocks and the carbon travels back to the sea.

C. Carbon in Fossil Fuels

1. Fossil fuels are formed from decayed plants and plankton.
2. Man adversely affects the carbon cycle by releasing more carbon into the air, contributing to global warming.

46.8 Greenhouse Gases and Climate Change

A. The Greenhouse Effect

1. The sun's heat is absorbed by the Earth's surface.
2. Some of the heat is reflected back into the atmosphere, but atmospheric gases send some heat back to Earth.
3. The greenhouse effect is a natural, necessary phenomenon to maintain reasonable temperatures on Earth.

B. Changing Carbon Dioxide Concentrations

1. When scientists began to measure carbon dioxide levels in 1959, they saw annual fluctuations.
   a. The carbon dioxide levels drop in the summer when plants use it for active photosynthesis.
   b. The carbon dioxide levels rise in the winter when there is less photosynthesis occurring.
2. Overall, the carbon dioxide levels in the atmosphere are rising.
   a. Scientists were able to check carbon dioxide levels in the past by drilling deep into glaciers or by examining fossil foraminiferan shells.
   b. The carbon dioxide level in the atmosphere is the highest it has been in 15 million years.

C. Changing Climate

1. Currently a global climate change is occurring, which can be defined as a long-term change in the Earth's climate.
   a. Global warming is causing a warmer ocean temperature, which results in melting glaciers and more severe storms.
2. Scientists in 2007 determined that the rise in temperature was due to human activities.
   b. Efforts are underway to reduce the use of fossil fuels as energy sources.

46.9 Nitrogen Cycle

A. Nitrogen exists in the atmosphere as N_2, which is not in a usable form for plants.

1. Some natural processes such as lightening and volcanoes can convert the nitrogen to a usable form.

2. The bacteria rhizobium that exists in nodules on legumes also converts the nitrogen to a usable form.
3. Plants obtain ammonium from the soil, and it is later broken down by fungi and bacteria in a process called ammonification.
4. Nitrification is the process that converts ammonium to nitrates.
    a. First, ammonia is converted to nitrite by bacteria and archaea.
    b. Then other types of bacteria change nitrites into nitrates.
    c. Nitrates and ammonium are used by producers.
5. Denitrification is the process in which bacteria convert nitrate to nitrogen gas in the atmosphere.

46.10 Disruption of the Nitrogen Cycle

A. Nitrous Oxide—A Double Threat
1. From testing the nitrous oxide level in ice core, scientists have seen the level rise from 270 ppb to 325 ppb.
    a. Increases in nitrous oxide are due to commercial fertilizers, livestock production, and the burning of fossil fuels.
2. Increased amounts of nitrous oxide in the atmosphere can lead to global warming and depletion of the ozone layer.

B. Nitrate Pollution
1. Nitrates are common contaminants in the water supply.
    a. They may result from fertilizer use or septic tank malfunctions.
2. Nitrates have been known to increase the risk of thyroid cancer, respiratory infections, diabetes, and other cancers.
3. The EPA has said that drinking water should contain no more than 10ppm of nitrate.
    a. Usually private wells go untested.

46.11 The Phosphorus Cycle

A. Phosphorus cycles between the land and the ocean.
1. Phosphates are necessary for major cellular components like nucleic acids, plasma membranes, and ATP.
2. Plants get phosphorus from the water and soil, and animals get it from consuming plants or other animals.
    a. Phosphorus levels are quite often a limiting factor for plant growth.
    b. A lack of phosphorus in the soil can be due to the absence of crop rotation.

B. An excess of phosphorus can result from water that runs off from fertilized fields.
1. Excessive amounts of phosphorus in a watery environment can cause eutrophication.
    a. An algae bloom occurs that harms other plant and animal species.
    b. Eutrophication is difficult to reverse.

46.12 Too Much of a Good Thing (Revisited)

A. Fertilizers are used heavily in agricultural areas to improve crop yields.
1. This causes excess nitrogen and phosphates to enter water supplies through runoff.
2. These increases enter the Mississippi River and ultimately flow into the Gulf of Mexico.

B. These excess nutrients produce a "dead zone" in the Gulf of Mexico.
1. Eutrophication causes low oxygen levels and, therefore, causes the death of many organisms.

Suggestions for Presenting the Material

- Approach the study of the various cycles of an ecosystem by first explaining the necessity of that particular component in the environment. Then examine the deleterious effects of too little or too much of that substance.
- Begin by showing a simple food chain and an example of a representative animal at each trophic phase. Then stress that life and nature are rarely that basic. Show the students an example of a complex food web and discuss the unlikelihood that an animal would have only one food source. Create a disruption in the food web by imagining the destruction of a population of one species of animal. Let the students see that a seemingly small change in a food web could have a dramatic impact on many other species. Students will become aware of the unity that joins all organisms.
- Have the students view the award-winning documentary "An Inconvenient Truth." This powerful film may help to launch a discussion of the consequences of global warming and the impact that this movie has created worldwide.
- Use as many local examples of ecosystems as possible in discussions, demonstrations, and lab work. While it may seem overly simplistic and sometimes inaccurate to identify and describe the different levels of an ecosystem, students should see that it is useful because it helps us to understand the functioning of an ecosystem as a whole. Such ecosystem descriptions provide a valuable baseline against which we can measure the effects of changes.
- Using an overhead transparency of Figure 46.4, clarify the fact that the primary consumer is actually at the second trophic level. This may be confusing to some of the students.
- Stress the fact that, in various sections of the chapter, the authors show how humans have altered the natural ecosystems and their functioning.
- Use overhead transparencies to present the biogeochemical cycles.
- Invite a representative of the EPA, the state coastal commission, or another environmental group to address the class.
- Use a "Jeopardy" or "Who Wants To Be a Millionaire" format to reinforce the definitions of the key terms. A template for these games can be found at: http://teach.fcps.net/trt2/links/powerpointgames.htm
- Go around the room and have the students name examples of producers, consumers, detritivores, and decomposers that would be in the area surrounding your campus.
- See if your students can devise a food chain (or better yet, a food web) for organisms in your area. This will serve to show them how complicated and intertwined these relationships are.

Classroom and Laboratory Enrichment

- Have some of the students choose a cycle discussed in this chapter and make a poster depicting the stages. Each participant should explain his poster to the class and how human intervention may alter the natural cycle.
- Set up aquatic ecosystems in the lab and monitor them throughout the semester. Identify the trophic levels of the ecosystem and analyze the cycling of materials and nutrients within it. In what ways are the aquatic ecosystems in the lab similar to, or different from, a real aquatic ecosystem?
- Discuss the primary productivities of different regions of the United States. How can human intervention change primary productivity?

- Each student could undertake a study near their home of an environmental issue regarding an upset of one of the natural biogeochemical cycles. Are there any reasonable solutions to this issue? If so, write to your senator or congressman expressing your views.
- Test various water supplies for the presence of nitrogen and phosphorus. Are they within the recommended standards? If not, how far do they deviate from a normal level? Use a nursing or anatomy text to determine if an excess of either substance would cause any short-term or long-lasting effects?
- Determine the pH of water samples from several local bodies of water in your area. How much does the pH vary? If you have suitable equipment at your school, you can use a Global Positioning System to create maps of exactly where you obtained your samples. Since you are somewhat familiar with the area, can you find a reason to explain these differences in pH?
- Fill an aquarium with water and organisms from a nearby pond or lake. Add amounts of phosphorus and nitrogen to mimic eutrophication. What effects do you see in your artificial ecosystem?
- Analyze local soils to determine the mineral and organic contents.
- Divide the class into small groups. Have each section debate the pros and cons of different energy sources. Each group should be prepared to discuss the merits and drawbacks of one of the following energy sources: oil, coal, natural gas, hydropower, solar power, nuclear power, or other alternatives. Can the class come to any consensus about the safest method or combination of methods?
- Assuming that a flat 10 percent of the energy in one trophic level is conserved to the next, and that the producer represents 100 percent, calculate what percent is received by the marsh hawk in Figure 46.4.
- Write down the models of cars driven by some of your classmates. Research online to see if you can determine the emissions from each of these models. When you announce the results to the class, will that influence anyone's choice for their next vehicle?
- Visit a sewage treatment plant. Discuss the biological steps involved in the treatment of your local sewage. In what way could sewage treatment be improved?
- Research the steps that will be undertaken to convert the astronauts' urine into drinkable water in space.
- Collect some soil from what appears to be a detrital food web in a forest or field system. Can you identify any organisms as decomposers and detritivores? Do you imagine that some of the organisms performing these duties may be too small to see?
- Contact the epidemiologist at your local hospital. Inquire how they handle their dangerous biomedical wastes. In the past it was sufficient for a hospital to simply contract with a company to dispose of hazardous wastes. Now hospitals are required know the pathway of the dangerous trash after it leaves the building. This makes it clear that all parties involved are responsible for proper environmental procedures.
- Design a simple survey containing a few concise questions relating to environmental concerns addressed by this chapter. Have each student poll 10 fellow students outside of the classroom. How do your peers feel about environmental issues? Do they consider this an urgent matter to address? And most importantly, would they be willing to put their money where their mouth is?
- Look online for an example of a biomass pyramid for an ocean ecosystem. How does it differ from those seen in Figure 46.8?

- Have your students bring in containers from detergents and fertilizers that they use in their own homes. Read the labels to see if there is a significant difference between them. Would your students be willing to switch to a brand that contains less phosphorus, even if it costs more?

Classroom Discussion Ideas

- Does anyone see the ironic dichotomy that Morgan City in Louisiana celebrates a shrimp and petroleum festival on the same day? The production of oil may be emitting pollutants into the air that are increasing the greenhouse effect. The result of the increasing greenhouse gases, as we know from the text, is contributing to global warming. As global warming intensifies, polar ice caps will melt and, therefore, raise the water level. The lowlands of Louisiana, with some of the lowest levels of coastal area in the United States, may disappear at an alarming rate. If this continues at this current rate, the shrimp festival may have to be moved to a city farther inland, where it will have become the new coastline!
- In addition, scientists have discovered that an increase in ocean temperature does not cause more hurricanes, but the ones we do have will worsen in intensity. As we know from Hurricane Katrina, the devastation from a strong hurricane can result in the displacement of millions of people, and many billions of funds are needed to attempt to repair the area.
- The Louisiana bayou area may be one of the areas that will show the early effects of global warming. We need to observe the damage that is being done now and address it dramatically before it is too late. The nations of the world must band together to consider global warming as a very serious worldwide problem that must be aggressively attacked with manpower and financial means.
- One consequence of global warming that may not be immediately evident is the spread of tropical diseases. As the Earth warms, the boundaries of where tropical diseases can exist may expand. Diseases such as malaria and dengue fever may eventually become common in the U.S.

Additional Ideas for Classroom Discussion

- Discuss the rapid deforestation of the rain forests. How does this impact the biogeochemical cycles that we have addressed?
- Discuss what would happen to an ecosystem if all of the producers disappeared. What would happen to the ecosystem if all of the consumers, decomposers, or detritivores disappeared? Can you think of examples of ecosystems in which any of these events has occurred? How can an ecosystem recover from such a disturbance?
- Show examples of various biomass pyramids. Can the students match them with the proper ecosystems? How would a biomass pyramid from the open ocean differ from the one in Figure 46.8?
- Describe several trophic levels of a typical ecosystem and ask the students to arrange them in the correct order.
- How and where do humans fit into a food web?
- The pesticide DDT is just one example of a substance that undergoes biological magnification as it travels through an ecosystem. Can you think of others? (One possible example is the movement of strontium 90, a byproduct of nuclear testing in the 1950s, through the food web.)
- Look into articles about the effects of biological magnification in Lake Erie? Which animals are affected? What steps have been undertaken to remedy some of the environmental issues there?

- What do you think were the first producers to evolve on Earth? Do we know what they might have looked like?
- Examine the composition of several plant and garden fertilizers. What are the major ingredients? What components provide the "miraculous" growth rates?
- Why is the term food chain rarely used when describing actual ecosystems?
- Why are humans at the top of nearly every food web of which they are a part? Are they ever at any other level? How has man's role in food webs evolved through the centuries?
- What would the personal and ecological advantages be to humans if they were to eat "lower down" on the energy pyramid?
- Why does a pyramid of energy usually narrow as it goes up?
- Research some alternative fuel sources for automobiles. Why do you feel these are not readily available?
- Is it environmentally wise to rely on large quantities of nitrogen-rich fertilizers for crop production? What are some alternatives? Discuss the pros and cons of commercial fertilizers.
- Try to locate examples of energy pyramids from various locations. It may be impressive for students to see the loss of energy at each phase. Contrast the amount of energy lost by endotherms and ectotherms, and explain why this difference occurs.
- Why is a pyramid of biomass a more accurate representation of an ecosystem than is a pyramid of numbers?
- Investigate the source of your home water supply. If applicable, see if you can find the name of the aquifer that supplies the water.
- Why does normal rain water have a pH of around 5.6? (Note: A pH of 7 is neutral.)
- How have coal-burning power plants changed in the past 20 years?
- Perform some research on the ozone layer above the Earth. Where did they first discover a hole in the ozone layer? Can anything be done to repair the damage that has occurred?
- Tropical forests are highly productive ecosystems, incorporating extremely large amounts of carbon and other nutrients into plant material. Yet, when cleared of vegetation, such areas make poor farmlands. Why?
- About 500,000 trees are needed for Sunday newspapers for Americans. Is this necessary? When will we no longer be able to afford such extravagance? How would the environmental and economical impact change if you received your paper online?
- In each of the biogeochemical cycles indicate the route each component takes in recycling. What invisible component is not recyclable?
- Make a list of renewable and non-renewable energy sources. Which method or combination of methods would you recommend?
- Draw a timeline indicating the dates of the different legislative actions relating to car emission standards.
- Ask students to make a list of ways in which they could modify their own lifestyles and behaviors to reduce environmental pollution.
- Make sure your students understand what happens to the energy that is lost at each trophic level. Who loses more energy, ectotherms or endotherms?
- There are lots of terms in this chapter that must be defined. Make sure your students know these before they attempt to learn the overall concepts.
- Contact the local weather service to determine which tests are performed on collected rainwater.

How Would You Vote? Classroom Discussion Ideas

- No one would argue that the major source of nutrient pollution is the result of agriculture and sewage systems. However, one improvement could be made rather easily by eliminating phosphate-rich detergents and home fertilizers that contain excessive amounts of phosphates. This would not be an extra expense for the consumer, but it would result in detergent and fertilizers that, perhaps, would not be as powerful as those on which the consumer has grown dependent.
- The question boils down to whether the public would accept products that are somewhat inferior for the sake of the environment.
- Probably the first step in the process would be to educate the public on the consequences to the environment of excess nutrients. An educated consumer would be much more apt to realize the ultimate damage caused by the current products. This would require a massive media campaign to enlighten the public. Ask the students to design a pamphlet or commercial that would effectively explain the issue to the average consumer. Do your students feel the public would comply if they really understood the process of eutrophication? Poll the class on this issue.

Term Paper Topics, Library Activities, and Special Projects

- Read *Silent Spring* by Rachel Carson and report a summary to the class. What specific species exhibited symptoms related to DDT exposure? Considering that it was written in 1962, do you find the material to be controversial? Do you feel the author made a significant impact toward the restriction of DDT?
- Write a report detailing the events at Three Mile Island in 1979. Were there any effects on the local ecosystems? How does the accident at Three Mile Island differ from that at Chernobyl?
- Write a report on ecosystems deep on the ocean floor at depths impenetrable by light. What kinds of organisms make up the first trophic level in such ecosystems? How are these organisms obtaining energy? Are these organisms well-studied by scientists?
- What happens to an ecosystem if any one of its levels is removed? Find descriptions of ecosystems in which this has happened and describe the results.
- Describe the chemical changes that occur during nitrogen fixation. Can you envision a way that this could be done in the laboratory?
- Name some other materials that could potentially be biomagnified as they move through the food chain. Are there any current regulations to prevent this from happening?
- Discuss farming techniques designed to minimize nitrogen loss in the soil.
- What are the biological effects of acid rain on fish populations?
- Obtain records of the yearly average temperatures and rainfall amounts from your local weather bureau. How far back do these records go? Graph the data. Are there any trends?
- How do you think greenhouse gases affect the respiratory system? Are there any statistics to back this up?
- Discuss the primary productivities of various regions around the world. Which areas have the highest and lowest primary productivities? Why?
- Read "Earth in the Balance: Ecology and the Human Spirit" by Al Gore. Summarize the book to the class and state the three facts that surprised you most from the book.
- Describe the history of the use and subsequent banning of DDT in the United States. Draw a timeline that shows the significant events in its usage.

- Write a letter to your congressman asking for more information about how one of the environmental issues in this chapter is being addressed.
- What were the commercial uses for chlorofluorocarbons? Why were they banned? What substances have served as safer alternative?
- Contact your local weather department to find out, on the average, how many days per year are rated as having an unsafe quality of air? What does this mean for humans and other animals?
- Discuss the environmental effects of strip-mining on biogeographical cycles.
- Read several articles on crop rotation. How does this help the farming industry? Name a series of crops that should be rotated through one field so that valuable nutrient levels are maintained.
- List and describe some of the primary producers in an open ocean ecosystem off of the United States coastline.
- Describe the biochemical steps used by chemosynthetic autotrophs to produce energy.
- Review Figure 46.14 and explain the causes of the different carbon levels, both in plants and in soil, to the class.
- In this chapter, nutrient levels are measured by sampling ice cores and sedimentary rock. Can you research where and how these measurements were obtained?

Possible Responses to *Critical Thinking* Questions

1. The vegetable gardens in Maine and Florida would differ greatly based on climate (e.g., rainfall, temperature, latitude, length of growing season, soil content, and perhaps proximity to the ocean), depending on their exact locations. All of these factors would greatly influence what types of crops would be best suited to each region. Florida would have a longer growing season, so I would expect the garden in that area to have a higher annual productivity.
2. The website listed takes you to a site that is sponsored by the United States Geological Survey Department. At this website you can click on a map to increasingly zoom down to about the county level. It will then give you information about your particular watershed, such as water quality, location of groundwater inventory sites, etc. In addition, it offers detailed definitions of all technical terms for the layperson's interpretation.
3. One would not be able to test the air in bubbles in frozen ice, because phosphorus does not occur naturally in that form. The best way to check phosphorus levels from the past would be to test the levels in sedimentary rock. This type of rock is the major reservoir for phosphorus.
4. If you increased the number of nitrogen-fixing bacteria in an aquatic ecosystem, it could result in an algae bloom and eutrophication. The additional nitrogen would encourage an overgrowth of algae, which may cause a hypoxic atmosphere for the animals that reside there. This eutrophication would lead to an increase in carbon production and an increase in carbon accumulation.
5. If the mycorrhizal fungi were used to provide plants with phosphorus and nitrogen, the risk of eutrophication would decrease dramatically. The runoff from the fields would not contain the excessive amounts of nutrients that would be seen in an area exposed to large amounts of fertilizers. Some research should be performed before such a widespread plan is initiated to ensure that the fungi in large amounts would not cause any significant disruption in the overall balance of nature.

Possible Responses to *Data Analysis Exercise* Questions

Scientists are attempting to show that human activities have impacted the amount of carbon dioxide in the atmosphere. In Antarctica, there is thick ice that can be used to measure the carbon dioxide level over time.

1. The highest carbon dioxide level between 400,000 and 0 A.D. was 300 ppm.
2. During this same time period, the carbon dioxide level never reached the level attained in 1980.
3. The trend in the carbon dioxide level for the 800 years prior to the advent of the industrial revolution was fairly constant, with some slight variations. After 1800 the carbon dioxide level began to rise dramatically.
4. The rise in the carbon dioxide level between 1980 and 2007 was much higher than the rise between 1800 and 1975.

47

THE BIOSPHERE

Chapter Outline

Objectives

1. Learn the patterns of air circulation that are formed due to the Earth's rotation, land masses, and elevation, which help to create different communities of organisms.
2. Understand how ocean currents are formed from temperature alterations of the surface water formed by the changing seasons and varying latitudes.
3. Know that a biographical realm is a large area characterized by the plants and animals it supports.

4. Be aware of how soils vary in different biomes and help determine the organisms that reside there.
5. Understand that deserts form a unique biome that receives little water and is usually located near 30° north and south.
6. Learn that grasslands form where there is more rain than a desert, but less than a forest. Areas with slightly more rain can also support shrubs.
7. Know that evergreen broadleaf forests are located from the equator to 10° north and south, and receive higher rainfall.
8. Understand that rainforests, which are located at tropical latitudes, provide a unique biome for vast biodiversity and benefits to mankind.
9. Learn that coniferous forests are found in cold climates where the rainfall fluctuates and the soil is poor.
10. Understand that the tundra consists of very cold, often windy climates, which are characterized by sturdy, low-growing plants.
11. Learn that freshwater ecosystems undergo seasonal changes in succession.
12. Be aware of how our water supply is vulnerable to contaminants and undergoes wastewater treatments.
13. Understand that coastal zones support mangrove wetlands and coastlines comprised of different zones.
14. Learn that coral reefs are a rich breeding ground for a variety of species and are particularly vulnerable to damage.
15. Know how upwelling occurs in the ocean to move water rich in nutrients along the coastlines.
16. Understand how excessive amounts of nutrients can adversely affect a lake or stream.
17. Know the life cycle of the cholera bacteria and how its effect on humans can be decreased.

Key Terms

climate
pollutant
monsoon
ozone layer
smog
acid rain
rain shadow
biogeographic realms
biomes
soil profile
deserts
grasslands
dry shrublands
dry woodlands
semi-evergreen forests
tropical rain forests
boreal forest
temperate deciduous forests
evergreen broadleaf forests
coniferous forests
arctic tundra
alpine tundra
permafrost
lake
spring overturn
thermocline
fall overturn
estuary
coral reefs
pelagic province
benthic province
seamounts
hydrothermal vents
upwelling
El Nino
La Nina
biosphere

Lecture Outline

47.1 Warming Water and Wild Weather

A. El Niño can cause drastic changes in the Pacific Ocean ecosystem.
   1. It is caused by warmer waters, which alter currents.
   2. El Niño has caused flooding and disrupted massive communities of organisms.
   3. El Niño typically increases rainfall, which has resulted in flooding and landslides.

B. La Niña is another climate event that produces less rainfall, but increases the likelihood of hurricanes in the Atlantic.

C. The biosphere refers to all of the places we find life on Earth.

47.2 Global Air Circulation Patterns

A. Seasonal Effects
   1. Climates vary based on wind and ocean currents.
   2. Climate is also based on the amount of sunlight, elevation, and proximity of land and seas.
   3. Seasonal changes occur because the Earth's axis is tilted 23 degrees.
      a. In summer, the Northern Hemisphere gets more sunlight and has longer days than the Southern Hemisphere.
      b. The opposite events occur in the wintertime.
      c. On the spring and autumn equinoxes, all locations have 12 hours of daylight and darkness.
   4. Changes in daylight occur according to a location's latitude.

B. Air Circulation and Rainfall
   1. Areas nearest to the equator are exposed to the most sunlight.
      a. This is due to the fact that particles and greenhouse gases reflect some sunlight back to Earth.
      b. Also, energy is spread out over a smaller surface at the equator.
   2. These changes in surface temperature cause air current patterns.
      a. Warm air rises, collects water, and rains north and south of the equator.
      b. Dry, cool air descends at around 30°, where deserts are often located.
      c. At around 60° latitude, moisture is again released.
      d. At the poles, the air again lowers and does not contain much water.
      e. When water travels over land, it rises and falls more quickly than it does over water.

C. Surface Wind Patterns
   1. As the air moves away from the equator, this causes the winds to take a curved path.
      a. In the Northern Hemisphere winds curve toward the right, and the opposite is true in the Southern Hemisphere.
      b. Winds are named for the direction from which they blow (e.g., Westerlies).
   2. When two air masses meet, the winds are sometimes unpredictable.

47.3 The Ocean, Landforms, and Climates

A. Ocean Currents and Their Effects
   1. The ocean at the equator is approximately 8 cm higher than at the poles.
   2. This difference in elevation moves the water toward the poles.
   3. Other influences on ocean currents are wind, the rotation of Earth, and topography.
   4. The Gulf Stream is a major current along the eastern coast of the United States.

B. Rain Shadows and Monsoons
   1. A rain shadow indicates that after air rises and cools over mountains, it rains on one side of the mountain and leaves the side away from the wind fairly dry.
   2. A monsoon occurs in areas north or south of seas and creates an intensely windy storm.

47.4 Biomes

A. Differences Between Biomes

1. Biomes are usually defined by having similar climates and distribution of species.
   a. The primary characteristics of a biome relate to temperature and rainfall.
   b. The soil composition also varies among the different biomes.
2. Primary production varies among biomes.

B. Similarities within a Biome

1. The organisms in the same type of biomes have faced similar selection pressures, so they tend to be similar.

47.5 Deserts

A. Desert Locations and Conditions

1. Deserts receive less than 10 cm of rainfall yearly.
2. Most deserts are usually around 30° north and south latitude.
3. The deserts are very hot in the daytime and cool down rapidly at night.
4. The soil in deserts has very little topsoil and tends to be salty.

B. Adaptations to Desert Conditions

1. The plant life seen in a desert biome is adapted to poor rainfall.
   a. The adaptations of desert plants include a waxy cuticle, thorns, a pulpy interior, extensive root systems, and active stomata.
   b. Typical desert plants are cacti and mesquite bushes.
2. Animals that live in the desert must conserve water.
   a. Animals of the desert include bats and kangaroo rats.

C. The Crust Community

1. A community of cyanobacteria, lichens, mosses, and fungi make up a desert crust that lies on top of the desert soil.
   a. The desert crust fixes nitrogen and holds soil in place.
2. If the crust community is disturbed, it may impact other organisms.

47.6 Grasslands

A. Grasslands are often located between deserts and temperate forests.

1. The characteristics of grasslands are: rich topsoil, strong winds, seasonal growth, and infrequent rain.

B. Temperate Grasslands

1. These areas receive more rainfall than deserts, but not as much as forests (around 25–100 cm).
2. This biome is characterized by periods of drought, winds, and occasional fires.
3. In the 1930s, extensive plowing caused soil erosion and the area was referred to as the Dust Bowl.
   a. Plants of the grasslands include short-grass and tall-grass prairie.

C. Savannas

1. Savannas are a type of grassland that contain some shrubs and trees.
2. This biome can be found in Africa, India, and Australia.
   a. In Africa, savannas host zebras, giraffes, elephants, wildebeests, and lions.
3. Temperatures are always warm, and there is a rainy season.

47.7 Dry Shrublands and Woodlands

A. Dry Shrublands

1. Dry shrublands receive 25–60 cm of annual rainfall and are prone to fires.
    a. Plants in this biome are adapted to recover easily from fires.
2. This biome is usually located on the western coast of continents.
    a. In California, the dry shrublands are called chaparral.

B. Dry Woodlands

1. This biome receives more rain in the wintertime than the dry shrubland.
2. Trees are short and provide little shade.

47.8 Broadleaf Forests

A. Semi-Evergreen and Deciduous Forests

1. Semi-Evergreen Forests
    a. Semi-evergreen forests are found in Southeast Asia and India.
    b. They contain both deciduous broadleaf trees and those that keep their leaves.
    c. Tropical deciduous forests have scarce rainfall and trees that shed their leaves in the dry season.
2. Temperate Deciduous Forests
    a. Temperate deciduous forests have 50–150 cm of annual rainfall.
    b. In this biome, trees are deciduous and dormant in the wintertime.
    c. In the temperate deciduous forests in North America, there are oaks, maples, deer, squirrels, bears, etc.

B. Tropical Rain Forests

1. Tropical rain forests of evergreen broadleaf trees are located between 10° north and south.
2. Rainfall here is 130–200 cm per year and humidity is high.
3. A dense canopy is formed of trees, vines, and epiphytes.
4. Tropical rain forests have the most species-rich biome and also the greatest primary production.
5. Deforestation is threatening the rain forests.
    a. This could lead to the destruction of habitats and eventually extinction of species.
    b. Some extracts from plants in the rain forests have proved beneficial to man.

47.9 Coniferous Forests

A. This biome contains many evergreen trees with adaptations to conserve water.

1. Common trees here are firs and pines, and certainly redwoods on the U.S. west coast.
    a. Conifers have needles and a thick cuticle to reduce water loss.
2. The term *boreal forest* refers to the coniferous forests across northern Asia, Europe, and North America.
3. The pine barrens of New Jersey contain pitch pines and scrub oaks, which have the ability to withstand frequent fires.

47.10 Tundra

A. Arctic Tundra

1. The arctic tundra has a harsh climate that receives less than 25 cm of rainfall per year, mostly in the form of snow.
2. This biome is located between the polar ice cap and forests of the Northern Hemisphere.
3. Arctic tundra contains permafrost, which is permanently frozen ground, and a rich reservoir of carbon.
4. This biome support lichens, wolves, voles, and caribou to name a few species.

B. Alpine Tundra

1. The alpine tundra is found in areas with very high altitudes.
2. Winds are strong here, so plant life consists of several species of low-lying plants.
3. Snow may exist year round, but there is no permafrost.

47.11 Freshwater Ecosystems

A. Lakes

1. Lakes are bodies of fresh water that contain several zones.
   a. The littoral zone is near the shore and consists of shallow water and algae.
   b. The limnetic zone is the open-water zone.
   c. In deep lakes there is a profundal zone, which does not receive sunlight.
2. Nutrient Content and Succession
   a. Lakes undergo succession by changing over time.
      1) Newer lakes are clear, low on nutrients, and contain a small amount of plants.
   b. As the lake matures, it undergoes eutrophication.
3. Seasonal Changes
   a. The upper layer of many lakes freezes in the winter.
      1) When the ice melts, the spring overturn causes the water on the top to move downward, and vice-versa.
      2) In the fall overturn, the top of the lake moves down and the water toward the bottom moves up.

B. Streams and Rivers

1. Streams and rivers are fresh-water areas that are in motion.
2. The factors that affect flow volume and temperature are: rainfall, snowmelt, geography, altitude, and amount of shade.
3. Cold water holds more oxygen than warm water.

47.12 Coastal Ecosystems

A. Estuaries—Where Fresh and Saltwater Meet

1. Many immature forms of species exist here along with algae and phytoplankton.
2. The constant influx of fresh water keeps an estuary nutrient-rich.
   a. Spartina is a plant that can withstand salty water and immersion during high tides.
3. A mangrove wetland is characterized by plants with noticeable prop roots.
   a. Man is infringing on this ecosystem by destroying trees and using the area for shrimp farming.

B. Rocky and Sandy Coastlines

1. Coastlines consist of an intertidal zone with three layers.
   a. The upper littoral zone is only underwater during high tide.
   b. The midlittoral zone is submerged during the regular tide and exposed at the lowest tide of the day.

47.13 Coral Reefs

A. Coral reefs create a unique ecosystem in which many species reside.

1. Coral is formed of calcium carbonate that is colored by dinoflagellates.
   a. When a coral reef is stressed, it expels the dinoflagellates, dies, and becomes bleached.
   b. Stresses include exposure to pollution, erosion, and over-fishing of the area.
   c. Coral reefs all over the world are in danger largely from man's intervention.
2. The coral reefs are usually located in warm waters between 25° north and 25° south.
3. The largest reef is the Great Barrier Reef off the coast of Australia.

47.14 The Open Ocean

A. Pelagic Ecosystems
   1. The open ocean is referred to as the pelagic province.
   2. The pelagic province includes a zone of much productivity known as the neritic zone.
   3. In the upper layers of the pelagic zone, there is a diversity of organisms.
   4. The deepest layers are largely unchartered since man cannot dive at such depths.

B. The Seafloor
   1. The benthic province is the bottom of the ocean, containing rocks and sediments.
      a. Near continents, the benthic province is an area rich in biodiversity.
   2. Seamounts are underwater mountains that serve as a suitable habitat for many invertebrates.
      a. Fishermen sometimes use disruptive trawling techniques to drag nets along the bottom and capture fish.
   3. Hydrothermal vents release warm water that is rich in minerals from the ocean bottom.
      a. Scientists theorize that life may have started in this type of environment.
   4. Animals called loriciferans have been discovered in the deepest waters, which are devoid of oxygen.

47.15 Ocean-Sea Interactions

A. El Niño Southern Oscillation (ENSO) is defined as changes in sea surface temperatures and in air circulation patterns in the western equatorial Pacific Ocean.
   1. This results in global repercussions on weather.
   2. El Niño brings about heavy rain and warm air.
   3. This weather pattern may last for 6–18 months.

B. Often the El Niño pattern is followed by another weather event called La Niña.
   1. La Niña is characterized by colder water.

C. The 1997–1998 season resulted in an El Niño/La Niña episode.
   1. An upwelling occurred that caused a massive algae bloom across the entire Pacific Ocean.
   2. Scientists also noticed an increase in cases of cholera in Peru.
      a. Scientists were uncertain where the bacteria *Vibrio cholerae* was between outbreaks.
      b. It was discovered that crustaceans called copepods house the bacteria.
      c. The number of these copepods varies with varying water temperatures.
      d. The cholera outbreaks may be prevented by filtering the water through cloth to prevent copepods from remaining in the water.
         1) This primitive preventative method has reduced the cholera outbreaks by 50 percent.

47.16 Warming Water and Wild Weather (Revisited)

A. The United States National Oceanographic and Atmospheric Administration (NOAA) collects temperature data from various areas of the Pacific Ocean.
   1. It is hoped that scientists can predict upcoming weather patterns, such as El Niño and La Niña.
   2. This data could help predict weather events such as droughts, flooding, hurricanes, and fires.
      a. This knowledge could enable areas to be better prepared for these weather emergencies.

Suggestions for Presenting the Material

- Make up a series of flashcards. Place different facts about biogeographic areas on each card, such as average rainfall, temperature, latitude, and major species found there. See if the students can put the various "fact cards" under the proper biogeographic area.
- The use of slides showing views of the different biomes may be helpful to enable students to visualize the specific areas.
- Now that we have discussed numerous cycles in nature in the last chapter and biomes in this chapter, we are setting the stage for the upcoming chapter on human interference.
- Discuss the characteristics of desert vegetation that makes them well-suited to that biome. Show some common examples so that these features are evident.
- If available, show a film that illustrates wind patterns and subsequent effects on the climate.
- Ask a speaker from the EPA, state coastal commission, or other environmental group to speak to the class.
- Use overhead transparencies to show worldwide patterns of climate and biome distributions.
- Discuss what impact, if any, El Niño and La Niña have on the weather in your area.
- Have a discussion about the different seasonal effects in the Northern and the Southern Hemispheres. Explain why these differences occur.
- What surface winds affect your area? How does the Earth's rotation help determine the direction of these winds?
- As a review of previous material, explain why leaves in deciduous forests turn different colors in the fall season.

Classroom and Laboratory Enrichment

- As each biome is discussed, ask students who have visited that biome to share their observations with the class.
- Discuss the educational requirements and experience necessary to become a meteorologist. How do they utilize satellites for weather prediction? If possible, invite a meteorologist to speak to the class.
- Use a globe and the information you have learned about global patterns of air circulation to explain the reasons for your latest weather conditions. Explain why your region has the weather it does.
- Prepare a diagram showing how the effects of increasing elevation are similar to those of decreasing latitude.
- A fisherman off of the New Jersey coast caught a butterfly fish (who is native to the Caribbean) in the beginning of the winter season. How could you explain this? Note: the fish was not released from anyone's aquarium.
- Using data from a local weather station. Graph the air quality ratings in your area over a several-month period? Do you see any patterns that exist? What would be the major contributors to air pollution in your area?
- Prepare a table listing: a) each biome, b) its principal location, and c) its chief plant and animal life.
- Study your own biome in depth. What animal and plant species predominate? What is the soil like? Describe the climate including average temperature and rainfall levels.

- What is a prairie? What happened to the American prairies? Are there still patches of prairie in the United States?
- Why is species diversity so high in tropical rain forests? Why do the rain forests make poor farmland?
- Perform a soil analysis on some different soil samples from your area. Which ones seem to hold water the best? Which seem richest in nutrients?
- If nearby, take a field trip to a lake, estuary, or coastline region. Can you identify the specific zones? Do you see any signs of man's intervention?
- Test water samples from any bodies of water near your school. Are any of these suitable for drinking water? What would a high coliform count in the water signify?
- Why do you think relatively little has been done to eliminate the greenhouse effect? What do you think is required before governments such as our own will pass laws regulating the types of human activities responsible for phenomena such as the greenhouse effect? Which other countries are enacting laws to reduce the emission of greenhouse gases? Which ones are negligent?
- From a map of the world, color in the six biogeographical realms as they are represented. List the latitudinal boundaries of each.
- Draw and label the major ocean currents on a world map.
- Prepare a list of environmental concerns in your area and state. Ask students what should be done and then ask them what realistically can be done.
- Why does precipitation tend to increase in towns that are on the eastern side of the Great Lakes?
- Stress the differences between arctic tundra and alpine tundra.

Classroom Discussion Ideas

- Scientists should study the past incidences of weather patterns such as El Niño to be able to predict the future course of weather. How have manmade activities altered these patterns?
- Relate the movement of hurricanes through the Caribbean and Gulf of Mexico to the ocean currents you see drawn in Figure 47.5.
- How have the intensity of storms such as hurricanes changed in the last two decades. How is the intensity of hurricanes in the United States related to the temperature in the Gulf of Mexico? What methods are being considered to remedy this problem? Research an idea suggested by Bill Gates and others. Does this idea seem feasible to you?
- Make a list of the major monsoons that have occurred in the past 10 years. Is there a strong seasonal link to these storms?
- Research some species of animals that you consider to be most affected by drastic weather patterns, such as El Niño.
- How much of an impact would another El Niño have on the world today?

Additional Ideas for Classroom Discussion

- Discuss some of the ways to improve soils considered too poor for agriculture. What are some of the characteristics of desert soils and tropical soil that make them poorly suited for long-term agriculture?

- What is meant when a lake is described as "dead"? How does such a condition come about? How can a "dead" lake be rejuvenated?
- Describe the rates of nutrient cycling in the tundra and in the tropical forest. How can you explain the different rates of nutrient cycling in these two biomes?
- Do you believe that prescribed burning of forests should be allowed? View the website: http://edis.ifas.ufl.edu for regulations regarding controlled fires in Florida.
- Should modern technology change desert habitats such as Palm Springs, California, where lawns are green only because they are maintained by artificial means?
- Visit a wastewater treatment facility in your area. Do they use traditional or natural methods to treat the water?
- We currently live in a disposable society—when something breaks, we simply get another. How has this shift in human values changed over the past 50 years? How has it impacted the environment?
- Discuss the ways in which animal morphology might differ from one biome to the next. What role does annual mean temperature play in determining animal morphology? What differences in plant morphology can you see among the different biomes?
- List the ways in which a city, especially a large one, represents one of the least stable of ecosystems.
- Why would it be unwise to clear tropical forests and irrigate arid lands for conversion to agriculture?
- Do some research on the disease cholera. When was it first discovered and where? What are effective prevention and treatment options?
- Look into monsoons. Where are they the most common? What was the worst monsoon in recorded history? During which season do they usually occur?
- Choose a biome that is not represented in the United States. What conditions are not present to support this biome?
- How would the unrestricted use of off-road vehicles impact a desert biome? Are there any laws to prevent this from occurring?
- Choose an organism that would be a part of the desert crust. What contribution does this organism make to the desert ecology?
- Contrast the characteristics of an oligotrophic lake and a eutrophic lake. Are there any examples of either of these in your area?
- Ask students to make a list of ways in which they could modify their own lifestyles and behaviors to reduce environmental pollution.
- Does your college have an ecology or environmental club? If not, would your class consider starting one?

How Would You Vote? Classroom Discussion Ideas

- How many people do you know who avidly watch the weather report just to see whether they need to carry an umbrella each day? If funding is spent researching climate cycles, meteorologists may be able to foresee violent storms and drastic changes in the weather.
- From an ecologist's standpoint, major catastrophes for animal and plant species could possibly be averted.

- It may be difficult to convince taxpayers that this is a prudent use of their funds. People are generally looking for the government to improve their lives today and they are less worried about long-term consequences.
- The secret will lie in educating the public about weather patterns and the effects that can result from events like El Niño. If we start teaching young children about these phenomena, they will hopefully grow up to be voters with ecological conscience.

Term Paper Topics, Library Activities, and Special Projects

- Research the biomes on Mt. Washington in New Hampshire. Because of its extremely high and windy altitude, it is a highly studied area for observing a tundra biome "close to home." What animal and plant species would you expect to find there? Which biome would you see at the base of Mt. Washington?
- Write a description of your local climate in all seasons. List and describe all of the factors responsible for your climate.
- Write a report about historical descriptions of the Dust Bowl.
- Irrigation has brought "bloom to the deserts." But is there a negative side to this practice?
- What characteristics do you see in vegetation of the tundra? How are those features adaptive in that harsh environment?
- What changes in plant species composition would you see among deciduous forests as you traveled from the eastern United States to the western coast?
- What would happen to some northern U.S. lakes if global warming raised the temperature so that they did not freeze? How would this affect the flow of nutrients?
- Use soil science textbooks to help write a description of local soil types.
- Discuss the condition of Lake Erie in the 1970s. What has been done since then to undo the damage?
- Using Styrofoam balls, have a student demonstrate that the Earth's axis is not perpendicular to the plane of the elliptical pathway. In addition, show the position of the Earth at summer and winter solstices and at the autumn and spring equinoxes.
- Prepare a colored map of the United States showing which areas of the nation provide the most and least food; superimpose shading to show the areas of the most dense consumer (human) populations.
- Describe the role of estuaries in commercial fisheries. Discuss the ecology of one of the commercially important estuaries in the United States.
- Locate the following website http://www.braziltourism.org/ecosystems.html. It shows a map of the various biomes contained in Brazil. What types of plants and animals would exist in each of these areas?
- Describe where prairie remnants are found today in the United States. Prepare plant species lists of the short-grass prairie and the tall-grass prairie.
- Look up historical records of thermal air inversions that resulted in significant numbers of deaths due to air pollution.
- Discuss the environmental effects of strip mining.
- Describe what happens when a lake undergoes eutrophication. Discuss examples of situations in which eutrophication was reversed. What changes in aquatic species composition will occur as a result of eutrophication?

- Research one of the chemotherapy drugs that are obtained from the rain forests. How was its medicinal value discovered? Are the plants that supply this extract bountiful in the rain forests?
- Look up information on one of the rare species that are found in the deep ocean. What is their diet? What adaptations allow them to survive in this unusual environment?
- Look on NOAA's website at http://www.elnino.noaa.gov. They discuss how they go about predicting the arrival and impact of El Niño and La Niña events.
- Who are your local polluters? Find out which industries release pollutants into the atmosphere. List the pollutants, and describe what steps the companies have taken to reduce emission of pollutants.
- Require each student in the class to write a letter to a government representative or company executive about an important environmental issue. Did they receive a satisfying response?

Possible Responses to *Critical Thinking* Questions

1. The climate of London is heavily influenced by the Gulf Stream, which brings warm water, and therefore air, northward. Calgary has no such mechanism providing it with warmer weather. Scientists are concerned that the Gulf Stream could shut down, due to global warming and the melting of polar ice caps. This would have drastic consequences on the temperatures and biomes it affects.
2. China is becoming a major source of air pollution on the western coast of the United States. Air pollution does not respect political boundaries and air currents bring the Chinese pollution to the U.S. The EPA has performed studies that verify that 25 percent of the pollution above Los Angeles originated in China. This is not surprising since the Chinese add a new coal-burning factory every week and the percentage of automobiles increases by an average of 10 percent per year!
3. Even though a desert looks desolate and empty, it actually supports an entirely unique ecosystem. If off-road vehicles are allowed to ride in all areas of the desert, plants and animal habitats will be destroyed. Although it may be easy to destroy the flora and fauna of the desert, it would take much work and time to restore it to its natural state.

Possible Responses to *Data Analysis Exercise* Questions

The National Oceanographic and Atmospheric Administration monitors the sea surface temperatures to see if climatic events coordinate with El Niño, La Niña, or just neutral conditions.

1. The greatest positive temperature deviation occurred in 1998.
2. El Niño occurred during the winter of 1982/1983, whereas La Niña occurred in the winter of 2001/2002.
3. The longest interval without a La Niña event was from 1990 to 1995.
4. La Niña was present in the fall of 2007, when California had severe wildfires. The region would have been well-suited for fires, since a La Niña event tends to produce less rainfall.

48

HUMAN IMPACTS ON THE BIOSPHERE

Chapter Outline

Objectives

1. Realize that there have been five mass extinctions that occurred naturally and we could be heading to an era of a manmade extinction.
2. Be able to describe how many species are endangered or threatened due to deforestation, desertification, hunting, and species introduction.
3. Know that we are aware of many threatened species, but there are probably many more than we think.
4. List the efforts made to protect habitats and regions at risk.
5. Know that many species are affected by our process of overdevelopment and over-use of non-renewable resources.
6. Realize that many grasslands are changing into deserts due to poor farming techniques that lead to soil erosion.
7. Understand that plastic trash and acid rain harm animal species.
8. Know that humans can positively impact organisms by appropriate farming and by educating the public at large about environmental issues.

Key Terms

mass extinction	pollutant	ecosystem biodiversity
endangered species	ozone layer	indicator species
threatened species	biodiversity	hot spots
endemic species	conservation biology	ecoregions
acid rain	ecological restoration	desertification
bioaccumulation	genetic biodiversity	riparian zones
biological magnification	species biodiversity	

Lecture Outline

48.1 The Long Reach

A. Far-reaching impacts of man are felt in areas like the North Pole.
   1. Greenhouse gases are causing global warming, which melts polar ice caps.
   2. Animals in arctic regions have high levels of mercury and other toxic substances.

B. All areas of the world have evidence of human intervention.
   1. Many animal and plant species are suffering the effects of man's activities.
   2. We now have the knowledge to understand man's influence on the environment and to attempt to minimize it.

48.2 The Extinction Crisis

A. Mass Extinction
   1. Extinction is a natural process.
      a. Scientists estimate that 99 percent of all species that ever existed are extinct.
   2. The Earth has already had five natural mass extinctions.
      a. The greatest mass extinction was at the end of the Permian era.
         1) This extinction was caused by the consequences resulting from volcanic activity.
      b. Sometimes a decrease in the numbers of one species encourages expansion of another species.
         1) For example, when the number of gymnosperms decreased, angiosperms became dominant.

B. The Sixth Great Mass Extinction
   1. A sixth mass extinction caused by man's interference may be underway.
   2. The arrival of humans coincided with the extinction of many large animals.
      a. Hunting animals contributed to the demise of many species.
   3. Other causes of extinction are: climate variation, comet impacts, and diseases that are introduced by humans.
      a. Animals such as the dodo bird are extinct due to destruction of their habitat and hunting by man.

48.3 Currently Threatened Species

A. An endangered species is one that is in immediate danger of extinction, whereas a threatened species is one that is likely to become endangered.

B. Causes of Species Declines
   1. One common cause of the decline of a species is overharvesting.
      a. This is the case in the Atlantic codfish population, and also with the invertebrate the white abalone.
      b. Scientists are using captive breeding techniques to attempt to rejuvenate the species.

2. Endemic species are most vulnerable because they live in a limited area.
    a. Panda bears are an example of an endemic species.
3. Destruction of their native habitat is a major reason why species become endangered.
    a. This affects plants (e.g., prairie fringed orchid) and animals (e.g., ivory-billed woodpecker).
4. Man has hindered natural habitats by introducing foreign species.
    a. Examples of predators that are interfering with natural environments are: rats, brown tree snakes, kudzu, and Japanese honeysuckle.
5. Often the decline in one population will lead to a decrease in another population.
    a. An example is the decrease of both bison and buffalo clover.
6. The use of biological controls can affect species other than the intended target.

C. The Unknown Losses
1. A great number of species are either currently evaluated for threats or found to be threatened, as noted by the International Union for Conservation of Nature and Natural Resources.
    a. It is unknown how many other species, such as microbes or protists, are also endangered.

48.4 Harmful Land Use Practices

A. Desertification
1. Grasslands can develop desert-like conditions in a process called desertification.
    a. This can be caused by over-grazing, improper farming, droughts, and heavy winds.
    b. An example can be seen in the Great Plains or in the Gobi desert.
2. The best method to avoid desertification is to restrict farming from areas with drought conditions and high winds.

B. Deforestation
1. Deforestation destroys habitats, encourages flooding, and increases the chance of landslides.
2. This destruction of forests reduces the nutrient content of the soil and affects weather.
3. The most deforestation is occurring in Central and South America.

48.5 Toxic Pollutants

A. Pollutants are defined as natural or man-made substances that are released into soil, air, or water in greater-than-natural amounts.

B. Acid Rain
1. Acid rain is primarily caused by the emission of sulfur dioxides and nitrogen oxides into the air.
    a. These gases are released from coal-burning plants, cars, and power plants.
2. When these acidic gases combine with precipitation, it is called acid rain.
3. Acid rain harms aquatic organisms, trees, and plants.
    a. Acid rain disrupts nutrient cycles in the soil.

C. Biological Accumulation and Magnification
1. Some plants can be used to help eliminate pollutants from the environment.
2. Animals tend to accumulate toxins in fatty tissues, so older animals show more effects.
3. The amount of toxins increase as you move up the food chain, so those animals exhibit biological magnification (increased levels of the pollutant).
    a. An example of biological magnification occurred when fish-eating birds accumulated a very large concentration of DDT.

D. The Trouble with Trash
1. Plastic trash can kill organisms.

a. Birds, fish, and other marine organisms are particularly affected by ingesting or becoming tangled in plastic.

2. Many plastic products do not biodegrade for decades or more.

48.6 Ozone Depletion and Pollution

A. Depletion of the Ozone Layer

1. The ozone layer refers to the area about 10–17 miles above sea level that contains lots of ozone.
    a. This layer helps shield us from harmful UV radiation, which can cause mutations.
    b. Exposure to UV rays also increases the incidence of skin cancer.
    c. Plants are also affected by additional UV exposure.
2. In the 1970s, scientists noticed that the layer was becoming thinner, and a decade later it appeared so thin that it was referred to as the hole in the ozone.
3. Chlorofluorocarbons (CFCs) are the main culprit in the destruction of the ozone layer.
    a. In 1987, many nations agreed to phase-out the use of CFCs.
    b. Even though the CFCs are not being released in great amounts, they are still breaking down and impairing the ozone layer.

B. Near-Ground Ozone Pollution

1. Ozone near the ground is considered a pollutant.
    a. This type of ozone is formed when organic compounds are burned or when exposed to sunlight.
    b. To reduce ozone as a pollutant, avoid any activities that release gas into the air where they will be exposed to direct sunlight.

48.7 Effects of Global Climate Change

A. Average temperatures are increasing due to global warming.

B. Climate changes have a huge impact on the environment.

1. The water level rises due to the rising temperature and glacial melting.
2. The salinity and acidity of the water is also affected.
3. Rainfall levels change.

C. Many animal and plant species utilize temperature clues to know when to flower or reproduce.

D. Humans may be more prone to infectious diseases and heat strokes.

48.8 Conservation Biology

A. The Value of Biodiversity

1. Biodiversity includes genetic diversity within a species, species diversity, and ecosystem diversity.
2. Conservation biology serves to monitor biodiversity and find ways to protect it.
3. Biological wealth includes benefits that can be derived from the environment.
    a. Some plant and animal products may produce valuable chemicals and medicines.
    b. Plants produce oxygen and use up carbon dioxide.
    c. Plants hold soil in place to prevent erosion.
    d. Other organisms decompose and detoxify wastes.
    e. Natural species can be combined with farm crops to produce an improved type of plant

B. Setting Priorities

1. Conservation biologists chose the areas that need protection first, called hot spots.
2. Conservation biologists also defined 867 ecoregions and specified those that are the most in need of ecological efforts.

C. Preservation and Restoration
   1. A scientist studying the birds of Costa Rica purchased some of the land as a sanctuary.
      a. This encouraged others to donate land and money so the area flourishes.
   2. Ecological restoration is the renewal of a severely damaged ecosystem.
      a. Restoration efforts are underway to improve conditions in the Louisiana marshlands.

48.9 Reducing Negative Impacts

A. Helping society to understand sustainability is a major initiative today.
   1. Supplies for newer, extravagant homes may damage the environment.
      a. For example, copper wiring must be mined and may create ecological dead zones in its wake.
   2. The recycling of goods prevents the need for more extractions of materials from the environment.
   3. Reduction of energy use, especially of fossil fuels, is a prudent practice.
      a. Walk, ride a bike, car pool, or take public transportation.
   4. Consider carefully the impact of all renewable resources.
   5. Support environmental causes through your votes and also with your wallet.

48.10 The Long Reach (Revisited)

A. Ice sheets in the arctic are breaking up as a result of global warming.
   1. These melting conditions will make it easier to remove minerals and fossil fuels from the area.
   2. Since these materials are in short supply, pressure is mounting to excavate in this area.
   3. Conservationalists warn that these processes may destroy a valuable biome.

Suggestions for Presenting the Material

- Now that we have completed the ecology section of the book, it may be time to review some of the past chapters. This chapter deals entirely with man's interference, but some of the previous chapters deal with some of the concepts in more detail. Review concepts such as acid rain, crop rotation, greenhouse gases, and global warming before beginning the chapter.
- You may want the class to see the movie "An Inconvenient Truth," which deals with many of the ecological concepts that we have discussed in this section of the book. The movie does a great job of visually representing statistics and views of the actual biomes.
- Start the discussion with some slides of animals in trouble due to man's influence (e.g., a polar bear on a melting ice cap, a bird caught in plastic netting, etc). These types of powerful images may open up the discussions.
- Have each student write a short essay concentrating on the environmental issue from this chapter that really stood out in their minds.
- Use a "Jeopardy" or "Who Wants To Be a Millionaire" format to review the key terms from this chapter and the previous ecology chapters. A template for these games can be found at: http://teach.fcps.net/trt2/links/powerpointgames.htm
- Design a questionnaire for students to use outside of your classroom. Each student in the class should poll 10 non-science-major students. Have the questionnaire ask a few simple questions relating to information from this course about air pollution. Your survey will be assessing the layperson's knowledge of basic facts about pollution. Tabulate your results—where they what you expected? Keep in mind that the average college student may be better informed that an

older individual with no formal environmental education. What can be done to heighten awareness about air pollution?

- Obtain a map of the United States showing the areas of highest cancer rates. Do you see any clusters of high cancer areas? Ask the students to speculate as to why certain areas are more at risk than others.
- Why does normal rainwater have a pH of around 5.6?

Classroom and Laboratory Enrichment

- Assign each student an endangered or threatened species to investigate fully. What is the major reason for its decline? What could be done to save this species? Refer to http://www.iucnredlist.org/ for lists of endangered and threatened species.
- Look into the previous five mass extinctions. If the humans of today with their advanced technology had lived during any of these extinctions, do you think the extinctions would have been preventable?
- Research some animals that are extinct. Do you think the animal could have developed an adaptation that would have enabled it to survive?
- Take a field trip to a local zoo. Do the animals seem to be in their natural habitat? What changes could be made to mimic their native surroundings? Why do you think caged animals do not always reproduce successfully? Could anything be done to improve this?
- Research some extinct plants. Why couldn't these plants be artificially maintained?
- When you observe the number of species on Table 48.1, the number of insect species really stands out. What features of insects make them so successful?
- Focus on one of the critical or vulnerable ecoregions in Figure 48.14. What circumstances have lead to the deterioration of these areas?
- Why are Americans the major users of all the resources of the world? What country do you think would rank second?
- Look into the events leading up to the Dust Bowl in the Great Plains. When did this take place? How could better farming methods have avoided this occurrence?
- How could we avoid the plastic trash from being consumed by marine animals? What can we do about this?
- Do you think by educating the public about the economic value of some biological products, we can do more to save ecosystems?
- How is strip logging superior to normal logging techniques?
- Interview the director of physical plants at your school. How does your school recycle products? Do you recycle glass, plastics, and paper? Are there recycling containers at prime locations throughout the campus? If not, how can this be improved?
- Invite an environmental speaker to your class from the EPA, state coastal commission, etc. Have each student prepare a question to ask this expert.
- Research federal laws regarding air pollution passed in the last 10 years. Do you think these laws are too lenient? What changes would you recommend?
- Divide the class into small groups and debate the pros and cons of different energy sources. Each section should be prepared to discuss the merits and drawbacks of one of the following energy sources: oil, coal, natural gas, hydropower, solar power, nuclear power, and other alternatives.

- Look at the website http://www.epa.gov/superfund/ to see if there are any superfund sites near your home or college. These sites are targeted by the EPA for clean up since they are considered to be uncontrolled hazardous waste sites.

Classroom Discussion Ideas

- Scientists have begun to realize that events that occur in one part of our planet may have profound consequences for the entire planet and its inhabitants. Nowhere is this more evident than in the Arctic regions. Previously, man was only concerned with stripping all of the natural resources from this uninhabited area. No one noticed, or cared to notice, changes in the Arctic environment. Only in recent history has man really studied the loss of the polar ice caps and the effect this has on the rest of the Earth.
- The polar ice caps are melting due to global warming, which affects everyone on our planet. In most areas of the globe, an increase in temperature of a few degrees goes unnoticed, but when one looks at the effects this has on our polar environment, it is shocking!
- We need to find ways to extract oil and minerals from the Arctic without damaging their ecology. If this is not feasible, then perhaps we should abandon our mining of these substances to preserve the valuable ecosystem there.
- Let's hope that we can find a way to study the Arctic habitat without damaging it further.

Additional Ideas for Classroom Discussion

- Name some indicator species. What traits make these species able to signal adverse conditions in the environment?
- Choose one area of the country and plot the average yearly temperatures as far back as these statistics were measured. Does your graph show signs of global warming?
- Many grocery stores use the word "organic" to describe their products. Are there any laws defining the term? How about the term "green"? Is that term legally defined? Could some companies try to falsely market their products by saying they are environmentally friendly?
- Are there any steps you could personally take to decrease plastic trash, other than recycling?
- In Brazil, they utilize sugar cane as a common energy source. Why do we not use these methods in the United States?
- There is a very large island of trash that has accumulated in the Pacific Ocean. See if you can find out further information about this and how it is being addressed.
- Desertification is a natural process. In manmade deserts, a vicious cycle occurs. As the ground becomes dry, species die off. With less vegetation undergoing transpiration, the rain decreases. Look at events in a newly formed desert and see if this cyclic process has occurred.
- How do we determine which endangered species have the greatest value to the planet? Do animals always take precedence over plants? Should the animals that are not "warm and fuzzy" be given the same attention as those that we consider to be "cute"?
- When building a new home, what practices could you follow to make the house a "green" home? Are there any houses in your area that have adaptations that are environmentally friendly?
- Why is the ozone layer of the Earth's atmosphere shrinking at the same time that excessive amounts of ozone at the Earth's surface are present in photochemical smog?

- How many students in the class recycle their aluminum cans? Newspapers? Glass? Take a hand count. Ask students for reasons they do or do not recycle? Does your school collect recyclables? If not, could this be suggested at a student government meeting?
- What is low-sulfur coal? How is this better environmentally?
- What is thermal pollution? What are its effects?
- What nations are actively enacting laws against air pollution? Are they stricter or more lenient than those in the United States?

How Would You Vote? Classroom Discussion Ideas

- Monitor the voting for the online question. Point out to the class that the environment at the poles is extremely unique. If it were to become damaged further, species may become extinct or at the very least endangered. If this environment is permanently destroyed, there is nowhere else on Earth that can support many of these species.
- Perhaps more emphasis should be place on renewable resources. What are some renewable resources that could replace petroleum? Why are they not currently being used?
- At some point, our energy needs will have to be supplied by renewable resources. Why not now, before we lose valuable ecosystems like that of the Arctic?
- The sixth mass extinction will be the first that is driven by man. What is our moral obligation to other species to prevent this?
- Have each student write a letter to their congressman or the CEO of a company to ask about environmentally friendly practices that are underway.
- Currently some of the species that live in the Arctic are endangered. The devastation produced by additional assaults on the area could mean the end for these organisms. In addition, we need to send the message to other countries that we highly value the diversity of nature and hope that they do the same.

Term Paper Topics, Library Activities, and Special Projects

- Scientists have been boring into ice caps to test ice cores for environmental factors of the past. Recently they feel more pressured to complete this study. Why?
- By looking at past examples of major extinctions, about how long do you think it takes an environment to return to the previous level of diversity?
- Review a study done in New Jersey to see if pollution is harming the mosquito species. Although most people are not too concerned about the welfare of the mosquito, it can be used as an indicator species. What trait of a mosquito make it well-suited as an indicator species?
- Many parts of Florida have been particularly vulnerable to the introduction of non-indigenous species. Is this making southern Florida a threatened ecosystem? What can be done about this?
- Look in your daily paper or weekly news magazine for an article about an environmental issue. Summarize the article for the class.
- Do you see that defining areas for ecotourism is a mixed blessing? These areas are set aside to be protected, yet lots of tourists are passing through and possibly damaging the environment. Pick a particular area that is used for ecotourism and see if its human visitors have had an impact.

- Some individuals feel that all of the environmental problems we experience can be boiled down to one cause—overpopulation. How do you think the population explosion should be addressed? Would legislation like that in China work in the United States?
- Research malformations that have been widespread in amphibians recently. They have found other amphibians with malformed limbs, etc. Do you relate this to pollution? How can this be determined? Are frogs an indicator species in their environment?
- Research the case where some samples of Tylenol were poisoned. What permanent impact did this case have on our environment due to the creation of tamper-free products? How much did our plastic trash increase?
- Can we classify the Gulf Stream as an endangered ecosystem? Does it appear to be disappearing?
- Read a book about environmental topics and do a report for the class.
- Locate articles that discuss the deforestation of the rain forests. At what rate are they being destroyed? If deforestation continues at this rate, how long will it be before there are no more rain forests?
- Describe the actual contents of industrial smog or photochemical smog in the nearest city with an air pollution problem. Describe the ways in which the air pollution affects the health of area residents.
- Biological magnification of mercury may occur in humans that ingest large quantities of certain fish. Which fish are most likely to contain high mercury levels? Are these species restricted from the diets of pregnant women?
- What are the effects of acid rain on fish populations?
- Have a student choose one type of energy source. Is it renewable or non-renewable? Do you expect this type of production to increase or decrease over the next 25 years?
- Countries like India and China are major contributors to air pollution. Has there been any correlation between their increased air pollution levels and respiratory diseases?
- Some people say that China's biggest export is air pollution. Do you agree with this statement? Why is the western United States the recipient of much of this pollution?
- Pick a species that is damaged by acid rain. How does the acid rain impact the lives of these organisms?
- Are there sustainability courses available at your institution? Suggest the significance of adding some environmentally friendly courses.
- Write a letter to a company that you feel uses excessive packaging. Do you have suggestions for how the packaging materials could be more environmentally friendly?
- Join or start an ecological club on campus. What should be your first project? Or start a "green club" at a local middle school. Have the students publish a newsletter with ecologically prudent ideas for improvements in their homes, their school, and their community.

Possible Responses to *Critical Thinking* Questions

1. As we know from this chapter and the previous ones, greenhouse gas emission causes global warming. In my area it is evident that many migratory birds are traveling further north due to the problem of increased temperatures. This requires that the birds establish new zones of habitat, and they may be displacing birds indigenous to that new locale. As you know, displacing one animal species may disrupt an entire food web. Also, if the average temperature rises significantly, animals may be subject to diseases that were previously only found in tropical locales. Plant

species may also have difficulty adjusting to the new temperature range. As you can see, temperature changes could have a major impact on the species residing there.

2. Often the amount of dangerous toxins in an animal's body depends on their diet. If the organisms consumed by an animal, such as a ringed seal, contain the pollutants, then the toxin becomes biologically magnified in the larger animal. A bowhead whale consumes plankton, which would not retain the toxins as well as the marine animals that are the diet of the seal.
3. In any area, it seems as though the species that naturally lives in that environment should take precedence over an introduced species. People are obviously opposed to destroying the feral cats since they envision cats as friendly house pets. It would be best if feral cats were captured and neutered before their release. Hopefully this would decrease the feral cat population sufficiently to let the bird population recover adequately.

Possible Responses to *Data Analysis Exercise* Questions

Harmful chemicals travel to Arctic locations via wind, where they enter food webs. Through the process of biological magnification, the toxins enter the bodies of the Arctic people. This study was performed to see if the level of PCBs influences the sex of unborn children.

1. More males were born to women with less than one microgram per milliliter of PCB in their serum.
2. Women were more apt to have daughters when their PCB concentration was greater than 4.0 micrograms per milliliter.
3. If a village had an inordinate amount of female newborns, one would expect the PCB levels to be above four micrograms per milliliter.